Peter Norton's

New Insid the PC

Scott H. A. Clark

SAMS

201 West 103rd Street, Indianapolis, Indiana 46290 USA

Peter Norton's New Inside the PC

Copyright ©2002 by Sams Publishing

FIRST EDITION

International Standard Book Number: 0-672-32289-7

Library of Congress Catalog Card Number: 2001093561

Printed in the United States of America

First Printing: March 2002

04   03   02   4   3   2   1

Trademarks

Warning and Disclaimer

Associate Publisher
Michael Stephens

Acquisitions Editor
Kim Spilker

Development Editor
Steve Rowe

Managing Editor
Charlotte Clapp

Project Editor
Matt Purcell

Copy Editor
Kezia Endsley

Indexer
Tina Trettin

Proofreader
Andrea Dugan

Technical Editor
John Gosney

Team Coordinator
Lynne Williams

Interior Designer
Gary Adair

Cover Designer
Aren Howell

Page Layout
Rebecca Harmon

Overview

Contents

Dedication

For My Parents, Whose Love Has Never Faltered.

Acknowledgments

Many people and companies dedicated a great deal of time and resources to putting this book in your hands.

We would first like to thank Andrew Wadish and Michael Yu, who researched and contributed to the new material. Andrew also spearheaded the re-organization of the entire text. Both men are talented writers and technology experts who have focused their skills on network engineering and security.

Sincerest thanks to our literary agent, Matt Wagner, of Waterside Productions.

Thanks also to everyone at SAMS Publishing.

Scott would like to extend a special thanks, in alphabetical order, to Christopher, Don, Glynn, Kacie, Nancy, and Scott, and also to Brien, and Jacob—all for their mentoring and tireless support.

We couldn't have completed the project without the generosity of many different companies. I'd like to thank them each, individually.

Sincerest thanks to SGI/Silicon Graphics, for the use of their F180 flat panel display. In our opinion, it's simply the best display on the market, period.

Thanks to Dell Computer, for a Dell Dimension 8100 desktop PC and a Dell Inspiron 8100 laptop PC. We have worked with Dell for many years now, and continue to be impressed with the quality of their products and their excellent service and support.

Our thanks goes to Xerox and to Alexander Ogilvy, their public relations representatives, for the use of a Xerox Tektronix Phaser 860 DP color printer. This may be the best color printer available today.

Thanks to Lexmark for the use of their C720N color laser printer, truly the best of its kind.

Thanks to Agenda Computing for allowing us special access to their Agenda VR3, Linux-based handheld PC.

Thanks to Palm Computing for the loan of a Palm m500.

About the Author

Scott Clark has been the director of Peter Norton's computer books for over twelve years. He has written for many of them and has edited almost every book in the series. He was the primary author for the best-selling sixth edition of *Peter Norton's Inside the PC*, and made major contributions to the seventh and eighth editions. He has among his other titles, *Peter Norton's Complete Guide to Norton SystemWorks*, and *The Effective Executive's Guide to Microsoft Access 2002*. Scott has been a visiting professor of website design and Internet technologies at Fullerton College. He lives in Southern California in a house full of Stickley furniture and Disney memorabilia.

"For a successful technology, reality must take precedence over public relations, for Nature cannot be fooled."
– R. Feynman

Tell Us What You Think!

As the reader of this book, *you* are our most important critic and commentator. We value your opinion and want to know what we're doing right, what we could do better, what areas you'd like to see us publish in, and any other words of wisdom you're willing to pass our way.

As an associate publisher for Sams Publishing, I welcome your comments. You can fax, e-mail, or write me directly to let me know what you did or didn't like about this book—as well as what we can do to make our books stronger.

Please note that I cannot help you with technical problems related to the topic of this book, and that due to the high volume of mail I receive, I might not be able to reply to every message.

When you write, please be sure to include this book's title and author name as well as your name and phone or fax number. I will carefully review your comments and share them with the author and editors who worked on the book.

Fax:	317-581-4770
E-mail:	feedback@samspublishing.com
Mail:	Michael Stephens
	Sams Publishing
	201 West 103rd Street
	Indianapolis, IN 46290 USA

Introduction

You're about to embark on an amazing voyage of discovery, understanding, and productivity. Welcome!

From the day it first appeared, the IBM PC stirred excitement and fascination: The PC marked the coming of age of "personal" computing, a drastic change from the days when all computers were managed by other people who doled out computer power to users on an as-needed, as-available basis. Today, the PC is the tool without equal for helping business and professional people improve their personal performance and the quality of their work. Students of almost all ages and other home-based users have successfully expanded personal computing into near ubiquity. The home-PC market encouraged the development of an ever-growing range of applications from word processors for homework, to technologies that allow people to actually work at home. Users also have utilized the technology to find recipes, play with games, enhance their education, and research topics.

The original IBM PC also spawned a great many other computers—some from IBM, but most from the makers of IBM-compatible computers—that make up the PC family. In fact, when I first wrote this book, it was actually called *Inside the IBM PC*, but the strong influence that companies other than IBM now exert on the PC industry inspired me to change the title a few years ago. The term *PC* is now universally used in the computer industry to refer to any IBM-compatible computer, and that's exactly how the term is used in this book.

I am excited and enthusiastic about the PC family; I want you to be, too. I want to lead you into understanding the workings of this marvelous machine and to share with you the excitement of knowing what it is, how it works, and what it can do. Armed with that knowledge, you'll be positioned to make intelligent decisions about computers for yourself, your family, or your company.

My Approach

If you know anything about me or the first edition of this book, you know that I made my reputation by explaining the technical wizardry of the PC. In the early days of the PC, that was what PC users needed most—an inside technical explanation of how the PC worked. The world of the PC has matured and changed since then—a lot—and so have the needs of mainstream PC users. I haven't changed my approach, however, and it occurs to me that you might want to know how I look at what I do.

From my perspective, the most useful approach to a subject such as this one has always been to assume that you, my reader, are an intelligent, curious, and productive person. That means that you'll never find me endlessly repeating elementary stuff, as though my books were "for dummies," and you're spared from all the dysfunctional oversimplification and condescension that such writing makes inevitable.

I like to write in the same way that I talk, and you might already know that my conversational approach was something of a novelty back when this book was first published. I don't mind saying that I'm proud to see my basic belief—that people can talk about technology like people, not like machines—has been adopted by hundreds of other writers, including my competitors. I think you'll intuitively agree that you'll learn more about your computer from "talking" with me about it than you would if I just handed you pages of technical lists and hieroglyphic diagrams and told you that the test will be on Wednesday. But, when this book premiered, that's exactly what most computer documentation was like.

Today, many companies have taken steps to empower everyday computer users to make many of their own decisions, to solve their own problems. You might not be employed by a large multilevel company—you might work in a small company, or be a student, retired, self-employed, or not employed at all—still, this book will lead you to the same power and enable you to make the same sorts of productivity jumps by giving you a personal, direct, and complete understanding of the essential technologies used in your PC.

About This Book

This isn't a book for people who are having trouble finding the on/off switch on their computers. Instead, it's for people who have some experience and the curiosity to begin examining these wonderful machines in greater depth. My goal is to make understanding the PC easy and fun.

This is, more than anything else, a book written to help you learn what you really need to know about the PC. You can successfully use a PC today without really understanding it. However, the better you understand your PC, the better equipped you are to realize its potential and—don't forget this—to deal with emergencies that almost certainly will arise. After all, when something goes wrong, the better you understand the machine, the more likely you are to make the right moves to fix the problem and reduce its adverse impact on you and your business.

Vitally important, too, in today's economy, is the realization that by understanding what goes on inside your PC, you'll be much better equipped to make intelligent decisions when it comes time to pull out the wallet. You won't end up paying for what you won't use, and you'll really minimize your risk of "driving home with an Edsel," when you can look at technological trends and understand where things are and where they're likely headed. With high technology, more than anything else, advances tend to antiquate much of what came before. Last year's innovation will probably be this year's low-end model, and in the grand scheme of things, I wouldn't want it any other way. For you and me personally, however, this type of evolution-by-replacement can make buying equipment extremely stressful. By the time you're finished here, you'll be in a strong position when it comes time to analyze all of your purchase options and make a purchase choice that will give you the most for your buck—the greatest longevity.

Finally, PCs are now an integral part of our lives. Children learn to use them in schools, at home, or at a public library. Even some very casual users now have "home pages" on the World Wide Web.

You might not see yourself becoming all that heavily invested in computing as a part of your life, but it certainly is an ever-increasing part of most of our lives, and it appears that computers will be even more at the core of our children's lives. Thus, to understand your PC is in a way to understand more fully the social and technical environment in which you live. That puts the contents of this book right up there in importance: on a par with that to be found in books on politics, economics, and the history of our civilization.

Why Change a Bestseller—For Readers of Previous Editions

If you already own a copy of a previous edition of *Peter Norton's Inside the PC*, some natural questions you'll be asking yourself are these: "Do I need yet another version of this book? What's new here that I want? And if I do buy this version, is there any reason to save the previous version(s) I have?" Here are my answers.

This book is unlike any previous edition of *Inside the PC*, except for the first two editions.

In some ways, it's true, this is an update from the eighth edition, so if you have carefully read that version you might recognize the occasional familiar passage. However, the world of computers—which includes you and me, of course—has changed dramatically. I might go so far as to say that it has changed *again*. Today's users—and the tools they regularly use—are more stratified than ever, simply because there's now too much for any one person to know it all.

This new edition reflects that evolution. It is a complete reorganization that, really, is closer to the first edition than it is to the recent seventh and eighth editions with which you might be more familiar. The original plan for this book, as I've said, was to take you, the reader, from where to are to where you want to be—giving you the understanding of your PC that you really need to get the most out of your hardware. This new edition reflects the fact that where you want to be depends on who you are, and what you need to know depends on where you are now. All of the content you've come to expect from *Inside the PC* is here, but I've sorted it out to make the experience of reading this book more useful and more enjoyable, whether you're a novice, advanced, or an expert reader.

PCs are not hackers' toys, nor merely programmer's tools. They have become nearly universal. That this has happened is no accident. Many companies have expended enormous effort trying to make PCs so easy to use that you won't have to think about how they do their jobs—you'll just use them.

Still, your effectiveness will increase with your understanding. The more savvy you are, the less likely you are to be taken in by unwarranted hype over the "latest and greatest" innovations. Also, having a sound understanding of the technologies equips you to have more influence on the companies that create all the new products, both hardware and software, that we all want to see made as useful as possible. These companies actually do listen quite carefully to the "end users" of their products—but they listen much more attentively when they think these customers actually understand what they are talking about, and aren't merely making the mistakes of the misinformed.

Acquiring that understanding now can be harder than ever. In part this is because there is so much more to know; and in part it is because some of the new ideas are so complex and arcane. However, I firmly believe that any intelligent person who wants to understand these topics can, if only they are willing to give them some focused attention, and if only someone—in this case me—is there to guide their learning.

Look at the Table of Contents. I've divided this one book as if it were actually three. The first book is called "The Glass Box." This name goes back to the first edition of *Inside the IBM PC*, when the real goal was to escort readers from thinking of the PC as a sealed "black box" to thinking of it as a glass box—one they could see into clearly and understand the inner workings. For beginners, this is still my goal. Book One will give you a solid grounding in the world of the different parts that make up PCs, the different types of PCs that exist, and the different technologies that can enhance your experience as a user.

Book Two, "Inside The PC" gets closer to the heart of the matter, taking you deeper into the core technologies that make your PC actually work.

Book Three has the somewhat circular name "Inside the Black Boxes in the Glass Box," but you'll see that name fits very well. This third section moves you towards an expert's understanding of the little "black boxes" like processors and memory chips and video accelerators that are the real heart of how your PC does what it does.

Throughout each book, you'll find references to the other books, showing you exactly where to look for information that is more—or less—advanced than what you're currently reading. This new organization means that you can use the book now in your hands in whatever way best serves your needs. If you're starting out, you can begin on page one and read straight through. At each level you'll gain an understanding built on what you've already read—and you don't have the rather unpleasant experience of suddenly finding a highly technical—or fundamental—discussion interrupting the flow of the text. It makes no sense to explain, for example, that memory chips exist, and then discuss their operation on a subatomic level, and then go back to mentioning that they happen to be distributed on plastic cards that are usually green. Such a thing can make new users feel like they've stumbled into a tedious physics lecture while, at the same time, making expert readers frustrated with the need to read hundreds of pages to find what they really want. In fact, if you're an advanced user, you can turn directly to Book Two or Book Three and get to work. If you come across something that sounds foreign, you'll find references back to pages in the earlier Books. You can jump, quickly come up to speed, and then get back to the original discussion. I hope you'll find that all of this makes getting inside the PC a fulfilling experience.

New Topics, New Angles

There is a tremendous amount of new material in this edition. I explore portable and hand-held PCs and PDAs in depth for the first time. Wireless networking—a technology that barely existed when I wrote the previous edition—gets almost its own chapter. In fact, I help you explore all manner of networking topics in a way I've never done; these technologies have matured from being excursions to being essentials. The same is true of other new technologies which you'll find here for the first time: recordable DVDs, DSL and other broadband connections, and on and on.

Much has changed in the two years since the previous edition was published. Some of it was predictable, and some of it—as you'd probably expect—has caused things that would be "available in ten years" to be in your hands today. So, this new edition is a complete update. What you'll now find here will serve you well today and into tomorrow. Again, welcome!

Navigation Aids for Your Journey

Some people think they'll get lost in a book as big as this one. Well now, I wouldn't want that to happen. So I've made sure you have plenty of ways to keep the big picture in view, and to find each nook or cranny that especially interests you.

I've already talked about the new way this edition is organized. You'll see that new structure reflected in the table of contents. The Table of Contents is also the first place to look if you want information on a specific topic. Or, if you want to find something very specific, check the index. That is an especially good way to find something when you remember reading it, but can't recall where in the book you found it.

The glossary, which was reintroduced in the previous edition, is still here, dramatically expanded to cover the new technologies you'll find throughout the whole book. I've tried to give you a very concise definition of each term.

Technical Note: Technical asides are handled somewhat differently here than what you might be used to from previous editions. They're still detailed, technical information—the "real goodies," you might say. But Technical Notes have been written so that they now reflect the tone of the discussion in which they appear. Just look for paragraphs that look like this one, with this icon beside them.

Tip: Looking for some hot tips? I have them in here, too. This is how they will appear in the body of the book.

Note: Some times I have a note flagged in the manner of this paragraph. These are not necessarily technical points, nor are they asides. They are just something I found—well—noteworthy.

Warning: Speaking of tripping up, there are some important cautionary notes. These are warnings help you avoid hurting yourself, your PC, or your data. Please read them carefully, also, and follow them every time they apply. You'll be glad you did.

Peter's Principle

Finally, there are a number of what I hope are useful ideas scattered through the text. These are discoveries I have made that I want to share with you—the fruits of my experimentation that might when shared in this manner save you some painful learning experiences.

PART I

The Glass Box

1

The Desktop PC

Welcome to the first stop in your adventure inside the PC! You might have noticed that this first section of the book is called "The Glass Box." This is an idea of mine that originated from the first edition of this book. It seemed to me that mainstream PC users and business people were unable to get the most out of their computers because they fundamentally didn't understand them. PCs were, essentially, "black boxes," with all sorts of equipment and components hidden away inside. Who knew what they did? Who knew how to do anything to maximize their performance? Who knew whether that black box contained all sorts of expensive options, which might never be used?

The answers to those questions, I thought, and I think, should be "anyone who wants to know." But, like the black boxes in commercial airplanes, PCs were viewed as sealed environments. Woe to anyone who should dare lift a screwdriver and peer inside!

And so I wanted to write about the PC—about what's inside the PC—in such a way that anyone who wanted to know could know about and actually understand everything that happens inside the box. My goal then, and now, is to change the black box into a glass box, with all of the PC's innards exposed and laid bare.

Presumably, because you're holding this book today, you are someone who wants to know. Perhaps you're tired of spending money on features you never use, or tired of chasing the latest techno-trends only to find you were directed—perhaps by individuals meaning well—into a dead end. Perhaps you've simply got an exciting curiosity to understand the tools you use. There are a myriad reasons why you might want to really "see" inside the PC. Whatever the reasons you're here, they're why I'm here, too. Together, we'll take a journey that will empower you to make the best PC-related decisions for yourself, your family, your business, or your corporation.

PCs come in a huge variety of shapes and sizes, and have many levels of capability. You'll start your journey by taking a look inside the most common configuration: the desktop PC. From there you'll go on to look at other popular styles of overall systems, like portables and handheld PCs. In effect, you'll start outside the glass box, looking in. Then you'll actually step inside the glass box—inside the PC—and take an ever-closer look at what makes it all work.

The Three Main Parts

A desktop PC is actually made up of three main parts. And here I'm talking about parts that can be internal or external. Strictly speaking, the average desktop PC would have to be called three black boxes. First, of course, is the system unit. That's what we all think of when we say "the PC" or "the computer." Second is the display. Third is what I'll call input, but that you can think of as the keyboard and mouse, or some other pointer. These three systems make up the minimum hardware needed for what is called a PC. Even a handheld or palm-sized device has these three parts, although they are found in one box in that case. (You can buy desktop PCs, too, in which all three parts are found in one or two external cases.)

Because most people think of the system unit as the PC, it's good to take a look at what's inside it first.

> **Caution:** If you want to open your PC and actually look inside as you read through this chapter, I think that's a great idea. Before you do, you might want to take a look at Chapter 5, which gives you a quick but complete introduction to the issue of safety—both for you and your PC—when it comes time to open the system unit case.

The System Unit

When you think about a PC, it's probably the system unit you're thinking about, for the most part. People talk about upgrading their computers, but sometimes only that one box shows any changes. And although the display and the input hardware are absolutely part of any PC, the system unit really is "the computer."

What's In Here—The Five Systems in a PC

What's inside the system unit is just about everything that does what you bought a PC to do. (For the moment I'll ignore external devices and peripherals. You'll take a look at all of them later in the book.) But what really is inside the PC?

In fact, there are five major systems inside the system unit. Although each of these five systems functions as a complete subsystem of the PC, none of them is worth anything on its own. As you'll see, they work together to create, collectively, the PC.

Let's take a look at each of these five systems. In case you didn't read the introduction, I'll mention here again that what you'll find in this chapter—indeed, in this first section of the book—is introductory material. You'll see what's inside your PC without getting too far into how it all works. As you move to the second and third sections of the book, you'll get an ever-deeper understanding of these systems, their parts and components, and how they interact on your behalf. That said, the five systems inside a PC are the logic system, the display system, the storage system, the input/output system, and the communications system.

The Logic System

As anyone who's spent any time working with a PC will tell you that "logic" on a PC isn't the same as human logic. Logic, in the sense of philosophy, is only indirectly related to a PC. The term "logic" refers to the major circuitry inside a PC because that circuitry often evaluates whether certain things are true or false. What sorts of things? Well, whether an electrical circuit is completed in a certain way, and so forth. Or, more often, whether certain collections of circuits are completed whereas certain others are not. The logic in your system's circuitry can also make certain types of analyses and then act on them. For example, "if this is true, then do that," or "if this is true and that is false, then do the other." All of this is called *Boolean logic*, and it can get pretty complex. Consider:

IF ((X AND Y) AND (NOT Z) AND (Y AND NOT W)) THEN DO A

And that's really a simple example. These sorts of analyses—which are called *logical evaluations*—are completed by the circuitry in the PC's logic system billions of times each second. Those evaluations make your computer compute. Underneath Microsoft Word and Quake III is an endless parade of AND NOT NAND NOR OR IF and THEN.

For the moment, you don't need to know anything more about a PC's logic than that. The question this section wants to explore now is: Which major parts of the PC actually perform and facilitate those endless billions of evaluations?

The logic system is actually comprised of five main parts.

The Motherboard

The first part of the logic system is the PC's motherboard. It's the large, usually green, piece of plastic that's covered with copper lines (they're called *traces*, by the way) and that has most of the PC's chips, sockets, and connections soldered to it. The copper traces connect the components and systems on the motherboard to each other. In the following sections, you'll be introduced to all of these components.

Unless your PC is more than three or four years old, your motherboard—although it might be made by any one of several manufacturers—is almost surely a "plug-and-play" compliant motherboard. What that means is that your motherboard was designed to support the industry standard called "plug and play", which is a set of rules governing how different pieces of hardware should interact with the motherboard and with other pieces of hardware. (By the way, a *standard* is a set of rules regarding some aspect of the PC that all major manufacturers agree to live by.)

Before plug and play existed, each manufacturer determined how its products would work, and it was very common for many products to be incompatible. That really limited the consumer's choices and it made the PC harder to configure and use. Plug and play wasn't a panacea, but it has definitely moved things along the right path. Today, it's most likely that you can use whatever brand of video card you like in conjunction with any modem, sound card, or network card...and so forth.

The support for this flexibility and freedom has to exist in the devices themselves, in the operating system, and in the software that controls the motherboard (which I'll talk about in a moment.) For the time being, let's continue looking at the motherboard.

As I said, the motherboard is the PC's backbone—the part of the PC that everything branches from and connects to, usually directly, but sometimes indirectly (as in the case of USB or SCSI devices, which you'll read about later in this book.) The motherboard is also responsible for maintaining the basic settings necessary to keep the PC working. Thanks to plug and play, most of your PC's settings are established and confirmed while your PC is starting up. But there are some settings that are more basic, and that need to be maintained differently. These are controlled in two ways: in hardware and in software.

Hardware today is, for the most part, plug-and-play compliant. That means that it has flexibility in terms of how it works with the PC as a whole and can be set in a number of ways during the startup (or *boot*) process, depending on the other hardware you have installed. There is of course older hardware that doesn't comply in this way, and there are still other aspects of your PC—like the speed of your main processor, as one example— that usually never change, and that needs to be set the moment you turn on the power. To maintain these sorts of settings, your motherboard often has *jumpers* and *jumper wires* on it.

Jumpers

Jumper wires look like two or more comparatively long, straight wires that stick up directly from the motherboard. By completing a circuit between certain of these wires (or *pins*, if you prefer), certain settings are made and maintained. You complete this sort of circuit by using a small, rectangular connector called a *jumper*. When a jumper is properly seated on two pins, a piece of copper inside the jumper completes that circuit (and the circuit is *closed*.) This will, as I said, determine features like the speed of your main processor, or how fast your main memory operates.

If there is no jumper between a set of pins, the circuit is *open*, and the motherboard interprets that situation as representing a different setting. For example, a jumper over a specific set of two pins might mean that your main system bus runs at 66MHz, whereas the absence of that jumper—or a jumper between other pins—might mean the bus runs at 133MHz. (Don't worry about these terms for now. What's important is that you understand that the speeds of key pieces of hardware are sometimes set using hardware jumpers.)

BIOS

Although jumpers are still used for specific tasks, it's more common today that the majority of your PC's basic settings are maintained in software. That software is part of a system called the BIOS (Basic Input Output System), and those settings are stored in a special type of memory, called CMOS or FlashMemory, all of which you'll read about later in the book. These special types of memory allow your PC's configuration settings to be maintained even when the system is off or even unplugged. The BIOS performs many jobs, but among them are keeping track of how many drives your PC has, what type and size they are, and how they're installed. The BIOS settings also commonly include fundamental information like how many of each type of external port (or connector) your PC has, and whether you're using certain types of older hardware that need to be treated with kid gloves.

A small program (also part of the BIOS) called the *BIOS setup* lets you view and modify these settings. They're then saved and maintained until you change them again (or change the hardware in such a way that these settings automatically update themselves.) Every system is different, but many systems allow you to access the BIOS Setup program by pressing the Delete or F2 keys right after you power up your PC.

Main Processor

Central to your PC, although not usually physically "central" to your motherboard, is the *CPU* or *Central Processing Unit*. This is the Pentium III, Pentium IV, Athlon, or whatever main processor your PC uses to perform the tasks you ask of it, from running Windows or Linux to sending e-mail or composing music. The main processor even runs the programs stored in the BIOS—which is why your processor speed often can't be maintained in that software. The CPU needs to know how to run so that it can get to the BIOS settings and work with them.

Technically, the main processor isn't part of the motherboard, although the socket that the CPU sits in is. CPUs connect to motherboards in a variety of ways, depending on the model. In the main, this socket is called a *ZIF* or *Zero Insertion Force* socket. That means that it takes no pressure to get the hundreds of pins on the bottom of the CPU chip to drop down into the socket. Once the CPU is properly seated, a lever at the side of the socket moves the socket's electrical connectors into place. These bind against the CPU pins and lock it down.

Memory

In order for your PC to be able to do anything, it takes more than just a CPU. The PC needs room to work, if you will: Room to store the programs it runs and room to store your information while you're manipulating it. That room is provided by *memory* chips, which are also plugged into their own type of socket on the motherboard. Memory chips have evolved a lot since the first PCs, in which they were usually permanently soldered directly to the motherboard. Today there are several types of memory that perform their jobs at a variety of speeds and in a variety of ways, all of which you'll read about later in the book. Regardless of these types, most memory today is physically packed in what are called *DIMMs* or *Dual In-line Memory Modules*.

DIMMs are small cards that consist of several memory chips, all wired together. Connectors on both sides of the bottom edge of the card complete the link between the memory sockets on the motherboard and the memory modules.

The memory that I'm speaking of now is called *main memory*, because it's where most of your PC's work is kept while it's working. Main memory, unlike the BIOS's memory, is emptied and erased when you turn your PC off. That's why you lose work you haven't saved if you suffer a power outage. So why not use memory like the BIOS's CMOS or FlashMemory for all the memory in the PC? Because that type of memory is extremely expensive. Also, that type of memory was designed to maintain its contents—not for rapid-fire performance. The newest types of chips used for main memory focus on providing the best possible performance and reliability. So there are different types of memory in your PC, all of which are used for different purposes, as you'll read about later. (There is also *video memory,* which is usually connected to a graphics card that plugs in to the motherboard. This memory is extremely fast and is dedicated to supporting your PC's display needs.)

The Bus

The final major component of your PC's logic system is the *bus*. According to one writer, the term is a derivative of the Latin word *omnibus*, which means "for all purposes." Whether that was the original source or not, it's certainly plausible, because the system bus is the structure on the motherboard that connects everything together.

In fact, there are many buses in every PC and on every motherboard, and you'll read about all of these in the different parts of this book. One of the two most important buses in a PC is the *system* bus, which is the connection between the main processor and main memory. But what's generally being talked about when you hear people saying, "the PC's bus" is the set of components and connectors that make it possible to install hard disks, optical drives, and plug-in cards into the main system unit.

The earliest bus of this type was called the *ISA (Industry Standard Architecture)* bus. This was later augmented into what's known as the *EISA (Extended ISA)* bus. Your hard drives and DVD connect to the EISA bus through dedicated connectors that support their IDE electronics. Your PC might also have one or more sockets or *slots* into which you can plug EISA-compliant cards that provide new capabilities for your PC, like an internal modem or network card.

As components got faster and faster, the EISA bus became a bottleneck to improved performance. The *PCI (Peripheral Component Interconnect)* bus was the solution to that problem, and it remains the bus of choice in today's PCs. PCI is a major improvement over EISA in that it operates much faster, can work with more bits of data simultaneously, and is designed to support the needs of plug and play. PCI also provides a direct connection to main memory for the devices that are plugged into it, further enhancing overall performance.

Closely related to the PCI bus is the *AGP or Advanced Graphics Port*. This is a somewhat recent development that provides excellent performance potential for the next system inside your PC, the display system.

The Display System

The display system consists of all the circuitry and connections that make it possible for your PC to produce visual output. In other words, it makes the screen work. The screen is of course part of the display system, regardless of what type of screen it is. PCs today commonly use either CRT (cathode ray tube) monitors—which are glorified television sets—or some type of flat display, usually LCD (liquid crystal diode) like those used in notebook PCs and handhelds. You'll read about all the types of displays later in the book, as well as get a detailed understanding of how the display system produces the images you see.

The display system consists of a video card, now more commonly called a *graphics adapter* or *graphics accelerator*. In order for such a card to perform optimally, it will almost always now be designed to plug into an AGP slot. The AGP slot provides a direct, high-speed connection between the graphics accelerator, the main memory, and the main CPU. This connection makes it possible for the graphics accelerator to use main memory, rather than memory located on it, to store and manipulate graphic images. This allows for the storage and use of a very large number of complex graphical textures that are key to producing realistic 3D images. AGP's direct connection also makes it possible for the PC to support *streaming video*. Streaming video refers to a video signal coming off of the Internet or a disk in a continuous manner (like a stream of flowing water.) In order to display that kind of imagery so that it doesn't appear to skip, jump, or flicker, the PC needs to be able to handle the streaming data very, very quickly. The direct, isolated connection between an AGP video card and main memory makes that possible.

The latest version of AGP, still under development, is known as AGP 3.0 or AGP8x. This forthcoming version will provide dramatically accelerated performance over existing versions of AGP, and will also eliminate obsolete features. That last factor should lead to a more powerful, less expensive graphics accelerator.

Before AGP was developed, all video cards were supported by one of the other buses, either PCI, ISA, or the VESA local bus, which was a precursor of PCI. PCI graphics accelerators are still available, but market forces have recently made them more expensive to buy than the better-performing AGP cards, because ever fewer consumers are buying them. It's likely that PCI display adapters will be a *legacy item* (that's PC jargon for "obsolete") by 2002.

The Storage System

Neither the logic system nor the display system are worth much if there's no way to store your work, whether it's still work-in-progress or the final job. Main memory can't be used for this purpose because it's too expensive to buy in large enough quantities, and because all of your work disappears if the power fails.

The solution to that problem, originally, was magnetic tape. The same sort of electrical signals used to store audio were adapted to store the digital content needed for computing. The greatest limitation of tape, of course, is that you have to fast forward and rewind it to get to the data you need. This type of storage is called *sequential access*, because you can't just jump directly to any spot on the tape, one bit of information after another. To say that this method is slow is an understatement.

And so the idea came about that magnetic material could be formed onto the surfaces of either hard platters or floppy plastic, and the data stored on them could be accessed on demand. With the right way of reading and writing, you could jump directly, even randomly, to any piece of information you wanted. And so disks as a whole are a type of *random access storage*. Different types of disks evolved to meet different needs. For the most part, all of these attach to the PC through one of the available buses. The ISA (EISA) bus is the most common way. (Most hard drives and optical drives are also known as IDE or ATA drives, and ATA evolved as a way to connect to the original ISA bus, as you'll read in later chapters.) It's also possible for drives to connect via the USB, SCSI, or IEEE 1394 serial buses.

Hard Disks

The first type of disks to come into existence were what are now called hard disks— an accurate, if not too creative name. Essentially, the magnetic material that stores information is fused onto the surface of a hard metal platter. Several of these are bound together on the same central spindle, which spins them very rapidly. (Hard disks today spin at speeds from 5400 RPM up to over 10000 RPM.) Very small recording and play-back heads—not unlike those used in tape machines—are mounted on metal levers and float above the disk platters. As the ability to store more and more information on a disk increased, the size of these units shrunk. The first disks had a diameter of over 14 inches. Today's IBM Microdrive packs 1GB of data on a drive with a one-inch diameter. You'll read about how hard drives work in detail later. Fundamentally, however, they're used to store data for the long haul, but to keep that data quickly accessible. (Tape is still commonly used to archive data that will not need to be retrieved quickly or often.)

Floppy Disks

The second major development in disks was the floppy disk. In fact, floppy disks, or floppies, were around in the PC world before hard disks, but the hard disk was the first disk storage ever developed (for mainframes.) You couldn't even get an original IBM PC with a hard disk. It came, instead, with one or two floppy disk drives.

Floppy disks use the same basic principle of storing data as hard disks do, but they do so at lower capacity, speed, and cost. Instead of using hard platters, the magnetic material is fused on flexible plastic sheets, which give the floppy disk its name. Floppy disks have the added advantage of being portable and more durable than hard disks, which, even today, generally break if you drop them on the ground.

CD-ROM

The CD-ROM was the first type of optical disk to be developed for use with PCs. Unlike hard disks and floppies, which store data through the use of magnetic impulses, CD-ROMs store data by using a laser to read patterns of bumps and pits pressed into the disk's metal component. (This is sealed inside plastic to make it durable and prevent oxidation of the metal.) CD-ROMs are, in fact, made in much the same way that old vinyl LP records were made: a master disk is struck and its data (pits and bumps, called *lands*, instead of a wavering groove) is pressed into the raw material for new disks. CD-ROM drives originally had a maximum speed of reading 150,000 bytes of data per second. The first increase in speed was by a factor of two, so those 300k/second CD-ROMs were called 2x. Nowadays, it's common to see 52x CD-ROM drives, which have a maximum potential of 7,800,000 bytes/second.

CD-R and CD-RW

Not long after the CD-ROM was introduced, the market began to clamor for a CD that was writable. The first of these was the CD-R ("R" for "recordable"), which can store 640MB (megabytes, or millions of bytes) of data. These disks can be written to only once. This involves a process that you'll read about at length later in the book.

After CD-R became common, demand for a CD that could be written to many times, and even erased, led to the CD-RW ("RW" for "re-writable".) These disks have the same capacity as their read-only or recordable namesakes, but writing and rewriting speeds are generally still limited to 12x, with 4x still being the most common rewriting speed.

DVD

The latest type of disk storage is the DVD. As you'll read later in the book, DVDs now come in several varieties, all in a number of competing, incompatible formats. This includes read-only DVDs, like the video movies you can purchase, as well as recordable and rewritable DVDs. These have a capacity as high as 4.7GB (gigabytes, billions of bytes) per side.

The Input/Output System

Naturally, none of these systems for manipulating, viewing, or storing data is of any use if you can't get data into the PC. As it happens, a dedicated system handles that sort of thing, too. The input/output system consists of first the PC's keyboard and mouse, because those are the main tools you use to get data and commands into the PC. It also includes the PC's primary communications ports and buses. This means that the printer, or parallel port, the serial ports, and the entire USB subsystem are also part of your PC's input/output system.

Keyboard and Mouse

Even if you're new to using a PC, it will be no surprise to you that keyboards and mice are the basic ways users interact with their computers. This terminology is part of the general culture, and even people who *never* use computers usually understand what's up when they walk into the middle of a conversation and hear, "... but the mouse wasn't responding, so I couldn't select the right text." You'll learn all you might want to know about these pieces of hardware later in the book. For the moment, just be aware that the functions they perform are part of a larger whole, all of which makes it possible to interact with your PC.

Parallel Port

The parallel port has changed a number of times over the years, but it still primarily serves its original purpose: to provide a connection between your PC and your printer. As you'll read later in the book, the term *parallel* refers to the fact that data is moved through the port across a number of parallel connections, so that entire bytes move at one time, rather than the parts that make up a byte (which are called *bits*) being moved sequentially, or serially, one after another, until an entire byte has been transferred.

The first parallel ports were useful for sending data only one way—to the printer. After all, printers are used exclusively for output, right? Well, as time passed, it turned out that this was a shortsighted view. It has proved very useful to have the parallel port evolve bi-directional capabilities, so that a printer can send status messages—things like "Hello! I'm out of paper!"—back to the PC and its user.

The bi-directional parallel port also opened up a whole other world of capabilities because it became possible to make hard drives or other storage devices that could connect to a PC externally via the parallel port. This provided a simple connection that was much faster than the other external connections available on PCs at the time. Implementing a parallel port interface was quite inexpensive, so with factors of ease, performance, and cost coming together, how could it fail?

In fact, it failed on a number of grounds. First, a parallel cable is thick and heavy. Small tape storage units sold for performing inexpensive backups were literally dragged off the desk by the weight of the cable that connected them to the PC. Second, each manufacturer came up with its own set of instructions and commands for interacting with these external devices. Consequently, some of these devices were incompatible —which made claims that you could chain them together rather fruitlessly. Worse, many of these devices were incompatible with the printers with which they shared the parallel port. All of this made using parallel-port peripherals about as convenient as, say, having to shut down your PC and rewire everything before backing up, and then repeating the process so you could print a letter.

Serial Port

The second major part of the PC's input/output system is the serial port. Most PCs come with two, actually, and these are most often used for connecting an external modem (which allows a PC to connect to remote systems across a normal telephone line.) Another major use for serial ports has been to connect a mouse to a PC. Unlike parallel ports, serial ports move their data one bit at a time across as little as one wire (plus a ground wire.) This is slower than a parallel port, but it's also cheaper and uses a much smaller, lighter cable.

Because of its dismal performance, the serial port has never been used to attach peripherals like storage devices. In fact, it hasn't been useful for much other than connecting the most rudimentary of hardware. But, because serial hardware is so much less expensive than parallel, and because a parallel cable is such a pain to use, it was natural that a high-performance serial port would evolve.

USB and IEEE 1394

In fact, two high-performance serial systems have evolved. They are the Universal Serial Bus (USB) and IEEE 1394, or FireWire. You'll encounter these in depth soon. They provide a high-speed way for data to move serially in and out of the PC. USB makes it possible to connect a huge range of equipment, from external drives to modems, to network interfaces, to specialty video devices, as well as mice and keyboards. If you want to connect more USB devices than you have USB ports, you simply add a small box called a *hub,* which has many USB ports on it, each of which supports more devices or even another hub.

IEEE 1394, which Apple Computer calls FireWire, is also a high-speed serial system. It doesn't use hubs, but allows you to connect many devices together, one after another, in a chain. Unlike the chaining together of parallel devices you read about a few moments ago, all IEEE 1394 peripherals must comply with a set standard that determines how they can operate and inter-operate. You don't have any worries about one box not liking another, or end up having to reboot over and over.

In fact, almost all USB and IEEE 1394 peripherals are *hot swappable*, which means that you can plug and unplug them at will without turning off the PC or rebooting. This is tremendously useful. The only question about the whole affair is why did it take so long to come into being?

The Communications System

The last of the five big systems inside your PC actually overlaps with the input/output system in a lot of ways. That probably doesn't surprise you, because people commonly think of input and output as a way of "communicating" with the PC, and the name of this last system is the communications system.

Strictly speaking, the type of communications I'm talking about here are not between you and the PC. I'm thinking more about the ways your PC is able to communicate and share information with other PCs and other users. The two primary ways that happens is through the use of modems and network interfaces.

Modems

I've already mentioned modems. They allow you to connect to remote PCs or networks (like the Internet) over a standard phone line. You'll learn all about how they work and what their strengths and limitations are. For the most part, they're usually serial devices (that is, they connect to the PC either through a serial port or the USB system.) They can be housed in external boxes or they can be a card inside the PC.

If your modem is on an internal card or on the motherboard (which does happen), it generally creates its own serial port that functions in addition to the physical connectors that can connect your PC with the outside world. For example, you might have a serial mouse on the first of two physical serial ports and a label maker on the second physical port. Just because you've used both of your serial ports doesn't mean you can't install a modem in your PC. The software that controls the modem almost always works in conjunction with Windows by establishing a third serial "port" that the new modem uses all for itself. Because modems use serial ports, this system and the I/O system really do cross over.

Regardless of how it connects, your modem takes the digital information you want to send to a remote location and converts it into sound impulses. These impulses are transmitted across the telephone lines. It also listens for data coming in, in the form of other sound impulses, and it translates those back into data for you. The infamous "squealing" you hear when your modem connects is just those sounds transmitted through a built-in speaker (mostly so you know the modem is working.) Once the connection is established—thankfully—the speaker turns off and the modem works silently. (And you can configure almost any modem to work silently all the time, too.)

Network Interfaces

Network interfaces are the second major way for your PC to connect to the outside world. As you'll read in Chapter 11, "Networking: Wired and Wireless," there are quite a few types of networks and different ways for data to be sent across them. The bottom line: A network is a collection of PC and other computers connected either by wires or wirelessly. This connection allows users to move data from one location to another. That data can be Web pages you're viewing off the Internet, or it can be e-mail you're sending. It can also be high-quality video conferencing with pictures and sound, or it can be documents you work on while you telecommute from home.

Network connections have traditionally been faster than serial connections, but they've been more expensive and complex to implement, too. With consumer demand for high-speed (*broadband*) access to the Internet—which, after all, is just a gigantic network—

those factors have recently changed a lot. Even small homes often have a small network established between rooms and most major printers come with a network connection as a standard option. That type of connection makes it easy for anyone on the network to make use of the printer without interfering with anyone else's work.

The Five Systems as a Whole

In truth, it's not just the input/output and communications systems that overlap. All of these five systems work together inside the system unit to provide the total computing experience that you expect and need.

In addition to the system unit, there are two other main parts that make up your PC. Let's take a quick look at them, and then move directly on to getting a deeper understanding of this exciting world.

The Display

Whether your monitor is a CRT or an LCD, and whether you know how it works or not, you likely understand that the display makes it possible for you to see what's happening inside the PC. We're a very visual species, and it seems inevitable that the display will remain the main tool we use to understand and benefit from what computers can do.

Not too many years back, computers didn't have displays. Instead, they had flashing lights and teletype printers that spewed out endless reams of paper, printing hardcopy of every bit of the PC's output and our input. It was a costly, unreliable way of doing things, and the CRT, or cathode ray tube, became part of computing just about as fast as it was embraced for entertainment through television. Because that's really all a computer's CRT is: a glorified television. Just was with a TV, a beam of electrons causes phosphor on the inside of the glass tube to glow, effectively "painting" a picture of what the PC is doing.

The other major technology used to make a PC display is LCD, or liquid crystal diodes. You've probably seen LCD watches all over the place, in which an electrical signal from the watch causes little black numbers to display the time. An LCD display is much the same system, on a grand scale. Electrical signals from the PC's display adapter (or graphics accelerator) cause the liquid inside an LCD flat panel display to arrange itself in such a way that a light, shining through the liquid from behind, presents a full-color image of what you would otherwise see on a CRT.

You'll read lots about CRTs and LCD panels. Each has its advantages. CRTs are a lot cheaper, without question, but LCD panels present a much clearer image. CRT's are great for showing full-motion video, but take up a huge amount of desk space. LCD's are small, light, and very energy efficient, but, at least until very recently, have been less than satisfactory for viewing video.

Input Devices

The third main part of your overall PC is the collection of input devices that make it possible to interact with the computer. Earlier, I talked about the input/output system that works inside the system unit. This section discusses your keyboard, mouse, and other devices such as joysticks, trackballs, graphics tablets, touch-screens, and so forth—all of which give you a way of getting the PC's attention, telling it what you need done, and providing it with the data it needs to accomplish those tasks.

As you'll see, keyboards and mice come in many types and sizes. There are 104- and 101-key keyboards that come with most new PCs and that most folks use. There are also weird, spread-apart keyboards that are designed to cut down on repetitive stress injuries that come from typing all day, every day.

Mice are responsible for moving the pointer around on the screen, so that you can take full advantage of Windows' graphical environment. Rather than memorizing and typing commands to get work done, you can just point with the mouse to a graphic representation of some tool you want to use, and then do whatever you need to do. You can select commands from graphical menus, again by pointing and clicking one of the buttons on the mouse. You can use the mouse to draw, as though you were using a pen on paper, or to select text you want to format or move.

A mouse might work by using a mechanical system, or an optical one, and you'll learn about both.

Inside the PC

Believe it or not, if you've read these first pages, you've really glimpsed most of what is inside the PC. Every PC, no matter how slow or fast, humble or powerful, mammoth or portable, has these three main parts, and the same five systems working together inside the main unit. Depending on your configuration, all three parts might be inside the same case, but all the parts are there, nevertheless.

Certain types of PCs do have their own unique characteristics, though. So, before delving deeply into how processors work and how hard drives store data, you need to take a look at the two special-case (pun intended) situations in which the pieces and parts that make up your PC might seem very different. In the next chapter, you'll take a look at notebook and laptop PCs. Chapter 3 introduces you to the variety of handheld and palm-sized devices that might not seem like PCs, but really are. Finally, Chapter 4 gives you a sound introduction to how all computers actually work. With that under your belt, you'll be ready to tackle the rest of everything I have to offer here.

Once again, welcome! You're well on your way to getting the most out of your PC by really understanding what's happening inside.

2

Portable PCs

Your intuition probably tells you that what makes a PC effective on the road, in the air, or at a trade show is considerably different than what you look for in a basic office or home desktop unit. With the exception of some new best-of-both-worlds systems, you'd be right. Of course, taking a desktop PC from one location to another has always been possible, but it certainly isn't a convenient thing to do. You can use an ordinary desktop PC only when it and its display are set up somewhere, with all the pieces attached and plugged into a live wall socket supplying appropriate AC.

As a result, there has long been a need for a special kind of PC—one that can be moved from one place to another conveniently, and for some uses, it must also be able to operate wherever it is located, without needing any outside source of power. These are called *mobile PCs*.

From Luggables to Laptops and Beyond

The first PCs were exclusively desktop machines. They had at least three parts: a system unit, a keyboard, and a monitor. Early PC users who needed to use the PC in more than one location either got more than one machine (and carried their data back and forth on floppy disks) or went through the inconvenience of taking their 50-plus pound PC with them from location to location, enduring the effort of setting up the PC in each new place.

Luggables

Some manufacturers, including IBM, realized early on that the portable PC market was viable. The first of these so-called portables were single-box units. They included the keyboard, the display, and all the system unit pieces in one handle-equipped case. They were about the size and weight of a sewing machine, so one rather strong person could lift them—although no one would want to lift and carry them far. Once you arrived at your workplace, all you had to do to get to work was open the lid—which often contained the keyboard—and plug in the power.

The early manufacturers called these machines *portable*, but folks now refer to them as *luggable* to emphasize the fact that you certainly wouldn't choose to carry this type of load around if there was any easier way to get the job done.

True Portables

Technology itself limited the development of true portables. The state-of-the-art electronic circuitry was insufficient to produce the lightweight components required. When it became possible to make really compact circuitry that contained the necessary functionality, the first true portables emerged.

These early portables were heavy and bulky by today's standards, and carrying them all day was no fun—not all that much better than the earlier *luggables*. But many people, including me, did just that because it was the best way to get PC computing capability on the go.

These portable machines had one important thing that the luggable PCs never had: a rechargeable battery. This meant that not only could you take your PC to your destination and plug it in and use it there, you could even use your portable PC en route—for a short time, at least.

Early battery-powered PCs could only operate for a short time before their batteries needed recharging. Later models got better and better, and today's best units perform quite impressively. But the issue of battery life between charges remains a key feature that distinguishes competitors in the market.

Laptop PCs and Our Dell Inspiron 8100 Example

Miniaturization hasn't stopped, of course. If anything, its rate has accelerated. The second generation of portable computers were small enough to rest comfortably on your lap while being used—the appellation *laptop* was born.

Today, laptops are the most common type of mobile PC. These machines are small enough and light enough (about four pounds) to be carried easily, yet they essentially can be as powerful as a good desktop PC. (They aren't so small or light that you can just stuff them into a purse or pocket, but they will fit inside a briefcase or attaché case, or a similar sized computer case.)

These machines are typically about the size of a piece of letterhead (8.5 by 11 inches), and perhaps one to two inches thick. In fact, these are sometimes called *notebook* computers because of their similarity in size to a student's paper-filled binder. There are several reasons why this size has evolved as the more-or-less standard size of a laptop PC. There are two good reasons for not making machines smaller than this size. One is to ensure that the keyboard is large enough to use comfortably and naturally. The second is to make the screen the same size as a desktop monitor.

This size is the best compromise between an adequate-size keyboard and readable screen, yet still small enough to carry easily. Still, there are many smaller mobile PCs being made. You'll look at them in a moment.

Figure 2.1 shows a Dell Inspiron 8100 portable computer. This is effectively the state–of–the-art in 2001. (If any of the terms you're about to encounter are confusing, don't worry. You'll find each of them defined very briefly in the Glossary at the end of this book, and you'll also find detailed discussions of the technologies they represent elsewhere in this book. I've included references in the text so you can learn more about each of these technologies.) I'm going to talk about an example unit's features at some length because they are indicative of the capabilities you'll find in today's mobile PCs.

This unit (on which most of this book was written, incidentally) has a 1.13GHz mobile Pentium III processor, a 15 inch (diagonal measurement) 1600x1200 pixel active matrix screen (with an nVidia GeForce2 Go 4X AGP graphics processor), 32MB of DDR video memory, 128MB of PC133 RAM, a 48GB ATA-100 hard disk, a floppy disk drive, and a DVD drive (which can play DVD movies, read DVD-ROM discs, and also read CD-ROMs and audio CDs)—all that and battery power, too! It has built-in standard serial, parallel, S-video, IEEE 1394a and IrDA ports, two USB ports, plus two PC Card slots (both of which support CardBus and one of which also offers Zoomed video support.) It has an internal V.90 modem, and built-in support for 10/100 Ethernet networking. It contains built-in Harmon Kardon stereo speakers and a microphone. It can even output digital audio in the S/PDIF format.

Figure 2.1 shows the laptop with its top open. The first callout points to one of the two included pointing devices (a touchpad) with two large buttons below it. This laptop also has a DualPoint pointing stick which functions simultaneously with the touchpad, so it's easy to use whichever device satisfies you best. Note the DVD-ROM, located on the left side of the machine, and the floppy disk drive, installed in the notebook's front media bay. In the case of this notebook, the DVD drive can instead be a combination DVD and CD-RW (CD recording) drive, or simply a CD-RW. (You'll learn all about DVD and recordable CD technology in Chapter 8, "Removable Storage".)

Figure 2.2 shows a close-up view of the back side of the Dell notebook. Here you can see, beginning at the left, the twin *fans* that are the center of a unique heat-management system that Dell calls HyperCool. Effectively, the system acts like a radiator for the notebook— most particularly for its super-fast CPU, which generates a tremendous amount of heat.

To the right of the fans is a standard *PS/2 port*. This allows users to attach an external keyboard or mouse, just in case the provided touchpad and pointing stick aren't sufficient. A VGA port follows, which allows users to display the notebook's video on an external monitor or projector. Unlike many notebooks, which support VGA video-out at only limited resolutions, this unit can output its full 1600x1200 pixel display. (For a good deal more information on VGA and PC video, explore Chapter 6, "Video and Monitors".)

Figure 2.1
This Dell Inspiron 8100 laptop computer is typical of the best of today's portable computers.

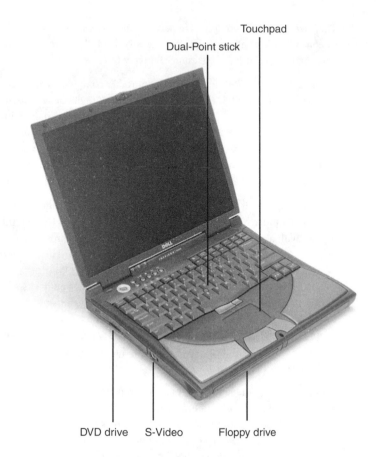

Touchpad

Dual-Point stick

DVD drive   S-Video   Floppy drive

Figure 2.2
The back of the Inspiron 8100 provides a wealth of connectivity.

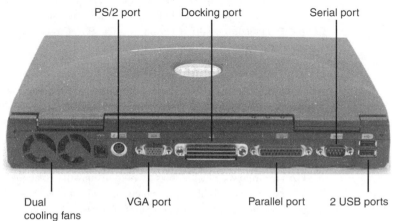

PS/2 port   Docking port   Serial port

Dual cooling fans   VGA port   Parallel port   2 USB ports

Next to the VGA port is a proprietary connector that allows this notebook to "dock" with what's commonly called a *port replicator*. More about this in a moment. Next to the docking connector—and almost as large—is a standard *parallel port*, next to which is a standard *serial port*. These provide connectivity with the majority of printers and external modems, respectively, along with other devices such as light pens and barcode scanners. (For an in-depth look at serial ports, take a look at Chapter 9; you'll find a good deal more about parallel ports in Chapter 10, too.)

The usefulness of these *legacy ports* (that is, ports that have been around since the beginning of the PC's evolution and work as well with devices that are 20 years old as they do with the latest options) is brought into serious doubt by virtue of the last two ports you can see in Figure 2.2: the twin *USB ports*. As you'll read about in Chapter 9, "Serial Ports," USB (Universal Serial Bus) provides high-speed access to a huge variety of devices, including those traditionally requiring the older, larger, and slower parallel and serial ports. Indeed, even the latest printers provide USB connections, making the familiar name of the parallel port—"printer port"—seriously antiquated. The USB ports allow you to add and remove external devices on the fly, without rebooting or powering-down the notebook.

Figure 2.3 shows a close-up view of the right side. Expandability and connectivity are the name of the game here. On the left you can see the two ports—technically, they're an *RJ-45* and *RJ-9 port*—that provide this unit's integrated Fast Ethernet and modem support. Fast Ethernet is a networking standard that provides connectivity at either 10Kbps (bits per second) or 100Kbps, as you'll discover in Chapter 11, "Networking—Wired and Wireless," and the modem is a called a 56K V.90 modem, which you'll learn about at length in Chapter 12, "Modems and Broadband."

Next to the modem port is a panel that provides access to the notebook's removable hard drive. The hard drive has a 48GB capacity, and spins at 5400 RPM. In Chapter 7, "Disks and PC Data Storage", you'll learn a great deal about hard drives and why their rotation speed is important. Integrated into this panel is a port that provides fast *IR (infrared) connectivity* to devices such as printers, PDAs, cellular telephones, as well as some networks. You'll learn all about IR ports in Chapter 9, "Serial Ports." Briefly, the IR port uses pulses of light in the infrared range (like what your television and VCR remotes use) to transfer data between devices.

Further to the right are the unit's two *CardBus PC Card* slots, which you'll learn more about later in this chapter. These slots enable you to temporarily install a wide variety of devices—anything from a network interface card to a SCSI interface (which you'll learn about in Chapter 7, "Disks and PC Data Storage") to a hard disk. The lower of the two slots supports zoomed video, which you'll read about later in this chapter. This basically is a high-performance way to get live video into a notebook.

Figure 2.3
Expandability and communications are featured on the right side of the Inspiron 8100.

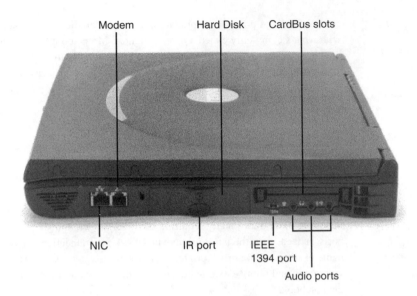

Directly beneath the two CardBus slots is an *IEEE 1394* (FireWire or iLink) *port* and a set of audio in and out ports. You'll learn a lot about IEEE 1394 in Chapter 9. Fundamentally, it's a high-speed serial bus—similar to USB, but a good deal faster, at least, than USB 1.1—which is most often used to get digital video and digital still images into and out of a PC and digital camcorder or camera.

Fitting everything into this case was something of a tour de force for the engineers. The only way it could be done was by using the very smallest standard parts, and in many instances, custom-designed parts. Also, these designs leave out some things that are standard on desktop PCs. For example, there are no slots into which you can plug either a standard ISA or PCI option card.

After they put all the pieces in place, the manufacturers do not encourage end users to open up the case. This is unlike the situation with desktop PCs, but makes sense because the parts in a portable are often not only smaller but also more fragile than those used in desktop units.

Yet, the makers of notebook PCs like this one do allow for some upgrading. For example, in this portable you can add more memory (up to a total of 512MB) if you like. When this machine came from the factory, the memory sockets were empty. Figure 2.4 shows the door on the bottom that you remove to access the add-on memory sockets. Also shown is the modem/NIC (network interface card) panel that allows the user to install or change networking options from the configuration originally purchased. (For example, this unit supports an optional internal wireless networking card that can replace the integrated modem/NIC.)

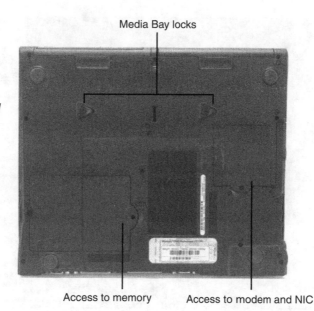

Media Bay locks

FIGURE 2.4

The bottom of the Inspiron 8100 provides access to its media bays and to upgrade it—with memory, modem, and so forth.

Access to memory   Access to modem and NIC

Many of the parts in this computer were modified in order to save weight or space. For example, in Figure 2.5, the DVD drive drawer is shown open. You'll notice that almost one-third of the drawer has been cut away. The missing part of the drawer is not important, either for supporting the DVD or CD disc or for giving the drawer sufficient strength, so it could be omitted safely. The small amount of mass it represents could be shaved off the weight of the machine. Being concerned with such minor amounts of weight might not seem important, but if you trim away a little bit here and there, the overall weight savings can be quite significant.

The hard disk drive in this PC is an industry-standard model, but it's smaller than almost any hard drive you've probably ever seen. It is, in fact, smaller than a deck of standard playing cards. The drive is mounted in a custom holder that slips into the case and locks in place. Figure 2.6 shows the drive in its bracket, facing backward. (Note the deck of playing cards. You might be interested to know that this 48GB hard drive has the same capacity as approximately 72 CD-ROMs or 33,333 floppy disks.)

FIGURE 2.5

The DVD drive drawer comes out from the left of this portable PC. Notice how the base has been cut away to save weight.

FIGURE 2.6

The hard disk for this portable PC, removed from its normal place in the right-center of the case.

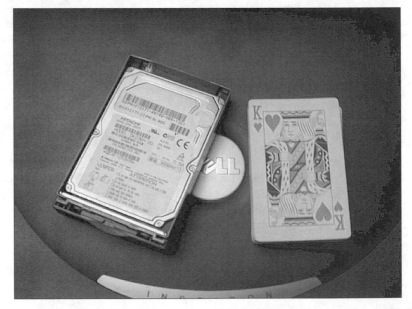

The battery in this laptop is an intelligent Lithium-Ion battery. It actually contains circuitry inside the battery case. This enables the PC to learn all about the battery's requirements for charging, as well as its present state of charge. Then it can do an optimum job of keeping the battery charged, without overcharging it, and it can keep the user informed very accurately about how much longer the battery can keep the laptop running.

Figure 2.7 shows this battery. Notice the five LEDs, next to the small round button. Press that button and the appropriate number of LEDs light up, depending on the amount of charge in the battery (from 20 percent to 100 percent in 20 percent steps.) At the right, you see the connector by which the battery links itself to the PC. The multiple terminals supply power and communicate with the notebook.

FIGURE 2.7

The intelligent battery used in this laptop.

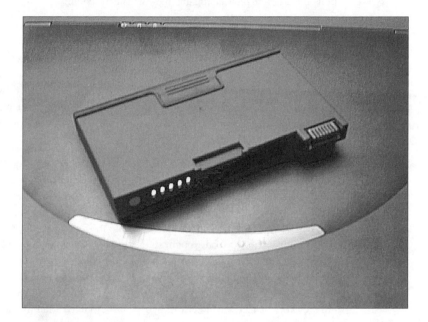

The lengthy list of features you've just read covers just about everything you might want from a mobile PC. There is a cost to this broad functionality, of course, and not just in dollars. Full-power multimedia notebooks like this example unit commonly weigh in at the top end of the mobile PC scale—the Dell Inspiron 8100, for example, weighs 7.9 pounds in a standard configuration. This isn't a lot of weight in absolute terms, particularly if you travel with your notebook PC in a roll-on bag. But if you don't ever use the multimedia capabilities, you have the option of selecting a mobile PC that leaves those features—and their weight—behind.

New, Thinner Laptops

Although laptops got smaller and were packed with ever more features—in the process becoming more and more capable of replacing desktop PCs—"road warriors" who needed only a very good PC for doing a limited number of tasks have convinced manufacturers to offer an entirely new category of laptop computers.

These are the ultra-thin laptops. Sony pioneered this trend with its Vaio model, but now all the major laptop makers are jumping on the bandwagon. These machines all have good keyboards and screens that can be nearly as large and nice as the high-end "regular" laptops, although they are generally several inches smaller. The overall size of these new machines approaches that of a normal laptop in all but thickness; they are approximately half as thick as a regular laptop and they are much lighter.

To achieve these benefits, they have been designed without built-in DVD (or even CD) or floppy disk drives, and they also lack many of the other features common in today's high-end laptops such as our example Dell Inspiron. For most of these units, DVD or CD support is available, but you have to purchase the hardware separately, and it connects to the laptop through what is usually a proprietary cable. (The upshot of which is you must buy the external devices made by your laptop's manufacturer. This can be annoying if another manufacturer produces a comparable device that sells at a much lower cost.)

The availability of a docking bay is also a much more significant issue for this type of mobile PC than it is for our example unit, because this type of laptop simply doesn't include the functionality and connectivity that you find built-in to our example. In fact, some of the smallest and lightest units have only two connectors: one for headphones and one for an external docking unit. Traditional PC functionality like serial ports, parallel ports, USB, and CD or DVD drives are built into the docking units. Of course, to have this functionality on the road, you must travel with both the laptop and its docking bay. Ironically, the total weight can easily exceed the weight of an all-in-one unit like our example from Dell. If you never use those features, you can always leave the docking unit at home or at your office, but if you suddenly encounter the need to load software from a CD or connect with a network, you'll have to have a family member or employee ship the docking unit to you.

Peter's Principle

These lightest and smallest mobile PCs are fantastic if you're a member of their target audience, but before you select such a unit and leave its docking or expansion bay at home, allow me to relate an experience of a friend of mine. Last year, on a certain two-week recreational trip, she took a small laptop with her, figuring that its internal modem would be all she'd need while on the road. She'd be able to check e-mail and communicate with anyone who really needed to be in touch. When she arrived at the hotel, she found that their all-digital telephone system was not compatible with standard modems. They provided, however, broadband Internet access in every room through a standard Ethernet connection. Had she owned a full-featured notebook, she could have plugged in her network connection and been on her way. As it was, she had to phone her office and have her docking back shipped overnight to her.

This isn't a clear-cut situation, of course. What you carry and what functionality you leave behind is a matter of preference and personal need. My suggestion is just to remember that flexibility is always important when you're on the road.

Sub-Laptop PCs

Smaller than these smallest laptops are the wide variety of handheld devices, like the Palm m505 and a variety of Windows CE units. We'll take an in-depth look at this hardware in the next chapter.

Hardware That Is Almost Unique to Mobile PCs

I've talked about how a full-featured notebook, like our example unit, can provide all the functionality of a desktop PC. Let's take a moment to look at hardware found in almost every mobile PC, but very few desktops: *PC Card* and *CardBus slots*.

What's In a Name: PCMCIA, PC Cards, and CardBus

Earlier, I mentioned that our example notebook comes with two *CardBus* slots. You probably know these devices by the name *PC Card*. Originally, they had the cumbersome name *PCMCIA cards* (sufficiently cumbersome, in fact, that it spawned the false translation, "People Can't Memorize Computer Industry Acronyms".) The "PC Memory Card International Association" began as a trade association of several manufacturers of RAM and ROM chips. They designed a credit-card sized carrier for memory chips with a connector on one end, and they published a specification for these cards, as well as the slot into which they would fit. When it became clear that this was a convenient form factor for adding something to a portable PC, other manufacturers joined the PCMCIA, and they began the push to broaden the applicability of this standard.

For example, Hewlett-Packard and Western Digital, among others, produced miniaturized hard disks that fit on these cards and determined how to support them through appropriate device driver software. Manufacturers of other PC peripherals, including modems and network interface cards, also saw an opportunity here like the CardBus modem shown in Figure 2.8.

The PC Card design has undergone many developments, leading to two fully standardized form factors, called Type I, and Type II, and one proprietary form factor, called Type III cards. They share the same dimensions, except for thickness. A PC Card slot can accept a single Type I card, a single Type II card, or a pair of Type I or Type II cards. Many PC makers, especially Toshiba and others focusing on mobile PCs, provide oversize slots that can accept a Type III card.

Any PC Card slot must support the original 16-bit bus (based on the ISA bus.) Newer cars and slots support *CardBus*, which is simply a 32-bit version of that interface, derived from the PCI bus standard. The 32-bit CardBus standard was developed to facilitate the implementation of high-speed functionality in the small PC Card form factor.

FIGURE 2.8
*A CardBus
modem.*

It All Began as Memory, and Not Just for PCs

Memory chips (RAM and ROM) are useful in many devices. This book focuses on PCs, but the makers of those chips are well aware that automobiles, game machines, and other products also use up lots and lots of their output. Several of the major memory chip makers got together and decided to create a standard specification for how to package some small add-on memory modules for use in game machines and other applications. Because they were interested in memory cards and were an international group of companies (and because PCs are one of the major target uses of the products they met to discuss), it is perhaps not surprising that they named their group the PC Memory Card International Association (PCMCIA.)

They settled on a *form factor* (size and shape) for these modules that is roughly that of a calling card (business card) and a third of a centimeter (which is about an eighth of an inch) thick. They published a standards document, which is a lot fatter than the cards it describes.

Broadening the Range of Uses

One especially important group to adopt this new standard module for memory add-ons were the laptop PC makers. They received this new form factor gratefully, because it fit well with their goal of making laptop computers ever smaller while still providing the amount of memory that their customers wanted.

Type I cards are the original size, about 85×54×3.3 mm (which in English units is about 3.3×2.1×0.13 inches.) Type II cards are 5 mm thick. Type III cards are 10.5 mm thick. Allowing for the space between cards, this works out so one can build a card bay that will hold one Type II or one Type I card, or a larger card bay that will hold one Type III, or two of any mix of Type I and Type II cards.

The thinnest cards (Type I) work well for RAM or ROM (or Flash RAM), and very clever manufacturers have even managed to insert a modem or a network interface card into this size PC Card. The thickest (Type III) cards have been used for such relatively bulky items as miniature hard disks.

What's a CardBus and What Is Zoomed Video?

As I mentioned, CardBus was developed to replace the 16-bit PC Card with a faster, 32-bit cousin. Having twice the number of data lines meant, in fact, that the new Card Bus interface could transfer data twice as fast as the original PC Card interface.

Even that wasn't fast enough for some. So another innovation emerged. This is a special new system bus that goes directly from a CardBus slot to the video subsystem. It enables the video accelerator to use the memory (or other resources) on a CardBus card without the delays of going through the main system bus. This new bus has the rather whimsical name of *zoomed video port*. (This apparently refers more to the zippy way data can move from PC Card to video frame buffer, rather than anything about actually "zooming" a video image. So far, MPEG decoder PC Cards are one of the few kinds of PC Cards that actually use zoomed video connection.)

The Future of PC Cards

It seems unlikely that PC Cards will disappear anytime soon, but there is no question that their functionality is limited. It's often the case that the same—or even better—capabilities can be provided through external devices plugged into a USB or IEEE 1394 slot, which you'll read about in Chapter 9. Probably the single most popular use of PC Cards has been to add modems or network connections to mobile PCs that lack them. The appeal of this will remain, especially with the ultra-light laptops, some of which have a single PC Card slot as their only expandable connection when away from their docking unit. But, for the majority of notebooks, modems and NICs are now built-in, so they don't need this type of PC Card anymore. What remains are cards that appeal to niche markets—such as TV tuner cards—and cards that provide notebook connections to external SCSI devices (which you'll read about in Chapter 7, "Disks and PC Data Storage".)

Lessons Learned from Portable PCs

As mobile PCs have evolved—and particularly as the number of people who use them has grown from thousands to millions—both users and manufacturers have learned some really valuable lessons. Let's look at a few that will most likely impact you.

Space Constraints Lead to Proprietary Parts

As I previously said, cramming all the power of a desktop PC into a package as small as a laptop is no easy feat. Just look at your desktop PC a moment. Think about all the space it takes up. Notice, if you will, the mass of cables and connectors it contains. Now consider what you might have to do to put all those pieces into such a tiny box.

The only way to do that (so far) is to use at least *some* proprietary parts and some industry-standard parts designed especially for mobile PCs. This means that it isn't possible to build your own laptop as easily as it is to build your own desktop PC. You can't just go to the nearest computer superstore and buy a case plus a bunch of parts to go in it and end up with a laptop PC.

This means laptop parts aren't as prevalent, because each part may be used only in a particular model of laptop or mobile PC. This fact drives up cost.

As just one example, memory modules for desktop PCs are a commodity item; they are made by many companies, and for the most part, are interchangeable. For a given type of memory, there is only one physical model and size. However, until recently, memory modules for laptop computers came in many shapes and sizes, and they often cost several times as much per megabyte as the standard memory modules used in desktop PCs. Many of the newest laptops use industry-standard SODIMM memory modules (which you'll read about in Chapter 17, "Understanding PC Memory".) Although there are proprietary versions of SODIMMs as well, the development of these standard modules is a huge step forward in terms of reducing the cost of laptop memory.

This is only one example of the main reason why laptop computers cost more (for a given level of performance) than their desktop brethren. It is the direct result of their having to use proprietary miniaturization in order to put all the pieces a particular manufacturer wants to include into such a compact space.

Space Constraints Limit Upgrade Possibilities

When you build a desktop PC, you put its "guts" into a system unit case. Normally, that case is noticeably larger than needed. This is done so there's room for unused slots and bays for optional cards and drives, making upgrading easy.

The only upgrades that are possible on a typical mobile computer are ones that the manufacturer built room for. Other than functionality that can be added via PC Cards, there are no optional slots here for additional technologies. Rarely are there spare drive bays, either. In top-quality models like the Dell Inspiron, you can swap the floppy disk drive for another hard drive, a CD-RW drive, or another battery, but economy models don't usually offer this flexibility. Indeed, they rarely even offer swappable bays.

Mobile PC makers have addressed this limitation in two ways. The oldest is by offering *docking stations*, as I've mentioned previously. In the case of the Dell Inspiron, a docking unit can replicate the already-present serial, parallel, PS/2, USB, video, headphone, and networking ports. Such a unit is more commonly known as a *port replicator*.

You've already read about the big drawback to using a docking unit: They are sufficiently non-portable that you likely will opt to travel without them. Really, docking units are a way to temporarily convert your mobile PC into a deskbound PC. (Additionally, as in the case of the example system, the docking unit merely replicates functionality already present in the main unit.)

Because of ever-smaller and more capable electronic devices, it's possible, now, to pack nearly every conceivably useful port right into the notebook. Consider again the Dell notebook. Its list of built-in connectivity is just about all-inclusive. It provides:

- Standard PS/2, serial, parallel, and video ports
- An internal modem and network card
- Digital video and audio input and output
- USB and IEEE 1394 connectors
- S-video (television) and surround stereo audio output, plus microphone

There's almost nothing remaining for the two CardBus slots to do! The built-in networking card can even be replaced with an internal wireless networking card, complete with integrated antenna.

The point to take from all of this is that expandability remains a major issue when you're considering which mobile PC will best meet your needs. An all-inclusive unit will initially weigh more and cost more than models with more limited functionality, but you come away with essentially everything you might ever want in a mobile—or, indeed, a desktop—PC.

Space Constraints Mean Greater Control

A flip side to all these limitations to the design of mobile PCs is that the manufacturer has greater control over what they contain and how they work. This is because laptops are mostly fixed in their features by the manufacturer and use proprietary parts.

Therefore, mobile PCs aren't subject to nearly as many weird problems as desktop PCs. They just don't have the chaotic mix of parts from different manufacturers tucked inside, so the makers can feasibly test almost all the variations of each of their models before shipping them to customers—which makes them easier to support once they're purchased, too. A general-purpose desktop PC can contain any of several thousand add-on pieces after it is shipped from the factory, so this kind of testing is simply impossible.

For this reason, mobile PC makers have been much more successful in getting their products to work well with energy-saving features than have the desktop PC makers. Of course, the fact that battery power is such a precious resource has also impelled the mobile PC makers to work harder on this goal.

When Enough People Want Something...

As electronic devices continue to shrink, it becomes more feasible for laptop manufacturers to include more and fancier devices inside their machines. And as the market for these machines expands, the number of folks demanding certain features increases. The inevitable result of this is that "full-featured" laptops are getting more like desktop PCs all the time. One way that happens is simply by including more of the desktop PC items, which now are small enough to fit. Another way is that manufacturers now have enough of a market to justify creating custom parts that implement popular functionalities that were formerly unavailable in such small form factors or with such low power consumption.

Indeed, soon the price, performance, and functionality distinctions between a "pretty good" laptop and a "pretty good" desktop PC might vanish. You can see one example of this trend in the rapidly falling price and improving size and performance of high-resolution, active-matrix LCD screens. Laptops now have screens as good as desktop PCs. Flat-screen LCD panels are becoming more popular on some desktop machines than conventional CRT (cathode ray tube) screens.

Extending Your Battery's Life

Whatever type of mobile PC you have, whatever type of battery your laptop uses, and no matter how long it lasts between recharges or battery replacement, you probably wouldn't mind if it lasted a little while longer. At the very least, you could save some hassle and money. So, you'll find some steps you can take to extend your battery's life. It also warns you when not to use methods that might compromise your efficiency. Not every power-saving idea that you find in your favorite computer magazine makes good sense for the way you use your computer.

Use AC Power Whenever Possible

Use AC power whenever you can. Shouldn't that be obvious? No, it really isn't. Almost every PC that can run on rechargeable battery power includes a battery charger. That is true even when you might think it isn't. If your PC has a battery eliminator or any other way to run from the AC line instead of from its internal battery, most likely the power supply inside it is really a battery charger. Often, these chargers reside in a box in the middle of the power cord or in a cube at the end of the power cord that goes into the wall.

Does this make a difference? Yes. First, this means that while you are running on AC power, you are at least trickle-charging your PC's internal battery. When your PC is full of charge, they will not shut themselves off completely; they will supply a slight trickle of current to keep the battery topped off. This is done because rechargeable batteries lose some of their charge over time just sitting there. You may think of it as if there were a small load on the battery inside its case. Even if you don't pull any current out of its external terminals, the battery will slowly lose power on its own.

Most of these power supplies assume that your PC has its battery installed (and that the battery isn't *really* dead—by which I mean that the battery is still capable of accepting a charge even if it doesn't currently have much of one in it.)

Normal PC power supplies convert AC power from the wall into DC power. This involves taking the alternating current (AC), which is simply alternating positive and negative waves of electric power, and turning them into a steady supply of direct current

(DC.) To dothis, however, they must store some electrical energy internally to bridge the times when the wall socket isn't supplying any voltage or current. Normal power supplies store this energy in capacitors. Because these capacitors enable the power supplies to filter out the pulses inherent in AC power and thus provide a steady DC output, they are called *filter capacitors*.

PC Power supplies with internal batteries can enable the internal battery to do most of this energy-storage task. In effect, they enable the battery to run the PC for short periods of time, 120 times each second. After each one of these intervals, the power supply replaces the charge that was withdrawn from the battery.

> **Caution:** Here's the point of all this: You must have your PC's battery in place (and it must not be dead) if you are going to run your portable PC on AC line power. That is true for almost every PC with a rechargeable battery. It is not true for a mobile PC that doesn't have a charger type of power supply—its AC power supply won't be depending on the battery to help it do its job.

One big benefit you get from the strategy I have just described is that when you run this type of PC from the AC power line, you are in effect running it on a UPS. Thus, you are automatically protected against brownouts, surges, spikes, and power failures.

Don't Recharge Inappropriately

Clearly, if you run your PC on battery power for very long, you will have to recharge that battery at some point. Most manufacturers recommend that you discharge the battery all the way, then recharge it fully. They don't approve of partial discharge and recharge cycles.

This is most important if you have an older-style NiCad battery in your PC, because partial discharge and recharge cycles cause the battery to lose capacity through the "memory" effect. It also is a good idea to use a full discharge and recharge cycle even on batteries that are built using one of the other popular chemistries.

Having a spare (and fully charged) battery with you if you are using your PC away from AC power is a good idea. That way when the first battery is depleted, you can swap batteries and keep on computing. Then at the next convenient time, you can recharge the depleted battery, making it ready for use when the swapped battery becomes depleted.

> **Caution:** If your mobile PC manufacturer doesn't advocate the use of generic batteries, think long and hard before replacing your notebook's battery with one that purports to be compatible. Doing that could damage the new battery, the PC's power supply, or both.

Use Power-Saving Settings

The battery in your mobile PC supplies power so your PC can do its job. If your PC can be configured to require less power, the battery will be capable of supplying it with adequate power for a longer time. This fairly obvious insight has been implemented in most mobile PCs; you can make the PC use less power whenever you don't really need it to be using the maximum.

In practice, this means that if you aren't currently accessing your PC's hard disk, there is no reason for it to be spinning; this is also true for your CD-ROM drive. Also, if you aren't doing anything with your PC, the display can be turned off. Perhaps the most exotic approach is that you can slow down the CPU clock speed any time it is waiting for you to press a key or move your mouse. Each of these strategies reduces the total power consumption by the PC.

However, these savings don't come without some associated costs. For example, it takes a few seconds to get a turned-off hard disk back up to speed. So if it has been shut down to save power, you will have to wait those few seconds before you can access it again.

What Must Be Done by the Hardware

All of this sounds fine, but what actually happens when your mobile PC implements its variety of power-saving features? In order to be able to power down different parts of your PC selectively and using software, the parts in question must be able to interact appropriately with that controlling software. Naturally, you can never completely turn off power to a component that must be able to respond to a software signal asking it to turn on, but you can let it power down all but the tiny part that listens for that wakeup signal.

A common example in most homes is a television set that can be turned on using a remote control. Some part of the TV set must be listening for the infrared signals from the remote control in order to respond to them.

Energy Star monitors can be commanded to go into any of several states of reduced power, from nearly all the way off (except for that tiny monitoring part) up to almost completely on but with the screen image blank.

The reason for having several levels to which the monitor can be powered down is that it takes different amounts of time to "recover" each. The lower the power, the longer it will take to get back into full operation.

Most of the components and subsystems in a mobile PC are designed to power down when they're not being used. The hard disk can be turned off when it isn't needed, and modems can be powered down (with just enough circuitry left powered that they can come back to full operation when they detect an incoming call.) Printers also now have power-saving modes that drop their consumption to nearly nothing.

Perhaps the most interesting of the various power-saving features is that the clock speed of the CPU can be reduced. All modern PC processor chips (and many of the other chips used in a PC) are made using the complementary metal-oxide semiconductor (CMOS) process for manufacturing integrated circuit chips. One important fact about a CMOS circuit is that it uses almost no power to sit in one state. Every time you change the state of a portion of the circuitry, however, some small chunk of electric charge will make its way through the circuit from the power lead to the ground lead. The size of the chunks of charge that fall through each time are fixed. So the average rate at which charge flows, which is to say the average current through these devices, is directly proportional to the number of state changes that are taking place within them during each second.

The power dissipated as heat in the chip is simply the average current through it multiplied by the voltage on the power lead attached to the chip. Therefore, power is also directly proportional to the number of state changes per second.

One thing CPU manufacturers have done and continue to do is work to lower the needed voltage to power their chips. Originally, all the chips used 5 volts (except for a few that used 12 volts.) Now, most of the key circuits are a great deal less than that. Indeed, the CPU at the heart of the example unit is a Mobile Intel Pentium III processor, which uses between 1.1 and 1.7 volts. This is an amazingly tiny amount of power. The lower the voltage applied to the chip, all other things being equal, the lower its power dissipation.

Some CPU chips can have their clock slowed down arbitrarily. They can't go any faster than the rated maximum speed without risking errors, but they are capable of going as slowly as you like without any bad consequences. As you reduce the clock frequency, you also reduce the power they draw from the battery or other power source.

Other CPU chips have some minimum speed they must go. They are like a person riding a bicycle. Depending on the person's skill, it is possible to ride quite slowly, but most people can't actually stop the forward motion of the bicycle completely without having it fall over. The reasons are different, but many CPU chips cannot run at less than some minimum speed without failing to remember what they are doing.

Furthermore, PC memory is mostly SDRAM (which stands for Synchronous Dynamic Random Access Memory.) The data in these chips must be refreshed at least a few thousand times per second in order not to forget the information they are holding.

However, it is often possible to reduce the clock speed of the CPU from several hundred million cycles per second to perhaps one million. Doing so will reduce the power of the CPU chip, the memory chips, and all the other CMOS chips that are running at the same frequency by the ratio of the normal operating clock speed to the slowed-down clock speed.

Reducing the clock speed of the CPU can save you up to 99 percent of the energy drain in those chips when you aren't actually using them. Really sophisticated energy-saving circuits can apply this strategy not only when you walk away from your PC, but also any time that it is waiting for you to do something.

Each time you type a key, the PC must do something with that. If it finishes its work before you press the next key, it can slow down its clock until you press the next key. In effect, you make the PC run just fast enough that it is always working, but never faster than necessary. This clever trick works with virtually no downside to it. The reason is that you can slow or speed the clock any amount you like in almost no time, and the circuitry needed to do this is minimal.

On the other hand, powering down the monitor or stopping the hard drive from spinning means that when you are ready to use them once more, you have to wait up to several seconds for them to recover and get back up to speed. So you really don't want to do that every time you aren't using them for just a few seconds or a few minutes. The hard disk might stop turning if you don't access any files on it for many minutes. If it does, you will experience a possibly annoying delay when you next want to save a file or load a new program.

These are some of the ways that hardware can reduce the average power it consumes while still enabling you to compute at more or less full speed whenever you want to do so. If your PC can take advantage of all these features, you might be able to leave it on almost all the time with very little energy wasted. However, the hardware cannot do this job by itself.

What Software Must Do

In order to make the hardware pieces turn off or on or slow down at just the right times, some program must tell them what to do and when. Part of the motherboard BIOS is dedicated to this purpose. These programs can only activate or deactivate the hardware; they don't know when you want those strategies applied, so you need some way to tell those programs what you want.

You can do this in two ways. One is through some entries in the motherboard BIOS setup program. (Normally, you access this program with some special keystroke at a prescribed point in the bootup process.) Here, you might be able to specify, for example, whether you want the hard disk to stop spinning when it hasn't been accessed for the length of time you specify. (Usually, you can't enter just any time you like, but rather you must pick from among several fixed options.)

Another level at which your PC can be programmed, or configured, for power savings is through an operating system applet. Thus, the operating system might monitor the programs you are running and decide which of the energy-saving options it should invoke. Again, you can tell the PC (by making some choices in the Windows Power Control Panel, for example) how you want it to do that job.

Summary

Mobile PCs are different from other PCs intended for desktop or file server use. Mainly, the mobile PCs have been carefully designed to be the absolute minimum size and weight possible for their feature set. This means they generally are less flexible about accepting upgrades than other PCs and often are more stable as a result.

Mobile PCs use batteries. Battery technologies are complex and constantly improving. If you can get a PC that accepts standard size batteries or, even better, smart batteries (and your PC knows how to use those smarts), you will be much happier with the results.

Whatever battery strategy you use, reducing your PC's power needs helps extend that battery's life. Modern mobile PCs are pretty good at doing this in several ways. Many of those same strategies can be applied to desktop PCs, but for now you might want to pass on most of them because they also often bring along some additional instability.

Mobile PCs are so good now that with a docking station and an external keyboard, mouse, and monitor, they can serve very well as a desktop PC replacement. No longer is a mobile PC useful only when you are on the road.

Smaller PCs and PDAs have their place in our computing world as well. As the technology improves, they might come to assume ever larger roles in our lives. But for now, nothing smaller than a laptop is likely to serve all the uses people have for their PCs.

3

PDAs and Handheld PCs

As you move through almost any environment today, you encounter people using—or, at least, carrying—mobile PCs. The portable PC has become an extension of our lives. It's not just a portable filing cabinet; it's an entire office, complete with workspace, connectivity, and even the digital equivalent of an executive assistant, in many cases. And it's a very well-equipped entertainment center, too. It provides digital audio and video, and even satellite or cable and broadcast radio reception. It's no surprise that the mobile PC has replaced an astounding collection of equipment that used to weigh-down every traveler's luggage. If you have a full-featured notebook computer, you don't need a clock radio, a CD player, a personal video unit, a dictation device, or video game unit. You might not even need an attaché case, except for storing your PC. The full-powered notebook has also reduced the need for travelers' business centers, with fax machines and telephones and high-speed Internet connections.

All of this potential does come with a price. In fact, it comes with a two-fold price: the dollars you must initially pay to purchase the PC and the burden you incur by having—as it were—all your eggs in one, eight-pound basket. Having everything you could possibly need in one box definitely adds to the weight of that box. And with all you need in one unit, you're likely to need that unit everywhere you go.

In some instances, this latter price—dragging your notebook around with you—is simply overkill. In others, it might be totally impractical, or even unsafe. Even the super-slim and light units that cut down both weight and functionality won't do you much good if you absolutely need your hands free most of the time. Wouldn't it be marvelous if you could put a PC in your pocket? Wouldn't it be even better if that pocket-sized PC could do most of what a full-sized PC can?

Put a PC in Your Pocket

You probably figured out that, of course, this device does exist. The market has given them a variety of names, from *handheld*, to *portable digital assistant* (PDA), to *palmtop* (a mildly humorous pun on *laptop*), but as this class of device has evolved, they've largely come together to achieve one purpose: to put a PC, or its nearest equivalent, in your pocket.

Ancient History

The history of the PDA/palmtop is, in many ways, the history of failure. Entire companies have come and gone in their attempts to produce a successful and useful PC on this small scale, and there are previous few PC manufacturers today who don't have at least one of these embarrassments to leave off of their corporate timeline. But, to understand why PDAs are the way they are now, it's useful to understand their history. Let's take a look at a few of this genre's successes and…well, "not successes."

The Psion Company

In 1984, a company called Psion produced a small handheld device that looked a lot like a pocket calculator on steroids. The Psion 1 organizer, shown in Figure 3.1, featured a single line display, capable of showing 16 characters at a time. It had basic database capabilities, making it useful as a place to store contact information, and not surprisingly it also performed all the basic math functions. It could be programmed by the user to run actual (very small) computer programs using a simple, proprietary language called POPL. This programmability made the Psion similar to the many handheld advanced calculators that Hewlett-Packard has produced for decades, but its database capabilities distinguish it as the earliest form of the *personal digital assistant* (PDA).

FIGURE 3.1

Psion's original Organizer, called Psion 1. It is roughly the size of a standard deck of playing cards.

Apple's Newton

The 1993 release of the Apple Computer Newton NotePad device gave the world the first arguably handheld. It is readily recognized as an ancestor of today's PDAs. I say *arguably*, because at roughly five by eight inches and weighing in at a full pound, the NotePad wasn't exactly tiny. It was, however, a revolutionary combination of technologies. The NotePad had a touch-sensitive screen, which covered a four-by-three inch backlit LCD panel. Although touch screens had been around for over a decade, Newton was the first attempt to use them on this portable scale. Additionally, the Newton featured something that even most of today's PDAs do not: handwriting recognition. A vocabulary of over 93,000 words (expandable to include 1,000 words defined by the user) enabled the Newton to read what you wrote. Your writing was then stored as text, rather than as graphical images, which require tremendously more storage space. Newton also allowed for external connectivity through a PC Card modem (which you read about in the previous chapter) and it provided a software intelligent assistant that automated frequently performed tasks.

At least, it did all of these things in theory. Apple Computer was correct in its declaration that a huge market would exist for very small, powerful computers. Unfortunately, Apple's timing was about seven years off, and the ability of the Newton NotePad to actually *perform* its promised feats lagged sadly behind Apple Computer's ability to make those promises. Newton's main processor—even in its later incarnations—was underpowered relative to the tasks demanded of it (in particular, the job of handwriting recognition, which was interminably slow and inaccurate). At the same time it ate power like nobody's business. Battery life was sorely disappointing. Apple's own problems with manufacturing quality control sealed the Newton's fate. Sales for the Newton were so poor that it seemed the market had rejected the very idea of a handheld computer.

The PalmPilot

It was three years before anyone else premiered a handheld PC. This time, in 1996, it was a small new company called Palm that, back in 1995, had been purchased by U.S. Robotics (now 3COM). Their first device, the PalmPilot, shown in Figure 3.2, was about half the size and one-third the weight of the Apple Newton, and worked far better. Like the Newton, it had no keyboard. Instead, PalmPilot relied on a touch-sensitive screen. But Palm did not follow Apple down the treacherous path of strict handwriting recognition. Instead, Palm was responsible for two major innovations in this regard.

First, the PalmPilot could display a graphic of a keyboard on its display. Thus displayed, the graphic allowed users to "type" data, one letter at a time, into the PalmPilot using a pen-like stylus. Although you certainly wouldn't want to write the great American novel using this method, it worked quickly and accurately. It was, therefore, two steps ahead of Apple's Newton on this point, alone.

FIGURE 3.2
The PalmPilot was the first handheld device to enjoy real market success.

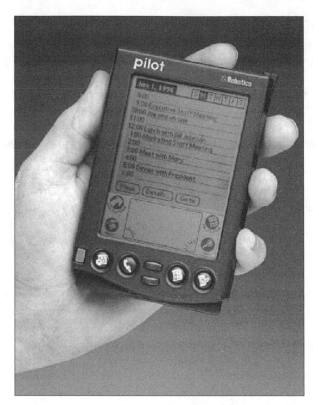

More dramatic was Palm's realization that handwriting recognition—true handwriting recognition—was simply beyond the power available in any handheld device of the time. (Indeed, it remains a niche technology to this day because of the impractical processing power it requires.) The reason this is true is simple, and it's one you'll understand intuitively: everyone's handwriting is different. That might sound glib, but the fact is, it's hard enough for a human to read another human's handwriting—think of what your doctor's penmanship looks like on a prescription. For a computer, it's *extremely* difficult. No one writes characters exactly the same way, every time. We leave gaps where lines should touch; we angle letters strangely; from time to time we combine printing and cursive writing, like the examples in Figure 3.3.

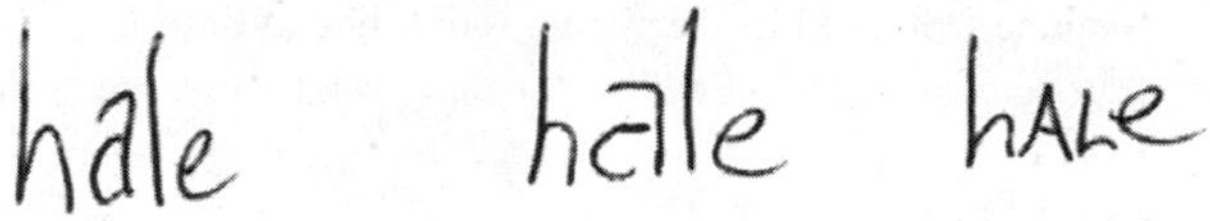

FIGURE 3.3

Variations in how one person writes letters make handwriting recognition a complex and demanding task. Trying to write a piece of software that can universally recognize human writing is almost— although not quite—impossible.

hale   hale   hALe

Write Right

In Figure 3.3, you can see common variances in my own writing. Looking at my associates write assures me that I am not unique in this regard. If a handwriting recognition application is going to be able to decipher what I write, it has to be able to understand these variances. If it can't, it's going to either make recognition errors that I'll have to correct—which is annoying—or it will demand that I stop and re-write what it was unable to understand—which is even more annoying. Imagine for a moment the task of creating a piece of software that can understand not only my own writing with its nuances and changes, but *everyone's* writing.

Look just for a moment at my examples, showing different ways I might write the word "hale." At the extreme left, the word is likely recognizable by almost everyone reading this book. I've written slowly and carefully, using strict letterforms similar to those taught to children in elementary school. But what about the word to the right of that? Here, I've been quicker and more casual, and that allowed for a gap between the two lines that make up the letter "a". Did I write an "a," or did I write "cl"?

Knowing the word "hale," you can almost surely still read what I wrote. This, in fact, is why systems like the Apple Newton came with built-in dictionaries. When the system analyzed a user's writing and came up with gibberish, "hclle," for example, it turned to its dictionary. If your choice of words coincides with the system's vocabulary, you may be in luck. The recognizer will work with the dictionary to laboriously check for a word that matches a variety of handwriting oddities. Of course, if you know words that the system doesn't—which, I guarantee, you do—or if your handwriting is unique in unexpected ways, you might be out of luck. Look at the right-most example in the figure, where I have combined upper- and lowercase letters, as many people do when printing. The recognizer might understand "hale," but it will likely appear as "hALe," which, almost surely, is not what you want.

In any event, you need to stop and tell the system that it either has or has not correctly ana-lyzed what you wrote, and you need to correct the error. Worse still, you might be unable to continue writing while the system is devoting most of its processor power to trying to turn your penmanship into English. Anything you try to write during this time is simply lost.

Graffiti

Palm solved the problem in a way that was originally as controversial as it is genius. In order to maximize the PalmPilot's ability to recognize its users' handwriting, Palm created a standardized way of drawing characters. This system, called *Graffiti*, is shown in Figure 3.4.

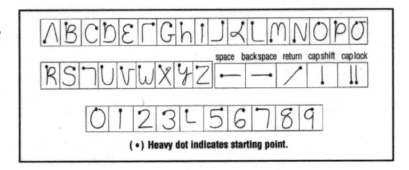

If you want a Palm device to understand what you write on it, you must write using Graffiti. It takes only about 15 minutes to learn proficiently, and eliminates the majority of problems faced by handwriting recognition. Everyone who writes on a Palm device writes basically the same way because of the uniqueness of each Graffiti character and the simplicity of their style. Every time a user writes a given character, she writes it essentially the same way. No letter requires that the writing stylus be raised in the way that I had to raise my pen to write the letter "a" in Figure 3.3. So, a Palm device isn't going to have to worry about what "hclle" means. A memory-hungry dictionary and a power-thirsty analyze-and-search system aren't necessary because the Palm device doesn't need to understand the *words* I write, only the *letters*.

Actually, the Palm devices don't even understand the letters. Instead, they understand the actual pen-strokes I make. Let me explain what I mean, because this is a key feature of the usefulness of Graffiti. When you or I look at a letter, we see the letter as a whole. If you look back at Figure 3.3, in the left-most example, you see the letters "h," "a," "l," and "e" which come together to spell "hale." It's only when I get sloppy, as in the middle example, that you might start to think about how letters are written, rather than the letters themselves. In that example, I wrote the "a" of "hale" carelessly, so that it closely resem-bles the two letters, "c" and "l" in close succession. You can use context to put the two pen strokes together in this example, but other examples using other words might produce ambiguous results.

The Palm device's Graffiti engine doesn't wait for the user to lift the stylus between characters before it attempts to recognize the writing as a whole letter. Instead, it watches the *process* of writing, and matches movement of the stylus with Graffiti characters. If you look at the Graffiti lettering chart in Figure 3.4, you'll see at first glance that the character representing the letter "a" is a triangle with no base. This is not what the Graffiti engine sees. It sees that the user's pen starts at some point on the screen, then moves up and to the right, then turns sharply down and moves further right—a step-by-step process which corresponds to the Arabic letter "a", as shown in Figure 3.5. This method—looking at the process rather than the result—frees Palm users to write as they will. So long as users create their own versions of the individual Graffiti characters by moving the stylus *basically* in the correct pattern, the Graffiti engine will recognize anyone's writing successfully.

FIGURE 3.5

All of these pen strokes are successfully recognized as the letter "a" by Palm's Graffiti engine.

The Graffiti system further simplifies recognition by assigning an area of the screen to letter recognition and another area to number recognition. Palm determined, probably correctly, that people would want to be able to enter numbers quickly and would object to learning a new way—or even a modified way—to write them. Consider, for example, the letter "T" and the number "7." They share the same Graffiti pen strokes. By restricting the recognition of pen strokes to either letters or numbers, depending on where the user writes, numbers can be entered by writing them as humans are used to, and recognition errors won't occur.

Finally, the Graffiti engine can be changed from recognizing lower- or uppercase letters, as well as punctuation marks.

I mentioned previously that Graffiti was controversial when it debuted, and that's true. Asking people to buy and use a device that demanded they learn a new way to write seemed a tall order for 1996. What users soon discovered was that Graffiti is simple and intuitive. The performance of Palm's Graffiti engine is excellent. Handwriting recognition was, finally, a useful feature and not merely a frustrating idea ahead of its time.

PIMs, Not Palms

The PalmPilot, and the many models that have followed it, like the m505, shown in Figure 3.6, are now called PDAs, or Personal Digital Assistants, but they were originally thought of as belonging to a class of devices known as PIMs, or Personal Information Managers. The name PIM describes a set of basic features. Telephone book, scheduling calendar, and calculator are the key components of a PIM, and it is the first two of these that distinguish the PIM branch of the tree from the branch occupied by Hewlett-Packard's line of programmable calculators, such as the venerable HP-41C. (Of course, HP now produces PDAs, too.)

FIGURE 3.6

The m505, the atest offering from Palm, is a trim, elegant, full-color device with enough memory, computing power, and connectivity to make it viable as the only com-puter some users will need.

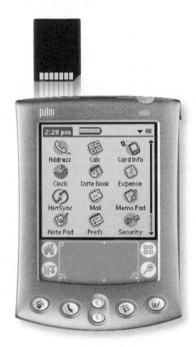

It really wasn't until about the time of the first PalmPilot that the idea of the PIM really caught on. A popular question asked about early PIMs was "Who would ever need this?" and a common observation was "Anyone who would need this has already got better ways of handling these same tasks." Consequently, wide arrays of PIMs have failed. At the time of this writing, PIMs that would have been considered top of the line only two years ago are now marketed to children and are sold for under $40 in the toy departments of major discount stores. For the most part, PIMs feature a small, marginally usable keyboard and an LCD display capable of showing between one and four lines of text.

PIMs usually have no, or limited, connectivity, like the original model of the credit-card sized, ill-fated REX, which was seemingly designed to definitively answer the question,

"Is it possible for a computer to be too small?" The first REX could be plugged onto the back of a Motorola cellular telephone, expanding the phone's available contact directory, but was useful for little else. The emergence of PIMs targeting children with promises of being able to "beam" secret messages across math class might be the death knell for this branch of strictly limited devices. The market has spoken and requires a great deal more than a phonebook and electronic diary from any device that it's going to, effectively, carry around in its pocket.

Palms, not PIMs

Fortunately, Palm and PalmOS-based devices from other manufacturers are ready to provide what the market is demanding. Before I start exploring the features that distinguish Palms from PIMs, let me explain what I mean by PalmOS.

PalmOS

An *operating system*, as you read in Chapter 1, "The Desktop PC," is a program or set of programs that provides the basic functionality for a device. Everything the device can do is built upon features provided by the operating system, or OS. Microsoft Windows is an operating system that runs on a certain type of Intel and compatible hardware. Windows gives this hardware the ability to execute programs and also provides those programs with a regimented way of interacting with the hardware. How elements appear on a display, how a PC is able to connect with other computers online, how to read data from a DVD, and when it's time to crash are all elements controlled by Windows.

From a programmer's perspective, a well-designed operating system includes a set of tools that make it easy to create new software that shares fundamental ways of interacting with users. This is what makes it allegedly easy to learn any Windows-based application, once you understand how the windows, the menus, the mouse, and other Windows graphical user interface (GUI) features work.

PalmOS is the operating system that runs on hardware created by Palm Computing, Inc., which is a former subsidiary of 3COM. It also runs on hardware made by other manufacturers, including Handspring and Sony. However, whereas a PC can have a variety of general-purpose OS's run on it—Windows, Linux, and so forth—these small, handheld devices need a specialty OS designed exclusively for their hardware. (A notable exception to this is the Agenda VR3, which runs Linux, and which I talk about later in this chapter.) So, the PalmOS can only run on hardware specifically designed for it, and hardware designed to run the PalmOS can *only* run the PalmOS.

Within the PalmOS is all the core functionality of what are generally called "Palm-based" devices, including the Graffiti engine you've already read about. In this way, if a user wants a particular set of features that are offered only by a single hardware manufacturer, she can buy the hardware that fits her needs and still use the familiar Palm interface. A Sony Palm-based device might offer functions not available on a Palm brand PDA, but it will work like every single other PalmOS unit on the market. You'll read about hardware options that exist in the Palm world in just a few pages.

So Much More Than a Phonebook

The PalmOS differentiates the Palm from being a PIM. Although the PalmOS does require a specific type of hardware on which to run, it isn't discriminating about what types of *software* it will run in turn. The PalmOS is a full-featured operating system that provides software developers with all the basic tools they need to design programs that will do just about anything. Games, financial calculators, user-definable databases, GPS (global positioning satellite) locator software, Internet connectivity with e-mail and Web browsing—all of these and more are available for Palm-based devices. Palm devices do include PIM-type software, providing a scheduling calendar, to-do list, and, of course, a phonebook, but they also come with games, notepad software, and an expenses management application. It's this general-purpose functionality and expandability that puts Palm (and similar) devices in a completely different class from PIMs. As far as most users are concerned, Palm-devices were the very first handheld computers that were really useful.

HotSync

A feature that further distinguishes PalmOS-based devices from the PIMs that came before and have come after is the ability to connect a Palm handheld to a more traditional desktop or notebook PC. Using special software that runs on the PC and the Palm, the data on a Palm device can be backed up and updated in one step. The Palm device rests in a cradle like the one shown in Figure 3.7, which, in turn, connects to the PC through a USB port. The process is initiated when the user presses the single button on the cradle. The process is called HotSync.

FIGURE 3.7
The Palm HotSync cradle.

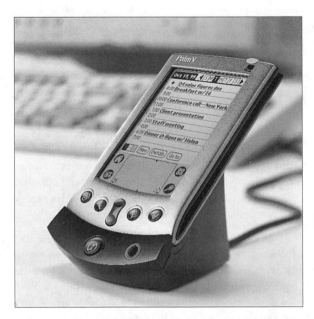

Data and application software can be moved to and from the Palm device during the HotSync process. This is achieved through the use of one of two types of *conduits*. As the name suggests, conduits are pathways along which data travels. The PalmOS provides the first type of conduit to all Palm applications. This is a general-purpose backup and transfer conduit, which makes a desktop-based copy of data stored on the handheld unit and installs new software on the Palm. The general conduit can also extract data from Palm's default desktop companion software (which mirrors the handheld's basic PIM functionality) and update it on the Palm device. In this way, if you have an appointment in your calendar that you modify through the desktop software, when you HotSync next, the appointment will be updated on your Palm device. In order to move data across this conduit, an application on the handheld need only change a single identifying bit from zero to one, and the PalmOS does the rest. (Users can configure whether certain applications are backed up during every HotSync, and that configuration manually changes the bit I'm referring to here, but the software itself can also tell HotSync, "Don't back me up next time.")

The second type of conduit is not provided by the PalmOS, but it is *supported* by the operating system. These are custom-programmed conduits that are created by the developers of the individual pieces of software that the conduits manage. Custom conduits are actually small programs that run whenever the handheld unit is HotSync'd. These can be designed to perform many tasks according to the needs of their software application. For example, a handheld database program can allow you to search for content on your business's master database and then move that data to the handheld. Perhaps it's a subset of the products you stock, showing part numbers and the number you have on hand. Your Palm device can easily go with you to the loading dock and serve as a data-entry point for receiving new parts. As equipment is checked in, you update its record on your Palm. When you get back to your office, you HotSync the handheld. This runs the database conduit, which knows how to look at the database entries on the Palm, search your company's database for corresponding records, and update the master database.

Power in the Palm

As the years have passed, the capabilities of Palm-based devices have exploded. The first such explosion was the introduction of the Palm keyboard, shown in Figure 3.8. The Palm keyboard plugs into the bottom of a PalmOS device, using the same connector that device uses to plug into its HotSync cradle.

With the keyboard in place, users do not have to use either Graffiti or the screen-based keyboard to enter data. Touch-typing on a full-size set of keys allows for the quick and convenient entry of a huge amount of data into the Palm device. The keyboard makes the Palm as useful for note taking or letter writing as a full-featured notebook computer.

FIGURE 3.8

The second major expansion and improvement in Palm-based devices is in their internal memory and processor power. The original PalmPilot came with 128KB of memory and was not expandable. This is roughly enough data to store fewer than 50 contacts—and that's it. Today's Palm-based devices commonly have between 2MB and 8MB of RAM, plus 2MB to 4MB additional ROM memory in which core features are stored. That gives users room for all the information they could want to store for their 3000 closest friends, and still have room left for solitaire and travel expenses. (The Palm's ROM is actually FlashROM, which you'll read about in Chapter 17, "Understanding PC Memory." This is read-only memory (ROM) that can be written to in certain circumstances.)

The power of the Palm has increased dramatically, too. Although MHz figures are never the last word in processor speed—because one processor might be far more efficient than another, even if the second chip has a higher MHz—it is true that the first PalmPilot had a 16MHz processor and current offerings come with a 33MHz one. In the case of the Palms, however, the faster chips are also newer and a great deal more efficient than their 16MHz ancestors, so the actual increase in processor power is *more* than it seems on the surface.

The external power of Palm-based devices is the third area that has exploded in the last few years. You'll look at Palm connectivity in a moment, but what I'm talking about here is the capability to actually perform additional hardware-based tasks.

Companies like Handspring have pioneered PalmOS devices that include a proprietary expansion port, called the *Springboard*. Springboard is a port that's located on the back of Handspring's line of PalmOS devices (collectively called the Handspring *Visor* family of handhelds). This port can be used to install additional memory into the Visor, but is more popular as a feature port. Over 70 Springboard modules are available from different companies, providing a wide range of new capabilities. An example is the VisorPhone module, shown in Figure 3.9.

When mounted on the back of a Handspring Visor, as shown in Figure 3.10, the VisorPhone (which is now free under certain circumstances when you purchase a Visor directly from Handspring) gives full cellular telephone capabilities to the handheld. Rather than carrying around your PDA and your cell phone, you can have both devices in one unit. Similar, the IDEO EyeModule digital camera, shown in Figure 3.11, adds the basic capabilities of a full-color still-image camera to the handheld device.

Figure 3.9
*The Springboard
VisorPhone mod-
ule brings cellular
connectivity to
the Visor line of
PalmOS hand-
helds.*

Figure 3.10
*The VisorPhone
Springboard
module turns a
Handspring Visor
into a cellular
telephone.*

FIGURE 3.11
*The EyeModule
Digital Camera,
from IDEO,
converts a Visor
into a full color
still-image camera.*

Other modules expand the Handspring Visor devices into a GPS (Global Positioning Satellite) tool, an MP3 music player, a voice recorder, a scoring device for your golf game, or even a universal remote control for every IR device in your home. Although Handspring pioneered this type of expandability for PalmOS-based devices, Palm has, itself, followed accordingly, by adding their own proprietary expansion port to their latest m500 and m505 models. Earlier, in Figure 3.6, you saw the Palm m505 with a memory expansion module above it. Palm's expansion port also provides for future expansion devices similar to those currently available for Handspring's Visor line. Regrettably, Visor's products are not compatible with Palm's handhelds.

Connectivity

In addition to being able to expand into whole new worlds of hardware, the Palm-based devices also have a strong foothold in the world of connectivity. Beginning with the Palm III series, all Palm handhelds support integration with Web-based content through TCP/IP. Specially designed "Web clipping" applications allow users to pull content from the Internet or from a company's Intranet to the PalmOS handheld. Additionally, PalmOS handhelds can be expanded to provide a wired or wireless modem connection to the

Internet. In fact, an e-mail client is a standard part of the Palm complement of resident software. Palm handhelds are compatible with all of today's popular e-mail software, including Eudora, Microsoft Outlook, Microsoft Exchange, and Lotus cc:Mail.

Of course, all of the recent PalmOS devices support IrDA (infrared) connectivity, which allows both data *and* programs to be "beamed" from one Palm device to another, or from a Palm device to some other compatible device, like a cellular telephone. I even have a small program on my Palm handheld that allows me to compose ring tones for my Nokia cellular telephone and then beam them directly through the phone's IR port. (It's a useful feature now that most cellular providers are charging for the ability to download ring tones over their networks.)

Linux By the Handful—Agenda

This discussion of the PalmOS shouldn't lead you to the conclusion that it's the only game in town. That's far from true. You'll learn about the major competition to the PalmOS—Windows CE—in just a moment. Before exploring Windows CE, I wanted to take a little time to introduce the latest development in the handheld world, from a company called Agenda. Their handheld device, called the VR3, is the world's first Linux-based PDA. That is, rather than running the PalmOS or some other operating system, the VR3 runs Linux.

The idea of running Linux on a PDA is a step forward in several ways. First, Linux makes the VR3 the first PDA that is capable of true multitasking, not merely task-switching. Users can retrieve or enter contact information or take meeting notes while the VR3 retrieves data from the Internet through a network connection. Additionally, Linux makes the VR3 the first truly open-source PDA device. In a world where need traditionally mandates proprietary solutions to hardware and software problems, the VR3 will actually run any Linux software that fits on it, and developers can use standard Linux tools and libraries to create applications for it.

The VR3, although the first device of its kind, comes with a feature set that is appealing to users as well as developers. It has 16MB of *Flash memory* (that is, memory that holds its contents permanently, except under special conditions in which it can be modified or erased) and 8MB of RAM, giving it ample room for software and data. It supports audio input and output, giving it the native ability to serve as an MP3 player or digital voice recorder. It also features a built-in high-power infrared port, making it suitable as a remote-control device without requiring the purchase of an external IR module. Like PalmOS devices, the Agenda can be expanded to support a modem, and it provides synchronization with a desktop or notebook PC.

Windows-Centered Devices

This section is called "Windows-Centered Devices" because there are several classes of devices that compete with the PalmOS-based handhelds, all of which use one or another version of Microsoft Windows as its embedded operating system. You'll read about the different types here and do a little feature and functionality comparison. Before you dive into that boiling pot, however, note first that the answer to which class of devices is better is very subjective. It's fairly common to read that PalmOS devices excel for their clean interface and ease of use, whereas Windows-based devices (Pocket PCs and Handheld PCs, or HPCs) have a stronger "wow" factor. But "wow" can mean "wow, that's exciting," or "wow, that's hard to use," so it's not as simple as deciding whether you want bells and whistles or a workhorse, as you'll see.

Let's first take a quick look at the history of Windows-based handhelds, and then you'll explore Pocket PCs and Handheld PCs.

Windows CE 1.0 and 2

Windows CE first premiered in late 1996 as a handheld version of the standard Microsoft Windows operating system. From what you've already read in this chapter, you might remember that this date coincides closely with the successful release and marketing of the earliest PalmPilot device. Windows CE attempted to provide handheld users a scaled-down Windows interface that was familiar and, thus, simple to use. But there were numerous problems.

First, Windows seems to have been somewhat ill-suited to the small device format. Users of the earliest Windows CE devices complained—with justification—at the huge amount of screen space wasted by the size of window scroll bars, frames, and menus. Most of these first devices did not support rechargeable batteries, and after about 20 hours of use—or after about two weeks sitting idle—the system's alkaline batteries had to be replaced. The earliest Windows CE devices supported only four shades of gray, limiting the apparent resolution of their LCD screens. When support for 24-bit color was implemented in Windows CE 2.0, the added functionality came with a high cost in battery life.

Many people were of the opinion that, although Windows CE devices *looked* like they were running Windows, they operated differently enough that the seeming similarity actually made them harder to use. (Consider the pleasure of finding a handheld device that uses the familiar Windows check boxes, windows, and menus, and the frustration of finding that those graphical elements don't work the ways you're used to. Every time you switch from desktop to handheld, you have to remind yourself how each environment operates, even though they look the same.)

Windows CE 3.0, or Pocket PC

The latest version of Windows CE, 3.0, has improved functionality and performance to the point that it provides serious competition to PalmOS-based handhelds. Windows CE 3.0's name has been changed, too, to Pocket PC, apparently in an attempt by Microsoft to encourage the notion that this is a whole new ballgame. In some ways, it is. The Pocket PC natively supports a wealth of multimedia capabilities including playback of MP3 files and digital voice recording. Web browsing is possible through the inclusion of Internet Explorer for Pocket PC. E-mail, with attachments, can be sent and received through a reduced version of Microsoft Office called, not surprisingly, Pocket Outlook. Pocket PC devices include more powerful, updated versions of core Windows CE software, too, including Pocket Word and Pocket Excel. These give the Pocket PC devices the native ability to directly read and create files in the standard, desktop formats. (For the record, software is available for PalmOS devices that provide similar capabilities.) These Pocket Office programs also provide for tight integration between the desktop and Pocket PC. On the other hand, Microsoft has decided to provide *no* support for using a Pocket PC device with an Apple Macintosh or Linux/Unix-based computer.

Pocket PC devices also include native support for true handwriting recognition, as well as their own version of a Graffiti-like shorthand. Unfortunately, true handwriting recognition is, today, little better than it has been for years. Most users find it easier to jot a quick note into the Pocket PC notepad and then transcribe the note to text later, rather than relying on the device's recognition engine.

Finally, Pocket PC devices uniformly use a display that runs at a higher resolution than do the PalmOS devices, and color Pocket PCs use a higher color depth as well. This makes graphic images brighter and sharper on Pocket PCs than they are on Palm-based handhelds. What it does not do, however, is give you the extra workspace you might think it would. PalmOS applications have been designed to make the most of that hardware's display, with no waste. Much of the time, the Pocket PC's screen is being used by the OS, and is dedicated to providing an interface that looks like Windows (with menus and scroll bars and window frames) rather than providing the maximum possible user area. Nevertheless, if you want a handheld to view digital images or other multimedia content, the Pocket PC is your best bet.

On the downside, Pocket PC devices are still attempting to do what some have called impossible: trying to get Windows to run in a small, low-power environment. It turns out that the Pocket PC OS is just as memory and power-hungry as its predecessors, although, of course, today's hardware comes with rechargeable batteries. The memory hunger is really more of an issue. Although Pocket PC devices commonly come with at least twice as much memory as PalmOS devices, the Windows interface that makes Pocket PCs work also *uses* much more memory than does the PalmOS. This means that the reality of

Pocket PC devices—that they have about the same or less usable memory than comparable PalmOS devices—is a great deal different from how their specs appear in marketing copy. One consultant I know recommends that no one purchase a Pocket PC device unless they can comfortably afford to add a 32MB or larger memory expansion card, too.

The power-hungry aspect of Pocket PC devices extends also to the demands they place on their processors. It's common for Pocket PC devices to have CPUs that run at 206MHz, compared to the 33MHz processors found in high-end PalmOS handhelds. Yet, for the majority of tasks, users find that the PalmOS performs faster than does Pocket PC.

Handheld PCs

Handheld PCs are also Windows CE 3.0 devices (although CE 4.0 is on its way at the time of this writing), but their hardware configuration is a good deal different from Pocket PCs. First and most obviously, Handheld PCs have a physical keyboard, not just the on-screen simulation provided by the PalmOS or Pocket PC. For the most part, these are so small that users end up typing with just two fingers, taking short notes that they expand when they can sit down with a full-size keyboard on their desktop or laptop. Handheld PC screens are larger than those on Pocket PC devices, and screen and keyboard together lead to a device that weighs in at one pound, or slightly more. Handheld PCs offer the same suite of Microsoft Pocket Office applications and similar e-mail and Internet connectivity as do Pocket PCs, although the physical keyboard makes for an arguably more productive writing or e-mail composing experience. It's not uncommon for a Handheld PC to include an internal modem, and they often support external connections to Ethernet networks if you plug in a PC Card network adapter.

Comparisons

Although it might sound like it, I don't side exclusively with PalmOS devices. I introduced the idea of making a comparison between the two platforms by saying that choosing one over the other can be a very subjective thing. Naturally, as with any PC, you need to be certain that the software you want to run—and the tasks you want to perform—are supported by the hardware you intend to purchase. The best way—and really, the only reasonable way—to select a handheld PC or PDA is to actually work with the models you're considering, at least for a few minutes. Most major computer and discount electronics stores are now set up to let you do this.

For the most part, if you want a fully capable multimedia device, you'll want to look hard at the Windows-based products. Excellent among them is the Cassiopeia line of Pocket PCs from Casio. Figure 3.12 shows their E125 model, the top of the line color device at the time of this writing.

Figure 3.12
Casio's Cassiopeia Model E125.

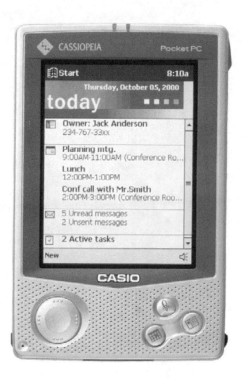

This unit is roughly the size—and cost— of comparable PalmOS products, although its display is far superior to most everything on the market. It can be read in direct sunlight, which is practically unheard of for color PDAs, and supports 16-bit color, so digital images appear true and sharp. It comes with 32MB of RAM right out of the box—ample room to run the Pocket PC OS, plus applications, plus store your data.

If, instead, you want a hardcore business tool that can be expanded to support multimedia capabilities if and when you decide you want them, look to the PalmOS-based devices. These are better optimized for handheld use and aren't hobbled by an attempt to move a full-screen environment to a 240 by 320 pixel screen. Although the PalmOS interface might be new to you, I think you'll find that it is easy to learn. This eliminates the "buy what you already know how to use" factor and lets you focus your purchase decision on the features/cost balance. In this way, you'll buy a device that you'll actually use, and not just one that seems particularly "cool" in the store.

Understanding Bits and Bytes

You've learned a lot already about the hardware that makes up your desktop PC and the portable and handheld PCs you might also work with daily. To really understand how the hardware is built and how it works, you first need to come to terms with what *information* is. I've said that computers are used for processing information, but what is information, *really*? In this chapter, you learn what makes up the information in your computer. You'll also explore the many ways that information is represented inside a PC. Overall, you'll explore how the real world and the PC world relate and interact.

You might think this is all very arcane stuff that only a geek would want to know. Actually, this topic is very important for anyone who wants to know *how* computers work. If that's your goal—and presumably it is, because you're here—there are two aspects of digital information you need to understand:

- The fundamental language of digital computers is written in binary numbers. That language is often presented in ways that are much easier for humans to understand and work with comfortably.
- Most data documents contain redundant information; knowing this enables you to compress those data files.

The purpose of this chapter is to explain each of these fundamental and significant concepts. This chapter concludes part I of this book, and as such, it helps bridge the gap to part II, where you really start to dig into how your PC actually does what it does and, of course, why that knowledge is useful to you.

What Are Information and Data?

Most people have an intuitive sense of what information is. You've worked with it for years, and these days, not a day goes by that you don't encounter the word. But can you define it precisely? In truth, most people can't. In the day-to-day workings of the world, most people never need to define it, and so they've never thought about it.

On the other hand, people whose daily business *is* information tend to think about such things, and it turns out that there is a clear way to carefully define what information is. Information can best be understood as *what it takes to answer a question*. That is, given any question conceivable, *information* is the content—in whatever form—necessary to answer that question meaningfully.

There's an advantage to putting it this way: it becomes possible to determine exactly how much information is needed to answer particular questions. It has enabled computer designers to build information-holding places that are large enough to hold the needed information. It has also enabled these folks to create processing systems that are fast enough to manipulate the required quantity of information in a useful amount of time.

How Big Is a Question?

The simplest type of question is one that can be answered as either yes or no, because you only need the minimum amount of information to specify the correct answer. The minimum amount of information in a PC, or you can say the smallest unit of information, is called a *bit* (short for *binary digit*).

In mathematical terms, the value of a bit is a 1 or a 0. These values can represent true or false or yes or no. In electrical engineering terms, a bit's value is represented by a voltage somewhere that is either high or low. Similarly, in a magnetic storage medium (such as a disk or tape, for example), a bit's value can be stored by magnetizing a region of the medium in some specified direction or in the opposite direction. Many other ways to think about bits and other means for storing them are also possible, and you'll meet at least a few later.

How Big Is an Answer?

Certainly, the world contains questions that cannot be answered with simple yes-no answers. So, if a computer's fundamental unit for working with information is the bit—which can only have two options—there must be a way of putting bits together so that they can represent answers to more complex questions. And naturally, the world contains tasks to accomplish that aren't strictly questions. Consider the everyday task of writing a letter. A letter is filled with numbers and words, and they are made up of letters separated by spaces and punctuation symbols. How does the yes-no world of the computer meet the needs of letter writers?

Well, if you write down all the possible letters, numbers, and symbols in a representative language, you'll see how many different ones of these there are (disregarding how often each one occurs). Consider giving each of those unique symbols a numeric label. If you have a letter that contains 43 unique symbols or characters, you have a *character set* with 43 members. The order of the symbols in your character set means nothing—although you might want to write the symbols down in alphabetical order, because, as humans, we're used to working in that order.

If you do this, the letter "A" might get the label 0. The letter "B" might be 1 and perhaps, the question-mark character would end up being 37. Recall that the fundamental unit of information in a computer is a bit, and a bit can have a value of either 0 or 1. If you list two or more bits together, you'll be counting in the *binary number system*. We're much more used to the decimal number system, where we use 10 distinct symbols to count from zero to nine, and then start over, adding places to the left as we count higher and higher. In the computer's binary world of ones and zeros, you don't have 10 symbols to count with—you only have two: one and zero. But counting works the same way. You can count from zero to one using one digit. You can then add a place to the left and continue counting. Just as there is the "ten's place" in decimal counting, there is a "two's place" in binary counting. The two systems translate like this:

Decimal	Binary
0	0
1	1
2	10
3	11
4	100
5	101
6	110
7	111
8	1000
9	1001
10	1010

You probably already have worked with this sort of thing in past mathematics classes. The point here is that it's not difficult to represent decimal numbers in the binary number system that PC's use.

Going back to the letter-writing example, you saw that it's also no problem to represent things like letters and punctuation by using numbers. The letter "A" as zero, a question-mark as 37, or what have you. By extension, then, you can now see how letters can be manipulated in the PC's binary language. Text is converted into numbers by assigning every possible text character to a number-label in a character set. The PC simply works with the binary representation of those numbers. Reasonably enough, this is what people mean when they say that information in a computer is just a string of ones and zeros. The ones and zeros work together to represent real-world information.

A Little Bit Is a Little Bit Too Little

The binary nature of computers cuts both ways. On the one hand, it's a very simple, unambiguous world. There are millions of switches inside your PC's main processor, each of which can be on or off, representing a one or a zero, in turn. (You'll read much more about processors in the next chapter.) There are no "somewhat on" or "maybe" states inside your PC. On the other hand, endless strings of ones and zeros are pretty cumbersome. Let me show you an example.

Using one common character set, called ASCII, which you'll read about in a moment, the following table shows a name with its decimal and binary equivalents.

Common Text	S	C	O	T	T
Decimals	83	67	79	84	84
Binary	1010011	1000011	1001111	1010100	1010100

All those 1s and 0s are far too cumbersome for humans trying to program and design computers, so you don't, in fact, have to deal with bits one at a time. Instead, you look at collections or groups of bits. For historical reasons—the first chips designed to work in PC-like computers moved eight bits of data at a time—bits are grouped into eights, which are called *bytes*.

When considering how information is represented and stored inside the PC, people consider the number of bytes needed to make that representation happen or to make that information fit. In the ASCII character set, each letter or symbol is represented by a single byte. With eight bits in a byte, and each bit able to store a zero or a one, eight bits together store up to 256 values. (With one byte, you can count from 00000000—a byte with the value of zero—up to 11111111—a byte with the value of 2^8, or 256.) The extended ASCII character set, then, has 256 members.

Bytes can store more than just text characters, however. In the world of graphics, you can use one byte to store a color value for each dot of light in an image (which, as you'll read in Chapter 6, "Video and Monitors," are called *pixels)*. This allows you to have up to 256 colors in that image. This is where the term *eight-bit image* comes from.

Bytes can represent sound, too. Using just one byte, you can represent every note on a piano almost three times over. A different byte can represent how long each note plays, one of up to 256 lengths. It's easy to conceive of a rudimentary music program that uses just these two bytes to send instructions to your PC's sound card to play a recognizable tune.

But human eyes can see many more than 256 colors. And, when it comes to digital music, we all want something that sounds better than a buzzy tootle-toot. To represent the complex real world more accurately inside the PC, we need to group again, using collections of bytes.

Note: Depending on the environment that you're working in, a collection of two, four, or sixteen bytes is sometimes called a word, but that's a bit of jargon that has fallen out of use, for the most part. Have you ever heard anyone advertising "one word graphics"? No. But have you heard of 32-bit graphics? Absolutely. This is one of those delightful, too-rare instances where PC jargon has lost out to clarity.

Naturally, by combining bytes, you dramatically increase the number of things you can represent. One byte—eight bits, each of which can have one of two values—can keep track of 256 (2^8) colors. Two bytes, sixteen bits, can keep track of up to 65,536 (that's 2^16) colors. When you put three bytes together, the sixteen million-plus colors allow you to store enough color information to produce a realistic-looking photographic image. Note the example in Figure 4.1.

FIGURE 4.1

The qualitative difference between 2-bit, 8-bit, and 24-bit color images.

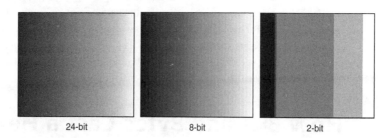

24-bit   8-bit   2-bit

Taking all of this into consideration, perhaps you can now understand the relationship between information in the real world and how that information is represented and stored inside the PC. The term *digital data* is often used when those bytes are working together. The distinction between data and information is a subtle one. Data is the raw resource that, when combined with a specific context, creates meaning. A seemingly endless string of numbers is just data. The same string of numbers manipulated so that it creates a graphical chart showing your company's five-year growth relative to market performance—that's information.

To keep track of all the information in your PC, however, requires a *lot* of those seemingly endless strings of bytes. Thousands of them, in fact. So it's common to talk about large collections of data. When you have roughly one thousand bytes, you have one *kilobyte*.

Note: In fact, a kilobyte is exactly 1024 bytes. Bytes exist in the world of binary numbers, in which exactly 1000 isn't a very convenient number. 1000 is a simple number in the decimal world, because it's 10^3. But the closest equivalent in binary counting is 1024, which is 2^10.

Kilobytes are usually represented by KB, so 100KB means roughly 100,000 bytes. The PC file that contains this chapter is about 200KB. A standard 3.5" floppy disk originally had the capacity to store 740KB bytes. Today, they can store 1200KB, but that starts to become a cumbersome way of talking about things. So, it's time to group yet again.

A collection of one thousand kilobytes—that is, one million bytes—is a *megabyte*. Megabytes are usually represented by the abbreviation MB and it's common to call them "megs." Rather than saying you have a 1200KB floppy disk, you might say instead that you have 1.2meg floppy disk. Similarly, 20 years ago, an absolutely huge hard disk drive costing about $10,000 was capable of storing 10MB (or 10 megs) of data. That's $1000 per megabyte. Today, an audio CD can hold about 80 minutes of digital music in roughly 700MB of space.

In the last few years, two additional terms have become common. A *gigabyte* is a collection of one thousand million bytes (1000MB). (In the United States, this is one "billion," although that term has different meanings in Europe.) Gigabytes are usually called "gigs" or "jigs," depending on whether you prefer the hard or soft "g" sound. Gigabyte is usually abbreviated GB. Today's hard drives, costing about $150 at the time of this writing, normally have capacity for about 100GB of data. That's $0.01 per *hundred* megabytes. The other relatively new term is *terabyte*, which refers to 1000GB of data, can be abbreviated TB, and is usually called unbelievably expensive.

How Bits and Bytes Cast a Hex on ASCII

In order to start exploring how bits and bytes are actually used, let's return for a moment to the idea of character sets. Early teletypewriters used five or six bits per symbol. They were severely restricted, therefore, in the number of distinct symbols a message could contain (to 32 or 64 possibilities, respectively). To see just how restrictive this is, consider that there are 26 letters in the Latin alphabet, and every one of them comes in an upper-case (capitalized) form and a lowercase (uncapitalized) form. In addition, there are 10 numerals and quite a few punctuation symbols (for example, the period, comma, semicolon, colon, plus and minus signs, apostrophe, quotation mark, and so on). Count them and just the ones I've mentioned here come to 70 distinct characters, and this is too many for a six-bit code. Even leaving out the lowercase letters, you'll have 44 characters, which is too many for a five-bit code.

For about the first half of modern computing history, all these symbols were in fact accommodated by using seven bits. That allows 128 symbols, which is enough for all the lowercase and uppercase letters in the Latin alphabet, all 10 digits, and a generous assortment of punctuation symbols. This standard (which now has the formal name of the American Standard Code for Information Interchange, or *ASCII*, pronounced "ask-ee") uses only 96 of the 128 possibilities for these printable symbols.

The remaining 32 characters are reserved for various *control characters*. These values encode the carriage return (start typing at the left margin once again), the line feed (moves the paper up a line), tab, backspace, vertical tab, and so on. The ASCII standard also includes symbols to indicate the end of a message. ASCII, then, is a way to *encode* text characters so they can be represented by bytes.

Symbols and Codes

Codes are a way to convey information. If you know the code, you can read the information. Naturally, the more general purpose a code is, the more useful it will likely be to a large number of people. (Paul Revere's "one if by land, two if by sea" was a perfectly valid code; it's just not especially helpful today.)

Any code, in the sense I am using the term here, can be represented by a table or list of symbols or characters and their alternative (coded) meanings. The particular symbols used, their order, the encoding defined for each symbol, and the total number of symbols define that particular coding scheme.

> **Tip:** In order not to be confused by all this talk of bits, bytes, symbols, characters sets, and codes, keep in mind that the symbols you want to represent are *not* held in your PC. Only a coded version of them can be put there. If you actually look at the contents of your PC's memory, you'll find only a lot of numbers. (Depending on the tool you use to do this looking, the numbers might be translated into other symbols, but that is only because the tool assumes that the numbers represent characters in some coded character set.)

You'll encounter two common codes as you work with increasingly technical documentation on PCs:

- Hexadecimal
- ASCII

The hexadecimal code makes writing binary numbers easier. ASCII is the most common code used when documents are held in a PC.

Hexadecimal Numbers

The first of the two common coding schemes is *hexadecimal numbering*, which is a base-16 method of counting, often simply called "hex". It takes 16 distinct symbols to represent the "digits" of a number in base-16, hence the name. Because there are only 10 distinct Arabic numerals, those have been augmented with the first six letters of the Latin alphabet (usually capitalized) to get the 16 symbols needed to represent hexadecimal numbers (see Table 4.1).

Table 4.1   The First 16 Numbers in Three Number Bases

Decimal	Binary	Hexadecimal	Decimal	Binary	Hexadecimal
0	0 0 0 0	0	8	1 0 0 0	8
1	0 0 0 1	1	9	1 0 0 1	9
2	0 0 1 0	2	10	1 0 1 0	A
3	0 0 1 1	3	11	1 0 1 1	B
4	0 1 0 0	4	12	1 1 0 0	C
5	0 1 0 1	5	13	1 1 0 1	D
6	0 1 1 0	6	14	1 1 1 0	E
7	0 1 1 1	7	15	1 1 1 1	F

Hexadecimal is nothing more than an economical way to write large binary numbers. Programmers and other technical people often prefer it to simply using base-10 numbers because Hex is much closer to the PC's native world of binary numbers and eight-bit bytes.

You can recognize a hexadecimal number in two ways. If a number contains some normal decimal digits (0, 1, … 9) and some letters (A through F), it is almost certainly a hexadecimal number. Sometimes authors will add the letter *h* after the number. When speaking of hex values, it's common to say, for example, "hex forty-three" or "hex thirteen-a" for *43h* or *13Ah*, respectively.

Although converting between binary, decimal, and hexadecimal is a good skill for programmers to have, it's not something that most people want to get involved with, mathematically. Fortunately, there's an easy solution to those times when you might want to convert between the different number systems.

The small calculator application (usually called an *applet*, incidentally) that comes with Microsoft Windows can instantly convert any value from any of these bases to any other. To use it, just launch the Calculator, which you'll usually find under Accessories in the Programs section of your Start menu. In order to use the base-conversion features, you'll need to change the view from the standard calculator to the scientific one. To do this, simply select Scientific from the Calculator's View menu. At this point, you can perform any mathematical operations you choose—or you can simply key in whatever number you want to convert. Keys labeled "A" through "F" allow you to key in hexadecimal numbers directly. To change the base at any time, simply click one of the radio buttons in the upper-left, selecting "Hex," for Hexadecimal (base-16), "Dec," for Decimal (base-10), "Oct," for Octal (base-8, which you don't need in the context of any mainstream PC use), or "Bin," for Binary (base-2).

Try an example, if you like. Follow these directions, and then key in 10,111,967. Click the "Bin" radio button and there you have it: 1001 1010 0100 1011 1101 1111.

The ASCII and Extended-ASCII Codes

The other very common code you'll encounter in the world of PCs is ASCII. As you've already read, ASCII has been the almost-universally accepted code for storing text information in a PC. If you look at the contents of one of your documents in memory (or on a PC disk), you usually must translate the numbers you find there according to this code to see the document. Of course, because ASCII is so commonly used, many programs exist to help you translate ASCII-encoded information back into a more readable form. Among others, this class of software includes word processors and notepads.

True ASCII uses only seven bits per symbol. This means there can be only 128 characters (symbols) in the ASCII character set. About one quarter of these (those with values 0 through 31, and 127) are reserved, according to the ASCII definition, for control characters. The rest are printable. (Some of the control code characters have onscreen representations. Whether you see symbols or have an action performed depends on the context in which your PC encounters those control code byte values.)

> **Note:** They're called control characters because, back in the ancient days of teletypes, they actually controlled the teletype's print-head and paper handling. In order to underline a letter, for example, you had to transmit the letter, and then a control character that signified "backspace the print-head one space" and then the underscore character. In order to make it easy to enter these characters, the Control or Ctrl key was added to electronic keyboards. You would hold down Ctrl and then press the appropriate letter key. ASCII code 7, for example, stands for Ctrl+G, which would audibly ring the teletype's bell. Ctrl+H, ASCII code 8, is the backspace control character.

Those symbols and the ASCII control code mnemonics are shown in Figure 4.2. You add the decimal or hexadecimal number at the left of any row to the corresponding number at the top of any column in order to get the ASCII code value for the symbol shown where that row and column intersect. Table 4.2, later in this chapter, shows the standard definitions for the ASCII control codes.

Because PCs do use full bytes of information, they are able to use a character set (that is, a code) with twice as many elements as pure ASCII (which, recall, used only seven bits). Each manufacturer of these small computers was free to decide independently how to use those extra possibilities. Many companies made many different choices for how to use what are now sometimes called the *extended-ASCII* characters (those with values from 128 through 255). In the world of IBM's PC family they allowed DOS-based text programs to include common foreign-language symbols like é and ñ. Some also provided the means to draw lines or other non-letter shapes on DOS's restrictive "character only" display. In this way, what were actually ASCII characters 200, 205, and 188 would appear on the screen like this: ___ (You'll read more about PC displays and how they have evolved in Chapters 6 and 20, "Video and Monitors" and "Video Acceleration".)

FIGURE 4.2
The ASCII character set, including the standard mnemonics and the IBM graphics symbols for the 33 ASCII control characters.

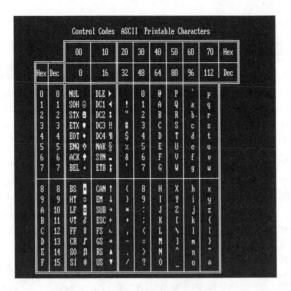

In the past, printing these extended-ASCII characters from DOS was difficult if the printer manufacturer didn't use the same set of extra symbols that IBM did. Today, of course, most people do all of their printing through Windows, so what you see on the screen is usually exactly what you get on paper. This convenient fact is described by the acronym, *WYSIWYG* (pronounced "wizzy-wig") meaning "What You See Is What You Get."

Not everything in your PC uses ASCII coding. In particular, programs are stored in files filled with what might be regarded as the CPU's native language, which is all numbers. Various tools you might use to look inside these files show what at first glance looks like garbage. In fact, the symbols you see are meaningless to people. Only the actual numerical values (and the CPU instructions they represent) matter. These numbers are, in fact, the machine language that you'll read much more about in Chapter 5, "A First Look at Motherboards and Processors."

Control Codes

Any useful computer coding scheme must use some of its definitions for symbols or characters that stand for actions rather than for printable entities. These include actions such as ending a line, returning the printing position to the left margin, moving to the next tab (in any of four directions—horizontally or vertically, forward or backward).

Only the special codes indicate the beginning or the end of a message. Another special code lets the message-sending computer ask the message-receiving computer to give a standardized response.

Four important PC control codes include the acknowledge and negative-acknowledge codes, the escape code, and the null code. These are used when data is being sent from one PC to another, for example, by modem. The first pair are used by the receiving computer to let the sending computer know whether a message has been received correctly, among other uses. The escape code often signals that the following symbols are to be interpreted according to some other special scheme. The null code often signals the end of a string of characters.

Table 4.2 shows all the officially defined control codes and their two- or three-letter mnemonics. These definitions are codified in an American National Standards Institute document, *ANSI X3.4-1986*.

Table 4.2   The Standard Meanings for the ASCII Control Codes

ASCII Value Decimal (Hex)	Keyboard Equivalent	Mnemonic Name	Description
0 (0h)	Ctrl+@	NULL	Null
1 (1h)	Ctrl+A	SOH	Start of heading
2 (2h)	Ctrl+B	STX	Start of text
3 (3h)	Ctrl+C	ETX	End of text
4 (4h)	Ctrl+D	EOT	End of transmission
5 (5h)	Ctrl+E	ENQ	Enquire
6 (6h)	Ctrl+F	ACK	Acknowledge
7 (7h)	Ctrl+G	BEL	Bell
8 (8h)	Ctrl+H	BS	Backspace
9 (9h)	Ctrl+I	HT	Horizontal tab
10 (Ah)	Ctrl+J	LF	Line feed
11 (Bh)	Ctrl+K	VT	Vertical tab
12 (Ch)	Ctrl+L	FF	Form feed (new page)
13 (Dh)	Ctrl+M	CR	Carriage return
14 (Eh)	Ctrl+N	SO	Shift out
15 (Fh)	Ctrl+O	SI	Shift in
16 (10h)	Ctrl+P	DLE	Data link escape
17 (11h)	Ctrl+Q	DC1	Device control 1
18 (12h)	Ctrl+R	DC2	Device control 2
19 (13h)	Ctrl+S	DC3	Device control 3
20 (14h)	Ctrl+T	DC4	Device control 4
21 (15h)	Ctrl+U	NAK	Negative acknowledge
22 (16h)	Ctrl+V	SYN	Synchronous idle
23 (17h)	Ctrl+W	ETB	End of transmission block

Table 4.2   Continued

ASCII Value Decimal (Hex)	Keyboard Equivalent	Mnemonic Name	Description
24 (18h)	Ctrl+X	CAN	Cancel
25 (19h)	Ctrl+Y	EM	End of medium
26 (1Ah)	Ctrl+Z	SUB	Substitute
27 (1Bh)	Ctrl+[	ESC	Escape
28 (1Ch)	Ctrl+\	FS	Form separator
29 (1Dh)	Ctrl+]	GS	Group separator
30 (1Eh)	Ctrl+^	RS	Record separator
31 (1Fh)	Ctrl+_	US	Unit separator
127 (3Fh)	Alt+127	DEL	Delete

As you now know, Ctrl+X means press and hold the *Ctrl* key while pressing the *x* key. Alt+127, which enters the Delete code, means to press and hold the Alt key while pressing the 1, 2, and 7 keys successively on the numeric keypad portion of your keyboard.

Unicode

You understand now why the early five- and six-bit teletype codes weren't adequate to do the job of encoding all the messages and data being handled on your PC. What might be less obvious is why even an eight-bit code like extended-ASCII isn't sufficient. If everyone on the planet spoke and wrote only in English, eight bits might be plenty. But that clearly is not reality. By one count, there are almost 6,800 human languages. Eventually, someone will want to be able to communicate in each of them using a PC.

The importance of this is becoming clearer and clearer. At first, people tried some simple tricks to extend extended-ASCII. That was enough for a while, but soon the difficulties of using those tricks outweighed their advantages. And in any case, it was becoming apparent that these types of tricks just wouldn't do at all for the broader task ahead.

In the beginning, the heavy users of computers of all kinds were people who used a language based on an alphabet, usually one that was similar to English. Simple variations on the ASCII code table were worked out, one for each language, so that the set of symbols included all the special letters and accents used in that country. These "code pages" could then be loaded into a PC, and it would be ready to work with text in that language.

However, this strategy can work only if two conditions are met. First, the computer in question must be used for only one of these languages at a time. Second, the languages must be based on alphabets similar to the English alphabet.

Some very important languages use too many different characters to fit into even a 256-member character set. This is clearly true for the Asian languages that are based on ideographs, and for many others. At first, people thought they could solve this problem by devising more complex character sets, one per language to be encoded. And the really difficult languages were handled by combining groups of characters that would together stand for each of the more exotic characters.

The solution ultimately was to devise an entirely new encoding scheme—one that has enough capacity to hold all the symbols used in any of the 6,800 languages of the people on this planet. This new system is called *Unicode*.

The basic approach is to represent each symbol in Unicode with a 16-bit (that is, a two-byte) number. Normally, this means one can represent at most 65,536 distinct characters or symbols. (Remember you can use two bytes together to represent up to 65,636 colors. Unicode is simply another system that represents real-life information with 16 bits of computer data.) This 16-bit set of possible symbols is called, in Unicode jargon, the *Basic Multilingual Plane* (BMP). A little more jargon: using this BMP system is called *UCS-2 encoding*. Another Unicode standard exists, called *UCS-4*, which, naturally enough, uses four bytes for each character, rather than two.

Figure 4.3 compares the extended-ASCII way of representing a character with the Unicode UCS-2 and UCS-4 methods.

FIGURE 4.3

Three ways characters are represented in PCs.

How Characters Are Represented in a PC

Extended-ASCII Representation

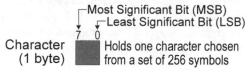

Character (1 byte) — Holds one character chosen from a set of 256 symbols

Unicode (UCS-2) Representation

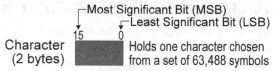

Character (2 bytes) — Holds one character chosen from a set of 63,488 symbols

Unicode (UCS-4) Representation

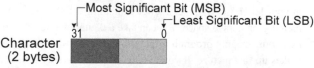

Character (2 bytes)

Each of the two 16-bit words that makes up a UCS-4 character holds a number within a special 1024-number range in the UCS-2 Basic Multilingual Plane. The combination of these two numbers specifies a location in a million-plus location plane for custom characters that don't fit within the UCS-2 BMP.

Why not simply use four bytes per character from the outset? The answer is that this is too wasteful of space. You can almost always get away with two-byte characters, and only when you need to use something more exotic do you have to dedicate four bytes per symbol. This still means that a document that is all stored in Unicode will be at least twice the size of that same document stored in ASCII (assuming it could be represented accurately in ASCII), and possibly just a little bit more if it includes some of those special characters that require four bytes.

> **Note:** The details of Unicode are well beyond the scope of this book. If you are interested, you can find most of them on the Internet. Point your browser to the Unicode home page at:
>
> `http://www.unicode.org/`
>
> and follow the links you find there.

In Windows 98, Windows Me, Windows 2000, and Windows XP, you are using Unicode (probably without knowing that you are). Every directory entry pointing to a file on your disk drives is stored using Unicode. Directories on certain optical disks also use Unicode. And Microsoft Office applications use Unicode extensively in the document files they create. This makes it much easier for these programs to support users with different language needs. You set your language preference once (and it is recorded in the Windows Registry). Thereafter, every program you use, including Windows Explorer, shows you displays in your language, interpreted from the Unicode representation. And surely this is only the beginning. No program can claim to be truly international unless it supports Unicode.

Reducing Bits, Bytes, and Real Life

At the beginning of this chapter, I asked the questions "How big is a question?" and "How big is an answer?". You've seen that, as far as the PC is concerned, the answers to those questions depend on how many bytes of data it takes to accurately represent whatever it is that you want from the PC: text, sound, visuals, and so forth. You can very easily type a letter in an ASCII text editor. That editor uses one byte of data to represent every character in your letter. In principle, a letter containing 1000 characters can fit into 1KB of PC memory or storage space. You can take a digital picture of your family and open it on your PC. Your imaging program might use two bytes to store the color of each dot of light that makes up that picture. If you assume a common array of 640 horizontal dots (pixels) and 480 vertical dots, you come up with a total of 307,200 dots. Representing the color of each dot with 16 bits of data should make such a picture take at least 614KB (that's two bytes for each pixel).

In fact, modern software is a lot more sophisticated than that. There is a lot of repeated information in almost any photograph, for example. Remember that a big patch of blue sky is really nothing more than lots of bytes all storing a numerical code that means "blue". If you've got a bunch of these blue bytes together, you don't actually need to store every single byte. Instead, you can simply use three or four bytes to say "the next 243 pixels are blue." When your imaging program encounters that data, it translates the abbreviation back into 243 blue pixels and perfectly reproduces the photograph. But you've used three or four bytes rather than 243.

Similarly, a short story about home life might contain the word "Mother" 958 times. Using ASCII, it takes six bytes to represent "Mother," which equates to 5748 bytes throughout the manuscript. What if, instead, you use a single byte—one of those extended-ASCII values that you're not using in the document, like ASCII 207, perhaps—to represent every occurrence of the word "Mother." By using one byte to represent the value of six bytes, you've reduced that 5748 bytes down to only 958.

This kind of replacement is called *compression*, and, specifically, it's *lossless compression*, because appropriate software can perfectly reproduce the original photograph or document. Compression is used throughout the PC world, and especially in preparing to send data across the Internet or over a phone line. Naturally, the less data you have to move, the less time it takes. (You can read more about compression, including a second important type, *lossy compression* in Chapter 18, "Storage: How Does Data Get There?". It's an important factor inside the PC.)

Summary and Looking Ahead

Everything to do with your PC comes down to bits and bytes. The programs you run are written in high-level computer languages that are convenient for people. But those programs are reduced to nothing more than bytes that represent the instructions the PC's processor can understand. Data that moves between modems (which you'll read about in Chapter 12, "Modems and Broadband") is turned into sound waves so that it can be carried by the telephone system. But your modem just turns those sound signals back into strings of bytes.

Your PC doesn't know anything about music, or literature, or art. It only knows how to manipulate binary numbers. The use of bits and bytes to represent data is arbitrary. There's no such thing as a byte of music, or a byte of video. People do usually think about data this way, though.

Try an experiment and you'll see why. Try to open, say, a picture file using a text editor, or a digital music file using an illustration program. In either case, if you get anything at all, you'll just get junk. (In Windows, you'll most likely get nothing but an error message.) Now open the file again using appropriate software. Everything is fine. So people sometimes think "this data is music" and "that data is a picture of the dog." But if you examine the raw contents of those two files using a utility program called a Disk Editor, all you'll see is bytes. The values of the bytes in the two files will differ, but otherwise, the files will look the same. That's because all data is the same. What differentiates bytes of blue and bytes of Beethoven is the software you use—the *context* you impose on that data. It's that amazing relationship that makes it possible for users to do everything they do with their PCs, turning raw *data* into the *information* that is their world.

This is the last chapter in the first part of your journey inside the PC. I've tried to introduce you to basic PC hardware and to the main types of PCs you'll encounter. With this chapter, you've learned how the world you experience every day is translated and encoded in ways PCs can understand. It's my strong hope that the following three points will take you a long way on your exploration inside the PC:

- Knowing what kinds of PCs are out there
- Knowing what physical components they all share
- Knowing how familiar human things like music and art can be made to exist in the PC's world

The book's ultimate goal, as I said in the Introduction, is to unveil the mystique of the computer by making its boundaries transparent and revealing its secrets. It's that level of knowledge and the comfort that comes from it that will propel you towards being a powerful, efficient PC user. When you grasp what a PC can do for you and how it does those things, your own creativity will be unlocked. Uncertainties like "I'm not sure I can do that on a PC" will change into "Yeah, I can make that happen," or, in some cases, "No, the technology for that isn't here yet." Being able to make those distinctions keeps the right tools in your hands and can save you and your business *tremendous* amounts of money.

The next step—and the next part of this book—takes you deeper inside these newly transparent boxes. You'll gain a solid understanding of the hardware to which you've now been introduced. The next chapter gives you an in-depth look at the backbone of every PC—the motherboard. It's here that all of a PC's components come together. You'll also learn about the PC's main processor, which quite simply runs the show.

PART II

Inside the PC: A Closer Look at Components

A First Look at Motherboards and Processors

In the first chapter, you got a snapshot of the whole PC as the sum of its parts. Chapters 2 and 3 gave you a look at two special types of PCs, also as the sum of their respective parts. Then, in Chapter 4, I talked about how PCs—of whatever type—turn information into the kind of data they can manipulate and how data turns back into information again.

The following chapters take you through a more intimate look at each of the parts of the PC, one at a time. In this chapter you will become familiar with two of the primary components that make up any typical PC, and you will see the schemes by which they are interconnected. After that, you'll continue exploring inside the PC. I think you'll find this approach very helpful. The fact is, there's a lot inside the PC. Breaking up these wonderfully capable multifunctional machines into their many parts makes a complex world very manageable and understandable. You'll come to understand the parts, one by one, in as much detail as you want, and see how they fit together and work as a whole. This is the most direct route to an overall understanding of the total PC.

Most PCs have a lot in common. As I said in Chapter 1, the essential core of the typical desktop PC comes in three pieces: a keyboard and mouse, a display, and the system unit. Of course, you might also have a printer and other things, but nearly every PC has these three pieces, and it must have them in order to do anything useful.

You might very well want to open up your PC and look inside as you read through this chapter. Before you do that, allow me to give you some tips—safety tips, in particular—that will make it much easier to get your PC running again after you open the case.

Safe System Unit "Surgery"

This section introduces you to some basic considerations that are relevant to a physical exploration of your PC. Some of what follows will seem obvious to you; some of it won't. But there are a few simple precautions to take whenever you're going to open your computer. These precautions will protect your PC's components and you as well.

The first thing to consider is the potential for hardware to be damaged by stray static electricity. Fortunately, the best defense is simply common sense. The second and equally vital line of defense is a heightened awareness of exactly the impact you have, both electrically and physically, even if you just reach inside to touch something with no intent of moving it.

Of the three principal pieces that make up your PC—keyboard, monitor, and system unit—only the system unit is something you will want to open. The keyboard contains little of interest (and often a whole lot of tiny springs that might fly all over the place if you aren't careful). I suggest opening the keyboard only if you need to clean it after a very bad liquid spill into it. (Even then, it often will be better simply to replace the keyboard.) The monitor presents a different issue. At least it does if it's a typical *CRT* (*cathode ray tube*) monitor—that is to say, one that somewhat resembles a television set.

> **Warning:** You *really* don't want to open your monitor. There is actual, physical danger there—high electrical voltages can remain on the cathode long after the monitor is turned off and unplugged (this includes old monitors that you have not used in a long time). If these discharge into your body, **you could die**. At best, you'll have the worst day you can remember. Furthermore, there is nothing going on inside a monitor that is relevant to your understanding of how a PC works. If you have a monitor that is not working correctly, replace it with a new one or have a certified technician fix it for you. The price of a new monitor is much less than the price of personal injury.

The system box, in contrast to the keyboard and monitor, is designed to be opened by anyone. And opening it is going to be necessary to fully understand its construction and workings.

Other pieces of your PC can be opened, too. Printers, scanners, mice, and so forth, are usually designed so that you can get inside to clean them, to unjam stuck pages, and so forth. Naturally, there's nothing wrong with opening this kind of device for those established purposes. Keep in mind, of course, that your laser printer probably wasn't designed for you to take a screwdriver and reduce it to all of its individual pieces, so use your good judgment. Your safety and health are your most valuable properties.

Guidelines for Avoiding Static Electricity Damage

You might have heard or read that PCs are very sensitive to damage from static electricity. It turns out that you are a lot more dangerous to your PC than it is to you; at least in terms of what could go wrong when you open up the system unit. The voltages used by the integrated circuit chips in your PC's system unit are anywhere from a little less than

3 volts up to 12 volts. These are so low that you won't hurt yourself touching any of them. On the other hand, people normally walk around with static electric charges of several hundred volts, or up to several thousand on a dry, cold day. That's more than enough to totally fry the delicate innards of your computer.

An electric current won't flow unless there's a voltage difference to drive it. Therefore, the actual voltage of your body isn't very important by itself. What matters is the difference between the voltage at your fingertip and the voltage at the places you're about to touch. If you first touch the power supply or an unpainted portion of the metal chassis of your PC system unit, and then touch whatever you want inside, you will, by this first step, have brought your entire body (including your fingers) to essentially the same voltage as the chips you'll be touching. In this case, no damage will be done.

> **Warning:** It might seem counter-intuitive, but it's vitally important that you keep your PC plugged-in to its grounded power outlet whenever you're working inside it. The ground is central to carrying dangerously high voltages away from both you and your PC. You should, however, unplug your motherboard from the power supply if you have an ATX-based system.
>
> You might read the opposite instruction elsewhere, but don't be swayed. Your PC should remain plugged-in and turned off.

If you get one of those nasty "static on a cold winter morning" shocks when you touch the case, be glad. That shock might have pained you, but it could have killed your PC's inner workings.

There are several steps you can take to eliminate the harmless nuisance of these "scuff your feet then touch the cat" shocks. First, think about reducing the static electric charge you carry around. You can get static-reducing carpet or a chair pad and put it where you sit or stand when you work on your PC. An even easier solution is to get some fabric softener, dilute it with three to four times as much water as softener, and then spray the diluted mixture on your carpet. Repeat this as necessary, probably no more often than once a month, and then only in especially dry weather. (Make certain that you test the solution on a small, out-of-view section to guarantee that it doesn't stain your carpet.)

You can reduce the bite of these little shocks another way. Purchase a static-guard wrist strap. The simplest of these are disposable: They're made of paper with a conductive strip attached. You attach one end to your PC's case (it's self-adhesive) and place your wrist through a loop in the other end. And static that builds up across your skin while you work is drained down the wrist strap. If you do a lot of work inside PCs, a non-disposable variety is also available.

When you move around a room, you're potentially picking up more static charge. This is why you must discharge yourself *each and every time* you are about to reach inside the PC. Likewise, if you're carrying an option card and are about to install it, by touching the case while you hold the card you are ensuring that the card and the case are at the same voltage. It is then safe to insert the card. (Of course, you should be discharged before you pick up an option card, too.) Additionally, while you're working on your PC, endeavor to keep a hand on the case at all times (or use one of the static straps I mentioned, above). This will provide a route for continuous discharging of any static electricity that might build up around your body while you're working.

Beware Line Current—It Can Kill You!

To be totally safe working inside your PC you must not only guard against static electric discharges, you must also be sure that the electricity from the wall socket doesn't come out and bite you. There are two easy ways to guard against this. First, if your PC has a power switch in back on its power supply, in addition to the power-switch or startup-switch on the front, make sure that this switch is off. Many modern PCs don't turn off completely until and unless you turn this switch off, too. The second way merits some special attention.

> **Warning:** Never, under any circumstances, for any reason, *ever* open up the sealed power supply inside your PC. Like your monitor, the power supply contains voltages *that could easily kill you*. It's sealed for a reason. Leave it sealed.

If you ever hear strange sounds coming from your power supply—weird fan noises or what sounds like electricity shorting out—replace your power supply if you know how to do so, or pay someone who does know how. Never open your power supply for *any* reason.

Keeping Track of Changes—And Reversing Them Correctly

Once your system is well and truly powered-off, and any static has been discharged from your body, you can start looking or working inside, making changes if necessary. If you do choose to unplug something, or to unscrew something, you'll want to carefully record just what the connection looked like before you made the change. (Some people find taking digital camera or Polaroid photos a handy way to capture some of this information.) Then, if something you change doesn't work out, you can at least put it back the way it was.

Often a particularly troublesome kind of connection in this regard occurs where flat, multi-conductor ribbon cables attach to printed circuit boards. Typically, there is a field of gold-plated pins sticking up from the board. On the end of the cable is a rectangular block of plastic with some holes in one side. You plug in the cable by pressing the block down over the pins.

Two types of problems can arise. One is when the plug is turned around 180 degrees. The other is when it gets offset from the correct position by exactly the spacing of one pair of pins (typically just one-tenth of an inch). Doing either of these things means that the wires in the cable connect with the wrong pins, or they fail to connect with any pins.

Two things can help: First, the usual practice is to identify one of the pins as the *number one* pin. This is often shown by a small numeral 1 printed next to that pin on the printed circuit card. (It is usually indicated by having a square bit of copper on the bottom side of the circuit board around the hole into which the pin is soldered, instead of the round ones used for all the other pins.) Ordinarily the number one wire in the ribbon cable has different color insulation than the rest of the cable. (Sometimes this stripe of color on one edge of the cable is blue, sometimes black, and sometimes red. Or you might find that all the wires are different colors, in a rainbow pattern. In that case, the brown wire will be number one.)

If you're lucky, the manufacturers of both the cable and the board with the field of pins will have taken one or two more precautions to keep you from plugging in the cable incorrectly. If they did the first good thing, there will be one or more missing pins and one or more of the holes in the block will be plugged up (at locations that match up with the missing pins). This arrangement of missing pins and matching plugged up holes ensures that the block can only be plugged onto the pins in the correct position and orientation. If they did the second good thing, there will be a housing around the pins so the block cannot be offset by a pin-spacing distance. (And sometimes the block will have a small bump on one side that fits into a slot in that housing, preventing you from plugging in the cable backwards.)

Figure 5.1 shows just such a ribbon cable and its connectors. In this case one pin is missing and one hole is plugged up. This cable is *keyed* to ensure that it is installed correctly. There is also a housing, with a slot, but there isn't any bump on the connector so the plugged hole *key* is the only way to make sure the connector isn't turned around.

Notice in this figure the indicated small triangle on the motherboard that shows you where pin number one is on the post and header connector. Also visible (only barely visible in this figure, but easily seen when you can see the actual colors) is that the number one wire in the ribbon cable is colored red instead of gray. (This cable and connector must be turned over 180 degrees to the right in order to fit into the connector on the motherboard.) I've shown that "sandwich" opened like a book to let you clearly see the mating keys.

Post and header connector with a
missing pin to match the key on plug

Matching "keys"

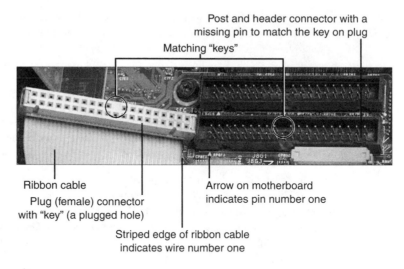

Figure 5.1
*Ribbon cables
and the header
connector can be
tricky to align. But
keys (missing pins
and plugged or
missing holes) can
make it easy.
Shown here are
the two EIDE
connectors on the
motherboard of
the example desk-
top system and
one of the EIDE
cables that attach
to them.*

Ribbon cable

Plug (female) connector
with "key" (a plugged hole)

Striped edge of ribbon cable
indicates wire number one

Arrow on motherboard
indicates pin number one

Another trouble some people have, closely related to the difficulty I just described with ribbon cables, has to do with placing or moving shorting *jumpers*. These are little blocks that contain a metal insert. You slide them down over a pair of pins and the metal insert shorts those two pins together. (They are sort of like a two-wire ribbon cable connector without the ribbon cable.) But, of course, if you miss the correct pair of pins, you won't short what needs to be shorted, and you may short something else that shouldn't be shorted. The only solution to this problem is to get a bright light and, if you need it, a strong pair of glasses or a magnifying glass. Then look very closely at what you're doing. You might also find that a pair of needle-nose pliers, commonly available at hardware or electronics stores, enhance your physical dexterity when you're working with these little nuisances.

> **Warning:** Something to remember whenever you're working inside your PC is that, with very few exceptions, the force needed to seat connectors and cables inside your PC is slight. In fact, the amount of pressure you exert on a key when you type will usually be sufficient to put things in their place. If you encounter resistance, first pull back and double-check that everything is aligned properly before you try pushing harder.

Figure 5.2 shows one such jumper. Here there are three "posts" (just like the pins in a post-and header ribbon cable connector) and a metal-lined sleeve that can cover (and in the process short together) two of them. The jumper is normally installed either over the left and center posts or over the right and center posts.

FIGURE 5.2

At the top you see a jumper from an example motherboard. This type of switch is often used to enable the user to select various fundamental features.

A Platform to Build Upon: The Motherboard

Enough talk about how or how not to open up hardware. Let's take a look together at what's inside every PC on the planet. Every PC has one printed circuit card in it that serves as its foundation (logically, and often mechanically as well). This circuit card is commonly called the *motherboard*.

There are two common *standards* used in the design of PC motherboards today. They go by the names ATX and micro-ATX. These standards are agreements made between many motherboard manufacturers. They guarantee that all motherboards which bear certain descriptive names (which are usually the name of the standard to which the motherboard adheres) will work perfectly with any other components that adhere to the same set of design rules. These begin with the design of the motherboard and then specify a chassis and various other features designed around the needs of that motherboard for housing, cooling, and power—plus the space needed for plug-in cards and disk drives.

The first of these standard designs, the ATX, arose as a simplification and standardization of the several slightly different ways in which PC makers made motherboards a few years ago. Their designs all stemmed from the design of IBM's PC model AT—hence the name ATX for the new, more standardized, and easier to manufacture PC desktop motherboard. The second common design, the micro-ATX, is simply a further simplification and reduction in size of the ATX design.

In all cases, the motherboard has a socket or slot connector for the computer's main processor, or CPU, and most or all of the computer's memory chips, plus a number of circuits whose job is to convey information to and from all the other circuits on the motherboard and to the connectors leading to the plug-in cards and the disk drives. The most common generic name for these circuits is the motherboard *chip set*.

Figure 5.3 shows an ATX motherboard. The callouts indicate where you can find various key features. In this figure, you see the motherboard removed from its case and viewed from a position above and in front of it.

FIGURE 5.3

An ATX motherboard with several key features marked. Don't worry if you're not yet familiar with some of these features—you will be, soon.

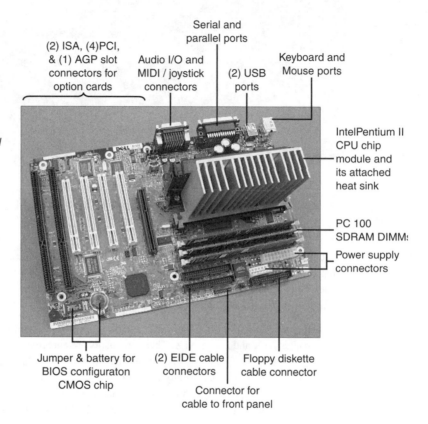

(2) ISA, (4)PCI, & (1) AGP slot connectors for option cards

Serial and parallel ports

Audio I/O and MIDI / joystick connectors

(2) USB ports

Keyboard and Mouse ports

IntelPentium II CPU chip module and its attached heat sink

PC 100 SDRAM DIMMs

Power supply connectors

Jumper & battery for BIOS configuraton CMOS chip

(2) EIDE cable connectors

Floppy diskette cable connector

Connector for cable to front panel

The largest object, sticking way up above the board's surface, is the heat sink attached to the CPU module. That is a vital part. It's designed to draw away the tremendous heat generated by the normal operation of the CPU. Without it, the CPU would simply cook itself to death. (In fact, it's called a *heat sink* because its purpose is to "drain" heat away.)

The long rectangular objects at the left are the *I/O (input/output) slot connectors*. (Recall from Chapter 1 that data moving into the PC is generally called *input*; data coming out of the PC is generally called *output*. The two processes together are usually just called "I/O".)

This motherboard has three types of I/O slots, which is common among all of today's PCs. The two black slot connectors are the older, so-called Industry Standard Architecture, or ISA design. This slot was the first of its kind, implemented back in 1984 in the first IBM

PC AT models. By today's standards, ISA slots are very slow performers, and they can only move a maximum of 16 bits of data at a time. In the main, ISA slots are included in today's PCs simply to provide backwards compatibility with old plug-in cards.

The four smaller, white, slot connectors are called PCI slots, for *Peripheral Component Interconnect*. These first premiered about 10 years ago, and they can move up to 32 bits of data at a time. For this and several reasons which you'll learn about in Chapter 15, "Motherboard Magic," PCI slots are a lot better performers that ISA slots ever were. When you read about plug-and-play, later in this chapter, you'll learn other reasons why PCI was a major step forward.

Finally, the newest type of motherboard connector slot is the black connector (on the right in Figure 5.3), and set farther back from the rear edge of the motherboard), which is an AGP (Advanced Graphics Processor) slot connector. A plug-in card with any of a wide variety of functional parts can be plugged into any of these slots other than the AGP slot; AGP is reserved for video display adapters. Like the PCI slot, an AGP slot can move 32 bits at a time, but AGP has certain characteristics that make it a real speed demon. Chief among these is the special relationship the AGP slot shares with a PC's main processor. You'll read about AGP in detail in Chapter 20, "Video Acceleration."

Behind the CPU module in this figure are some special-purpose input-output connectors that are stacked up along the rear edge of the motherboard. We'll look at those in more detail in a moment, in connection with Figure 5.4, which shows this motherboard from the other side.

Let me finish getting you acquainted with the components on the sample motherboard before I start talking about them in any detail. Just in front of the CPU module are three memory modules plugged into special *DIMM* (Dual In-line Memory Module) sockets. (You'll learn a lot about these in Chapter 15, and more about memory in Chapter 17, "Understanding PC Memory"). And in front of them, on the left, are the connectors I talked about earlier. These connectors are part of this motherboard's IDE (Integrated Drive Electronics) controller, which manages the functioning of hard drives, floppy drives, and CD or DVD drives that are connected to your PC internally. (You'll read a lot more about IDE and the different kinds of data storage drives and devices in Chapters 7, "Disks and PC Data Storage," and 8, "Removable Storage." For an advanced look at PC, storage, take a look at Chapter 18, "Storage: How Does Data Get There?".)

To the right of the two IDE connectors are two white connectors for power cables, and at the very front of the motherboard are two more black connectors. The smallest one is for a cable that goes to the front panel indicator lights and the switches for power and reset. The other connector is for the cable to the built-in floppy disk drive. Even though the PC's IDE controller manages the traditional, 3.5" floppy drives as well as hard and optical drives, floppy drives plug into the motherboard through these separate connectors. They don't share the same cables or connections with your hard drive.

Finally, in the lower-left corner of the motherboard is a round battery and the jumper you saw close up in Figure 5.2. This area contains the circuits that must run even when the PC is disconnected from the power supply. That includes the CMOS memory chip that holds configuration information about this PC, as well as the clock circuit that keeps track of the date and time of day. (You first read about CMOS briefly in Chapter 1, when you learned about the PC's BIOS. You'll find much more on this topic in Chapter 16, "Kick Starting: The Boot Process.")

This motherboard is indicative of modern boards in that it doesn't have a whole lot of jumpers on it. It's designed for use with a specific set of CPUs at certain speeds. Many older or economy motherboards have lots of jumpers, so the PC can be made to work correctly with any of a variety of CPUs and memory modules.

Still, this motherboard is like most in that it has a lot of setup options you can choose to alter. They are accessed through the BIOS configuration setup program instead of by moving jumpers around. (More on the BIOS setup program in Chapter 16 where you'll learn about everything your PC does every time it starts up.)

Figure 5.4 shows this motherboard from the rear. Now you can see the front face of the CPU module as well as the details of the rear-mounted special-purpose input-output connectors.

FIGURE 5.4

The example ATX motherboard, here seen from above the rear edge of the board, with several key features marked.

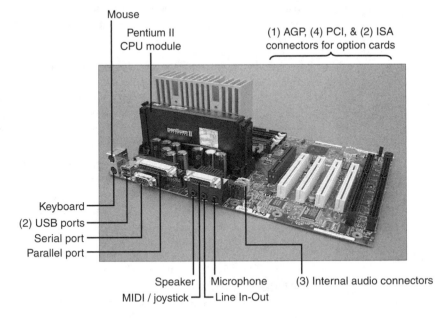

Mouse

Pentium II
CPU module

(1) AGP, (4) PCI, & (2) ISA
connectors for option cards

Keyboard
(2) USB ports
Serial port
Parallel port

Speaker
MIDI / joystick

Microphone
Line In-Out

(3) Internal audio connectors

I've labeled each of the individual, special-purpose input-output connectors in Figure 5.4. The three internal audio connectors serve the same purposes as the external ones (line, microphone, and speakers), but they are used with cables from built-in devices, most commonly a DVD or CD drive or a television tuner card. One feature that might not be immediately obvious about this motherboard—but which you'll soon appreciate—is that this motherboard incorporates within its own circuitry many features—like audio support—that used to be supplied only on plug-in cards.

Playing Host to the CPU

Most CPUs are held in place in the ZIF (Zero Insertion Force) sockets I mentioned in Chapter 1. On the side of the CPU's socket is a small lever, locked in place under a tab at the side of the socket. Gently pull the lever outward slightly, and then tilt it up. This will release the lock on the CPU so that you can remove it.

And when you do remove it, lift the CPU module straight up. Don't rock it back and forth or side to side. If it doesn't come out quite easily, don't simply tug harder. Look very carefully at the module and its connector and see where you are encountering resistance. Follow those tips and you are unlikely to cause any damage to either the motherboard or the CPU.

> **Note:** By the way, these tips also apply when you are removing an AGP video card or, to a lesser extent, any plug-in card. You can damage them if you rock them side to side, laterally. They do often take a strong push or pull to get them into or out of their slot connector. This can be facilitated by pushing in one end at a time. However, you *must* be certain to push the card in (or pull it out) perfectly vertically. Lateral rocking or bending can easily damage the card and your motherboard.

Incidentally, if you do ever want to remove the CPU from your PC, be certain to wait until your PC has been turned off for a good while, to let the CPU module and its heat sink cool down. CPUs get hot enough to burn you quite badly!

You Must Feed Your PC: The Power Supply

In some ways, the most fundamental piece of equipment attached to the motherboard isn't the CPU—it's the power supply. After all, without electricity, the computer does nothing. And actually, the PC's power supply has two important jobs:

- Convert wall outlet AC electrical power into suitable DC voltages. (Which is another way of saying that the power supply supplies power.)
- Remove the heat that results from the consumption of that electrical power.

The power supply's first job is to accept energy from the electric utility company using the power cord. It converts this AC power to direct current (DC) at several different voltages, because different components inside your PC have different power requirements.

Figure 5.5 shows a typical PC power supply. Notice that it has a lot of wires coming out and ending in a number of power output connectors. The largest two go to a pair of connectors on the motherboard.

The rest of the connectors are for powering drives of various sorts and, in some PCs, additional fans. The cables carry different voltages, depending on their intended purpose. Most modern PCs can accept at least one or two floppy disk drives and up to four EIDE hard disks, and/or CD or DVD, or other drives. Each of these devices needs electrical power to do its job, and none of them gets that power from the motherboard. Instead, they use power connectors that hook directly to the power supply. (The drives do connect to the motherboard through one or more cables that carry data to and from the drives.) Typically, modern PC power supplies provide between 250 and 350 watts of power, adequate to meet the needs of a PC with a variety of drives, plug-in cards, and other components all working together.

Peter's Principle

PC power supplies are equipped with built-in fuses or breaker-switches. Just like the fuses in your home, if the amount of power being demanded is more than the amount that can be safely and reliably delivered, the power supply's fuses will burn out—and your PC will suddenly turn off.

Not too many years ago, it was common for PC power supplies to be underpowered for the drives, sound and video cards, modems, and other devices. It's rare, today, to need to worry about whether your PC's power supply is putting out enough wattage to keep all of the PC's components well fed. Nevertheless, there are a few things to watch out for. If your PC suddenly behaves erratically, with distorted video, or a malfunctioning storage device—especially if you've just installed some new component—you might want to double-check the manufacturer's specifications for everything you're asking your PC to power. It might just be that you can solve all of the problems and avoid possibly losing important work just by upgrading your power supply.

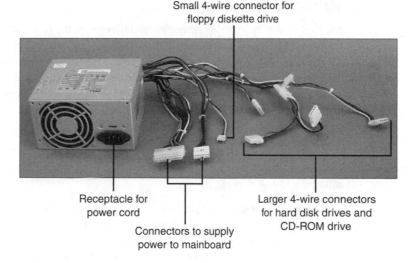

Small 4-wire connector for
floppy diskette drive

Figure 5.5
*The power supply
of a typical desk-
top PC.*

Receptacle for
power cord

Connectors to supply
power to mainboard

Larger 4-wire connectors
for hard disk drives and
CD-ROM drive

Room to Grow: Slots and Bays

Any functional part of your PC that lives inside the PC system unit and that isn't on the motherboard must be attached to the motherboard to let information flow between those pieces and the circuits on the motherboard. Normally that means the parts in question will be mounted in a drive bay and connected to the motherboard or an adapter via ribbon cables, or they will be mounted on printed circuit cards that are plugged into one of the motherboard's I/O slot connectors.

The pieces of the PC that go outside the box also must connect to the motherboard. They do so either via ports on the motherboard that stick through the back panel or by plugging into connectors on the backs of printed circuit cards. These printed circuit cards are themselves plugged into one of the motherboard I/O slot connectors.

I have already shown you a fairly comprehensive collection of special-purpose input output connectors on the back of the example motherboard. The only ones that aren't there and that you are likely to find on other PCs are an *IrDA* (infrared data communications) port and a FireWire (IEEE 1394) connector.

It wouldn't be possible to give a comprehensive list of all the types of plug-in cards that you can add to a PC. Suffice it to say that if you can imagine something a PC might do, somebody has probably made a plug-in card to fill that need.

A few of the most common plug-in cards are video display adapters, network interface cards, SCSI adapters, digital video cards... and the list goes on and on.

Who's On the Bus?

So, the I/O slots and various connectors and sockets are the physical means by which components plug into a motherboard. But any time you connect one piece of computer hardware to another, if you expect them to work together, there must be an *interface* between the two that fulfills certain needs. An interface (a place where things plug together) must meet three conditions: The two halves of the interface must be physically, logically, and electrically compatible.

Let me explain each of these points in turn. The first one is pretty obvious—physical compatibility. If you try to push a plug with fifteen pins into a socket with only nine holes, it just won't go. Likewise, two plugs with 15 pins won't connect; one of them must be a 15-hole socket.

The second one—logical compatibility—is less obvious. Even when the connectors mate properly, there must be agreement between the manufacturers that, for example, data is going to go out of device A on pin number three and come into device B on socket hole number three. You'll encounter the term *logical* in many different parts of the PC world, and it can have subtly different meanings.

The way I'm using this term for the PC means very closely the same to what logical means for people. Logical, in this sense, basically refers to how parts of the motherboard and attached devices "think," if you will. In order for the two to communicate with each other, they must "think" alike. There must be an agreement between what types of inter-actions can occur and how each will be handled. The logical compatibility provided by any interface really, then, makes certain that both halves of the connection "speak the same language," in a broad sense.

The third condition—electrical compatibility—is really the simplest of the three. Fundamentally, it means that devices that use the interface will be made so that power and data are sent back and forth on certain physical wires, and not others, and so that they operate at expected voltages in expected ways. If you like metaphors, you might say that "electrical compatibility" is a bit like two people having a polite, formal conversation at a sound level that's both audible and comfortable for both of them. Metaphors aside, you're already familiar with the idea of electrical compatibility if you've ever traveled internationally. Devices made to work on one country's AC current need *adapters* to work on a different system. At the simplest level, that adapter is a kind of interface.

Any time you have an agreement among computer hardware makers for an interface like this, it's called a *bus definition*. This applies especially when the agreement is not just between a few companies, but is shared by the entire industry. (Recall that I first talked about a PC's "buses" in Chapter 1.)

Some bus standards are created after a lengthy negotiation between companies, possibly under the aegis of some national or international standards organization. Others just happen when one company makes a lot of one kind of device, call it a widget, (and, at first, all the other devices [gizmos] that can connect to it) and then many other companies jump into the marketplace, offering their alternative gizmos to connect to the first maker's widget.

The first way, using a standards committee, is necessary when many companies want to enter a new marketplace more or less at once.

The second way standards arise, by a *de facto* standard-creating process, is easiest to explain by way of a little history. IBM defined most aspects of what we today call a PC by publishing its design for the original PC in 1981 (and again in 1983 for the PC/XT, and in 1985 for the PC/AT) with the hope of inducing others to make plug-in cards that would work with it. Not only did that happen, but the PC clone makers also used that information to help them make products that would directly compete with IBM's PCs. And thus was born what we now call the *industry standard architecture* (ISA) bus standard definition, and more generally, the standard notion of what constitutes a PC.

Recently a third way to create a standard—a full-system standard, however, not merely a bus standard—has emerged as the most common method. In this variation, one company solicits input from several other companies. Then the first company publishes its notion of a new standard. If the company doing so is very prominent (for example, Microsoft or Intel), very likely this new standard will be adopted by a lot of companies (including at least those who were consulted during its creation) and a new industry standard will have been born.

I *am* using the term *bus standard* a bit more broadly than some authors have. I include any standardized interface between two kinds of PC hardware that must be able to connect and work together. Other authors have limited the term to only a few of the more famous buses, such as the I/O bus, which in its several forms is called by the jargon acronyms ISA, EISA, VESA, MCA, AGP, and PCI. (There's a great deal to know about all these different buses. It's easily enough to fill a book of its own. But you will read much more in depth about them and their differences in Chapter 15.)

In the wide sense that I'm using the term here, there are a lot of buses in your PC. A *bus*, quite simply, is just a path on which data can move, either between parts of the PC, or between the PC and components and peripherals plugged into the PC. Some buses have received a lot of attention, and their names are, if not household words, at least relatively familiar jargon, others you might never have heard of before. The ISA bus and PCI bus variant forms of the I/O slot connector are two examples of famous PC buses, and the USB (Universal Serial Bus, which you'll explore a lot in Chapter 9, "Serial Ports") is another. Along with USB, FireWire (IEEE 1394) is the newest of the important buses. In time they might be the only widely used bus connections from a PC to the outside world, and thus might become the only ones most people will care about.

Controlling Chaos by Leaving the Legacy Behind

The most wonderful fact about PCs is that their open design, with so many different bus standards and interfaces to choose from, has led to a truly vast marketplace where a huge number of vendors have made a rapidly expanding variety of both hardware and software. The resulting mix-and-match environment has given PCs enormous flexibility and power. But it also has, inevitably, edged us close to chaos. This chaos must be managed or PCs will be so complex and difficult to set up and keep running that only a tiny fraction of the potential users will be willing to endure the needed effort.

To prevent this near chaos from curtailing a booming market, industry leaders have tried several things. Some of those companies proposed new standards for how a PC should be built. Other times, these companies—normally fierce competitors—have cooperated in the development of new industry standards for PC design.

Why ISA Means Chaos

The biggest headache for the designer of any new PC is the success of all the earlier designs. That success means that many millions of prospective customers for the new PC design will already have a PC and that most of those PC owners will want to move some or all of the peripheral devices and plug-in cards from their older machine to the newer one. The headaches come from trying to make the new design accommodate those older parts.

This is a particular problem for plug-in cards designed for the original ISA bus. That bus design, unlike many newer I/O bus standards, didn't allow for the sharing of vital PC resources and control channels. And the cards designed for the ISA bus in the past typically didn't have any provision built in to let the motherboard turn them off or reassign their resource usage if that usage conflicted with another card in the system. A recent trend, even with so-called legacy ISA cards, is for them to include some plug-and-play control-lability.

The ISA bus design didn't contemplate having the system configure the cards, nor having it disable them. But if the cards themselves include the proper provisions, a more modern PC can use those cards as compatible plug-and-play (PnP) cards, even when they're plugged into an ISA slot. (More on plug-and-play in just a moment).

Modern PCs are expected to spot any new hardware and adapt themselves to it, and sometimes they can. But ISA cards, in particular the older, non-PnP compatible ones, are resource consumers that the newer PCs can't control. Even worse, the PC motherboard can't know, without some help, what resources this type of card is using. That means the use of these cards can defeat the automatically self-configuring PC.

This specification needed to be improved before a truly modern PC could emerge. These improvements have evolved through several intermediate standards (with variable market success) before reaching their present state. And, of course, even that is just a weigh station on the way to some future, even-better PC design, with the next step being the total elimination of ISA-bus connected devices.

Plug-and-Play

There is a constant theme to all of these enhancements to the original PC architecture. It is to make the machine do more of what it is good at (detail work) and let the human operator concentrate on what humans are good for (seeing the big picture and the general application of the PC to some task humans value).

This means that PCs are more and more capable of performing well out of the box, without requiring extensive tweaking by the users. That makes for a better OBE (out of box experience), and hence for happier purchasers—and it also allows for easier upgrades.

All of these developments have been guided by a vision of a PC that's fully automatic in its configuration. The name the PC industry has given to this vision is *plug-and-play*. The difficulty in implementing this vision has been two-fold. One is to incorporate backward compatibility—which means the capability to use older, legacy devices with even the newest PC—and the other is preserving the open marketplace with all its wild and woolly freedom for innovation.

The Essentials of Plug-and-Play

Plug-and-play is first and foremost a philosophy describing how a PC should operate. The simplest form of this philosophy is creating a PC infrastructure that works without needing much in the way of user setup effort. More formally described, plug-and-play is a whole series of formal standards describing a number of ways to achieve this goal. And only PCs that conform to these standards are entitled to be described, by the trademarked term, as plug-and-play.

Essential to this effort is the notion that every part of a PC (whether it's built onto the motherboard or is added to the PC on a plug-in option card or by plugging it into some other connector) needs a device identifier. This *device ID* implies all the technical details that the PnP-controlling software (either the BIOS itself or an operating system like Windows) must know about the device. For some devices, the ID identifies them as capable of being turned on or off and perhaps of having their resource usage controlled by the PnP-management software. For other devices it indicates that they are old (legacy) ISA cards or otherwise are inherently unable to be disabled or controlled.

The PC must learn about all of the PnP devices it contains. So one of the jobs that must be done during the bootup process is detecting all those devices. Responsibility for this task is divided among several players. The PCI controller chip has this job for devices plugged into PCI slots. Other controller chips perform this task for other buses and their hardware. The PnP BIOS coordinates all this information and adds to it information about devices that are built into the motherboard, attached across the IDE bus, plus the keyboard and a few other devices.

> **Note:** If you happen to be running Windows, you can see how your system organizes its PnP devices. Simply go into the Control Panel, System dialog box. Click the Device Manager tab, and select the View Devices By Connection radio button. Now click the plus sign in front of Plug and Play BIOS to see all the sources of this information and how the BIOS brings them all together.

After the devices in the system have been detected, two more tasks remain. One is to decide which device gets which set of resources. The controller of each of the PC's buses performs this arbitration and allocation job first. A system-level arbitrator will do the rest.

Finally, a *configurator* program must go out and set up each configurable PnP device so it uses the resources that have been assigned to it. The configurator also configures the device drivers for any non-configurable legacy ISA devices (at least for those for which the necessary information has been supplied) so they will access those devices using the resources they are known to use.

Resolving Windows PnP Device Resource Conflicts

If, when you look at the Device Manager tab in the System Properties dialog box, you see any device listed with an exclamation point in a yellow circle on top of it, that device is in conflict with some other device. (So you will likely see either none of these symbols or more than one.) That is a sign that you must help the system resolve these conflicts because it has tried and failed to do so on its own.

Alternatively, you might see some devices listed with a red X or a black X in a red circle over them. These are disabled devices. If you didn't choose to disable them yourself, Windows did so to resolve some resource conflict.

By highlighting one of the devices with the exclamation point or red X over it and then clicking the Properties button, you'll call up a dialog box that might tell you just what the problem is. Go to the Resources tab and see if it lists the conflict.

Sometimes you can remove the conflict by altering the resource usage manually in that dialog box. Other times, after you have discovered the conflict, you can resolve it quicker if you have a general knowledge of which resources different devices use and of how those uses can be altered (by jumpers, switches, or running some software program). In order to try to manually allocate resources, you'll need to uncheck the Use Automatic Settings check box you see in the device's Device Manager window. In some instances, Windows won't allow you to make manual changes, in which case you'll need to try to re-allocate the resources used by other devices, or you'll need to make resource-setup changes in your PC's BIOS. That topic is beyond the scope of this chapter, but you'll read about the BIOS in detail in Chapter 16.

The more worrisome cases are when Windows hasn't even noticed there's a conflict. This can happen when you have legacy devices that haven't been described properly to Windows. Only by knowing which resources those devices use and then making sure that Windows is reserving the required resources for those devices, can you eliminate that source of problems. In most cases, you'll find information about the resources demanded by older devices in their user manuals or on the manufacturer's Web site. As a final option, you can remove the card from your PC and look for jumpers on it that are labeled with the IRQ or memory settings the card is configured to use.

Understanding PC Processors

You've learned a lot now about the components on a PC's motherboard, and some of the different ways in which they are connected. Of all the components in your PC, however, the single most important is unquestionably the central processing unit (CPU). In the 20 years since Intel released its first CPU for a PC, it has produced eight generations (including several dozen models) of CPU chips that are closely enough related to the original chip (which was given the name "8086") that they deserve to be called members of a "family" of chips. Because the first member of that family was the 8086 micro-processor, every model before the Intel Pentium had an 86 at the end of its name. They are called the *x86* family of CPU chips.

There are other non-x86, yet clearly important, central processor chips being manufactured by other vendors for use in small computers. Most notable, perhaps, are the PowerPC G4 chips made by Motorola, which have been used in the recent members of the Apple Macintosh computer line. The chips in this family are powerful and important in their niche markets, but none of them is used in any model of what I am calling "a PC" for the strict purposes of this book.

The next sections of this chapter give you an overview of this crowd of PC processor possibilities and perhaps some insight into how you can navigate your way through the resulting confusion to find the perfect processor for your PC.

But what, really, is a central processor? Knowing what one is and what it's used for would certainly contribute to finding that "perfect" processor out there. So, here's a whirlwind tour.

So, What's a Processor, Peter?

You've doubtless heard that a PC's central processor, or CPU, is its "brain." It would be much more accurate, and a closer metaphor, to say that a CPU is simply the main part of the several chips and circuits that collectively make up a PC's brain. Time has allowed our human brains to develop many different "subsystems" that automatically handle many of the processes necessary to keep us alive—and offload that work from our conscious minds. (Imagine if you had to think about breathing to keep your respiration going!) The PC has evolved in much the same way, and CPU's have achieved a lot of their ever-increasing performance by off-loading many management and operational tasks to other chips and systems in the PC.

So, that's what a CPU *doesn't* do. It doesn't personally control, if you will, the movement of every bit that flows through your PC. Like your human brain, however, the CPU does ultimately control most of the processes and sub-processes that a PC performs. The CPU chip is responsible for making sure that all of a PC's components are working in synchronization with each other. This is achieved through the use the *clock*, which is just a regular pulse that establishes tiny blocks of time during which actions inside the PC can occur. If you like, you can think of the clock as the drummer at the back of a marching band who makes sure that everyone is stepping along in perfect harmony.

When you ask your PC to do something—anything—your request eventually gets translated down into a series of *instructions* for the CPU to carry-out. These instructions are made up of a code that the CPU understands, called *machine language*. The set of instructions that all CPUs in the x86 family understand is called, naturally enough, the *x86 instruction set*. Different CPUs use different sets of instructions unless they use an *x86 compatible instruction set*, which usually consists of all the x86 instructions plus a few more that are unique to that specific CPU. In the earliest members of the x86 family of CPUs, at best, one instruction could be carried out with each pulse of the system's clock. Another way of saying this is that one instruction was processed during each *clock cycle*. Today, a variety of methods, which you'll read about in Chapter 15, allow for multiple instructions to be performed during a single clock cycle.

In order to pass instructions to the CPU, each component (or collection of components) in a PC must be able to get the CPU's attention. They must be able to interrupt what the CPU is doing and say, effectively, "excuse me, but I need some help here, then you can go back to what you were doing." Not surprisingly, these interruptions are made through signals called *interrupts*, and they're monitored and managed by a part of the CPU called the *interrupt handler*. Inherent in the CPU's design is the ability to suspend what it's doing for a moment, attend to some new thing, and then go back to the first task, without data being lost. The interrupt handler simply watches for interrupts to occur, and then passes them on to the rest of the CPU. When do interrupts occur? Every time you press a key on the keyboard, every time you send data to the screen or to a storage device—all the time. The system clock also has its own interrupt, which is how the CPU is made aware of each clock pulse.

The CPU can perform two basic types of instructions: arithmetic and logical instructions. *Arithmetic instructions* are precisely what you'd expect: the CPU adds, subtracts, multiplies, and divides integers that are passed through it. The logical operations give a CPU the capability to compare one piece of data to another and evaluate whether certain conditions are true or false. They also make it possible for the CPU to very efficiently perform one operation over and over (which is called a *loop*), or to jump from one instruction to another (which is called *branching*).

I said that the CPU's arithmetic instructions let it work with integers. That's because CPU's have a separate set of circuitry that's designed to manipulate fractional values very efficiently. Because fractional values are most easily expressed by humans by using a decimal point (as in 3.14159265, or 9.99), this specialized part of the CPU is called the *floating point unit*, or *FPU*.

As data is being actively manipulated by the CPU, the data is maintained in temporary storage spaces inside the CPU itself, called *registers*. The fact is, today's CPU's can manipulate data much faster than the PC's main memory can move that data to and from the CPU. In order to eliminate delays, in addition to the registers, CPU's today each have more of their own, built-in, very high-speed memory. This memory is called a *cache*, a term borrowed from common English, where a cache is a temporary storage place for valuables. (You'll read about FPUs and caches and much more in Chapter 15.)

All of what you've read so far is such a high-level discussion of what a CPU does; you might even call the whole thing a metaphor. I say that a CPU performs "instructions," and it would be reasonable for you to think of a child whose parent calls for her to come to the kitchen, and then gives the child some money and directions to buy some milk at the corner store.

As you know from Chapter 4, all that really happens inside a PC is that bits of data are moved around and manipulated. Bits, as you will remember, have only one of two values: zero or one. These two values easily correspond to whether electricity is flowing through a switch, or whether it isn't. And that, in fact, is really how a CPU works. A CPU is just a microchip made up of millions and millions of transistors, each of which operates like a switch. Electricity can flow through a transistor, or it can be prevented from flowing, and one transistor can control the flow of electricity through others, and on and on and on. It's the functioning of these millions of microscopic transistor switches together that gives you the ability to represent information inside a PC in the form of data, and to work with that data and turn it back into new, useful information.

The earliest PC processors didn't have very many transistors, and so they were very limited in their ability to work with data. They could only move between 8 and 16 bits of data at a time, they could only carry out a single instruction in each clock cycle, as I mentioned earlier. As CPUs evolved, it became possible to reflect on their increasing power as a function of the number of transistors in the chip. Consider the following table, for example.

Year	CPU Name	Number of Transistors	Clock Speed
1978	8086	29,000	5-10MHz
1982	80286	132,000	6-12.5MHz
1985	80386 DX	275,000	16-33MHz
1989	80486 DX	1.2 Million	25-50MHz
1993	Pentium	3.1 Million	60-66MHz
1997	Pentium II	7.5 Million	200-300MHz
2000	Pentium III Xeon	28 Million	866MHz
2000	Pentium 4	42 Million	1500MHz (1.5GHz)

The dramatic increase in the number of transistors in a CPU (and their requisite increase in processor power) is often attributed to a phenomenon known in the industry as *Moore's Law*. Gordon Moore was an engineer who, in 1965, said that the number of transistors in a microprocessor would double every 18 months. He believed this trend would continue through 1978, at which time he felt a threshold would have been reached. Many times throughout CPU history, such thresholds have been anticipated and pushed aside. Moore's limitation on his own prediction is the only part of that prediction that was false. Moore's Law still holds today.

The Pentium Family Tree

The best way to understand today's CPUs is to know a little about what came before them. The ancestors of today's Pentium family of processors are, of course, the members of the x86 family I mentioned earlier. Other than having vastly slower clock speeds and fewer transistors, how were these earlier chips—the 80386, the 80486, and so on—different from their offspring?

They were different in three very important ways and one additional, not quite as important, way. First, the 80386 and 80486 chips, before the Pentium processor, had what was called a 32-bit *bus width*. What that means is that they could only work with 32 bits of data at a time. (Earlier chips, the 8086 and 80286, could only work with 16 bits at a time.) Pentium-class processors have a 64-bit bus width, enabling them, in principle, to work with twice as much data in the same amount of time as their ancestors. The second major difference is that Pentium processors were the first PC CPUs that could perform more than one instruction at a time.

The third major change was the development of *pipelining*. Simply put, pipelining is just a way of making sure that the CPU is never left waiting for data—a waste of time called *lost clock cycles*.

The fourth change was the inclusion of a new set of instructions to augment the antiquated x86 instruction set. These new instructions made it possible for Pentium-family processors to be particularly efficient when handling data for many of the then-emerging technologies of multimedia. These instructions, which were called *MMX*, or *MultiMedia Extensions*, have been incorporated into later CPUs made both by Intel and its competitors. The limitation to their value, however, is that a piece of software must be specifically written to use the MMX capabilities. Multimedia products that are not written for this instruction set gain no benefit.

Improving a Good Thing—The Pentium Pro

Intel's next step in the development of CPUs was called the Pentium Pro. The Pentium Pro incorporated both a slightly improved Pentium CPU and a separate chip that held the Level 2 (L2) cache memory.

This was the first time that cache memory was located physically inside the CPU module and the change had some very significant echoes, both in later Intel x86 designs and in the offerings from the clone x86 CPU makers.

The Pentium Pro also introduced a variation on pipelining, called *speculative execution* or, as Intel prefers to call it, *dynamic execution*. This feature enables the logic pieces inside the CPU to keep busy more of the time. If there is nothing to be done on the instructions that would normally come next (for example, because they involve some data that must be fetched from main memory), the logic unit will pick out a future instruction whose data is already on hand and determine what the result of that instruction would be. That result is held in reserve, and if that instruction actually gets to be executed with the anticipated data, the result is instantly made available. Otherwise, that result is discarded, and the logic unit's efforts are wasted. Then again, that unit couldn't have been doing anything more useful, so nothing really is lost.

Although instructions are often executed out of order, their results are always made available to subsequent instructions only in the originally specified order. That makes this process work transparently; the programmer and the user don't need to be concerned with how the CPU acts as though it is working more quickly—they simply notice that it does.

Finally, the movement of data into the CPU has priority over moving data out, which further eliminates lost clock cycles. According to Intel, this prioritizing of memory accesses sped up the overall working of the system more than any other method it has tried.

Pentium II

In the middle of 1996, Intel brought out its next *x*86 family member, the Pentium II, which you can see back in Figure 5.4. Effectively, the Pentium II simply is a Pentium Pro with some slight design tweaks that enable it to handle 16-bit programs more speedily, plus the MMX technology. Thus, it combined the best of both the Pentium MMX and the

Pentium Pro. On the other hand, to reduce the cost of the Pentium II relative to the expensive Pentium Pro, Intel chose to use cache memory in the PII that was only half as fast as that in the Pentium Pro. Economically, it was a move that definitely sped up adoption of the new chip, although some have called it a technological step backwards.

One very new change that came about with the Pentium II was how it was packaged and how it connected to the motherboard. Beginning with the 386-model chip, Intel had been packaging its x86 CPU chips in square, thin, black ceramic wafers with an array of gold-plated pins sticking out of the bottom. Those pins were then inserted into a socket on the motherboard.

Every new generation of x86 processor came in a larger package and it needed more pins than any of its predecessors. Intel kept designing new sockets to accept them, and it labeled those socket designs with sequential numbers. By the time we got to the final Pentium releases, the socket was called Intel's Socket 7. But Intel departed from that, putting the Pentium II into a much larger module with an edge connector. And that edge connector fits into what Intel termed its Slot 1 CPU connector.

These Pentium II CPU modules were given the name Single Edge Contact Cartridge (SECC). Essentially, they were composed simply of a box surrounding a printed circuit card with an edge connector. That printed circuit card carried, in the case of the Pentium II, the CPU chip, the L2 cache memory chip, and a few other components (such as bypass capacitors) that were necessary to make it all work well.

The Pentium II Xeon Series

In addition to introducing new Pentium II models with ever-higher clock speeds, Intel also brought out a minor variation on the theme that it termed the Xeon series. This was one step in its plan to divide the PC marketplace into server, workstation, desktop, budget, and mobile segments, and to offer products for each with features chosen to appeal especially to that segment.

The Pentium II Xeons were essentially Pentium II processors, with even more cache memory included in the CPU module (and, more importantly, with that cache running at the full CPU clock speed). Also, some other minor features were added to facilitate *multiprocessing* (using more than one CPU in a single PC) and enterprise system management.

The Pentium III and 4 Series

The latest members of Intel's x86 family are the Pentium III and Pentium 4. These are, in many ways, not very new designs at all. They are both gradual updates the Pentium II design. Many models of these two processors are being offered at various clock speeds, and with various amounts of cache.

The real news about the Pentium III design was its inclusion of some new registers and a new set of instructions that expanded on what MMX added. The Pentium III and Pentium 4 also each have an additional FPU (floating-point mathematics unit) that allows them to perform a great deal more of this type of complex mathematics than their predecessors.

Most of the remaining changes between the Pentium III and Pentium 4 are simply accelerations of the Pentium III's capabilities. Pentium 4 supports far faster system bus speeds (that is, the speed at which data can move across the PC's main bus) and performs fundamental arithmetic operations faster than the PIII. Pentium 4 also includes Intel's new "NetBurst" architecture, which is supposed to give the P4 new intelligence in terms of selecting the order in which multiple processes should be executed. All of this boils down to making a more efficient processor.

Attacking the Low-End Market—Intel's Celeron Models

As the number of PCs sold each year grew, and Intel's sales along with it, Intel decided to segment that market. Intel introduced a lower-cost version of the Pentium called the *Celeron*.

This differently named product is, in fact, just a repackaged Pentium II with a couple of feature differences. First, these CPUs are designed to work only with a 66MHz system bus, rather than the 100MHz speed supported by the "full" Pentium II and later processors. Second, the initial Celeron models (which worked at clock frequencies of 266 and 300MHz) came with no external cache built into the CPU module. Finally, these processors arc packaged in such a way as to make them cheaper to manufacture. This was of primary importance, because Intel was facing very serious competition from AMD (and, at the time, from the now-defunct Cyrix), in particular, for the low-end of the PC CPU market. Even with the omission of the L2 cache and reducing the packaging costs, Intel could not lower prices quite far enough to effectively counter AMD's pricing. As a result, Intel's market share plummeted to an unprecedented less-than-a-majority of all sales in this segment.

Also contributing to Intel's poor sales showing was the very poor computing performance of the initial Celeron models, compared to their competition. This mainly was caused by the omission of the L2 memory cache in the CPU module and the failure to provide that cache on the motherboard.

Intel rectified this error in later Celeron models, which included a 128KB L2 cache, which is smaller than the Pentium II cache, but which works even better because it is located on the same chip with the CPU and thus works at the full CPU clock speed. In effect, Intel upgraded these Celerons to be nearly as good as the Pentium chips—the only significant way in which they fell short was in their limitation to the slower system bus speed.

As with the Pentium III and Pentium 4, Intel also went back to a socketed design for the Celeron. The newest Celerons come in a package that looks exactly like the original Pentium, but with more pins. The socket these new Celerons fit into, now termed Intel's Socket 370, is very much like the earlier Socket 7, with (of course) more holes into which those pins can go. A Socket 7 accepts 321 pins; a Socket 370 accepts 370, which is just what the Celeron package has.

The Intel Itanium

Intel's latest development in PC CPUs is actually a step away from the x86 family. In fact, it's a huge step. Intel calls this new family of chip the Itanium, and it uses a new architecture. Instead of being part of the 32-bit x86, Itanium is the first processor to use Intel's new 64-bit IA-64 architecture.

On the simplest level, that means that these new chips will use 64 bits instead of 32 to address memory—which means a *much* larger amount of memory can be supported. IA-64 also makes use of Intel's new EPIC (Explicitly Parallel Instruction Computing) technology. This gathers together related processes and executes them within a single clock cycle. This is rather tantamount to producing a CPU that can do several things at once. If programs are designed to use EPIC technology, they'll let the processor focus on executing as many instructions as quickly as possible, rather than using today's technology which requires the processor to spend time analyzing and deciding which instructions will benefit the most from simultaneous execution—and then, finally, carrying them out.

At the time of this writing, both the future and the success of the Itanium processor remain uncertain. Itanium processors are being targeted primarily for use within huge system servers, where their capability to process instructions in parallel is well suited to respond to hundreds or thousands of client/server requests. Intel is itself focusing on this market, labeling the Itanium as the processor of e-commerce. In its own tests, Intel has shown the Itanium to perform a good deal faster than competing chips (such as the UltraSparc III, which is used to provide access to monolithic online database systems). The chip is supposed to be especially good at performing the millions of floating-point calculations that are required by highly encrypted systems, like those used for secure data retrieval and online shopping.

In order to benefit from the Itanium's 64-bit architecture, operating-system support is required. You won't get breathtakingly superior performance simply by plugging an Itanium processor into your current PC (even if such a thing was possible). Microsoft is preparing 64-bit versions of Windows at the time of this writing; which will likely be available to the high-end corporate server market by the time you read this. What really remains to be seen is whether this new architecture will be embraced, and by whom. Stay tuned!

What If It Isn't Intel Inside?

A few times so far in this chapter—and then only briefly—I mentioned another maker of CPU chips for PCs besides Intel. That is mostly because Intel has such a lion's share of the market. But this isn't the full picture. There are alternatives to having an Intel processor inside your PC.

Another reason I have emphasized the Intel designs is because they exemplify most of the industry's trends. When you understand all that Intel has to offer, you'll find yourself well prepared to evaluate where the competition's offerings fit. (Recently the clone x86 makers have innovated in significant ways, but those innovations are easily understood in terms of what Intel did previously or what Intel has done since then in response.)

When you are number two in a market dominated by the number-one supplier, one of your main tools for convincing people to buy your product is to offer a lower price for the same quality and quantity of goods. The clone processor market nicely exemplifies this concept.

Advanced Micro Devices (AMD)

Advanced Micro Devices (AMD), Intel's primary second-source supplier for its earlier x86 chips, has offered faster, yet cheaper and fully compatible CPU chips for many years. Its 386 designs were essentially identical to Intel's. The AMD 486SX was different but arguably a better design than Intel's, and it certainly ran faster and cost a lot less. AMD's next offering, the AM5x86, used a 486-like 32-bit I/O bus, but had an instruction set that more nearly resembled that of the Pentium. This began the real departure from the Intel x86 standard to one of AMD's own devising.

AMD's next design, called the K5, was fully a functional equivalent to a Pentium. It followed this with a K6, which used a radically new architecture that resulted in an improvement over Intel's Pentium Pro and Pentium II designs. However, manufacturing difficulties kept AMD from taking full advantage of those design superiorities.

AMD's latest design, the Athlon XP processor, is a whole new world, and will likely give Intel their first real competition in the last five years. This processor, which has been designed from the ground-up with Microsoft's newest Windows XP operating system in mind, is optimized to, AMD hopes, perform more real work per clock cycle than an Intel processor operating at the same speed. The Athlon XP takes advantage of Intel's innovative pipelining, a term which you encountered earlier when you read about the Pentium chip.

In pipelining, the various stages of performing an instruction are broken up, with dedicated circuitry on the chip doing each instruction. The chip is designed so that, as one section is executing an instruction, another section is gathering the data to be processed by the next instruction and a third is determining (decoding) what is to be done to perform the instruction after that.

In a way, pipelining is similar to an assembly line or an automated car wash. When some local group assembles a group of volunteers to raise money by washing cars, the cars usually are washed one at a time. However, automated car wash machines do several cars at once. As one is being rinsed, another is being washed, yet another is dried or waxed, and so forth. It is a production line. The time to wash any one car remains about the same, but more cars can pass through the automated car wash each hour than can be washed by a single team of people working on one car at a time.

Intel's CPU designs have incorporated pipelining in varying degrees almost from the very beginning. The extent and sophistication of the pipelining has, however, been greatly increased with each succeeding generation. And now with what amounts to multiple assembly lines in parallel, each is fed from a set of preprocessors that decode instructions and gather data. Then, through feeding a set of postprocessors that put the processed data back into memory, the Pentium raised the performance that is possible much more than you would expect if you only looked at the clock speed.

AMD claims its Athlon XP processor takes all of this to the next level. The number of pipelines available to send instructions to the CPU is known as the *depth* of the pipelining. By balancing a high clock speed with full pipelining, AMD claims that this chip, forthcoming at the time of this writing, consistently delivers more real-world performance at each clock cycle. If so, AMD might give Intel some serious run for its money. Another bit of processor technology, called speculative buffering, should allow the Athlon XP to move data *which it is likely to need in the future* from main memory into the CPU's own, high-speed, Level 1 cache. Based on these innovations, AMD claims that its Athlon XP 1800 is 30% faster than an Intel Pentium 4 running at 1.8GHz.

In its own press releases, AMD has been fond of making an analogy between its Athlon XP chip and automotive performance. A six-cylinder car, AMD observes, produces less performance than does a nine-cylinder car. At high RPMs, the six-cylinder car is going flat out, but still doesn't trundle down the street very impressively. The nine-cylinder car can move just as fast at lower RPMs. However, take the nine-cylinder car and make it operate at the high RPMs of the six-cylinder, and the smaller engine gets left in the dust. Naturally enough, AMD is hoping that end users will fall in love with its nine-cylindered Athlon XP.

The real bottom-line is this: The Athlon XP will put a "nine-cylinder car" in your "garage" for the same cost of a "six-cylinder" Pentium 4.

Major and Minor Improvements

Over the decades, PC processors have improved in two ways: They have become faster, and they have become more complex.

The chips made today run a lot faster than their predecessors do. The first PC used a 5MHz clock frequency. Today's best machines run at better than 2000MHz, (2.0GHz, or gigahertz), with still faster ones promised very soon.

The Pentium II, for example, was hugely more complex than the 8086. The Pentium II had nearly 7,500,000 transistors on the chip; the 8086 had only 29,000. Today's Pentium 4 has over 42 million. But not every improvement is a major one. Some are valuable, yet only minor in nature.

The two biggest landmark events in the *x*86 family's history were certainly the introduction of virtual 86 mode and memory paging in the 386 and the development of the Pentium chip with its dramatic changes in internal design and, accordingly, performance. Everything else pales by comparison.

For the PC user, this means that when software became popular that exploited all the 386 could do, any older CPU-based PC really was obsolete.

Summary

You first read about the PC's CPU and motherboard in Chapter 1. Here, you've gone deeper and learned about the different models of Intel processor that brought us gradually to where we are today. Essentially, you've learned about the PC's central workhorse. The remaining chapters in this section of the book take you deeper into the other subsystems that make up the PC. As I promised in the introduction, moving towards the end of the book will bring you ever closer to a high-level understanding of the PC, one piece at a time.

So, let's move forward and dive into the world of PC video.

Video and Monitors

In Chapter 1, "The Desktop PC," I introduced the five key parts of any computer, and in the previous chapter, you started to explore those parts. That chapter reviewed the characteristics of motherboards, main processors, and memory. The part you're going to examine in this chapter is the PC's mechanism for information output. In almost all cases, that means the PC's *video display,* also known as the *monitor* or the *screen*. This chapter introduces you to most of the technologies that are now in use, or might soon become important, in PC display subsystems, including the cards or chips inside your PC that make it all work. Although my goal is primarily to help you understand these different technologies, you will find that such an understanding comes in very handy when you evaluate different options for the display on your next PC, or if you are considering upgrading the display on your present PC.

It's Just No Good if You Can't Get the Information Out

What good is a computer that can process information, but cannot display the results of that processing? Not much, which is why your PC has a video display screen, or monitor, attached to it. And that's why you spend most of your time while you are using your PC looking at that screen.

What Is the Display Subsystem?

The PC display subsystem is the sum of several parts that work together in the attempt to give you visible results from your computing efforts. Every PC's display subsystem consists of three parts. One part creates and holds the image information; this is the *video display adapter*. Another part displays that information; this is the *monitor*. The remaining part is the *cable* that goes between the other two parts.

The video adapter can be either specialized circuitry that's already part of the motherboard itself, or—and this has always been the most common option—it can be a plug-in card. In the latter case, it is usually called the PC's *video card*. The terms *graphics adapter* and *graphics accelerator* are sometimes used, but these are essentially new jargon, and they usually refer to the video card.

> **Technical Note:** As is often the case with new jargon, these terms do little to add real meaning to discussions, and they blur the only real difference in this market. A video card can be easily unplugged, which allows you to upgrade your system to provide new video features or improved performance. Video circuitry that's part of the motherboard can sometimes be overridden by installing a plug-in video card, but it can't be upgraded or replaced in the traditional sense. It's also common to be able to add memory to a plug-in video card (you'll learn about this later in the chapter), but you can rarely do that with motherboard-based video.
>
> Today, motherboard manufacturers are adding some of the same brand-name video chips to motherboards that you can purchase as popular plug-in boards. So, if you anticipate wanting to upgrade your PC's video when new technology is available, it's not enough to know that the PC you're about to purchase comes with a "MightyVid 3000 4xAGP Graphics Accelerator". You need to inquire whether that graphics accelerator is built-in, or whether it's a plug-in card that can be removed and replaced at will.

The monitor itself consists of an internal *display device* (the hardware that actually creates the image you see—loosely referred to as the *screen*) and some electronics that controls and makes that display work. Normally, people use the terms *monitor* and *display* interchangeably. Once upon a time, it was something of a chore to select a video card and a monitor that worked well together. Today, most any monitor will work successfully with any video card or motherboard video. The characteristics that used to make such a big difference are still around, but people think of them today as the *range* of capabilities a monitor can provide when it's coupled with any given video card. These same factors commonly appear in marketing and in technical reviews of various video hardware, so it's wise to understand them. Let's dive right in now.

Basic Characteristics of Video

Now that you have been introduced to the physical components that make up the display subsystem, there are several basic ideas about images and how humans see, plus some critical jargon, you'll want to understand in order to make sense of any discussion of PC video technologies. I'll define each one here briefly, and then go back and describe some of them in more detail as I tell you more about how they are used. The first you will encounter is the *pixel* and its role in computer displays.

Peter's Principle:

As you move forward, you'll find increasing amounts of technical terms, much of which might seem like jargon when you first encounter it. And, in fact, some of it is *just* jargon, designed to support experts' expertise and to keep competition at bay. But, for the most part, technical terms in computing are a bit like the specialized language of medicine. In the words of James Burke, doctors speak mumbo-jumbo "because they need to be precise; or would you rather be dead?" Like the thousands of pieces that make up you and me, there are so many different bits and pieces to both the hardware and software that make PC's work, it's advantageous to use words that have certain, unambiguous meanings.

As you encounter new technical terms, I'll do my best to make sure that you know what I mean when I use them. The point is not to impress you with what I know about PCs; I want to share that knowledge with you. I hope that, as you find yourself comfortable with more and more computing jargon, you'll get more and more excited about what the world of PCs has to offer you.

Pixels

Today's PCs make images one "picture element" (or *pixel*) at a time. These pixels are simply small parts of the overall picture—if you like, you can think of them as "dots". Each dot, or pixel, in an image is of one color and has a certain level of brightness across its entire area. The neighboring pixels can differ in color and brightness, but each of them has only one color and brightness. To store these colors and brightness levels, the computer computes and holds in its memory a number, or a small group of numbers, that specifies the color and brightness of each pixel in the image. A very large number of pixels placed so closely together that the human eye sees them as touching, makes up the images we see. The number of pixels used to create a given image is commonly called that image's *resolution*, although you might know that this term also has another meaning. You'll explore this other meaning later in the chapter when you read about resolution in more depth.

The number of pixels that create an image greatly determines the amount of detail that image can show. You probably understand this concept intuitively. If I asked you to draw a picture of your face, but allowed you to make only four marks on a blank 8x10" piece of paper, the drawing wouldn't resemble you at all. You might even refuse the task, arguing that four dots isn't enough "information" to show what you look like. If I told you that you could make several hundred dots, you might be able to produce something that, in the vaguest ways, looked a little bit like your own face. You'd be giving me a little more "information," and, if I already know what you look like, I will probably be able to see the resemblance. If I told you that you could use millions of dots, the way that photographic film uses millions of crystals, you would have no technical limitations preventing you from showing me what you look like with sharpness and great accuracy.

I'm using the term "information" here for a specific purpose. Recall from Chapter 4, "Understanding Bits and Bytes," how computers use bits and bytes to store data, and how that data, when it's used in certain ways, becomes what we call information. As you continue reading this chapter, you'll see how your PC manipulates special collections of bytes in certain ways—the end result of which is an image on the PC's monitor. You'll see that images appear fuzzy or distorted when the PC isn't using enough bytes to represent them—that is, when the resolution is too low; when there isn't enough information.

Sometimes, there isn't enough information about an image because you're not using enough dots—not using enough pixels, that is—to represent it. Another factor that contributes to how sharp and accurate an image on a PC can be is not so much the number of the pixels themselves, or even their size, but the size of the space between them. The space between pixels is a property of the display hardware, and it goes by the name *dot pitch*. Let's take a deeper look at resolution and dot pitch and their roles in computer video.

Resolution

I mentioned that the term resolution has two meanings, both related to video. The simplest of these two meanings is that resolution is the total number of pixels (dots) in the entire image. Because it would get cumbersome to talk about "786,432 pixel images," people usually break resolution down into the number of pixels horizontally and vertically. Thus, we say images have a resolution of 1024×768 pixels, or a width of 1024 dots, and a height of 768 dots. You can relate how this is more useful to everyday life, too. If I offer to rent you a banquet space that is 1000 square feet, it might be difficult for you to visualize how big that is. At the same time, you don't know whether my room is 100 feet wide and only 10 feet deep, or whether it has more useful dimensions. So, just as people speak of the dimensions of a room, this particular definition of *resolution* is actually a statement of the dimensions, if you will, of an image. A room might be 20 by 30 feet; a particular image might be 1024×768 pixels.

Before I explain the second meaning of "resolution," let's think for a moment about what you just read. You might be thinking that my comparison of room dimensions and image dimensions has a fatal flaw. We can all talk about the size of a room because we all agree on how big a "foot" is, and we agree on how "feet" are laid out and measured. But who knows how big a dot is? And doesn't that matter?

The answer is that dots can be many sizes, and it both does and doesn't matter.

You do have to concern yourself with how big each pixel in an image is, but you don't usually talk about pixel size directly. Just as it's awkward to talk about 786,432-pixel images, it's also awkward to talk about 0.002-inch pixels. Instead, dot size is measured by how many pixels fit in a given amount of space—usually an inch. So, you'll read about 2400 dot-per-inch (that is, pixels per inch) images, and so forth. As you likely expect, having more pixels in a fixed amount of space means that you can squeeze more information into that space, which translates into a sharper, more accurate image. In this sense, pixel size matters. Divide an inch by the number of pixels per inch and you've got the size of each pixel.

At least, that method works when referring to an image printed on paper. That's because printers generally lay down each dot as close as possible to the adjoining dots. It's not necessary to go into all the details of how printers work now. You can find those topics discussed in Chapter 14, "Printers." What's important at this stage is understanding that this second meaning of *resolution*—the dots-per-inch meaning—applies more to printers than to video. This is because the dots on traditional television-like CRT (Cathode Ray Tube) computer monitors aren't, in fact, right up against each other. Because they're not, their absolute size doesn't matter as much. To understand why all of this is so, you need to consider two more characteristics of video: dot pitch and beam spot size.

Dot Pitch and Beam Spot Size

If you've worked with a modern laser printer, you might have seen that it can print an image at different dot-per-inch resolutions. By altering the size of the dots it prints, the printer produces more or fewer dots-per-inch and, so, an image with higher or lower resolution. A traditional TV-like PC monitor doesn't usually have this capability. How close each pixel is to its neighbor (the *dot pitch*) and the size of each pixel (*spot size*) are set at the monitor's manufacturer. You can use software to change the number of pixels used to display any given image, but you cannot actually change the size of the smallest-possible dot of light, nor of how closely packed the dots are. (You can, however, "fake it" and simulate this kind of change, as you'll see in just a moment.)

Let's look at spot size more in-depth. Imagine that you want the monitor to display an isolated dot of light surrounded by blackness. How small of a dot can it create? This depends wholly upon how the monitor causes dots to appear. The most common type of monitor, a cathode ray tube (CRT), squirts a beam of electrons onto the back of the monitor screen. The monitor glass is coated with a material that glows when electrons stimulate it; this coating is called "phosphor". Wherever the electrons hit the phosphor, light is emitted. So, a monitor's spot size is the smallest single dot of light the monitor can create. And that size is set by the diameter of the beam of electrons. An analogy, although not a perfect one, might be the metal, focusable flashlights you can buy everywhere today. Focus the beam of light in one way, the spot it makes on the wall is small; focus another way, the spot is very large. In the case of a CRT, the "focus," if you will, is fixed.

I mentioned earlier that dots on a monitor don't abut each other like do those on a laser printer. The reason for this is that light waves spread out in a way that a laser printer's solid toner doesn't. The implication is that one spot of light on a display has a tendency to bleed into its neighboring spots in a way that dry toner on paper doesn't. Naturally, if you have two spots onscreen too close to each other, they'll bleed and blur together. If you've got two dots acting as one, you've lost information and, as you'd expect, you'll lose sharpness in your image.

In fact, all monitors cheat. They don't really make single spots of arbitrary colors. Instead, a monitor makes individual spots of color that are arranged in very tight triplets. Each spot in the triplet glows with a single pure color (red, green, or blue). By controlling the relative brightness of the different colored spots, the computer can create what to your eyes appears as a single spot of almost any color you want. One set of these triplets functioning together creates one visible pixel on your side of the screen.

And so, the question is how close can the display's dots of light be to each other, side by side, and still remain two distinct dots with different colors and brightness? The answer to that question—how close two dots onscreen in fact are—depends on how tightly packed the sets of red, green, and blue triplets are, and that measurement is called the monitor's *dot pitch*. It might seem that a monitor's dot pitch is just another name for its dots-per-inch resolution, but people don't usually speak of it that way, and dot pitch isn't measured in that way. Instead, we use the term "dot pitch" to mean the distance onscreen from the center of one element in a pixel's triplet (say, the center of a pixel's green component) to the center of an adjacent pixel's green component, measured in millimeters. A monitor with a .26 dot pitch is one in which the center of one of each pixel's three parts is only 0.26mm from the center of that part of an adjacent pixel.

You've probably intuited that dot pitch and spot size are related. Naturally, the more tightly focused a spot of light is, the more densely you can pack several identical dots. The better focused a monitor's electron beams are, the smaller each part of a pixel's triad can be, and the more densely these can be packed. At the same time, it is possible for two monitors to have the same spot size but have different dot pitch. In this situation, the higher-dot-pitch monitor simply has more black space surrounding each component of each pixel. This makes each pixel seem less sharp which, naturally, makes each image less sharp. This fuzziness often leads users of high-dot-pitch monitors to suffer frequent headaches and eyestrain. Today, a quality monitor can have a dot pitch of as little as 0.21mm, although 0.26mm is very common. I personally recommend against using a monitor with greater than a 0.28mm dot pitch, and even that can cause eyestrain in some people. As concern for safe, ergonomic computing has grown, so has the importance of a monitor's dot pitch. It's a statistic you shouldn't ignore.

Most of this discussion assumes that the monitor uses a CRT as its display device. What about liquid crystal display (LCD) panels? They also are built with triplets of single-color spots that can each glow with an adjustable brightness. So the concept of dot pitch is the same for them as for CRTs. We'll look at flat panel displays in depth later in this chapter.

Image Resolution Versus Dot Pitch

You now know that dot pitch and spot size are fixed characteristics of a monitor. That being the case, how do these factors relate to the idea of resolution? And, more to the point, what does it mean when you read about "changing the resolution of a monitor"? How can you change resolution if the factors that go into resolution can't be changed?

In fact, this sort of change requires the "faking it" that I mentioned earlier. Resolution can change in one of two ways, depending on whether you want to change the resolution of a single image or everything the monitor displays. Let's consider the single-image option first. Perhaps, when your monitor is working optimally, it can display 1024 pixels horizontally and 768 pixels vertically. When your daughter sends you a digital picture of your grandkids that has a resolution of 2048×1536 pixels, must you only see half of the image, or is there an alternative?

Depending on what software you're using to view the image, you *might* only see 50% of the image at first. But almost all imaging software has a "zoom" feature that allows you to see the whole picture. How? The software analyzes the pixels in the image and it throws pixels out by averaging the color and brightness values of adjacent pixels together. In the example of your grandkids' photo, the software would average pixels together so that 50% of them can be discarded. That allows for a close approximation of the original, huge photo to fit on your screen.

> **Note:** I've cheated a little and myself, by setting up an example that's exactly twice the size of the monitor's resolution. In fact, the "averaging" of pixels that takes place is some rather complex computing, and it's not really as easy as saying "This pixel is red and the one next to it is blue, so I'll replace them both with one purple pixel." But it's close.

You *do* lose information in this process (although you only lose it on the screen—the original file isn't altered unless you explicitly make that change), but the end result is one that most people will consider very good. And most people will prefer seeing 100% of a very-good image over seeing 50% of an excellent image. When we use a piece of software to make this kind of "zoom" alteration, we say that the "effective resolution" of the image has been altered. (The *effective resolution* of an image is the number of pixels used to actually display it onscreen. You can contrast this notion with the *inherent resolution* of the image, which is the resolution at which the image was actually stored on disk. In the grandkids example, the image's 2048×1536 inherent resolution has been reduced to an effective resolution of 1024×768.)

The second type of resolution change—and the second way PC video "fakes it"—is made when you want to alter the resolution of everything your monitor displays. This is the sort of change that takes place when you open up your Display control panel in Windows, select the Settings tab, and move the Screen Area slider towards Less. Let's consider a PC monitor that, when it's operating at its best potential, displays 1600×1200 pixels. You use the Display control panel and change the Screen Area from 1600×1200 to 800×600. Suddenly, some things (icons, windows, and so forth) that were on the right side of the screen have disappeared, and everything you can see is bigger. What's happened, and how?

What's happened is that the PC has basically done the opposite of the type of change you read about a moment ago (when I talked about changing a single image's resolution). Rather than throwing out pixels and averaging pixel values, you're seeing pixels combined. Let me explain. You know that dot pitch and spot size don't change. So, in order to display only 800 dots across and 600 dots down, rather than 1600×1200, the PC's video system uses two physical pixels on the screen to show you a single spot of light (because 800×600 is half the resolution of 1600×1200). Everything on the screen looks bigger because twice as many physical pixels are being used to display it. Icons that were on the right edge of the screen have disappeared because the screen is now, effectively, half as wide as it used to be.

Of this second "fake", two points should be mentioned. First, Windows knows enough about this sort of change in resolution to cause programs to reformat themselves for the new settings. That's why the icons in your lower-right corner System Tray don't disappear. Windows knows to "move them to the left," when you reduce the monitor's effective resolution. Menus, too, reformat themselves, usually, although some older software might not behave properly unless you actually re-start Windows. (That's why Windows asks you if you want a resolution change to be implemented immediately or only after you restart.) The second point I want to mention is that today's best video hardware and software work together, performing some sophisticated mathematical tricks that are actually a lot more complex than the "2-for-1 pixel exchange" I gave as an example. More complex averaging is used, combinations of more than just two pixels are analyzed, and better actual results are realized.

Figures 6.1 and 6.2, will, I hope, make this clearer. In Figure 6.1, you can see the Display Control Panel with its Settings tab selected. From here, you can use the slider labeled Less and More to change the screen area of your entire monitor. Figure 6.2 shows the effect of making such a change. At the left, you see a normal 1600x1024 display. At the right, I've reduced the screen area to 800x600.

FIGURE 6.1

The Display Control Panel allows you to quickly change your monitor's screen area.

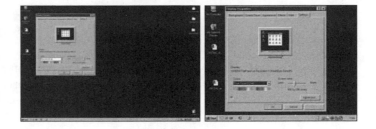

FIGURE 6.2
At the left, my screen's normal 1600x1024 resolution. At the right, the screen area has been reduced to 800x600. Objects that have a fixed size (in pixels), like the Control Panel, take up much more onscreen "real estate" at the lower setting.

How Images Are Painted on the Screen (Overview)

I've talked a lot about pixels and dots and so forth, but I've only mentioned in passing how pixels actually work. The pixels that make up an image are "painted" on the screen. I think you'll find that the following analogy to this process will make some important facts about this process clearer.

Imagine that you are holding a hose and directing a stream of water at the side of a building. The wall surface is rough, and it reflects a lot of sunlight. But where the water hits the wall, the wall reflects less light. This means that you can "paint" darkness on a region of the wall simply by directing your stream of water there. As long as any place on the wall stays wet, it will also stay dark, and you'll be able to see that you had pointed your hose there. But suppose that it is a very hot day and the water evaporates from the wall quickly. Now you can see only the places you have most recently played your stream of water. Finally, suppose that you modulate the amount of water that is flowing out of the hose as you sweep it across the building. This makes some places it passes get very wet and others hardly get wet at all.

This method of "painting" water on a wall is very much like the way most PC display technologies make images. In CRTs, the water stream is replaced by a beam of electrons hitting phosphor. Where the beam is intense, with many electrons hitting the phosphor each microsecond, the spot will glow brightly. Where the beam is weaker, it will produce less light. By varying the intensity of the electron beam as it hits the red, blue, or green component in each pixel's triad, the apparent color of that pixel is controlled. (A strong beam hitting the red and blue components and a weak beam hitting the green component will produce a bright purple pixel, and so forth. For more information about color mixing and color theory, take a look at Chapter 14, which covers PC printers.) In an LCD panel, the pixels are addressed one after another, each one being set to the appropriate color and brightness in its turn, thus achieving a similar effect.

How does the notion about each spot on the wall drying up shortly after the water stream leaves it translate to PC displays? CRTs and some other display technologies have images that naturally fade after some short period of time. These devices need the PC to "refresh" the images—repainting them, if you will—many times per second. If they aren't refreshed often enough, you'll experience a flickering image, and it might also be too dim to see clearly.

The number of times each second that the image gets refreshed is called the *refresh rate*. Typical PC CRT-based displays have their images refreshed at least 60 times each second and sometimes more than 100 times per second. Like dot pitch, this also is an ergonomic consideration. Our eyes and brains are remarkably sensitive to flickering light. For sensitive people, like me, a monitor that refreshes too infrequently seems to actually flicker, like an old movie. Too much of that, and eye strain and serious headaches are on their way. Many people are comfortable with a refresh rate as low as 60Hz (that is, 60 times per second). I used to get headaches from using any monitor with less than an 80Hz refresh rate—which, at the time, meant almost any monitor or television. LCD panels, on the other hand, are capable of displaying images indefinitely, without refreshing. This factor has made LCD panels the monitors of choice for me, even as long ago as 1998, when they were *far* more expensive than comparable CRTs.

> **Technical Note:** I just used the term Hz, which you might already know is an abbreviation for Hertz. In the worlds of electronics and computing, Hertz is a measurement of how many times something electronic happens in a second. So, if you read that AC current fluctuates at 60Hz, that means it fluctuates 60 times per second. (And, for the record, engineers call that kind of fluctuation a "cycle," so you may hear or read of Hertz measurements as being measurements of cycles per second.)

This process of "painting" every pixel on the screen and then repeating the process over and over—a process used in virtually every PC display—is called a *raster-scan display* process. Some raster-scan displays use a CRT; others use an LCD panel. I will describe the details of how each type is built later in the "Raster-Scan CRT Images," and the "LCD Panel Images" sections. For now, I just want to focus on the nature of the images being displayed.

> **Note:** Just in case you're wondering, it's called a *raster* because of the way the electron beam sweeps across the screen. *Raster* comes from a Latin word " rastrum," which is a rake, like a garden rake which scrapes across the lawn, drawing straight lines in the grass.

In a CRT display, the electron beam is painted across the screen from left to right in a straight, horizontal line on the very slightest of downwards diagonals. The downward drift is just enough that, when the beam reaches the right edge of the screen, it is at the proper height to begin painting the next row. The beam moves back to the left edge and again moves smoothly across the screen. This continues until the lines have been painted in succession all the way down the screen.

A different type of display, used very rarely in the PC world, is called a *vector-scan* display. Here, the path of the beam forms the lines of an image, one stroke at a time. (When the beam must be moved from the end of one stroke to the beginning of the next, the intensity is simply turned down to zero.) By drawing just these lines over and over again very quickly, an image is produced, much in the same way that a laser-light show draws shapes. Raster-scan displays, in contrast to this, use a regular pattern of horizontally sweeping the beam to draw any image. The image is drawn while the beam sweeps by modulating the beam intensity very rapidly in an appropriate pattern.

Figure 6.3 shows how both types of display might draw a triangle. The top of the figure (a) shows the strokes that make up the triangle using the vector-scan approach. The bottom-left portion (b) shows how a raster scan can accomplish the same effect. The bottom-right section (c) shows graphs of the raster-scan beam's horizontal and vertical positions, each as a function of time.

Figure 6.3
How vector-scan and raster-scan displays form images.

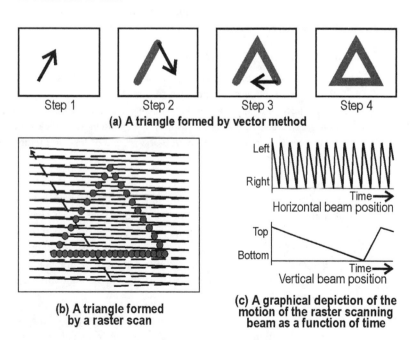

Step 1   Step 2   Step 3   Step 4
(a) A triangle formed by vector method

(b) A triangle formed by a raster scan

(c) A graphical depiction of the motion of the raster scanning beam as a function of time

A Little More About Scanning Frequencies and Refresh Rates

Your PC display subsystem draws and redraws the screen image constantly, and at very frequent intervals. It must do this. If it didn't, you wouldn't know it when the information to be displayed changed.

How often must it redraw the screen image? That depends on what type of image it is. In all cases, you want to have the feeling that you aren't waiting to see the new information. That requirement alone means that the screen must refresh at least 10 times per second. If you are looking at a movie, it will appear jumpy unless you see at least 24–30 new images each second. If the scene has any objects that change their brightness significantly from one screen image to the next, those images better be painted on the screen at a rate of at least 60 images per second. Otherwise, you will see a flickering, and soon you will get a headache.

To be sure that your PC display works well for all purposes, manufacturers usually try for a refresh rate of at least 72 times per second. Indeed, most video cards and CRT monitors today are capable of operating at refresh rates in excess of 80Hz, all the way up to 120Hz. You'll discover more about Hz refresh rates later.

Let's consider some of the requirements that this refresh rate imposes on the display mechanisms. Consider the example of a screen image with a resolution of 1024×768— that is, an image with 768 rows of pixels, each row containing 1024 pixels.

Raster-Scan CRT Images

A raster-scan image on a CRT is painted one pixel at a time, and the display must paint all those pixels 60 or more times per second. This implies some pretty tough requirements on the speed of the display system. PC displays form raster-scan images in what is called a *progressive* manner. That means they sweep down the screen from top to bottom once per image. They must do this in 1/60 of a second or less, so the minimum *vertical sweep rate* is 60Hz.

To get all 768 lines of pixels drawn 60 times each second, the lines must be drawn at a rate of 46,080 lines per second (760*60). Actually, the required rate is a little bit higher than this, because there must be some time equivalent to that required to draw several lines for what is called the *vertical blanking interval*. During this time, the electron beam is shut off and the beam steering mechanism moves it vertically up from the bottom of the screen to the top. So, the actual rate at which lines are drawn horizontally is probably at least 48KHz (48,000 lines per second). This line-drawing rate is called the *horizontal sweep rate*.

As it is drawing a single line, the display mechanism in a CRT must be capable of changing the strength of the electron beam rapidly enough to set the correct brightness for each pixel, independently of the brightness of its neighbors. After all, the beam is painting individual pixels at a rate of around 48 million per second. Because it takes a little time for the electron beam to move from the right side of the screen back to the left side, the actual rate of pixel drawing might be around 50 million per second. This means that the electronics in the monitor (and those on the video display adapter) must be able to perform at rates in excess of 50MHz.

The CRT display must, therefore, be capable of synchronizing its electron beam sweeping to the vertical and horizontal drive signals that are, in this case, coming to it at around 60Hz and 48KHz, respectively. These are the minimal numbers to look for if you want to have a CRT that is capable of displaying good, clear, 1024×768 graphic screen images.

After the electron beam has painted an image, that image will immediately start to fade away. In fact, with the type of CRTs used in most PC displays, the pixels in any given region of the screen fade essentially to black in a small fraction of the time it takes the system to draw an entire image. The technical term for this effect is the *persistence* of the phosphor in the CRT, and for most PC displays it is at most a few milliseconds and perhaps much less than that.

LCD Panel Images

LCD panels come in several types.The different types create their images in different ways. (I'll describe the principal types in some detail later in this chapter.) All of them use a raster scanning procedure, but some allow the individual pixels much more time to be set to the correct brightness than is the case with the others. That is good, because LCD panel pixels cannot be turned on or off at anywhere near the rate at which pixels are painted on a CRT's screen. On the other hand, the pixels in an LCD panel have, effectively, an infinite persistence time. That is, after the pixels are set to some brightness or color, that image tends to remain on the panel as long as power is applied or until it is replaced by some other image.

Character Versus Bitmapped Images

The original IBM PC display subsystem that most people bought was what IBM called its Monochrome Display Adapter and Monitor. This monitor was a simple green screen cathode ray tube. The video adapter that drove it created images that consisted solely of letters, numbers, and a few graphic symbols. The screen image was divided into 25 lines with 80 character positions on each line. Any symbol could be placed in each of those 2,000 character positions, and each of those symbols could be either bright or dim, or it could blink. This was a pure character display system.

An early alternative to this green screen, character display was the IBM Color Graphics Adapter (CGA) and its monitor. This displaysystem took a different approach to forming its images. Instead of putting character symbols into character cells on the screen, the CGA display painted 64,000 individual pixels. Each one could be made to glow in any one of four colors. Far less detail exists in an image formed this way, but what detail there is can be specified more arbitrarily. IBM dubbed this type of display an All-Points-Addressable (APA) display. Today, it's usually called a *bitmapped display,* because one or more bits in the video image memory is assigned to each pixel on the screen. Any new PC monitor you'd purchase today is a bitmapped monitor.

Where and How Is the Image Formed and Maintained?

As I just mentioned, screen images for PCs come in two forms: character images and graphic bitmapped images. Each of these forms requires storing the image information in memory in a different form. For a character image, all you must store in RAM is two bytes of information for each character position on the screen. One of these bytes holds the extended ASCII code for the character to be displayed in this position. The other byte holds attribute information. (These attributes specify such qualities as the color for this character, how bright it is, and whether it is blinking or underlined.)

If, on the other hand, the image is bitmap, much more detail must be stored. The color of every pixel must be described. Just how that is done depends on what *color depth* this image is to have.

Color Depth

Color depth refers, indirectly, to the number of possible colors for each pixel in a graphic screen image. If all the pixels are either black or white, you need only one bit to specify in which of these two colors a particular pixel is to be shown. If the image allows each pixel to have any one of four colors, you need two bits per pixel to define which of those four colors is to be used. By similar reasoning, you can see that four bits suffice to select any one of 16 colors. Eight bits can specify any one of 256 colors. The color depth is simply the number of bits needed to specify the color of each pixel. (For a refresher on how the number of bits relates to the number of colors, look back at Chapter 4.)

The most commonly used color depths in PC images are 2, 4, 8, 15, 16, and 24.

Consider an old-fashioned VGA graphic display. The resolution of the entire image is 640 pixels per line and 480 lines. This says there are 307,200 total pixels. Normal VGA specifies that each pixel can be given any one of a specified set of 16 colors. That means that the color depth is four bits. So, for each pixel you must have 1/2 byte (four bits) of video image RAM, for a total of 153,600 bytes (exactly 150KB). Because RAM chips always hold a number of bits that is some integer power of 2, VGA video cards normally had 256KB of video image RAM.

Where Physically and Logically Is the Video Image RAM?

I just mentioned in passing that the video image RAM is typically on the video card. Is that always true? Why?

Screen images for a PC need to be maintained in some very special memory locations. These locations must be accessible to the CPU, but they also must be accessible to the video image output circuitry. The CPU needs rapid access to them, but the video output circuitry needs even more rapid access. This dictates where the chips that make up that memory must be placed physically.

If you have a plug-in video card, because the video image output circuitry is on the card, it only makes sense to put the video image RAM there also. If your PC has its video display adapter circuitry located on the motherboard, you will find the video image RAM somewhere very near it. In any event, in all but the cheapest systems, the video image RAM consists of a totally separate set of chips from those that make up the PC's main memory. A PC's main memory simply doesn't perform fast enough to provide the speed necessary for high-quality bitmapped images at a high color depth. Furthermore, the necessary speeds are so fast that even the distance the electrical impulses must travel between video memory chips and the other video output circuitry becomes significant. It's necessary, therefore, for video RAM to be as close to the other video circuitry as possible, and for it to be very fast RAM, indeed.

> **Note:** There are a few exceptions to this, incidentally. Silicon Graphics, Inc. has developed a Visual Computing architecture for their Visual Workstation systems that enables nearly the entire system's main memory to be used for video-related purposes. Of course, one aspect of how this is achieved is that all memory in these systems must meet the higher performance and tolerance specifications that are reserved for dedicated video memory in more standard-use PCs. At the other end of the financial spectrum are the lowest-quality "economy" PCs, which attempt to trade quality for price. These systems use a portion of main memory for video and are extremely unsatisfactory performers.

Exceptions aside, the newest mainstream PCs separate things even more. They use an Advanced Graphics Port into which one plugs an AGP video card. This AGP connector carries the data from the CPU over a different set of wires than those serving all the other plug-in cards, so the AGP video signals never have to share those wires with—and, therefore, never have to wait for—any other hardware. The CPU is also able to send data to the AGP card at the same time as other data are going to the other plug-in cards (for example, on the PCI bus) and several times more rapidly than the data flow in the PCI bus. (You first encountered the AGP bus in Chapter 1, and you will read about it in depth in Chapter 20, "Video Acceleration".)

The video image RAM is located *physically* on the video card (or in the near vicinity of the video circuitry). *Logically*, things seem quite different. From the perspective of the CPU, this block of memory is just more memory, like any other it can see. When images need to be processed, the CPU can access and manipulate the data stored in this memory and then send the result out to the monitor. Unfortunately, this sort of work uses a *lot* of CPU time and processor power.

Accelerated Video Cards

A better solution for creating complex graphic images is to have a *graphics coprocessor* as part of the video card. This is a small, dedicated computer located on the video card itself, unless your PC has its video circuitry all on the motherboard. The sole job of a graphics coprocessor is computing pixel color values for graphic images, thus taking these time- and resource-consuming duties off the main CPU.

In this sort of system, the program that is creating the image can describe that image in fairly broad, high-level terms. For example, it might specify that a triangle is to be drawn and give the coordinates of the corners, the width, and color of the line to be used, and perhaps a color to use to fill the interior of the triangle after it has been drawn. The PC's main CPU won't compute the pixel information for the images to be displayed, but will instead pass instructions at this high level to the graphics coprocessor. That device will then compute which pixels in the image must be set to the color of the border and which are to be set to the fill color. And, it will load all those pixel values into the video image RAM. All the while, the main CPU is free to do other work.

Figure 6.4 schematically shows these two approaches to graphic image generation. The upper panel shows a block diagram of how images are created and then displayed when a graphics coprocessor is not involved. The lower panel shows how this changes with a graphics coprocessor. This figure doesn't show any details for the video image readout hardware. I'll talk about the video hardware in a moment.

Perhaps the most significant point to see here is that the speed of data flow from graphics coprocessor to video image RAM and the flow from there to the screen are controlled only by the details of how the video card is built. Most modern video cards are very fast and are capable of moving a huge amount of data very quickly between the graphics coprocessor and the video RAM.

FIGURE 6.4

Two ways to gen-erate a graphics image.

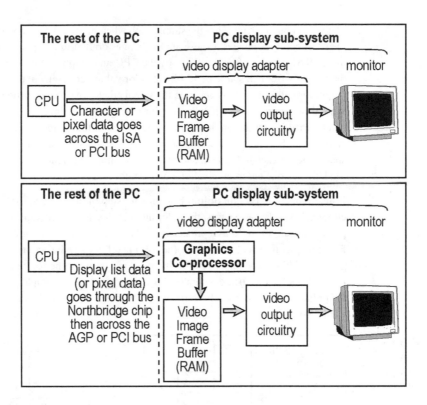

What Paints the Image on the Screen—and How?

I have mentioned many times now, but I haven't yet explained, the actual video display circuitry. It makes up one essential part of any video card. Allow me to remedy that. You will find additional details on a much more technical level in Chapter 20.

Modern display adapters can operate in a huge number of contexts, which are called video *modes*. The particular mode you are using determines three features. First, it specifies whether the image you are creating is composed solely of characters, like a DOS-mode screen, or whether it is a bitmapped graphic. Second, it specifies the effective resolution of the image (how many pixels per line and how many lines). Third, it specifies the color depth (how many bits per pixel are stored in the video image RAM). The video display circuitry has from one to three separate jobs to perform, and these are determined by the video mode in which the video display adapter is operating.

The video output circuitry has the simplest job when in modes that support, paradoxically, the most complex images. (These are the images crafted in full-pixel detail in the video image RAM—or the *frame buffer*—by the CPU and graphics coprocessor, and for which the frame buffer holds at least 15 bits of color value per pixel.) In this case, all the video output circuitry must do is generate the signals that move the electron beam, and at the same time pump out each pixel's tri-color brightness. The brightness for each part of a pixel's triad is sent out on one of the three analog output wires going from the video circuitry to the monitor. (Recall that each pixel is actually made up of a triad of three spots, one for each red, green, and blue. The combined brightness of the elements of this triad creates one onscreen pixel of a given color and brightness.)

If the color depth is eight or four bits, another step often is added to the video output circuitry's job. In these cases, the color number doesn't directly specify the color of the pixel. Instead, it is used as a pointer into what is called a *palette* or *color lookup table*. For example, if the color number of a given pixel is four, the actual amounts of red, green, and blue to be displayed for that pixel are found at the fourth line of the palette. Figure 6.5 shows a block diagram of this circuitry and also a sample palette table showing the default values for 16-color standard VGA images. (A 0 in the table represents none of that color; a value of 63 represents the maximum amount of that color.)

FIGURE 6.5

How a VGA display creates colored pixels through translating numbers from the frame buffer.

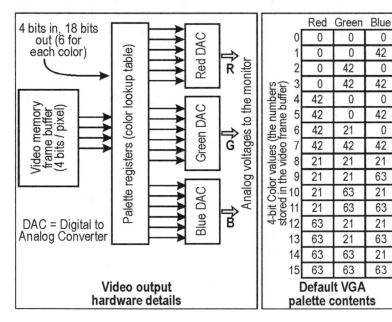

	Red	Green	Blue
0	0	0	0
1	0	0	42
2	0	42	0
3	0	42	42
4	42	0	0
5	42	0	42
6	42	21	0
7	42	42	42
8	21	21	21
9	21	21	63
10	21	63	21
11	21	63	63
12	63	21	21
13	63	21	63
14	63	63	21
15	63	63	63

Video output hardware details   Default VGA palette contents

A palette mechanism is used for four-bit or eight-bit color modes because when you have so few colors, you might not like the ones you get. By using a palette, you can still have no more than 16 or 256 simultaneous colors, but the particular ones you get on a given image are determined by the contents of the palette table, which can be altered any time you (or a program you run) want to change it.

For example, GIF images typically use this strategy. They have at most 256 colors in any single image, yet sometimes they look stunningly like a photograph. The reason is that GIF images normally contain a palette that has in it a set of well-chosen colors that best represent whatever image the file contains. Graphics image display programs read that palette out of the GIF file and load that set of colors into the hardware palette in the video display adapter whenever they are displaying a GIF file.

Getting the Colors Right

Including color in an image makes a huge difference. Color displays convey information more compactly than monochrome displays, because colors can be used to convey subtext to various items on the screen. Because color printers are quite affordable and capable of quality prints now, preparing documents in color has become far more commonplace, and sometimes expected by recipients of your printouts.

Colors are slippery beasts, however. Colors in images onscreen often don't match what is printed, and all color display devices (monitors or printers) are not properly adjusted when they come from the factory. These factors combine to make it difficult to be sure when you look at a screen image whether its colors are the same as what you will see when you print it.

You can take two approaches to get the colors in an image just right. One is to tweak how the monitor displays colors, and the other is to alter the stored information in the image until the monitor colors look however you want them to. (In addition to what you're about to read, you will learn more about colors and color theory in Chapter 14 when you look more in-depth at color printing.)

Adjusting the Monitor

If you plan to print some computer-generated color images, or intend them to be viewed on more than just your PC, you probably will want to adjust your monitor until each color appears at least very nearly correct. That is, white pages should look white, and red should look red.

The first level of accomplishing this is called *aligning the monitor*. This is simply making sure that the electron beam that carries information for the red subpixels in the image is hitting only the dots or stripes of phosphor that glow red (and, of course, doing the same for the other two colors of subpixels). When that is done, any field of pure color will appear to be the same hue and saturation. This color might or might not be right, because of some details of both how humans see color and how display devices create colored images.

You can make some other useful adjustments to an image that can make its colors appear more correct. An adjustment known as *color temperature* is used to make a white page seem white rather than bluish or yellowish. (This is also sometimes called *white balance.*) You can also generally adjust the color strength, or brightness, of each of the three primary colors that work together to generate each pixel. This allows you to tweak the red, green, and blue output of your monitor until images look as you want them to. Professional graphics artists commonly use expensive hardware that actually looks at the monitor output and aids in adjusting it until the color values are perfect. The rest of us, who are mere graphics mortals, might find this type of adjustment more useful as a way to make what we see on the screen match the color of a test pattern we've printed on our color printer. (That's what the pros use it for, too, but it's possible to "eyeball" the adjustment if your job isn't resting on your settings being perfect.) Most monitors today are equipped with a built-in menu function that allows you to make these, and other, adjustments rather easily.

Adjusting the Image Information

The alternative way to adjust the color appearance of an image is simply to alter the color values that are stored in the image itself or in its palette table. This is the way to go if you want to adjust an individual image to match certain values for a specific purpose, but you would not want to use this method ubiquitously and have to manually adjust the appearance of every image you view and print.

How to Talk to a Video Display

Now you know pretty well how a PC creates, stores, and outputs a video image. But, in fact, I haven't yet told you the newest wrinkle in how that output step can be done.

The original PC displays sent purely digital data to the display over several wires in parallel. (The signal on each wire was either ON or OFF at every instant.) Monochrome displays used two wires to get four brightness levels. CGA displays used four wires to get potentially 16 colors. EGA used six wires to get up to 64 colors.

This approach ran out of steam right about there. So IBM introduced an analog approach with its VGA display (three wires with variable voltages representing variable amounts of red, green, and blue). All PC displays up until very recently used a refinement of that approach.

Now, with LCD digital flat panel displays in particular, and someday in the not too distant future with all displays, the market will be returning to a truly all-digital interface—but with a big difference from the old way.

PC users still want to have many levels of brightness for each color element in a pixel's triad of dots, and they cannot have dozens of wires in the cable. So the industry is moving toward using a very high-speed digital serial bus. The brightness information for each triad element will be digitized and sent as binary numbers over this bus.

What's the advantage to doing this? There are several. First is the usual advantage of all things digital; you can send the information without fearing that any noise will get into it and degrade the signal. As long as the signal is received and regenerated properly, it will be a perfect copy of what was sent. Second, the images on a fully digital display potentially can be better than on the present generation of analog-brightness-for-each-digital-subpixel displays. Certainly they should be more reproducible, meaning that you won't have to adjust them to get the image to look right, nor will the image differ noticeably from one display to the next. Finally, when the industry has this all worked out, the interface will be cheaper to build than the present all-analog interface.

Why aren't people using all digital video interfaces already? For one, if you switch to a purely digital flat panel display, you have to replace your analog output video display adapter, and there are still few all-digital video cards on the market. Their number is growing, however, and, as I mentioned earlier, the card in our example unit from Dell can output both analog and true digital signals.

Second, it is only recently that competing digital standards have been ironed out into one. With that debate settled, it's now economically more sound for manufacturers to produce all-digital cards, knowing that any new digital monitor will be compatible with those cards (in other words, the market is finally big enough to justify the investment). You'll read more about digital flat panels later in this chapter.

Understanding Display Technologies

Up to this point, I have told you a great deal about color vision and color images, but not actually very much about exactly how the display devices you use create the images you can see. There are two principal categories of display devices for PCs, and several others that are not yet in common use. As mentioned before, the most common for desktop PCs are CRTs. Virtually all laptops use some version of an LCD panel. Projection display devices (for use in showing PC presentations to large audiences) can be built using either type of technology, or using a new, third technology from Texas Instruments, called Digital Light Processing (DLP).

Cathode Ray Tubes (CRTs)

You've already read a lot about CRTs. A CRT is a big glass bottle with a vacuum inside. It also contains three electron guns that shoot focused beams of electrons, some apparatus (either magnetic or electrostatic) that aims these beams both up and down and side to side, and a phosphor screen upon which these beams impinge. The vacuum is necessary to let those electron beams travel across the tube without running into air molecules that could absorb them or scatter them off course.

Color CRTs also have one of two mechanisms, either a *shadow mask* or an *aperture grill*. The phosphor is not a continuous sheet of material, as it is in a monochrome monitor, but instead consists of the triads of dots or stripes, which you've already read about. These dots are made of three materials. All three materials glow when an electron beam hits them, but each glows in its own color (red, green, or blue).

In the first kind of color CRT, a *shadow mask* is located a short distance away from the phosphor. This mask is simply a metal sheet with a regular array of holes punched in it. The electron guns are arranged in a triangle at the back of the tube, and the phosphor has a triangle of dots of different color phosphors in front of each hole in the shadow mask. Because of this geometrical arrangement, each of the electron guns can "see" only the dots it is supposed to illuminate. The beam deflection apparatus deflects all three beams together to form the raster scan pattern. As the set of three beams sweeps across the shadow mask, the holes guarantee that each beam lights up only phosphor dots that glow in the correct color for that beam.

The alternative arrangement uses an *aperture grill*. In these CRTs, the electron guns are placed side by side, just as you see in Figure 6.6. The aperture grill is simply an array of parallel wires, shown in this figure as the dashes in the dashed line near the phosphor. The gaps between those wires enable the beams from the three electron guns to illuminate three adjacent stripes on the tube surface. At just those locations behind each gap are three stripes of the corresponding phosphors.

FIGURE 6.6

A simplified schematic of a typical color CRT which uses three electron guns and a shadow mask or aperture grill to illuminate triplets of phosphor dots or stripes.

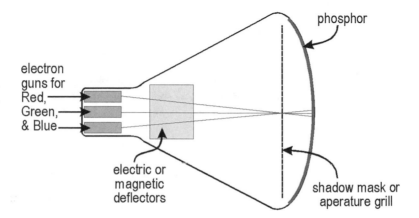

Sony patented this second technology under the name *Trinitron*. That patent has now expired, and many manufacturers use it.

Thinner CRTs

With the popularity of flat panels, like our example unit from Silicon Graphics, the amount of desk space taken up by traditional CRT monitors has suddenly started to seem inordinate. I suspect that the "cool" factor has a lot to do with this, but there's certainly no question that CRTs are big, and big CRTs are *really* big.

CRT manufacturers have thus begun to develop traditional CRT monitors that are not nearly as deep as their predecessors. These "short-neck" models use advanced deflection mechanisms so that the electron gun no longer needs to be the distance from the screen that was required by previous beam-control technology. Because the gun doesn't have to be as far away, the tube can be shorter.

Liquid Crystal Displays (LCDs)

The second category of PC display devices LCD panels. These devices come in many variations, but the fundamental method of operation is the same for all of them.

Figure 6.7 shows a simple LCD panel. Here, a light source shines through a polarizer. Like polarizing sunglasses, this sheet only passes light waves that are radiating in parallel to the lines of polarization. This light travels through a special liquid crystal fluid. The property of the molecules in this container, or cell, is such that an electric charge adjusts the transparency of the fluid and, thus, the brightness of the light passing through it. By controlling the transparency of each liquid crystal cell, the video circuitry controls the brightness and color of each pixel on the screen.

FIGURE 6.7
A typical LCD panel.

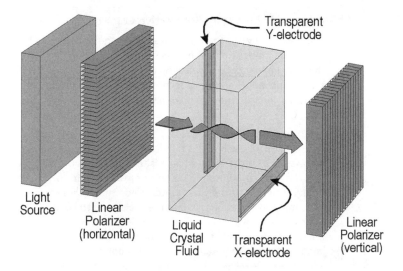

Light Source — Linear Polarizer (horizontal) — Liquid Crystal Fluid — Transparent X-electrode — Transparent Y-electrode — Linear Polarizer (vertical)

This design describes a *passive-matrix* LCD panel. That means that each pixel just sits there and responds when you address it, but does not respond at any other time. This technology is considered old now, and is used almost exclusively in small handheld PDAs. I'll describe how an *active-matrix* LCD panel differs from this next.

Active-Matrix (TFT) LCDs Are the Only Way to Go

Active-matrix LCD panels differ from the passive-matrix panels in one simple-to-state, but, for many years, very hard-to-build way: They have a small circuit (with one or more transistors) for each subpixel, or three per pixel in a color screen. (These subpixels are analogous to the triads that make up a single color pixel on a CRT.) These circuits are built by a process that carries the name "thin-film transistors" (hence the acronym you commonly will see added to the name: active-matrix/*TFT* LCD panel).

Because these are essentially electronic memory circuits, they respond very quickly to a signal telling them what value to store. Then, they drive the appropriate voltage across the cell and hold it there until they are told to change that value.

The raster-scanning mechanism in an active-matrix LCD display goes very rapidly over the whole array, setting brightness values into each transistor on the entire screen. In fact, it scans those displays at the same rate as a CRT.

All of this explains why passive LCD panels have been discontinued in notebook computers, where users more and more want displays capable of displaying movies, not merely simple static graphics or text. Because an active-matrix display remembers each pixel value, it isn't necessary to "refresh" the display rapidly in order to keep from having the image flicker.

Additive Color Versus Subtractive Color LCDs

There are two ways to modify this design to make a color LCD panel. One way uses three times as many intersections as the number of pixels to be formed in the final image. Each subpixel is covered with a colored plastic filter. Then the signals applied to each intersection adjust the brightness of each subpixel. This creates a color image in a manner that is essentially identical to that used by color CRTs.

The other way to modify the design is to layer three liquid crystal panels on top of one another. Each one is filled with a colored liquid crystal. Each one has its own set of x- and y-electrodes, this time just one intersection per pixel. Each layer absorbs an adjustable portion of just one color of the light passing through it. This is similar to the way printed color images are created. The principal advantage to this design is that it enables you to create as many pixels as intersections, thus making higher-resolution LCD panels possible. The principal disadvantage is that the light must pass through three layers, and so the resulting image is fainter, or you must use a stronger back light.

Replacing Your CRT with an Active-Matrix LCD Panel

With passive LCD displays soundly antiquated, and with the cost of manufacturing active-matrix displays always dropping, these very nice flat screen displays are now becoming common in offices, on desktops, at point-of-sale terminals, and elsewhere. They are still more expensive than a CRT of the same size and resolution, but not by a huge factor. LCD panels are delightfully lightweight—less than a quarter of the weight of an equivalent CRT—and they take up very little desktop space (because they don't have to have the big CRT "bottle" poking out of the back). Those two factors alone have made them highly desirable in many places where there either isn't room for a big CRT or where the display needs to be moved often from one place to another.

Figure 6.8 shows our test display: the truly breathtaking 18-inch (diagonal measurement) F180 flat panel from SGI. It can display photo-realistic (24-bits per pixel) color images at an actual pixel resolution of 1280×1024. You can use it to display images with lower resolution by using only a portion of the screen. Alternatively, the display can stretch the image to more-or-less fill the screen. If you try to display a higher-resolution image, the display will simply not show it at all. You can, in that case, reduce the resolution of the image in software and then display it, as discussed at the beginning of this chapter.

FIGURE 6.8
The SGI F180 flat panel display.

The SGI F180 display is significantly brighter and sharper than a comparable CRT monitor and, truly, it's about the sharpest image I've ever seen, outside of my beloved SGI 1600SW digital flat panel (which is the F180's ancestor). SGI uses a unique four-tube lighting system that produces accurate and uniformly illuminated colors immediately after being turned on. Other LCD monitors use simpler lighting techniques that lead to hotspots at the edges of the monitor and improperly balanced color as the lighting tubes warm up to their full temperature.

Additionally, the F180 has inputs for both analog VGA and true-digital DVI-I signals, so that the panel can be connected to two computers simultaneously, or so that one user with a digital video card can take advantage of the higher quality image that true-digital output creates.

The new display uses less than half the power of a 21" CRT, too, and it generates only one-third the heat. The implication—particularly given the power crises that are plaguing the electric bills of people as I write this—is that the monitor can actually pay for itself in a little over three years.

Off, or Rather, On The Wall

As you can imagine, more developments in PC displays will occur as time goes on. None of the displays used now are perfect, so there is ample room for improvements. For now, CRTs and LCDs are the primary display technologies in use. In addition to CRTs and LCD panels meant for direct viewing, there are products that use displays of either of those types in a projection mode. These projectors can fill a large screen with a PC-generated image, and they might seem quite exotic compared to a simple desktop or laptop PC's usual monitor. With one exception, though, PC projectors are merely the same types of display made superbright and imaged on a screen. The exception is Digital Light Processing (DLP) technology from Texas Instruments, and it's changing not only how you'll see your PC, but how you see movies, too.

Digital Light Processing

One of the most promising and exciting new display technologies to come down the path recently is Digital Light Processing (DLP) from Texas Instruments. This isn't a monitor technology, per se, but it is a projection system that is perfectly suited to the digital PC projectors of the near future, as well as the big-screen displays that might finally unify the television and the PC monitor into one device.

How DLP actually works is a bit hard to visualize—and even harder to believe—so I've included Figure 6.9, which is Texas Instruments' own illustration of the process.

FIGURE 6.9

Digital Light Processing (DLP) relies on TI's ability to create a digital micromirror device (DMD) which contains, among other things, 1,310,720 mirrors in the space of one square inch.

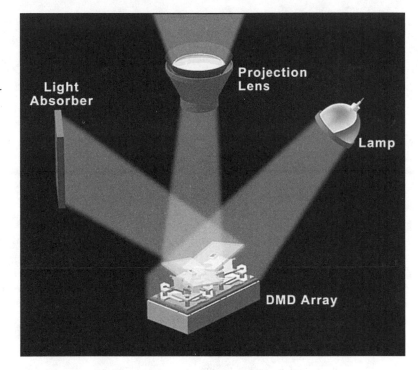

Here's how it works in a nutshell. The digital representation of some image (or a continuous series of images) is sent from the computer to the DLP processing chip. This chip controls the movement of each of the 1,310,720 micromirrors on the digital micromirror device (DMD) itself. In Figure 6.9, the DMD is that weird thing at the bottom center, and an actual DMD is shown in Figure 6.10. What you're actually seeing in Figure 6.10 is just two of those one million-plus mirrors. Each mirror is mounted on a flexible stalk that causes it to "float" above the DMD's base.

Beneath the array of mirrors is another array—of electrodes, two for each micromirror. In response from instructions that come from the DLP processor, these electrodes are charged or discharged in such a way that they cause the mirrors above them to tilt. In Figure 6.9, you can see that both of the two sample mirrors are tilted, one in such a way that light from the source lamp is transmitted through a projection lens. The other mirror is tilted so that the source light is sent into an absorbing surface (and is, thereby, "lost").

Here's where it gets both amazing and a little complicated. You read earlier in this chapter how CRTs and LCDs create pixels of almost any conceivable color by combining triplets of red, green, and blue subpixels. The brightness of each of the three colored subpixels mixes together with the others and a single spot of light is perceived on the screen. The brighter the red subpixel is, the more red the resultant pixel is. If the green subpixel is very dim, the pixel it contributes to will seem to have very little green to its color, and so on. This process is used over the space of the entire display, and you're able to see solid, full-color images.

FIGURE **6.10**
*The DMD fits in
the palm of a
hand.*

DLP builds on this idea, but works completely differently. Texas Instruments discovered that, if you change the color of a single spot of light fast enough, over and over again, a person looking at that spot will see what appears to be a solid (not flashing) dot of light. The color of that dot will be the combination of the different colored flashes, just like the color of each viewable pixel on a CRT is the combined color of its subpixels. This might sound strange, but, really, it's the same way that motion pictures seem to move. Flash different images in front of the human eye fast enough and the person watching will see the images combine. At the movies, this creates the illusion of smooth motion between the individual frames of film.

Now, one micromirror is responsible for the color of each pixel that gets projected. But wait, you say, don't you need three micromirrors, one for each red, green, and blue? No. Instead, every image that is sent to the DLP processor is split into its red, green, and blue components. A color wheel, spinning at more than 120 rotations per second, sits between the light source and the DMD. When the red gel of the color wheel is in the light, the DLP processor activates thousands of electrons through the DMD so that the mirrors move. Mirrors that are responsible for pixels that have a lot of red in them are tilted so that the red filtered light is sent towards the projection lens. Mirrors responsible for less-red pixels are angled towards the absorber.

The color wheel turns to its green gel, and the DLP moves the mirrors so that the proper amount of green light is reflected through the lens, and then the process repeats for blue. This all happens over 120 times per second, which is sufficiently fast that the human eye blends the light from the three color bursts into a single, solid spot of light that is the combined color of the bursts.

(In other words, rather than using three spots of light that are so close to each other they appear to mix, DLP uses one spot of light that changes to different intensities of the three primary colors so fast that they appear to mix.)

Because each micromirror is only 16 square microns, and because they are less than one micron apart from each other, the images DLP produces are far sharper than are those of their only competition, LCD projectors. (Saying the same thing using the CRT terminology you learned earlier in this chapter, the DLP's beam spot size and its dot pitch are infinitesimal compared to those of LCD projectors.) And, because light is reflected right off of the micromirrors (rather than transmitted *through* an LCD, where much of it is absorbed), DLP images are brighter than any produced by any other projection technology. They're even brighter than images from traditional film projectors.

DLP is very new, and, as you might expect, it's still quite expensive, but prices are already dropping and demand is very high. For the businessperson who travels from seminar to seminar, lugging a PC projector along, the DLP projectors—with their weight of as little as 2.2 pounds—are a very welcome innovation. Combine that convenience with the impact of a DLP image, and cost becomes relative. It's all but a given that you'll see DLP in more and more places, including in the home and executive office.

Summary

When it comes to PC display subsystems, you have a lot of choices. Many different technologies exist, as well as many implementations of each one. Armed with the information in this chapter (and the additional information in Chapter 20), you will be able to understand each new PC display product. You will know why it works as it does, and therefore which ones will be of interest to you and which you can quickly pass by.

7

Disks and PC Data Storage

If you've read the previous chapters, you now understand how your PC thinks, so it's time to talk about how it remembers. Storage—that's where all the programs your computer uses and all your data are kept. *Storage* is the collection of places where information is kept, long-term. It is in sharp contrast to RAM *memory*, which is the place where you must put that same information (programs and data) before the CPU can do anything with it.

The concept of storage is a broad one. It covers many kinds of long-term information-holding devices. Because the first storage technology that was commonly used on PCs was the floppy diskette drive, the PC has been designed mostly to view all the rest of these holding devices (including CD-ROMs, Flash memory cards, and tape drives) as though they, too, were disk drives.

In fact, at least if you're using the online tools developed for Windows, this generalization has been taken so far that distant computers you access over a network or over the Internet often appear onscreen as just additional disk drives attached to your local PC. This makes using those diverse resources much simpler.

Traditional PC Disk Drives

Before going into non-disks that look like disks to a PC, you should first understand actual PC disk drives. The first drives were floppy diskette drives. Later came hard drives, and then removable drives of various types. In the next section we'll explain a little bit about the floppy diskette technologies used in PCs, followed by a section discussing hard disks.

STANDARDS

You might have noticed that we use the term *diskette* whenever we refer to a floppy, and *disk* only when we refer to a hard disk. This usage is common, although not totally standard. We use it to help keep clear the differences between these different technologies.

Diskette Drives for PCs

The essence of any magnetic disk storage device is that it contains one or more circular disks. These disks are coated with a material that responds to magnetic fields that enables information to be stored there. The disks are mounted on a spindle and they turn under a head (or heads) that can move radially in toward the axis of rotation or out toward the edge of the disk. Normally in PC disk drives, the head is moved to the location of the data your program needs, and it sits still while the disk spins past it and the information is written to or read from the surface in bursts. Figure 7.1 shows this arrangement, albeit with a much exaggerated scale. Normally the head is tiny, and the bursts of magnetic data recorded in the surface, even if they were visible (which they aren't), would be so tiny and close together that they wouldn't be clearly distinguishable in this figure.

FIGURE 7.1

As the disk turns under the stationary read-write head, that head passes over a track past sectors of recorded information on the surface of the disk.

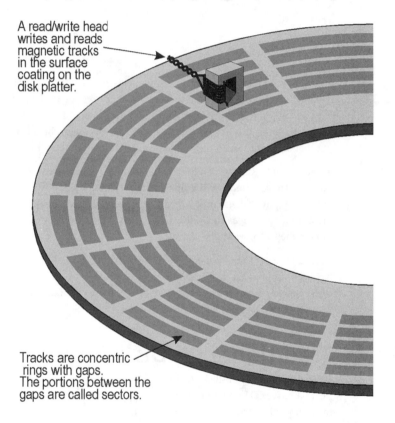

A read/write head writes and reads magnetic tracks in the surface coating on the disk platter.

Tracks are concentric rings with gaps. The portions between the gaps are called sectors.

Getting a diskette drive was an extra-cost option for buyers of the first PCs (and hard disks simply weren't available). Having a floppy diskette drive (or even two of them) quickly became standard. Not only did these devices provide a means for storing programs and data for the long haul, they were also a convenient way to exchange information with other people.

The original PC floppy diskette drives are physically larger than the ones used today (5 1/4-inch instead of 3 1/2-inch) and yet they could hold only a small fraction of what modern diskettes can. What you see when you pick one up and remove it from its protective paper jacket is a stiff, square paper folder with a large hole in the middle and several small notches on some of the edges.

Inside the square paper folder is a thin disc of clear plastic (usually Mylar) that has been coated on both sides with a very thin layer of magnetic iron oxide. This magnetic coating is similar to the coating on an audiotape. The disc actually is floppy—it's very flexible. But when it is in its sleeve the whole assembly is moderately rigid. The diskette drive spindle grabs the disc through the large, round center hole. The read-write head slides on the surface of the disc as it moves toward the center or away from it, along the length of the oblong hole you see at the bottom of the sleeve. (The details of how data is stored on a diskette, in terms of tracks and sectors, are similar to how it gets stored on a hard disk. We will explain both in the section "DOS Disk Overview," in Chapter 18, "Storage— How Does Data Get There?".)

The original PC diskette drives could only read and write data to one side of a diskette, and they didn't use the available surface area as efficiently as later models. This meant those drives could store at most 160KB on a diskette.

We've come a long way since then. The most common diskettes today use 3 1/2-inch diameter discs that are much better protected in hard plastic housings, with a metal shutter to cover the hole where the read-write head contacts the vulnerable surface of the disc, and with a metal hub bonded to the disc to let the drive hold and turn it more precisely.

One result of these improvements is that these 3 1/2-inch diskettes can hold 720KB or 1.44MB of information per diskette. Indeed, with simply an alteration in how the data is recorded, Microsoft and IBM each came up with (different) ways to push that capacity to something closer to 2MB per diskette, while still using standard diskettes and standard diskette drives. (Microsoft called their format MDF, for Microsoft Distribution Format, and they intend that it be used only for their distribution of programs to save themselves the cost of more diskettes. IBM called their new format XDF, for Extended Diskette Format, and they also use it only for software distribution.)

A few manufacturers introduced a higher-density standard diskette that held 2.88MB per diskette. Unfortunately, a special drive was needed to use them, because the magnetic coating on these special diskettes requires stronger magnetic fields for writing, and special circuitry was required to understand their different read-head signals as well.

This uniqueness was fatal. Very few people wanted to replace their floppy drives just to double the capacity. Furthermore, if they did start using those special extra-high density diskettes, their diskettes wouldn't be useful for giving files to other folks who didn't have those special drives in their PCs. This theme of "we don't want it if it isn't compatible with everything that has gone before" has been a resounding chorus from the PC user community to the manufacturers. It took them a while, but now most of the manufacturers know the folly of trying to give people something that isn't fully backward compatible. We'll explain the latest attempt, the LS120 drive, later.

Floppy diskette drives attach to the motherboard via a 34-wire ribbon cable. You can attach zero, one, or two floppy diskette drives and how you physically connect each determines whether a drive becomes A: or B:. The ribbon cable has two connectors; a floppy diskette drive hooked up to the middle connector becomes B:, and the one at the end of the cable is A:. This little feat is accomplished because certain control wires within the ribbon cable, when reversed from their normal orientation, cause the PC to recognize the second device on the cable as a second drive. This physical difference eliminated the need for expensive control electronics on the floppy drives. Some PC BIOSes now allow software swapping the drive-letter designations.

Hard Disks for PCs

Hard disks are like floppies except that the media are, well, hard. Called a *platter*, these rigid disks are made of aluminum or glass (see Figure 7.2). They are much thicker than a floppy's disc, but the coating of magnetic material is comparably thin. Some hard disks have just one platter. Some have several; all are mounted on the same spindle and spun together.

FIGURE 7.2

The location and numbering of disk heads (surfaces) and cylinders on a logical hard disk.

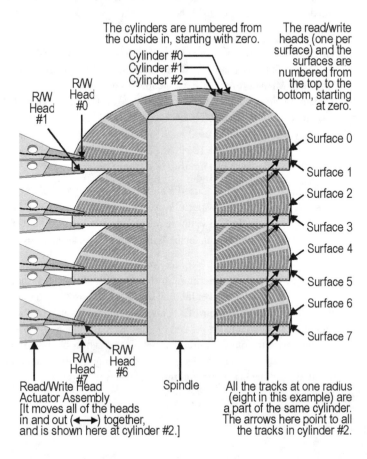

The cylinders are numbered from the outside in, starting with zero.

The read/write heads (one per surface) and the surfaces are numbered from the top to the bottom, starting at zero.

Cylinder #0
Cylinder #1
Cylinder #2

R/W Head #1
R/W Head #0

Surface 0
Surface 1
Surface 2
Surface 3
Surface 4
Surface 5
Surface 6
Surface 7

R/W Head #7
R/W Head #6

Read/Write Head Actuator Assembly
[It moves all of the heads in and out (◄—►) together, and is shown here at cylinder #2.]

Spindle

All the tracks at one radius (eight in this example) are a part of the same cylinder. The arrows here point to all the tracks in cylinder #2.

The huge significance of the rigidity of a hard disk's platters is that after you have recorded some information on it, it's relatively easy to find your way back to the same spot to read the information. Floppies stretch and swell with changes in temperature and humidity. Hard disk platters don't—or at least they don't do so nearly as much. This fact has allowed the makers of hard disks to use read-write heads that are much smaller than those in a floppy diskette drive, and that allows them to pack the information on the disk surface much more densely than is feasible on a floppy.

When PCs were new, adding a hard disk wasn't an option. Hard disks existed and were sometimes installed on small business computers, but only the priciest of those pre-PC machines sported them. Adding a 5MB hard disk to a PC could easily double its cost. By the time the second major PC model came along, the IBM PC/XT, IBM realized that the larger capacity and speed of hard disks was becoming a necessity.

The earliest PC hard disks were two-part contraptions. The drive itself, with an attached printed circuit card, sat in the disk drive bay. It connected via two data cables to a controller card that was plugged into one of the I/O slots on the motherboard. In its earliest form, these drives and the drive-controller interface were often described by the acronym for the data-encoding technology, MFM (Modified Frequency Modulation), which is the same data-encoding strategy that was used then, and is still used for floppy disks.

Technical Note: *Data encoding* refers to a method of representing magnetically (in this case) the 1s and 0s that make up a string of bits. You might have a picture in your head that is overly simple of how magnetic data recording is done. You might think that the bits of data are recorded directly in the surface of the medium with 1s represented by little regions of north magnetization and 0s represented by little regions of south magnetization.

Unfortunately, disk heads excel at seeing changes, say from north-pole to south-pole magnetization, but aren't so good at detecting the state itself. Thus, any time you pass the head of a disk drive over a spot where the magnetization changes in direction or strength, the circuitry gets a clear signal that is easy to spot and to which it can then respond. But if you try recording a long string of the magnetic equivalent of 0s (or of magnetic 1s), the drive doesn't see any changes in the magnetic recording, and has a tendency to get lost.

So, a necessary part of magnetically recording digital data is to first encode it, replacing long, unchanging patterns of 0s and 1s with patterns that do change regularly.

Many encoding schemes have been used over the years. They sported monikers such as *MFM* and *RLL* (*run-length-limited*). Each scheme was better than the ones before it, in terms of how much data it could cram into a given space on the disk.

All floppy diskette drives use MFM encoding exclusively. Hard disk makers have now pretty well settled on some form of RLL, with 2,7 RLL being the most popular.

The next generation of PC drives used an improved data-encoding method called *RLL* (*Run-Length-Limited encoding*) (these names are just jargon and don't really matter; we mention them because you may encounter them elsewhere), and those drives required new controller circuitry as well. Although some further improvements in data encoding were made after that generation, essentially all modern hard disks use a version of RLL data encoding.

Drives were improved in other ways. The MFM and RLL drives were followed by *ESDI* (*Enhanced Small Device Interface*) and *SCSI* (*Small Computer System Interface*) hard drives. ESDI is much like the MFM or RLL interface, but with some improvements that make it possible for these drives to have larger capacity and greater speed.

IDE/EIDE Hard Drives

ESDI was popular for a short time, but it died away quickly when IDE (Integrated Device Electronics) drives appeared on the market. This trend was greatly accelerated when the improved EIDE (Enhanced Integrated Device Electronics) drives came along. These drives have the matching controller electronics moved from the plug-in I/O card to the circuit card on the side of the drive itself.

The initial IDE interface was merely a subset of the IBM's original 16-bit Input/Output bus for their PC/AT model computers. This subset had just those signal wires that were needed to service a hard disk. Soon, with all the clone PC makers using the same design, IBM PC/AT's I/O bus became known as the *ISA* (*Industry Standard Architecture*) bus. And in a similar manner (but with formal blessing of an official standards committee), that original IDE interface was declared an industry standard called the *AT Attachment* (*ATA*). A later, improved version of that standard is what we now call the *EIDE* interface.

Another enhancement, known by the name *ATAPI* (*AT Attachment Packet Interface*), extended the workings of the EIDE interface to accommodate other sorts of devices than just hard disks (for example, CD-ROMs).

SCSI Hard Drives

SCSI is not so much a way of interfacing to a hard drive as it is a tiny, one-computer local area network. Attaching a SCSI device of any type (and hard disks are only one of the many kinds of devices that can have a SCSI interface) to a PC requires the use of a *SCSI Host Adapter*. This is a plug-in card that mediates between the activity on the SCSI bus and that on the PC's I/O bus. Generally, if you only want one or two hard drives in your PC, and you don't have any other use for any SCSI-interface devices, the easiest solution is to use EIDE hard drives. But using SCSI hard drives can give you even greater performance, and they can allow you to add many more drives as well as other peripheral devices.

EIDE and SCSI each have certain advantages, and so both will probably be around for a long while. Let's take a look at how these systems evolved, how they work, and why you should care.

The Origin of IDE, EIDE, ATA, ATAPI, and More

If you want to understand, in a general way, what all this IDE, ATA, and ATAPI stuff is about, a simple telling of the tale will do. The IDE bus is that part of the ISA bus needed to support disk drives and the like, redirected to a special connector to save on the use of ISA slots. The ATA standard describes how to deal with hard disks over this IDE channel. The ATAPI standard extends ATA to CD-ROMs and certain other devices on that same channel. You say that's too brief? Okay. Then here is a little more detail.

> **Note:** For perspective, note that the IDE "channel" (to give it the technically correct description) is intended only for use inside a PC's system unit. Any devices hooked to this channel will be internal ones, unlike what is possible with the SCSI expansion bus, the USB, and with IEEE 1394 (FireWire).

The Early Days

When PCs were young, electronics could not be as densely integrated as they can today. It took a lot of room to fit in all the chips needed to do useful tasks. This meant that hard disks had a lot of electronics built on them and still required a plug-in card plugged into an expansion slot and connected to the drives by ribbon cables, just as with the floppy diskettes you've already seen.

Electronics evolved. As mentioned earlier, the electronics needed to operate and interface a PC with a hard drive was put onto the drive. The first version in which this showed up were products such as the HardCard. That was Plus Development's trademarked name for a hard disk controller card with the hard disk actually mounted on the card. These cards were huge. They completely filled an ISA slot and physically obstructed the ISA slots around it. But, when you plugged one of them into your PC, voila! You had just installed a working hard drive. No having to match a controller, cables, and a drive. No having to low-level format the drive. Just add DOS and go.

The next hard drive evolutionary stage was closer to what we have today. The electronics were further reduced in size to the point that they were all placed in the hard drive. This drive didn't need a separate controller. As mentioned earlier, because all the electronics are on the drive, this was called an *Integrated Device Electronics* (IDE) hard drive, and was the first of the breed of today's most popular hard drives.

These IDE hard drives didn't need any external controllers, but they did need to connect to the ISA bus. So we got things called *IDE paddle cards, IDE host interface cards,* and so on. These looked a lot like the old hard disk plug-in cards. They fit into an ISA slot and had a 40-pin connector that accepted a ribbon cable from the drive. Most of the time these cards—like those that preceded them—also had a floppy disk controller and often two serial ports and one parallel port on them, and that meant having at least a little bit of circuitry, including one or more integrated chips.

The next move was pretty obvious. Makers of motherboards knew their customers were always going to want to plug in a floppy disk drive or two, and also one or two hard drives. So they moved the floppy disk controller to the motherboard. Plug in your floppies to one connector, plug in your IDE hard drives to another, and you were off and running. (But note: This solution enabled you to attach, at most, two floppy diskette drives and two IDE hard drives.)

EIDE, ATA, and ATAPI

The IDE connectors on motherboards were linked separately to the ISA bus lines so each of these connectors (or *channels*) could support one or two IDE devices. This change also required other aspects of the motherboard—specifically its BIOS—to evolve.

Later modifications made it possible to have the four IDE devices be any mixture of slow CD-ROMs and fast hard drives you wanted, with the hard drives significantly larger than was previously possible. This new, faster version of the IDE interface is called *Enhanced IDE*, or EIDE.

Better I/O for Better (Faster) Devices

EIDE interfaces enabled much faster communication than the original ISA interface, even though the bus clock was still "stuck" at a slow 8.33MHz. The speed increase came about through the improvements in the protocol that describes how the clock cycles will be used to address devices and transfer data.

Appropriately, modern EIDE hard drives—and in particular those termed *Ultra DMA hard drives*—are indeed much speedier devices than their ancestors.

The *AT Attachment* (ATA) standards are the formal specifications for how IDE and EIDE interfaces are supposed to work with hard drives. The *ATA Packet Interface* (ATAPI) is an extension to that standard to describe how the interface will work with non–hard drive IDE devices, such as CD-ROM drives. These ATAPI devices use an almost completely different set of commands, but they function electrically and in terms of the timing for those commands just like the ATA devices.

Details About Speed Issues and ATA-2

The typical use for the IDE channel, in all its variant forms, is to transfer a block of data between a peripheral device and some location in the main memory address space of the CPU. There are several ways in which these transfers are made. Some of these ways require a lot of attention by the CPU, essentially involving it in each transfer of one or a small group of bytes. Other methods permit transferring larger blocks of data as a single transaction.

Every transaction carried with it some amount of overhead. Naturally, the best performance was achieved when this overhead was kept to a minimum, which was not really possible with these earliest IDE protocols. (Recall that a *protocol*, like the *standards* discussed in Chapter 5, is simply an agreed-upon way of achieving some goal.)

Because the IDE interface used 16 parallel data wires, it was possible to move two bytes of data through the IDE channel at a time (one byte per wire). A protocol was introduced in which each of these 2-byte data transfers could be accomplished in only a single clock cycle. Because the bus speed was 8.33 million clock cycles per second, each cycle allowed 2 bytes to be transferred. This protocol (formally called ATA-2) allowed a maximum of 16.6 million bytes to be transferred each second. For many years, this was the fastest you could move data across any IDE channel.

ATA-4 (Also Known as UDMA)

When hard disks were relatively slow, the 16MB/sec maximum data transfer rate was ample. As disks became larger and faster, this data transfer rate was a serious bottleneck to the smooth flow of data inside PCs. The industry's first response was the introduction of yet another variation on the data transfer protocol, formally called ATA-4.

This first variation doubled the number of data transfers from 8.33 million per second to 16.7 million. Because each data transfer carries 2 bytes of data, the new maximum data transfer rate was 33.3 million bytes per second, normally written as 33MB/s. You might have encountered drives that comply with this standard but are called by other names. The terms "Ultra DMA," "Ultra ATA," and "ATA/33" are all synonymous with the correct name, "ATA-4."

Virtually all hard drives being made today conform to the requirements of this new protocol, as do the EIDE channel controllers on all modern PC motherboards. Thus, this is now the standard (maximum) speed of EIDE channel data transfers. Of course, many drives today also exceed this standard dramatically.

ATA-5

The next standard developed was formally called ATA-5, but it's now more commonly called UDMA-66, or Ultra ATA/66. This standard was the first that actually required a change in the EIDE channel hardware. The cable between the drive and motherboard must have 80 wires instead of the normal 40.

There were also some changes necessary in the host controller electronics and in the device electronics. When all these changes are in place, the channel clock frequency is doubled to 16.7MHz. This, combined with the Ultra ATA data transfer protocol, enables up to 66.7 million bytes of data to be transferred each second.

This works only if all the devices on the channel are capable of operating at the higher clock speed. If they are not, devices will be forced to operate at the slower rate, and the whole channel will function only as an ATA-4 channel. Similarly, if you plug an ATA-5 capable EIDE device into a channel with only an ATA-4 capable host controller, the device will function as if it were only an ordinary ATA-4 device.

Nothing is lost, but also nothing is gained by having ATA-5 capabilities in only some of the devices on a specific EIDE channel. The only real gain comes when all devices are ATA-5 compliant, and at that point the gain is a very significant one—a doubling of the maximum speed at which the channel can convey information.

Ultra ATA-100 and Ultra ATA/133

As of this writing, the latest news in hard drives produced by many companies is known as "Ultra ATA-100." As its name suggests, the primary improvement in this technology over that defined in ATA-5 is a dramatic improvement in maximum data transfer rate: from 66MB/s to 100MB/s. This technology—and we aren't calling it a *standard* because it hasn't been formally standardized throughout the industry, and each manufacturer is handling certain issues proprietarily—requires the use of the 80-wire cable, first introduced with ATA-5. The PC's motherboard and drive controller must also be ATA-100 capable, or the drive will operate only at ATA-5 (66MB/s) or ATA-4 (33MB/s) speeds.

We said that Ultra ATA-100 is the latest news *in drives manufactured by many different companies* because there is even later news, but it reflects the innovations of one company alone. In June 2001, Maxtor, one of the largest manufacturers of hard drives of all types, introduced a new specification that they call "fast drives," and which is also known as Ultra ATA/133. As of this writing, the technical details of Ultra ATA/133 are both proprietary and confidential, but Maxtor has released that these drives will, as their name suggests, boost the maximum transfer rate of data from 100MB/sec to 133MB/sec, and these drives will be backwards compatible with ATA-100 and earlier controllers. They'll also require the use of the 80-wire connector cable.

IDE Connectivity

Extended Integrated Device Electronics (EIDE) devices are connected to the PC motherboard via another special connector, or they can be connected to an option card plugged into the PC's I/O bus. The latest version of the EIDE specification enables, theoretically, four EIDE channels, each one capable of supporting two EIDE devices.

Most modern PCs support two EIDE channels on the motherboard. They also usually have one or more EIDE internal hard drives. A jumper on each drive's circuit board determines whether the drive functions as a *master* or as a *slave*. The first hard drive you install on each of the EIDE channels must always be set as that channel's master. It is important that only one device acts as master and one as slave on each EIDE channel, so you must pay careful attention to the settings of these jumpers. These designations primarily serve to identify each drive at the hardware level, much as the SCSI ID of each device in a SCSI chain identifies that device uniquely.

The cable that connects hard drives to the motherboard is similar to a floppy drive cable without a twist. Additionally, hard drive cables contain more wires and are, thus, wider than floppy drive cables. A hard drive cable will have either two or three connectors (one for the motherboard and either one or two for drives), and most are keyed to prevent plugging it in backward. If no key-tab is present, one of the wires of the cable will be marked with a color—usually red. As you have likely already read, on the motherboard and the drives, one end of the connection socket will be marked 1, 2 or with a small triangle; the red side of the cable always connects closest to the marked side of the socket. Unlike floppies, however, each hard drive's jumper settings identify it and it doesn't matter whether a drive is plugged into the end or middle of the cable.

In most PCs, the primary and secondary EIDE channels are nearly equivalent. You might put any device you want on either cable, making sure you have only one master and one slave on each one.

Nevertheless, you might still want to put fast devices on one EIDE cable and slower ones on the other cable. Some PCs can send messages only as fast as the slowest device on any one channel (cable). Thus, if you put your fast hard drive and your slow CD-ROM on the same EIDE channel, you might find your hard drive crawling along, slowed down by the CD-ROM's inability to keep up.

The Really Good Bus with the Really Bad Name (SCSI)

The *small computer system interface (SCSI) bus*, pronounced *scuzzy,* is a relative old-timer in the industry. But it didn't achieve much popularity in PCs until fairly recently. There were several good reasons for this, among them the perceived difficulty in setting up a SCSI bus on a PC and making it work correctly.

In contrast, a SCSI bus has always been built into every Macintosh computer, so Apple aficionados have had the advantages of this bus available to them for much longer. Now, after some years of struggle, the SCSI bus is also well supported in the world of PCs. For those situations in which the SCSI bus outperforms all the alternatives, PC owners can take advantage of it easily.

The SCSI bus is the preferred way to connect hard disk drives with the largest capacity and highest data transfer rates (although this preeminence is constantly being challenged by developments in EIDE drives). It also provides a convenient way to attach several types of external PC peripherals (such as CD-ROM, Zip, and other removable media storage devices, scanners, video cameras, and so forth) and get maximum performance from them. These advantages are offset to a degree by a slightly higher price for SCSI-enabled versions of all these devices and by some added complexity in the setup process.

The SCSI Architecture

In a sense, you can think of a SCSI bus as a small local area network. The main difference between the SCSI bus and the ordinary LAN is that rather than being a means of communications between multiple PCs (and perhaps a file server), the PC to which the SCSI bus is attached is the only general-purpose computer on this bus. Each SCSI device has, in fact, a small special-purpose computer in its SCSI interface portion. That computer has only one task to perform, and that is to manage communications on behalf of the peripheral device to which it is attached with the SCSI plug-in card (called a *host adapter*) and with other devices on the SCSI bus. (Much more on LANs in Chapter 11, "Networking—Wired and Wireless.")

As with most standards that have been around a while, SCSI has grown and changed over time. So there are, in fact, several versions of SCSI. By now it has evolved into several distinct flavors of bus. The overall definition of SCSI has not changed, but the details of its design have, and along with those changes have come a range of performance possibilities.

The Several Flavors of SCSI

The original source of the SCSI standard was a proprietary protocol developed by Shugart Associates (an early maker of hard drives) and the NCR Corporation at just about the same time as IBM's introduction of the first PC. They called it the *Shugart Associates Computer Interface* (SASI). A short time later this standard was adopted (and somewhat modified) by the American National Standards Committee, giving it at that time the name *Small Computer Systems Interface* (SCSI).

SCSI-1

The original version of SCSI, now called SCSI-1, required a cable with eight data wires plus one wire for parity. (Recall from earlier that *parity* is a method of error-checking.) This cable connected from the host adapter to any SCSI peripherals in a *daisy-chain* fashion. This means that each device had two SCSI ports on it. The first device was connected to the host adapter directly. The second device was connected to the first device. The last device on the external chain had its second SCSI port filled with a terminator (or else it must terminate the SCSI bus internally). This termination is necessary to reduce the confusion caused by signals "reflecting" off the end of the SCSI bus cabling.

All the devices attached to the SCSI bus operate independently. Each has its own, unique SCSI ID number (from 0 to 7). Any of them can put a message on the bus requesting permission to transfer data from itself to another specified device on that bus, or to receive data from another specified device. If the bus is not otherwise occupied, these two devices "have a conversation" all on their own, without any intervention on the part of the SCSI host adapter. The host adapter is involved only when it is the target (or source) of such a conversation.

Note: It is vital that each device on the SCSI bus has its own ID, because that is the only way it knows when it is being "spoken to." Normally, the host adapter is given the SCSI ID of 7. The other devices can usually have their ID set by the user. There are two common ways this is done.

Most external SCSI devices have a switch of some kind on their back panel to enable you to set their SCSI ID. Some will enable you to choose any value you like; others will enable you to choose from among only a few preselected options. One common design for such a switch has a number showing in a window and two tiny buttons above and below that window. If you press in the button above the window with a piece of wire (an unrolled paper clip works nicely), the switch will move to the next higher number. Pushing on the other button lowers the number. A different kind of switch that is also popular for SCSI ID settings is one that looks like a miniature clock face, with a pointer you turn with a small screwdriver.

Internal SCSI devices normally are connected slightly differently, and their SCSI IDs are also set differently. All the internal SCSI devices are simply plugged into a common ribbon cable. The last one on the cable (the one physically farthest from the host adapter) must terminate the bus or be followed by a separate internal SCSI terminator.

The original version of the SCSI bus allowed data transfers at rates of up to 5MBps (1 byte on each clock cycle, with a 5MHz clock frequency). That is faster than the ISA bus could support, and so was thought to be amply fast for the time it was introduced.

SCSI-2 and Wide SCSI

In 1991, ANSI (the American National Standards Institute, an independent industry body responsible for, reasonably enough, defining national standards) came out with an update called SCSI-2. This version of SCSI included everything in the older version with some additions. First, it endorsed a new, more compact cable-end connector. Second, it enabled the use of multiple cables to support 16- or even 32-bit data transfers in parallel. Third, it established a complete software-control system for SCSI, called the Common Command Set (CCS).

SCSI-2 also provided support for doubling the clock speed on the SCSI bus. This variation was called *Fast SCSI*. With Fast and, later, *Wide SCSI* (which meant 16 bits in parallel over two separate cables), it became possible to carry out data transfers at rates up to 20MB per second.

SCSI-3

As soon as SCSI-2 was officially approved, the committee began work on SCSI-3. This update made several significant changes in the standard. First, it decoupled the CSS (software) definition from the hardware definition. That means it is now possible to have different competing hardware that are all a form of SCSI simply because they use the same command set.

In fact, the SCSI-3 standard is a whole collection of standards, each covering one aspect of the interface. Because these are each a part of the standard and don't exist independently of it, they're called "layers." The lowest layer is called the *physical layer* and it defines the cables and connectors to be used. The next layer, referred to as the *protocol layer*, describes how the electrical signals are organized to send packets of information. The third layer is called the *architecture layer*, and it covers how command requests are organized, queued, and responded to. Primary commands are the top-level set of commands that all SCSI devices must support. Device-specific commands are optional ones used by particular classes of device (for example, CD-ROMs or hard drives).

The second major change in SCSI-3 was the formal endorsement of a new kind of cable-end connector, with more contacts to support 16-bit data transfers over a single cable. Today, this style of cable is referred to as a *Wide-SCSI connection*.

Third, SCSI-3 adds 1 bit to the SCSI ID, thus allowing up to 16 devices on a SCSI bus. The host adapter is still given the SCSI ID of 7 by default, but now other devices can be given any ID from 0 to 15.

With Ultra Wide SCSI, another name for SCSI-3, it is possible to transfer 40MB of data per second on a single SCSI (wire) cable. Ultra2 SCSI achieves the same throughput by doubling the speed of the SCSI bus itself, not just increasing the potential of the drives or other connected devices. (Of course, the devices must also be Ultra2 compliant and be capable of outputting data at this rate, as well.) Ultra2 Wide SCSI is a further extension that moves 16 bits, rather than 8 bits at a time across the Ultra2 accelerated bus. This technology makes an 80MB/sec maximum transfer rate possible.

In 1998, the SCSI trade association formalized Ultra3 SCSI, but it was a sufficiently loose standard that Ultra3 devices made by different manufacturers were not guaranteed to meet their potential. Adaptec, the largest manufacturer of SCSI interface devices and cards defined a variant of Ultra3, called Ultra 160 SCSI, and this unofficial (but very "standard" standard) boosts the potential of SCSI to 160MB/sec, in ideal conditions, using compliant devices.

SCSI Devices

What, exactly, is a SCSI device? It can be almost anything: a hard disk, a CD-ROM drive, a Zip drive, a recordable CD drive, a printer, a mouse, a tape drive, an image scanner, and a graphics tablet. Really, just about any PC peripheral device can be given a SCSI interface. The defining characteristic of all SCSI devices is that they have a SCSI interface. This is a small computer that "speaks SCSI" out of one side (across the SCSI bus) and understands how to operate the peripheral device(s) to which it is attached out of the other side.

Because of this "intelligent" aspect to SCSI devices, and because the SCSI standard allows multiple, simultaneous, independent conversations between SCSI devices across a single SCSI bus, it can have a high degree of multi-processing in a PC with a SCSI bus and a suitable array of SCSI devices. This won't happen automatically, but it can happen, with suitable software support.

The SCSI Host Adapter

The SCSI *host adapter* is composed of interface circuitry that sits between the internal system bus of the PC and the SCSI bus. Its job is to send and receive messages in the SCSI fashion on the SCSI bus and simultaneously to send and receive messages on the PC system I/O bus in its native protocol.

Some PCs have a SCSI host adapter built onto the motherboard (as is the case for all Macintosh computers), but most use a separate plug-in host adapter. If it's on a plug-in card, the host adapter could be on an ISA card, a VESA VL bus card, ór a PCI card. To get the highest performance out of SCSI devices, it is important that the data transfers not be limited by the slow ISA bus. Most of the good SCSI host adapters sold today are PCI cards.

Because SCSI functionality has not been built into PCs from the beginning, the motherboard BIOS does not contain software support for that function. This means that to operate a SCSI bus, the host adapter must either have an on-board BIOS ROM chip, or you must load a suitable software driver from a non-SCSI hard disk before using the SCSI bus.

Furthermore, the software in the BIOS ROM on a SCSI card (or in the lowest-level software driver that might have been provided on a disk with the host adapter) is probably only barely adequate to set up the SCSI host adapter for minimal operation. To get the full benefit of the SCSI bus, and in particular to support multiple devices hooked to it, you probably must load at least one more driver program. This might be a CAM (Common Access Method) driver, or it might be an ASPI (Advanced SCSI Programming Interface) driver. You must use whatever your SCSI host adapter and the devices attached to it require.

You can have more than one SCSI host adapter in your PC. However, if you have many of them, you likely will find yourself running out of IRQ levels to assign to them. The practical limit is probably two.

Tip: Another job the host adapter has is to determine at powerup which SCSI devices reside at which SCSI IDs on the SCSI bus. For this to work, all those devices must be powered on when you boot your PC. If you plug everything into one power strip or power controller, you can easily ensure that this is so by having the entire system turn on with one switch. Otherwise, just get in the habit of turning on the external SCSI devices before you power up your PC.

Mixing IDE and SCSI Disk Drives

The most common kind of hard disk in a modern PC is one that connects to an IDE bus. You can have up to four IDE devices (hard disks, CD-ROM drives, and so on) in most PCs, and, using special plug-in cards, you can add up to four additional IDE devices.

You also can use SCSI hard disks in a PC. There are two advantages to using SCSI hard disks. One is that the best of them are capable of higher data transfer rates than even the best of the IDE drives, and the other is that you can have more SCSI hard disks than you can IDE drives. You can easily add seven hard disks—or 15 on a SCSI-3 host adapter—and with the use of logical units, you can push that to as high as 56 (or 240 with SCSI-3). This might be of little interest to you unless the operating system you are running is capable of supporting that many hard disks—which certainly rules out DOS and Windows 95 or 98—or at least as many hard disks as you want to use, which could be much less than those higher numbers, yet more than four. SCSI also has other performance benefits for operating systems such as NetWare, Windows NT, and most flavors of Unix, which can take advantage of them.

What if you want to use both IDE and SCSI hard disks in your PC? In that case, you must know some special tricks. First, some older motherboard BIOSes will require that you boot your PC from one of the IDE devices. (That can be a hard drive or it can be an EIDE CD-ROM.) The only other alternative supported by most PCs is to boot from a floppy disk. Most newer BIOSes incorporate support for booting from any EIDE or SCSI drive.

Less standard is which drive will show up with which drive letter. The boot drive will always be C:, but from there things get much murkier. The most common BIOS strategy places the primary EIDE channel's master first, and then the primary EIDE channels slave, and then the secondary EIDE channel's master, and then its slave, and then the SCSI hard drives, if any. But we have seen many variations on this. The BIOS assigns a numerical physical address to each hard drive. Later, Windows will assign a drive letter to those hard drives in numerical order, with C: being associated with drive number 80h, D: with 81h, and so on (assuming each hard drive has a primary DOS partition on it).

Summary

In this chapter, you've explored the two primary technologies on which PC hard drives are built, IDE/AT/ATAPI and SCSI. In the next chapter, you'll read about removable storage devices, including hard drives. Hard drives are among the most popular and best-selling devices in the PC world today. If you're interested in learning the technical details about how hard drives actually *work*, turn to the third section of Chapter 18.

Removable Storage

The previous chapter introduced the different types of hard disk drives and the different ways they attach to and communicate with the rest of a PC. This chapter focuses on a different aspect of long-term data storage: the many removable technologies that allow you to conveniently take your data with you.

Variations on the Theme of PC Storage

Until fairly recently, floppy disk drives and hard disks were the only widely used PC data storage hardware. It doesn't appear likely that either floppies or hard disks will *totally* disappear from PCs any time soon, but a plethora of new products have become popular. These products use many different technologies—some new, some new versions of old. This chapter gives you a broad overview and enough depth on the most important of these products so that you can understand where each one fits into the picture. That understanding is critical in guiding your future PC storage purchase decisions, and my emphasis on the basics will stand you in very good stead when you are confronted with even newer storage options.

The Multiple Dimensions of PC Storage Technologies

All PC storage technologies can be classified in one of several dimensions: speed (performance), capacity, whether a device can write as well as read data, and the technology behind the technology (what makes it go). Keep these dimensions in mind as you read the following sections, which are organized based on the technologies behind the technologies. Thus, I talk first about removable magnetic data storage devices (other than the hard disks and floppies that I have already discussed), followed by optical, magneto-optical (MO), and electronic PC data storage devices.

Primary versus Secondary Data Storage

Almost all of these devices are used most often for *secondary data storage*. This is as opposed to *primary data storage*, which is perhaps best exemplified by your PC's hard disk. When you use your PC, the programs you run usually come from your hard disk. The data comes also from your hard disk, and the data you generate goes to your hard disk—almost always. Thus, hard disks are your primary storage devices.

Secondary storage devices are the ones to which you copy data from the primary device (or vice versa). A floppy disk is one of the most common secondary storage devices. A tape drive, Zip drive, or most any other data storage device you can name is most often treated as a secondary storage device.

DVDs, CD-ROMs, CD-Rs, or CD-RWs are good examples of PC storage devices that are most often used as secondary storage, with some exceptions. You probably use CD-ROMs to install programs, but you might also use them to run those programs if you don't want to give up the hard disk space the programs require. Most people, for example, use DVDs and CD-ROMs as primary data storage when viewing a reference disk (an encyclopedia, atlas, and so on) that comes on one of those media.

Going the other way, some people actually use hard disks as secondary data storage. They'll remove a hard disk from one PC and carry it to another, or store one that is loaded with archival data in a closet. Such things are, or were, common for large companies, but less so for individual users.

Removable Magnetic PC Data Storage Devices

The same basic magnetic recording technology used in hard drives is also used in several removable PC data storage devices. The most common example is a tape drive. Others include removable hard disks, hard disk drives with interchangeable media, and various types of super-floppy disk drives.

Tape Drives

The one removable magnetic storage device, besides floppy and hard disks, that has been used for PCs from the beginning is the magnetic tape drive. A few of the earliest PCs used an audio cassette tape drive to store data. Audio cassette recorders were designed to record audible sound—analog signals. In order to make them suitable for digital data recording, the data must be encoded as tones. (Modems do this to encode data for transmission over the voice telephone network, for the same reason.) This worked, but not well. It was slow beyond belief, and not much data fit on a standard audio cassette.

Soon, those tape drives were supplanted by special-purpose drives meant just for digital data recording, which worked much better. They used another form of data encoding, storing the information as magnetized regions on the tape and reading that information back as the tape passes over the read head. These drives went through many generations of improvements, with special 4mm wide digital audio tapes (DAT) in Digital Data Storage (DDS) drives representing the present state of the art. Many manufacturers, including Seagate and Hewlett-Packard, make this kind of tape drive for PCs, and tape capacities per cartridge go up to 40GB or so.

One thing is constant here. All the types of tape drives are sequential access devices. That means that all of the tape must pass the read head from the beginning of the reel or cassette to wherever the data is that you want to read. When you want to write to a tape, you must again scroll past all the previously recorded information before you can start recording (unless, of course, you want to tape over the previously recorded information with the new data).

Because tape drives are sequential devices, they are best suited for situations in which you want to read or write a great deal of information at once, but won't need to retrieve it repeatedly or instantly. Backing up your hard drive's data is a perfect example. If the tape controller, tape drive, and PC are all matched properly, data can flow continuously, or "stream," off the hard drive and onto the tape without having to stop the tape movement until the entire task is complete.

If, however, the whole system isn't properly tuned, you might have to move the tape a short distance, and then stop it while you wait for more data to be prepared for writing. To keep from having a gap on the tape, you might even have to back up the tape and let it take a running start before resuming recording where you left off. Such a lack of streaming performance can make an otherwise relatively speedy tape drive into a real sluggard.

Peter's Principle:

Generally, tape is the cheapest form of PC data storage available, but it also is the slowest. Unfortunately, it is not always as reliable as you might want. Every good tape system comes with software that includes an option to verify the tape. Whatever that option does, it doesn't catch all the mistakes the tape drives make. So my recommendation to you is this: If you use tape as a critical backup medium, verify your backups on your own, by restoring a sample backup set to a different drive letter and checking that every file made that round trip (hard disk to tape and back to hard disk) flawlessly. Then repeat this test occasionally on at least a random sampling of your backed up files.

Because their operating characteristics are so different, the software that initially operated tape drives was totally different from the disk drive software. More recently, some manufacturers have created device drivers (the software that handles talking to the tape drive) for their products that make them emulate a disk drive. If you use one of these products, you might think you are performing random access to some DOS logical drive that acts just like all the others in your PC—except that it will be horribly slow.

The largest PC installations, with many dozens of gigabytes of storage, are most commonly backed up to tape libraries. These devices have multiple tape cartridges and one or a few drives, plus robotic devices to load and unload the tapes as needed. With these systems, you can readily store many terabytes (that is, thousands of gigabytes) of data. Indeed, there are few viable alternative options today for storing those huge quantities of data.

Removable Hard Disks

At the opposite extreme in terms of speed and cost is the removable hard disk. You can, of course, use any ordinary IDE or SCSI hard disk and (after turning off your PC) remove it and take it to another PC or store it away as archival storage. It is much more convenient, however, to add a docking bay to your PC. This is simply a box that goes into a space in a PC that is meant for a floppy disk drive, with an opening in the front into which you plug suitably designed swappable drives. The docking bay connects internally to the PC's power supply and also to an IDE channel or a SCSI host adapter.

With this type of device, you can swap drives in the bay while the PC is on, although you might have to reboot the PC before it will recognize what you have done. A PC with full plug-and-play support, on the other hand, might be able to immediately recognize the new device and use it properly.

Aside from the mechanics of the docking bay, these devices are just like a normal hard disk you might install inside your PC or through an external SCSI cable.

An alternative approach is to make a hard drive subsystem that can be attached to a PC's parallel port. This works, but it has an inherently lower performance than a drive that is attached directly to the PC's I/O bus using an IDE channel or a SCSI host adapter.

The newest types of removable hard disks attach to a PC using a USB or an IEEE 1394 (FireWire) port. On PCs running Windows, these devices are automatically recognized when they are plugged in. There is the possibility of losing data if you improperly unplug one of these devices, so most come with the capability to eject their media—if the device uses removable media, naturally—or to "shut down" the device before you simply pull the plug. This process ensures that all data you think you've saved to the disk has actually been written securely. The USB port is not really fast enough to support hard disks as satisfactorily as a direct SCSI or EIDE connection, but the IEEE 1394 ports are amply fast.

Hard Disks with Interchangeable Media

You can gain most of the benefits of a removable hard disk at much lower cost by using a special kind of hard drive that can accept interchangeable platters. It isn't easy to make this approach work well—primarily because even tiny dust particles can foul up a hard drive, and keeping a removable cartridge clean is hard—but with good design, it can be done. The newest example of this approach is the Peerless drive from Iomega, which stores either 10GB or 20GB per cartridge. This drive solves the former problem of dust contamination by having the drive surface *and the recording heads* both sealed inside the cartridge case. This device connects to a PC using the USB or IEEE 1394 FireWire bus, which you can read about in Chapter 9, "Serial Ports."

Super-Floppy Disk Drives

The super-floppy disk category covers several technologies. All of them differ from the simpler technologies used in standard floppy disk drives. Ordinary floppy disk drives position the read/write head using a *stepper motor*. Any system that aspires to store a much greater amount of data cannot afford to do this because the stepper motor cannot support the necessarily higher data density. Thus, all super-floppies use the same type of advanced head positioning mechanism used in hard drives.

> **New Term:** A *stepper motor* is a specialized type of electric motor that turns a precise, pre-determined amount every time it receives a unique electrical signal or "pulse". For example, each pulse might mean "turn one rotational degree," so 45 pulses would turn the motor exactly and precisely 45 degrees. By translating the stepper motor's rotation into linear movement, it's possible to align a floppy drive's read/write head with the tracks on the disk. Unfortunately, this kind of motor—in contrast to a servo or a linear motor—isn't capable of providing any feedback, so you never know with certainty that the recording head is exactly where you want it to be, or that you'll be able to move it to a precise location repeatedly. These limiting factors make stepper motors completely inappropriate for the kind of high-density recording used in hard disks.

Another difference is in how the head is positioned relative to the surface of the medium. A normal floppy disk drive presses its two heads against one another, with the floppy's disk in between. This means that these drives are actually dragging the heads across the surfaces of the disk. To keep wear to an acceptably low level, the drives cannot turn the disk quickly. Again, to get high capacity and higher performance out of a super-floppy, these issues must be addressed.

Iomega's Zip Drives

By far, the most popular of the floppy-disk-like technologies is the Zip disk from Iomega. These are just slightly larger than the now-standard 3 1/2-inch floppy disk, and they come in both 100MB and 250MB capacities. The 250MB drives also support the antiquated 100MB disks. Naturally, because the physical size of the disks is different from a standard floppy disk, a Zip drive reads and writes only Zip disks. So if you have a PC with a Zip drive, you will probably also want to have a normal floppy disk drive.

Zip drives come in both internal and external SCSI interface models for both PCs and Macs, as well as external models that attach to any PC's USB or parallel port and an internal model that connects to a PC's IDE bus. When connected, the Zip drive simply appears as an additional logical drive, with its own drive letter. (I'll discuss how Windows assigns drive letters in Chapter 18, "Storage: How Does Data Get There?".) This is one way to carry small amounts of data from PC to PC when a LAN is not available.

The performance of a Zip drive over a parallel or USB port is not very high. Over a SCSI port—an option no longer available—however, it approached the performance of a (slow) hard drive.

LS-120—Another Floppy Drive Replacement

A number of other manufacturers produce drives that are competitive with the Zip technology. Perhaps the most successful at this time are the LS-120 Superdisk drives and disks.

These Superdisks are actual magnetic and optical hybrids, but not in the same sense as magneto-optical disks, which you'll read about in a moment. In the LS-120, recording takes place magnetically the same way as on an ordinary floppy (but at a reduced scale), but the head positioning is done by the same optical method as is used in an audio CD player (even using some of the same parts as in an ordinary CD drive). To make this optical positioning work, the disks have an optical track impressed on them at the factory. The head positioning mechanism uses this to locate the head, and then the reading and writing are done in exactly the same manner as any normal magnetic disk drive.

The LS-120 drive's capability to work with normal floppy disks as well is explained by its two heads. One is an absolutely ordinary floppy disk read/write head. The other is the smaller read/write head needed to work with the more densely packed data on the Superdisk's 120MB format.

The LS-120 drive acts very much like a floppy disk drive, only when it is used with its special disks, it can store much more information and it can deliver the data to and from the special LS-120 disks much faster than is possible with normal floppy disks. This last point implies that one must attach the LS-120 drive to the PC in a different way than floppy disk drives, because the standard floppy interface works too slowly to keep up with these drives.

Most internal LS-120 drives are connected as IDE drives, just like a CD-ROM drive. This presents one possible problem for folks who want to use an LS-120 drive as a replacement for their PC's floppy disk drive. That is the problem of how to boot from a standard floppy disk. Until recently, hardly any PCs could boot from a CD-ROM drive or any other IDE devices. Now, to allow booting a PC using a freshly formatted hard disk directly from a distribution software CD-ROM, most new PCs permit users to select any suitable ATAPI-compliant IDE device as the boot device. And if your PC's BIOS is LS-120 aware, it might even allow you to make that drive your A: drive.

Hooked up in this manner, an LS-120 drive can serve as your PC's main floppy disk for booting from a safety boot disk or from a system disk, in case your hard disk dies, and it can be used to install programs that expect to be loaded from the A: or B: logical drive. It also can be used for backups; with 120MB per disk, it won't take too many of them to back up all the files you have changed recently for all but the most active PC user. However, be aware that an LS-120 drive, although much faster than a normal floppy disk drive, is slower than a Zip drive or many of the other alternatives on the market.

The LS-120 drive makers have had some success in convincing some PC makers to include them as an option (in lieu of a normal floppy disk drive). But they still haven't nearly as much market presence as the Iomega Zip drives, which also can be purchased as an internal option in many new PCs (but in that case, in addition to, rather than in lieu of, a normal floppy disk drive).

PC Card Hard Disks, Magnetic Stripe Cards, and Other Similar Devices

There is a constant push from consumers for smaller devices. In part, this trend is driven by the increasing power of portable PCs and folks' natural reluctance to lug along lots of heavy add-on gadgets for what is getting to be a rather light and compact computer.

The removable magnetic data storage industry continues to create more and better gadgets to serve this market. In addition to creating adapters that let PCs read magnetic stripe credit cards, there are devices that read special-purpose cards. These cards have magnetic stripes that hold more data than a normal credit card.

The memory suppliers to both the PC and the game machine world created a standard some years ago for small cards to carry add-on RAM. This was first called the PCMCIA card (for PC Memory Card International Association, the name of the trade group that published the standard). They are now called PC Cards. They come in one size, but three degrees of thickness, and are called Type I, Type II, and Type III, depending on how thick they are. Type III PC Cards were primarily used to make small hard drives portable, but are obsolete because of IBM's introduction of the Compact Flash-based Microdrive, which is covered shortly.

That doesn't mean that there are no magnetic data storage options for miniature computers. There are, in fact, many. For example, Iomega offers a super-small storage device called PocketZip, which is just slightly larger than a mounted 35mm slide (about 2×2×1/2 inches). Each of these minidisks holds 40MB of data. Initially targeted for use in digital cameras and personal digital assistants (PDAs), they didn't really catch on, and are now found mostly in MP3 players. Iomega also offers a small external PocketZip drive, which enables you to transfer files to or from a PC.

IBM has also released their Microdrive. This tiny hard drive has a capacity of either 340MB or 1GB. The drive fits within the confines of a Type II Compact Flash card, which is a technology you'll read about at the end of this chapter.

Other miniature magnetic recording options include magnetic strip cards. These are similar in size to credit cards, but can have a larger data storage capacity than is typical of a credit card with a single magnetic stripe on one side. This greater capacity is achieved by using more of the card's area for recording data. At this point, these are hardly mainstream products, but they do exist, and if you really want a small, rugged, yet magnetic data storage device, this is one candidate.

A variation on this theme is laser data cards. These are like the optical discs I discuss in the next couple of sections—but in a flat form, just as magnetic stripe cards are like magnetic disks, but in a flat form. In both cases, you need specialized reader/writer devices to utilize these cards.

Removable Optical PC Data Storage Devices

The most common optical PC data storage device is the CD-ROM (compact disc, read-only memory). As the name suggests, this is a form of read-only storage. A CD-ROM comes from the factory with its content already in place; you cannot alter that content later.

CD-ROMs are, however, far from the only kind of optical data storage available for PCs. There are also the recordable (write once) and rewritable versions, called CD-R and CD-RW, plus the DVD (also available in read-only, recordable, and rewritable versions). Some companies with very large archival data storage requirements have been using larger laser discs (LD) and magneto-optical (MO) disks for many years, and these too are now being used with PCs, but only in selected applications.

To explain how a CD-ROM drive works, and also to explain the many alternatives now on the market, I must first start the story where it actually began, with music CDs. Or in a sense, even earlier, with vinyl records.

Music CDs Set the Standard

In "the old days," when someone made a new audio recording, the electrical signal from a microphone vibrated a needle while it dug a spiral groove into a master vinyl record. (In the *very* old days, the microphone's diaphragm was simply connected mechanically to the needle—no electronics were involved!) Next, this master record was duplicated in two steps. The first step was to cast a mold of the master. The next step was to stamp out huge numbers of identical copies of the master using this mold.

CDs Are Made Almost the Way Vinyl Records Were

The process for making music CDs is similar to its predecessor, the vinyl records, with one tremendous difference. The master disks for music CDs are made in a different way.

The first step in making a music CD is to convert the analog signals from the microphone (or from synthesizers and other sources) into a string of numbers. This analog-to-digital conversion captures the music into a form that can be reproduced over and over again without any loss of quality (very much *unlike* analog music recordings on tape or vinyl records).

The binary digital data is recorded on the master disc in a manner I describe in a moment. From this master, molds are made and multiple copies stamped out much as vinyl records are made. The differences are these: Only one side of a CD is available for use; the opposite side is silk-screen with the disc's identifying label. Additionally, the binary data is read optically instead of mechanically (by passing the data under a beam of light instead of dragging a needle across it), and the data bits are stored more densely on the CD's surface than the wiggles in the grooves of a vinyl record.

Because the data is read optically, the surface of the CD that has the data impressed into it is coated with a mirror-like metal film (aluminum or gold). That surface is then protected by a clear plastic coating. Because the data is so dense, the mirror-like surface is broken up with tiny spots that might appear to be imperfections but are actually the data, arranged in a spiral. The spiral has its turns so closely wound that the resulting disc acts like a diffraction grating, breaking white light into a rainbow.

How CDs Store Digital Information

The way that music CDs store information digitally is both simple and stunningly clever. It uses the fact that lasers produce highly directional light beams of a single wavelength. You can focus such a beam onto a small spot. If that spot has a mirror-like surface, the beam bounces back essentially unchanged. If, however, that spot has a pit of exactly—or almost exactly—the right size and depth in the mirror, the light bouncing from the bottom of the pit will be out of phase with the light bouncing off the surface around the pit. These two out-of-phase components will interfere with each other, and the resulting reflected beam of light will be noticeably different from the original.

Manufacturers have developed a way to use a moderately high-powered laser to burn these pits in a spiral on the master disc. Your CD player has a (relatively low-powered) diode laser that tracks this spiral as the disc turns, shining a tiny spot of infrared light on the spiral to detect the data stored there. It then converts the digital information it reads into analog signals that can drive your headphones or be routed to your stereo system.

The pits serve two purposes in this scheme. First, they encode the digital data. Second, their presence signals where the spiral track goes. The read head follows the pits like a trail of bread crumbs and reads the data encoded in the exact placement of those pits.

CD-ROMs Aren't So Different; CD-ROM Drives Are

The data CD-ROM emerged when someone realized that if an audio CD player *didn't* convert the information it read from digital-to-analog form, it could store huge amounts of digital information.

Data CD-ROMs are made in the same way as music CDs. That is, they are stamped out as exact copies of a master disc (subsequently coated with metal and then protected with a plastic coat), and they contain purely digital information. The only difference is that the CD-ROM drives don't convert that information to another form; it remains digital. These drives simply present the data they read to your computer and let it decide what to do from there. (CD-ROM drives can also play music CDs, and for that purpose they have the digital-to-analog conversion circuits built in. But now, with fully digital sound systems in some PCs, it is possible to play audio CDs in a wholly new and better way, avoiding the digital-to-analog conversion step until the last possible moment, when the information reaches the speakers.)

Partly because of the demands of the music industry for music CD players, manufacturers have learned how to make CD-ROM drives inexpensively. (This same technology is also used as a part of the new super-floppy drive technology known originally as a *floptical* drive, and now called the LS-120 Superdisk drive.)

The key to this success is the fact that all CDs—including audio CDs, CD-ROMs, and the CD-R and CD-RW discs I describe next—and their drives are built to a set of exacting specifications. These standards (variously called Red, Orange, Yellow, Green, White, and Blue Book) guarantee that the different styles of discs share many properties in common. This enables designs and even some parts to be shared among the different kinds of CD drives.

Having a CD-ROM drive, or more than one, is a great boon to the PC user, and an even bigger boon for software companies. With a maximum storage capacity of around 650MB per CD, huge amounts of data and some large programs can fit on a single disc. This disc can be used directly at modest access speeds, or PC users can load those programs (and perhaps some or all of the data) onto their PC's hard drive for even quicker access.

However, there is still one major limitation to CD-ROMs: They can't be used to store new data.

Recordable CDs (CD-R) Are Different

The next logical step was to create a CD that could also be written to. The resulting device is called a compact disk, recordable (or CD-R for short). Expensive at first, at the time of this writing these blank disks cost only about 30 cents for 700MB of storage. Except for digital tape cartridges, the cheapest medium around.

A CD-R disc looks largely like a CD. Although all pressed CDs are silver, CD-R discs are gold or silver on their label side and a deep green or cyan on their recordable side. The silver/cyan CD-Rs, known as Type II, were created because the green dye used in the original CD-R design does not reflect the shorter-wavelength red lasers used in new DVD drives. The cyan dye used in the Type II format will allow complete compatibility with DVD drives. Either way, CD-Rs act like a CD-ROM (in that you can read the contents of a CD-R in any normal CD-ROM drive). Put one in a special CD-R drive, however, and you can also write to it.

This trick is achieved by making the blank CD-R disc and the CD-R drives a little more complicated than their ancestors. The CD-R disc has four layers instead of three (see Figure 8.1). The CD-R drive's laser operates at three or more power levels. At the lowest level, the laser light detects the presence or absence of pits or marks on the recording surface in order to read the disc. At the higher level, it can actually burn marks into that surface.

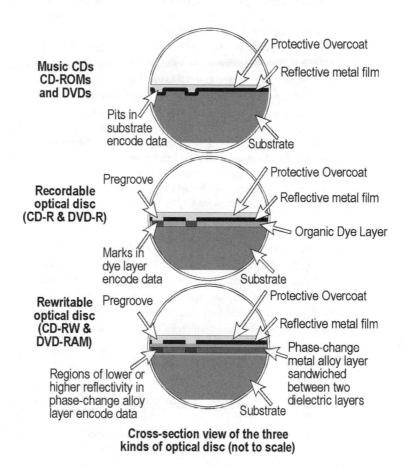

FIGURE 8.1
A CD-R disc has one extra layer and a slightly wobbly spiral pregroove.

Music CDs CD-ROMs and DVDs

Protective Overcoat
Reflective metal film
Pits in substrate encode data
Substrate

Recordable optical disc (CD-R & DVD-R)

Pregroove
Protective Overcoat
Reflective metal film
Organic Dye Layer
Marks in dye layer encode data
Substrate

Rewritable optical disc (CD-RW & DVD-RAM)

Pregroove
Protective Overcoat
Reflective metal film
Phase-change metal alloy layer sandwiched between two dielectric layers
Regions of lower or higher reflectivity in phase-change alloy layer encode data
Substrate

Cross-section view of the three kinds of optical disc (not to scale)

You might not have thought about it, but the machines used to make a master CD (for an audio CD or a CD-ROM) must have one complexity that the corresponding players don't need. The recorders must be capable of creating—not merely tracking—the spiral pit pattern. They do this by having a carefully machined mechanism that moves the burning head away from the center by a fixed amount each time the disc makes one revolution.

To keep from having to build that type of mechanical complexity into all CD-R drives, the designers of this new medium added a slightly wobbly spiral pregroove to the disks. The laser light that reads or writes information to this disk can sense this groove and follow it. The wobbly bit about that groove means that the light reflected from it will vary in time, giving the tracking mechanism an always changing signal to grab hold of and lock onto. This helps not only with following the pregroove, it also helps keep the disc turning at just the right speed. (Some disks have information modulated onto that pregroove signal to tell the drive about the optimal power level for recording, and so on.)

> **Technical Note:** Until recently, most CD drives turned their discs at a speed that varied depending on how far the portion of the spiral they are currently reading was from the center. The purpose for doing that was to keep the head moving over the surface at a constant linear velocity (CLV). This is in contrast to the way a hard disk turns at a constant angular velocity (CAV)—a behavior that is also referred to as a constant number of revolutions per minute (rpm).
>
> The newest high-speed CD-ROM drives (above 52X) use a mix of CAV and CLV, but there are no new standards for doing this, so far.
>
> The main way this affects users today is that manufacturers are free to call a CD drive (of any variety) a 52X drive (for example, if at its peak speed it passes the head over the surface 52 times faster than is standard for music CDs). If the disc turns with CAV, that means its top linear velocity occurs only for the outermost turns of its spiral track. Because CDs record from the inside out, only a full CD will benefit from the advertised speed of the drive, and then only when reading from its outermost portion of the spiral track.

By the nature of the process used to record data on a CD-R, recordable discs are write-once objects. You can burn marks into the surface, but you cannot remove them later. This makes a CD-R best suited for archival storage of information. It is not a candidate for day-to-day temporary and reusable storage, like a floppy disk. The fact is, however, that most floppies are recorded on once, and most paper is written on just once. Therefore, there are many situations in which a CD-R is an almost ideal recording medium.

CD-RW Adds Reusability

As nice as CD-R disks are, you can't reuse them. Folks value reusability in a disk, so inventors and engineers toiled and came up with a still more complex version of the CD. A CD-RW (Read/Write) disc contains two more layers than a CD-R. What really matters is that the recordable layer is made of a special material, an alloy of several metals. As it comes from the factory, this layer is formed of some highly reflective crystals (refer to Figure 10.4).

Instead of burning marks into it with a high power laser, a CD-RW drive uses its highest power to melt a small region of the recording layer. After it is melted, that material freezes into an amorphous form that doesn't reflect light nearly as well as its crystalline form. The laser's middle power level warms the layer to something less than its melting point, but a high enough temperature to change those spots from the amorphous to the highly reflective crystalline form.

This strategy allows the CD-RW media to be written to and erased many thousands of times. The erasing can happen as new data is written, unlike the earlier rewritable optical disc technology now called MO (magneto-optical). One downside to this technology is that the marks created on a CD-RW disc are not quite as good at light scattering as the marks on a CD-R disc or the pits on a CD or CD-ROM, so they are not readable in all CD drives. Only drives with *automatic gain control circuitry* can handle them correctly, and so far this feature is far from ubiquitous.

CD-RW is a relatively new technology, but it has been gaining market share rapidly. The drives now cost little more than CD-R drives, which means that the drives, at least, are a good purchase because they can be used to play audio CDs and CD-ROMs, as well as play and record CD-RW discs. Sales of the CD-RW media have also been healthy; apparently a great many people are willing to pay around three times as much per disc to get the reusability of the CD-RW media rather than buying the less expensive, but nonreusable, CD-R media.

There are just these four types of CDs (audio CD, CD-ROM, CD-R, and CD-RW). But there are a number of additional types of optical discs that matter to PC users. The newest, and becoming the most important, are various flavors of DVDs.

Digital Versatile Disc (DVD)

Essentially, a DVD is a higher capacity version of a CD, but that difference has made quite an impact. DVD technology is, in some ways, very different from CD technology; in other ways, it's very similar. DVDs, like CDs, are optical discs read by a laser. But the DVD laser, unlike the traditional CD laser, produces a visible beam and is tuned to the red band of the visible light spectrum (635 or 650 nanometers). If you have a red laser pointer, it almost surely operates at this same wavelength. Consequently, its operating wavelength is considerably shorter than the infrared lasers used for CDs. This shorter wavelength makes it possible to read the far more densely packed data on a DVD disc. As you've already read, the different laser frequency also mandated the creation of CD-R Type II discs. Some DVD systems, notably from Sony as of this writing, actually employ two lasers: an infrared laser (790nm) for CDs and CD-R discs, and the shorter-wavelength laser for DVDs. Most DVD drives also contain two lens systems, one for CDs and one for DVDs.

In addition to a significantly shorter wavelength laser, DVD data points, or pits, are a good deal smaller than CD pits. These pits are packed together tighter and also span a slightly larger area of the disc than do their CD cousins. More fundamentally, major improvements in error-correction methods have made all of these other improvements practical. Finally, DVD discs can—unlike CDs of any variety—be double-sided, with up to two recordable "layers" per side. By simply refocusing the laser's lens, the device can read the data from either layer. (Actually, in some systems it's more complex than that, but at its simplest, refocusing is all that's necessary.) A double-sided, double-layered DVD designed under today's specifications has a capacity in excess of 17GB.

Why All the Excitement?

Why is this so exciting to so many people? Audio CDs were first devised to record music. DVDs started out as digital video display, and their primary claim to fame was that their data capacity was sufficient to permit recording an entire feature movie (in MPEG2 compressed form) on one side of these high-density optical discs. That got Hollywood (and the rest of the movie and television industries) excited. And the plans didn't stop there.

You've already read that DVD formats exist with as many as four "sides" (two layers of data on each of two physical sides). One proposed standard would make the spiral of pits go from the inside to the outside on one of those two layers and in the reverse direction on the other. This could enable users to play a movie (or other streaming content) nearly continuously from inside to outside and back to the inside again. That's why movie makers got excited by the DVD. But before they could formulate a standard that met only their needs, the computer industry weighed in to be sure that the needs for digital data storage would be equally well served. Soon what had been the "digital video disc" became the "digital versatile disc," capable of holding either computer data or a movie.

Incidentally, the player used to show a DVD movie need not be different from the drive you would use to "play" digital data into a computer, but several other factors must be met before a PC DVD-ROM drive can play DVD-video movies. Among other things, a DVD-ROM drive must have either internal or external hardware support for decoding the MPEG2 combined video and audio data stream. Additionally, your hardware will have to contain the copy-protection circuitry that's part of the DVD-video standard.

Movies aside, with this much capacity and with backward compatibility insured, it was almost a given that PC makers would rapidly adopt the DVD drive (in a read-only version for DVD-ROMs) in place of the CD-ROM drive that had become ubiquitous. You can still get a CD-ROM drive, but why would you want to when you can get the more capable DVD drive for nearly the same price? The DVD drive will play all the discs the CD-ROM drive will and also the newer, more capacious DVDs. Indeed, it's now very common to find a DVD drive and a CD-RW drive in the same unit, so you can play DVDs and CDs, as well as burn CDs.

Overall, these developments were so exciting that many manufacturers didn't even wait for the standards committees to finish their work. Because of this, several types of recordable DVDs have emerged, and the two chief hardware contenders are Pioneer and Hewlett-Packard.

DVD State of the Art

In fact, as of the time of this writing, five versions of burnable (that is recordable, as opposed to professionally pressed for mass distribution) DVDs exist: DVD-R, DVD-RAM, DVD-RW, DVD+RW, and DVD+R. Of these, DVD-R is like CD-R in that it can be written to one, and only one, time. The other four formats can be written to and erased over and over, although each works in a slightly different way with different levels of compatibility. The formats are not, in general, compatible with each other, nor are they even all compatible with home DVD players already in wide distribution. Indeed, DVD-RAM is basically a backup format for computers, and can't be read in any other type of DVD drive. DVD-RAM drives can *sometimes* read discs created in DVD-R drives, but not always. Some DVD-RAM drives can also read discs created by the rewritable-format drives, but that, too, is not reliable. There is also some incompatibility between variant types of DVD-R drives, which can read most DVD discs, but cannot read DVD-RAM or DVD-R drives created in their competitor's format.

DVD-R drives work the same way as do CD-R drives, which you read about earlier in this chapter. DVD-R has a capacity of 4.7GB per side. (One of the two DVD-R formats, DVD-RG—for "General"—supports two-sided discs, increasing each physical disc's capacity to 9.4GB. In addition to the two incompatible formats of DVD-R, there is further incompatibility between DVD-R media and hardware. Recently released drives comply with version 2.0 of the DVD-R specification and can handle the 4.7GB discs I mentioned a moment ago. Earlier drives cannot use these discs, and have a maximum capacity of 3.95GB, but the 3.95GB discs are more universally compatible with other hardware—including later drives and home player units. Finally, DVD-R has been known for persistent problems with data loss. DVD-RW is the rewritable version of this technology.

DVD+RW and DVD+R are closely related technologies—not only are they similar to each other, but they're similar to the CD-recording methods with which they share names. DVD+RW uses phase-change technology lifted from CD-RWs, and DVD+R uses the same type of dye material that makes CD-R units work. They each have a capacity of 4.7GB per side, and both support dual-sided media. The first DVD+RW to market was Hewlett-Packard's DVD100i, which hit the market at the time of this writing for the phenomenally good price of $599.00. The nearest competition is the inferior DVD-R technology with drives priced between $200 and $500 more than the HP unit. DVD+RW can store computer data as well as video, and can be played back in any home DVD player. This technology has been embraced by many of the biggest names in the PC industry: Dell, Sony, Philips, Ricoh, Yamaha, and Mitsubishi, to name a few. Notably absent are Compaq and Apple, which have allied themselves with DVD-R and DVD-RW.

DVD-RAM drives also support a capacity of 4.7GB, and use a combination of the magneto-optical (which you'll read about in the next section) and phase-change technologies. DVD-RAM discs are generally sold in sealed cartridges, which makes them incompatible with any other type of DVD drive. Of all DVD technologies, DVD-RAM will probably be the first to leave the market.

The most important thing to remember when you're looking at DVD hardware is the difference between "+" and "-". DVD-RW and DVD+RW (and DVD-R and DVD+R, for that matter) are different technologies supported by different companies, with different levels of compatibility and apparent reliability. Before you purchase a unit, make sure you have explored whether you want a DVD drive to be a big "+" or a minus.

Magneto-Optical PC Data Storage Devices

In addition to devices that use a purely magnetic or a purely optical technology for data storage (and DVD-RAM, which uses both), there is one more important hybrid of the two. This is the magneto-optical (MO) disk. These were developed many years ago in large platter formats. They haven't made more of a splash in the PC world because the drives tend to be expensive, and other, newer technologies are as reliable. The media are not that different in construction or price from CD-RW discs, but the MO drives cost a *lot* more than a CD-RW drive.

Basics of Magneto-Optical Data Storage

When I described how hard disks work, I skipped over many of the more arcane details. You can read about those in Chapter 18. One detail will, however, help you see how MO recording is nearly the same as, yet very different from the other magnetic-data recording technologies.

That detail is how the physical characteristics of the magnetic recording medium dictate the design of the recording device. Three properties of the magnetic recording medium are used in MO recording: two for recording and another one for reading back the recorded data.

MO Recording

All magnetic storage devices, and this includes MO, use as their medium a material that can be permanently magnetized in either of two directions. The material is always magnetized—at every place in the medium it merely is sometimes magnetized in one direction and sometimes in the opposite direction. There are several key properties of any such magnetizable medium. The most important one, for your purposes, is how easily you can switch the magnetization from one orientation to the other. The name for this property is the medium's *coercivity*.

If the material's coercivity is low, magnetizing it is easy. This helps when you are trying to design a tiny write head for a miniature disk drive. The small head can generate only a fairly modest level of magnetic field. However, a low value of coercivity also means that it is relatively easy for the magnetization of the medium to be reversed accidentally. If you have ever damaged data on a floppy disk by inadvertently passing it near a magnet, you have seen a vivid demonstration that the coercivity of the magnetic material used in floppy disks (and, as it happens, also that used in most hard disks) is not very high.

Magneto-optical disks, in contrast, use a medium whose coercivity is over 10 times higher. This means that after you record something on an MO disk, it is almost completely invulnerable to any stray magnetic fields. That higher coercivity also means that

MO disks require recording magnets that can generate fields that are over 10 times stronger than those used in other magnetic data storage devices. Those fields just can't practically be made in the tiny sizes needed to pack lots of data into a small space.

The solution to this dilemma is a clever one. It takes advantage of a second important physical characteristic of the magnetic recording medium, the *Curie temperature*. All permanently magnetizable materials have a coercivity that falls as the temperature rises. In fact, after a critical temperature is reached (called, as you might now have guessed, the Curie temperature), the material stops being a permanent magnet. After you cool it off below that critical temperature, however, its permanent magnetic properties return.

So if you use a laser to heat the surface of an MO disk, you can easily set the orientation of its magnetization with a small magnetic field from the write head. A blast of light from a focused laser of a suitable power quickly heats the magnetizable material in just one tiny spot almost to its Curie temperature. Simultaneously, the write head generates the field necessary to change the magnetization of this spot. Soon after, as the spot cools off, that new magnetization will be locked in place. The laser spot can be very small— smaller even than the magnetic recording head, which means MO disks can hold more than a magnetic disk of a comparable size.

Reading Data from an MO Disk

Reading data back from an MO disk uses the third curious property of the magnetic recording medium: its capability of twisting the polarization of light. A laser beam consists of light of a single wavelength, moving in a single direction. It also is strongly polarized, which means that the magnetic fields for each quantum of light (each photon) are parallel to one another (and at right angles to the direction the beam is traveling). Bounce such a beam off a magnetized surface, and the angles of all those photons' magnetic fields will rotate a small amount. The direction of rotation depends on which way the magnetic field points in the surface from which the light beam bounced.

The returning light beam is passed through a linear *polarizer*. (You can think of this device as being like a comb that passes only photons whose magnetic fields are aligned so that they can slip through the teeth of the comb.) If the polarizer is set just right, it will pass many or most of the photons bouncing off places on the surface that are magnetized in one orientation and pass almost none of the ones bouncing off places where the magnetization is oppositely oriented. Detect this change in light amplitude, and you have, in effect, read the orientation of the magnetic field on the surface of the medium.

There are now two standard sizes for modern MO media: 5 1/4-inch and 3 1/2-inch. The larger ones can hold about as much as a CD-ROM. MO disks come permanently housed in much thicker and sturdier cartridges than even the smaller floppy disks. This is important because they are often used to store valuable data, and keeping the surface of the media clean and undamaged can be key to giving data a long life.

Electronic PC Data Storage Devices

One other group of electronic data storage devices is used in or with PCs. This group uses electronic means for data storage. They look like disk drives, but they really aren't. Therein lie both their strengths and weaknesses. Ordinarily, electronic memory is volatile, but there are several ways to make nonvolatile electronic data into storage devices.

PC Card Flash RAM

Portable computers need storage, just as much as desktop PCs, but they can't always accommodate the same kinds of storage devices. One solution to this need is to use PC Card Nonvolatile RAM. These devices are roughly the size of a credit card, but somewhat thicker (approximately 86-54-5 millimeters, or about 3.4-2.1-0.2 inches in English units).

These PC Cards, formerly known as PCMCIA cards, have some nonvolatile RAM chips inside them. This memory is made of erasable electrically programmable read-only memory chips (EEPROMs), ferro-electric random access memory chips (FRAMs), or simple DRAMs with a small battery attached to preserve their contents. The latest models use what is termed *Flash Memory,* which is a kind of inherently non-volatile electronic memory similar to EEPROMs. These devices don't lose their contents when their battery dies.

Whatever their technology, PC Cards enable you to permanently (or close to permanently) store information rapidly, and you can read it back even more quickly. The only drawbacks are that their capacity is small and their cost is high. Still, if you have a PDA, you might find that PC Card Flash Memory is your best option. This is especially so if you treat your PDA roughly, because a Flash Memory card, with its lack of moving parts, is inherently more rugged than any kind of hard drive, and even more rugged than most floppies.

Tiny Storage Cards

It can never be too small, can it? PC Cards are nice and fairly small, but not small enough for some folks. So, there are now five more formats that have become popular with the digital camera makers—CompactFlash, SmartMedia, Sony MemoryStick, Secure Digital, and MultiMedia Cards.

CompactFlash and SmartMedia

The first two of these are essentially the same Flash Memory you get in a PC Card, but because they are smaller you get less space to store your data. The CompactFlash cards are about one-third the area of a PC Card and two-thirds as thick. The SmartMedia cards are about the same area as a CompactFlash card, but much thinner. If you have a digital camera or other device that uses one of these, you can use only the one type of card, because they are not interchangeable. You can also easily get a reader for either of these types of Flash Memory card, which plugs into your PC to allow speedy data transfers from the flash card to your PC.

If you've got a notebook, you can purchase a simple adapter for CompactFlash memory that enables it to be inserted in a PC Card (PCMCIA) slot. Windows will automatically install the card as another drive on your system.

The main reason that the CompactFlash card is so much thicker than the SmartMedia card is that CompactFlash includes the electronics to manage the process of recording images to the NVRAM (non-volatile RAM) chips and of making this device appear to be a disk drive. The SmartMedia cards depend on having that controller electronics built into the camera or other devices into which these cards are inserted.

Sony MemorySticks, Secure Digital, and MultiMedia Cards

All three of these technologies are also Flash Memory, and the original Sony MemoryStick was, in fact, not much different from CompactFlash or SmartMedia cards, about which you've just read.

In its latest incarnation, however, known as MagicGate MemorySticks (MGMS), it belongs to a new class of digital storage cards: protected and encrypting storage. The two other players in this new field are Panasonic, with its Secure Digital (SD) cards, and the MultiMedia Card Association's MultiMedia Card (MMC). Although these devices implement proprietary technologies to achieve certain ends (which I'll talk about in just a moment), they are also new implementations of Flash Memory technology. (The exception to this is some MultiMedia Cards actually ROM (read-only) devices. This type of MMC distributes reference data. The FlashRAM versions of these units are available in a wide range of capacities, from 8MB up to 128MB, depending on the device. Like other Flash devices, there are no moving parts, nothing to wear out, and they weigh in at about the same weight as two US quarters.

These devices distinguish themselves in their implementation of security and encryption processes. Secure and private data is, of course, a great thing alone, but the security features are not targeted at directly protecting the consumer.

Instead, these devices provide copy protection and performance management so that content providers, such as recording and media companies, can prevent consumers from sharing files and also regulate how many times those files can be accessed before they become unavailable. These ideas are in compliance with the SDMI-2 (the second version of the Secure Digital Music Initiative) and the wishes of the RIAA (Recording Industry Association of America).

The idea works on two levels.

The plan requires consumers to use Internet-enabled devices (MP3 players, cellular phones, and so on) to download media. As the consumer, you would pay a fee—say $2.00, about what it used to cost to purchase a 45rpm vinyl record and permanently add it to your collection. This fee would allow you to listen to the song a few times, or it might entitle you to listen to it as many times as you like for a limited number of days, perhaps a week. At the end of that time, the file will self-destruct. If you want to listen to that song again, all you have to do is go back online, pay another fee, and wait to download it again. Once you've done this a few times and are sure you really like the song, you can go out and pay the full price to purchase an audio CD, or you can pay a larger fee online and download a copy of the song that will never self-destruct (at least not on purpose).

The plan also uses serial numbers in the MGMS, SD, or MMC to encrypt the downloaded media.This encryption prevents the consumer from sharing the file with anyone else— either you won't be able to copy the file, or else it won't work if you do copy it to another device. Encrypted files would also be unable to be transferred to another true digital media, so content providers don't need to worry about their copyrighted material being burned onto CD-ROMs and shared in that manner. A further proposal links a second serial number in the card-reader device (the phone, MP3 player, and so on) to the one in the card, so that consumer's can't share the file by simply passing the memory cards around. Under this scheme, a song I download on my MP3 player wouldn't play on your MP3 player, even if you have the same make and model.

Historically, copy protection has been universally bad for the consumer and largely bad even for content providers. In the past, it was fraught with problems. Software copy protection commonly made it impossible to make backup copies of mission-critical programs and applications. If the original was lost, the purchaser might have to buy a new license for the product—in the worst case—or, at least, spend time trying to convince a telephone representative that he/she was honestly not trying to obtain an illegal copy of the product.

Serialization has also been used, both through the use of external hardware attachments— called *dongles* because of the invasive way they dangled off the back of the PC to which they were attached—and through complex analyses of system hardware and characteristics, similar to what Microsoft has purportedly implemented in both MS Windows XP, not yet released at the time of this writing. The former technique often created incompatibilities with other external hardware, like modems and printers, and if a disgruntled employee stole the dongle, the application simply would not run until a replacement was purchased and obtained. The latter technique promises to create difficulties for any lawful owner who significantly modifies the configuration or installation of hardware in the PC. If, for example, a product uses the serial number of a hard drive and the serial number of a network card to generate a protection scheme, that scheme will fail if the owner replaces the hard drive or network card. (The software would assume it had been illegally transferred to a second computer, because the new components would have new serial numbers).

In the end, the market alone will determine the success or failure of this latest resurgence of copy protection and of the software and hardware that implements it.

Summary

In this chapter, you learned about the variety of removable storage available for PCs. From magnetic media of all kinds—tapes, disks, cards, and more—to optical media, to purely digital electronic media, the options are many. Which you choose depends on your own needs and budget. Tape devices provide secure long-term storage of huge amounts of data, but trade off quick accessibility and quick data transfer rates. Removable drives and cartridges are faster than tape in all respects, have similar capacity, but are more fragile than tape, and might not have tape's proven longevity.

Optical media has neither the capacity of tape or removable hard drives, but has the feature of convenience and near-universal compatibility. The longevity of optical media continues to be a subject of debate. Analog laser discs were originally said to oxidize and become unusable after 10 years, but this proved to be untrue. CD-ROMs were originally given an estimated life span of 10 years, too, but that has recently been bumped to 20. It is proposed by manufacturers that recordable DVDs will have a life expectancy of over 45 years. If true, that would set DVD up as the "ultimate" in storage media, so long as universal standards for reading and writing eventually emerge. Even tapes cannot claim a failure-free longevity in excess of four decades.

It's my hope that this chapter has given you sufficient familiarity with these options and their technologies so that you'll be an informed user when it's time to make purchase and implementation decisions. If you want to learn about how hard drives and optical drives actually *work*, then turn to Chapter 18.

Serial Ports

Computers are useful only if information can get into them and back out of them. In this chapter, you'll learn about several of the most important interfaces used to get information into and out of PCs.

To get an idea of how an interface works, take the keyboard as an example. It has, from the beginning, had its own special-purpose interface for inputting data. PCs also have two major types of general-purpose input and output interfaces. In this chapter, you'll learn about one of those: the various types of serial ports—including USB and FireWire ports—and how they work.

Talking Through a Tiny Pipe: Serial Ports

PCs move information around internally either a byte at a time (on eight parallel wires) or several bytes at a time (using even more wires). This is practical inside the PC, and valuable because all the bits of a byte arrive at their destination together at the maximum speed. This is how the various internal buses—PCI, ISA, and so on—work.

However, this isn't as practical outside the system unit. If you are sending information a relatively short distance—say to your monitor or perhaps even to a printer nearby—you can use a multiwire cable to carry data in many parallel paths similar to those inside the system unit. But what if you want to send information a longer distance? It's often more practical to use a different strategy called *serial communication*.

The name "serial" comes from the fact that data is communicated in a series of bits, one after the other. This serial approach has been used, traditionally, when there is no pressing need for speed. Historically, serial connections are slower than parallel connections (you'll read about parallel connections in Chapter 10, "Parallel Ports.") Understand that there is nothing inherently slower about a serial link relative to a parallel link. It just so happens that, as these methods have been implemented on PC ports, parallel data has traditionally moved faster than serial data. If you like metaphors, you might compare serial to parallel in this context by considering that you can move more water through, say, 32 one-inch pipes than you can through only one.

Later in this chapter, you'll learn about two much higher-speed versions of the serial bus, the *Universal Serial Bus (USB)* and *IEEE 1394*, sometimes known as FireWire or iLink. But first let's explore the basics of serial communication and learn how they apply to the traditional, not-terribly-fast, standard PC serial port.

Serial Communications Basics

The idea behind serial communication is simple: Just send one bit at a time. To send a byte, send each of its eight bits, one after another. If you want some insurance that the byte gets where it's going without any of the bits being changed, you can have the serial link also send along a ninth (*parity*) bit. This extra bit provides a way for the connected serial devices to check for errors in the data. In its simplest terms, by checking to see whether the value of the parity bit is zero or one, it's possible to perform a calculation that will let you know whether the previous 8-bit byte was transmitted correctly, or whether its values were corrupted.

In principle, you should need only a single wire, or actually a single pair of wires, for serial communications. In practice, separate wires are normally used for the outbound and the inbound data, for a minimum of three wires in a serial communication cable (send, receive, and ground). Usually, several more wires are added to signal controls, such as whether the receivers at each end are ready for incoming data.

Two common connector styles are used for standard serial ports on PCs. One is the DB9 (9-pin) connector; the other is a male DB25, which is essentially the same except that it has 25 pins instead of 9. Both are shown in Figure 9.1.

FIGURE 9.1
The DB9 and DB25 serial connectors.

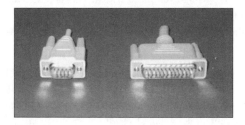

What's a UART and What Does It Do?

Data moves through parallel wires inside the system unit, and then moves along a single wire through the serial port. So, PCs needed a way to convert a data stream from parallel into serial and back again. Before PCs existed, the circuitry necessary to make these conversions was available. The module that does this conversion job is a Universal Asynchronous Receiver/Transmitter (UART).

There have been several generations of UART. The earliest converted a single byte into serial bits and back again, and it did this at a maximum rate of 9,600bps. Faster models soon emerged that converted a single byte at a maximum (guaranteed) rate of 115Kbps. Today, an even later model of UART, called the 16550, can transfer data at rates up to around 400Kbps, and has some other even more important advantages. I'll talk about those briefly in the "How the 16550 Saved the Day" section later in this chapter.

How Serial Data Is Sent

The serial data-sending process occurs like this: The CPU addresses the UART and sends a byte of information to it over the system's (internal) I/O data bus. The UART picks up the data and stores it temporarily. At that point, the CPU is free to go back to using the system bus for other purposes.

Now the UART serializes the bits that make up the byte it received and sends them out one at a time over the serial communications link's outbound data wire. When the entire byte has been sent (with or without an extra parity bit), the UART will wait between one and two bit-times before it begins to send the next byte. That waiting time is referred to as the stop bit (or bits).

How Serial Data Is Received

At the other end of the line is another UART. Its job is to undo what the first UART did. It must notice each incoming bit and store those values internally. After it has received the entire byte (plus its parity bit if it has one) and checked the parity, the UART is ready to present the complete byte to the receiving CPU.

At this point, the UART effectively "rings the CPU's doorbell." (Technically, it asserts an interrupt request, which you'll read about in Chapter 15, "Motherboard Magic".) When the CPU requests the data, the UART sends the data byte onto the receiving system's internal I/O bus. The CPU reads the data from the I/O bus.

> **Note:** The CPU is not required to accept the byte immediately. It normally waits until it is finished with the current instruction it is processing, and it might wait much longer than that. However, if the CPU waits too long, it might lose some of the incoming data. Most of the time, the first few bits of the next byte will already be arriving across the serial link. If the CPU fails to pick up that received byte in time, the UART simply discards it and replaces it with the next byte it received, after telling the CPU that data has been lost.

How the 16550 Saved the Day

Keeping up with the UART used to be quite a burden on the CPU, especially at higher rates of data transmission. Every time a byte is received or a byte has been sent, the CPU stopped whatever else it was doing, switched to the communications program that sends and receives data, and then switched back.

To help reduce this burden, an improved UART called the 16550 was created. This UART has additional data buffer space—16 bytes worth of space—which the CPU can quickly fill and get back to other business. Only when the UART has handled all 16 bytes of data must the CPU stop its other work to dump another 16 bytes in the UART.

Both for incoming and outgoing data, the buffering of data on the UART saves a lot of overhead time that the CPU would otherwise have to waste as it constantly jumps between servicing the UART and whatever else it was doing. (Incidentally, shortly after the 16550 was released, problems relating to how it handled data in its buffers were detected. These were rectified with the 16550A UART, and its subsequent models.)

Modern PCs often have the serial port interface electronics included in the motherboard chip set. In today's systems with their large-scale integrated circuits, you probably won't actually have a 16550 or other UART chip on the motherboard. You will probably have the functionality of one or more such chips hidden away inside a Very Large-Scale Integrated Circuit (VLSI) chip, which is part of the motherboard chip set. The UART circuitry is there, but is only active when it needs to be.

A Series of Serial Ports

Fundamentally, what you've just read describes how serial communications work. With that understanding, let's now take a look at the variety of serial ports found on today's PCs. Although each of these types of ports adheres to its own standards of how data is to be transferred, all of these ports move data in a serial fashion.

Serial Links Without the Wires—IrDA

Serial links usually include a serial port interface on the PC, a cable from the PC to some peripheral device, and a serial port interface on that peripheral device. Sometimes you can have the effect of all that without using a cable. Several physical technologies are used in lieu of passing an electrical current down a copper wire.

The oldest technique uses infrared light—essentially the same technology used in most TV and VCR remote controls. A port and related circuitry converts electrical signals into light signals and back again. This type of wireless serial port is now ubiquitous on laptop computers and PDAs, and is also found on many cellular telephones and even on some printers.

The Infrared Data Association (IrDA) has defined a standard called, appropriately, *IrDA*. Devices that are compliant with this standard are capable of transferring data at any rate up to the normal maximum for such ports of 115Kbps. This standard has been subsequently expanded to support what is commonly called *Fast IR*, but is more accurately called IrDA 1.1, and provides transfer speeds up to 4Mbps (megabits per second). IrDA ports can transmit across an area as far as four meters, but as the distance increases, so do the errors. In practice, distances of less than one meter have proved extremely reliable.

Another limiting factor is where the devices are with respect to each other. Infrared light, like all light, travels in a straight line (spreading out as it does so). In order to communicate reliably, the infrared ports on the sending and receiving devices need to face each other directly—ideally with less than a 17-degree angle of deviation. This is a good deal less tolerant than TV remotes, but a good deal more data is being sent, too.

Incidentally, don't confuse infrared serial communications with what's generally being discussed under the aegis of "wireless communications" or "wireless networking." These use radio signals, not infrared light, for the most part, and can move data a good deal faster than does an IrDA port. You'll read about wireless networking in Chapter 11, "Networking—Wired and Wireless."

The Universal Serial Bus (USB)

Although IrDA ports are found everywhere in the mobile world, almost all PCs—even desktops and servers—now come with one or two connectors for a newer type of serial communication. The hardware and industry standards involved are collectively called the *Universal Serial Bus*, or *USB* for short.

The USB port is in many respects a traditional PC serial port, but there are some important differences—ones that have a profound impact on how it feels to use a USB-connected device. It is much simpler to set up and use USB devices, and using them avoids all the nightmares associated with configuration conflicts that plagued users in the past when adding new peripheral devices to a PC.

Key Differences Between USB and a Standard PC Serial Port

A USB cable has only four wires. Two carry data (in both directions), and two carry power (to allow the use of at least some USB peripherals without having to plug them into wall power or run them off batteries). This is in sharp contrast to the nine or 25 connections required for the older-style serial port.

Despite having fewer wires, USB can transfer data much faster than the original PC serial port— at either 1.5 or 12Mbps. Even the lower of these two speeds is over 10 times faster than the traditional PC serial port's top speed. USB switches dynamically between these two speeds as needed to accommodate all the devices that are attached to it. If you use only low-speed devices, the bus will never rise to the upper rate. If you attach any high-speed devices, the bus will continue to operate the slower devices at the slower rate, but will quickly shift into high gear when the faster devices need attention.

USB cables are designed to be nearly goof-proof. The end that connects to a PC, or to a hub through which it will send data toward the PC (and receive data from the PC), has a flat, rectangular shape. (You can see these connectors in Figure 9.2.) At its other end, a USB cable has a very different, nearly square connector. This marks the end that spits out data to a peripheral device or accepts data back from that device.

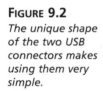

FIGURE 9.2

The unique shape of the two USB connectors makes using them very simple.

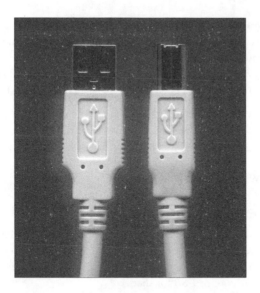

USB Hubs

The USB strategy for connectivity permits devices to be connected either directly to the PC, or indirectly through one or more hubs. Each hub has a hub controller, a signal repeater (which boots the strength of the data signal as needed), and multiple inputs for attaching USB devices, called downstream ports. It also has one output called the upstream port, which connects back to the PC or to another hub that is closer to the PC on the USB "tree" of hubs and devices.

Each USB-enabled peripheral device can have a hub built into it, but it's more common to purchase a standalone USB hub. You can use as many hubs as you need in order to attach all the USB peripherals you want (up to the limit of 127 USB peripheral devices and hubs).

What sorts of peripheral device might have a built-in USB hub? The first, and most obvious, candidates are USB-enabled devices that sit in front of your PC. For example, you might have a USB-enabled keyboard with ports into which you can plug a USB mouse and possibly some other USB devices. But a hub can be built into any PC USB device, into which you can plug still other USB devices. (Unused USB hub inputs are simply ignored by the system, and thus cause no problems.) An example of a USB hub is found in Figure 9.3.

The USB ports on your PC are connected to what is called the *root hub*. Each external hub can run off the power it receives from the root hub over the USB bus, or it can have a power supply that plugs into a wall outlet—the latter is by far the most common configuration. Individual USB devices can also draw power from the root hub or an external hub, or can have their own power supply. Again, the latter is the most common.

FIGURE 9.3
USB hub.

Using USB

The most wonderful thing about USB is how it works when you use it. You simply plug in the devices and they work—almost instantly. No fuss, no muss, no bother. They just work. You might need to install device drivers for some devices, but, in the main, USB truly can be plug and play. The second wonderful thing about USB is how few resources it uses. A USB port, with as many as 127 devices attached, nevertheless uses fewer computer resources. For instance, it might use only one IRQ and one port address. Compare this to the traditional serial port, which requires the same resources to support only one device. (You'll read about IRQs and port addresses in Chapter 15.)

The USB Communication Protocol

How is it possible to have so many devices, yet use so few computer resources (compared to traditional serial devices)? The answer to that lies in how communication is managed over a USB bus. In short, your PC thinks it's supporting only one device—the USB host, which is the collection of software and hardware inside the PC that basically "is" the USB bus. That host, in turn, supports all the attached peripherals over that bus.

The host is in charge of the USB bus. It is the sole master. No other USB devices are permitted any real control; they are, effectively, slaves. When you plug in a USB device, the host notices this fact and then starts a "conversation" with that device to determine what it can do and what software support it requires from the PC. The host then loads any needed device drivers on the fly. Likewise, when you unplug a USB device, the host notices this, unloads any drivers it had loaded, and otherwise notifies the system that this device is no longer available. Resources that the device was using can be released for other uses.

Furthermore, when an attached device wants to send data to the host, it must wait for the host to give it clearance. The host polls each of the attached devices constantly to be sure it permits any pending data to be sent to it. With all of the external devices connected to the host through one or more USB hubs, the entire setup gets the name "hub topology." You can see what this hub topology looks like in Figure 9.4.

FIGURE 9.4

USB uses a hub topology, with a master root (host) hub controlling all of the slave devices and secondary hubs.

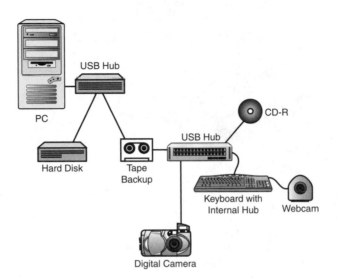

Messages on a USB bus are always one of four kinds. The first are *control messages*. These are how the host learns about the peripherals and also how the peripherals alert the host to their needs for service. The second type of messages is the *interrupt message*. The third type of messages is the *isochronous message*, and the last message type is the *bulk message*.

Interrupt messages are the least important and least common. For the most part, these are sent by only the simplest devices, like a keyboard or a mouse, which needs to be able to function while other processes are happening, but which don't send or receive any significant quantity of data. Because their data-flow needs are so small, it's reasonable for them to be able to interrupt the flow of other data through the USB.

The essential idea behind isochronous and bulk messages is that all the data transfers can be divided into two data transfer types, based on the data's *urgency* needs or their *need for accuracy*.

Isochronous data transfers are used for the first of these two kinds of data transfer. If you are sending digital information that represents music or video, getting the message there in a timely manner is very important. There is little problem if you lose a few bits now and then, just as long as the data is reaching its destination in the allotted time. Each device that requires isochronous communications can inform the host how much guaranteed bandwidth it desires. The host allocates available bandwidth to accommodate the request as best as it can, which ensures that data indeed reaches its destination in a timely manner.

On the other hand, if you are transferring a computer program or a critical data file, accuracy is your preeminent concern. The transfer can take as long as it must, but the data absolutely has to get through without any lost or altered bits. Bulk data transfers are used for this transfer need.

The host will not allow any more than 90 percent of the bus's available bandwidth to be used by isochronous requests. That ensures that bulk transfers, control messages, and interrupt messages always get through. They might be delayed somewhat, but this delay is typically not too bad.

USB 2.0 (or USB Hi-Speed)

Although USB 1.1 has been a huge success in the PC world, it has proved to have at least one shortcoming that threatens to limit its life: performance. At best, a USB connection offered bandwidth of 12Mbps. Although this is a tremendous improvement over older, traditional serial ports, it falls a good deal short of today's needs. It also falls short of the performance of its primary competition, IEEE 1394, also known as FireWire, which is discussed in the next section.

To compete, USB had to evolve, which it has begun to do with the new USB 2.0 standard (sometimes called USB Hi-Speed). USB 2.0, even as this is being written, is only just seeing its first actual products emerge. USB 2.0 has a potential bandwidth of 480Mbps, placing it at roughly 40 times faster than USB 1.1 (now sometimes called USB Basic-Speed), and nosing just slightly past the performance of IEEE 1394, at least theoretically. The USB 2.0 standard has the very attractive feature of being compatible with not only all existing USB devices, but also with their cabling and connectors. So owners of those devices don't need to do anything to make them work on a new PC that supports USB 2.0. Older PCs will be upgradable simply by replacing the existing USB ports with new ports containing the USB 2.0 circuitry, and updating operating system drivers. (Microsoft says that it will not support USB 2.0 in Windows XP, which is almost ready for release at the time of this writing. Subsequently, they reversed that decision, and drivers are available for Windows XP, although not every manufacturer's products support them.)

New USB 2.0 root hubs and external hubs support old and new devices in any combination, and will automatically switch speeds to provide each device with the maximum performance it can support. Everyday users should notice no variance in the performance of USB 2.0 devices that are sharing the same hub with legacy USB 1.1 devices.

Of course, USB 2.0 devices must be connected to a USB 2.0 root hub, or to an external hub that connects to a USB 2.0 root hub. Legacy USB 1.1 hubs can also be connected to the same external USB 2.0 hub, with a complement of USB 1.1 devices connected to them.

USB 2.0 might dramatically expand the range of devices that can be connected to PCs through the USB port, although whether this will happen remains to be seen. Given the dramatic difference in performance between USB 1.1 and IEEE 1394, it's been pretty obvious so far when a device warrants USB and when it warrants IEEE 1394. Items not needing quicker transfer rates, like keyboards and mice, will continue to use USB 1.1. On the other hand, peripherals needing a fast, efficient transfer rate, such as digital video cameras, use IEEE 1394. With the coming of USB 2.0, that distinction is blurred at best.

IEEE 1394 FireWire

Around the same time that USB first became really popular, another new serial port also came on the scene. This other serial port is known as the IEEE 1394 connection. This type of serial connection is meant for high-speed, serious-capacity data-transfer work. The starting speed for this bus is around eight times faster than the top speed of a USB 1.1 bus, up to 400Mbps, with developments in the works to expand that speed to 800Mbps, and faster still.

What is now the industry standard, IEEE 1394 began its life in 1986 in Cupertino, California, at Apple Computer, which called this high-speed connectivity FireWire. The name, trademarked b Apple, allegedly came about partly because the technology allowed data to move so fast, and partly because, when data did move that fast, the wires and connectors actually got hot. Whether the legend is true or not, Apple's FireWire was the first really high-speed serial communications technology. It wasn't until nine years later, however, that Sony started implementing a version of FireWire on their digital video cameras, and, eventually, the technology was adopted as the IEEE 1394 standard.

Different from USB

Even though they are both high-speed serial busses, IEEE 1394 is distinct from USB—even from the high-speed USB 2.0—in a few key ways. On the hardware level, of course, IEEE 1394's connectors and cabling are distinct. USB uses a total of four conductors, two carrying power, and two carrying data. The IEEE 1394 standard calls for two pairs of wires for data and one pair for power—a total of six wires. USB cabling also uses a unique connector at each end, whereas IEEE 1394 cables can be reversed freely, as shown in Figure 9.5.

FIGURE 9.5
IEEE 1394 and USB cabling and conductors are very different.

USB Connector

IEEE 1394 Connector

More important than the fact that they look different and are wired differently, the two standards work quite differently. As I've said, USB is a hub-based, master-slave topology, with the root hub polling all attached devices, watching for devices that need to send or receive data, and controlling the entire process. Figure 9.6 shows how IEEE 1394 is connected. IEEE 1394 devices can be connected in a variety of ways, creating "branches" off of which multiple devices are connected. Don't confuse IEEE 1394's physical appearance with a hub topology, however.

FIGURE 9.6
IEEE 1394 is wired as a daisy chain of equal devices.

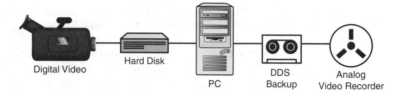

Digital Video   Hard Disk   PC   DDS Backup   Analog Video Recorder

IEEE 1394 uses a *daisy-chain topology*, very similar to the SCSI chain you learned about in Chapter 8, "Removable Storage". IEEE 1394 is composed of a series of linearly connected (that is, daisy-chained) equal devices working together. It's commonly called a *peer-to-peer* configuration, and you'll encounter that term in a similar context in Chapter 11, when you read about networking. IEEE 1394 supports up to 63 devices chained together, over a maximum distance of greater than 70 meters. Each IEEE 1394 device has sufficient internal electronics to function without a computer-based controller. Two IEEE 1394 video cameras can, for example, exchange video without being anywhere near a PC. Similarly, many IEEE 1394 devices, like video cameras, can send content to an IEEE 1394 hard drive, even in the absence of a PC. Contrast this with USB devices, which don't work without the control of a root hub.

Note: You can contrast IEEE 1394 with SCSI, too, even though their topology looks similar in its simplest form. IEEE 1394 devices are all plug-and-play, and are all *hot-swappable*. This means that you can add or remove IEEE 1394 devices from the chain at any time, without powering-down the device you're removing or other devices in the chain. This is not true of SCSI. When multiple devices are connected to a PC, each device's unique identifier is created on-the-fly, as devices are detected, added, or removed from the chain, SCSI devices must be assigned an identifier in hardware, usually through the use of a physical push-button switch or dial, and this identifier cannot change while power is applied. If two SCSI devices with the same ID are added to the chain, the entire system will not work. In contrast, IEEE 1394 devices will simply accept a new identifier each time they are interconnected, so that "identity crises" never occur. (You also learned about termination when you discussed SCSI; no such issue exists for IEEE 1394.)

More Alike than Different

All of the previous notwithstanding, USB and IEEE 1394 have more in common than they have differences. They handle bandwidth intelligently. That is, they will enable any device to have as much data transfer capacity as it needs—up to a point. But they will reserve enough of their overall capacity to enable them to service the other devices on the bus. A device, such as a video camera, that simply must have all its data passed down the bus because it has nowhere to store it, can request and be assured of receiving enough data transfer capacity to keep the images flowing down the wires. Other devices that can afford to wait might be forced to do so, but their data transfer needs will ultimately be accommodated.

Also, both buses enable devices to talk to one another, without having to involve the host in the conversation. That is, after the host has assigned addresses to everyone on the bus, any device can ask the host about who else is on the cable, and subsequently can address messages directly to a desired target device. The host might be carrying on a separate conversation at the same time with some other device.

The commands supported on these buses are modeled after those used in the SCSI-3 standard, which you read about in Chapter 7, "Disks and PC Data Storage". Indeed, IEEE 1394 was explicitly modeled on SCSI-3, and certainly the lessons learned in the SCSI development have influenced how USB's commands work, too.

And, as I've already mentioned, both buses enable power to travel alongside data. Each cable design includes power wires separate from the data wires. That enables devices such as the keyboard or mouse, which need only a little bit of power, to get power from the data cable.

What if You Need Lots of Serial Ports?

Despite the flexibility of the newer USB and IEEE 1394 serial ports, there might be times when you need to use traditional serial connections—and you might need more than your PC has available. Unfortunately, the design of PC serial ports (and parallel ports, for that matter) imposes some severe limits on how many ports you can have. You can have up to four serial ports, although finding enough free system resources to support all of them is often a problem. How do you get past these limits if you really need more ports?

The Option Card Solution

The usual solution to this need has been to fit a plug-in card with a microcontroller that can handle many (up to 64) serial ports in one of the ISA bus slots. This board comes with a specialized software driver that runs in your PC and communicates with the on-board microcontroller to cause it to route messages to and from all these ports appropriately.

Essentially, that solution involves putting another computer inside your PC. A number of vendors have made cards with this sort of functionality for many years.

The LAN Solution

An alternative solution to a shortage of printer or serial ports on a PC is to hook it to one or more other computers. Connect them through a local area network (LAN) of some sort and then use all the serial (or parallel) ports you want as long as you use no more than four serial and three parallel ports per PC on the network. You'll learn more about LANs in Chapter 11.

The Ultimate Solution

You have another way to solve this problem. You can now purchase USB devices that provide support for several traditional (DB9 or DB25) serial ports. You plug your legacy devices into the USB device, and the USB host takes care of making everything work. This approach enables you to attach up to 127 of these USB devices (including those hubs) and thereby get all of them to work using no more resources than a single device attached to a serial port.

Summary

In this chapter, you've read about the serial port and its many flavors. The traditional serial port has been around from the beginning, and only now, 20 years after the creation of the PC, is its mastery waning with the ubiquity of USB and the phenomenal growth of IEEE 1394. In the next chapter, you'll read about the "old PC port," the parallel port, traditionally used to connect a PC to a printer. After that, you'll continue your exploration of PC connectivity by diving in to the *real* topic of the times: networking.

Parallel Ports

In Chapter 9, you read about one of the two oldest types of ports on the PC—one of the two oldest ways to get data into or out of your computer. This short chapter continues that exploration by giving you an in-depth look at the *parallel port*, the second of those two "old fogies."

The Faster Path

When IBM introduced the PC, it offered an optional printer interface card and printer—a parallel interface. Such an interface uses a separate wire for each bit of the data being sent to the printer. Thus, an entire byte can go to the printer at once. (Recall from the previous chapter that a serial connection moves one bit at a time, sequentially, until all of the bits in a byte have been transferred.) This approach enabled IBM's printer adapter to pump characters to the printer much faster than was possible with a traditional serial communications link.

People now use parallel ports on PCs that have far greater capability than the original IBM PC printer port—but all of them are built on the same foundation. We first explain that original port in some detail, and then discuss the several ways in which that original design has been elaborated and improved upon in recent years. These later versions are part of an industry standard called IEEE 1284-1994.

The Original IBM PC Unidirectional Printer Port

Clearly, if you're going to move eight bits at a time, you need at least eight wires (one for each bit in a byte) for a parallel port. In fact, many more than just eight wires are needed for this type of parallel-data-transfer interface. In the original IBM printer port design, 17 wires are used for signals plus several more ground wires. Why so many signal lines? The printer port sends data to the printer by first putting the data bits on the eight data lines. Then, it sends a signal on another line to tell the printer that the byte is ready to go. The printer then reads that byte and, after it has finished, sends back an *acknowledge* signal on yet another wire to the PC. This tells the printer port that it's okay to prepare the next byte for transmission. Because of this tightly interlocked handshaking protocol, the printer port can send data to the printer just as fast as the printer can accept it (and it won't send it any faster than that).

Five status wires enabled the printer to ask the PC to wait if it was busy processing the data it has already received. They also allowed the printer to tell the PC when it was out of paper or when some error (such as a paper jam) had occurred. Four control wires enable the PC to send commands to the printer, to tell it, for example, to reset itself or to move to the top of the next page.

Bidirectional Printer Ports

The intent of the original IBM PC printer port was simply to pump data to a printer. Soon it became clear that there were times when it was highly desirable for the parallel port to be capable of receiving data as well as sending it out. These times would support interactive communication between a PC and its printer and would also make possible entirely new uses of the parallel port itself—such as for data backup. IBM included this capability in its next generation of computer, the PC/AT, publicizing it aggressively when it introduced the PS/2 line later. In fact, there are two ways to make a standard PC parallel port function in reverse. The method used by IBM in the PS/2 computers is to modify the circuitry so the data wires can be driven either by the port or by the peripheral device to which it is attached. This method enables data input rates that are comparable to those achievable on data output.

Enhanced Printer Ports

Despite the limitations of parallel ports, they have been the fastest standard I/O hardware available on just about any PC. For this reason, people have developed lots of additional uses for them beyond printing.

There are two classes of use for parallel ports that go beyond its original purpose. Because these two kinds of use involve different patterns of data transmission, they have led to the development of two improved standards for parallel ports.

One of these classes involves a fairly well balanced use of both input and output, with data transfers in both directions needing to go as fast as possible. These uses include hooking up a CD-ROM drive, external hard drive, Zip drive, or other mass storage medium to the parallel port. This strategy always runs slower than if these devices were directly connected to the PC's general-purpose I/O bus using a plug-in card with interface circuitry that has been optimized for that use. On the other hand, it was convenient to be able to hook up such an external peripheral device to a PC parallel port, perhaps load a driver program off a disk, and then use the device. For one example, this makes backups a breeze, and it also enables easy transfers of rather substantial amounts of data between PCs that are otherwise not connected. These two possibilities help explain why the Zip drive was such a smashing success.

The other class of extended use is for printers that must get much more data for each page they print than just the characters you might see there. (In particular, this describes page printers, especially those printing large bitmapped graphic images.) These printers might occasionally need to send data back to the PC—sometimes even a fairly substantial amount of data—but those occasions are fairly rare compared to the times they need huge amounts of data shipped out to them. You'll read about the various types of printers at length in Chapter 14, "Printers."

The two new designs for "super parallel ports" were combined with the two methods for using standard parallel port hardware bidirectionally into an official standard published by the Institute for Electrical and Electronic Engineers (IEEE) in 1994. They named this the IEEE 1284-1994 standard.

Any peripheral device that conforms to the IEEE 1284 standard connected to a parallel port that also conforms to that standard is capable of operating in any of five modes. Of these, the two new, "advanced" modes are referred to as EPP (Enhanced Parallel Port) and ECP (Extended Capability Port).

EPP Ports

The EPP super parallel port design was developed to focus on supporting fast data transfers, both in and out of the PC, and also enable easy switching between the two directions of data flow.

After the parallel port hardware has been configured through the PC's BIOS to operate in EPP mode, additional system resources are allocated to the port. (Technically, these are CPU port addresses, which you'll read about in Chapter 15, "Motherboard Magic.") With these additional resources available, the port can function at a much faster rate than otherwise. The main reason it can do this is because the hardware of the parallel port has been enhanced so it is now able to handle all the separate steps for a single byte transfer by itself, freeing the PC's CPU for other work. The CPU can execute just one command and the byte transfer happens. The CPU doesn't have to be involved in the handshaking described earlier.

Right away this means that EPP data transfers can go as much as four times faster than traditional ("compatibility mode") transfers. In some circumstances, the port's top speed can be boosted to nearly 2Mbps. This is over 10 times faster than the compatibility mode.

ECP Ports

Hewlett-Packard and Microsoft were interested in a different kind of parallel port improvement. They focused on speeding up huge block data transfer rates and lowering the demands on the software driver and CPU even below those needed for EPP operation. The result of their work is now a part of the IEEE 1284 standard, and is called the Extended Capability Port (ECP).

Among other features, ECP includes a provision for data compression using run length encoding (RLE). This is a data compression scheme that is particularly effective if the data being sent has long runs of a single value. For example, if you are sending a bitmapped image of a page and there are big areas of white, RLE will just say, in effect, "Okay now, white goes here for such-and-such a distance." That is much more efficient than sending a single white "spaces" over and over again. Combining this efficiency improvement with the high data rates (comparable to EPP) yields the highest possible data transfer rates for large blocks of data all going in one direction.

ECP is a more loosely coupled mode of operation than any of the other 1284 modes. Unlike standard compatibility mode and EPP operation, the handshaking is not tightly interlocked. This makes the ECP protocol suitable for devices with large data buffers at either end of the connection.

ECP can accomplish data transfers in either direction, but the channel must be "turned around" before it can be used in a direction opposite to its most recent use. This turnaround requires several steps of time-consuming negotiation. Perhaps the greatest delay involved is that the turnaround cannot happen until any in-progress transfer is completed. This restriction makes the ECP port mode less suitable than EPP for external mass storage devices in which reads and writes are often intermixed.

ECP also has the drawback that it requires the exclusive use of certain system resources (technically, a *DMA channel*). If you have resources to spare, go ahead and work in ECP mode. But if you are running short of DMA channels (as seems pretty often to be the case in a modern, fully equipped PC), you might have to forgo the advantages of ECP and fall back to EPP operation instead.

Finally, there is one other way in which an ECP port can be used that goes well beyond what is possible with a parallel port used in any other mode. This involves the use of *ECP channels*. In effect, ECP channels are subdevices within the peripheral device attached to the ECP port. By designating different data transfers as going to or from different channels, it is possible to communicate with one channel over an ECP port even when another channel in that same peripheral device is busy. For example, in a combined ECP printer/fax/scanner device, it is possible to receive a fax while the printer was busy printing a separate document.

The Physical Side of Things

You've read in the previous chapter and this one about how physically different the various serial ports and cables and the parallel ports and cables are. Actually *seeing* the differences might prove to be both informative and entertaining.

Figure 10.1 shows first what you also saw back in Figure 9.4—the different conductors used by the new USB and IEEE 1394 serial connections. The right side of the figure shows the main type of IEEE 1284 connector, on the same physical scale.

This is a standard DB25 connector. It is the IEEE 1284 connection that usually mates with the port found on your PC or notebook computer. It consists of a D-shaped frame (hence the name) with 25 individual pins inside.

What you normally find at the opposite end of a cable with a DB25 connector is a Centronics connector, named after the printer manufacturer that first implemented it. The Centronics connection doesn't attach to a printer or other device by use of the screw-in terminals you see on the DB25. Instead, wire braces come off of the connected device and interlock with the brackets on each side of the Centronics connector. Should either of the wire braces fail—a sadly common occurrence—the weight of the parallel cable can easily pull the connector away from the printer or other device, severing the connection and forcing users into troubleshooting mode. The connector itself consists of 36 conductors.

In an attempt to reduce the size of the Centronics connection, the Mini-Centronics connector was developed. There's no question that it is smaller than its big brother, but, after all is said, it's not really *that* much smaller. It, too, has 36 conductors, and has the added benefit of latching and locking on to devices. The locking mechanism is a definite improvement over the old Centronics wire braces, but it is still less reliable than it might be, and, when it fails, the weight of the parallel cable again can pull the connector off of its host device.

FIGURE 10.1
A comparison of IEEE 1394, USB, and IEEE 1284 connectors.

Even as the size of the connectors themselves is reduced, there is a limit to how densely you can pack the 18-plus wires and shielding that run the length of the various parallel cables. There's also a limit to how thin you can make those wires and have them remain reliable and strong. Because these many parallel wires are inherent to the very nature of a parallel interface, it is their weight and bulk that are the interface's greatest drawback.

"Printer" Ports Aren't Just for Printers

As noted before, what were first called printer ports (and now are referred to more generically as parallel ports) are often used for much more than just shoveling data out to a printer. Indeed, these ports became one of the most-used means of connecting external peripherals to a PC.

It's so easy to get a peripheral to work when it is plugged into a PC's parallel port that, for many years, this was the preferred way to hook up almost any device for which you want a substantial data transfer rate, as long as you are willing to put up with suboptimal data transfer rates.

Printer Ports Aren't Even for Printers Anymore

Today, however, that circumstance is changing radically, through the development of the USB and IEEE 1394 connections and networking. Most of the high-speed devices that could be connected using parallel ports—external backup tape drives, hard disks, image scanners, and so on—can now be connected using one of the two new serial ports. Indeed, the vast majority of printers today come equipped with USB connectivity. Even a high-end Xerox Phaser 860 color laser printer can connect to a PC in a matter of seconds using a standard USB port and cable. The reason for this change is two-fold.

First, as easy as it was, relatively speaking, to connect external devices to a PC using the parallel port—and, indeed, even to chain multiple devices in a long line—it was obviously necessary to make these connections using parallel cables, which are thick, heavy, not especially bendable, and very expensive, foot-for-foot. It wasn't uncommon to have a small external tape drive that was tilted up off its feet by the weight of the parallel cable hanging off its back.

Second, and far more serious, is that, although the functionality for IEEE 1284 (parallel) ports is very well established and standardized, there was no standardization among the devices that used the port. In some circumstances, you might need every device connected to the port powered-on in order to make use of any of them. This might mean that, to print a brief memo, you might need to have your tape drive, scanner, and external hard disk all turned on. For the most part, if these sorts of devices weren't powered-on at the time the PC was started, turning them on later wouldn't make their port daisy-chaining work, so you'd have to shut down your entire PC, power-up all the devices, and then reboot—just to print a one-page memo.

Similarly, there was never any guarantee that a command that might tell your scanner to scan an image would not interfere with another device. It wasn't uncommon to hear your tape drive re-initialize itself every time you tried to print through it, and it wasn't unheard of for a tape drive to not pass data on until that initialization was complete. Obviously, this isn't how it was *supposed* to work, but with no industry standard regulating the combined functionality of different devices, this is sometimes what you got. We know more than a handful of people who purchased tape drives, only to return them after finding they were simply incompatible with the printer they also needed to chain off their PC's parallel port.

As you read in the previous chapter, USB and IEEE 1394 change all of that. Both of these serial buses use delightfully lightweight cables that can bend willy-nilly and won't drag hardware right off your desk. They both also use highly reliable device addressing schemes that guarantee that equipment—a tape drive, a hard drive, a mouse—entirely ignores any commands that are not meant for it alone. USB and IEEE 1394 devices are entirely hot-swappable, so there's never a concern of powering-up devices before you start your PC or needing every USB device you own to be on so that you can move digital pictures from your camera.

The combination of devices—including printers—moving to these new serial busses and moving to directly networked connections (which you'll read about in the next chapter) is really sounding what seems to be the death-toll for the parallel port. As manufacturers continue to work to reduce the size of PCs, especially mobile PCs, the huge parallel port is increasingly impractical. We can't foresee the future, of course, but don't be surprised if you start to see PCs and printers that sport all of the new serial connectivity, but have no parallel port in sight.

Summary

This brief chapter has acquainted you with the fundamental issues that surround the history, development, and ongoing changes of the familiar "printer port"—the IEEE 1284 parallel port. Although modifications and improvements continue to be made to the port and its connectors, the idea of a parallel port has, itself, gradually moved towards being a casualty of progress. With the high-speed performance of USB 2.0 and IEEE 1394, there is really nothing that a parallel connection can do that these smaller, lighter serial connections can't provide—and, really, provide better. It might be some time before we see the parallel port actually vanish, and it might be that some unforeseen development makes it suddenly invaluable, but the greatest likelihood is that parallel ports will prove to be among the dinosaurs that "evolve" out of existence.

Networking—Wired and Wireless

If you asked any number of industry experts about the most important issue in computing today, I have little doubt that every one of them would give you an answer that centered on the notion of connectivity. Connectivity between computers, between users, between companies, and between governments. And connectivity means networking.

So, what exactly is networking? And why, just because industry experts say it's important, should you care? What can network technology actually do for you or your business? How can you get the most out of it? And, isn't it terribly expensive?

What Is Networking?

If you put together everything that everyone is talking about when they talk about computer networking, you can boil it all down to this: networking is everything that goes into connecting computers together. In practice, that means everything from electronic cards to hundreds of millions of miles of wire, to satellites, to cell phones, to chat, to security measures, and so on. This chapter explains the critical aspects of networking. By the time you're finished, you'll have a really solid understanding of networking, what it takes to put it all together, and how it can impact your own productivity. Then, when you're ready, you can turn to Section III of this book and check out Chapter 19, "Advanced Networking," where we'll talk at length about the underpinnings and foundation of network technologies, about TCP/IP, which is the networking standard (known as a *protocol*—more about protocols in a moment) that makes the Internet of today work. That chapter will also show you IPv6, the successor to TCP/IP, and introduce you to *Internet II* (just when you thought it was safe to go back on the Web).

In this chapter, we'll break networking down in much the same way that Chapter 1 broke down the entire PC—with the same goal of making transparent what seems like a "black box" to a lot people. If you ask people about networking, many will tell you that it's complicated, confusing, frustrating, annoying, and absolutely vital to everything their business does. And all of that can be true. But a little understanding goes a long way in the networking world, and we think you'll find that "complicated, and confusing" won't be your personal view of networks when you're finished reading here. So, after a brief introduction about why everyone is so "big" on networking, we'll look at the different types of networks, and then break those down into their composite parts and different configurations. After that, you'll be introduced to the different ways to implement networking in your home or small-to-medium-sized business. We'll end this chapter with a discussion of the new and very exciting wireless networking technologies.

Why Network?

It's a somewhat sad but true fact of business social life that, if you don't network, you don't get anywhere. Today, the same is even more true—although less sad—of computing. Networking makes it possible for people inside your business (or home) to work with each other, and to work seamlessly with people in other locations or other businesses. It has brought the world right into the homes and offices of people with limited mobility or limited funds. You'll probably never turn to your partner, give a tight hug and sigh "At least we have Paris," waxing nostalgic over an online excursion the two of you took through the sounds, images, and video of France online, but, really, it's infinitely better than never seeing Paris at all.

Networked resources haven't replaced books, per se, but why purchase an encyclopedia when the latest edition—complete with illustrations, video of famous speeches, and events, and more—is at your fingertips? Why spend thousands of dollars to buy a laser printer for every office in your corporation when entire workgroups of users can share a single printer? Indeed, why buy two expensive color pre-press systems when you can print to the networked pre-press computer in the office across town—or across the country? Why spend the thousands of dollars it costs to annually subscribe to the various multi-volume industrial-supplier catalogs, when you can access them over a network, sharing them with co-workers throughout your company while you teleconference? Indeed, why spend the time, money, and risk of business flight when teleconferencing will put them across the table from you? Why struggle and fail, trying to make a go of it as an entrepreneur in a tiny town when you can enjoy living in the same town, but become a millionaire, selling your goods or services to the entire world, online?

Teleconferencing, sharing resources, sharing and collaborating on documents, expanding your personal library to include millions of books, musical recordings, video—and, really, expanding your personal world to include the *entire* world—that's why people use networking. It lets you do all of the things we mentioned, and far more. Networking has made it possible for people to do anything remotely that we used to have to do together.

Well, almost anything.

Not that networking is a source of isolation. It's not. The point isn't to avoid human contact, but to think about contact in an entirely new way, on entirely new levels. I have friends with whom I live and work, here in Southern California. I also have close friends

who live in Chicago and Durham. One of my two best friends often lives in Paris—
networking made it possible for us to talk everyday, at little or no cost. Networking
makes it possible for film crews in Europe to send dailies to Hollywood. It also allows
talented, struggling musicians in New Dehli to share their art, get a recording contract,
and actually make a career of what they love to do. Networking can make the "American
dream" available to the citizens of the entire world who want it.

What's Wrong with Networking?

Of course, networking isn't a golden egg available to anyone. Nor is it the silver bullet
for all a person's, business's, or people's ills. Just as networking shrinks the world and
brings desirable things closer, so, too, does it bring danger closer, in many ways.
Networking has organized and brought people together whom it would have been far
better to leave isolated and individual. It's also made it possible for bored, malicious
children to get in the way of the honest business of multi-national corporations and
individuals, alike. In the early rush to embrace networking, resources were placed
online—and made available to *anyone*—that probably should have had their availability
regulated, if not actually restricted.

In a lighter vein, networking isn't the best solution to certain problems, either. If you
have two computers at home, and you need to move small files between then on rare
occasions, it probably doesn't make sense to take the time and spend the money to network
those PCs together. And if you have information that is *highly* confidential, moving that
data across a network might not be the smartest and most secure way to get it from point
A to point B. And if you only need to conduct business meetings with remote co-workers
or suppliers on rare occasions, the cost of installing—or even renting—teleconferencing
hardware is outrageous, relative to the cost of, perhaps, two or three plane tickets each year.

So it's not a great idea to just run out to the computer store and purchase networking
hardware and software willy-nilly. The decision to network is one that you should give
some consideration. Before you can do that, you need to know the facts. And that's what
we're here for. So, let's take a look at networking from the outside in, and build your
understanding.

Types of Networks

In fact, there are many different types of networks out there, depending on just what you
mean by "types." Regardless of all the competing hardware and software out there, there
are really three basic types of networks, into which all of the paraphernalia fit. On the
simplest level, these types describe the number of people served by the network. The
types are LANs, WANs, and what we'll call "the Net," consisting of both the Internet and
intranets. If these terms are unfamiliar to you now, don't worry. They won't be in just a
few pages.

LANs

LANs are probably the most common and most familiar type of network in the world, today. The name is an acronym for *local area network*. As that implies, LANs are designed to serve the needs of users in a limited physical area. That doesn't mean that LANs can only service a small number of people; hundreds of people can be connected together on a LAN, or on a series of LANs, which are themselves connected. This will be touched on more later.

A LAN doesn't require the use of any specific type or brand of hardware or cable—and wireless LANs are the latest, greatest thing, as you'll soon read. You can have a LAN between Windows PCs, or between Apple Macintosh computers, or you can have both types of computers sharing the same LAN with an SGI graphics workstation. Setting up a LAN doesn't mean that you have to use a particular networking protocol, either. The only thing it really means when someone refers to a LAN is that, in general, the computers and resources that are connected are closer than about 3000 feet away from each other.

> **Technical Note:** Recall from a few moments ago that a *protocol* is simply an organized, standard way of doing something. A "network protocol" is just a collection of rules, ways, and means that people adopt to make it possible for them to connect to and interact with each other electronically.

LANs make it possible for everyone in an office to share a single printer. They can share files, work on projects together, send instant messages, and even e-mail, with the right software. A LAN is, truly, just a small version of a big network. What you lose with a LAN is almost exclusively distance.

Peer-to-Peer LANs

Now, having already said there are three main types of networks, we need to clarify that and mention that there are two ways of setting up a LAN. One of these ways is also used in larger networks, as you'll see in a moment. Of the two kinds of LANs, the type most often used in a home office or small business, is called a *peer-to-peer* LAN.

Your peers, of course, are people like you—people who share interests, experiences, or characteristics. It's in this last sense that we talk about peers on a network. Your network peers are computers like yours. They're probably computers under people's desks or kitchen tables that are used regularly for the main tasks of computing: Peers are used for writing term papers, preparing your tax return, or blowing the smithereens out of the Dramboozles from Karthrax IV. In a peer-to-peer network, your computer has resources that you share with others on the network, and their PCs have shared resources you can access too. If you want to access a file on Drew's computer, you connect to it, and his PC is responsible for providing the processor power and time needed to retrieve the file from his hard disk and send it to you. (Your PC uses processor time in this, too, but the big point here is that retrieving a file from Drew impacts Drew's computer. If the file is very large, Drew might notice that his PC slows down, or might even appear to lock up while the file is being sent.)

You might have a laser printer that is directly connected to your desktop PC, which is shared on a peer-to-peer LAN. If someone else wants to print, his or her PC uses the shared connection to spool the document to your PC. You then bear the burden of processing that file and sending it to the printer. If you're running a lot of programs at the same time and are running out of memory, you might not have the resources available to print. In that situation, your co-worker can't print anything until you shut down some applications, and your PC might even crash when it tries (and fails) to print.

What's fantastic about peer-to-peer networks, however, is that (at least today) it doesn't take any special or dedicated software to control the network. Nor does it require expensive extra hardware. If you have two PCs running Windows 9x or later, with an available internal slot or with a USB connector, for about $30.00 ($10 dollars for each of two network interface cards and $10 dollars for 20 feet of cable), you have everything you need to set up a peer-to-peer LAN. The steps that go into actually connecting and configuring a network are, unfortunately, beyond the scope of what we can cover here, but, these days, it's not too complicated. Some of the wireless systems you'll read about near the end of this chapter are truly plug-and-play. They come with software that does most the work for you. We say "most" of the work because in almost all cases you, as the individual user, will still need to configure your system's security settings, providing passwords to people you consider authorized users, and so forth.

Client/Server

The other kind of LAN—and, just so you know, the technical term for "kind" of LAN is *architecture*—so, the other architecture that's used to put together a LAN is called *client/server*. In this framework, all the desktop computers on the network are still each other's peers, but they're not directly connected to each other, and the resources they all share are usually (although not always) managed very differently.

The best way for me to describe client/server—although certainly not an analogy of our own invention—is to say that client/server works a lot like a restaurant. When you go out to eat, you're a *client* of the restaurant you select, and the restaurant, as a whole, is responsible for serving your needs—that is, it's your *server*. If you want something from the kitchen, you don't get up and get it yourself, nor do you go and talk to the cook, pull him or her away from someone else's meal, and ask the cook to prepare your desert.

Instead, you make use of the resources the restaurant has available for getting you fed. You tell a server what you want, and the server goes back to the kitchen (where all the food is kept), where your request is handled in one of two ways. If what you need is quick to provide or an emergency, someone in the kitchen grabs it and sends it back to you, via the wait staff. If you're just ordering your meal, unless you're someone very important, your order goes into the kitchen queue, and you get fed, basically, when it's your turn. If you want something that isn't available, the service staff is responsible for telling you. They might even offer an alternative, or tell you how long the wait will be.

That's really *exactly* how client/server networking works. Although everyone on the network—the clients—might have files on their own hard disks, the files and resources that are really intended for sharing are connected to a standalone computer, the *server*. When you want to use a shared resource, you contact the server across the network, and it is responsible for locating the resource, checking its availability, checking that you have permission to access or use that resource, and then sending it to you. If a resource is offline or busy, the server will send you a message letting you know about the situation. If the server itself is busy, your request will go into a queue, which the server will process at the first opportunity. The exception to this relies on something called *priority*. If your PC is designated as "an important person," the server will, when possible, delay serving the needs of others to take care of you first.

In order to make this all possible, extra hardware and software are required. You might use the same $10 network interface card in each PC on the network, but you have to designate one computer as the server, and leave it to serve the network's needs. In order to do that efficiently, it needs some special characteristics of its own, which amount to huge amounts of memory, huge amounts of hard disk storage, and the fastest possible processor (or even multiple processors). Although this sort of equipment cannot yet be classified as inexpensive, it's by no means as expensive as it recently was, and it's not necessarily any more costly to buy a small server than it is to buy a reasonably powerful desktop PC.

The real benefit of client/server computing is that resources are controlled centrally, and they can be backed-up and archived easily. The server bears the burden of processing the network's requests, so your own productivity isn't impacted (as with a peer-to-peer network) when Lori wants to work on the huge presentation that you champion. The client/server architecture is also better suited—far better suited—to accommodating the needs of many users (clients). It's possible to set up a big peer-to-peer network, but it's a nightmare to manage. Centralized resources, such as those provided by the client/server architecture, are reasonable to administer, and generally prove to be more practical on many levels. For these reasons, and many others, client/server is the architecture that's used for any network of any real size or complexity. With enough users vying for resources, the payback in productivity usually covers the initial investment in very little time.

WANs

WANs, or *wide area networks*, are usually, naturally enough, big LANs. A LAN is also composed of a large network that connects multiple LANs together. WANs are a lot less common today than they once were, because the ubiquity of the Internet has made available other, far less costly, solutions to far-range networking. In the past, however, it was common for a company to rent a dedicated, high-performance telephone line from the phone company (at astronomical cost) and use that to connect, say, the network in its Toledo office with the network in its Manhattan office. WANs were also used to connect smaller distances, such as from one building in a corporate park to another, which were just too far for a LAN setup.

Linking Two LANs

Often, people want to link several LANs together. This is most often done to let any computer on any of the linked LANs exchange data with any other computer on those linked LANs. In many instances, two LANs can be connected simply by installing a cable between them. Then you'd have simply one larger LAN.

But directly connecting multiple LANs is often not a good idea. It's better to link the two LANs by an interLAN connection box (called a *router* or *bridge*) of some sort.

This is particularly vital if you want to link two networks that use different physical setups, or *topologies*. (More on what topologies are in just a moment.) When linking dissimilar topologies, you absolutely must have some type of router to pass signals from one LAN to the other.

A *router* is, in fact, a computer running a suitable program to examine each arriving data packet's *envelope* (the portion of the packet that specifies who sent it and where it is s upposed to go) and then send it on its way to the correct attached LAN. This routing function effectively isolates a connected network from packet traffic that is not addressed to it, providing a considerable efficiency savings. A router might also translate the physical protocol (the method of handling data packets). A *bridge* connects two networks with the same topologies (which contrasts a bridge with a router's capability to connect networks with differing topologies).

One reason for using a router between two LANs rather than directly connecting them is that the router can isolate data traffic on one LAN from that on the other. That is, any data packets that originate on one LAN and are addressed to another computer on the same LAN have no reason to leave that LAN.

If you can keep all the "local" packets within each LAN and only exchange the "long-distance" packets, you will keep the data traffic congestion on each LAN to the minimum possible value. For this reason, one of the most common prescriptions for speeding up a sluggish LAN is to break it into segments and connect them to one another with routers.

To factor into this equation, however, you need to pick a "routable" protocol to run on your network. (Just in case you don't remember the jargon, a *protocol* is simply a way of achieving some task that all participants agree to follow. A networking protocol is, then, an agreed-upon way of moving data across the network from place to place.) The simplest networking protocol of all—NetBEUI—has the smallest overhead due to a number of reasons, key of which is its inability to be routed. The following list shows common protocols in alphabetic order and their ability to be routed:

Protocol	Routable	Protocol	Routable
CLNP	Yes	PPTP	Yes
DECnet	Yes	SLIP	Yes
DLC	No	SNA	Yes
IPX/SPX	Yes	SNAP	Yes
LAT	No	TCP/IP	Yes
NetBEUI	No	X.25	Yes
PPP	Yes	XNS protocols	Yes

The inability to be routed substantially restricts the size of a network you can grow to by preventing the protocol from being transmitted across a router. Nonroutable protocols can be used only on a LAN or across a bridge or router. Bridges and routers are discussed in more detail in Chapter 19.

Intranets and the Internet

The third major type of network is the Internet and its private sub-type, the intranet. Entire books have been written on the Internet, and that's certainly more than we can cover here. Bottom line: The Internet isn't actually any *one* thing. It's a collection of LANs and WANs from all over the world, connected together in a way that facilitates the sharing of resources. There is no central server that runs the Internet and accommodates the needs of everyone connected to the network. There are systems called *core routers* that manage the flow of data throughout the Internet. But the *servers* on the Internet are legion, each accommodating the needs of a group of network customers or a given business or corporation. (In fact, any given business or entity might have *many* servers, which provide different resources.)

Access to the Internet is made available through *ISPs*, or *Internet Service Providers*, which can be telephone companies, or can be other companies, like AOL or Surfcity Networks, in Huntington Beach, CA. Subscribing to the services of an ISP usually provides a *user account* through which you can receive and send electronic mail (e-mail) and that identifies you as a paying customer, entitled to use the service. That, in turn, puts the Web and all manner of resources at your fingertips.

Intranets are just private connections that are maintained across the same physical connections used by the greater Internet. Companies use intranets to make internal resources—databases, reference libraries, e-mail, and so on—available to employees within the company's walls, but none of the Intranet content is available to the greater world of Internet users. (Intranet content *can* be made available to authorized users on the Internet, but it requires special configurations, hardware, and user authentication.)

The advantage of an intranet is that it allows companies to use the many tools available for creating and managing Internet content on a more local scale. There's no need to devise your own way to display content internally if you can simply create Web pages and make them accessible through any Web browser, like Microsoft Internet Explorer, on any PC inside the intranet.

You don't have to purchase a custom e-mail solution, either. Just set up an e-mail server as if it were for use across the Internet, but configure it for internal, intranet access only. This saves additional investment in training time, both within the IS departments and throughout the company. Any employee who can play an online game at home knows enough to work with their company's intranet resources. (And the same configurations and hardware that establish and protect an intranet from outside invasion can limit internal access to the Internet. Don't want employees searching for inappropriate content while they're using your network? Just shut them out.)

ISPs

What type of ISP you choose really depends on what you need and what you want. If you want specialized content all gathered together and organized for you, and you don't mind being one of millions of customers all waiting for help when something goes wrong, using a large ISP might make the most sense. Of course, when malicious individuals attempt to impair Internet traffic, they usually focus on these huge ISPs, because they can then "enjoy" ruining someone's day on an unprecedented scale. For myself, I've found that a carefully selected local ISP is the way to go. I've used the same ISP for a number of years. Although they are small, relative to ISPs like AOL or GTE, they provide me with fast, courteous, and *reliable* service whenever I need it, whatever the problem. I never wait on hold with 13,214 others for an underpaid part-time "business computing" student to try to take care of the question as quickly as possible by providing the most convenient, often wrong, answer. My ISP, Surfcity Networks, actually knows who I am, so I don't waste my time explaining that I understand PCs better than checking to see that the network is plugged in, and so forth. They don't super-simplify their answers, so I get less information than I need, and they are willing to take the time to make sure I do understand. Essentially, they *care*.

The Parts of a Network

You've learned about the three main types of networks. In this section, you'll get acquainted with the parts that make up any network.

Many Topologies

For the world of LANs, *topology* refers to how each PC is connected to all the others in a logical sense, without regard to the physical arrangement that accomplishes this connectivity.

Figure 11.1 shows several common LAN topologies. In each case, we have also indicated one or more of the common network cabling schemes that use that topology. The USB LAN is in fact designed for connecting peripheral devices to a host computer rather than for connecting computers to one another.

FIGURE **11.1**

Some common LAN topologies.

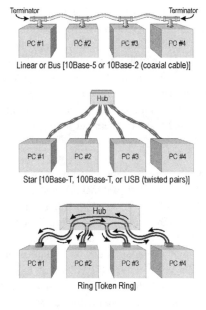

Linear or Bus [10Base-5 or 10Base-2 (coaxial cable)]

Star [10Base-T, 100Base-T, or USB (twisted pairs)]

Ring [Token Ring]

Bus or Linear Networks

The top portion of Figure 11.1 shows what is sometimes referred to as a *bus topology*. The most common examples of this scheme are the antiquated 10Base-2 and 10Base-5 wiring schemes used in the earliest Ethernet LAN installations. (We'll explain Ethernet in a moment.) 10Base-2 used a thin, flexible coaxial cable. The nickname for this wiring scheme was *thinnet*. The 10Base-5 wiring scheme also used coaxial cable, but this was thicker, and more rigid. This made setting up such a network complex, but the larger cable could carry the network signals much farther than the thinnet cable.

> **Note:** Incidentally, the "10Base" part of these names refers to the maximum data transfer rate of the network (10Mbps). The numbers 2 and 5 are numeric designations that identify the length and type of wire used for the connections. 10Base-2, for instance, is good for approximately 200 meters on coaxial cabling. Likewise, 10Base-5 is good for approximately 500 meters on thick cabling.

Figure 11.1 shows the taps (connections) for each PC as BNC T-connectors attached to the PCs (or actually to the network interface adapters installed in those PCs), with the cable made up of short pieces going from PC to PC. At each end of the bus, the open side of the T-connector was capped with a *terminator*. This is a device that connected an appropriate resistor between the center conductor and the shield of the coaxial cable. The result was that any electric signals arriving at the terminator were fully absorbed; none of those signals were reflected back along the bus. (Reflected signals are sometimes confused with genuine data, which is why terminators were required.)

Star Networks

The middle portion of Figure 11.1 shows a *star network*. This is the most common way to connect multiple devices to a central one. Here, you see a *hub* (a device that serves as a centralized connection point) connected to each PC by a set of twisted-pair cables (so called because they house two pairs of wires that are twisted around each other). These wires (essentially high-grade telephone lines) are inexpensive to manufacture and very easy to install.

It's important to realize that although the hub is shown as if it were at the center of the network, in a star wiring scheme, all the signals that arrive at the hub on any cable are immediately sent back out on all the other cables. This means that the hub is a data interchange point. In effect, all the cables are simply wired in parallel, and thus any signal put onto one shows up on all. That makes this logically very much like the bus topology shown at the top of this figure.

Star topologies are used for many kinds of networks (meaning different cable designs as well as different methods for using those cables). This variety of Ethernet is usually called 100Base-T, and each cable (referred to as Category 5 or better cable) has four unshielded twisted pairs (UTP) of copper wires. As with 10Base-2 and 10Base-5, the name 100Base-T implies a maximum Ethernet data rate—in this case, 100Mbps. The same wiring scheme, if it is of a high-enough quality, can also be used to carry 1000Mbps (1Gbps), also known as gigabit Ethernet.

Modified Star Networks

A simple star network has every node connected directly to the hub. But in many cases it is more practical to have a multilayer, modified star network. In this form of networking (which is used for Ethernet and USB networks), each device that is connected to the hub can be a controlled device, another hub, or a combination of the two. The wiring in these networks can, thus, be a multiple branched tree rather than a pure star network in which every device connects back to the root hub, such as is used in medium- and large-sized Ethernet LANs.

Ring Networks

The bottom portion of Figure 11.1 shows a *ring network*. The most common example of this, now dated technology, was a token-ring network. Here, you see a MAU (Multistation Access Unit) and a cable from it to each of the PCs. MAUs are analogous to hubs, which were mentioned just a moment ago. In a token-ring network, data must go into each PC and back out again, through the MAU and on to the next PC, until the data has made a complete circuit around the ring.

The MAU just connects the outbound data path from each PC to the inbound path to the next PC; it does nothing to the data as it goes by. In fact, you can build a ring network without a MAU just by connecting each PC to both its neighbors. The reasons to use a MAU (besides the fact that the token-ring specification calls for one) are that it makes setting up the network easier and the network itself more robust. MAUs automatically disconnect PCs that are powered off, and in certain types of network card failures.

The token-ring specification is also frequently referred to by its name of the defining standard organization's name, IEEE 802.5. (You'll encounter the IEEE 802 designation again later in this chapter when you read about the new, wireless networking.)

Network Interface Cards and Devices (NICs)

In order to connect an individual or other device to a network, it's necessary to have somewhere to actually plug in the network cable. This "somewhere" is usually provided by either a port on the PC's motherboard, itself, a card that is plugged into one of the motherboard's expansion slots, or a USB device. These cards and devices are responsible for establishing communication between the PC and the network as a whole—whether it's a peer-to-peer network or a client/server environment. They provide a way for each device on the network to identify itself, so that as data is moved, it knows where to go. This identity is provided through the NIC's own MAC address (Media Access Control). This code is permanently wired into each NIC and functions like an unchangeable serial number.

Network cards and devices also take responsibility for correcting errors that occur as data is moved over the network. The NIC's own processor will automatically resend data that a receiving NIC indicates was not transmitted correctly. Naturally enough, the NIC also makes this evaluation, so, in many instances, your PC's CPU doesn't have to be bothered.

Network Cabling

The cabling used to connect networks is, in the main, made up of glorified telephone cable. It's called *UTP*, or Unshielded Twisted Pair. In the standard network cable, there are eight wires that are twisted together in pairs—hence the name. Network cabling is rated in terms of its maximum performance (that is, the highest speed at which it operates reliably and the longest distance over which a single length of it can be used) by the term *Category*. Currently, *Category 5* is the most commonly used network cabling, providing reliable connections of up to 328 feet per segment. Newest is *Category 7*, which is not yet a standard at the time of this writing but which, if accepted as a standard, will provide very high-speed connectivity through more bandwidth.

Ethernet—The Everywhere Network

The wiring plan alone doesn't fully define a network. The next level of definition specifies how those wires will be used. In particular, it specifies the signals the wires will carry and how they are to be interpreted. All networks organize data into packets. The purpose of this packaging is to enclose each message in an envelope that describes (at a minimum) who is sending it and who is supposed to be receiving it. This envelope is then passed across the network to its intended recipient. The job of making all that happens falls on the shoulders of the network protocol.

I mentioned the notion of a network protocol several pages back. A *network protocol* is a standardized method of sharing resources. The beauty of using network protocols is that you can buy any hardware and any software you like and have guaranteed compatibility with any other hardware and software, as long as anyone you want to connect to is using the same network protocol.

Today, two protocols reign supreme. TCP/IP is the protocol of the Internet—in fact, it's an entire stack of related protocols that facilitate sharing different kinds of resources over the Internet or an intranet. You'll read about TCP/IP in depth in Chapter 19.

The other protocol that's used practically everywhere goes by the generic name of Ethernet. Every computer on an Ethernet network has an address. In some networks, each computer is assigned an address by some central arbiter or based on which segment of the network it is hooked to. Ethernet is different in this regard. We mentioned that every network interface card ever made has its own, unique, MAC Address. That is the address that Ethernet uses to route each packet of information that is sent to that device.

The cleverest concept in the Ethernet protocol is its means of resolving an inevitable conflict that will arise whenever you have multiple "speakers" that can each start speaking at any time. On a network, this means that their signals will be mixed, and the result is a muddled mess that none of the "listeners" can understand.

A part of the Ethernet protocol, known as carrier sense, Multiple Access with Collision Detection (CSMA/CD) takes care of this problem. Here's how it works. First, an Ethernet NIC will listen to the signals on the network to be sure no one other device is, if you will, "talking." Then, if it wants to speak, the device will start doing so.

If some other device starts speaking while the first device is waiting, the first device won't begin speaking until the network is quiet once more. If, by chance, two devices start at virtually the same instant, both will soon realize it and they'll each stop and wait a random (and therefore probably different) amount of time before they attempt to speak once more.

In polite conversation, people take turns and wait to speak. This works fine, unless too many people suddenly decide to express themselves. Similarly, on an Ethernet, if there isn't too much data "traffic," it all works splendidly. But if the network is almost always busy, some devices might find it hard to "get a word in edgewise." Because the Ethernet NIC sends out data only when it has some message to convey, the size limit of an Ethernet network is set by how much total conversational content the entire collection of connected computers wants to exchange, rather than the number of connected PCs. In other words, it doesn't matter as much how many PCs are connected as it does how much data those PCs need to transfer across the network. Consider a box of books that you need to ship across the country. The cost of shipping doesn't depend on how many books you put in the box, but on their total weight. One giant book costs as much as many little paperbacks. A few PCs with huge demands for moving data will impact the network much more than several PCs that only move a few KB per day.

Ethernet has some other excellent qualities. In Ethernet's 10Base-T (or 100Base-T or 1000Base-T) star configurations, the failure of any one of the connected computers or of any one segment of cable will not cause the network as a whole to fail (unlike a bus topology, which relies on the successful operation of each PC along its length). Only the one computer that failed (or whose cable to the hub failed) will drop off the network. Of course, a hub failure would bring down the entire network, but because the hub is just a simple connection block, failure is a rare event. Support of a star network is simpler, too, because it's most likely that the one computer that isn't working is the only one with a problem. In a hub topology, you need to work through each connected PC until you find the problem.

Some other aspects of Ethernet's popularity have to do with the fact that its competition had major drawbacks. ArcNet preceded Ethernet into general usage but was much slower. IBM's token ring was just that—IBM's. Their proprietary attitude did much to discourage its adoption. What probably pushed Ethernet over the top of the acceptance curve was its general adoption by operators of minicomputer systems running under the Unix operating system.

The main drawback to Ethernet, however rarely it manifests itself, is that there is no guarantee that every PC will "get its turn to talk" as soon as it needs to. Thus, a super-congested Ethernet can simply fail to convey some of the messages it is supposed to convey in time to satisfy the timeout requirements of the software attempting to use it. This prompts more attempts to send the data, which ultimately result in a broadcast storm. This makes it essential that the next higher level of organization of the communication over the network uses some form of error detection and correction. (That job is done by any modern operating system that supports Ethernet.)

Note: A *broadcast storm* is a sudden flood of messages that clogs your transmission medium, reaching or nearing 100 percent of your bandwidth. A broadcast storm slows down the network and can even prevent clients from using it. The most common cause of a storm is a malfunctioning NIC, but high levels of traffic can also cause a storm.

If your network ever suffers a broadcast storm, the best tool for troubleshooting is a *protocol analyzer* that can identify the source of the storm. If it turns out to be a faulty NIC, you must immediately remove that machine from the network until the card is changed. However, if you determine that the problem is due to high utilization, you need to use switches, bridges, or routers to segment your network.

Alternative Small Networks

Although the vast majority of networks in homes and small business today use a combination of the Ethernet protocol and Ethernet-compatible hardware, there are alternatives. In fact, one alternative is TCP/IP, which can function on the same hardware as Ethernet with operating system support (which any major operating system today provides).

Other alternatives are the different proprietary networks. The idea driving these is straightforward: An Ethernet network is still too complex for home and small business users to set up. Additionally, Ethernet hardware is so popular that nobody is making any serious profit from it anymore. So, it would be great if there were a system that would trade an outrageous cost (relative to Ethernet) for simplicity.

We don't personally believe that Ethernet is too hard for the average home or small business user to set up, and for that reason we aren't mentioning any names. We think that it *might* be true that there are some people who would rather spend money than spend time. For them, these proprietary network solutions are just the ticket.

Although each of these different systems uses a proprietary protocol for moving content and sharing resources, and each requires the purchase of proprietary hardware for each PC on the network, they have broadened their marketing appeal through their use of common and familiar connections. Specifically, some of these networks can connect via the USB bus that's now built into every PC made. Even though it's possible to establish a small network via USB by using software and regular USB cables (no expensive hardware necessary) the hardware systems come with software that it supposed to make installing and troubleshooting them far easier.

Other proprietary networks make use of your home's existing telephone wiring to share resources. Their manufacturers say that you can establish a network from any point in your home (or office) to some other "any point" by connecting their hardware to your PCs, and then just plugging in to a wall jack. The performance of this kind of network is considerably slower than that of Ethernet 100Base-T—in fact, they function at about 1/10th the speed, at about six to eight times the cost, per PC. That performance depends on the quality of your home's telephone wiring, too. If you commonly hear static when you talk on the phone, you'll probably need to rewire your home before you get anything that even approaches ideal performance out of this kind of system.

Incidentally, this kind of network doesn't interfere with your use of the telephone. You can use both at the same time, because the network's digital data moves through different bandwidth than does your spoken conversation. (For more on this idea, take a look at Chapter 12's discussion of ADSL.)

Wireless Networking

The very latest in networking is networks without wires. The term "wireless" has turned into something of a buzzword meaning two different things. The sense in which we aren't talking about "wireless" here is the sense that refers to using your cellular telephone to send and receive e-mail or using your handheld or palm-sized PC to access content on the Web from wherever you happen to be at the time.

What we are talking about is, simply, networks of the type we've been discussing, but that use transmitters and receivers instead of wires. There are, roughly speaking, three main types of wireless networking available today: proprietary solutions, IEEE 802.11b networks, and Bluetooth networks.

Proprietary Wireless Networking

We feel much the same about proprietary wireless networking that we do about its wired proprietary cousins. By definition, using a proprietary system locks you in to that hardware, and might limit your ability to expand or upgrade the network later. But that isn't necessarily a bad thing, if you aren't worried about those issues. Proprietary wireless networks perform, in general, at about 1/50th the maximum speed of a standard, wired Ethernet 100BaseT system, and they cost about six to eight times what 100BaseT hardware can cost. With the advent of 802.11b (and the alleged coming of 802.11a) and Bluetooth, proprietary systems are rapidly disappearing—as they should be.

IEEE 802.11b (and 802.11a) Wireless Networking

The original name is something of a mouthful, so IEEE 802.11b wireless networking has recently been renamed "Wi-Fi," which stands for *Wireless Fidelity*. This is a protocol, like Ethernet (which, you might recall, is also known as IEEE 802.3), and any hardware manufactured in compliance with this protocol should be able to freely share resources with any other Wi-Fi certified hardware. Wi-Fi networks cost about 10-20 times what Ethernet 100Base-T hardware does, and that soars to 40-60 times, if you want to be able to share your Internet connection across the wireless network (a capability inherent in any Windows 98 and later-based Ethernet configuration). You can move data at a maximum rate of 11Mbps, around 1/10th the performance of 100BaseT Ethernet, but more than fast enough to serve up any Internet connection and share it with others on the network. Wi-Fi hardware connects to your PC using the USB port or through a CardBUS slot (for notebook PCs).

IEEE 802.11a is yet another standard that provides a faster connection than Wi-Fi (about five times faster) but that isn't compatible with Wi-Fi hardware. 802.11a hardware isn't yet available, but already industry insiders have expressed some concern. First of all, wireless networking is what marketers call "a hot technology." Unfortunately, it's a rather expensive, hot technology. The sorts of users who adopt new products (like today's 802.11b Wi-Fi products) early on might be loathe to repeat their entire investment a year from now, when 802.11a products are available. Additionally, 802.11a hardware uses four times the power to transmit than Wi-Fi uses—so your notebook computer's battery will definitely feel the drain. Finally, although it can move data faster, 802.11a can't transmit over the same distances as Wi-Fi. Because your home office and your bedroom aren't likely to change how far apart they are, that might not seem like an important factor to you, but it can be. The capability to transmit over distance closely relates to the capability to transmit through solids—like through the walls, ceilings, and floors of your house. The Wi-Fi connection that works fine today might be a connection you can't successfully or reliably establish with 802.11a.

Security Risks of 802.11b and 802.11a

These two wireless networking technologies also pose significant risks to the security of the data and resources available across them. When you install them, it's not mandatory to set up any kind of password. If you don't, anyone with 802.11b hardware in range of your network can access the data on your network. And do you really want your neighbor reading the complaint letter you wrote to the homeowner's association about his loud parties?

Bluetooth Wireless Networking

Bluetooth is a competing standard to 802.11b, which, like 802.11b, is only just emerging at the time of this writing. It also uses wireless transmissions (radio frequencies, or RF) to move data across the network, but the manufacturers of Bluetooth-compatible hardware are focusing on a somewhat different market. Bluetooth only operates at about 1/10th the speed of Wi-Fi (that's 1/1000th the speed of Ethernet 100BaseT) and it only moves data over a distance of 10 meters or less. But, it's hoped, Bluetooth will find its way not so much into your home as into every aspect of your life. Imagine that you have your bank accounts connected to a Bluetooth-enabled wireless phone. You can make purchases at Bluetooth stores by "beaming" money from your phone to the store's Bluetooth cash registers. You can pay for your meal at a Bluetooth restaurant in the same way—possibly even beam your waiter's tip directly to her bank account.

The question that remains at the time of this writing is, "Does anybody really want that?" *Wired* magazine identified Bluetooth some time ago as #1 on one of its monthly "Hype" lists. Whole Web sites dedicated to Bluetooth haven't been updated for the past year because, well, there's not been much to say. It's going to take time before the answers are entirely clear, but we won't be surprised if, when the world *has* embraced wireless technology, nobody remembers the name Bluetooth.

Summary

Networking is a huge topic, but it's just one part of the total capability of your PC. We've looked at the basics of networking in this chapter. You've seen that there are basically three kinds of networks—LANs, WANs, and the Internet—and that they are, in turn, supported by two different architectures: peer-to-peer or client/server. You've learned about protocols and seen that they regulate how information moves across the network—it's not the NIC hardware or the cabling that determines what type of network you have.

We ended with a glimpse at the latest news in networking—wireless networks. Whether that news proves to be a turning point in computing, or the latest, greatest vaporware, only time will tell.

Related to networking—very closely related, because connecting to the Internet is one of the main things people are using networking for these days—is the topic of the next chapter. Modems and, even more, broadband connections are how we're reaching out from the networks in our homes to the networks of the world.

Modems and Broadband

The previous chapter talked about bridging between isolated PCs, bringing them together in a networked environment to make a better use of available resources—including people. In this chapter, we will look at different ways of connecting PCs to other computers: with modems and other technologies that bridge gaps even bigger—sometimes far bigger— than those bridged by LANs.

In the last chapter, we mentioned that one old type of network connection was a permanent wired link between a mainframe computer and its many terminals. Modems are commonly used to make transient links (wired or wireless) between PCs and other computers. You probably already knew that. Now let's look into exactly what modems are and how they work.

Reaching Out

Motorola used the phrase "Reach out and byte someone" in its advertisements for modems. We've always rather enjoyed this clever play on the slogan used by the telephone company to promote voice calls: "Reach out and touch someone," because modems are the most common way to send bytes of digital data over a normal voice-grade telephone line.

A modem is an interface device. It connects your PC to a telephone line (or in some cases, to a number of other types of connection systems).

The name *modem* stands for *mo*dulator and *dem*odulator (once capitalized in the acronym MODEM, but now more commonly written simply as modem) because a modem has both a modulator and a demodulator built into it. What, you ask, are those? A good question. And why are they needed? That's another good question.

"Yodeling" PCs

Most PCs sold today include a modem, usually built-in but sometimes externally attached to it. When you use the modem to connect your PC over the phone line to a distant computer, you are likely to hear many strange sounds coming from the modem's speaker. You might have wondered what they are and why you need them.

The sound you hear when your modem begins a remote connection session is essentially your modem "talking" to another modem at the other end of the phone line. The different strange tones normally go on for several seconds, and then the modem shuts up. Actually, the modems continue singing their strange song. You just don't hear them because normally the communication software application that operates the modem tells it to turn on its loudspeaker until the two modems have successfully "negotiated" a connection, and then to shut off its speaker for the duration of the call.

This enables you to hear that your modem is trying to connect—and if you understand what you are hearing you can tell how successful the attempt is. After the connection is established properly, by shutting off its speaker, the modem saves you from having to listen to all that screeching the entire time your PC is connected.

Why Modems Are Needed

The standard telephone network was designed for one purpose: carrying human voices in spoken conversation. It's now being used for a totally different purpose: carrying lots of digital data back and forth. The important characteristics of these two types of communication are very different. The telephone network functions acceptably for human voices; it simply cannot carry digital data as such.

> **Note:** You'll read later in this chapter about technologies that allow your telephone line to do what has never before been possible—technologies like DSL. For the time being, let's see how modems have made digital communication possible on the normal kind of telephone line—called a Plain Old Telephone Service (POTS) line—which simply can't "speak" digitally.

Why can't ordinary phone lines carry digital data directly? Human voices are sounds that cover a range of frequencies from roughly 30Hz up to about 10KHz. That is, we make vibrations in the air that fluctuate no more often than 10,000 times per second and no less than around 30 times per second. Any sounds outside that range are inaudible to most of us. We don't even need to hear all those frequencies in order to understand what someone else is saying.

To save money, and for other technical reasons, the phone companies have limited the bandwidth—that is, they have limited the usable frequencies—of their normal voice-grade lines to a maximum of about 3KHz and a minimum of around 100Hz. This lets enough of the sounds we make get through for most normal conversational purposes. (You'll read later in this chapter about what the remainder of a telephone line's bandwidth can provide.)

You might be wondering if the fact that a human voice produces an analog (that is, a continuously variable) pressure wave as opposed to a digital signal is somehow important here. It's not. As we will explain in a moment, modems create tones (including sometimes very unmelodious tones) to represent the digital bits you actually want to transmit.

Digital data is sent over a phone line in a serial manner. That is, the data is sent one bit at a time. You can have either synchronous or asynchronous connections. A *synchronous connection* just pumps out the bits of each byte one after another, all in synchrony with a regular pulse produced by the internal computer clock. An *asynchronous connection* sends out all the bits for one byte, plus some start and stop bits to tell the receiving computer where the data begins and ends (and perhaps a parity bit to verify its accuracy), and then waits a little while before sending out the next byte. There is no necessary connection between the computer clocks at the two ends of the link.

> **Technical Note:** Traditionally in PC applications, modems operated asynchronously. The exception to that today is if you are running an error-correcting protocol such as V.42; then the modems switch to a synchronous data transfer mode. This change is invisible to the user, but it results in some improvement in data throughput (as well as a lot more assurance that your data made it across the link okay, thanks to the error-correcting aspects of the protocol).
>
> The use of error correction requires that the modems on both ends of a connection support the same protocol (V.42). Fortunately, this compatibility is now ubiquitous.

The limit on the frequencies at the low end is no problem for people talking, but it is as much of a problem as the limit on the high end for the transmission of digital data. To see this, consider a digital message that consists of 1 million 0 bits followed by a 1 bit, and then another million 0 bits, and then a million 1 bits. If this message were converted into voltages in the synchronous serial manner, it would be a constant voltage almost all the time. This long time between voltage alternations constitutes a very low frequency signal and is equivalent to silence. Nothing would be happening on the link, and the receiving end wouldn't know whether it was still connected or not.

One solution to this problem is simple enough: Use the data values to modulate a tone signal. The tone for a 0 bit is different from the tone for a 1 bit, but at all times there is some tone being sounded. That way, there is never any silence: the signal is always present for the receiver to hear.

This is how early modems worked. But this strategy doesn't allow pushing the maximum number of bits over the phone line in each second. Essentially, it uses only a few of the many frequencies the phone line is capable of carrying. By using more of those frequencies simultaneously, we can send many more bits each second—which is what high-speed modems do today.

In order to understand just how a modern modem does this trick, we'll first distinguish between two terms that are commonly confused: *bits-per-second* (bps) and *baud*.

What's a Baud?

In honor of Emile Baudot, a 19th-century French telegrapher who invented an early transmission code, we use the term *baud* as the unit of speed in data communications—or misuse it, as is more often the case in writings and conversation about PC communications.

Technically, one baud means one symbol per second. A symbol can represent any number of bits—the maximum number for a particular connection is set by the characteristics of the transmission medium (wires, optical fiber, radio waves, string between two tin cans, and so on) and of the transmitting and receiving devices. At very low data rates, each symbol is normally used to represent a single bit.

In antiquated, slow modems (carrying data at 300bps or fewer), each bit was represented by one of two tones, one for a 0 and the other for a 1. At higher data rates, more tones are used. If you used 512 tones, you could encode nine bits simultaneously. (In fact, instead of using 512 discrete frequencies, modern modems use fewer individual frequencies but delay some of those signals by a variable fraction of a cycle, which phase modulates them, in order to convey more information.)

A 300-baud modem uses one symbol per bit, so the baud rate and the bits per second are both 300. At higher data rates, the common practice is to send signals that stand for one of a larger set of possibilities. That means that each "symbol" carries several bits of information. If there are 512 possible symbols (signal states), each one carries nine bits of information. This is what was done in a V.34 (28.8Kbps maximum data rate) modem when it operated at its maximum data rate. In this case, the actual baud number is only one-ninth of the number of bits per second. Thus, a 28.8Kbps modem is actually just a 3.2 kilobaud modem. But you'll never see that in an advertisement for these products—it just doesn't sound impressive enough!

When Modems Talk to Each Other and to Their PCs at Different Rates

For the most part, PC modems use a serial port to connect to the PC itself. (The few parallel port modems were an ancient exception. Even the very few USB modems, which don't plug into a traditional serial port, are using a version of serial data transmission—as the full name for USB, Universal Serial Bus, suggests.)

The serial port hardware does two necessary things. First, it converts the data from parallel bytes into a serial stream of single bits. It also adds some very necessary start, stop, and parity bits. The modem converts these bits into tones (called "modulating the carrier with data") and sends them over the phone line.

At the other end must be a similar modem that will convert the tones back into digital bit levels (called "demodulating the data"), and the serial port at that end will convert those bit streams back into parallel bytes. (Refer to Chapter 9, "Serial Ports," for a detailed discussion of how serial ports and USB work.)

Note: Internal modems are built on plug-in cards you put into a slot inside your PC's system unit, usually on the PCI bus. They include all the hardware for a serial port on the plug-in card. External modems attach to a serial port either on your PC's motherboard or on some other plug-in card. Internal modems draw their operating power from the PC's power supply. External modems use a separate power supply.

There are some important implications in these differences. If you put an internal modem into a PC, you must be sure that its serial port doesn't conflict with one that is already in the machine. Conversely, if you want to use an external modem, you must be sure your PC has a serial port available for it, and it must be one that will work fast enough to support the modem. A serial port that supports data rates of 57.6Kbps or greater is preferred for 28.8Kbps modems, and a minimum of 115Kbps is required for 56Kbps modems.

Why must the serial port be able to work more than twice as fast as the modem? There are several reasons. First and often, the controlling fact is that data compression is often used in modem protocols. That means that more bytes of data are sent from the PC to the modem than the modem sends out to the receiving modem at the other end. When receiving data, the decompression the modem does means it must be able to send more bytes to the PC than came across the telephone line. Second, there is some operational overhead because the PC must sometimes send commands to the modem. These are additional bytes that must flow over the PC-to-modem link that don't also have to travel over the telephone line.

What's important in all this is that the modem-to-PC link must not be a bottleneck. If the modem is ever frustrated in sending its data to the PC, some of the incoming data will be lost. So, we routinely set the serial port speed to at least twice the modem's maximum data rate—and even sometimes *that* turns out to be not quite good enough.

Most external modems have a feature that internal modems do not—a feature that has endeared them to computer support people for years—they have status lights on their front panels. These are wonderfully informative about the modem's activity and state and provide extremely useful troubleshooting information.

An external modem's separate power supply provides another nice feature: you can turn off an external modem without turning off your PC. This is sometimes useful to reset a modem that gets "hung." It also can be a security precaution, because if the modem is turned off there is no way anyone can "reach into your PC" via the phone line.

The data serializing and the bit-stream modulation are two distinct processes. The first process (serializing the outbound data) occurs in the serial port, as does the deserializing of the inbound data. The second process (modulating the outbound bit stream onto the carrier and demodulating the inbound tones into an inbound bit stream) occurs in the modem.

These two processes might not run at the same rate. Often, we run the connection from our PCs to our modems at one rate, and run the modems at a different rate. In order for this to work, the modem and the serial port must be able to buffer some of the information, and also to tell one another when they are ready to send or receive additional data. All modern modems have those features.

Sometimes modems "compress" the data they send over the phone line. That is, they look at a stream of bits and determine a way to encode that information more compactly (getting rid of redundancy) by using a standard method. The receiving modem uses the inverse of that method to reconstruct the original bit stream. This lets the modem send more data across the link (more bits per second) than the physical baud rate it is using would seem to allow. But it can do this only if the data it is receiving has redundancy in it. The general concept of data compression was covered in Chapter 7, "Disks and PC Data Storage".

In order to keep a data compression modem busy—that is, to keep it sending "compressed" information across the link at the maximum speed of which it is capable—you must send the data to it from the PC somewhat faster than it will be going across the modem-to-modem link. You also must take the received data away from the modem just as fast. Again, this is why we commonly set our serial port data rate anywhere from two to four times faster than the nominal maximum bits-per-second data rate the modem can support over the telephone line.

> **Note:** You also should be aware that often, when you see a message from your communications software about how fast you are "connected," the speed refers to the number of bits per second (even if it called the "baud") at which data is flowing between your PC and your modem—it doesn't mean the speed at which the modem is sending and receiving bits on the phone line. So, if the connect speed you see reported seems to be faster than you thought your modem could go, that's the reason.

A factor that bears on this is the wide use of the V.34 modulation, which negotiates the actual data transmission rate independent of PC interaction and does so continuously during transmission. Although this is an excellent line noise compensation feature, it leaves the computer able to report only the data rate at which it communicates with the modem.

Standards—The More the Merrier!

In order for a modem link to work, the modems at both ends of the link must be compatible. That is, they must use the same methods for modulating and demodulating the carrier signal, compressing the data, and so on.

Over time, modems have changed a lot. Even simple, inexpensive modems today are vastly more capable than the best (and most expensive) ones were just a few years ago. This means that many modem standards exist.

Initially in the United States, the Bell Telephone Laboratories defined all the standards used for modems. Now, however, the usual standards are set by an international standards organization. For many years, the relevant organization was the CCITT (International Telegraph and Telephone Consultative Committee—the letters are reversed because the organization's actual name is *en Français*). That role has now been taken over by the International Telecommunications Union (ITU), which is an organization that serves in an advisory capacity to the United Nations. Thus, the new designations for modem standards carry the prefix ITU-T (instead of CCITT). The CCITT's successor organization, the ITU, is headquartered in Geneva, Switzerland. As a consequence of this heritage, virtually all ITU documents have been written originally in French and later translated to English with the occasional interesting results.

The ITU-T standards don't just spring up out of nothing. Usually, one company comes up with what it regards as a "breakthrough" that lets it make a modem that outperforms previous ones. That company will, of course, market the idea and try to get everyone to buy its modems. But this wonderful new feature will work only when one of these special modems is talking to another of the same kind of modem. Eventually, the manufacturer decides that it is in its interest to get a formal international standard to cover this new feature. Then (if it *is* a commercially successful feature) every modem maker will put it into their products, and at that point all of those modems, no matter what brand, will be able to use that new feature when talking to any of the other modems that include support for it. That is when an international standard develops. (Sometimes the process works in a slightly different manner, too: companies get together to discuss new technology *before* any product premieres with that new capability in place. Agreements are made and market segments divided-up, and then the international standard is announced with products following close behind.)

Some of the commonly used data communication standards for modems include these: V.32 for 9600bps; V.32bis for 14.4Kbps; V.34 for 28.8Kbps; V.42 for error control; V.42bis for data compression; V.FC, a proprietary version of 28.8Kbps (now superseded by V.34); MNP2-4 (various error control protocols developed by Microcom and given to the industry); MNP5 (data compression; less efficient than an alternative standard called LAPM, but both are used by V.42bis); and MNP10 (data compression optimized for cellular telephony). The best known of the ITU-T standards is V.90, which is for what are called "56Kbps" modems. (See the section later in this chapter on "Modem Speed" for a full discussion of these modems.)

Modems can also be used to send and receive faxes. When they send and receive faxes, they conform to a different set of ITU standards, bearing such monikers as V.17 for 14.4Kbps faxing and T.30, the fax protocol itself. (And, incidentally, one of the ITU standards that's only now really taking off is the ITU-TE30 standard for sending and receiving color faxes.)

A quality, modern modem will support all of the standards just listed (and probably several more). Usually, each time you go online, the software you're using will send configuration information to the modem. This sets values in a series of registers, and those values tell the modem which of those standards to support during the present call.

Even if you ask the modem to work at its maximum possible speed, it might discover that the modem at the far end isn't capable of working that fast, or that the line between them is too noisy or distorts the signals too much.

In that case, the two modems negotiate some slower speed at which they will carry on the conversation. They do this unless you (or the person at the far end) have instructed your modem (again through commanded register settings) to accept no less than some high standard. In that case, the modems will just hang up the phone whenever they run into a problem.

Similar configuration issues apply to error correction and data compression protocols. You must tell the modem to use them, and the other modem must agree to do so. (Another useful trick—if your modem refuses to connect—is to try to connect at a slower speed. If that succeeds, it's likely—although not certain—that there's nothing wrong with your modem, but you do have a noisy telephone line that's impeding the connection.)

Must you configure your modem? Probably not. Many people use communication software that is either built in to their PC's operating system or supplied by their modem manufacturer, an online service (such as America Online), or an Internet service provider. In any of these cases, that software is probably preconfigured. Note however, that these preconfigured settings are more likely to be biased toward trouble-free modem installation rather than optimal performance.

Varieties of Fancy Modems

When you go shopping for a modem, you are likely to feel overwhelmed by all the jargon and features of the various models. Because this is such a rapidly changing field, it's impossible to tell you about every one of the terms you might encounter. But we can tell you about some of the more popular and important ones.

Data, Fax, or Voice?

First, you must realize that modems frequently perform at least two and sometimes three jobs in PCs. One is data communication. This is what you use when you surf the Internet. It also is what you need to send and receive e-mail or to transfer files. The second main use is for sending and receiving faxes. A third use is for handling voice phone calls (with the help of an additional telephone handset or other equivalent hardware). A voice-capable modem can be used for simultaneous voice and data communications on a single phone line if the other modem supports this mode of operation.

A modern variation on this idea is called *Voice over IP* (VoIP) and refers to routing voice phone calls placed on ordinary (analog) telephones—with their signals converted into digital data—over the Internet to an appropriate receiving box that can convert that digital data back into analog form and deliver it to another person's normal telephone that is connected to that receiving box. This was one of those niche applications that was certain to be the "next big thing," but remains a niche application as of this writing. It is possible that within a few years almost all voice calls will be handled in this fashion instead of going over the traditional public switched telephone network (PSTN), but that seems increasingly unlikely. Certainly, VoIP is almost sure to remain a niche product until and unless it fully leaves the world of traditional modems and is embraced by broadband hardware manufacturers and service providers. Even then, current experiments in providing VoIP via broadband cable have failed in two ways. First, the quality of sound they provide leaves much to be desired. Second, and more damningly, consumers simply don't seem interested in the ability.

Knowing this, you must decide which of these tasks you want your modem to do. You don't have to buy a modem that does all three unless that is what you want. On the other hand, if all those capabilities come at an acceptable price, there's no drawback to your modem being able to do something you don't need or want it to do. Someday you might change your mind.

Most modems advertise in big type their maximum speed when used for data communication. The present standards for fax transmission don't permit sending that sort of information quite as fast as the newest and fastest data modems, so the lower fax speed is not usually mentioned on the box. Be assured that if you buy a "data and fax" modem it will support the relevant standards and will send and receive faxes at the proper speed.

One kind of data, fax, and voice modem just routes different calls to the appropriate software or hardware. That is, if this type of modem is in your PC, and if you are running the appropriate program to monitor the modem, when a fax call comes in your fax software will be launched and the fax will be received. If a data call comes in, some data communications program will be launched. For voice calls, your PC might start ringing.

Modem Speed

Analog modem speeds have pretty much peaked. The present standard best advertised speed is 56Kbps, but these modems are not quite what you probably think they are.

Older 33.6Kpbs models transferred data simultaneously in both directions at up to 33.6Kbps. This requires all the bandwidth that is commonly available on a standard (POTS) voice-grade telephone line. In fact, it requires a very good connection to get this full speed. Many times using these modems doesn't result in any faster file transfers than if you use a 28.8Kbps modem, and possibly hardly any faster than a 14.4Kbps mode.

The ITU V.90 standard "56Kbps" modems achieve their faster speed for downloading (data inbound to your PC) by receiving data faster than in the outbound direction. This uses more of the available voice line bandwidth for the high-speed direction, at some limitation to the speed in the reverse direction. Also, even at their very best, they cannot pump data across the line at the full, theoretical maximum of 56Kbps. The telephone regulatory agencies won't allow that. Thus, the actual download speed is limited to, at the very best, around 53Kbps (with line noise often limiting it to a good deal less than this).

The most common application of this lopsided data rate arrangement is for connection to the Internet. In this instance, you will usually send short strings of commands and receive large image-laden responses. But, only if you are using these beasts with an optimum quality telephone line will you get more than 33.6Kbps throughput, and then only in one direction at a time.

In fact, the only way to guarantee high-speed access to online resources is to connect via one or the other of the different broadband methods that are spreading as we speak from "metropolitan centers" to "nearly everywhere." Cable TV systems and digital satellite services have taken to providing Internet access over the connection they have respectively been using to provide homes with television programming. And the telephone companies, themselves, have jumped in to the broadband consumer market with technologies like DSL. We'll explore all of these in the remainder of this chapter.

Cable Modems

Many of the cable television companies are now in the Internet service provider (ISP) business. They usually offer a small box that splits your TV cable in two. One branch goes to your normal television cable box for tuning channels and displaying them on your television set. The other cable goes to a second box that will connect to your computer via a USB port or an Ethernet networking card. These latter boxes are commonly called "cable modems" because they perform the job of demodulating the data signal off the cable so your PC can make use of it, and modulating your PC's output so that it can be carried back on the cable.

An alternative to this method is known as "Telco Return," in which data is delivered to your PC via thecable system, but any data your PC sends—that is, anything you upload, including your requests for Web page content—is sent to the ISP via a standard modem, using the traditional telephone line. The obvious limitation of this latter approach is that your upload speed is limited to whatever level of performance you can get out of your standard modem.

Data delivery via cable modem is possible because the ISP effectively transmits a group of data streams as though it were simply another channel on the system. Any single "television channel" of this type can support up to approximately 2000 simultaneous users. Although that sounds like a huge amount of bandwidth, the reality is that, as more users log on, performance of the entire system rapidly degrades. If you are the only person in your area who is using your cable modem at 3am, you should be able to expect superb speed. On the other hand, if you're trying to surf the Web at 6pm, when everyone in your entire neighborhood is doing the same, it's possible that your actual performance might slow down to speeds you'd expect from a traditional modem over the telephone line.

Here's why. A cable company's main plant consists of a number of parts, which are located around the service area. The most important of these parts is called the *head end*, which is where the cable signal originates. From the head end, the entire analog cable signal is transmitted via fiber optic cable to regional *nodes*. At each node, the signal is demodulated off the fiber, turned from light into an electric signal, and is sent out via one of several coaxial cables, known collectively as a *cluster*. These coaxial cables carry the signal to a particular area. The advantage to this setup is that, should a regional cable fail, only the customers in that small area are impacted. (Similarly, if a node should fail, the outage is limited to only the customers served by that node.) Each customer in the area will attach to one of these large, coaxial cables via the smaller coax that comes into the home or business. This entire system is referred to as HFC—*Hybrid Fiber Coax*. A diagram of this configuration appears in Figure 12.1.

FIGURE 12.1
A typical cable modem system.

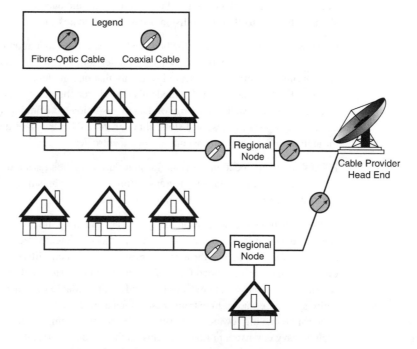

As you'd expect, the cable signal coming to your home—the "downstream" signal—is continuous, because this is required to give you television programming. The outbound, or upstream signal is another matter entirely. In order to send data from your PC out onto the cable (and, presumably, to wherever in the world you want it to ultimately go)

your cable modem has to share the available bandwidth with other cable modems. Data is sent out from your cable modem in bursts. Each burst is contained in a system time slot, and is handled in one of three ways.

Ranging slots occur periodically throughout the system and are used to keep all cable modems properly synchronized with the head end. Because the physical distance between each modem and the head end can vary greatly, and because time is required for a signal to move across that distance, ranging slots provide a clock mechanism that compensates for the variances and that defines the two other types of time slot. Ranging slots also tell individual cable modems what power they must use for transmitting so that all upstream signals arrive at the head end at the same power level. (Again, this is because signal strength degrades over distance.)

Contention slots are open for use by any modem on the system, on a first-come, first-served basis. These are normally used to allow a modem to alert the head end that it has data to transmit that requires a time slot of the third type: a reserved slot. Effectively, contention slots are the means by which the modems on the system say, "Excuse me, could I have your attention, please?" Should more than one modem attempt to transmit data at exactly the same moment, the two bursts collide and the data in them is lost. The system alerts both modems that the collision occurred and invites each to try transmitting again.

Reserved slots are assigned by the head end to a specific modem on the system. This occurs in response to a modem's request for attention, which was sent in a contention slot. During the time of the reserved slot, only that one modem can transmit. The system notifies all other modems in that modem's shared area that they cannot transmit until the reserved slot expires. The majority of data that is uploaded from individual users to the cable system is sent in reserved slots, although very short bursts of data might be allowed through the system within contention slots, themselves.

Because only one local modem can transmit during a given reserved slot, all other users in the shared area must take turns transmitting. This mechanism can dramatically impact the upstream performance of the entire local area.

At the same time, all modems on the system are watching the continuous downstream flow for data that is addressed to them. Every modem actually receives all of the data being sent to every user in the area. Your own cable modem filters out and throws away everything that isn't intended for it. If one user on the system suddenly receives a huge stream of data, that stream reduces the bandwidth available for other users' data, and the entire system degrades. In extreme cases, such as in denial-of-service attacks, so much data can be moving towards one user that the entire system effectively shuts down. With such a heavy downstream flow, modems on the system are unable to receive reserved slots from the head end. In a sense, it's a little like the head end saying, "I can hear you calling me, but I don't have time to respond." Even under normal operations, as more and more modems compete for available bandwidth, everyone's performance suffers.

Technical Note: What's in the head end? Lots of stuff, but the single most important piece of equipment for data communication is the Cable Modem Termination System, or CMTS. The CMTS acts as a connector between the entire cable system and the Internet. It is responsible for receiving the cable company's inbound Internet data stream (usually routed via a T3 or similarly high-bandwidth connection). It modulates this data stream on the cable signal by transmitting it into the frequencies reserved for several cable television "channels," at anything from 50 to 860MHz. (It also demodulates the upstream transmissions from the system's cable modems by receiving signals across those channels.)

The CMTS also creates the time slots that every modem on the system synchs to, and that every modem uses to transmit data upstream. As modems log on to the system, they search for the digital downstream signal from the CMTS. Once the signal is found, the modems listen for the CMTS to transmit an identifying packet that indicates the digital stream is data, and not a digital television signal. If that packet doesn't arrive in a period of time, the modem goes back to searching for additional digital signals. When that identifier is finally found, the modem locks on to that signal and begins listening for additional configuration information from the CMTS. This information consists of, among other things, the "channel" on which the modem should continue listening for actual data, the "channel" on which it can establish its upstream, return path, and how much data fits in the system's contention slots. All of that handled, the modem uses one of those contention slots to let the CMTS know it's now ready to actually work with the data in the downstream. The modem then watches for ranging slots, so that it can synchronize its clock and power levels with the entire system.

When the modem and the CMTS are communicating reliably, the CMTS authenticates the modem as a valid system user, and provides it with an IP address via DHCP.

The CMTS is also responsible for dynamically compensating for power fluctuations so that connected modems stay connected.

Keeping It Purely Digital

The POTS voice-grade telephone lines that you probably use in your home, and might be using in your office as well, are analog communication channels. A *wire pair*—two copper wires, separately insulated and normally twisted together in a loose helix—carries electrical signals in an unbroken local loop from the telephone company's central office to your telephones, fax machines, or modems, and back. As you've read, for these lines to carry digital data, it has traditionally been necessary to modulate that data into an audible form that can be carried through this loop.

All major phone companies have now converted their central offices (CO) and long-distance lines from analog to digital. This means that the analog signals sent from your home are turned into true digital signals when they reach the CO. Thus, when you use a POTS line for digital communication, the signals will almost certainly be converted back and forth between analog and digital forms more than twice. This takes time, introduces errors, limits transmission potential, and only strengthens the case for switching to a purely digital approach. There are many purely digital approaches available, each of which operates at its own rate, and comes with its own costs. Table 12.1 shows a variety of the more popular approaches and their respective performance (with an old analog standard at the bottom for comparison). In the remainder of this chapter, we'll take a look at a select few of these.

Table 12.1 Connections and Their Performance

Connection Type	Maximum Transfer Rate	Transfer Time for 1GB
OC3072	160.0 Gbps	0.05 seconds
OC192	10.0 Gbps	0.80 seconds
OC48	2.5 Gbps	3.00 seconds
OC3	0.156 Gbps	51.00 seconds
T3	0.045 Gbps	178.00 seconds
T1/DSL 1.5	0.00154 Gbps	5208.00 seconds
DSL 640k	0.00064 Gbps	14060.00 seconds
56K	0.00005 Gbps	139500.00 seconds

Just to give you a more common frame of reference, 5208 seconds is roughly one and a half hours; 139500 seconds is 38 hours, 45 minutes. At the time of this writing, you can count the number of organizations that need the performance of OC3072 on your fingers, but new high-speed digital approaches to moving data continue to out-perform all that have come before, and the need for speed seems to be growing almost as fast. Nevertheless, at their astronomical cost, these have a fringe appeal at best. Let's examine the more down-to-earth digital approaches that you'll definitely encounter, and not just hear about in "gee whiz!" magazine articles.

The Many Flavors of DSL

Of the purely digital approaches that telephone companies have begun to offer in the last few years, one stands out for its value. In fact, there are several flavors of this approach available, but they all fall under the general name of DSL (*Digital Subscriber Line*). DSL services are, collectively, a way of transmitting a purely digital signal on top of the regular analog telephone signal, so that the same physical wires can be simultaneously used for data and voice. The varieties differ, primarily, in their bandwidth—that is, the biggest difference between them is how fast each can be in each direction of data flow. Although the intricacies of DSL technology are extremely technical and beyond the scope of this book—indeed, entire sets of books have been dedicated to *really* explaining how it all works—let's take a higher-level look at DSL and its various flavors.

ADSL

The oldest form of DSL, the most widely utilized, and the only form that has become a fully open standard is called ADSL, or *Asymmetrical Digital Subscriber Line*. ADSL was first developed in the research lab in 1989, but only in 1998 did it become commercially available, and only in 2000 did it really begin to become widely affordable. ADSL was made possible because the frequency of signals on a POTS line has traditionally been filtered to cut out anything over 4KHz (with a rolling-off of the signal through 20KHz). This filtering left a tremendous amount of bandwidth unused and available. ADSL layers a digital signal on top of the analog voice signal, using frequencies from 25KHz through 1.1MHz. Because the two signals use exclusively different frequencies, they do not interfere with each other and, so, can coexist.

A box called a *DSL modem* connects to the line at both the user's end and the telephone company's end—within the telephone company's closest switching station. The modems divide the available digital bandwidth into an upstream and a downstream channel, and are responsible for moving data across the line. At the user's end, the DSL modem connects to a PC or PCs via an Ethernet or Fast Ethernet LAN connection. PCs that are networked together through a hub can all simultaneously use the single DSL connection as if they were directly connected to the DSL modem. Of course, doing so reduces the performance of the connection on each machine somewhat, but, unlike cable modem service, DSL performance will not suffer if everyone in your neighborhood has DSL and uses it at the same time. (DSL performance will drop if a given ISP's users are demanding more traffic than the ISP can handle, but this is a factor of the ISP, not of DSL service as a class.)

One limitation of ADSL is that it requires the user to be located within a maximum distance of 18,000 feet to the telephone company's nearest digital switching station.

The word "asymmetrical" in ADSL's name indicates that data moves at a different speed in each direction. That is, the upstream and downstream data flow at different rates, upstream always being significantly slower than downstream. The justification for this is simple: much of the time, users connecting to the Internet will be retrieving files or surfing Web pages. When you request a Web page, it takes *much* less data to make that request than it does to fill it. Web page requests consist largely of "This is who I am, this is where I am, and this is what I want," whereas the Web pages themselves contain images, sound, and other large elements. It's reasonable, then, to send those requests much more slowly than they are filled, because there's so much less data to send. In the case of ADSL, the downstream "pipe" can flow data at speeds of eight megabits per second (8mbps), whereas the upstream flow tops out at speeds approaching only 1mbps. One important factor of ADSL is that service providers do not universally guarantee actual performance. Some do; others promise a "range" within which your mileage, as they say, can vary.

Varieties of ADSL also exist. Until recently, the most highly promoted (which is not to say the most popular or most promising) of these was known as G.Lite, or, more properly, ITU standard G.992.2. Considerably slower in performance than full-rate ADSL, G.Lite never quite overcame its obstacles. Its primary appeal was that it was supposed to be fully installable by the user, requiring no visit from the telephone company to implement. (Full-rate ADSL once required the installation of filters outside the home and, usually, the use of a microfilter plugged into the user's wall jacks. ADSL technology has dramatically improved, however, and external filters are no longer necessary in many installations.)

G.Lite was also supposed to be able to provide DSL service to customers who are too far away from the telephone company switching station to receive ADSL. In practice, however, G.Lite constantly interfered with the voice calls whose wires it shared, and telephone companies had to roll trucks, install filters, and provide microfilters to make the worst of the interference disappear. In short, the appeal of G.Lite has proved—as of this writing—mostly smoke and mirrors. Proponents swear that the technology isn't yet dead, but industry consultants have already been indicating their view that, although they won't say so, G.Lite has proved to be too "lite" to satisfy.

SDSL and HDSL

SDSL, or Symmetric Digital Subscriber Line, is in general, more expensive than ADSL, but offers certain appealing features to business users. Primary among these, as the name suggests, is a guaranteed performance both downstream and upstream. Although asymmetric DSL provides a downstream path (that is, a path for downloading data to the user) that can be many times faster than its upstream (that is, uploading from the user) path, SDSL clocks along in both directions at a fixed rate—up to 1.5Mbps. Because of this uniformity, SDSL is a much better way of connecting a Web site to the Internet than is ADSL. SDSL also offers a lower cost than the faster HDSL, which we'll discuss in a moment. Why does uniform performance imply better suitability for Web site hosting? The average user downloads far, far more data *from* the Internet than he or she uploads *to* it. In the case of a Web site, however, this isn't the case. Every time the average user downloads something from the Web, the site that hosts that data is naturally uploading it to the user. SDSL speed is maintained in both directions so that the subscriber can provide acceptable Web performance to its customers while simultaneously benefiting from DSL's high-speed downstream potential. (Of course, Web hosting isn't the only reason why companies select SDSL, but it is the reason the average person is most likely to encounter.)

HDSL, or high-speed DSL, provides symmetrical performance, as does SDSL, but at a fixed 1.5Mbps transfer speed. HDSL is being implemented widely as a replacement of the older T1 service that many companies have been using for years (and which you'll read about below). The advantages of HDSL over T1 are numerous. HDSL can provide duplex transmission—that is data can be moved upstream and downstream simultaneously—which T1 connections cannot do. For a variety of technical reasons, HDSL lines are also far less temperamental than are T1 lines, requiring no special equipment for line conditioning or filtering, no repeaters to keep the signal strong as it moves over the copper wires, and HDSL signals can travel up to 12,000 feet from point to point—twice as far as T1.

Integrated Services Digital Network (ISDN)

An older way of stepping from analog to digital is to use an ISDN (Integrated Services Digital Network) line. ISDN has been around for many years, and is still popular in certain circumstances—most particularly in areas that are too far from a telephone company switching station for DSL service to be an option. But the ever-increasing availability of DSL has definitely whittled ISDN's market share down. For the most part, today, ISDN is a good deal more expensive—and slower—than comparable DSL offerings, so many metropolitan residents who once turned to ISDN for their only affordable access to broadband have now embraced DSL.

There are several flavors of ISDN. First is the so-called Basic Rate Interface (BRI). This offers you two data channels at 64Kbps (B-channels) and one control channel (D-channel) at 16Kbps. The combined data rate on both B-channels is 128Kbps. The D-channel cannot normally be used for data connectivity; it is used to provide information and call management. With this service, you will usually get two phone numbers. You can receive a call on either number, and even receive two simultaneous phone calls, using both channels at the same time. If you do this, each call will get one of the B-channels, and data can flow across this channel at 64Kbps if the data channel is not in use, or at up to 56Kbps if it is. If you place only one call from your computer, and if your computer software and ISDN "modem" support channel-bonding (and if the modem at the other end of the connection does also), you can get a single channel of 112Kbps or 128Kbps, depending on the state of the D-channel.

A more expensive version of ISDN is the Primary Rate Interface (PRI). This offers 23 B-channels and a 64Kbps D-channel, with a total data transfer rate of about 1.5Mbps when all channels are used at once. ISDN PRI is commonly provided on lines that have been conditioned for T1 service (which you'll read about later).

There are some significant drawbacks to using ISDN. One is cost. In most places, it costs anywhere from a little bit to a lot more than a POTS line to get an ISDN line—and where DSL is available, as mentioned, DSL service is almost always cheaper. A normal analog telephone service line usually costs $30 to $40 per month. An ISDN line typically costs two to three times as much. The first-time setup charge for an ISDN line can run anywhere from free (if you get a special offer—almost unheard of nowadays, when the special offers are all targeting the DSL camp) to $500 for a remote location. The greatest cost is actually using the ISDN connection once it's installed. All calls—even local calls, and even *incoming* calls—are metered. This means you pay for each minute you use, unlike almost all DSL service that comes attached to a monthly, unlimited-use fee.

Additionally, channel bonding doesn't always work. Some ISPs won't guarantee that it will work for every call, though it might. Many ISPs charge you double for calls when channel bonding happens, but only the normal rate if it fails. This variability means you can't count on getting the full 128Kbps data rate just because you want it. Naturally, your ISP must offer ISDN connectivity for you to make use of it. This option is decreasing in its availability as the DSL grows exponentially. Unless you find that you simply can't get DSL service in your area, ISDN is rarely your best choice.

T1 and Other Very High-Speed Connections

Before DSL was available, the phone companies routinely leased special high-bandwidth, continuous-connection lines to companies that needed that service. These lines, which are still available, come in several denominations. One of the most popular is called a T1 line. This line can handle 1.544 million bps, the same as some DSL lines. Some companies have leased T1 lines from the phone company and then turned around and leased a fraction of their bandwidth to other companies. That allowed companies with a smaller appetite for bandwidth to get it at a lower cost than a full T1 line. T1 connections require specially conditioned physical lines and are only functional over short distances, usually up to only a little more than a mile.

Very large companies need even faster data rates. The phone companies offer something called T3 service (45Mbps capacity), and for the super-hungry, OC3 through the breath-taking OC3072 (160Gbps) services (optical fiber service standards, which, at the time of this writing, can cost well in excess of $500,000 a month, even for the slower connections). If you really need one of these levels of data capacity, you will need very specialized assistance, indeed. You must talk to the phone company, and you definitely want to hire a consultant to help you define your needs and the best solution to them.

Which Way Should You Go?

Analog or digital, which way should you go? Maybe you can have it both ways. Some Internet service providers offer both digital (DSL) and analog service—this option enables you to connect with a traditional modem to your ISP when you're on the road, where DSL service is likely to be unavailable. (On the other hand, increasing numbers of hotels are offering broadband connectivity in their guest rooms. In general, what you need to connect in these situations isn't a modem at all, but an Ethernet connection so that your laptop can jump on to the hotel's broadband network. You read about Ethernet in Chapter 11,"Networking—Wired and Wireless.")

A different choice is whether to use one of the always-connected options or a dial-up connection. You get a lot of advantages from a constant connection—and one big disad-vantage. Some of the advantages are that you don't have to make a conscious choice to connect to the Internet—it's just there, all the time.

The disadvantage is simply the flip side of that same coin. Your system is wide open to outside intruders all the time, and some program on your PC might decide to reach out to the Internet and get something and bring it in. You won't necessarily be aware of what these outside programs are doing to your PC until it is too late to stop them. So if you do opt for a constant connection, you'll likely need also to invest in a firewall or other secu-rity measure to control what comes into your PC when you aren't looking.

Summary

Connected PCs offer capabilities that standalone PCs simply cannot match. This chapter described the most common ways that PCs are connected to other computers and networks through a modem or broadband link, and briefly described some of the things they can do when they are connected in that way.

Input Devices

You've read about the fundamentals that make up your PC, including the variety of connections and ports that exist to allow you to connect peripheral devices and add new capabilities. In this chapter, you'll take a look at one class of peripherals that are probably the most important around: input devices.

Your PC is only useful because it does what you want it to do. Before that can happen, you need a way to *tell* it what you want. It's equally vital to be able to give your PC material to work with, whether that material is the text of a book, the notes of a song, or the pixels of a digital photograph. You work with input devices to make it all happen. The keyboard itself is the input device that you use with your PCs most often, but it is by no means the only one. In this chapter, you'll explore these vital devices; you'll see how they work, and how they can make *your* work easier, too.

The focus here, broad or narrow, is on the devices that give you the means to get data into a PC, and not on the conduits through which that data is conveyed from the input devices into the PC. You've already read about that topic, particularly in Chapter 9, "Serial Ports," and Chapter 10, "Parallel Ports." You also read about the keyboard's and mouse's legacy port, the PS/2 port, back in Chapter 1, "The Desktop PC." We will talk about these various connections in this chapter, as we explain how your keyboard and other devices work, but you should look back to those earlier chapters if you want an in-depth refresher on PC ports.

Let's begin this journey by turning back the clock a few decades—back to the time when, in a manner of speaking, the keyboard seemed like it *was* the computer.

The Keyboard Is "Key"

All computers, including PCs, began as character-manipulating devices. The earliest business computers, as you've already read, had no ability to output text other than to endless reams of paper, making them seem truly like "super typewriters." Now, of course, we routinely use our PCs to create and modify images, and even when we use them for "simple" character-oriented tasks like letter writing, we work with much more than just the letters, numerals, or symbols our documents contain. But if you strip away all of the fonts, formatting, and other special features supported by today's word processing software, you're left with the text itself—the core of the communication. And even today, 20 years after the invention of the PC, no one has yet perfected a better way to enter text into a PC than the keyboard.

Keyboard Basics

Computer keyboards descended from typewriters, which is the reason for the general placement of the keys (including the QWERTY key layout). This way, people who learned to type on typewriters can type on computers of all types equally easily. Of course, computer keyboards must do more than typewriter keyboards. So your PC keyboard has more keys than most typewriters do. And, as PC keyboards have evolved, today's keyboards have additional, specialized keys that yesterday's keyboards didn't have.

The additional keys on a PC's keyboard—those not found on standard typewriters— enable you to perform some control functions. These include navigation keys (up, down, left, and right arrow keys, Page Up, Page Down, Home, and End), the Delete and Insert keys, two Control (Ctrl) keys, and two Alternate (Alt) keys. Control and Alt keys are used in conjunction with other keys, pressed simultaneously, to modify the meaning of a keystroke. Many keyboards now also have a key bearing the trademarked flying Windows logo which, when pressed, automatically opens the Windows Start menu. Of course, like any typewriter, a PC keyboard has two Shift keys.

These facts apply to almost every PC keyboard, but PC keyboards differ greatly in many other ways. The next section discusses some of the details about how keyboards work. Then you'll learn how keyboards sometimes differ in how they convey information to (and, in many cases, receive information from) the PC to which they are attached.

Different Keyboard Technologies

The purpose of a PC keyboard at its lowest level is to tell the PC each time a key is pressed or released. Knowing about the key releases is just as important as knowing about the key presses. This is especially true with the Shift keys (which modify the meanings of other key presses as long as the Shift keys are held down), but it also can be true with keys that can be used together in sets (called *chords*), such as the ever-popular Ctrl+Alt+Delete.

Different Keyboard Key Switches

Regardless of the keys or the configuration, what every keyboard needs is a way to sense when the person using it presses or stops pressing a key. Many methods have been used, as described in the next sections.

Domed Elastomer Key Switches

The most common key switch design in use today is one made with a sheet of artificial rubber placed between the keys and a printed circuit board. This rubber sheet has a dome formed in it directly beneath each key. When you press a key, it pushes down on the dome. When pushed far enough, the dome buckles and the key pushes the rubber dome into contact with the circuit board below. A conductive spot on the inside of the dome completes a circuit, signaling the computer that the key has been pressed.

Correctly designed, this type of keyboard has a very satisfying touch-responsive feel, and is cheaper to make than many previous keyboard technologies with similar tactile feedback.

Inexpensive "Dry-Contact" Key Switches

A common alternative keyboard switch is what is sometimes called a *dry-contact switch*. This is a switch designed for use in circuits that carry very little electrical current.

At its simplest, a dry-contact switch might be just a spring wire that the key presses against another wire. When they touch, the switch is closed. When they come apart the switch is opened. Nothing snaps, no sudden movements occur, and there is no noise. Nothing about this type of switch actually lets you know when the computer sensed your key press or release.

Some PC makers include in their BIOS setup an option to have the PC beep or click every time you press a key. That feature is included in case you are using a keyboard with no other means of giving you feedback (and not to make you lose your mind, as you might otherwise suspect).

Snap-Action Key Switches

The very first IBM keyboards used special, miniature snap-action switches. If you press on the key very gradually, the key presses back with a force that increases as you press it down farther and farther. But at some point (the *break-over point*), the force with which the key stops pushing back ceases for an instant. Instead, the key lunges forward a short distance after which it resumes pressing back on your finger. Shortly after that you will reach a point at which the key simply cannot be moved any farther, no matter how hard you push.

As you then slowly reduce the pressure of your finger on the key, at first the key moves slowly back up. Then, at some point the pressure on your finger falls briefly to almost nothing, and the key snaps upward. After that it continues to follow your finger until it returns to the full-up position. The snap action in these switches guarantees that their contacts will snap together rapidly and decisively when they are turned on, and also snap apart very rapidly when they are turned off. This helps keep the switches from burning out from *arcing*—which could otherwise happen during the brief times when the switch contacts are nearly, but not quite, closed.

This is a non-issue for switches used in today's PC keyboards, and making switches this way costs much more than almost any of today's alternative methods.

However, IBM did tests and discovered that typists were more accurate when they received both tactile and auditory feedback for every keystroke. Therefore, they chose to use these more expensive, but in this respect, better quality, snap-action switches in their initial PC keyboard.

Snap action is important for the key switches on a keyboard being used for a lot of typing. When only a few keystrokes need to be entered at a time, this tactile feedback is not nearly as important as certain other keyboard characteristics (such as cost, durability, or resistance to liquid spills).

Membrane Key Switches

PC keyboards that are intended for use in very hazardous environments often are sealed and use membrane or simple capacitive switches. This is a switch similar to those often used on microwave ovens. Instead of keys that move, these keyboards have sensitive regions called *keypads*. Push on one, and they notice it. Stop pushing and they notice that also.

Again, you get no direct feedback from the switch when it closes or opens. Even if you have your PC beep or click for each keystroke, you'll find that you simply cannot type as quickly, nor will your typing be as accurate with this type of keyboard as with either of the preceding two. But these keyboards last far longer in places where they are likely to get abused, or where the environment is too hostile for an ordinary keyboard.

Regardless of How it Works, How Does it Work?

When you press and release a key—on any type of PC keyboard—that action generally only closes and opens one electrical contact (and perhaps gives you some tactile feedback). By itself, this action doesn't cause any messages to go to the PC. Those messages come from some electronics that are built into the keyboard. In fact, an entire computer exists within every PC keyboard. This is an example of an *embedded computer*. It runs a single program all the time—the program that causes this keyboard computer to watch all the keys to see which are pressed or released and to send appropriate messages to the PC to inform it about those events.

Ordinarily, the keys on a PC keyboard are arranged in five or six rows. The keys in each row are offset to the right from the ones in the row just above. Internally, the keyboard has a wire that goes to each row of keys and other wires that go to each (angled) column of keys. This forms a matrix, with each key at the intersection of one row and one column wire. The keyboard electronics activate one column at a time and look briefly at the signal on each of the row wires (or vice versa). In that way, the keyboard can examine the state of each switch in the entire matrix. It does this scanning so rapidly that it can examine every switch on the keyboard many times each second.

Besides noticing the switch closings and openings, the keyboard's computer creates and sends appropriate messages to the PC. Also, it turns on and off the lights that indicate to you whether the Scroll Lock, Num Lock, or Caps Lock states are in effect.

What the Keyboard Computer Does

The conversations between keyboard and PC are very simple and boring. At the time of boot, the PC tells the keyboard to reset itself, thus restarting its internal program. Later, the keyboard sends a message to the PC every time any key is pressed and every time any key is released. The PC, in turn, tells the keyboard any time a program wants to change the state of the Caps Lock, Scroll Lock, or Num Lock (so it can update the little lights on the keyboard). The PC also tells the keyboard computer what time delay and repetition rate to use for its *typematic action*.

The typematic action is what happens when you hold down any key (other than a Shift key). The keyboard's internal computer notices when you first press a particular key and sends a corresponding message to the PC. Later, if it notices that you have been holding down that key for more than a set time—which by default is half of a second—the keyboard computer will start spitting out multiple messages to the PC—10 times each second by default—each of those messages saying that this key has just been pressed againnnnnnnnnnnnnnnnn. When you finally release the key, the keyboard computer sends a final message saying that key has been released (and, of course, it stops its typematic action with respect to that key).

> **Tip:** What do you do if the default typematic rate isn't to your liking? The Keyboard control panel lets you to easily adjust the typematic rate and the typematic delay at will.

Scan Codes and the System Unit's Keyboard Controller

The messages from the keyboard to the PC's system unit enter that box through a special dedicated keyboard serial port, which was introduced in Chapter 1. From there, the messages go to the *keyboard controller*. The PC system unit's keyboard controller is almost always included as a part of the motherboard chip set.

The keyboard controller then gets messages about which keys have been pressed or released. Every time it gets such a message, the keyboard controller places a scan code that identifies the keystroke into a buffer. It also issues a hardware interrupt request (IRQ) on interrupt level 2. (Interrupts are discussed in detail in Chapter 15, "Motherboard Magic.")

It's important to remember that the scan codes indicate which key has been pressed rather than which symbol you intended to type. Thus, the scan codes for *a* and *A* are identical. Each scan code is interpreted in light of the present state of each of the three keystroke modifiers (Shift, Control, or Num Lock) to determine what the typist intended that keystroke to actually mean.

The original PC keyboards sent out 1-byte scan codes. All modern PC keyboards do that for the keys they have in common with those earlier keyboards, and they send modified forms of some of them (indicated by a prefix byte or bytes) for keys that have been added to the keyboard layout since those early days. This includes, for example, the second Ctrl and Alt keys. (As a technical aside, the scan code for a key release is identical to the scan code for that key being pressed, except that the most significant bit is turned on.) The interrupt handler retrieves the scan code from the buffer, and also the state of the Shift and Shift-locks. It then converts this information into an ASCII or extended ASCII character code—or if the key pressed was a Shift or caps-lock key, it alters the key's state stored in the BIOS data area.

How Application Programs Learn About Keystrokes

You can see now that pressing a key on the PC's keyboard does not directly cause a character to appear on the PC's screen. The process is much more indirect than that. Indeed, many times you will be typing and nothing will appear on the screen. Then, suddenly, a burst of characters appears. Other times, the keystrokes get "swallowed up," and you never see them on the screen.

The only way any program finds out that a keystroke has arrived at the keyboard is by looking for an appropriate message from the Windows kernel. On a basic level, though, you want to understand that, when keystrokes happen, two embedded computers (one in the keyboard and one in the system unit) have a conversation. This conversation triggers one of the CPU's interrupts (discussed in detail in Chapter 15). What happens from there is determined not by the hardware, but by whatever software is running at the time.

A Variety of Keyboards for a Variety of Needs

PC keyboards come in a range of sizes and styles. Before you look at some of them, you'll benefit from understanding a little bit about keyboard history.

When the first modern typewriter keyboards were developed in 1860, they were a major advancement on over 40 years of attempts to produce a practical typing machine. With many earlier typewriting machines, typists were easily able to jam the machine by typing quickly. A man named Chris Sholes determined that jams could be avoided by re-organizing the typewriter keys. This idea worked because of something called *digraphs*—combinations of keys used together, like *sh* or *th* or *er*, and so on. By moving these letters to keys that controlled typing-arms that were less likely to jam if typed in rapid succession, typists could actually type faster—not slower, as is often erroneously claimed of Sholes' system. It's called QWERTY, after the arrangement of letters in the top row of alphabetic keys. An illustration of QWERTY from Sholes' original patent is shown in Figure 13.1.

FIGURE 13.1
The QWERTY key layout, as illustrated in Chris Sholes' 1868 patent.

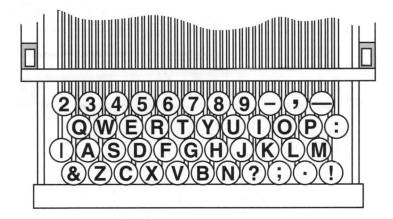

In the 20th century, several other keyboard layout styles and hardware designs were developed with the aim of reducing repetitive stress injuries and allowing the fastest typists to type truly fast—electric typewriters and computer keyboards not being subject to the limitations of one hundred years earlier. We'll look at keyboard hardware in a moment; first let's look at key layouts. Best-publicized among these is the Dvorak keyboard layout.

The Dvorak layout (shown in Figure 13.2) was developed in 1839 by August Dvorak, ostensibly to achieve all of the goals just mentioned: increased speed, reduced fatigue and injuries, and so on. The Dvorak layout's claims to success in these areas have not entirely withstood the test of time, however. Many recent studies have indicated no clear advantage of the Dvorak layout over QWERTY, although individual typists do sometimes prefer it. (Dr. Stan Liebowitz of the University of Texas and Dr. Stephen Margolis of North Carolina State University have studied the matter extensively, should you wish to pursue an interest in the debate.) The details are beyond the scope of this book, but the point is that determining which keyboard layout is best is a good deal more subjective than advocates suggest. If using a traditional QWERTY layout seems to tire your hands, first consider whether you're taking sufficient breaks and giving your hands time to rest. If you are, you might then consider exploring alternative key layouts, but don't expect them to be the panacea that they're often claimed to be.

The claims of alternative hardware designs seem to be based more in fact than are those of alternative layouts, and many user-friendly (ergonomic) keyboards have been produced in recent years. Here's a brief exploration of two of them.

Ergonomic Keyboards

Figure 13.3 shows the original Microsoft Natural Keyboard. This is a very popular ergonomic design. Instead of a flat keyboard or one that slopes up toward the top row, this design actually has the top row of keys slightly closer to the desktop than the bottom row and it includes a flap you can raise to tilt the front of the keyboard up even more. Furthermore, the keys are arranged in three groups. The left and center groups where your left and right hands spend most of their time are turned slightly in toward one another. The right group has the dedicated navigation keys and the numeric keypad, and it is oriented in the same way as a non-ergonomic keyboard.

Front edge of keyboard is raised
to ergonomically correct angle

This is referred to as an ergonomic design because research has shown that using this type of keyboard tends to keep your hands in a more neutral position, and that reduces the likelihood that you will develop a repetitive strain injury.

Figure 13.4 shows a very different keyboard design. This is the Evolution, from Kinesis.

FIGURE 13.4

This very different keyboard design, the Evolution, from Kinesis, can provide significant relief for sufferers of repetitive stress injuries, and may be able to prevent them.

This keyboard is really unique, and can be a tremendous boon to both victims of RSI (repetitive stress injuries) and to individuals with limited use or mobility of their arms or hands. Kinesis has divided the keyboard into two segments, with a touch-pad pointing Cirque device integrated into either the right- or left-hand segment, or both. In this way, users who are left-handed or who have finer motor control of their left hand than their right have a pointer where they desire it. Similarly, limited-mobility users can have immediate access to a mouse, without ever removing their hands from the keyboard.

The two segments can be positioned independently, so that their angle and pitch are fully customizable. Users who experience pain when trying to angle their hands to match the orientation of traditional keyboards can now angle the keyboard to match their own comfort zone. Even the height of each segment is independent and customizable.

Additionally, the Evolution is available in a chair-arm mount model that allows the two key segments to be completely separated and affixed to the arms of many desk chairs or wheelchairs. In this way, office workers can type while keeping their arms in the most neutral, ergonomically safe position, and—again— individuals who are severely limited in their arm or hand/wrist mobility finally have an affordable option that gives them full use of any PC. Kinesis products can be found online at http://www.kinesis-ergo.com.

Keyboards and Laptops

Laptop computers have long presented many design challenges, not least of which was how to fit in a full-size keyboard. Most present-day, full-featured laptops have a screen size on the order of 14 to 15 inches, which is enough space to accommodate a full-sized— if usually somewhat re-designed—keyboard. Without exception, smaller notebooks and laptops use a compromised keyboard. They aren't quite full size, nor do they have all the keys you will find on a normal PC keyboard. But they are still large enough for touch typing and almost all have some means for simulating any keys that were excluded in the interest of space. (You learned about some of the other special challenges faced by laptop designers in Chapter 2, "Portable PCs.")

Of course, nearly all mobile PCs provide the capability, either directly or through a docking bay, to attach a full-size, external keyboard. This option is fine when you're at home or in an office and want to work with your notebook—probably also using an external monitor—for long periods of time. But traveling with a full-size keyboard just isn't a realistic option, so this isn't really a useful feature while you're actually on a plane or train.

Keyboards for Handheld PCs and PDAs

When a PC is too small, there simply isn't room for a normal keyboard. Still, that functionality has proven to be important for many users. Virtually all hand-held devices use a touch screen and handwritten, stylus-based system for most of their input. In one mode, however, that screen displays a miniaturized keyboard, and you can point with its stylus at keys there, one at a time.

If you intend to do any serious amount of text entry into a handheld device, however, you will want to seriously consider one of the many external and collapsible keyboards like the one shown in Figure 13.5. This is nearly full-sized keyboard plugs in to the Palm's HotSync port whenever it's needed, and folds up—as shown on the left—into a space no larger than the Palm, itself.

FIGURE 13.5
The Palm Keyboard provides a collapsible, full-size keyboard for use with Palm PDAs.

Alternatively, products like Silkyboard, from NovaSIB, shown in Figure 13.6, provide a combination of software and hardware solutions—in this case, a silk-screened image of a QWERTY keyboard that adheres to the handwriting-recognition area of Palm OS-based devices—that gives users an always-available stylus-based keyboard for text entry.

FIGURE 13.6
The Silkyboard is a combination of hardware and software that provides an onscreen keyboard for PDAs using the Palm OS.

Alternatives to Typing: Voice Recognition

For those who aren't touch-typists or who might find even the most ergonomic of these keyboard styles to be unusable for whatever reason, voice recognition may be a pathway to efficient data entry. This technology has been in development for over 20 years, and it has been dreamed about for 50 years or more. Certainly, the popular *Star Trek* television series in the 1960s moved the idea of talking to your computer into the mainstream. But when manufacturers tried actually making a computer that was capable of understanding user's voices, they found that the task was much, much harder than they had expected. (Many "experts" in the field predicted that speech recognition would be common to computers "within the next five to ten years"—and this same phrase kept popping up time after time for more than 25 years.) It seems that even the experts couldn't believe that this task would turn out to be as hard as it really is. Even today, I know of a 30 year old engineer who says she expects to be able to "ride the speech-recognition gravy train all the way to retirement." It's one of the most complex tasks we have ever asked of computers.

You can divide the things a PC must do in order to converse with a user into four subtasks. It was obvious to researchers early on that these were the tasks to be performed, although just how each one is performed by a computer turned out to be not quite so obvious.

First—and by far the easiest—the PC must speak. By this we mean it must be able to produce sounds that resemble what one person might say to another.

> **Note:** We say that this task is the easiest of the four, but it is by no means easy. At the time of this writing, the state-of-the-art voice emulators have been developed, not surprisingly, by AT&T. The fruit of their labors can be heard on the Internet at http://www.naturalvoices.att.com. You can put their technology to the test by entering any English text you want and listening to it speak the content you've chosen.

Second, the PC must be able to listen and to recognize what it hears. By this we mean that if you speak into a microphone, the PC must be able to convert the electronic signals from the microphone into a stream of data that it can manipulate. This has proven to be one of the most difficult parts of the overall job.

Third, the PC must be able to understand the speech it has heard. This means taking the sentences it recognizes and figuring out how to respond. The sentences might be commands it is to perform, or they might be data it is to process. Combinations of these two are also possible—even likely. You might say to your computer "Find Joe Jones' phone number." The PC must understand that this sentence is both a command (find a phone number and display it, recite it, or perhaps offer to dial it) and data (the name of the person whose number is being sought).

Finally, the PC must be able to compose relevant responses, in a human language form. Then it can use its speaking capability to deliver that response. This chapter focuses on the second and third of those tasks because they are input-related: listening to and understanding human speech. This involves two tasks: Hearing the words and sentences, and then determining what those sentences mean.

Hearing and Understanding Are Both Hard Work

Most people don't give much thought to how they understand what people say to them. If you have, you probably realize just how complex it all is.

First, realize that you don't hear words. You don't even hear phonemes, which are the building blocks of words in a given language. You hear sounds. Your brain interprets the sounds—sometimes correctly, sometimes incorrectly. When we speak clearly to each other, our brains usually interpret what we hear correctly. But speaking clearly is actually something of a learned skill.

There are, it turns out, two very different ways to speak to a computer. One is the natural way people talk. The other is a highly artificial way to talk that is much, much easier for a computer to understand, but much more obnoxious for people to produce. We'll explain the distinction—which is the *hearing* part of the process—then we'll take a look at how to make a computer *understand* what it hears.

Natural Versus Interrupted Speech

If you've tried to learn a foreign language, you have no doubt noticed that one of the very hardest things to learn is to hear what a person speaking that language is saying. That is, what exactly are the words being spoken? Leave aside their meaning for a moment; just try to recognize the words the sounds represent.

The reason this is hard is that usually we speak rapidly. Speech seems even more rapid if you aren't familiar with the language. We do this because we all want to convey content as quickly as we can. So we speak essentially as rapidly as a trained listener can comprehend us. If you aren't yet a well-trained listener in that language, you will have difficulty discerning the words being spoken.

This suggests that the most difficult aspect of understanding is the task of deciphering the words from the stream of sounds. Research involved in making a PC understand speech leads to this same conclusion.

Breaking It Up Makes Hearing It So Much Simpler

Think about what speakers do when they want to be understood by someone who doesn't speak their language. No, we don't mean that they shout. They slow down. They speak each word clearly and distinctly. That is essentially what people had to do until very recently to get a computer to understand speech. Separate each word by short bits of silence—in effect, make the speaker pronounce the spaces between words.

This is called *interrupted speech*. With this strategy, the computer's task is made much simpler. Each burst of speech represents one word. So the computer can compare that burst of sound with a stored sample of all the words it understands and pick the one that matches most closely.

Flowing Speech Is So Much More Natural

Speaking for an extended period in an interrupted fashion is exceptionally annoying. Clearly the goal must be to have PCs that can listen to a human speaking as humans normally do, and still be able to pick out the words. For many years this was an unattainable goal.

Now, finally, we have arrived—sort of. In some situations, it is now possible to use natural, connected speech when speaking to a PC. This really only works for single-speaker recognition. Each user of the system must train the PC to understand his or her specific voice. This process can take as little as 30 minutes or as long as several hours, depending on the speaker and the system being used. Recently, Apple Computer has demonstrated speech recognition technology in its MacOS that exceeds 99% accuracy when properly trained for an individual speaker.

The Nutshell: How it Works

Whether you are attempting to make a PC program to recognize interrupted or connected speech, the first step is to attempt to identify the phonemes from the sounds the PC receives. Phonemes, again, are building blocks of sounds that form the words of a given language. Interrupted speech helps, mainly because the program knows where at least some of the phonemes start (right after each pause). With continuous speech, the problem of deciding when a new phoneme begins is a fairly tough one.

All natural human languages are redundant. We say quite a few more words than we need to say, just to represent our thoughts. One reason we do this is to give some contextual clues to help listeners identify the words we are speaking from the sounds they are hearing. Naturally, this suggests that a PC program that interprets speech should also be looking for these same contextual clues. Fortunately, all the good ones do.

In fact, they take this notion somewhat further—and often a bit more rigidly—than we do. Speech recognition systems have a dictionary of all the words you are most likely to say (with their pronunciations), but they don't assume that every word is equally likely. Instead, they take careful note of what you have just said to make predictions about what you will likely say next.

This means that a speech recognition program has at every moment a fairly fixed notion of what you are about to say, based on what it has already recognized. If you suddenly change topics, you can expect that the recognition accuracy will fall until the system figures out once more what the relevant context is.

If you think about it, this is not much different from what happens to people. If you suddenly jump to a new topic, you can expect to hear something on the order of, "Whoa. Huh?" People have the same problems as PC speech recognition programs—although we are much better at hearing unexpected words correctly the first time.

Most speech recognition programs aren't that conversational yet. They make their best stab at recognizing whatever is said, but mistakes enter the text they generate. Users must go back later and clean up those messes manually.

Understanding

So it now is possible for a PC to recognize what a person says to it. What's the next task? Understanding what those spoken words, phrases, or sentences are telling the PC to do (and then doing it).

The level of difficulty depends on the context in which you are doing it. If you plan to let your PC listen and then take actions based on what you said to it, you can limit the possible actions enough that it can recognize each command with a very high probability. Today's commercial voice recognition programs at quite masterful at responding to sequences of voice commands like "Format, Font, Italics, Size, Ten," and so forth.

But what if you want the PC to engage in a normal, flowing human conversation—with all the interrupted sentence fragments, sudden changes of subject, "ums" and "ahs," and other extraneous noises that this implies? You'll have to accept a lot less reliability in the recognition you'll get, and you will probably have to build in a lot of confirmation loops to check the accuracy. Even worse, your PC won't have many clues to let it know whether the speaker's utterances are commands or simply data to be stored.

How Far Along Are We Now?

What is the current state of the art? Progress in speech recognition has been very dramatic. More recent applications include untrained recognition of interrupted oral input. There are also a couple of excellent single-speaker (trained) recognition programs for uninterrupted speech. These programs work best when the speaker has had a chance to "read" a lot of text to the system so that it can learn that speaker's habits in terms of how he or she puts words together.

IBM's ViaVoice is one example of a product that can do this job acceptably. It requires a reasonable assemblage of PC hardware: a 600MHz Pentium III, and memory to work with (at least 128MB of RAM). ViaVoice can do a decent job as a dictation assistant with an internal vocabulary of up to 160,000 words in its main dictionary, and an additional 280,000 words in its secondary vocabulary. Words that are not part of ViaVoice's default vocabulary can be added by each user on an as-you-use-them basis.

Apple's Speech Recognition (ASR) technology, mentioned earlier, is a core operating system component. Developers can write their own software which uses Apple's speech engine, thus avoiding having to reinvent the wheel. Until recently, ASR has been most useful for issuing voice commands only. Today, however, it brings quite respectable dictation capabilities to Apple's Macintosh product line (when used with supporting software).

Both of these systems are capable of producing trained results in excess of 99% accuracy. Although that sounds fantastic, bear in mind that "99% accuracy" means that one in one hundred recognitions is wrong. Personally, we've been able to train the ViaVoice system to understand me at an accuracy level of about 99.6%. That reduces the average error rate to approximately four mistakes in every 1,000 recognitions. We find the errors vexing, but still use the product. For individuals who cannot, for whatever reason, readily use a PC keyboard of any variety, these speech recognition systems unlock and open otherwise impassible doors.

The Point Is Pointing (Mousing Around)

It might be impolite to point, but pointing is also the best method developed, so far, for controlling a PC. Keyboard input (or an alternative) is still vital to getting content into computers, but some type of pointing device is an essential complement to a keyboard. The most common pointing device is, of course, the mouse. Whatever pointing device you use, its function is to indicate (by pointing) some item and then select or act upon that item (usually by clicking or double-clicking a button on the mouse).

Many Kinds of Mice

Compared to a keyboard, a mouse is a very simple device—as it should be, for it has a very much simpler job to do. Essentially, a mouse is an object that you move around on your desk (or some other surface). As you do so it reports to the PC its motion. The PC uses these signals to move a pointer around the screen. When the *mouse cursor* points to some object of interest to you, you can signal your interest in that object by pressing one of the buttons on the mouse.

Mechanical and Opto-Mechanical Mice

The original mouse was a box with a small rubber ball sticking out of the bottom. Pushing the box around on the desk caused the ball to roll, and that in turn made some shafts turn and switches close to indicate the amount of motion in each of two perpendicular directions. This mouse design has been copied and refined in many ways.

Figure 13.7 shows three mouse designs. All of them are considerable improvements on the original mouse design, each in its own way.

FIGURE 13.7
Three PC mice, showing some of the differences in design for what is, functionally, the same in all four devices.

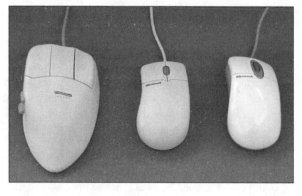

Contour Mouse   Original   Microsoft
(Size Large   Microsoft   Intellimouse
Right-handed)   Intellimouse   Pro

The mouse at the far left is a large, right-hander's mouse from Contour Design. (They affectionately call it "the big rat.") This mouse slopes down to the right and toward the front (the end with the cord coming out of it, where the buttons are), and it has a rest for your thumb on the side. It also has three buttons, which is one more than many PC mice offer.

The intention of this mouse design is to almost force you to grasp the mouse with your entire hand, and to move the mouse with your hand and lower arm as a unit. This is in contrast to how most people use mice, by flexing our fingers to move the mouse small distances, and only moving our arms for larger mouse movements. The slope also rotates your hand into a more normal position than is common for the majority of mouse users. (Think of how you hold your hand when you reach out to shake hands, or when your arms are hanging at your sides. The palms of your hands are facing in, toward your body. Any rotation from that position is stressful on your wrist.)

The mouse in the middle of the figure is Microsoft's Intellimouse with wheel. We will discuss the wheel and the number of buttons in a later section of this chapter. This mouse was Microsoft's first asymmetrical mouse, and like most, it is better suited to right-handed use than to left-handed use, although it can be used with either hand. (Microsoft suggests that you change hands from time to time in order to rest your dominant mousing hand for a while.)

On the right is a later Microsoft design. The Intellimouse Pro is not only asymmetrical, it is also sloped to one side somewhat. This grip enables you to move the mouse in a very controlled fashion—a delicacy vital for serious graphics work—but it does put more stress on one's fingers and wrist.

All these mouse designs work the same way internally. They all have a ball that rolls on the table top (or on a mouse pad), and that ball transfers its motion to two rollers that are inside the mouse. These rollers measure the motion of the mouse in two perpendicular directions (referred to as the X and Y directions, which you might also refer to as side-to-side and forward-and-back, respectively).

Figure 13.8 shows the Microsoft Intellimouse turned on its back, with the ball removed. The ring that you see beside the ball holds that ball in place normally. You can just barely see the two black rods that serve as rollers in this design to sense the motion of the ball.

FIGURE 13.8
A Microsoft Intellimouse Pro from the bottom, with its ball removed to reveal the shafts that sense its motion.

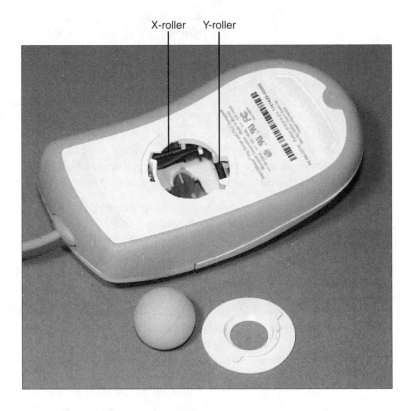

All these mice open up in some similar way. This is important, for you must be able to clean out dust and hairs that get caught on the ball and rollers. Otherwise, the mouse will not accurately sense and report its motions to the PC.

Most modern mice use a combination of optical and mechanical mechanisms. Some of them have a ball that rolls on two shafts, which turn optical shaft-angle encoders to convert those motions into electrical signals for the PC. These mice get dirty, but they are much easier to clean than the original, purely mechanical models.

Purely Optical Mice

The best mice today use no ball at all. An example of these is Microsoft's Intellimouse with IntelliEye. It uses a red LED to illuminate the desk or table surface on which it is resting. A small digital camera inside the mouse actually photographs that surface, over a thousand times a second. A tiny embedded computer inside the mouse itself then compares those images, detecting changes in the mouse's position. These changes are translated into exceptionally accurate X and Y movements of the mouse cursor on the screen. The mouse is sealed, so it never gets clogged and its accuracy never wavers. Its movements are more precise and easily controlled than are those of traditional mice.

Mice That Don't Look or Work at All like Ordinary Mice

Touchpads and pointing sticks are some of the most widely accepted innovations in the pointing device marketplace. We already mentioned the Cirque touchpad that is embedded in Kinesis' Evolution keyboard. This looks like a small, black space, just over two inches wide. You merely slide your fingertip across the window and the mouse cursor moves. You tap the window and it reacts as if you had clicked the primary mouse button. Tap and then slide your finger and it interprets this as you having pressed and held the primary mouse button and then dragged the mouse, thus enabling you to resize a window or drag an icon or other object around on the screen. The example laptop PC, shown in Chapter 2, comes, like most laptops, with a touchpad as its primary pointing device.

The majority of touchpads work by using semi-conductive or resistive pads that sense the location and pressure of one's touch. They need little if any cleaning and stand up well to most environments, including many that would be intolerable to an ordinary mouse. They also take up much less room, and, with no moving parts, tend to last longer than ordinary mice in the relatively hostile conditions often encountered by portable PC users.

The pointing stick, the other principal pointing device of laptops, is a force transducer. It was developed by IBM, which gave it the name TrackPoint, and first appeared on that company's line of ThinkPad notebook computers. A similar device appears on the example Dell Inspiron notebook, in addition to the touchpad. The pointing stick is a small post in a keyboard that usually sticks up between the F and G keys. When you push on it with your fingertip, it doesn't bend appreciably, but it does tell the computer the direction and pressure with which you are pushing. Software translates that information into the equivalent of a mouse motion, with more pressure corresponding to higher speed. In addition to the stick, there must be a couple of buttons somewhere nearby that you can press to get the effect of mouse button-clicks.

One Button, Two Button, Three Button, Wheel

"One Button, Two Button, Three Button, Wheel"—this sounds like the start of a child's rhyme. This also describes the number of buttons you are likely to find on a PC's mouse or other pointing device. (Well, graphic tablet pucks sometimes have as many as 16 buttons, but they are a special case.)

One-button mice (or other pointing devices) are used on Apple Macintosh computers, and not on PCs. When there are two buttons, as is most common in the PC world, one (usually the left button) is designated as the primary button, and the other is the secondary button. This is the most common arrangement. Other mice have three buttons. Because most PC mice have only two buttons, most PC software ignores the third button. However, the mouse driver software that comes with three-button mice almost always can be programmed so that pressing the third mouse button activates some user-defined feature. In the absence of such special drivers, a software package responding to the third button often is also capable of responding in the same way as pressing both buttons on a two-button mouse.

Many newer mice include a wheel located between the two buttons. This can be rolled forward or back, and you will feel it click from position to position as you do so. With support that is built into the Microsoft Windows operating system, this wheel motion can scroll a document, file list, or other window's contents up or down the screen. (This is different from moving your insertion point or selection cursor up or down within the document or list, which is what the arrow keys do.) The wheel also has a switch that is activated when you press on it. This serves as a normal third mouse button, or with software that is specially programmed to use this feature, it can activate an automatic scrolling mode.

How Far Can a Mouse Run?

As we end this discussion of mice, we'd like to draw your attention to a delightful, if whimsical, program that can actually keep track of how far you have moved your mouse over the years.

Mouse Odometer from Introspect Software, shown in Figure 13.9, normally runs in the background. Whenever you desire, it can display how far your mouse has traveled, along with some comparative details—just how far *is* 1823.43 miles, after all? The product can also produce much more detailed printed output similar to the "What has happened on your birthday" sort of thing, shown in Figure 13.10, indicating what you might have achieved had you moved the same distance as your mouse.

FIGURE 13.9

The Mouse Odometer will show you just how far your mouse has traveled.

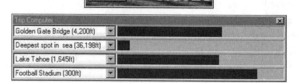

FIGURE 13.10

Mouse Odometer's distance analysis, showing you what your humble mouse has achieved.

Some Other PC Input Devices

A keyboard and a pointing device are the most common and most often used PC input devices. Many others sometimes are just the ticket for what you must do.

Scanners

Easily the most common other input device is a scanner. These come in several forms. Originally, most were black-and-white-only devices, just capable of seeing light or dark areas at each point on the scanned document or object. Today's color scanners are inexpensive, and black-and-white scanners are almost ancient history.

Physically, there are two types of scanners: one can scan only flat sheets of paper or film (called a *sheet-fed scanner*) and one that can scan bulkier objects, such as a page in a book (called a *flatbed* scanner). Most scanners of either type accommodate full letter (8 1/2-by-11-inch) or legal (8 1/2-by-14-inch) pages. Some special-use scanners can scan flat objects no larger than a business card, and still others can scan only 35mm transparencies or negatives (often called *slide scanners).*

In all cases, the output of the scanner and its associated software is a bitmapped image file of the document or object that was scanned. The file can then be converted in any of several ways.

Figure 13.11 shows a typical flatbed scanner. It uses a moving mirror and some focusing optics to capture a line of the document lying on its window onto a linear array of light sensors called a *charge-coupled device* (CCD). A bright white light inside the scanner illuminates a band on the window that moves along with the mirror's motion, thus permitting the scanner to read the contents of the object (sheet, book, or whatever) that is placed on top of the window, under the cover you see in the figure.

FIGURE 13.11
A typical flatbed scanner can read in pages or three-dimensional objects placed on its window.

An alternative flatbed scanner design uses what is called a *contact image sensor* (CIS). This is an array of light sensors that move along the underside of the window (alongside a linear light source) and receive reflected light from the document directly, without focusing optics. That design is simpler and makes for thinner scanners.

The two essential numbers that describe a scanner (besides its type and the maximum size of the objects it can scan) are the resolution of the images it captures (in dots per inch) and the color depth (in bits per pixel) in those images. As you might guess, manufacturers often quote these numbers in ways that mislead you rather than simply explain the capabilities of their products.

Common scanners meant for use with pages of text and illustrations are likely to have a resolution of at least 1200 dots per inch, up to perhaps as much as 2400 dots per inch. This is the *optical resolution,* which measures the fineness of the actual process of capturing information from the page or other scanned object. Many scanners have a different resolution in the direction across the page (which is based on the spacing of the light sensors in its CCD or CIS array) and along the page length (which depends on how often the unit "takes a picture" as it moves the sensing array or imaging point down the scanned object).

Most scanner makers also brag about what is called their *interpolated resolution*. The software can be directed to generate images with many more pixels than the scanning hardware has actually seen. The extra pixels are merely given values between the values at the actually seen pixel locations. (In an alternative methodology, the scanner *oversamples*, reading each pixel more than once and averaging the values. Either method is of dubious benefit in most applications of these devices.)

Scanners meant for scanning 35mm slides must have a very high resolution (in dots per inch), but only over a relatively short distance (across a normal slide's width). This can be accomplished either by having a very high-resolution scanner that can actually see all the detail in the slide directly, or by optically throwing a magnified image of the slide onto a larger area that will be scanned by a lower-resolution scanner.

The *color depth* is another slippery term in scanner descriptions. Scanners convert the analog light values falling on their light sensors into binary numbers. The more bits in those numbers, the more sensitively the scanner can discriminate between nearly similar colors. Often, scanner makers will boast that their units convert the images at 36-bit or even higher color depth. But when you read more carefully, you see that they might send out only a 24-bit color value to the PC. This might be adequate, especially when the hardware in the scanner makes an intelligent choice about which 24-bit numbers to send, depending on the overall brightness and range of brightness in the object being scanned. The best scanners not only convert the analog light into 36-bit (or higher bit-value) numbers, they also provide the PC software with every one of those bits.

Digital Cameras

Image capture is not solely the province of scanners and fax machines. Cameras do this job, also. Just as the typical office copier has changed from being an analog device to a fully digital one, digital still image cameras are beginning to replace their analog cousins. All motion picture cameras used to be analog devices, capturing images on film. Then came television and we had semi-digital cameras for motion pictures. (A TV image is generally captured, transmitted, and displayed as an analog signal representing the brightness of the pixels, but it is displayed on well-defined lines that can be thought of as a digitally defined location within the image.) Now we are beginning to see fully digital television cameras (with digitized brightness values as well as digitally precise pixel locations) and to have fully digital television broadcast transmissions.

Digital Still Cameras

Until very recently, if you wanted a good photograph—one with high image quality, color fidelity, and resolution—you had to use an analog still image camera. But if all you wanted was a low-resolution snapshot image you could get a digital camera. This market is changing very rapidly, and at last you can get reasonably priced, all-digital cameras that produce quite acceptable quality images for many uses.

Figure 13.12 shows the Canon PowerShot S20 digital still image camera used to take almost all the photographs you see in this book . This camera has a 2:1 zoom lens, and it takes images at a variety of resolutions and levels of compression: 2048×1536 pixels, 1024×768 pixels, or 640×480 pixels. In either case, it captures them in 24-bit color. Unlike earlier generations of consumer-level digital cameras, this camera can perform varying degrees of image compression.

The resulting images are amazingly good. Being able to produce really good images requires two things, and only recently have both been available in affordable digital still image cameras. First, you need a good lens system. Without that, you'll get only mediocre images no matter what else the camera offers. The second requirement is enough memory and processing power built into the camera. An uncompressed 2048-by-1536-by-24-bit image file occupies approximately 9MB. Fortunately, images can be compressed in well-understood ways without losing much in terms of visible quality—provided the camera has enough processing power built in, plus an adequate amount of data storage to hold the resulting image files.

There are three ways to use most digital still image cameras with a PC. In the case of the S20, the images are stored on a CompactFlash (CF) memory card that is inserted into the camera. (The camera is supplied with a 16MB card, and additional memory cards are available with capacities up to 340MB.)

You can leave that memory card in the camera and connect a USB cable between the camera and a PC. Using suitable software on your PC you can download pictures from the camera.

FIGURE 13.12
This Canon PowerShot S20 digital still camera was used to take most of the photographs in this book. It has an effective resolution of 3.24 million pixels.

This camera also fully supports both the 340MB and 1GB IBM Microdrive, shown in Figure 13.13. These provide a tremendous image capacity at an extremely low cost per megabyte.

FIGURE 13.13
The IBM Microdrive is a full-featured, shock-resistant hard drive, providing up to 1GB of storage in the space of a small stack of postage stamps.

The range of available digital cameras includes some with other, different and possibly quite valuable features. For example, some are capable of taking short video clips, or of capturing a brief audio recording to associate with each still image. This is one of the fastest moving areas of PC-related, consumer- and business-oriented technology today.

Joysticks and Other Game Port Devices

The *game port* is meant for use with a joystick (or a pair of joysticks) to enable one or two players to control a game on the PC. A *joystick,* in its original form, was a post that wobbled in any direction, plus one or two buttons. The stick was supported with springs to make it pop back in position when you released it. The joystick innards sense the amount and direction in which the joystick has been pushed off of straight up, and they indicate this to the PC via the game port. Of course, they also indicate when each of the buttons is pressed.

Why would you want such a device, when you already have a pointing device in your mouse? Because joysticks are designed for game movement that's impractical using a mouse, such as when you need to move in a particular direction for a long period of time.

Modern game controller devices are much more complex than the original joysticks. Some of them still can be connected to a PC via the game port, but others must be hooked to a USB port.

Summary

In this chapter, you learned about some aspects of the most common PC input device technologies. Far more can be said about these devices. Still, after reading this chapter, you should have an understanding of the various PC input devices, and you should have a fairly solid knowledge about the most important characteristics of several "key" ones, if you'll forgive the pun.

Printers

Over the past chapters, we have taken a look at all of the different parts that make up your PC. We've covered getting data into your PC via a mouse and the keyboard, what happens to that data inside your computer, and getting that data back out by looking at it on a display. We've even explored how to move data from one place to another by using a network or some form of removable storage, but there's one major component missing. All of these methods help you get data from one computer to another, but you haven't examined getting your data into a simple printout so that you don't need to have a computer to see your data.

Understandably, printing does have its limitations. A screen image, when coupled with animation or video imagery and audio, expresses much more than a plain paper printout. But, it's not expected that your printout will suddenly leap off the printer and start to sing and dance on its own. We haven't figured that out yet. However, through the latest generation of color printing technologies, you might swear that the photograph of a grey wolf you printed just winked at you.

The Purpose and Power of PC Printers

The printed page is probably the most universal way that humankind has left its mark, if you will, for future generations. A page of printed output can display considerably more information than a single screen image, and it's obviously much more portable than even the smallest laptop. You can take a piece of paper into environments that would destroy even the most hardened computer equipment, and the page looks and behaves the same. Plus, a printed page can have a mind-bogglingly long life. The Gutenberg Bible has been around for nearly 600 years! Now, we aren't not saying that those digital pictures of Aunt Martha that you just printed will be around for that kind of timeframe, but you can tell that the printed page has a long history and lifespan.

For this reason, and many more, PC printers are one of the most ubiquitous peripherals in the computer world. Over the last couple of years, there have been numerous break-throughs in printing technologies—most especially in color printing. It is possible today to create printed images that rival photographs in quality, all the while using printers under $300. Two years ago, to obtain this same image quality, you had to use a printer that cost well over $15,000 or more, and might have waited an hour for your print to emerge.

The point of a printer is to make marks on paper or some other similar medium. There are printers that can print on canvas, metallic sheet, plastic, and even glass. Some printers are designed to only print text at extremely high speeds, some printers are focused squarely on photo-realistic image printing, and there are many different types in between. We're going to take a look at the five main printer technologies: impact, inkjet, xerographic (commonly known as laser), solid-ink, and dye sublimation. But first, you need to take a quick look at how your computer tells your printer what to print and where to print it. Your computer and printer have to speak the same language, otherwise your printed output could be, shall we say, interesting? What you see may not be what you get.

Page Description Languages

A page description language (PDL) is exactly what it sounds like—a means for the computer to tell the printer what it needs to do to properly output a file onto paper so that it looks as close to the image displayed on the screen as possible. However, some printers (such as impact) have no need for a PDL, because they print from an ASCII text stream. These printers are a niche market, and are rarely seen in general use anymore. There have been many different PDLs used, but the three most common now are PCL, PostScript, and HP-GL/2. Of these three, 95% of the printers on the market use some form of PCL or PostScript. A detailed explanation of how each of these languages work is beyond the scope of this book, but we will explain the basic features and differences between each of these three major languages.

PCL

PCL is one of Hewlett Packard's page description languages—and probably the most common in general home and office printing. There have been several versions since PCL's inception in 1984—as of this writing, PCL6 is the most current. The easiest way to explain PCL is that it treats an entire page as one huge collection of dots, known as a bitmap. Primarily, PCL uses bitmapped graphics, which are sent to the printer as dot patterns. PCL also handles fonts in this manner—requiring the computer to download these fonts to the printer as individual images for each letter as the job is spooled. Besides describing how to print text and graphics, PCL commands tell the printer to use various features and capabilities to create the final output.

PostScript

PostScript was designed and created by Adobe Systems in 1985, and quickly became the de facto standard for the desktop publishing and graphic arts world. As of this writing, the most current version from Adobe is version 3. Unlike PCL, PostScript is very much like a typical programming language, using real English words to describe a printed page. The biggest difference between PCL and PostScript is that PostScript produces a page as a collection of geometric objects, known as *vector images*. An easy way to understand this concept: In PostScript, a line is just that—a continuous line. In PCL, a line is a group of dots. PostScript is an extremely powerful language, containing routines and commands that can even control a hard disk in a printer and many other advanced features.

HP-GL/2

HP-GL/2 was first created as a plotter language. Since a plotter draws its images one stroke at a time using a pen held by an arm controlled by the computer, the PCL method of treating pages like large arrays of dots won't work. Therefore, plotter control languages were born, describing pages as a series of lines and curves that the plotter arm could trace and create the final printout—almost like PostScript. Later, major pieces of the vector graphics functionality in HP-GL/2 were integrated into PCL version 5, giving PCL-based printers some vector-based functionality.

Printing Technologies

Now that you have a basic understanding of what your computer is telling the printer when you click that Print button, let's examine what the printer does to create your printed page.

Impact Printing

About the only method that hasn't been tried in a PC printer is using chisels to carve marks in stone tablets. However, some printers work almost along the same line. These printers are known as impact printers. These printers come in two families—character and line printers and dot-matrix printers.

Character Printers

The first computer printers positioned a ribbon soaked with ink in front of a piece of paper. The ribbon was then hit by a hammer that had a letter's shape on it. The impact drove ink out of the ribbon and onto the page. These printers produced output that looked like it had been typed on a typewriter. (Basically, it had been typed on a glorified typewriter.) These printers were very slow, very loud, and limited in that they could only print the characters that were on the hammers. If you wanted something different (like some other font or some specialized character), you were out of luck.

Line Printers

The other principal type of formed-character impact printer is the line printer. On the line printer, the print heads stay stationary, printing an entire line of text at a time, and the paper moves past the print heads at great speed. In one variation, a line printer has a solenoid-driven hammer for each column of type on the page. Each hammer has a vertical strip of metal raised and lowered between it and the ribbon. On that strip are formed all the different character shapes it can print. When the strip is raised to the correct height, the hammer strikes it and the character is printed. This can be going on simultaneously for every column on the page. An alternative design uses either one or two lines of hammers that operate along the same principle as a dot-matrix printer—each hammer creates a dot rather than a complete character, allowing the printer to print graphics.

The principal advantage of the line printer is its speed. A line printer can crank out up to 1,800 lines of text per minute (which works out to be approximately 30 8.5×11" pages per minute,) and up to 180 inches of graphics each minute. The disadvantages are inflexibility, noise (unmuffled, the noise levels are over 90 decibels), extremely high cost, weight, size, and yes, even their speed.

Because these printers are feeding a continuous strip of paper at high speed, the chance of someone being injured by being in the wrong place at the wrong time is a serious consideration. There are reports of serious injuries inflicted upon careless users who tried to grab the fast-moving paper and lost a finger, or at least were cut severely for their trouble. They are, however, durable as tanks and very good at what they do, which is why many large businesses still use them.

Dot-Matrix Printers

The older style character printers had one major shortcoming from the day they were invented—they couldn't handle graphics. Some inventive souls (with very little else to do, seemingly) did get around this limitation by creating ASCII art. ASCII art is just what it sounds like—pictures using standard alphabetic characters. However, this wasn't a very workable solution, and the dot-matrix printer was born. Like the character printer, it used a set of hammers and a ribbon to transfer ink to the page, but unlike the character printer, the hammers are a set of pins arranged in a column.

> **Note:** The name *dot matrix printer* comes from the notion that these printers form characters out of a rectangular array of dots. That array is called the *matrix*. The particular dots in that array that are printed define the character's shape. A dot matrix printer normally prints an entire row of characters each time it passes the head across the page. Each pass, therefore, corresponds to a line of "type," as is the case with the predecessor technology, the typewriter.

These printers produce text or graphics one row at a time by moving the print head across the page and firing the hammers against the ribbon where needed to create output. These printers are confined almost exclusively now to businesses and others who need to print multi-part forms, because there is no other print technology that can properly print these types of jobs.

Squirting Ink Printers

Another traditional way to make marks on a surface is by painting them. That means, in its essence, by putting a colored liquid on the surface and letting it dry. This is the basic technology behind *inkjet printers*. These printers spray a liquid ink onto the page. Most of them are descended from the dot matrix impact printers, and so the design of much of their internal mechanisms are similar to those earlier generation printers. (Most inkjet printers have multiple jets vertically aligned on a carriage that moves horizontally across the page, for example. This is analogous to the matrix of pins on an impact-printer's print head.)

This category covers a large range in terms of both quality and cost, but even some of the best-quality inkjet printers—notably those from Epson—are reasonably priced. One reason for the range of prices is that the inexpensive printers in this category often rely on the PC's CPU to do much of the work and the PC's memory to do the temporary storage. (In laser printers and more expensive inkjets, there is actually memory in the printer itself, so the PC can *spool* the image out to the printer and then get on with other things while the printer concerns itself with printing.) The trade-off in this is that you save money on the printer, but you might find that you can do very little else with your PC while it is printing—and these are some of the slowest PC printers, so you might find that you are locked out of other productive uses of your PC for longer than you can tolerate. Finally, realize that a lower initial cost often translates into a higher cost to operate. Ink is used in high quantities at high resolutions, and is often expensive.

Monochrome Laser Printers

Probably one of the most popular printer technologies in use today, the laser printer has come a long way since Xerox introduced its $350,000 model 9700 in 1977. (For reference, this machine was capable of 120 pages per minute with full-duplexing capabilities.) IBM also got involved, releasing its model 3800, which was capable of 20,000 lines per minute (roughly equivalent to 333 pages per minute.) However, neither of these were going to be much use to the PC market, and the first desktop unit was introduced by Canon in 1982 when they unveiled the LBP-10. Hewlett-Packard entered the fray in 1984 with their LaserJet (which coincidentally, used a Canon print engine, as do almost all HPs built up to the time of this writing), and the laser printer took off like a rocket.

How They Work

Black-and-white laser printers work on the same principle—the *xerographic* process—used in copy machines. Xerographic printing in a laser printer consists of a series of six steps, all revolving around a photoconductive surface. Photoconductive surfaces are unique in that they are excellent insulators when kept in a dark place, but when exposed to light, become highly conductive and can then hold an electric charge. Inside a laser printer, this photoconductive material is either a drum or continuous belt. For purposes of this example, we'll refer to this surface as the drum. The other important component in this process is a powdery material known as toner. Toner consists of a mix of highly colored particles and a powdery plastic bonding material, and is used as "ink" to create the desired output on a piece of paper.

1. First, the drum is wiped clean of any remaining toner particles, and then charged with a static charge.

2. After the drum is evenly charged, some type of light source is selectively shined onto the face of the drum, discharging the areas of the drum that make up the printed image.

3. The drum continues to rotate, and passes by another roller covered in toner particles. Because like charges repel and opposite charges attract, the toner sticks to the surfaces of the drum, forming the image to be printed.

4. After the image is formed on the drum and the toner is applied, the printer feeds in a piece of paper, which passes by the drum. The toner particles leave the drum and are attracted to the paper (which has an opposite electrical charge).

5. The paper continues past the drum, taking the toner particles along with it. The drum is then fully discharged by exposing the drum surface to light, and the process starts over for the next page to be printed.

6. Meanwhile, the paper continues through the fuser and passes between two heated rollers, which melt the toner and press it into the paper fibers, fusing the image permanently to the page.

The paper is ejected out of the printer, and voila! You now have a crisply printed page that won't run or smear when the ink gets wet, because it's permanently adhered to the paper.

Laser, LED, and LCS Printers—What's the Difference?

The name *laser printer* is slapped on any computer printer that uses the xerographic process to create a printed page. However, the light source doesn't have to be a laser beam. There are several other light sources used in printers. Let's take a brief look at the three major light sources—laser, LED, and LCS.

A laser light source consists of the laser that produces the beam, a rotating mirror, and a focusing lens. The laser is permanently fixed, necessitating the mirror. The mirror rotates back and forth horizontally, scanning the beam back and forth across the page as the drum slowly rotates. The focusing lens keeps the beam's size uniform as it scans across the page. Printers that use this type of light source are the true laser printers.

The next common light source is the LED, or light emitting diode. In an LED printer, the light source is comprised of a bank (or array) of LEDs and a fixed focusing lens. An LED printer produces an entire line of the image simultaneously, unlike the laser light source we discussed above.

The third light source used is known as LCS, or liquid crystal shutter. This method is similar in basic concept to the LED source. LCS printers use a quartz lamp as their light source, which shines through a bank of liquid crystal shutters that open or close to expose the drum. Like LED printers, an LCS printer produces an image one complete line at a time.

Monochrome laser printers are perhaps the most popular of all the printer technologies in use today, at least for general-purpose office use. They are among the fastest printers and the quietest, and their per-copy costs are among the lowest. However, with the continuing refinement of color laser printing and the major strides made by solid-ink printers, we would not be surprised as time progresses to see more offices turning to a solid-ink or color laser printer for their general-purpose output.

Color Laser Printers

Now that you understand how a monochrome laser printer works, let's take a closer look at the up-and-coming world of color laser printing. The basic concepts are the same, but, of course, there's more involved to produce a full-color printout as opposed to a black-and-white one. Color lasers use one of two print engines: four-pass or in-line. Let's take a closer look at the particular operating characteristics of each.

Four-Pass Print Engines

The first color print engine, introduced in 1993, is QMS's $12,500 ColorScript Laser 1000. It has become known as a four-pass print engine. There are two designs of four-pass engines. One of these uses four colored toner cartridges mounted onto a rotating cylinder: one cylinder each for cyan, magenta, yellow, and black. (We'll talk more about CMYK printing in a moment.) Each cartridge rotates into place, and the printer then repeats the same xerographic process four times, once for each color. The paper passes through the imaging path four times, but only runs through the fuser once after all the toner has been deposited.

The other type of four-pass engine consists of four toner cartridges stacked one on top of the other next to a photoconductive belt. The Lexmark C720 printer pictured in Figure 14.1, uses this type of four-pass engine.

The belt makes four complete revolutions, one for each color, but instead of transferring the toner directly to the paper, the belt transfers the toner onto an accumulator drum. After all four colors of toner have been transferred to the accumulator, the printer then feeds the paper through once and deposits all four colors in one pass, transferring the toner off the accumulator and onto the paper, which then passes through the fuser while the printer resets for the next page.

FIGURE 14.1

Our example color laser printer, the Lexmark C720, is widely hailed as the best color laser printer on the market at the time of this writing.

The printer has to basically print four complete pages, one each for the cyan, magenta, yellow, and black layer, even though only one piece of paper exits the paper path. This explains why the color print speed of printers that use this type of engine is susually one quarter of their rated black-and-white speed. Because the belt only has to make one turn to print black, the printer can turn out pages much faster. As an example, the C720 can print 24 black-and-white pages per minute, but only six pages per minute in full-color mode. The Lexmark C720's type of engine is certainly preferable to the system that actually rotates the toner cartridges, and its output quality is stunning, as several independent industry journals have agreed. But both types of four-pass engine have found wide acceptance in the market.

In-Line Print Engines

The other type of color print engine that is in wide use in color laser printers is known as an in-line or single-pass engine, also referred to as a tandem engine. This type of engine is basically four separate print engines, in that each of the four colors has its own drum and laser. These four engines are positioned on top of an accumulator belt, which rotates past the drums and transfers all four toner colors onto the paper in one revolution of the belt.

This type of print engine can produce color and black-and-white prints at almost the same rate of speed, because the belt only turns once per page whether it is printing full-color or monochrome. Color print speeds are usually about 10 to 20 percent slower, due to the extra time required by the printer to process the larger amount of data. However, these printers do have some drawbacks. Due to the more complicated mechanism, these printers are usually more expensive than printers using the four-pass engine. The biggest short-coming of these printers is their susceptibility to misregistration, or misalignment of the four colors. This is a characteristic of this particular engine, and is caused by the internal printer mechanisms (specifically the individual drums) being out of alignment in relation to each other. Let me be clear, though—this is not common behavior if the printer is properly maintained and in good working order.

Advantages and Disadvantages of Color Lasers

Since the last edition of this book, color lasers have made huge leaps forward, both in capability and affordability. When the 8th edition was published, a color laser printer could weigh the best part of 250 pounds, produced 1.5 pages per minute, and started at nearly $10,000. Now, a unit like our example Lexmark C720N weighs only 110 pounds, can print six pages per minute in full-color, and costs under $2,000 at your local computer retailer. Quite the difference. Their output quality has improved dramatically as well. The older models maxed out at 300 dots per inch—our Lexmark C720N is capable of 600 dots per inch, and can simulate 2,400 dpi. The difference in printed output quality is *very* noticeable.

However, when compared to other color printing technologies, color laser still has some disadvantages, the most prominent of which is the huge amount of consumable supplies required to operate these printers. The Lexmark C720N requires no fewer than 13 different consumables, ranging from the four colored toner cartridges to an oil bottle. A color laser printer using a tandem print engine requires 17 consumables. In contrast, our Xerox Phaser 860 (which uses the solid ink technology we'll cover in a minute) uses four individual colored ink "sticks" and a maintenance roller. A typical color inkjet printer can have as little as a single four-color ink cartridge. The powdered toner used in color laser printers can also be a problem. It has a tendency to "migrate" when you replace a cartridge. Nevertheless, color laser printers are a relatively inexpensive way for a business to produce large volumes of high-quality color documents at a low cost per page. Now that some models of color laser printers have dropped below $1,000, we expect to see color lasers making a large dent in the general home marketplace, although the strong foothold of inkjet printers will take some time to dislodge.

Solid-Ink Printers

The major competitor of color laser printers, solid-ink printers have made great leaps forward since the last edition of this book. The unquestioned leader (and the innovator of this technology) is Textronix, now a division of Xerox. In our tests and in our subjective opinion, the Xerox Phaser 860DP, our example unit shown in Figure 14.2, produces the best color output we've seen. Period.

The term "solid ink" actually refers to the way the ink is packaged, as it were, in shaped wax sticks, a bit like giant crayons. This is a four-color printing process—with each ColorStik being uniquely shaped to make it impossible to put the wrong color ink in the wrong reservoir. You can see the ColorStik ink in Figure 14.3.

FIGURE 14.2
The Xerox Phaser 860 color printer produces the best color output we've seen, bar none.

FIGURE 14.3
The Xerox ColorStik ink is shaped to prevent misuse, and black ink is free for the life of the printer.

How It Works

Solid-ink technology is probably one of the simplest full-color printing methods out there, and produces some of the most photo-realistic prints available. In a nutshell, colored wax sticks are melted and sprayed onto a rotating heated drum, which then transfers the ink directly onto a sheet of paper. No fuser or other "fixing" method is required because the ink solidifies and bonds to the paper fibers upon contact. Of course, this is a very simplified overview of what actually happens. Let's take a closer look at what happens inside the printer when it prints a page:

1. As the drum begins to turn, a microscopically thin sheet of silicone oil is applied by a roller on to the face of the drum to keep the melted ink from sticking. (This roller is the only consumable in the printer outside of the ink sticks.)

2. As the drum continues to rotate, the full-width print head sprays all four colors simultaneously, creating a mirror image of the finished page in one rotation of the drum.

3. When the ink is fully applied onto the drum, the printer feeds in a sheet of paper which is pressed against the drum by a transfer roller. The ink transfers onto the page and "fixes" instantly without having to pass through a fuser. The ink actually embeds itself into the paper, making a permanent image with an incomparable sharpness and fidelity.

And that's it! The printer ejects the page, and resets for the next print.

Xerox's solid ink technology is a great deal faster than any color laser technology available. The Phaser 860DP can print its first page in less than 10 seconds (that's not a misprint—but it is faster even than the first-page-out speed of most black-and-white laser printers) and it can print at speeds of up to 10 pages per minute (ppm) in high-resolution mode and 16 ppm in fast color mode.

Our example Phaser 860DP has another neat feature called *duplexing*—the ability to automatically print both sides of a page. The printer accomplishes this feat by printing the first side, partially ejecting the page, and then pulling the paper back in, passing it into a second set of rollers. The print process then repeats using the other side of the page, and the completed print is ejected into the output tray.

Features and Advantages of Solid-Ink

As stated earlier, solid-ink printers have made huge strides over the past few years—with output that now rivals dye-sublimation printers in quality, at a much higher speed. Our example Phaser 860DP is capable of printing 16 pages per minute in either full-color or monochrome, at a true 1200 dots per inch. Like the in-line color laser print engine, the solid-ink engine prints a single full-color image in one pass, but it has *none* of the mis-registration problems that plague the in-line laser engines. Another usability feature of solid-ink is the ability to add ink while the printer continues to operate. With all other printers, whether it be color or monochrome laser, inkjet, or impact, the print process needs to be stopped or paused to add ink.

Although it might surprise industry old-timers to hear it, another advantage of solid-ink technology is cost. Until recently, this was far from true, but it's true now. Our example color laser printer (without duplexing) costs almost the same as the non-duplexing version of its Xerox Phaser 860 cousin—the color laser is $2469 and the Xerox is $2399 at the time of this writing. For that price, the Xerox printer comes with twice the internal memory of the color laser printer. (Expanding the memory of the color laser printer to match the Xerox Phaser costs an additional $550 at the time of this writing.)

Solid ink has a total-cost-per-page that is noticeably lower than all currently available color laser printers—even when printing in black-and-white mode. Solid ink printers have a total of two consumables: the ink sticks and a maintenance roller. Compare this to the 12-16 consumable parts of comparable color laser printers.

The Sublime Printers: Dye Sublimation

Some solid materials don't melt when you heat them. Instead, they turn directly into a gas. (So-called "dry ice," which is solid carbon dioxide (CO_2), is an example of such a material.) This process is called *sublimation*. In dye-sublimation printers, a ribbon carrying a special colored material that can be sublimed is placed in close proximity to a specially treated paper. A spot on that ribbon is heated briefly. The dye sublimes, and the resulting tiny gas cloud partially re-solidifies on the paper. This is the basic process used in dye-sublimation printers.

An important point to notice is that the amount of dye that is transferred to any one pixel can be controlled by controlling how much energy is dumped into the corresponding spot on the ribbon. Thus, this process inherently allows printing in a sort of grayscale fashion—something many of the other processes are inherently incapable of supporting.

The list of methods that have been used to produce the spot heating of each dot in this class of printers is essentially identical to the list of the hot wax printers that use a page-wide ribbon. In fact, some printers can be used for both kinds of printing with just a change of ribbons and paper, and perhaps resetting some parameters used in the spot-heating mechanism by the driver software.

This category includes some of the best printers for producing photographic quality color images, as well as some of the slowest. Speed notwithstanding, their image quality has made them favorites of graphics arts houses, both in the usual letter-size format and in large-format models capable of printing an entire tabloid page at once.

The superior image quality these printers can achieve at a relatively low cost makes them popular in very small formats (4-by-6 or 5-by-7 inches, for example), as well. These printers can, in some cases, be driven directly by a digital camera to produce "instant" color snapshots similar in quality to Polaroids.

Smart Page Printers

When HP introduced the LaserJet and when Apple introduced the LaserWriter, the common personal computers of the day were simply not very powerful. They were not nearly powerful enough to do all the computing needed to rasterize pages described in PCL or PostScript in a reasonably short time. (To *rasterize* a page is to compute the color for each of the pels on the entire page. The name comes from the notion that those pels can be organized into rows just like the pels on a raster-scan video display.) This is why those companies made their printers with a very powerful computer built into each one. Those computers were dedicated to just the one job of rasterizing pages.

This makes them *smart page printers*. You send such a printer a description of the page in either PCL or PostScript, and it will determine what the page is to look like and then print it. Not only does that mean that these printers need a lot of computing power, it also means that they must have a lot of RAM in which to hold the page image they are computing. Only after the entire file has been processed can they be sure it is safe to begin printing any portion of it. This is so because both PCL and PostScript describe pages in a way that is somewhat like the way a vector art file describes an image. They use the display list concept. That means that the very last item in the file might be telling the printer about a header line that goes at the top of the page.

Back when these printers first came on the market, enough RAM for a full page frame buffer cost a small fortune—more than the rest of the printer's parts put together. So a strategy was devised to print the page in pieces, called *bands*. In this strategy, the RAM buffer might be large enough to hold, for example, only one-tenth of a page. The computer that is rasterizing the image will pretend that it has a full page buffer to work with. It then merrily rasterizes the entire image and deposits that information into that imaginary frame buffer. Only one-tenth of those locations have actual RAM; in the rest of the locations, the information "written" is actually simply discarded. If that real RAM is located at the top of the page image, that top one-tenth of the page can be printed when the computer has completed rasterizing the entire page. Next, the RAM is cleared, and its addresses reassigned to the next tenth of the frame buffer. The computer then must redo the entire process of rasterizing the file, from the beginning to the end. When it finishes, the next tenth of the page can be printed. This continues, with the paper advancing through the printer in spurts, until the entire page has been printed.

That strategy works, and it saves on the cost of RAM, but it obviously also makes printing pages take much longer. Now that RAM is (relatively) cheap, it makes more sense to be sure your page printer has enough RAM so it can rasterize the entire page image just once and then print it as a whole. (Furthermore, this will ensure that you don't get lines across the page where the bands end, which can happen if the paper-moving mechanism cannot be stopped and restarted gracefully.)

All of these smart page printer ideas have been applied to page printers using each of the principal printing technologies. Thus, you can have an inkjet page printer, a xerographic page printer (using a laser, an array of LEDs, or an LCS array), or a hot wax or dye-sublimation page printer. In all cases, the most common way those printers are supplied is with a very powerful computer inside of them to rasterize the page images. Some of these printers come equipped to interpret PCL files; some "understand" PostScript files; a few can do either; and all of them also can accept a pure bitmapped image of the entire page, or of any portion of a page, if that is what you want to send it.

One advantage to PCL as a language for controlling a printer is that if you just send some ASCII text to a PCL printer, it will print what you send it in some default font. (You must be sure to include the form feed character to tell it when to print and eject the page.) A pure PostScript printer can print an ASCII text file only if you first wrap the text inside a short PostScript program.

"Dumb" Page Printers

PCs are much more powerful than they were a dozen years ago. Pages of text and images aren't all that much more complex than they were back then. So now PCs are capable of doing the rasterizing job every bit as well as the printers.

Some companies have capitalized on this fact. They point out that if you buy a very fast computer, you can then buy (from them) a very inexpensive printer that can print images that are just a good as those from a much more expensive printer. This will work because these inexpensive, "dumb" printers don't have any computer inside. They depend instead on a software program running in your PC to do all that work and then ship out just the pels to be printed to the printer. All it can do is print a bitmapped image from that string of pels.

These companies also point out that the money you are investing in your PC can be put to good use when you are printing and also when you are not, whereas the investment you make in a computer that is built into a printer can do you some good only when you are actually printing something. This argument has merit, and it certainly has convinced some PC owners to get a much more graphically capable printer than they otherwise would have afforded. There is a downside to this approach, of course. If all your PC's power is going to be consumed in the rasterizing task for the next hour, during that time you aren't going to be doing much of anything else with it. It also means that you must have a lot of free RAM and free disk space on your PC for this strategy to work.

For example, I have a Tektronix Phaser IIIPxi tabloid (11×17-inch page size) dumb page printer that uses the solid-ink printing process to print page images in full color at 300 dpi. This means that there are 11×17×300×300 pels per page. That is 16.8 million pels. For full color, I must store three bytes for each pel. This isn't possible unless I can give the software rasterizing program at least 51MB for its frame buffer, in which it will create the image. In practice, the program spools most of that information to a disk file, so I can get away with merely a few megabytes of free RAM. But I find that unless I have a couple of hundred megabytes of free disk space, the printer simply fails to print the page at all! Fortunately, this is almost a non-issue now, given the huge size of hard disks, but if you're using an older PC, and you find your printer isn't printing, this might be the solution to your dilemma.

Getting the Color (Almost) Right

We've talked about black-and-white and color printers and how they produce their respective images, but there are some special considerations that come into play when you're dealing with getting professional-quality and reliable color output from any printing device.

Color Models

All that monochrome printers need to know for each pel on a page is just how black it needs to be. Some older printers allowed each pel to be only fully black or fully white. Today, all permit gray values as well. If you print a color image on a monochrome printer, the printer driver software converts the various colors into relative shades of gray, which are used to produce the grayscale image you eventually receive on paper. It's a simple enough process.

Printing in color isn't as simple at all, even though you might think it should be. After all—if you have a color image and you send it to a black-and-write laser printer, there's a conversion that has to happen, as we just mentioned. If you're sending a color image to a color printer, naturally, the printer just needs to know that each pel has a given color and brightness, and it all just goes straight on through and you're good to go, right?

Wrong.

To understand why that's wrong—especially because it's so counter-intuitive—you need to consider how we *see* colors and how we can be fooled by the clever use of just a few colors into thinking we are seeing many more.

It is true, of course, that each pel in a printed image (or each pixel on screen, for that matter) has a particular color and brightness. We use several *color models* to describe the visual appearance of the pixels. This topic may seem unnecessarily complex and arcane. However, it turns out to be the key to understanding the difficulties in getting good color images transferred to a printed page without having the colors change appreciably.

RGB

The most common model for PC video displays is referred to as the *red-green-blue* (RGB) model. This says that you can describe any color of light coming from a spot within an image by saying how much red, green, and blue light it contains. This is an *additive color model*, because the total light that hits your eye from that spot is the sum of the amounts of red, green, and blue light. Because of the way in which most PC displays create their images, this is the most natural way to describe them.

In the RGB model, you can specify a pixel's color by giving three numbers representing the amount of R, G, and B light the screen emits on some suitable scale. Thus, a color of (0, 0, 0) would be black (no light of any color is emitted). A color of (255, 0, 0) would be a pure red at maximum brightness (assuming a scale of 0 to 255, which is the most commonly used scale). A color of (255, 0, 101) turns out to be a lovely rose, the color (162, 240, 0) is a vivid new-leaf green, and (0, 142, 61) is a dark forest green.

However, certain types of display, in particular LCD panels, don't emit light at all. Instead, they modify the light that is reflected from them or that passes through them. Some make color images by passing light through a clear liquid crystal that is covered with an array of colored dots. This results in an effect very much like the three-color emitting dot groups on a color CRT. Other LCD panels pass light through three layers of colored liquid crystals. Each layer subtracts an adjustable portion of one color only of the light that falls on it.

CMYK

This latter behavior is very nearly the same as what happens when you look at a printed image on paper. Colored images are formed from layers of color-absorbing dyes. The color you see is determined by the colors absorbed by those dyes. From this description you will understand why this is referred to as a *subtractive* color model. The primary colors—normally red, blue and yellow—are slightly skewed in this model into cyan, magenta, and yellow, so this model is called the *CMY model*. When black is added, it's called the *CMYK model* (the *K* standing for black to avoid using *B*, which might imply blue). Every modern desktop PC inkjet, color laser, and solid-ink printer uses this model. (A few inkjet printers that are designed for portability and use on the road have eliminated black ink from their color cartridges, and they produce a composite black—actually, a very dark brown—by combining the yellow, magenta, and cyan inks together in high densities.)

HSB

A third model for expressing color is termed the *hue-saturation-brightness* (HSB) color model. This model forms the basis for understanding color television signals. That means that if you want to display a television image on your PC monitor, the PC is going to have to do a "color space conversion" to get what is basically an HSB image (or a variant of that called YUV), into RGB. Conversely, if you want to display your PC's output on a large-screen TV, the PC must do the reverse color-space conversion to go from the RGB image it normally generates to the YUV image it must send to a normal television set. Near the end of this chapter, we discuss some of the ways in which PC images and television signals are being combined today, and also tell you about an exciting new possibility that is just beginning to appear.

Figure 14.4 shows these three color models. In all cases, the left portion of the model shows a range of colors, and the bar on the right indicates the brightness. In each drawing, the circled numbers 1 through 4 show where the colors mentioned previously would appear on those schematic color solids. Number 1 is the pure, bright red, number 2 is the rose, number 3 is the new-leaf green, and number 4 is the forest green.

Technical Note: One problem with all color image reproduction technologies is the issue of the total range of colors that can be reproduced. Human eyes can see an amazing range of colors, considering that we are only sensitive to about one octave (a two-to-one frequency range) of light waves. The technical term for the range of colors we can see, or that a given technology can reproduce, is the *color gamut*. It turns out that the color gamut for RGB (red, green, blue) video displays is markedly less than the total color gamut humans can perceive. Similarly, the color gamut for each printing technology is a subset of all the colors we might want to print—and worse, it is not the same subset as that of a video display.

One way printer manufacturers have dealt with this problem is by using more than three ink colors. Monochrome printers use a single color. Traditional color printing processes for reproducing photographs and the like use the four so-called *process colors* (cyan, magenta, yellow, and black). Recently, some printer manufacturers have introduced models that can print in six or even seven distinct colors. Each added color expands the color gamut that a printer can achieve, albeit by an ever-decreasing amount, so adding still more colors than seven is not likely to help noticeably.

FIGURE 14.4
Three common color models.

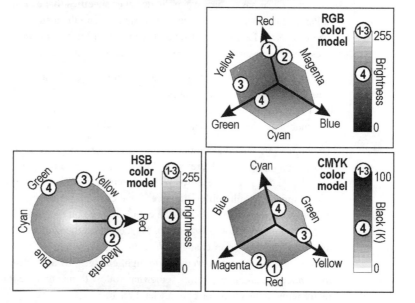

Printed images on paper (or on a transparency for use in an overhead projector) are subtractive images. That is, you shine nominally white light on them and the inks on the page subtract some of that light before it is bounced back to your eyes. To create the appearance of a red pel, for example, you must subtract most of the non-red color in the light that gets reflected from it. That is usually done in printing by the use of a suitable combination of cyan and yellow inks, with possibly some black thrown in to lower the overall brightness of that pel.

Note: There is another way to print colors, called *spot color* in the printing industry. Here, you use inks in each of the colors you care about. This can require the use of up to a dozen separate inks, and it is the only way to print documents with convincing golds and silvers, for example. But all common color printers for PCs do not use this approach. Instead, they use the more common four-color printing model with inks that are cyan (C), magenta (M), yellow (Y), and black (K).

Color Correction Programs and Printer Profiles

Just as with color displays, color printers won't always print images that look exactly alike. Our eyes can be very sensitive to even minor variations in color in an image. Some companies are extraordinarily concerned that their logos, for example, be printed in exactly the "right" colors.

One way the printing industry has coped with this problem is by the creation of a standard set of color swatches. The most famous of these sets is called the Pantone colors. This trademarked set of colors comes in a special book. If the graphic designer has a copy and the printer also has a copy, when the designer specifies that a certain area shall be printed in Pantone number whatever, the printer can compare the actual, final printed pieces against the copy of the Pantone color set and see whether the color came out right—and if it does not, make suitable adjustments to the printing press and ink supply so that it will.

That is how designers in one place can be sure printers in another place get the printed colors to be "just so." A different problem arises when the designer (or anyone who creates color documents) wants to design the document on a computer screen and then be reasonably assured that it will look the same when it is printed.

The colors you see on a computer monitor come from glowing phosphors. The colors you see on a printed page are created by absorption of a portion of the incident light by the inks on that page. These two very different ways of producing color often lead to the colors appearing quite different. Here is one example: If the incident light changes—for example, from white to yellow—the colors you see on the printed page will change (with every color shifting towards yellow). The colors on the computer monitor will change much less, and whatever changes do occur might seem to be in the opposite direction. This is because when the overall room light changes toward yellow, your brain attempts to compensate and now permits somewhat yellow things to appear to be white. And really white things then look somewhat bluish.

What you want is for the screen and page images to look the same in some specified set of standard conditions of room lighting, kind of paper, particular monitor, and so forth. This can be done, but it takes a bit of special modification of the video driver or the printer driver. These modifications go by the name *color correction*.

Color printers, just like the color monitors described in Chapter 6, often are supplied with a special *color profiles* file. This file contains information on just how much of each of the four colors it must be commanded to print to achieve certain standard, blended colors. Such a profile might be prepared separately for each individual printer, or it might be one that applies, in an average way, to all printers of a given model.

The International Color Consortium (ICC) has worked on this problem extensively. They have crafted a number of color models and color-model transformation strategies. Their work has led to a standardized set of color correction profiles for a wide variety of color image creation devices.

Windows incorporates color management support in what is termed its Color Management Module (CMM). The CMM contains ICC profiles for many monitors and some printers. Printers that qualify for a Windows-compatibility logo must, among other things, come with an ICC printer profile that you can add to that collection.

You can load a color correction profile for a monitor by going into the Display applet in Control Panel, selecting the Settings tab, and clicking on the Advanced button. Choose the Color Management tab, and you will see what has been loaded and have the opportunity to change it if you want. Similarly, the printer driver that sends color images to the printer will allow installation of a printer color correction profile. Figure 14.5, for example, shows the print driver for the Xerox Phaser 860 printer, which allows users to easily select from the many installed color profiles (including black-and-white/grayscale). The Lexmark C720 comes with a similar capability.

FIGURE 14.5

The print driver for the Xerox Phaser 860 allows you to select from among many installed and/or pre-defined color profiles, including a black-and-white setting which allows you to use exclusively black ink (which, incidentally, is free from Xerox for the life of the printer!).

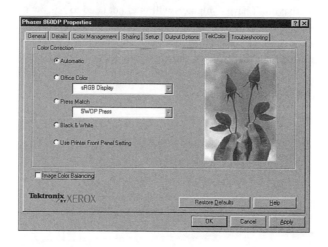

This informs that driver how to shade the colors in the image it sends out in order to make the resulting printed colors more nearly accurate representations of the image creator's intentions. Programs to create color images often also incorporate tools to compensate for the characteristics of your particular color printer.

By using some combination of all these tools (printer profile, driver adjustments, and image creation program adjustments), creating images both on your PC's screen and on paper that look very nearly alike should be possible, and in the case of ones that reproduce the appearance of some real objects, very nearly like those actual objects. Getting the colors almost right is, in fact, a relatively straightforward process with Windows and its supported output devices. But getting it exactly right on paper—which must include allowing for the slight individual deviations of the output of any given printer or monitor from others of the same brands and model numbers—is a tough job, even now, requiring specialized test equipment. When it is done right, though, the matching can be spectacularly good.

Summary

You now know the different mark-making methods used in PC printers. Each of the hundreds of models on the market uses only one of these. You know that printers often have a default font (and you know that this means a prescribed typeface, style, and size) in which they will print ASCII text. You also know that most are also capable of being commanded to print much more complex page images.

This chapter explained the difference between a formed-character printer and a dot matrix printer, as well as the difference between printers that print a single character at a time, a line at a time, or a page at a time. You have been introduced to some of the issues that are special to color printers.

You also read that most PC printers have some fairly powerful computers inside, and that printers that don't have computers will in effect need to borrow the power of your PC in order to get their jobs done. Armed with all this knowledge, you can now analyze any printer you come across and understand both what it is capable of doing and what it requires from you and your PC to work properly.

PART III

Inside the Black Boxes Inside the Glass Box

Motherboard Magic

In this chapter, we'll take a look at what many folks call the "guts" of a PC: its motherboard. This main board either already contains or directly connects to almost every major PC component, except for those that connect via an external bus like SCSI, USB, or IEEE 1394. Chief among the motherboard's components—and, really, the premier component of the entire PC and the component by which we most commonly classify different grades of computer, is the processor itself.

Processor Architecture

People who design computers often speak of the *architecture* of a given computer. What are they talking about? Isn't architecture something that applies to buildings and not to computers?

The dictionary defines an *architect* as "the designer of anything" or "the structure of anything." So the architecture of a computer is just a fancy way of referring to how its parts are arranged and how they have been designed to work together.

The core of any computer's design is its CPU. The designer of this chip ends up defining in many important ways what is possible for this computer. For example, the CPU has only so many pins on it. Their number, and their specific uses, define how much memory it can be connected to, what particular sorts of information manipulation it can perform, whether it responds to events outside itself when they occur, and so on.

The x86 CPU chips have many common features. It is that common set of features that defines the x86 architecture, and the PC architecture is a subset of the x86 architecture. Before we go into details on X86, let's talk about the difference between the two major CPU technologies: RISC and CISC.

RISC

RISC stands for Reduced Instruction Set Computer, and it supports a relatively limited number of instructions. Does this sound strange? Well, sometimes quality is more important than quantity.

Traditionally, computer manufacturers tend to design increasingly complex CPUs to cope with the new demand for fancy functions. With this design, more instruction types are supported at the expense of execution time. The more instruction sets to go through, the longer the delay it has.

Some computer manufacturers, with the intention to optimize processor performance and reduce production cost, reverse the technically sophisticated trend by building CPUs that support a very limited instruction set. PowerPC is one typical example of RISC processor. With simpler instructions, execution can be sped up without the need for fitting in more transistors.

Does this sound logical? Well, it depends. When the instruction set is simplified, the fancy functions will have to be handled by software, which might be counter-productive at the end of the day.

With the latest development in processor technology, RISC implementations become more and more complicated. They now include significantly more instruction sets than before. On the other hand, traditional processors are optimized by making use of design tricks commonly found in RISC platforms.

So, when you purchase a processor, should you go for one that is RISC based? We bet that the salesperson will not even be able to tell whether a particular processor is RISC. One thing for sure though, "RISC" is no longer a *must have* feature.

CISC and the Details of the x86 CPU's Architecture

CISC stands for Complex Instruction Set Computer. Most personal computers, including the popular x86 family, use this architecture.

We could easily fill the rest of this book with arcane details about how the various x86 processors work. But if we did, your eyes would glaze over, and in any case you don't need to know all those things in order to get an accurate, if general, notion of how the processors do their jobs. So this section is an overview of the most important architectural features of these chips. We will, in this process, blur some of the lines between different parts of the CPU or lump several related parts together. This will give you a unified picture that applies to all the members of the family that's clearer than if we described all the detailed ways in which the family members differ from one another.

Figure 15.1 shows a picture of the latest Intel Pentium 4 processor.

Figure 15.2 shows a picture of the Intel Celeron processor.

FIGURE 15.1
The Intel Pentium 4 is a latest-generation microprocessor.

FIGURE 15.2
Intel's Celeron family of micro-processors offers a balance between performance and cost.

Note: Do keep in mind that, for the rest of this chapter, we will be referring many times to the x86 chip family members. By this designation we mean the Intel family of microprocessor, including the variety of Pentium models, but we also include any of the clone CPU chips built by Intel's competitors, such as the AMD and VIA (Cyrix and IDT) chips. For simplicity, we don't mention this each time it applies. If your PC uses one of the clone chips, realize that what we are saying about the x86 chips probably also applies to the CPU chip in your PC. When there are significant differences between the different brands, we point them out.

Another important point to understand: even though the chips from AMD and VIA are considered to be X86 compatibles, some of them require the use of specific motherboard chipsets to function. Take AMD Duron and Athlon as examples; they do not work with Intel chipsets. Even worse, they require sockets of different sizes. We will get into details about the chipsets shortly.

The "Intel-Compatible" Chips

Starting from the early 80s, Intel was the only producer of X86 based processors. However, due to the explosive growth in demand, many manufacturers entered the market by producing "Intel-compatible" chips. These chips support the same X86 instruction set, and are often less expensive than the original Intel chips. In some cases, they even offer better performance.

The leading manufacturers of Intel-compatible chips were Cyrix and AMD. Cyrix was founded in 1988 to manufacture Intel-compatible microprocessors. Its 6x86 line of processors is comparable to Intel's Pentium chips in terms of integer performance, which is essential to running general office applications. However, due to its poor 3D computation performance, it failed to become the mainstream player. Cyrix was acquired by National Semiconductor in 1997, and then by VIA in 1999.

Figure 15.3 shows the VIA Cyrix 3 CPU.

FIGURE 15.3
The VIA Cyrix 3 is the newest of chips to come from a long line competing for market share against Intel's offerings.

AMD stands for Advanced Micro Devices. It is challenging Intel's leading position with its K7 Athlon processors. The Athlon series outperforms Pentium III in many respects, and is considered by most hardcore gamers the choice of 3D gaming platform.

Figure 15.4 shows the AMD K6-2 CPU.

FIGURE 15.4
The AMD K6-2 is another current-generation competitor of Intel's.

Figure 15.5 shows the AMD Duron processor.

FIGURE **15.5**
Another offering from AMD is the Duron family of chips.

Figure 15.6 shows the AMD K7 Athlon processor.

FIGURE **15.6**
The AMD Athlon family of micro-processors is the line of choice for users, like gamers, who demand the most from a PC.

The New IA64 Architecture

IA64 is the code name for the new 64-bit microprocessor technology being developed jointly by Intel and Hewlett-Packard. It is intended to become the commodity-computing platform for the next millennium. The IA64 architecture, due to its potential high performance, has resulted in endorsements from almost all major players in the computing industry.

Technically speaking, an IA64 processor can run software written for the original x86 architecture. However, for maximum performance, software optimized for 64-bit computing should be deployed.

IA64 provides a series of advanced techniques, including long instruction words, instruction predication, branch elimination, and speculative loading. The most interesting thing about IA64 is that it introduces a whole new computing paradigm called EPIC.

EPIC

EPIC stands for Explicitly Parallel Instruction Computing. It breaks the barrier of traditional CISC or RISC sequential programs through the use of explicitly exposed instruction-level parallelism. With this level of parallelism, a system can execute as many instructions as possible in parallel, when those instructions are properly bundled.

EPIC is a whole new way of computing. For effective performance, the OS must be re-written to take advantage of this new technology. A special 64-bit version of Windows 2000 is in development. Some versions of Linux will include support for 64-bit computing too.

AMD's Alternative: X86-64

One drawback of Intel's IA64 technology is backward compatibility. Technically it can run the old 32-bit applications through emulation. However, the performance of doing so is poor. In fact, running anything through emulation is slow.

Users who want to migrate to 64-bit and at the same time maintain optimal performance on the applications currently in use might need to maintain separate 32-bit processors. This puts a lot of weight on the consumer when making the 64-bit decision: they might never be allowed to have the best of both worlds!

AMD's 64-bit x86-64 architecture uses a different approach. Instead of redesigning the whole thing in 64-bit, AMD is adding 64-bit extension to the current 32-bit x86 architecture. This allows you to get the best 32-bit performance and obtain 64-bit compatibility, everything in a single core.

The new AMD's 64-bit extension to the x86 core adds eight new general-purpose registers (64-bit), 64-bit memory addressing, and 64-bit wide registers and instruction pointer. The extensions will be included in the upcoming K8 processors.

The Bus Interface Unit

Pretend you are "visiting" the CPU. Your first impressions will be a view from the outside, followed by what you see as you enter the "lobby." The actual CPU is connected to the outside world, in logical terms, by a portion of its internal circuitry we call the *bus interface unit*. This section "listens to" (monitors the voltage on) some of the pins, looking for input signals; "speaks to the outside world" (asserts a voltage) on some other pins; and for some pins can do either "listening" or "speaking," depending on the value of the voltage on yet another pin.

This section of the CPU is also responsible for *buffering* the input and output signals. This means that it contains amplifiers to make the output signals strong enough to be "heard" by any number of receiving circuits, up to some specified maximum. It also contains receivers capable of detecting the input signals while extracting very little power from their sources.

In some members of the x86 family, the bus interface unit also must translate voltage levels. In those chips, the external circuitry might operate from a 5-volt power supply, whereas the internal circuitry might be running on a 3.3-volt, or 2.5-volt power supply. This means that the valid voltage level to represent a binary 1 on any of the external pins is anything greater than about 2 volts, but on the corresponding internal connections the valid voltage level for a binary 1 is anything over about 1 volt. (In both cases, the level for a binary 0 is any voltage less than some threshold value that is very close to 0 volts.) The bus interface unit's receivers and output amplifiers are designed to accept and generate the valid voltage signals for each of its input and output connections, depending on whether they connect to the internal CPU circuits or to the outside world.

Finally, some members of the x86 family have internal clocks (occasionally known as the CPU's *frequency*) that run at some multiple of the external clock (also known as the *bus frequency*). The bus interface unit is also responsible for generating the internal clock from the external one, and for keeping information flowing into and out of the CPU in synchrony with both those clock frequencies.

Separating Instructions from Data

When the signals get inside the CPU, they must be routed to the correct internal parts. If you think of a CPU as analogous to an office, this job is the receptionist's.

The incoming signals consist of a mixture of two kinds of information: instructions and data. (Think of orders for finished goods and raw material, if you prefer the factory analogy. Think of employees who do the office work and clients on whom they perform their services if you prefer the office analogy.)

Instructions are placed in a queue for the instruction decoder. ("Go over to Window 3 and wait in line, please.") Data, on the other hand, is parked in some waiting rooms, called *registers*. ("Follow me. Now, please wait in here. Someone will be with you shortly.")

Figuring Out What to Do and Making It Happen

The instructions are taken out of the queue, interpreted, and put to work by a group of parts called the *code prefetch unit,* the *instruction decoder,* and the *control unit*. We refer to this collection of parts from here on simply as the *instruction handler*. This section of the CPU has several jobs to perform.

First, because the x86 processors are complex instruction set computer (CISC) machines, their instructions come in a variety of lengths. The shortest is a single byte; the longest can consist of well over a dozen bytes.

The instruction handler examines the first byte and from that value, it deduces how many bytes there are to this particular instruction. It must then make sure that the rest of the bytes of this instruction are ready for its use, and if they are not, invoke the help of other sections of the CPU to go out to main memory and fetch them.

Next, the instruction handler must decide what data this instruction needs. Some instructions carry some or all of their data inside themselves. These are called *immediate* data items. Other instructions operate on data that is already present in one or more of the CPU registers. Yet others operate on, or return results to, locations outside the CPU in main memory. The instruction handler must ensure that the data items needed by this instruction are in place and ready to be operated on. If they are not, the instruction handler must arrange for them to be fetched into the CPU.

Finally, the instruction handler has the job of determining just what the instruction is telling the CPU to do and then activating the relevant parts of the CPU to get that job done. The simplest instructions correspond directly to some elementary task that some element of the CPU's circuitry can do. The more recent members of the x86 family have specialized circuitry dedicated to performing even some of the more complex instructions if they are used often enough. This is done to make the CPU execute those instructions as fast as possible. In fact, most of the instructions an x86 processor understands require multiple actions by different parts of the computing machinery in the CPU. The instruction decoder looks up these steps in an internal library called the *microcode store*. It then delivers those microinstructions to the relevant parts of the CPU for execution.

Registers Are Temporary Information-Holding Places

Registers are important in any processor. Every computer and a microprocessor such as an x86 processor, which is actually a full computer in its own right, must have some place to hold information while it is being processed.

The many x86 family members have different numbers of registers and, in many cases, registers of different sizes. The original 8086 and 8088 designs include 14 registers, each capable of holding a single 16-bit number. The latest Pentium II has many more registers. Most of the Pentium II's registers hold 64-bit numbers; a few hold many more bits. In the case of these largest registers (called *translation look-aside buffers*), only a portion of the bits it holds is visible to a program running on the CPU. The rest are hidden from the program's view, but are accessible to the CPU to help it do its job more quickly.

One reason for the much larger number of registers in the most recent x86 family members is that they have become so complex that some special registers were needed to facilitate automatic testing of the processor at the end of its production cycle as the manufacturers attempt to make certain that their chips work before they leave their hands. Another reason is that these models include, in addition to the hardware needed to do the basic computing job they were designed to do, other hardware referred to as the *system management* hardware, which supports various special operations such as powering down to save power during times of inactivity.

To keep the story as simple as possible, we are going to focus at first just on the set of registers defined for the 8086. The registers added in later members of the x86 family are similar to these, at least in concept. We will introduce some of those other registers when discussing the functions that they serve. In the 8086 (and 8088), the 14 registers can be grouped into five categories. The following sections include a brief description of each category and the names of the corresponding registers.

General-Purpose Registers

Of the 8086's 14 registers, four are designated as general-purpose registers. These are mainly used for data values being processed. (That is, they can be added to, subtracted from, or multiplied by one another. They can be compared with one another, or a number in a general-purpose register can be combined with a number somewhere out in main memory. There are still other ways in which this data can be processed.)

If the instruction being executed needs only one byte of data, that byte can reside in either half of a general-purpose register, and it can be accessed by that instruction without altering whatever byte value is in the other half of that register.

These registers have simple names. These names are used within statements in what is called *assembly language programming* as a way to refer to particular registers. The names were defined by Intel, and they are based in turn on the names of the smaller, single-byte wide registers in Intel's 8080 generation of CPU chips (a generation that immediately preceded the first of the x86 family).

When a program refers to registers that are being used to hold 16-bit numbers, the names of the most commonly used registers are AX, BX, CX, and DX. (The older generation CPU chips had A, B, C, and D registers, which could hold only a single byte. You might think of X in this context as standing for *extended*.) When you want to refer to just one-half of one of these 16-bit registers, the lower half is called AL, BL, CL, or DL. The upper half is referred to as AH, BH, CH, or DH.

In more recent members of the x86 family of CPUs, there are a number of wider registers, and these often carry very similar names, such as EAX or EBX, meaning simply something twice as wide as the AX or BX register. Here, a letter (A, B, C, and so forth) alone used to refer to a byte-wide (8-bit) register; that letter followed by an X means a double-byte wide (16-bit) register. If that letter is followed by either an L or H, it refers to the lower or upper half of that register, and if the letter is followed by an X and preceded by an E, it refers to a 4-byte wide (32-bit) register with a similar purpose as the similarly named, narrower one.

You might think that these names were chosen just because they are the first four letters of the alphabet. That might be so, but they also have mnemonic value. (That is, they have longer names that are suggested by these short ones.) These four registers, despite being called general-purpose, have some restrictions on their use and some customary uses. Here are the details:

- The AX (or AH plus AL) register is most often used as the *accumulator,* which is the place where the result of some calculation ends up. For example, you can add the value in some other register or in a memory location to the value in the A register, and the result will wind up replacing the value originally in the A register.

- The BX register is often used to hold the segment portion of an address. When it is used for this you might think of it as the *base* register, because the segment address value indicates the beginning (or base) of a region of memory. The BX register (or BL or BH) can also be used to hold data of other sorts.

- The CX register is normally used to hold a number that indicates how many times some operation has been done. When that number reaches a specified target value, the program must jump to a different place in the program. Only if the *count* of operations that have been performed so far is held in this particular register, it is possible to do the necessary comparison and jump in a single instruction.

- The DX register (or DH and DL) commonly is called the *data* register. It sometimes is used to hold a port address. Other times it is used in combination with AX to hold a 32-bit number (for example, the result of multiplying two 16-bit numbers).

The Flags Register

One very special register is called the *flags register*. (Its mnemonic name is, quite simply, FLAGS.) This is a place that holds a collection of 16 individual bits, each of which indicates some fact. One of the simplest examples of a flag bit's meaning is the one that indicates whether the last comparison of two bytes found that they were or were not equal. Other flags indicate whether the result of the last arithmetic operation was positive or negative, whether it was zero, or whether it overflowed the capacity of the register. Still other flags indicate something about the state of the processor. Examples of this include the following: Is the processor supposed to respond to or ignore external interrupts? Is it supposed to run in single-step mode? When processing a string of bytes, is it working its way "up" the string or "down" the string?

Because the more recent members of the x86 family have wider registers for both data and flags, they can represent even more conditions by flags.

Generally, the values of these flags control the behavior of the CPU when it is executing what we term "conditional instructions." (This concept is explained more fully later in this chapter.)

The Instruction Pointer

Another special register holds the address in main memory of the instruction currently being executed. Its name, of course, is the *instruction pointer* register (and it is given the designation IP). The value in this register *implies* the location in main memory where the instruction being executed is held; to get the actual location, you must combine this value in a suitable fashion with a value in another register, called a *code segment register*. (You'll learn more about code segment registers later in this chapter when we cover segment registers as a class.)

The value that is held in the instruction register gets changed in either of two ways. One we refer to as the *normal flow* of control and the other as a *branch*.

The Normal Flow of Control

Unless the instruction being executed causes something different to happen, the value in this register, sometimes called the *Program Counter,* is automatically increased by the length of the current instruction each time an instruction is completed. This is done because in most cases the next instruction to be executed is held in main memory right after the current instruction. The complexity of needing to push the pointer up a variable amount comes from the fact that the x86 processors are CISC devices, with variable-length instructions. One of the implications of this is that they must handle instructions of different lengths. This variability makes it necessary to be able to push the pointer by alterable amounts.

Branch Instructions

About 10 percent of the time this is not true. In those cases, the current instruction might tell the CPU to fetch its next instruction from some other location. These instructions are called branch instructions, or *jump* instructions, and they come in two types: *unconditional branch* instructions, in which the next location is always different from the normal flow of control, and *conditional branch* instructions, which decide whether to jump to a new location or simply fall through to the next instruction after this one. These instructions usually base their decision on the value of some one of the flag bits.

One other way that the flow of control often gets altered is by execution of a subroutine call instruction. This is a way of effectively pausing the program execution briefly and instead invoking another program (or more accurately, a mini-program that has been embedded in some other place within this program). When that mini-program is finished with its task, it will execute a return instruction. That will cause the processor to resume execution of the original program at the instruction immediately after the subroutine call instruction.

This strategy of calling a subroutine is one of the ways programmers save themselves work. They can write a subroutine once and then use it from many places within their larger program, without having to copy all the instructions that make up that subroutine into the main program at each place it is going to be used. In fact, besides saving programmer effort, this also keeps the overall program size down, which can be another significant benefit in some situations.

Other Pointer Registers

Two more of the original 8086's 14 registers are also pointer registers. One is called the *base pointer register* (BP); the other is called the *stack pointer register* (SP). Each of them holds a number that is used as the segment portion of an address if the processor is running in real mode. In protected mode, that number is called a selector, but it serves a similar function. Either way it is used to point to a region of memory that is used for a stack. We'll explain just what that means later in this chapter.

Index Registers

Two of the registers were designed for use in moving strings of data (many-byte sequences of arbitrary length). One called the *source index register* (SI) might hold the address of the beginning of a string you want to move, for example. The other register in this class, called the *destination index register* (DI), holds the address to which that string will be moved. The number of bytes to be moved is usually held in the CX (Count) register. In addition to their use in moving entire strings of data, these registers can also be used to indicate a location within an array of numerical data or in a number of other ways.

Segment Registers

Finally, the last class is the *segment registers*. In the 8086 there are four of these. These are very special-purpose registers used only in performing address calculations. Later, in the section called "Calculating Addresses," we explain about some of the different ways in which the values in these registers get used in address calculations. Right now we simply want to tell you the names of the different registers and describe what types of addresses might be pointed to by use of their value.

The first is the *code segment register* (CS). CS holds a value that is combined with the value in the instruction register to point to the next instruction to be executed.

The next register is the *data segment register* (DS). Normally, DS is used to point to a region of memory in which data values are being held. It can be combined with a number in the BX, SI, or DI registers, for example, to specify a particular byte or word of data.

The third register is called the *extra segment register* (ES). It is, as its name suggests, simply an extra segment register provided for whatever purpose the programmer wants, although it most naturally gets used in connection with string operations.

The last register is called the *stack segment register* (SS). The value in this register is combined with the value in the stack pointer (SP) register to point to the word of data currently being processed in the stack. (More on the stack later.) The SS register can also be used in combination with the BP register for certain instructions.

Calculating Addresses

We mentioned in discussing the instruction pointer (IP) register that the value it contains, taken alone, doesn't indicate where in memory the instruction it points to is located.

Every time an x86 processor wants to refer to memory, whether to retrieve an instruction or to get or put some data item there, it must go through a more or less complex process involving at least two register values to decide where it must go. And often (in protected mode), the CPU must not only use those values from two (or more) registers, it must also access up to three different data tables in memory before it knows what actual, physical memory address is implied.

Going from Abstraction to Reality

There are several reasons for the complexity of address calculations in an x86 processor. Perhaps the most fundamental reason is that these processors deal in several kinds of memory address space.

At the physical level (what actually happens to real, physical objects in your PC), memory locations are addressed by voltages on wires that connect to each memory module or chip. These signals are derived from the voltages on corresponding pins of the CPU. If you look at the voltages on those CPU pins, labeling the ones that are high as 1s and the others as 0s, the binary number you get is referred to as the *physical address*.

Addressing Details

Some of those CPU address pins have their signals directly routed to the memory modules. (They pass through some other integrated circuits that amplify them, but they go straight through those amplifiers and are not mixed with other signals in the process.)

Others of the CPU address pin signals are combined in circuits called memory address decoders whose job it is to decide which, if any, of the memory chips or modules your PC has are supposed to be activated just now. All of those modules (or chips) get all the other signals, and the active module (or chip) uses them to decide which location to access.

The CPU, with its 64 data wires, connects to eight bytes of memory at a time. This means that the three least-significant bits of any address can be ignored in pointing to locations in main memory. They are used internally by the CPU to determine which of the eight bytes it just read is the one it wants to begin working with. Recalling that 23 is 8 and 225 is about 32 million, you can see that you need exactly 22 wires to address each 8-byte location within each 32MB memory module. Furthermore, it is possible (and usual) to make the address pins on the memory modules serve double duty. At one instant they read a row address and at a different instant a column address. That enables the module makers to get away with, in this case, just 11 address pins, plus one pin to indicate whether these address lines were reading the first 11 bits of the address (lines A3 through A13) or the remaining 6 bits (A14 through A24).

The signal lines on the memory modules, labeled chip enable, are used to turn the integrated circuits in this module on or off. The voltage on this line will either make the module responsive to signals on the rest of its input lines, or it will make the module go into a sort of stasis, whereby it ignores all its other inputs and creates no output signals.

The memory address decoder gets all the rest of the address lines; in this case, seven lines (A25 through 31). That is enough bits to point to any of 128 different "banks" of memory. This hypothetical computer, however, has only two banks. With 32MB in each bank, that is enough to run almost any one of today's programs (but it certainly is not enough memory to run more than one of the largest of today's programs at once). The memory address decoder must examine the signals on all seven lines in order not to activate those memory modules unless all of those lines except the first one have zero-level signals on them. The level on the first one determines which of the two memory banks to activate.

What Addresses Do Programs Use?

PC programs don't use physical addresses. The x86 family of processors doesn't enable them to. Instead, they must use at least one level of indirection. The actual physical address is generated by combining two or more numbers according to one of several strategies. Because of this complexity, you will run across the terms *logical address* (also known as the *virtual address*), *linear address*, and *physical address*. We'll explain each one of these concepts in the following sections.

Calculating Physical Addresses in Real Mode

You have already met the simplest of the x86 strategies for computing a memory address. Keep in mind that memory addresses in real mode are expressed in programs as logical addresses, each of which is composed of a segment value and an offset.

A segment value is multiplied by 16 (in hexadecimal that means simply shoved left one space) and then added to the offset value to get the physical address value. There are 65,536 possible values for the segment number and an equal number of possibilities for the offset. This means that a particular value for the segment portion of the address indicates a particular 64KB region of memory. The offset value indicates a particular location.

An important point to realize is that in real mode, there are many logical addresses (by which we mean a pair of 16-bit numbers, one for segment and one for offset) that point to each physical memory address. If you simply increase the segment value by 1 and decrease the offset value by 16, the physical address remains unchanged. Thus, the logical address 01A0:4C67h is exactly the same as the logical address 01A1:4C57h. (The lowercase letter *h* appears behind each address to remind you that these are hexadecimal numbers.) Normally, just having two four-digit numbers connected by a colon implies this, but we want to make this point very clear. That should also make it clear to you that the offset value 4C57h is exactly 16 less than the offset value 4C67h, because the two numbers differ by one in the "sixteens" place. As you will learn shortly, in *protected mode,* there can be even more logical addresses all pointing to the same physical address.

Calculating Physical Addresses in Protected Mode

All but the earliest members of the x86 family of processors have more than one operating mode. They all "wake up" in real mode, and in that mode they use the strategy just described for calculating physical addresses.

After several special and necessary data tables have been built in memory, it is possible for any member of the x86 family more advanced than the 80186 to go into some version of protected-mode operation. In these modes (there are three of them), the numbers held in the segment registers are not simply multiplied and added to the offset value to point to a memory location. The use of the numbers in the segment registers in any of the protected modes is so different from their use in real mode that they are called *selectors* instead of segment values.

Unlike a segment value, which points to a particular 64KB region of memory, a selector just points to one line in a data structure called a *descriptor table*. That line contains three facts about the "selected" memory region. One of them points to the beginning of the region. Another says how long that region is. The last "fact" is really a bunch of numbers that indicates certain special properties (called *access rights*) that region of memory has when it is accessed via that selector value.

The name *segment* still refers to the region of memory pointed to by a particular value in the segment register. But because the process for getting from the selector value to the segment position in memory address space is more convoluted, it is no longer appropriate to use the same name for both.

There are three advantages to this strategy. First, you can have any selector value you want point to any region of memory you want. (No longer is there any necessary connection between the regions of memory specified by two selector values that differ by some fixed amount.) The second advantage is that the size of the segment referred to by a selector value is not fixed. It can be as short as one byte in some cases, or as long as 4GB in other cases. Finally, the presence of the access rights in the descriptor table allows the CPU to control the kinds of access to this region of memory when it is accessed via this selector.

The name *logical address* is still attached to the combination of two hexadecimal numbers separated by a colon. The first one (which is always two bytes, or four hexadecimal characters, long) is now called the *selector* instead of the segment; the second one (which might be either four or eight bytes long) is still called the *offset,* and indeed it still means the number of bytes into the segment from its beginning, wherever that is.

We told you there were three versions of protected mode. The first version was introduced with the 286, so it is called *286-protected mode*. The second and third were introduced with the 386 and they are called *386-protected mode* and *virtual 86 mode*.

The only differences between 286-protected mode (which still is supported on even the latest x86 processors, for reasons of backward compatibility) and 386-protected mode (which is used almost all the time in modern programs) is merely the size of some of the numbers stored in the descriptors, and as a consequence, the possible size of the memory regions these descriptors "describe" and the number of access rights that can be specified for those regions.

Calculating Physical Addresses in Virtual 86 Mode

Virtual 86 mode is a strange sort of beast. In this mode, which is always used in conjunction with 386-protected mode, the running program thinks it is running on an 8086 processor in real mode, whereas in fact the processor is in protected mode, and the operating system is running in 386-protected mode and serving a role described as a *virtual 86 monitor*.

The advantage of this mode of CPU operation is that it enables you to run old DOS programs that were written to run in real mode, while having the advantages of protected mode. (We'll describe a bit of what those advantages are in the next section.) Furthermore, it enables you to run several such programs, each in its own DOS box, without any of them knowing that the others exist. This is done when you run an old DOS application in a window (which could be a full-screen window) under Windows 3.*x,* Windows 9*x,* or Windows NT, for example. (Booting in MS-DOS mode allows running the PC in real mode, which is possible in all versions of Windows except NT.)

How Paging Complicates Address Calculations

In the 386 and all later members of the x86 family, there is one more complication to memory address calculations. It is called *paging*, and it introduces the third kind of memory address. The selector value combined with the offset is still called the logical address, which is what programs actually use. If you add the offset to the base address, the resulting selector points to what is called the *linear address.* In the 80286, that was the same as the physical address. In the later x86 processors, it need not be the same.

The notion here is the following: A physical address is specified by the voltages on the CPU chip's address pins. It is one of some large number of locations in the processor's *physical memory address space.*

When paging is in use, the linear address is simply an abstract location in some hypothetical memory address space. Getting from a linear address to a physical one takes place by a process analogous to, but a bit more complicated than, the way we got from a selector value to a segment address.

The 32-bit linear address is broken into three parts. The most significant 10 bits are used as a directory index. The next most significant 10 bits are the table index. The least significant 12 bits are used as the offset.

You're probably used to hearing about *paging* as the paging to disk. This means that there's not enough physical RAM to contain all the code and data that the computer needs for every application.

By utilizing the processor's operation with an intelligent operating system such as Windows 95/98 or Windows NT, the same constructs that allow logical memory used by a process to be mapped anywhere in physical memory allow memory to be loaded and unloaded from portions of the hard disks on your PC.

This allows more programs to run at one time than there is physical RAM to run them. That's why operating systems that support paging to disk are often called *virtual memory operating systems* because they can use virtual memory as well as real physical memory.

Enforcing Protections

The name *protected mode* is suggestive. Something is being protected somehow. But what and how? The whole reason for protected mode is to facilitate good multitasking. In any multitasking system (think of a Windows machine running several programs at once), several programs might each think it is the only program in existence, and yet they all can run together in the same PC without interfering with one another. Or at least, that is the intention.

For this to work, it is necessary to keep the various programs from conflicting. Some master program must be in charge. That master program is the operating system (for example, Windows).

That is not enough, however. When an operating system launches an application on a PC, in real mode, the application program can do anything it likes. It can read or write to any portion of memory, can send information out any port, or write all over the screen. There is no certain way for the operating system to prevent this. That is why Intel devised the various protected modes for its x86 processors. The idea was not new; it was borrowed from mainframe computer experience (as was the notion of paging), but this was the first time it was applied at the microcomputer level.

The basic notion is that each program is assigned some protection level, and it can only do whatever that level of program is allowed to do. There are four levels of protection, from zero to three, and programs are assigned to one of these four rings. The core of the operating system runs in ring zero, and usually, in protected mode only that set of programs is allowed to run there. All application programs normally run in ring three. So far, no operating system has made much use of rings one or two, but they are there in every x86 processor, just waiting for some clever programmer to find a use for them.

Furthermore, each segment of memory (recall that now those are the regions specified by the contents of various lines in some descriptor tables) has certain access rights. Only programs that have the correct level of privilege can change those access rights, and only operations that the access rights permit are allowed to happen.

Who enforces all these rules? The CPU does. That is why this discussion is here, under the CPU's internal architecture, and why in particular under the discussion of address calculations. The same circuitry in the CPU that computes addresses also ensures that the instruction about to be executed doesn't violate any of the rules.

When a rule violation occurs, it is referred to as an *exception*. These are further classified as *faults, traps,* and *aborts*. When any of these exceptions occurs, the CPU stops doing what the program says to do, and instead it goes off and does something else. (Just how it does this is very similar to how it responds to external or software interrupts, and we will describe the mechanism in some detail later in this chapter.)

The most infamous of the exceptions is the one called a *General Protection Fault (of type 13)*. This generally results in an onscreen error message and leads to shutting down the offending application program. You might think that Windows crashes a lot. It does, but not nearly as much as it would without the hardware support that is built into every x86 processor for protection enforcement.

The Arithmetic-Logic Unit (ALU) and Its Kin

It is convenient, at this level, to lump together another collection of logical subparts of the CPU. These include the Arithmetic-Logic Unit (ALU) and some other portions that do similar things. The ALU actually adds, subtracts, multiplies, or divides integer values. It also can compare two numbers to determine whether they are identical and, if not, decide which one is larger.

Some Simple Integer Operations

Besides simple arithmetic (adding, subtracting, multiplying, and dividing) and performing logical comparisons, the ALU can also shift the bits around in a number of ways. Think of the contents of a 16-bit register as 16 individual bits sitting on 16 chairs in a row. The first kind of shift, called an *arithmetic shift*, just makes each bit get up and move one place to the right or left; the end bit that finds itself without a place to "sit down" simply is lost (and a 0 bit is moved in at the opposite end of the register).

Another kind of shift, called a *circular shift*, takes the bit that falls out of one end and stuffs it back in the opposite end. This type of bit shifting comes in handy when multiplying numbers, and also for certain logic operations. Trust me: Programmers often find this capability vital for their programs.

Dedicated Hardware for More Complex Tasks

We have now told you about all the important elements of an early x86 CPU. Later models mostly just have faster (and sometimes more) of these same units. But they also have a few other, specialized hardware units to do some additional tasks.

SMP

Short for Symmetric Multiprocessing, SMP is a special high performance computer architecture that makes multiple CPUs available to different processes simultaneously. "Symmetric" means that task can be assigned to any idle processor. Additionally, scalability is made possible by installing additional CPUs, provided that the motherboard has sparse sockets to accommodate extra processors.

For SMP to work, there are a couple of requirements to meet. First, your motherboard chipset must support multiple processors. Not all chipsets support SMP. Second, the processors you bought must be SMP capable. CPUs like Celeron, Duron, and some versions of Athlon are incompatible with SMP. Third, the OS must be able to detect and utilize the extra processors. You cannot run multiple OS using multiple processors. Therefore, all processors are going to be under the control of a single OS. Also, because all processors share the common memory and disk resources, the increase in performance provided by the additional processors is somewhat "discounted".

Unix, Linux, Windows NT, and Windows 2000 support SMP natively. Windows 9X and Me do not support SMP.

Figure 15.7 shows a section of a SMP capable motherboard with two processor sockets.

FIGURE 15.7
This motherboard is one of many that supports multiple processors.

Floating-Point Operations

Starting with the 486DX, a separate set of circuits is included in every x86 CPU to process floating-point numbers. This additional hardware consists of two parts. One is a set of eight very wide (80-bit) registers that are specifically designed to hold floating-point numbers. The other is the set of logic gates (and the special microcode instructions that activate them) that are arranged so as to perform the actual floating-point arithmetic.

The floating-point instructions were added to the instruction set well before the hardware to execute them became a part of the CPU. At first, the CPU would trap those instructions and invoke a special "emulation" program to perform those tasks; later, the CPU would trap them and pass them off to a subsidiary "numeric co-processor" chip. Finally, it was given the power to execute those instructions directly within itself.

Enhancements to the x86 Instruction Set: MMX, 3Dnow!, and KNI

The addition of paging and the additional protected modes in the 386 was truly revolutionary. The x86 instruction set was augmented with a whole raft of new instructions to take advantage of this new functionality. All later additions to the hardware had a less profound impact on the instruction set.

Until very recently, all the further additions to the x86 instruction set (for example, those for the 486 and early Pentium and Pentium Pro) CPUs were only minor tweaks on the previous set. But in the past couple of years, there were two significant new developments in the x86 instruction set and, if anything, change is accelerating. Interestingly, although some of these additions to the x86 instruction set were introduced by Intel, others appeared first in clone x86 processors showing the growing confidence of the clone CPU makers that their customers would respect them for new models that were "better" than Intel's, and not merely cheaper.

The first of these improvements was the addition of the so-called "multimedia extensions." Intel gave these the shorthand name MMX. These are a group of *single instruction, multiple data* (SIMD) instructions. The idea is that in a Pentium MMX, Pentium II, or any later Intel x86 processor, you can load *multiple integer* data items into the registers normally used for floating-point computation and then perform some operation on all of those data items simultaneously.

Specifically, an MMX instruction can use 64 of the 80 bits in a floating-point register to hold eight byte-wide numbers, or four 16-bit numbers, or two 32-bit numbers, and then it can act on all of them at once (for example, adding each one to the corresponding number stored in another of the floating-point registers).

This can be quite powerful. In many multimedia programs and certain kinds of business programs, precisely this sort of repetition of the same action on multiple, related data items is required. With MMX capabilities, these jobs can be sped up very significantly. Examples include digital signal processing (for example, a "Windows modem" program) and certain kinds of two-dimensional graphics processing (for example, "texture mapping").

One inconvenience to all this is that you cannot be using the floating-point registers to do floating-point and MMX calculations at the same time. (Ordinarily, in almost any modern x86 processor, there are integer instruction processing units and a floating-point unit working in parallel to speed the overall processing of your programs.)

AMD worked out a variation on this idea that they call 3DNow!. This involves both an augmentation of the x86 instruction set with some SIMD instructions performed in the floating-point registers, just like MMX, but now including ones for both integer and floating-point operations and some alterations to the actual registers to allow for more parallelism of computation. The particular instructions included in the 3DNow! set were chosen, as the name suggests, to speed calculation of 3D images, and also to speed the computations involved in advanced sound and video presentations.

All the recent CPU chips from AMD, Cyrix (a division of National Semiconductor), and Centaur (a division of IDT) include support for both 3DNow! and MMX.

Intel had to respond to 3DNow!, and rather than merely include what might be regarded as "me-too" support for that technology, they decided to enhance the MMX capabilities in future Intel x86 CPUs. At first called MMX2, this initiative is now referred to as the

Pentium III New Instructions (KNI), getting its name from the code name for the CPU model in which Intel will first debut these new instructions and the associated new internal CPU hardware.

KNI refers to improvements in three aspects of the CPU design: new instructions, new registers, and new ways to control accesses to memory.

The new SIMD instructions now include floating-point as well as integer operations. The instructions use some new, dedicated registers that are even wider than the old floating-point registers. This allows working with 128 bits (which could be eight double-byte integer values, or four single-precision floating-point values) at once. Furthermore, the new instructions include some things programmers told Intel they wanted, such as the capability to average by rounding down (used in video decompression for motion compensation), to sum absolute differences (used in video encoding for motion estimation), and some other instructions that have proven useful in speech recognition applications.

All previous x86 processors would first fetch an instruction, execute it, and finally store the results. It was not possible to begin fetching a new instruction until the previous instructions' results were being stored.

The new "streaming memory architecture" is a strategy incorporated into the Pentium III processor that permits a programmer to specify that several instructions be fetched in advance of their execution, and then have them executed, and finally store all the results as soon as possible, but without holding up the execution of additional instructions. This helps keeps the CPU from waiting for the delivery of data or instructions to or from memory. And that boosts overall CPU performance.

The advantages of all these new instructions only accrue to programs that are written to take advantage of them. The same thing applied to the floating-point hardware enhancements when they were new. Only programs that are aware of these processor enhancements, and have been redesigned to use them, will run faster. And only certain kinds of programs benefit from that sort of redesign.

In time, many, many programs have come to use the floating-point hardware. Running these programs on a 486SX- or a 386-based PC, which doesn't have the floating-point hardware built in, is horribly painful! The programs must invoke emulation programs to accomplish the effect of the missing special-purpose hardware, and those emulation programs are always tremendously slow compared to the dedicated hardware.

Even though MMX technology has been out for more than a year, it is still not used extensively in commercial programs other than games. The 3DNow! instructions are better supported, at least for Windows users, because Microsoft includes extensive use of them in the latest version of its DirectX driver program. Any program that uses the DirectX API to activate the hardware will benefit from this whenever that program runs on a CPU with 3DNow! support.

Presumably, Microsoft will support the KNI instructions equally in future releases of their driver and other system software. If so, and if the memory streaming architecture delivers the benefits Intel offers, their Pentium III CPU may leapfrog the competition once more. We can certainly hope so, for all our sakes.

The Level 1 Cache

There is one last key functional group in the CPU that we must discuss: cache memory. Some version of this idea has been an integral part of all Intel and clone x86 CPUs starting with the 486.

Actually, a form of caching (for addresses) was used even earlier in the translation look-aside buffers (TLBs) in the 386 and that form is also present in all later members of the x86 family. However, this caching is mostly hidden from view in a way that the data and instruction caching we are speaking about here is not.

The reason a memory cache makes sense is that modern CPUs are so very fast they can easily outrun the speed of main memory. So, by putting a small amount of very fast memory fast enough that it can keep up with the CPU actually inside the CPU (on the same integrated circuit chip), that cache memory can be used and reused as a temporary holding place for data and instructions on their way into the CPU and for results on their way back out to main memory. (Cache memory is also exceptionally expensive, because of its speed, which is why the two memory types—cache and main—coexist.)

This so-called *Level 1 cache* boosts performance in two ways. The first is when writes from the CPU to main memory are cached. The other way applies when reads are cached.

When information is to be written to main memory, the cache can accept that information and then let the CPU get on with its work immediately. The cache controller circuitry is then responsible for seeing that this information is later transferred to its proper place in main memory.

The second way a cache can speed things up is when the information in a given memory location is read by the CPU more than once. The first time there is no speedup. The second time (and any later times) the CPU asks for that same location's value. If that value is still in the cache memory, the cache controller can serve it up almost instantaneously.

The principal limitation on the effectiveness of cache memory comes from the fact that it is only a tiny fraction of the size of main memory. So only some small fraction of the most recently accessed locations in main memory will have their values still in the cache memory.

Memory Caching Didn't Always Make Sense

When PCs were new, building any cache memory into the CPU wouldn't have been worth it. That was true for two reasons. First, it adds complexity, and the manufacturing processes of the time could barely make chips complex enough to serve as CPUs. And second, those CPU chips ran so slowly that main memory could easily keep up with them. Now, however, the CPU chips can run several times as fast as the memory chips on even the fastest motherboards, and the needed additional complexity for at least a small amount of memory cache inside the CPU can be afforded relatively easily.

Careful study of actual everyday computer programs has shown that they very often reuse the same instructions, and even the same data items, over and over. This comes about because it often is very helpful to the programmer to use loops in the program in which some task is done over and over until some desired result is achieved. If the loop is small enough that all its instructions and all the data referred to within the loop fit inside the cache memory, during the execution of that loop the CPU can run at its top speed without having to wait for a relatively slow access to main memory.

In any case, if the running program wants to write some information to memory, it can simply hand it off to the cache unit and then continue its work. The cache unit will take care of getting that information to main memory eventually, as soon as the much slower external circuitry allows it to do so.

Making Cache Memory More Effective

A small pool of cache memory can be organized and utilized in several ways. Each of these techniques has different implications, both on how expensive the cache memory is to build and on how effective it is in operation.

Naturally, a lot of jargon is used to describe all the variations. Some of the names you will run across include *read caching, read-ahead caching, write-through caching, deferred write and read caching, fully associative caches, direct mapped caches,* and *set associative caches.* The set associative caches also come in two-way, four-way, and other subdesignations. Finally, the latest wrinkle is to separate the cache into two pieces: one dedicated to caching instructions and the other dedicated to caching data.

You can be pretty sure that the CPU makers are building in what their research says is the most effective kind and amount of cache they can include and still will permit them to make the chips using today's technology.

We'll return to memory caching in just a moment, because it also shows up in the architecture that goes around the CPU. And that is the next topic. At that time, we will also mention how some of what used to be called *external cache memory* is included inside the latest CPU designs.

The Architecture That Goes Around the CPU

At this point, you should have a pretty good understanding of the functional parts of the CPU and how they work together. To complete this discussion of the PC architecture, you still need to examine how the external parts of the PC are arranged. The most important of these is main memory. The next most important are the input/output ports. Everything else communicates with the CPU via one of these two structures.

Memory

Main memory and the CPU are the places in a PC where all the computing action takes place. This is true because data and programs must be in some portion of the main memory before the CPU can do anything with them. Some of the programs and a little bit of data might live there perpetually. Most of them are just brought into that space when they are needed and then either discarded (in the case of programs) or saved to a permanent storage location (in the case of data), after which the memory space they had occupied is once more available to be used by new programs and data.

Main memory in a PC is a mixture of RAM, ROM, and vacant potentiality. That is, your PC's CPU chip can address a physical memory address space of fixed size. At some of the locations in that space are random-access, read-or-write memory chips (RAM). At some other locations are read-only (or read-mostly) memory chips (ROM or non-volatile RAM, called NVRAM). And (usually) for most of the memory address space, nothing is there at all.

This hasn't always been so. When PCs were new, memory was a lot more expensive, per byte, than it now is, but the early PCs couldn't address more than a total of 1MB. Many owners of these early PCs had their machine's memory address space at least mostly filled with RAM or ROM.

The Maximum Size of Physical Memory

Modern PCs can address *many* more memory locations. Starting with the 386, they could potentially use up to 4GB of memory, and the Pentium Pro and Pentium II chips can, in theory, use up to 64GB of memory. Even at today's relatively low cost for memory, we know of very few folks who are pushing those limits very closely.

Modern members of the x86 processor family have two other address spaces, referred to as virtual (or logical) memory and linear memory. Linear memory address space is usually the same size as physical memory address space. The virtual memory address space, on the other hand, is enormously larger, as it is comprised of space provided by your hard drive.

The potential size of the CPU's physical memory address space is not the same as the maximum memory you can add to your PC, because PC makers don't connect all the address lines (either directly or via memory address decoders) to sockets. They don't need to, because none of their customers wants to put in as much memory as the CPU can address. (Even if they did, no current operating systems could use all that memory. Windows, for example, in all its flavors is, except for Windows NT, limited to using a maximum of 2GB of memory.)

Level 2 and Level 3 Cache

At the end of the discussion of the CPU architecture, we described the Level 1 (L1) memory cache included in all recent x86 family members. The idea of using a memory cache in a PC actually goes back even farther than the 486DX, which was the earliest of those L1-memory-cache enabled x86 processors. When the CPU chips became significantly faster than the fastest reasonably affordable DRAM chips, people started to be interested in having some cache memory, but at that point it still wasn't feasible for the CPU makers to put it on their CPU chips.

The first PC implementations of this idea were on 386-based machines. The motherboard in these PCs included some additional, extra-high speed (and extra costly) RAM chips, plus a specialized integrated circuit called a cache controller. For those PCs, this was the one and only memory cache it could have.

The size of this memory cache is mainly limited by how much money the motherboard maker thinks its customers want to spend for the performance gain which that much added memory will provide, rather than being limited, as the L1 cache is even today, by the amount of room and "spare" complexity available on the CPU chip. (The more cache the better, but after some point, the improvement in performance only grows slightly for even rather large additions to the size of the memory cache.) This meant that even when Intel and the other CPU makers started putting a small amount of cache RAM inside the CPU, motherboard makers found it helped their sales to include a second level of memory cache on the motherboard provided that this Level 2 (L2) cache was considerably larger than the L1 cache inside the CPU.

A given amount of memory in an L2 cache is not nearly as effective as the same amount of L1 cache for the simple reason that the external clock frequency on modern CPUs is only a fraction of the internal clock frequency. Still, it can be a useful addition to a motherboard, because it normally can deliver data or accept data in a single clock cycle, and often the DRAM that makes up the bulk of main memory requires two or more clock cycles to do those same things.

Intel's latest CPUs, starting with the Pentium Pro, have had two chips in the CPU module. One is the CPU itself, with its L1 memory cache onboard. The other chip is separate, L2 memory cache. This cache is connected to the CPU by a different bus than the one that connects the CPU to the outside world. Intel refers to this as its Dual Independent Bus (DIB) architecture.

There are two advantages to this strategy. First, the fact that transactions with this L2 cache are not taking up bandwidth on the main CPU-to-system ("front-side") bus means that bus can carry other traffic. Second, the CPU to L2 bus can run as fast as the L2 cache can support, and that has been, in various models, either half or all of the CPU core speed (in either case, much faster than the front-side bus). In a current Xeon system, for example, you might have the Pentium II CPU and its L2 cache both running at 450MHz while the front-side bus runs at a "mere" 100MHz.

Intel has announced plans to go one step further. In some upcoming CPU modules, they will incorporate both the L1 and L2 caches on the CPU chip and then put in an additional L3 cache on another chip in the CPU module. To minimize confusion (one must suppose), they also propose renumbering these memory caches so the smallest one, closest to the CPU, will be called L0 (Level Zero), the other, larger one on the CPU chip will be called L1, and the largest one (now probably several megabytes in size) co-located in the CPU module and connected via the DIB will be, once again, known as the L2 cache.

For those who want the ultimate in memory caching, a PC with a CPU module that incorporates both L1 and L2 memory caches could have a third level of caching (an L3 cache) on the motherboard. Each lower level of cache would be larger, in part to make up for its being slightly slower to access than the next higher level. The combination of all three levels of memory cache is the ultimate today in this technology.

The only way to buy that combination today is to get a so-called Super Socket 7 motherboard (which almost certainly will include some cache memory on the motherboard) and plug into it an AMD K6-3 processor with its L1 and L2 cache modules included in the CPU package.

Cache Coherency Problems

The whole notion of cache memory is that the local, small-but-fast memory contains an accurate copy of whatever is being held in some portion of the larger, more remote, slower main memory. This way, the CPU can deal with the cache copy as if it were the one in main memory.

That works well most of the time, but there are two situations in which it might not. First is if the information in the cache has not yet made its way to main memory before some other device in the PC attempts to read that information from its supposed location in main memory. The second case happens when the CPU wants to use some information from main memory but doesn't realize that because it was read into the cache, some other device has changed it out in main memory.

Every PC ever built, other than IBM's PC Jr., had a feature called direct memory access, or DMA. DMA means having a specialized micro controller that is capable of accepting a command from the CPU to move some data from one place in memory to another or to or from an input/output port. The DMA micro controller does this task while the CPU goes on about its business. Furthermore, large PCs that work as servers (and some particularly powerful desktop workstations) boast multiple CPUs, all sharing a common pool of main memory.

Either way, whether because you have multiple CPU chips or because your PC is using the DMA strategy (or perhaps some other "bus mastering" device such as a high-speed SCSI host adapter), it is entirely possible that at times the contents of main memory will be changed by something other than the CPU's cache controller (or the motherboard L2 or L3 cache controller if your PC has one of those devices). Whenever this happens, a cache controller that is connected to this memory must know about this fact and at the minimum, it must "invalidate" the image of those memory values that it is holding in its cache memory until it can replace them with a freshly read copy of the new values.

The only way that this *cache coherency* can be maintained is for the cache controller that is connected directly to the main memory pool to watch every access to that pool by whatever other device might be doing it. This enables the cache controller to see whether any address that is being accessed is one that is currently being imaged in the cache memory this cache controller is managing. So, every cache controller is, in fact, built to do this sort of *bus snooping* to see who else might be writing to memory.

The other type of cache coherency problem that can arise is, in a way, subtler. If the CPU tries to write to a memory address where there is some ROM or one where there is nothing at all, it clearly cannot make that location hold the value it sends out. If, however, the cache controller doesn't know that, it might hold the information written out by the CPU as though it were a valid image of what is actually in main memory at that address. As long as that image stays in the cache memory, the CPU will get that value any time it tries to read it back. If it waits long enough that the cache contents are completely replaced, however, the CPU will discover the real value (if any) that is being held in that location.

The only way to avoid this problem is to tell the cache controller up front which areas of physical memory address space are *cacheable* (meaning they have actual RAM there) and which are not cacheable (meaning either they have nothing there or they have ROM there). It almost always is very useful to do read-caching for ROMs, but it is *never* good to allow write-caching of memory locations that are occupied by ROMs.

Modern PC BIOS setup programs often include a section in which you can inform the cache controller which regions of memory you want it to cache. If that section is initialized properly, nothing will go amiss for this reason. But if you mess with those settings and get them wrong, you could be in for some nasty surprises somewhere down the road.

Stacks

We pointed out earlier that the CPU must have some temporary holding places for information it is processing. That is why it has registers. Sometimes, however, it doesn't have nearly enough registers to hold all the information it must have temporarily stashed somewhere.

This is especially true for a PC doing multitasking. This simulation of doing more than one thing at a time is accomplished by doing a little bit on one task, and then switching to another task and doing a little on it, and then switching to a third task, and so on.

Each time the CPU switches from working on one task to working on another one, it must save the values that are contained in every register for the first task and load those registers with the values it last had for the next task it is going to work on. The CPU accomplishes this by using stacks. This is not the only time stacks are used, by any means, but it is one of the most dramatic uses for them.

A stack is a simple concept. Think of a stack of dishes. When you want to put away freshly washed dishes, you stack them in a cupboard. When you want to take out some dishes, you take them off the top of the stack. The last dish you put on the stack becomes the first one you will take off.

In a computer, a stack is implemented simply as a region of memory plus a register that holds an address pointer. When an item is to be "pushed" onto the stack through an instruction understandably referred to as PUSH, the item gets written to the location indicated by the address pointer; then the value of the address pointer is reduced by one. That makes the next item to be pushed onto the stack go into the next lower memory address. Alternatively, when an item is "popped" off the stack, through an instruction with a similarly clever name, POP, it is read from the location pointed to by the register's contents, after which that register's contents are increased by one.

The maximum size of a stack is set first by the size of numbers the relevant register can hold, and second by the initial value of the stack pointer (which normally is the same as the size of the memory "segment" that has been set aside for that stack). Almost always, the latter limit is far more restrictive than the former, although it is possible to make a very large stack that would use almost the entire range of the relevant register.

If a program attempts to push more information onto the stack than it can hold, that stack pointer value will have to go negative, the CPU will notice this, and before it can happen, the CPU will cause an exception.

A PC must always have some stack ready for use. The CPU holds the pointer to the current location in the stack in its stack pointer (SP) register. That value is an offset into the segment pointed to or indicated by the value held in the stack segment (SS) register.

Any well-written program will create and use a private stack as one of its first actions. The reason for this is that the programmer cannot know how much space is left on the preexisting stack. A program creates a private stack simply by allocating some memory for the private stack, and then pushing the value presently in the stack pointer and stack segment registers onto the preexisting stack, and then loading the SP and SS registers with new values pointing to this newly allocated memory region. At the end of its work, the program will pop the old value off the stack and the CPU will be restored to its prior state. (It also is necessary to push onto the stack the contents of any register that the program will be altering and then pop them back off at the end.)

Any number of stacks can be defined in a PC at any moment, but only one of them will be the *current* stack. That is the one pointed to by the logical address ':[SS]. (This is the customary notation; read it as the hexadecimal numbers held in the two registers whose names appear inside the pairs of square brackets. Those numbers are joined by a colon.)

As an aside, note that there is another stack in all recent x86 processors. That is a special stack of eight 80-bit registers inside the CPU that are used in connection with floating-point number manipulation and in the Pentium MMX and Pentium II when executing MMX instructions. This special, hardware stack is normally used only by MMX (and 3DNow! on clone x86 processors) and floating-point math instructions, and it is different from the "regular" software stack created out of a portion of main memory and used by POP and PUSH instructions.

This notion of stacks is a very important one for PC programming. It allows programs to be written that are far more complex than would be possible if only the registers in the CPU could be used as temporary information-holding places. The whole idea of multitasking would be utterly infeasible without stacks.

Ports

When the CPU forms a physical address on its address pins, that address normally refers to some location in memory address space. But by simply changing the voltage on another pin (the memory or I/O pin) from high to low the CPU can signal that it intends the address pin value to be interpreted as a location in a different logical space.

Because the primary use for these other locations is to move information between the CPU and other parts of the PC, including some outside the PC, we call this logical space the space of the PC's input/output ports. And although the addresses in this new space are indicated by voltages on the same address pins that are used to indicate memory addresses, the I/O port space is quite different from the physical memory address space.

For one thing, I/O port address space is much smaller. Every member of the x86 family, from the earliest 8086 or 8088 to the latest Pentium II, has the same size I/O port address space, namely 64K (65,536) byte-wide locations. This is because when it is doing an I/O operation the CPU uses only the bottom 16 address lines.

Furthermore, none of the complexities of selectors or paging are associated with I/O port addresses. Because there are only 64K port addresses (each 1 byte wide), only a single 16-bit number is needed to point to a desired port. That number can be loaded into any of the general-purpose registers in the CPU, although some instructions assume that the port address will be loaded into the DX register.

Because all the x86 processors but the 8088 can read and write two or more (up to eight) bytes of information from memory at a time, they can also read or write the same number of successive port locations in one operation. And, as with memory locations, the processor can only address locations in the port address space with a resolution equal to the width of its data bus. (That is, the Pentium can only address ports in blocks of eight, although it can send information in or out any single byte-wide port if that is desired.)

What Makes I/O Ports Different from Memory Locations

The main distinction between an I/O port and a location in memory is what happens to data that is sent there. When you send a succession of bytes to a port, usually each of them will go on to some receiving hardware. When you read from a port, you might get a different value each time you read it (and none of them need be any of the values you sent out to that port), because what you see is whatever was last sent in to that location from the outside. This behavior is in stark contrast to that of a true memory location, where what is there is whatever you last wrote to that place, and that is what you will get if you read from that place.

That is not to say that it is impossible to put memory chips at I/O port locations. That is simply not done very often.

Memory Mapped I/O as an Alternative to Using Ports

What about the opposite "misuse" of an address, in which some I/O gadget is placed at a location in the memory address space instead of in I/O port address space? This not only can be done, it often has proven to be quite useful. No difficult trick is involved in making the port-like hardware respond as if it were memory. You just invert the signal on the MEM/IO# line and the port hardware will think all memory accesses are port accesses and vice versa.

The reason this can be useful has to do with the very different speeds with which the ISA I/O bus and the memory bus operate. To get maximum speed out of an I/O device, it used to be necessary to make it *memory-mapped,* which is making it appear in the CPU's memory address space. The most recent example of this is the Advanced Graphics Port (AGP) used for the highest-speed PC video display adapters.

Unfortunately, this also leads to some considerable complexity that is automatically avoided when the hardware is connected to a real port address. Because of the many ways that linear memory addresses can be shifted around in physical memory address space both by the selector/descriptor table strategy and by paging, it can all too easily happen that the port hardware will seem to bounce around all over the linear memory map or it might even disappear altogether. This is not at all what you want an I/O device to do, because the programs that intend to talk to it must know where to find it before they can function successfully.

Fortunately, now that we have fast I/O possible via the PCI bus, there is no longer enough gain in using this memory-mapped I/O strategy to make up for the complexity. Now almost all the I/O hardware that needs real speed is placed on the PCI bus.

Speed Issues for Ports

Originally, the ports were connected to the CPU data and address pins in exactly the same manner as memory chips. But as CPU and memory speeds increased, the paths for data flow to memory and to I/O became separate. They join in the motherboard chip set, but away from that point they operate independently and at very different speeds.

For example, a modern high-end PC uses a memory bus that currently runs at 100MHz (and an internal CPU clock of up to 500MHz), but the PCI bus runs at speeds up to 66MHz, and every PC that still supports the Industry Standard Architecture (ISA) input/output bus must run it at the same, sedate 8.33MHz or less. These speed limits are necessary to ensure that plug-in cards are capable of operating properly in even the newest and fastest PCs.

Interrupts: The Driving Force

At this point, you have seen all the essential parts that make up a PC. Thus, you have seen its basic architecture, at least in a static sense. What you haven't heard about yet are some of the key dynamic aspects to its architecture. In the rest of this chapter, we explain what these dynamic aspects are and how they work. The first of these, and in some ways the most important, is the concept of interrupts.

Polling Versus Interrupts

Imagine a small flower shop in a mall. The proprietor of this shop must serve the customers when they visit, but between customers she must go back into the back room and take care of paperwork. How does she know when to stop doing paperwork and come out to serve a customer?

The owner can use two fundamental strategies. One is to stop her work at regular intervals, get up from her desk and go out front to see whether there might be some customers desiring service. This is called *polling*. This strategy works, but it is terribly inefficient for two reasons. First, when a customer walks in, he or she must wait until the next time the owner happens to stop the paperwork and comes out to discover the customer. Second, when there are no customers, the owner cannot work steadily on the paperwork, but instead must waste time every few minutes coming out to look and notice that there aren't any customers waiting for help.

The obvious solution, in the case of a flower shop, is to install in a sensor that will be triggered each time a customer walks through the door. One common way this is done is by a light and photocell on opposite sides of the door. The light beam is broken by an entering (or exiting) customer, and that causes a bell to ring, alerting the owner in the back room that it is time to come out and help the customer. This costs more initially than the polling method. The shop owner must buy and install the sensor and bell, but it saves money in the long run by enabling the shop owner to work more efficiently.

Intel included something very much like this in the first 8086 processor and in every x86 processor since then. The details of how it implemented this idea are particularly clever.

Interrupt Vector Table

Intel built the x86 processors so that when they are operating in real mode and any one of 256 kinds of event occurs, the CPU will finish the present instruction it is executing, it will stop what it is doing, save a marker so it can pick up where it left off, and then start doing some specified task that is appropriate to the kind of interrupting event that just occurred.

Intel did this is by making the CPU, when it is interrupted, first discern what type of interrupt has happened and then go to a specific address very low in the memory address space. From that location it picks up a pointer to another location, and at that second location it finds a program that directs it in the proper handling of this kind of interrupting event.

Notice the indirection: Intel could have said, if an interruption of type 75 occurs, go to this specific address and do whatever the program there dictates. Instead, it said, pick up the pointer value in slot 75 of a special interrupt vector table (IVT) and execute the program to which that pointer points.

This indirection has several advantages, not the least of which is that it enables you to change how the CPU will respond to a given type of interrupt on-the-fly. All you must do is change the pointer value for that kind of interrupt from one that points to program A to one that points to program B, and the CPU will alter its behavior accordingly.

The location for the IVT is, in real mode, the first 1KB of the CPU's actual, physical memory address space. In virtual 86 mode, it is the first 1KB of the CPU's linear memory address space, which can be a very different region of the actual, physical memory. And in 286- or 386-protected mode, it is replaced by a similar structure called the interrupt descriptor table (IDT) that can be located wherever in memory the operating system wishes to put it. (For practical reasons the IDT must never be put in a portion of physical memory that might get mapped out of the CPU's view. But other than this limitation it can be anywhere.)

The details of how interrupts are handled in protected mode can become quite complicated, involving concepts such as "interrupt gates," "trap gates," "task state segments," and more. Fortunately, you can get a pretty good feel for how the overall process functions by focusing only on the way real-mode interrupts work. Then just trust that the designers of the CPU and the operating system did the appropriate more-complicated things to make the same ideas work in the more complex environment that occurs in protected mode operation.

How Do Interrupts Happen?

In our analogy of the small shop in the mall, we indicated that an interrupt might be used to signal some external event (in that case, the arrival of a customer). In PCs, some interrupts happen because of an external event. Others happen because a program says they happen. Yet others happen because the CPU says they should happen.

Hardware Interrupts

The first kind of interrupts, called hardware interrupts, is the principal means by which anything outside the CPU can get its attention. For example, each time you type a key on the keyboard, it sends a signal to the PC system unit. Special circuitry inside the system unit (called the *keyboard controller*) notices that signal, and in turn alerts the CPU to the arrival of a keystroke.

There are two pins on the CPU by which a hardware interrupt can be signaled: the normal interrupt input (whose pin name is INTR) and the non-maskable interrupt (with a pin name of NMI). However, many more than two hardware events might need CPU attention. This seems like a problem. Fortunately, the standard PC design (PC architecture) includes a solution to this problem.

A standard part of the motherboard circuitry that surrounds every PC's CPU is a subsystem called the interrupt controller. In the original PCs and PC/XTs, it could accept signals from any of eight input lines and send an interrupt signal to the CPU. Then, when the CPU acknowledged receipt of that signal, the interrupt controller would tell it from which of the eight possible sources that particular interrupt signal had come. In the IBM PC/AT and all later PC designs, the number of inputs to the interrupt controller has been increased from eight to 15 or 16. We say 15 *or* 16 because one of the interrupt inputs collects eight of the others, but in some situations it can also be used in its own right.

The input/output bus carries within it nine of these 16 interrupt request (IRQ) lines. Any device plugged into a slot on the I/O bus can inform the CPU of its need for attention via one of these lines. The rest of these IRQ lines are reserved for use on the motherboard by, for example, the keyboard controller.

Cards plugged into the ISA bus slots cannot normally share an IRQ line. Each IRQ line must be used for only one card. Cards plugged into the PCI slots, or into a CardBus slot, on the other hand, usually can share interrupts with other cards also plugged into these more modern buses. Any of the interrupts caused by a signal on an IRQ line ultimately arrives at the CPU on its INTR pin. The non-maskable interrupt (NMI) pin is normally used only for the PC's reset circuitry.

The difference between non-maskable and normal interrupts is this: When a maskable interrupt is asserted, the processor can ignore it if it has been told to ignore interrupts. The fact that an interrupt is pending is remembered until the processor is ready to act on the request. This is much like an adult who says to the child tugging on her sleeve, "Not now, dear. I will talk to you as soon as I finish talking on the phone."

The non-maskable interrupt is used when no delay can be tolerated. This is more like a fire alarm. The reset circuitry uses this means of interrupting the processor because it is sure to work, even if the processor gets totally confused and would otherwise stay in an "I don't wish to respond to interrupts right now" state indefinitely.

Software Interrupts

Intel decided it would also be a very good thing if a program could, in the course of its operation, cause an interrupt to happen. This would interrupt the running program and invoke another special program to handle the event corresponding to the interrupt.

The advantage of this approach is easy to demonstrate. The writer of an application program can know that at a certain point his or her program must send some information to the screen. But the program (and the programmer) need not know in detail just how to do that. All the program must do is assert the proper type of interrupt, with the correct values in the certain registers to indicate what is to be sent to the screen, and the program invoked by that interrupt will then do the job.

The programmer who writes the program that must write something to the screen need not understand anything about how that will be done. The programmer who writes the program that does that job needn't know anything about why this particular bit of information must be written to the screen at this time.

CPU Exceptions

After it had this mechanism in place, Intel found it convenient to use that mechanism to handle problems the CPU might detect on its own. For example, if a program attempts to access some memory it isn't entitled to access (often referred to as a general protection fault or a page fault), it will trigger a suitable interrupt. The corresponding program that is invoked can then invoke a dialog box telling the PC user what has gone wrong, and it can terminate the program that ran amok.

Interrupt Service Routines

The programs that respond when an interrupt happens are called, quite naturally, interrupt service routines (ISRs). One ISR must be designated for each of the 256 possible interrupts, or at least there must be one for any of them that might happen. However, nothing says these 256 programs all must be different programs. Usually, a great many of them are the same, single, simple ISR.

When an ISR is invoked, it runs until it is finished, at which point it executes a special RET instruction (which stands for return from interrupt). The CPU understands that instruction to mean, "Please resume doing whatever you were doing before."

The simplest ISR consists of nothing more than just one RET instruction. That is a "do nothing" ISR. After you have one such instruction in memory somewhere, you can simply make the IVT entries for any interrupts you want to ignore point to that RET instruction.

When Interrupts Interrupt an ISR

Nothing in what we have written so far indicates that ISRs are immune to being interrupted themselves. Sometimes they must not be interrupted for a very short time after they start executing, and in that case they can simply turn on the mask that inhibits interrupts. However, it is considered very bad PC programming practice to let that PC run in this state any longer than absolutely necessary.

As a result, it is quite common for an ISR to be interrupted. When that happens, it is suspended in just the same fashion as the original application program was suspended when that original ISR was invoked, and now a new ISR gets invoked. When it finishes its work and executes a RET instruction, the CPU will pick up what it was doing when it was last interrupted, which in this case means resuming what the first ISR was doing. Only when that one finishes its work will the CPU go back to the application program.

Layers Upon Layers of ISR

Not only can interrupts interrupt an interrupt service routine, it is also common for one ISR to call another one, which calls yet another one, and so forth. When each ISR is loaded into memory, it replaces the address in certain slots in the IVT with its own address. If it was written properly, it first copies the address that was once there into some holding place within itself. Then, if another ISR is loaded into memory that wants to handle that same type of interrupt, it will do all the same things. As long as these ISRs are written correctly, the whole multilayer assemblage of programs operates perfectly well and has the desired effects without the user being any the wiser about what all is going on deep inside the PC's memory.

BIOS Services in ROM

Where does your PC get its ISRs? Every PC ships from the factory with a motherboard BIOS ROM. This chip (or, often, a pair of chips) contains many things. Most of what it contains, however, is a collection of ISRs to do the most basic things every PC must be able to do, such as responding to keyboard input and writing to a monochrome (or the now obsolete CGA color) screen. As we will explain in more detail near the end of this chapter, the entries in the interrupt vector table (IVT) are initially set up to point to these ISRs.

Many PCs have some additional BIOS ROMs located on plug-in cards. One common example is a video card, which today almost always includes a fairly hefty BIOS ROM. This ROM contains alternative ISRs to handle screen output using the hardware on that card. A part of what must happen early in the boot process is for this card to place the addresses of its ISRs into the IVT in place of the addresses of the default screen handler ISRs in the motherboard BIOS ROM.

DOS and BIOS Services in RAM

Many additional ISRs are loaded into memory when you load the operating system. From one point of view, almost all of any operating system can be described as just one huge collection of ISRs. Most of the services that the operating system performs for programs are provided either by an ISR within the operating system, or by one that is located in some BIOS ROM.

When you load a terminate-and-stay resident device driver (for example, a mouse driver), that is yet another ISR. In almost every such case, not only is the program loaded into memory in a fashion that ensures it will hang around until it is needed, but also it must stuff its own starting address into the proper slot in the IVT, so that it will be activated at the appropriate moments.

The one common exception to this rule is the class of device drivers known as *block devices*. These are the device drivers that create phantom disks (for example, a RAM disk) or that activate special sorts of disks for use with your PC. They usually link themselves into the operating system both by stuffing some entries in the IVT, but more importantly by also inserting themselves into a *linked list* that is called the *device driver chain*.

Interrupts are one of the most important ways that things are caused to happen in a PC other than by direct action of the CPU. In fact, interrupts are so important that they have become a very precious resource. And there aren't enough different ones, especially of the hardware sort. This often leads to resource conflicts when you need to find an available interrupt for some new piece of hardware you want to add to your PC, but there simply aren't any.

Fortunately, as the ISA bus is phased out, and as the USB and FireWire (IEEE 1394) buses are phased in, we will at least be freed from this quandary. Those buses require interrupts to work, but just a couple each, and then they can handle a very large number of peripheral hardware devices with no additional interrupts being required.

Another special feature in the standard PC architecture that functions in a somewhat similar manner is the DMA channel. We mentioned this concept earlier in this chapter, in the discussion of cache memory. Now it's time to explain it in more detail.

What Is a DMA Channel?

For the most part, each time a byte of information is moved from one place to another within the PC's main memory or between a memory location and an I/O port, it gets there in two steps. The first step is for the CPU to read that byte into some register within itself. The second step is to write that byte back out to its final destination.

This works, but it has two drawbacks. The first is that the CPU cannot be doing anything else while it is moving that byte around. The second is the fact that it takes two distinct steps to make the move. For moving a single byte this is not so bad, but when you have a whole flock of bytes to move, it certainly isn't wonderful.

Several kinds of devices in a PC do want to do just that sort of many-byte information transfers. The floppy disk was the first. Sound cards do this a lot so much so that they often use more than one DMA channel. Likewise, scanners generally use a DMA channel, and who knows what new devices might want to do this as well?

Realizing this, the designers of the original PC decided to incorporate an additional microcontroller dedicated to solving exactly this kind of problem. This is a special-purpose microprocessor built to perform just the one kind of action needed for this job. It is called the Direct Memory Access (DMA) controller. With a DMA controller present, the CPU can hasten its work by telling the DMA controller that it is to move a certain number of bytes from successive memory locations starting at one address to successive memory locations starting at some other address. It also has the option of telling the DMA controller to send out a certain number of bytes from successive memory locations to a particular port address, again starting at some specified memory address.

The final option is that it can tell the DMA controller to receive a designated number of bytes from a particular port address and deposit those values in successive memory addresses, starting at some specified address. Each time the DMA controller sets up one of these transfers, it must do so over what is referred to as a DMA channel. That simply means that a particular portion of the DMA controller is assigned to this transfer task.

The DMA controller, however, doesn't get to pick which part does which transfer. Instead, the requesting device (the CPU or some I/O hardware) must specify the channel that will be used. This means that these channels are a precious resource, and conflicts in requests for them can keep them from being used to their full capacity.

So far, not many devices need DMA channels in a PC, so the issue of running out of DMA channels is not nearly as urgent as that of running out of IRQs. However, that happy situation might not last. As more and more devices that often must move large numbers of bytes are attached to our PCs, we might soon find ourselves wondering where on the DMA controller we can possibly find a channel to hook them up.

Why DMA Fell from Favor

At first DMA was wonderful. The floppy disk controller in the original PC used it, and it helped even that relatively slow device work more quickly and reliably. When they came along some years later, some hard disk controllers and SCSI host adapters used DMA as well.

Then things began to change. The CPUs got faster, but the ISA I/O bus couldn't speed up. Well, it did speed up a little bit, from the original roughly 4.77MHz to the PC/AT's higher 8.33MHz, but that was it. Any of the clone PC manufacturers who ran their I/O bus at a faster speed (and some did crank up the speed as high as 12MHz) were tempting fate, for surely some of the plug-in cards their customers would try in those slots would fail simply because they couldn't keep up with that higher-than-standard clock rate.

As CPU speeds have increased, so has the speed of main memory, although the latter speed hasn't increased quite as fast or as far. The speed of the bus from CPU to memory has crept up from 4.7MHz to 16MHz and then to 33MHz and finally to 133MHz, with some other steps along the way. The ISA bus, however, still must run at a measly 8.3MHz. This means that the DMA controller (in particular when it is sending information from memory to a port or receiving information into memory from a port over the ISA bus) is constantly and quite thoroughly frustrated by the slow I/O bus speed. Although it could do the job without needing constant attention from the CPU, it can't do the job nearly as quickly as the CPU could by tossing the bytes out to a memory-mapped I/O device. So a few years ago, *programmed I/O* to memory-mapped I/O devices became all the rage. (DMA was still useful for memory-to-memory transfers. These simply weren't needed as often as the memory-to-or-from-port transfers.)

How DMA Made Its Comeback

DMA has bounded back, and it is an even better solution now than it was in the first PCs. The reason is simply that we now have I/O bus technologies (the PCI bus, Universal Serial Bus [USB], and the CardBus) that can transfer data to and from I/O devices at speeds that are more nearly comparable to those on the main memory bus (although somewhat slower than before). Now, once more, the DMA strategy is a sound time-saver for the CPU and overall.

DMA also has been improved, so it uses the available bus bandwidth even more efficiently. The newest version, called Ultra DMA, can transfer data to IDE devices at speeds up to a full 33MBps twice the old maximum speed. It does this quite simply by transferring data on both the rising and falling edges of the (square wave) clock signal, rather than merely on the falling edges, as had been the custom and as is still the standard for most bus data transfers.

For the PC user, this means that DMA channels matter once more. They are once again the preferred way to carry large blocks of data into or out of I/O devices, and more and more we will see those devices using this strategy.

Keeping Up with the Clock

PC clock speeds are mentioned a lot. In fact, for many years one of the most prominent numbers in any PC advertisement was clock speed. ("Buy our nifty new 450MHz Pentium II Xeon dual CPU computer.") Just what is that speed? And what parts of the PC actually run at that speed? Are there other clocks in a PC? If so, what do they do? These are the questions we will answer in this section.

Asynchronous Versus Synchronous Computers

Although they are amazingly fast, electronic circuits do need some time to operate. Just how much time each one needs varies from sample to sample. It is possible to make a computer that has no clocks in it. Such a computer would run just as fast as each individual piece within it would let it. Data requested from memory would get used as soon as it showed up wherever it had been asked to show up. The results of calculations would be stashed back into main memory as soon as they were available. Never would any part wait unnecessarily long, just because it wasn't yet time to move on according to some central clock.

Such an asynchronous computer is *possible* to design and build, but it sure isn't easy. A far simpler way to design a computer is to synchronize each of the parts to some central clock or "heartbeat." As long as this clock ticks slowly enough, you can be sure that every part will have completed its assigned tasks before the next tick comes along and tells the parts to move on to their next steps. Synchronous computers are so much easier to design and build that nearly every computer built today is an example of such a design. Certainly every PC is.

Different Clocks for Different Purposes

This doesn't mean that all the parts must march to the beat of the same drum, however. It is possible, and has now become standard, to have a multiplicity of clocks in a PC, each one used for a different purpose. The following sections include a quick rundown on a few of the most important clocks in PCs. Your PC surely has all of these, and it might also have a several more.

The CPU Clock

The most famous clock is one that "ticks" inside the CPU chip. This is the 450MHz (or 300MHz, 100MHz, or whatever your PC has) that you hear so much about. It measures how fast the fastest part of your PC runs. Mostly these days, the CPU inner core runs at this speed and nothing else in the PC comes close. Well, if you have a Pentium Pro or a recent Pentium II Xeon CPU, its L2 cache, which is located inside the CPU module, also runs at this speed. In early Pentium IIs, the L2 cache runs at half the CPU clock speed. For all other x86 processors, the external cache runs at the same speed as the main memory bus.

The bus from the CPU to main memory commonly runs at some fraction of the CPU clock speed. Or, to put this more properly, the CPU runs at a multiple of the external bus speed. That is, the actual clock circuit that controls this speed is located outside the CPU and the CPU simply synchronizes its not-very-constant-frequency clock to a fixed multiple of that external clock signal.

For example, a 400MHz Pentium II machine, which is one of the fastest machines widely available as we write this, has a main memory clock speed of 100MHz. This means the internal clock is running at precisely four times the external clock. The somewhat faster 450MHz machines use the same external clock speed, but are designed to run with their internal clock synchronized at precisely four-and-one-half times the external clock speed.

The Main Memory Clock

The same clock that drives the CPU also drives the main memory modules and all the associated circuitry. (Remember, this is a clock that is outside the CPU itself and is running at a small fraction of the speed of the CPU's internal circuits, as explained in the previous section.) This clock's frequency is that of the front-side bus.

It might be, and commonly was the case in older PCs, that only the external (L2 or L3) memory cache (which is located on the motherboard) actually can keep up with this fast of a clock. In that case, the slower DRAM chips that make up the bulk of main memory must be enabled to run more slowly by the insertion of one or more "wait states". These are delays between the clock cycle in which the CPU or external cache controller asks something of a memory chip and the clock cycle in which it expects to find the result of the requested operation. Clever designers have sometimes managed to get around wait states for every main memory access by splitting the memory into "interleaved" banks, or in other ways. Still, if the main memory DRAM chips are simply unable to respond as quickly as the speed of the front-side bus clock would demand, wait states will be required, at least occasionally. This (at least occasional) inability of main memory to keep up with the CPU's demands is why it is useful to have an external memory cache (called Level 2 or Level 3 cache, depending on what is inside the CPU module).

Fortunately, in many recent PCs—especially those that are designated "performance" PCs—the DRAM chips used in the main memory can keep up with the front-side bus clock without any wait states, and for that reason a memory cache on the motherboard is not needed and is not included. (The L1 and L2 caches inside the CPU chip or module in these PCs is still needed and those cache memories run at substantially faster rates than main memory, as described in the preceding section.)

The Input/Output (I/O) Bus Clocks

As mentioned many times now, the ISA input/output bus is required to run no more rapidly than 8.33MHz. This signal is derived from the same clock as the main memory clock by dividing, in the case of our example systems with a 100MHz memory clock frequency, by a factor of twelve. The ISA clock speed is this slow in order to make sure that even very old ISA plug-in cards will function correctly when they are plugged into an ISA slot. Because this is so excruciatingly slow, and to avoid the problem of interrupt conflicts, some of the most modern PCs simply don't have any ISA slots.

Thank goodness today's PCs also have one or more additional I/O buses, and these buses typically operate at a faster speed than the ISA bus, although usually not quite as fast as main memory. The PCI bus operates typically at 33MHz and at 266MHz in the AGP slot in the fastest of today's PCs. These speeds are arrived at by dividing the main memory clock as needed.

Other Clocks in Your PC

Many of the subsystems in your PC must work in synchrony with a clock that runs at some different frequency and that isn't synchronized with the main memory, CPU, and I/O bus clocks. For one example, the video monitor scans the electron beam across and down the face of the display at a frequency set by the desired resolution of the image and the acceptable refresh rate.

The disk drives need clocks at special frequencies that are a fixed multiple of the rate at which their disk platters turn. A modem needs a clock that will make it put out or take in bits at the correct speed for the transmission rate it is trying to achieve.

There can be as many clocks as there are different pieces of hardware with differing speed capabilities and requirements. (You can't make the part go faster than it is capable of running, and in some cases you mustn't let it go either slower or faster than the standard speed for that sort of gadget.)

What Does Super-Scalar Mean?

When bragging about how much faster a new PC is than the older ones it has replaced, the manufacturers often point to its *super-scalar* performance. What does that mean? Quite simply, it means that if the clock speed on the new PC is the same as on the old PC, the new one will run programs faster anyway. If the new PC's clock is twice the speed of the old one, the new PC will run programs more than twice as fast as the old one. That is, the performance goes up faster than the clock speed. (If it went up in direct proportion to the clock speed, the performance would be scaled with the clock speed. Going up faster is, thus, super-scalar.)

There can be many reasons for super-scalar performance. Usually, it comes from some combination of improvements, such as having more instruction execution units (for integer and/or floating-point instructions); supporting newer, more efficient instructions (such as MMX and 3DNow!); having a bigger instruction pipeline; or having a bigger L1 or L2 memory cache. It might also come from having some part of the CPU "speculatively execute" instructions whose turn hasn't yet come, in the hopes that they will be needed later. At that future time, if those results are needed, they can be stuffed into the flow without waiting for them to execute. Or, perhaps the new PC actually uses more CPU chips than the older one.

Whatever the reason, super-scalar in simple terms just means the new PC works faster than you might have imagined. This is a good thing, but is not nearly as mysterious as the name makes it seem.

System Buses: ISA, PCI and AGP

A bus is a definition of how one part of a computer communicates with another. It defines a pathway for signals to flow between functional elements of the computer. If it's a full bus definition, it will be sufficiently detailed and complete for different manufacturers to make those different parts, safe in the assumption that their separately designed and manufactured products will work together properly when they are connected.

We will look into the many important standards that have defined PC hardware and architecture. Although the design of the CPU has been the primary driving force in the evolving design of PCs, the bus definitions have played an important supporting role.

The Original (ISA) PC I/O Bus

When IBM introduced the original PC, it used a CPU that had only eight data lines and 20 address lines. The CPU was connected to every other part of the PC over a common bus that carried those lines (and some other wires for control signals). Data moved on this bus at the speed set by the CPU's internal clock. Everything worked in synchrony, and it was all quite simple.

This simplicity was both intentional and necessary. At that time, it wasn't possible to put all the memory necessary on the motherboard. Often, some of the PC's main memory would end up on plug-in option cards. Certainly most of the other functions that required much in the way of integrated circuit support also had to be put on plug-in cards. That was true of the controllers for the floppy disk drives (and later for the hard drives introduced with the PC/XT). It also was true for the video subsystem and for the serial and parallel ports. Every one of these parts ran initially at a speed of 4.77MHz. Later, with the introduction of the PC/AT, that clock speed was increased first to 6MHz and later to 8MHz. But that is as far as it went.

Before CPUs started running significantly faster than this, the input/output (I/O) bus was divided from the other functions in a PC.

Growing Up ISA to Meet Modern PC I/O Needs

The ISA bus served the PC/AT well. But soon, clone computers that ran faster came on the market. With their faster CPU speed came a need for faster input and output capabilities as well as for faster ways to connect the CPU to the system memory chips. Many ways of meeting these needs have been tried over the years. IBM had its *MicroChannel*. Many clone makers made machines to an alternative standard called the *Extended Industry Standard Architecture* (EISA). An industry group called the *Video Equipment Standards Association* (VESA) was formed, initially just to help create new standards for how to build video display subsystems, but now serving to promote a variety of standards useful in many parts of a PC. That doesn't even exhaust the list of ways people have tried to improve on the good old ISA standard.

The PCI Bus

PCI stands for *Peripheral Component Interconnect* (PCI) bus. This mostly Intel-sponsored new way to connect the parts of a PC started as just a way to make motherboards more efficient. Later, it was extended to become a way to attach outside components as well.

An important point in the PCI design was that it could be adapted for use in many kinds of computers or other high-tech hardware. It was by no means limited to replacing the ISA bus, nor to working only in an IBM-compatible PC.

As we will explain in a moment, the PCI bus is not now a singular thing. There are several important variations. CompactPCI, for example, is a variant form of PCI that is used widely in industrial control and instrumentation. And the basic PCI bus is used as the main I/O bus for computers using many CPUs (x86, Alpha, PowerPC, and others). Finally, there are now four flavors of PCI for the PC, involving different data bus widths and different clock speeds. We'll explain all of these flavors, but for simplicity, we don't include any details on the CompactPCI standard, nor on the uses of PCI bus with other than x86-based PCs.

PCI Basics

Fundamentally, PCI involves a rethinking of the way the parts of a PC are interconnected. Initially, this included only those parts that were internal to the system unit, but in later versions of the PCI design it also encompasses ways of connecting to pieces that are outside that box.

PCI began as a means of interconnecting the chips that surround the CPU more efficiently, and of making those interconnections less dependent on which CPU chip the computer was using. Later, once Intel explicitly added a PCI bus connector, this became a viable replacement for (and vast improvement upon) the ISA bus.

Because it was a fresh take on the problems surrounding the ISA bus, the PCI bus could be made as good as the technology of that time would enable, without having to carry along all the "baggage" that the ISA bus carries even to this day. However, when the PCI bus was defined and widely adopted, it quickly acquired new baggage of its own. Still, it is proving to be a remarkably robust and flexible bus definition, as is shown by the variety of forms it takes and the widely different applications in which it is used.

Figure 15.8 shows a portion of a motherboard with six PCI slots.

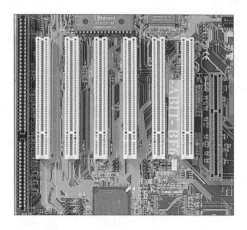

PCI Is an Efficient Bus

A PCI bus has only about half as many active lines as the ISA bus, yet those include twice as many data lines and can operate four times faster. To make the PCI bus work reliably at this speed, the connectors have a few more connections (124), with most of them being connected either to "ground" or to one of the power supply voltages. The main way that the PCI bus gets away with fewer lines is by using one set of them for both address and data information (at different times).

Also to enhance reliability, both address values and data are supplied with a parity bit. The PCI bus will notice whether either addresses or data get messed up. If that happens, the bus controller will notify the devices involved in the transfer, but it allows the devices to determine what type of error recovery procedure to take.

The PCI bus is designed to operate without termination (unlike a SCSI bus). This makes it easier for users because they don't have to think about termination issues. And it is designed to use the reflected signals that an unterminated bus implies. But these design choices also limit the length of a PCI bus segment to just a few inches, and the number of PCI cards or other components on a single segment of PCI bus to no more than 10. (However, one can extend the PCI bus's reach a lot by using bridge chips between segments.)

PCI Supports Plug-and-Play Automation

The PCI bus definition was crafted with automatic (plug-and-play) system configuration in mind. Each board plugged into a PCI slot (and each device connected to the bus on the motherboard) is required to have a local configuration data storage unit. The system reads and writes the data stored in these units as it configures the system.

PCI supports Multiple Masters and Shares Interrupts Gracefully

There are two challenges for a bus that ISA is simply not sufficient to meet. One is supporting multiple devices on the bus that might, at different times, want to take control of communication across that bus. The second is supporting multiple devices that all share the same few interrupt lines when they need to call for the CPU's attention. The PCI way of handling multiple masters is to have an arbitration unit as a required part of the host system. Its way of handling interrupt "conflicts" is simply to let every device that wants to tug on an interrupt line do so, determine which ones those are during an acknowledgement conversation, and then serve each of those requesters in turn.

What's a Mezzanine Bus?

The PCI bus (called a *mezzanine bus*) was designed to replace the ISA bus, but it is in fact a little different. Like the ISA bus, it routes signals between the CPU, various other chips on the motherboard, and cards that are plugged into its bus slot connectors. To do this it must buffer those signals and, in some cases, alter their timing.

Unlike the ISA bus, the PCI bus definition is not tied to any particular CPU chip or even to a chip family. The advantage to having a bus (or as Intel prefers to call it, an interconnection standard) that is processor-independent is that now many manufacturers can build PCI cards and potentially use them in a much wider variety of microcomputer-based systems. A larger market almost always means lower price products, as well as more variety of products both desirable outcomes from any consumer's perspective.

Furthermore, the PCI bus standard explicitly includes support for bridges. These can be bridges between PCI buses, or between a PCI bus and some other standard buses, such as the memory bus and ISA buses in a PC, or a VME bus in an industrial application.

The PCI bus was designed to run at what was, at the time, the full motherboard system bus's speed and to support what was then the full motherboard system bus-width parallel data transfers. Given the year it was introduced, this means PCI is clocked at 33MHz and has 32 data lines. That makes this bus four times faster and twice as wide as the ISA bus it replaces.

PCI was widely adopted very soon after its introduction. It was clearly a better idea than its predecessors in the PC bus arena. So much so that all the PC makers wanted to include it in their new products, and their customers were happy to buy these new products. Many companies started making PCI cards to go into these new slot connectors. (Most of them were video cards, hard disk interface cards, and network interface cards because those are the only kinds of card in most PCs for which the higher speed of PCI is crucial.)

When motherboard speeds jumped to 66MHz, the PCI bus stayed at 33MHz. And when CPUs starting handling data 64 bits at a time, the PCI bus stayed with 32 bits. Finally, just in the past year, the PCI standard has been extended to encompass both a 64-bit version and operation at 66MHz. And even better, these extensions have been made fully backward- and forward-compatible. That is, you can (with some resulting limitations on performance) use an old 32-bit, 33MHz PCI card in a new 64-bit, 66MHz PCI slot or vice versa. That two-way compatibility is really quite rare in standards-extension history.

This magic has been accomplished quite simply. The wider 64-bit PCI bus definition simply adds an extra section to the PCI connector, much as the 16-bit ISA definition extended the older 8-bit IBM PC I/O channel connector. Now, however, not only can you plug a 32-bit PCI card into one of these new connectors, you can even plug in a new wider (64-bit) PCI card into one of the older-style 32-bit PCI connectors and both ways work just fine. The trick is that the "wide PCI" (64-bit) card must configure itself to operate as if it were only a "narrow PCI" (32-bit) card when it is in a "narrow PCI" slot.

Similarly, the 66MHz definition for the bus works with older PCI cards because the PCI controller for a given segment will recognize whenever a slow PCI card is plugged into its bus segment, and then it will slow that segment down to 33MHz. In the other direction, any fast PCI card can run slower. The PCI definition generally supports cards or buses that run at any rate you want, down to 0Hz. Of course, most of them run at the maximum permissible rate for the version of the standard they support. Otherwise, they wouldn't get as much accomplished as they could in any given interval of time.

One exception to this generality is in a system configured to do power saving when it was not being used to its maximum performance. It could, in that situation, slow down the PCI bus and save some power. Not many of today's PCs do this, but they could be designed to do so, if the power savings were sufficiently worthwhile.

Thus, while mixing and matching PCI cards and slots between all four flavors is permissible, it will limit the bus performance a lot. So we can expect to see PCs sporting the new, faster PCI buses on one segment and still having a different PCI bus segment that runs at the older, slower rate. If the PC supports the new, wider PCI bus (probably on the fast segment), the user of that PC will be advised to plug all the narrow PCI cards into the other, slower segment, and reserve the wider and faster segment for only those cards that truly need that extra speed.

Finally, we'll mention that PCI cards can come in two voltage ratings. The older ones are all 5-volt cards. The newer ones are 3.3-volt cards, meaning that their internal circuitry runs at a lower voltage, which enables them to run cooler and helps make the faster PCI cards possible. There are differences in the places in the slot connector where the gaps are (and thus where the notches must be in the cards) to keep you from plugging in a wrong-voltage card for a given slot and there is a provision in the specification for making slots or cards that can run in a "universal" manner, indifferent to the voltage supplied in the slot.

The latest standard in the PCI family is called PCI-X. We introduce the PCI-X standard in the later paragraphs.

PCI As the "North-South" Axis In a PC

Precisely because PCI is a mezzanine bus and thus is intended to link between different types of bus it is a wonderful means of interconnecting different parts of a PC, both within the system unit and outside that box. Intel took advantage of this to separate the different functions of its motherboard chipsets into two groups and now the PC industry generally is supporting this separation in all the newer chipsets. This design innovation integrates one group of functions into the *Northbridge* chip. The other group of functions is integrated into what is called a *Southbridge* chip. The connection between the two chips is made using PCI.

The Northbridge Chip

The CPU connects to main memory via a faster and wider data path than it uses to connect to the PCI bus. This faster bus is the *front-side, system,* or *host* bus. The CPU is not capable of connecting directly to the memory modules. Some buffers and some memory address decoders are needed, at the least. Likewise, it cannot connect directly to the wires in the PCI bus. Thus, one of the jobs of the Northbridge chip is to buffer (strengthen) the signals from the CPU and then connect to the several places they must go.

The CPU "talks" with external I/O devices and with memory over the same set of wires. It just changes the voltage level on one of the associated control wires to indicate whether a memory or an I/O device access is happening. The Northbridge chip uses this control signal to separate messages to and from the memory modules from those going to and from the I/O devices.

The needed interface electronics to do these tasks (sometimes called a part of the *motherboard glue logic*) has been integrated into one very large integrated circuit chip (nearly as complex as the CPU), and this is now called the Northbridge chip. While they were at it, they also threw in support for another special-purpose, very high-speed data bus. They called this the Advanced Graphics Port.

Keep in mind that this description is primarily based on Intel's latest designs for a PC motherboard chipset. There are a number of other makers of motherboard chipsets, and they make some that are comparable to the Intel offerings, plus others that are quite different. Furthermore, Intel offers many chipsets, each optimized for a different set of uses. In this discussion, though, we are going to gloss over those differences and describe a hypothetical chipset that includes pretty much all the latest and greatest features (even though there might never be any single chipset that does all of these things).

AGP: The Side Trip to Better Video

The Advanced Graphics Peripheral bus (AGP) is fundamentally a specialized application of the PCI bus, with a number of improvements that are focused on what you need for a very good PCI video display subsystem. That video display subsystem will, of course, have a good video accelerator as its controller. Also, the video display system will doubtless have a large frame buffer in which to build the potentially very high-resolution and large color-depth images it displays on the screen. Such a video display subsystem needs two things from this new bus: a speedy connection to the CPU and a direct connection to some portions of main system RAM so it can move information into or out of locations there without having to involve the CPU. The AGP bus provides both of these capabilities.

An AGP video accelerator can be mounted on the motherboard, or it can be mounted on a plug-in card to go into a special AGP connector. Most common today are designs that use an AGP slot connector, because this enables the manufacturer or user to choose a different video card for different purposes (trading off, to name just one example, cost versus performance on 3D rendering).

When you have an AGP slot, it will always replace one of the PCI slots and in particular, the one that is nearest to the CPU.

AGP 1X, 2X, 4X, and Pro

Like the PCI bus from which it was derived, the AGP bus has now evolved into many related standards. The original bus standard supported single-speed (AGP 1X) and double-speed (AGP 2X) processing. The fastest version so far is AGP 4X. Most AGP video cards today support the 2X standard, as do most motherboards built today. However, very soon, we can expect to see many more motherboards and video cards supporting the higher-speed AGP 4X standard.

Figure 15.9 shows a portion of a motherboard with a PCI slot on the left and a standard AGP slot on the right.

The differences between these standards have to do partly with the voltage levels at which they work, and partly with how the clock signals are handled to make sure they stay in sync with the data signals. Many of the same ideas in connection with the new Rambus way of creating very fast system memory are also used in connection with the fastest of the AGP definitions. Also, the slot connectors for the various types of AGP card use the same strategies that all PCI buses use for working with different voltage cards.

Speed of communication with the AGP video card or subsystem is important, but it is not the only thing that matters. Also important is the processing power in that system. With today's levels of integration, it just isn't possible to put all the power and local RAM that you might want onto a card as small as a PCI or AGP card. If you did put that much processing power and RAM on an ordinary AGP card, it would overheat, or at least it would draw more power from the slot connector than the AGP standard permits.

The way around these limitations is yet another variation on the AGP standard, this time called AGP Pro. This standard proposes AGP cards that will be so "fat" (have so many components on them, and perhaps also have one or more daughterboards or other attached modules) that they cannot fit into the 0.8-inch space between PCI connectors.

An AGP Pro card is permitted to be thick enough to take up two slot spaces (the AGP slot and the nearest PCI slot), or three slot spaces. In either case the manufacturer of the AGP Pro card is permitted to make it plug into just the AGP slot connector, or also into the PCI slot connector(s) it spans. Having the card plug into more than one slot connector can provide several advantages, including access to more power and to some of the PCI bus connections that are not replicated in the AGP bus slot definition.

So far, we have the initial AGP Pro standard definition and some statements from manufacturers who intend to introduce AGP Pro video cards, but no actual AGP Pro products on the market. When they are, we can see just how much more powerful a PC can be when it is equipped with the absolute maximum in video processing and display power yet created for workstations or any other kind of standalone computer.

What's a GART?

We told you that one of the design goals for AGP was to give the video card direct access to the main, system memory. But it wouldn't make sense to allow it to access all of that memory. After all, the system RAM is partially used by the several programs running at once—some memory is used for each program's actual code, and some for each program's data. Only a tiny fraction of available system RAM is likely to be used by the video display adapter. The main use for this feature is to enable the AGP video card to store graphical "texture" maps in system RAM, thus enabling it to use nearly all of its local frame buffer for the actual image it is constructing and displaying. When it needs a texture map, it can reach out and grab it, and then apply it to the relevant portions of the image.

Thus, in the definition of the AGP bus there is the notion that the video display adapter will access only a portion of main memory. That portion is what it can see through a special AGP window. The *Graphics Address Remapping Table* (GART) determines which portion of the memory it can access.

The GART is a table, built either in some local memory on the AGP card, or in main memory, that specifies which regions of main memory are directly accessible to the AGP card. Just by changing the contents of this table you can alter which portion of main memory is being made available to the AGP card. There is specialized hardware on the AGP card to point to this table and to use its contents when accessing main memory through the Northbridge chip.

You Can Have Many PCI Buses in One PC

We just told you that the AGP bus is a PCI bus in disguise. It also is a totally separate bus from the PCI bus. That is, the AGP card can carry on a "conversation" with the CPU, or access main memory, independent of whatever the PCI bus is doing.

Further, it is perfectly possible to design a Northbridge chip with more than just an AGP bus and one PCI bus. There's no reason it couldn't have multiple PCI buses. After all, the functions of the Northbridge chip include being a bridge between the PCI (and AGP) bus and the front-side bus and it could just as well bridge several PCI buses, plus the AGP bus, to that front-side bus.

The main reason to expect this to be included in future PC designs is to enable you to have a standard, 32-bit wide, 33MHz PCI bus plus another 64-bit wide, 66MHz PCI bus. That way, as we explained previously, you can put in both older, slower, or narrower PCI cards and newer, faster, or wider PCI cards and have each of them perform up to their maximum capabilities. (You might someday have a PCI-X bus coming off the Northbridge chip in addition to one or more PCI buses.)

Alternatively, you could have a fast and wide PCI bus (or a PCI-X bus) come off the Northbridge chip and, after passing some fast-and-wide PCI (or PCI-X) slots, end in a PCI-to-PCI bridge chip that spawned another PCI segment, this time of the more traditional, narrower and slower sort.

Another reason for including multiple PCI buses coming directly off the Northbridge chip is to support more PCI slots than a single bus can have. Normally, by the time the loads on the bus represented by various parts of the motherboard circuitry are taken into account, a single PCI bus segment in a PC can have no more than four slots. The main place we'd expect to see more than this many PCI slots is in PCs that are intended for use as servers, or otherwise emulating a mini or mainframe computer.

Finally, there is yet another way to have multiple PC buses in one PC. That is to bridge from one PCI bus to another. Our example desktop PC does this in its quad video display adapter. That card has a PCI-to-PCI bridge chip on it, and the four video display adapters on that card are all located, logically, on the secondary PCI bus, across that bridge from the motherboard PCI bus.

The following table lists the various interface standards currently in use or ones that had been used before.

Standard	Applications	Burst Data Transfer Rate
ISA	Sound cards SCSI adapters Graphics cards Network cards Game Port cards Internal modems	2MBps to 8.33MBps
EISA	Network cards SCSI adapters	33MBps
PCI	Graphics cards SCSI adapters Sound cards Network cards Internal modems	266MBps
AGP	Graphics cards	528MBps

The Southbridge

At the "south" end of the PCI bus is a Southbridge chip. This chip contains all the rest of what normally comprises the *motherboard glue logic* or *motherboard chipset*, other than what is in the Northbridge chip. This is to say that the Southbridge chip has the needed interface logic to convey the signals from the PCI bus to the much slower ISA bus and all the other interfaces that a PC has. Today's motherboards provide only a couple of ISA slots at most, partly because so many of the things that once were done with plug-in ISA cards are now done with dedicated ports or with PCI cards.

The floppy diskette drives connect to the Southbridge chip. That chip usually supports two Enhanced IDE channels (primary and secondary) with up to two EIDE devices on each one, but it could support up to four EIDE channels. And it has a separate bus for keyboard, a bus mouse, a standard (possibly ECP or EPP) parallel port, and one or more standard serial ports. And it can have yet another bus interface for some Universal Serial Bus (USB) connectors as well as some IEEE 1394 (FireWire) connectors. Finally, the Southbridge chip will probably have an interface for a PC Card bay, in this case shown as a CardBus (32-bit) interface with a Zoomed Video bus connecting directly to the video subsystem.

If there is more than one PCI bus in a particular PC, it is possible to put one or more Southbridge chips on each of them. But that is not necessary.

If there are going to be any slots for ISA cards provided in this PC, their slot connectors will connect to a Southbridge chip. Thus, the ISA bus in this architecture is appended to the PCI bus, rather than being connected more-or-less directly to the CPU, as was the case for the original ISA bus.

The ISA, IDE, and PC Card interfaces run at 8.33MHz (exactly one-quarter of the original PCI bus rate). The only exception to that is if you were to have an ATA66 EIDE channel, in which case it would use a 16.7MHz clock, but only if the devices attached to it and the cable interconnecting them were all ATA66-compliant. The other ports connected to the Southbridge chip run at various slower speeds. (The Zoomed Video connection from the PC Card bay to the video controller runs at 33MHz, even though the connection from a PC Card bay to a Southbridge runs at only 8.33MHz.)

What You Gain From This North-South Division

By establishing a standard way to divide the electronics needed in a PC between what it calls the Northbridge and the Southbridge, Intel made it possible to do many interesting things. One is to have a docking station to which a (perhaps portable) PC could be connected. That docking station has its own set of peripheral devices that can augment the functionality contained in the PC.

Another possibility is that the Southbridge chip can be made by a different vendor than the Northbridge chip. As long as each properly interfaces to a PCI bus, they will work together flawlessly.

Finally, by having multiple Southbridge chips in a PC (and only one Northbridge chip) it is possible to have multiple pointing devices, each supported by its own port, and multiple other ports as well.

The Next Version of PCI: PCI-X

The new, 64-bit wide and fast PCI bus, called PCI-X, is four times as fast as the original PCI bus. That is still not fast enough for some purposes. To help push this technology yet another notch up, the PCI Special Interest Group (PCI-SIG) is considering and is expected to approve a variant form of the PCI protocol, named PCI-X.

In short, PCI-X is a compatible extension of the existing PCI Bus. The new architecture runs at speeds up to 133MHz, providing burst transfer rates above 1GBps (gigabytes per second) in addition to its fault isolation capabilities. This critical I/O bandwidth is targeted for industry standard servers running enterprise applications such as:

- Gigabit Ethernet
- Fibre Channel
- Ultra3 SCSI
- Cluster Interconnects

It is not an intention for PCI-X to compete with the AGP standard in graphics applications though.

This new, and very clever, protocol was developed jointly by Compaq, Hewlett-Packard, and IBM with the goal of making it possible to continue using a PCI-style connection in PCs where the amounts of data flowing would overwhelm even the fastest, widest PCI bus permitted by the previous standards. Most impressive is the fact that this new, higher data speed is fully compatible with existing 64-bit-wide-by-66MHz-clock-speed PCI hardware. The key observation these developers made was that the original PCI protocol was limited from going to higher speeds by a bottleneck that could be removed rather simply.

The speed-limiting bottleneck in conventional PCI systems is that within each clock cycle, each device is expected to notice what is passing over the bus, decide whether that is information intended for it, and then latch (grab) the data if it is. As the clock speed has risen from 33MHz to 66MHz, designers have found it difficult, but possible, to ensure that this could be done. A further doubling of the clock speed would simply have made this impossible with existing electronics.

The proposed solution to this bottleneck is very simple. Every device is modified by adding a register (a temporary electronic data holding place) that grabs the data off the PCI bus every clock cycle, whether it is intended for that device or not. Before the next clock cycle occurs, the device examines the data and decides what, if any, action it is supposed to take. This doubles the time it has to "make up its mind" and act. It also means that the responses come not one, but rather two, clock cycles after the stimulus thus adding one clock cycle to the overall transaction.

This permits doubling the clock speed to 166MHz. The added clock cycle cuts performance by only about 10 percent, because most PCI transactions take at least 9, and now will take 10, clock cycles. Overall, the gain is not quite a doubling of the speed, but it comes very close.

In order to implement PCI-X, each device on the bus must be PCI-X compliant. An important part of the PCI-X definition is the capability of sensing whether this is the case. Just as with the ATA66 enhancement to EIDE, PCI-X permits increased speed of operation only when all the pieces that are connected are capable of reliably operating at that higher speed. Because the physical connectors are not changed, nor are the electrical and logical aspects of the interface definition, you can plug older PCI cards into a PCI-X bus slot, or you can plug a newer, PCI-X card into an older PCI slot. Either way, if you do this these devices will operate only with the older PCI capabilities.

One of the advantages of the PCI-X architecture is backward compatibility. PCI-X is fully backwards compatible with conventional PCI products in the following ways:

- PCI-X cards can be used in a conventional PCI system. However, the PCI-X card will default to the speed of the PCI bus, which is either 33MHz or 66MHz.

- Conventional PCI cards can be used in PCI-X systems. The PCI card will run at its assigned speed, which is either 33MHz or 66MHz.

- PCI-X systems allow the use of both PCI and PCI-X cards on the same bus, with the bus speed default to the speed of the slowest card.

The PCI-SIG provides extensive information on PCI-X. Formed in June 1992, PCI-SIG is the industry organization chartered with maintenance of the PCI bus specification. It is led by a board of directors whose current members are the industry big players, including AMD, Compaq, Hewlett-Packard, IBM, Intel, Microsoft, Phoenix Technologies, ServerWorks, and Texas Instruments.

PCI-X and 3GIO

3GIO stands for Third-Generation I/O. PCI-SIG entered into agreement with the Arapahoe Work Group to manage and promote the 3GIO architecture specification. The Arapahoe Work Group is an independent industry work group comprised of Compaq, Dell, IBM, Intel and Microsoft. It drafts the standard for PCI-SIG to promote.

In short, 3GIO is a serial I/O interconnect that decreases interface pin count. The goals are to:

- Increase cost effectiveness
- Maximize bandwidth per pin
- Ensure high scalability
- Preserve customer investments
- Facilitate industry migration

So, why will people associate 3GIO with PCI-X? The key is that 3GIO leverages the PCI programming model. It is to be considered an extension of the PCI family. In fact, PCI SIG is considering a name that is more of a "PCI style" for 3GIO. The big question is, does 3GIO overlap with PCI-X?

The answer is NO. PCI-X is optimized for high-end bandwidth hungry applications that run on dedicated servers or workstations. On the other hand, 3GIO is of a general-purpose nature, for optimizing the SERIAL I/O performance of the lower end applications. They are targeting different market segments.

3GIO is using a layered approach for providing differential point-to-point high speed connections for I/O operations. The 3GIO layered model primarily consists of five layers:

- Configuration Layer: deploys the PCI plug-and-play model.
- Software Layer: deploys the PCI Software Driver model.
- Transaction Layer: uses packet based protocol.
- Data Link Layer: ensures data integrity.
- Physical Layer: the "fundamental" GIO links, with two differentially driven signal pairs known as the transmit pair and the receive pair. The embedded data clock has an initial transmission speed of 2.5GB per second per direction, which is expandable to 10GB or faster in the future.

One of the obvious advantages of this layered approach is that the impact brought by any change in the future speed and encoding techniques is restricted to the physical layer. The design of the end product can be simplified, and efficiency can be enhanced.

At the time of this writing there is not much solid working sample to demonstrate how 3GIO actually works in a real-world setup. It is estimated that we will see 3GIO products appearing in the market in late 2003.

Measuring Performance via Benchmarks

To compare the performance of your system, you rely mainly on the various benchmarks available in the market. Formally speaking, a benchmark is a test that compares the performance of different hardware and software. Different benchmark tests use different standards and mechanisms for execution, which can lead to un-intentional or intentional bias towards particular products. This is why you must know exactly what the benchmarks are designed to test when comparing their results.

The following list contains popular benchmark test software you can download from the Internet:

- Ziff Davis CPU Mark 99: `ftp://ftp.zdnet.com/zdbop/winbench/cpumk99.exe`
- Cli Benchmark: `http://www.ncpro.com/clibench/download/clibenchsmp.zip`
- Wintune 98: `ftp://wintune.winmag.com/wintune_43.exe`
- Winbench 99: `ftp://ftp.zdnet.com/pub/zdbop/winbench/wb9911up.exe`
- SiSandra 2000: `http://www.simtel.net/pub/simtelnet/win95/util/san649.zip`

FLOPS, SPEC, MIPS, and BogoMips

FLOPS is short for floating-point operations per second. It is a common benchmark measurement used to rate the floating-point performance of microprocessors. To be precise, it tests the strength of your processor's floating-point unit (FPU).

Floating-point operations include any operations that use fractional numbers for computation. Scientific applications and 3D software are floating-point hungry.

Because FLOPS does not take into account real-world factors like workloads, it is not being respected as a good measurement tool. And for this reason, a consortium of vendors created the Standard Performance Evaluation Corporation (SPEC) to provide more meaningful benchmark values.

MIPS is short for million instructions per second. It measures the number of machine instructions a computer system can execute per second. To be precise, it measures the computation speed of the CPU, and only the CPU. This means it might not reflect the true real-world performance, as real applications are often limited by many non-CPU factors. You can, however, use MIPS rating to give yourself a general idea of the system speed.

BogoMips originates from Linux. Every Linux kernel needs a timing loop to be calibrated to the processor speed of the system. To achieve this, the kernel has to measure, at boot time, how fast a busy loop runs on a computer. To be precise, the BogoMips value gives you a general indication of the processor speed. For the purpose of overall system performance evaluation, you are encouraged not to take this value too seriously.

For more information on BogoMips, please visit the BogoMips HOWTO documents located at `http://www.linuxdoc.org/HOWTO/mini/BogoMips`.

Summary

In this chapter, you've taken an in-depth look at motherboards—the backbone of any PC. In the next chapters, you'll delve into the worlds of the boot process, where your PC comes to life, and memory, which makes it all possible.

Kick Starting—The Boot Process

An awful lot happens when you turn on or restart your PC; more than you probably think. Myriad system checks verify configurations, look for hardware failures, and much more. At the core of all of these startup processes—which we'll explore in this chapter—is the BIOS.

What Is the BIOS?

One of the most vital PC programs is the one that starts as soon as the PC is turned on. This is the BIOS (basic input/output system), and it was commonly stored in ROM so that it would be essentially indestructible and available as soon as the PC's power supply stabilized. The BIOS is a set of hard-coded instructions—programs that perform the most basic, low-level control and supervision operations in your PC. It directly controls the hardware and works as a bridge between that hardware and the operating system and whatever software we run.

In order for the CPU to execute instructions, they must be kept somewhere the CPU can get at them quickly. The CPU is always in a hurry, and if you value your PC's speed, as most folks do, you never want its CPU to have to "twiddle its fingers" waiting for its next instruction to arrive. Likewise, for the CPU to process some data, it must be kept where the CPU can get at it again, quickly.

In practice, this means that every bit of data and all the instructions that the CPU executes to process the data must be in some part of the machine's RAM (random access memory) or ROM (read-only memory) at the time the processing takes place. RAM and ROM are very fast electronic holding places for numbers, and they are composed of small integrated circuit chips.

Every motherboard includes read-only memory chips. These ROM chips are separate from the main system memory. They contain the code of the BIOS, the abbreviation of Basic Input/Output System. This BIOS comprises several separate routines to serve different functions essential to the system boot process.

The reason to use ROM for holding the BIOS code is obvious: to avoid the code being corrupted by applications that have the capability to make changes to the wrong part of memory. Programs or data that are kept in RAM can be altered at will. But, unfortunately, they also can be altered in other ways that result in lost or unintentionally modified data. In particular, when you shut off your computer, or even merely reboot it, all the contents of RAM are lost.

For BIOS that is upgradeable, updates can only be performed via specialized floppy disks. This is generally known as a "flash upgrade" and requires that special instructions be sent to the BIOS chips to make them erasable; then the new BIOS code is written to the chips, and instructions are sent to make the chips "read-only" once again. The reason for all of this is to make it next to impossible to accidentally alter the contents of your PC's BIOS in ways which might render the PC completely unusable. Security and integrity of the BIOS code can thus be ensured.

The History of BIOS

Computers used to be seen as custom-made items tailored for specific needs. There came a need to perform large-scale production of computers for sale, and thus there had to be a way to standardize the computing environment but still allow room for accommodating some minor configuration differences. These differences include, and are not limited to, how much memory is installed, the size and address of the disk drives installed, and the installed devices. This is when people started to think of the concept of the BIOS.

With the introduction of the CP/M operating system for the IMSAI clone of the Altair 8800 computer back in 1977 by Gary Kildall, the concept of BIOS popped up. Shortly after that the BIOS concept was adopted by Microsoft, and many computer manufacturers started placing some parts of the BIOS in read-only memory.

In 1984, IBM introduced the IBM AT computer and its battery-powered RTC and CMOS memory. At this stage, the BIOS started to evolve. It used CMOS as a storage place for its configuration information. It had new features for security, power savings, and other options being added.

IBM AT has the RTC (Real Time Clock) added into the BIOS. This enhancement made the BIOS responsible for detecting and dealing with the movement from the end of the year 1999 to the start of the year 2000, which is the widely known Y2K problem.

BIOS Reverse Engineering

Reverse engineering is the process of analyzing software systems so that the software is more understandable for maintenance, evolution, or re-engineering purposes, or for analyzing a subject system to identify its current components and their dependencies so that design information can be extracted. With reverse engineering, the subject system is not altered. However, additional knowledge about the system can be produced.

Some people see reverse engineering as "the science of copying a technical function without copying the legally protected manner in which that function is accomplished in a competitor's machine or software." Whether reverse engineering is legal or not really depends. I would say, in the real world, it is better to judge on a case-by-case basis.

Is it possible to reverse engineer the system BIOS? Definitely yes. In fact, no password or BIOS facilities can effectively prevent reverse engineering from happening, as long as the BIOS/CMOS chip is captured. Physical security, in this regard, is more important. This means you should place your system in a secure place.

Reverse engineering can be viewed as an evil act that violates intellectual property. However, without reverse engineering, we might not have been able to see so many different PC clones available on the market.

The most famous instance of reverse engineering was Compaq Computer's cloning of the original IBM PC via BIOS reverse engineering. Why would Compaq need to do this? IBM invented the PC. To make the PC popular, IBM itself could not do the job. So, it published a technical reference manual openly for third-party manufacturers to provide add-ons for the PC. This way, third-party support could be obtained without the risk of having the design being copied.

In fact, the original PC was a combination of "off-the-shelf" parts from various sources, except for the ROM BIOS, which was IBM proprietary. The ROM BIOS was seen as a gateway that could discourage attempts to "copy" the PC.

In order to produce cloned PCs, one must figure out how the BIOS functions, and then reproduce the functionality. To avoid paying a massive IBM licensing fee, you cannot use any of the IBM's codes.

It is obvious that Compaq had received legal advice on how to circumvent the ROM BIOS problem. The engineers of Compaq broke down the original IBM design to find out the exact specification and function of that design, and then redesigned it to achieve the same specification and function. To be 100% legal, the engineers involved in the reconstruction process had to swear that they had never seen the original BIOS codes. It is now widely known that the process of reverse engineering IBM's ROM BIOS cost Compaq the efforts of 15 senior programmers and one million dollars.

CMOS and Other Programs

In addition to the BIOS, every motherboard includes another block of memory. This memory is made from low-power consumption CMOS chips. CMOS is the abbreviation for *Complementary Metal Oxide Silicon*. The CMOS chip is kept alive by constant battery power, without regards to the PC's power supply. This is generally supplied by a small disc battery mounted directly on the motherboard. Life expectancy for these little guys is about five years, but if you keep your PC for three years or more, you might need to replace the CMOS battery.

CMOS stores basic system configuration information, such as the number and type of drives, the memory size, the memory settings, the system time and date, and the hardware settings. The settings can be adjusted manually or be tuned automatically.

> **Note:** The key advantage to the CMOS chip manufacturing technology is the very low power needed to operate chips that are made using it. When PCs were young, this technology was relatively expensive, so it was used only when it really was needed. IBM decided when it introduced its PC/AT to use this technology to provide a small amount of ordinary "static" RAM that was made nonvolatile by adding a small battery. This combination of a battery plus a CMOS chip was soon nicknamed "the PC's CMOS." That name has stuck, even though now most of the integrated circuits in every part of your PC are manufactured by a variation of the same CMOS technology.
>
> Certain other programs are also kept in the motherboard BIOS ROM. In fact, it gets its name from these other programs. Their job is to activate the standard PC hardware, such as reading keystrokes from the keyboard, putting information on the video display, sending information to the printer, and so on. Such programs are called *device drivers*.

Changing the CMOS Settings

First of all, why would you ever want to make changes to the CMOS settings? Basically, you do this to specify the system configuration and to optimize the performance. In terms of hardware configuration, the most important configuration issue is related to disk drive configuration. In order for your IDE hard drive to work with the system, it must be configured in the CMOS setup. SCSI drives do not need to be configured, as their adapter cards are running with their own built-in BIOS.

Keep in mind that your PC's performance can be affected by the CMOS settings. Through the CMOS setup you can specify how fast the memory is running, whether or not cache is enabled, how fast the PCI bus should communicate, and so on.

You make changes to CMOS via the CMOS setup, which is a set of menus. It allows you to modify the parameters with which the BIOS configures your chipset. Usually, you enter the setup by pressing a special key combination at boot time, such as Del, Esc, Ctrl-Esc, and Ctrl-Alt-Esc (this key combination will vary according to your computer model). Different BIOS requires different key combinations, and the corresponding instructions are typically available onscreen.

If your PC doesn't display a message telling you how to get into the CMOS setup screens (and you can't remember how to do it), a simple trick might "fool" it into telling you that secret. Just hold down a key on the keyboard while the PC is booting. This will trigger an error and, usually, that will result in a message telling you to press some key to enter the BIOS and some other key to go on. Bingo! You now can enter the BIOS setup screens.

> **Warning:** Incidentally, unless you absolutely know what you're doing, your BIOS and CMOS settings are nothing to fool around with. If you make changes that aren't appropriate for your PC's hardware, it's guaranteed that your PC won't start—at all. You should always have your PC or motherboard technical manual close by when you're making changes. For the most part, modern BIOS's are auto-configuring if you leave them alone to do their job for you, but if you start making manual changes, you will need to change them back before the BIOS will properly re-auto-configure itself.

The NVRAM

Occasionally, you might need to change one or more of the programs that are kept in one of these ROMs. But if the motherboard BIOS were a true read-only memory chip, that just wouldn't be possible. On some older PCs, that is the situation. Therefore, for those machines you have to replace one such chip with another one that has been manufactured with the updated program in it.

All modern PCs use a variety of NVRAM (non-volatile random access memory) as their motherboard BIOS chips. Yet another term for this kind of memory is Flash ROM (or Flash RAM or Flash EPROM). This term comes from the notion that you can update an entire collection of locations in one fell swoop—an operation that is sometimes called "flashing" the chip. So to update the motherboard BIOS, you download a special program, start the PC in what Microsoft has termed MS-DOS mode (the "real mode" of CPU operation is the mode it starts in and remains in until the operating system starts protected mode operation), and then run that program.

There are two ways to make these changeable, yet semi-permanent memory devices. Most often they are integrated circuit chips that have been specially built to enable them to hold information indefinitely, even if no electrical power is supplied to them. Yet, by special means (involving higher voltages applied briefly to special programming pins), that information can change.

Alternatively, this facility might be provided simply as a small amount of normal RAM that has a tiny battery built into the chip package itself in order to enable it to remember its contents even when external power is removed. The choice of which kind of non-volatile memory technology to use is dictated by their relative costs, as well as the anticipated frequency of updates plus the anticipated time periods during which external power is unavailable. Each manufacturer must go through a design evaluation to conclude which kind to use in its PCs.

POST (Power-On Self-Test)

POST is short for *power-on self-test*. It is a series of diagnostic tests that run automatically when the computer is turned on. Generally, the computer components that will be tested by the POST process include the RAM, the keyboard, and the disk drives (these tests are not very in-depth though). Take the disk drive as an example. Until it has gone through quite the extensive test process, your PC doesn't know that it has any disk drives to work with at all.

When the tests are successful, and the PC knows its most-fundamental hardware is present and functional, the computer will boot. Otherwise, the computer will report the error by generating a pattern of beeps and displaying error messages onscreen if possible.

For the computer to load the test procedures, the startup program is kept in the BIOS ROM. The contents of this ROM are located in a special region of the CPU's memory address space where the CPU automatically goes (it actually jumps to address FFFF0h to start the program) when it first wakes up in order to find out what it is to do.

> **Note:** Sometimes the POST process can take quite a while to finish, especially when you have many devices attached to the computer. In fact, you can save yourself a little bit of time on subsequent bootings by altering a setting in the motherboard BIOS. Watch the screen when your PC starts up to learn how to enter the BIOS. The method varies from machine to machine, but most explain how to do it onscreen early in the POST process. (If that doesn't work, try holding down a key until the PC complains that there is a stuck key. After that message, there is usually a prompt telling you how to enter the BIOS.) In the BIOS, look for an option you can change to enable "fast boot" or to "skip testing memory on startup." In many cases, you will not only cut out the time normally taken to count all the memory locations (and test them), you also will skip testing some other parts that rarely fail, and so don't really need to be retested every time you restart your PC.

The POST Process

So what exactly happens when you turn your computer on and it starts up? Your PC performs a series of self-tests, configures itself, and then starts the operating system so you can get work done. Of course, this is an extremely condensed version of what exactly happens—so let's take a closer look at this process.

As soon as you turn on your PC's power, the power supply performs a self-test to make sure it is operating properly, and then signals POWER OK to the CPU. This signal clears any leftover data from the internal CPU memory registers, and resets another register called the program counter to F000, which tells the CPU where to find the next instruction it needs to process. F000 is the location of the BIOS, or Basic Input/Output System, which instructs the CPU how to interface with the other peripherals in the PC.

After the program counter is reset, the CPU performs an initial read and begins to process instructions. The CPU reads from F000 and loads the BIOS, which continues the boot-up. The CPU performs additional cross checks by reading data from different locations and comparing them against the correct values that are permanently encoded into the ROM BIOS.

Once the CPU is satisfied with the results of the cross-checking process, it proceeds to test the system buses, and then tests the RTC, or real-time clock. The RTC acts as the system's "heart," as it were, because all the system signals are synchronized to it.

At this point in the boot process, the PC begins to test the video card—and it is at this point where you first start to see some kind of output on your monitor. During this process, the memory on the video board is checked, and the video BIOS is read off the adapter and then inserted into the main system BIOS. After this process is complete, some type of splash screen appears on your monitor, usually containing information about the system BIOS version, processor identification, and other information, depending on your particular computer.

Another memory check follows, but this time, the main system RAM is tested. You might see a counter increasing to show you the progress of this test. During this process, the CPU is writing data to different locations in RAM, and then reading the data back from RAM and comparing it against the original values it stored. Once the RAM appears okay, the keyboard is checked-——at this point, you might see the lights for the number, caps, and scroll lock keys flash, and depending on your particular configuration, the number lock light might turn back on and stay on.

Once the keyboard checks out, the system then proceeds to transmit signals across the system bus to the hard disk drives and floppy drives, and then waits for a response. The installed drives answer back, and the drives are configured for use.

After everything is configured, the system then proceeds to crosscheck one last time, comparing the results of these POST tests against the values recorded in CMOS. The CMOS is basically the main repository where the system configuration is stored. If the system finds a different installed configuration than is recorded in the CMOS, the PC will prompt you to press a key and update the configuration on the CMOS setup screens.

If your particular machine has a SCSI controller card or other device that has its own BIOS code, it is also read into memory and added to the system BIOS. If present, the system then configures itself via plug and play, assigning interrupts, DMA channels, and other system resources as necessary. Once this final step is completed, the system then searches the disks for a particular piece of program code known as the *boot loader*. After the boot loader is found, the BIOS copies it into a particular location in RAM (address 7C00, FYI), and then hands off control to the boot loader, which then continues the system start up.

Device Drivers and Firmware

As mentioned earlier, certain programs are kept in the motherboard BIOS ROM for activating the standard PC hardware, such as reading keystrokes from the keyboard, putting information on the video display, sending information to the printer, and so on. These programs are called *device drivers*.

The device driver programs that actually command the hardware to work are so often called upon by application programs (and by the operating system, which is another kind of program that sits between the other two) that it is more efficient to always keep them in memory than to fetch a copy of them each time you want to operate the hardware. The collection of programs that performs the most basic information input (such as reading keystrokes) and output (such as writing to the screen) is the BIOS, and it is the main resident in the motherboard BIOS ROM.

No matter how the information-holding arrangement is constructed, and no matter which programs are kept there, these programs are called *firmware*. This name suggests their basic nature (in that they are a kind of software), yet they are intrinsically linked to some particular piece of hardware as well.

Apart from the device drivers on the motherboard BIOS, there are some other tasks performed by similar device driver programs located in other ROMs or from programs that are loaded off a disk drive, just like any application program.

One example of a program that lives in a special ROM is the video display adapter's BIOS. The original IBM PC came with device drivers to operate either the original monochrome character display or the earliest color graphics adapter (CGA) as a part of the motherboard BIOS ROM.

Now, though, almost no one uses either of these video display adapters. A few PC manufacturers have built in better video display circuits to their motherboards, and in those cases they have incorporated alternative device drivers to operate that alternative video circuitry right into the motherboard BIOS ROM.

More commonly, PCs are built with plug-in video display adapters. These option cards almost always carry a video BIOS ROM as well as the video display circuitry. By means of a special technique, each time you reboot your PC, the POST program looks for these "option ROMs" and, in effect, logically bonds them seamlessly with the programs in the motherboard BIOS ROM.

Still other augmentations to the BIOS programs don't need to be in a ROM. An example of this is the mouse driver. Normally when your PC boots, it loads from the disk (at some fairly advanced point in the boot process) a small program that knows how to take information from the mouse and convey it to application programs as well as how to put a mouse cursor on the video display. That bit of addition to the BIOS code ends up somewhere in your PC's RAM where it stays until the next time you reboot.

Which Strategy Is Appropriate?

If you always want your PC to do exactly the same task over and over, then it would be best if you simply put the program needed for that task into firmware. However, most of us use PCs to do many things. For us, the most sensible course is to store the programs for each of these purposes on a disk drive and load each of them into memory (RAM) only when they're needed.

Conversely, sometimes you might want a program that really must be in ROM to be somewhat inaccessible. One example is the computer's configuration or BIOS Setup program. If you could call that program up at any time with some hotkey sequence, you could summon it accidentally. Because most setup programs don't let you exit from them without rebooting, you could potentially lose a lot of work this way.

There are two strategies in this regard. Dell's Optiplex computers, for example, save the system state, including even the video display, before entering the Setup program. Then, after you finish making your changes, you can return to where you were before you entered the Setup program.

Dell used the other strategy in its Dimension line of computers. This is the more usual (and less expensive) industry practice whereby the user is forced to reboot the PC upon each exit from the Setup program. However, in these computers, Dell protects the user from the sort of accidental data loss described earlier by allowing them to enter the Setup program only during the boot process.

Just as some programs must be kept in memory all the time, either because the CPU can't access a disk to get them without already having them to use or because the CPU will be using them often, some data values must be kept always at hand. And, just as most programs are kept on disks most of the time, so is most data.

The only data your PC must have instant access to, or access to before it can access the disk drives, are details about how the PC is configured, including the parameters that describe the disk drives attached to it. This type of data typically is stored in the Complementary Metal-Oxide Semiconductor (CMOS), which is a particular kind of integrated circuit manufacturing technology. Although not exactly correct, common usage now refers to the data stored in this device as the "CMOS data."

You might wonder why this data isn't simply stored in the BIOS ROM along with the POST program that uses it. The reason is simple. The POST program never changes (except if you update it; something most users never do). This means that the POST program can be (and usually is) stored in an NVRAM or EEPROM chip whose contents are rarely, if ever, changed. However, the configuration data is subject to relatively frequent changes, so it must be stored in some easily alterable, yet non-volatile memory, which is exactly what the CMOS is. This chip also stores the date and time of day, and that information is updated every other second all day, whether or not the PC is on.

All the other data your PC uses is stored on some disk, somewhere. This might be the hard disk inside your PC's system unit or a floppy disk you put into the A: drive, or it might be on a disk on some remote computer you access across the Internet. From the point of view of your CPU, there is no difference. These are all examples of data that can be made available upon demand but that aren't where the CPU can use them instantly.

BIOS Fault Tolerance

BIOS is a critical component. When it is corrupted, your system can fail to boot. To provide a certain degree of fault tolerance, some motherboard manufacturers develop boards that deploy "Dual BIOS," meaning there are two BIOS chips on each board.

In a dual BIOS architecture, one BIOS chip serves as a backup in case the other one gets corrupted. During a failure of the primary BIOS, the system automatically switches over to the secondary BIOS chip and continues to boot. Note that the secondary BIOS will boot using only the default settings, meaning you will still have to manually tune the settings via CMOS setup. As far as I know, there is not yet a motherboard that provides BIOS "mirroring" function.

How Your PC Wakes Up and Prepares Itself for Work

One topic I want to cover in this chapter is a brief description of what your PC must go through between the time you flip on the power switch and the time it is ready for you to run your first application program. This process is called *booting* the PC, from the whimsical notion of the impossible task of lifting oneself by one's own bootstraps.

Fortunately, all PCs (as well as modern, larger computers) come with the capability of getting themselves started without all that fuss and effort by a human being. The reason they are able to do that lies in two features of their architecture. One is a portion of how the x86 processors are designed. The other is in the contents of a particular program that the motherboard BIOS chips contain.

Just as Intel hardwired the x86 processors to look in the first 1KB of main memory for the interrupt vector table, they also hardwired the address at which it will look for instructions when it first wakes up. The designated address is exactly 16 bytes below the top of the first megabyte. (An x86 processor can access only the first megabyte of memory address space when it first wakes up, because it always does so in real mode.)

So, if the PC maker arranges to have the motherboard BIOS ROM show up in the CPU's memory address space in the region just below 1MB, and if it contains an appropriate program starting at that special address, that boot program will automatically run each time the PC is turned on or reset.

Because a PC program normally progresses through memory from lower addresses to higher, and because the starting address is only 16 bytes below the absolute upper end of the first megabyte of memory, it would seem at first glance that the boot program would have to be impossibly short. In fact, the boot program first jumps unconditionally to some address a good deal further below this "ceiling," but still somewhere inside the motherboard BIOS ROM.

Next, the boot program determines whether all the standard parts of the PC are present and seem to be working normally. Before it gets very far into this process, it fills in the first 16 slots in the IVT with pointers to ISRs elsewhere in the motherboard BIOS. After that has been done, the boot program enables the maskable interrupts so the machine can respond to, for example, keystrokes from the keyboard.

Also along the way, the motherboard BIOS program determines whether a special video BIOS chip is located on a plug-in video card. If it is, the boot program transfers control of the PC to that program, which uses this opportunity to place its ISR addresses into the correct slots in the IVT. When that has been accomplished, the video card can display information on the screen. That video BIOS program commonly displays a copyright message as the first message on the screen. Then it returns control to the motherboard BIOS boot program.

The boot program now checks main memory to see how much of it there is, and to be sure it all works correctly. (Some PCs do a more thorough job of checking memory at this stage than others, which explains why some PCs can have flaky memory and yet pass this step in the boot process. They might reveal the deficiencies of the memory at a later stage, either when a memory management program loads and does a more careful check of main memory, or perhaps only by failing in the middle of some important task you are doing.)

Around this time, the boot program usually also offers the user a chance to suspend the boot program and enter the BIOS setup program. This enables you to go into a special set of screens that enable you to alter configuration settings stored in the motherboard CMOS.

The boot program continues by building some data tables in the DOS and BIOS data area, a region of main memory just above the IVT. This area holds, among other things, a concise record of the number of serial and parallel ports, floppy disks, and other standard pieces of hardware in this PC.

Now the boot program has finished its POST section, and it is ready to look for an operating system and load it into memory. If it succeeds in doing this, it will then turn over control of the PC to that operating system, and the boot program's job will be done. If the boot program cannot find an operating system, it typically will simply stop with a message saying that you should insert a bootable disk in the A: drive and press any key to restart the boot process.

In all PCs built more than a few years ago, the boot program would always look for the operating system in a standard set of places and always in the same order. It looked initially on the first floppy disk drive (A:), and then on the first hard drive (C:). If it didn't find an operating system in either of those places, it gave up (or in IBM-brand PCs only, it ran the BASIC interpreter located in a special motherboard ROM).

Many modern PCs are more flexible, and in their BIOS setup program, you can tell the PC which devices you want it to check and in what order. The possible boot devices now commonly include the A: and B: floppy disk drives (which could also be the new high-capacity super-floppy drives referred to either as a: drives or LS120 drives), the C: hard drive, or a CD-ROM drive attached to either the primary or secondary IDE chain.

Booting through a removable media like the floppy drive can be dangerous if the boot disk is infected with virus. One way to minimize the likelihood of infecting your PC with a so-called boot sector virus is to specify that it not try booting from A: or B:. When you must boot from a floppy, you can simply first enter the BIOS setup program and reset this choice to allow booting from the floppy disk drive, and then be sure that the disk you use is virus-free.

System Boot Sequence in Technical Details

Stage 1: Turn On Your System Power

It takes some time for the internal power supply to "warm up" and generate reliable power in the proper voltages for the entire computer system. In fact, it can take a half-second or longer for the power to be stabilized.

If the system is turned on prematurely, it can be damaged. To avoid the potential destruction, the motherboard chipset will generate a reset signal to the processor, which has the same effect of pressing the reset button on your chassis, until a power good signal is sent from the power supply.

What exactly is the Power OK signal? It is a signal sent by the power supply after it completes its internal tests and determines that the power is ready for use. The system's motherboard will not start the computer until this signal is received.

The nominal voltage of the power good signal is +5 V. Practically speaking, the allowable range is up to a full volt above or below this value.

Should a power surge or glitch occur, the power supply will turn off the power good signal until the problem is fixed, causing the computer to be reset.

Stage 2: The Processor Is Ready for Executing

When the processor first starts, it always looks into the system BIOS ROM for the start of the BIOS boot program.

The location that holds the BIOS boot program typically is at FFFF0h, which is at the end of the system memory. Note that these 16 bytes of memory space contain only a "pointer" that points the processor to the real startup program.

Stage 3: The BIOS Performs the Power-On Self Test (POST)

Keep in mind that POST takes place only during a cold boot, meaning the machine was off when started. During a warm boot, caused by pressing Ctrl+Alt+Delete, the POST is skipped entirely.

During the POST process, the BIOS looks for the video card's built-in BIOS program, which is normally located at C000h in memory. The system BIOS executes the video card BIOS and initializes the video card. At this point, you will see information onscreen about the video card.

When the system BIOS startup screen is displayed, the following information can be found:

- BIOS manufacturer
- BIOS version number
- BIOS date
- The key(s) to press to enter the BIOS setup program
- System BIOS logo
- "Energy Star" logo
- BIOS serial number

Keep in mind that the serial number is essential, as it can be used in many cases to determine the specific motherboard and BIOS version you use.

When the video card is initialized, the BIOS starts looking for the other devices' ROM BIOSes and executes them. For a typical IDE system, the IDE/ATA hard disk BIOS can be found at C8000h. A SCSI device controller might have its own BIOS enabled, and in such case, you will see its information being displayed onscreen as well.

There are two types of SCSI cards. Regardless of the card types, all SCSI adapters require the following local resources:

- IRQ
- DMA channel
- I/O address
- BIOS ROM memory

The older cards generally require manual jumper configuration to configure the IRQs, DMAs, and SCSI IDs. The newer cards use n-board BIOS to control the resource settings and automatic SCSI ID assignment. With plug-and-play capabilities, these cards can configure themselves most of the time.

Stage 4: Device Detection

In addition to running the device BIOSes, extensive checks are performed on other items, such as system memory. You can refer to this as a system inventory.

Nowadays all system BIOSes are plug-and-play compliant. All the plug-and-play devices are detected, configured, and displayed. A summary screen about the system's configuration then appears. Any device not shown hasn't been detected.

In order to truly support plug and play, the BIOS follows a series of steps to manage the plug-and-play devices. First, it creates a resource table that includes all the available IRQs, DMA channels, and I/O addresses, but excludes those reserved for the system devices. It then looks for the plug-and-play and non-play-and-play devices that reside on the PCI and the ISA buses, identifies them, and loads the last known system configuration from the ESCD.

ESCD (Extended System Configuration Data) is stored in a non-volatile CMOS memory area. This ESCD area is used to store configuration information about the hardware in your system. During the system boot, the BIOS checks this area of memory to determine whether changes occurred since the last boot-up. If nothing has changed, no configuration work needs to be done at this stage.

Another use of ESCD is to provide a communication link between the BIOS and the OS, as both of them use the same ESCD area to read and record the status of the hardware. In fact, Windows 9X and Me read ESCD to determine whether the hardware has changed so that they can take proper action.

The BIOS compares the current configuration to the last known configuration loaded from ESCD, takes the appropriate actions, and then continues with the boot. The BIOS settings are checked to determine whether any non-plug-and-play devices have reserved additional system resources. These resources are eliminated from the available resource table.

After all these steps, the resource table is pretty clean. The BIOS can assign resources to all the PnP cards from the resources left in the resource table.

The PnP devices that receive their resources are notified. The ESCD area is updated with the new system configuration. At this stage, you will see the message `"Updating ESCD ... Successful"` onscreen.

Stage 5: System Configuration Summary

Prior to booting the operating system from disk, a configuration summary is displayed. Typically you will see the following pieces of information:

- *Processor (CPU) Type*: Sometimes you see `-s` next to the processor type. This is a power management feature called SMM, which is short for System Management Mode. Note that, although the SMM circuitry is integrated into the chip, it is operating independently to control the processor's power use based on its activity level. Most modern processors support SMM.

- *Coprocessor*: This indicates the floating-point unit (FPU). Because all the latest processors have the FPUs built in, you will always see the value "Installed" or "Integrated".

- *Clock Speed*: This indicates the speed of the processor in MHz.

- *Floppy Drive A and/or Floppy Drive B*

- *IDE/ATA Drives*

- *Base Memory Size*: This value indicates the 640KB conventional memory.

- *Extended Memory Size*: This indicates how much extended memory has been installed in your system. The missing 384KB in between is the upper memory area. In the age of Windows Me, 2000, XP or Linux, you don't really need to pay attention to these base memory/extended memory values. These values are only relevant for DOS or the earlier versions of Windows.

- *Cache Size*: The amount of level 2 cache memory on board in the system.

- *Memory Type and Configuration*: Information includes the number of memory banks found as well as the type of memory installed.

- *Display Type*: This is only a generic value, and you will most likely see the value of "VGA/EGA."

- *Serial Port(s)*

- *Parallel Port(s)*

- *Plug-and-play Devices*

Stage 6: Boot Up

The BIOS starts searching for a boot drive. The typical settings found follow this sequence:

1. Floppy disk (A:)
2. Hard disk (C:)
3. CD-ROM drive (D:)

This sequence can be altered in the CMOS. How this is accomplished is different from BIOS to BIOS, but there is usually some setting named "boot sequence," or "boot order," which can be cycled through the available devices. Your motherboard or BIOS manual should identify this setting clearly and explain what options your specific PC has.

When the target boot drive is identified, the BIOS uses the boot information to start the operating system boot process.

Stage 7: OS Boot Process

Most likely your OS is installed on one of the hard disks. The BIOS will look for a master boot record at cylinder 0, head 0, sector 1, which is actually the first sector on the disk. This is the same if you are booting from a floppy—the floppy disk has a volume boot sector for booting purposes.

The BIOS boots the operating system using information contained in the boot sector. The code contained in the boot sector then takes over the control from the BIOS. If no boot device is discovered, or if the bootable hard disk partition is not set to active, the system will normally display an error message, and then will halt.

The Master Boot Record

Often referred to as the *boot sector,* the MBR exists in your hard disk, serving as a consistent starting point where key information is stored about the disk, such as how many partitions it has and what sort of partitions they are. Additionally, MBR holds the information required for the BIOS to load the initial boot program.

Located at cylinder 0, head 0, and sector 1, the master boot record contains both the Master Partition Table and the Master Boot Code. The Master Partition Table is a small table that includes the descriptions of the partitions contained on the hard disk. The Master Boot Code represents the small initial boot program executed by the BIOS. This code contains the instructions needed for transferring the execution control to the boot program stored on the OS partition, for the purpose of booting the OS.

MBR contains information essential to the boot up process. If it becomes damaged or corrupted, serious data loss can occur. Also, because the master boot code is the first program executed when the PC is on, this is a favorite target for a virus attack. You should install anti-virus software so that protection can be in place.

Active Partitions and Multi-Boot Setup

On a PC, only an *active* primary partition can be used to boot an operating system. There is only one active partition on each system. Logical drives within an extended partition can never be designated as bootable.

The most popular tool to configure partitions is the DOS FDISK command. You can create and remove primary and secondary partitions with this command. The most important thing to do, however, is to mark a primary partition as active, so that this partition can become bootable.

FDISK is available in DOS, Windows 3.X, Windows 9X, and Windows Me. It supports only the FAT family file systems, including FAT12, FAT16, VFAT, and FAT32.

> **Note:** The following functions can be performed with FDISK:
>
> *Create Partitions*: For creating primary or logical partitions.
>
> *Set Active Partition*: For setting the primary partition on your boot disk to active. Although this is a manual process, FDISK will warn you when none of the disks is active.
>
> *Delete Partitions*: For deleting the existing partitions.
>
> *Display Partition Information*: For displaying partition information without taking any actual actions.

In some cases you might need to host multiple operating systems on the same system. These OSes need to share the same file system in order to coexist. The recommended arrangement is to set up multiple primary partitions on a one-per-OS basis. You will then have to use a boot manager to control and manage this environment.

Boot managers, or boot loaders, are programs that insert themselves into the very beginning of the boot process. When your system boots, the boot manager runs immediately to analyze the primary partitions and present you with an OS menu. The primary partition that belongs to the OS of your choice is marked as active in real time, and the boot process continues.

In Windows, System Commander is a famous third-party boot manager product. On Linux, LILO is the de facto boot loader used in most of the Linux distributions.

The OS Boot Process

When the BIOS completes its startup activities, it starts loading the OS by searching for the boot device in the order specified by the CMOS setting. Once the boot sector is located, the OS continues the boot process.

DOS or any variant of Windows other than Windows NT or Windows 2000/XP starts out by booting the equivalent of DOS. For Windows, there are extra steps required at the end of the boot process after the underlying DOS has loaded, listed here:

1. The master boot code examines the master partition table to determine whether there is an extended DOS partition and whether there is a bootable partition specified in the partition table. Any primary and extended partitions must be loaded and recognized by the system.

2. The boot code next attempts to boot the primary partition that is marked active. If none of the partitions is active, you will receive error message such as `"No boot device"` or `"NO ROM BASIC - SYSTEM HALTED"` or `"Operating System Missing"`.

3. If an active primary partition exists, it is booted. The boot code loads the volume boot sector into memory and tests it before passing control to the volume boot code.

4. The volume boot code examines the disk structures to ensure that everything is correct, and then searches the root directory of the device being booted for the operating system files that contain the operating system. In the case of DOS, the following files are the search targets:

   • IO.SYS

   • MSDOS.SYS

   • COMMAND.COM

5. If the corresponding operating system files do not exist, you will receive error message such as `"Non-system disk or disk error - Replace and press any key when ready"`.

6. If those operating system files are present, they will be loaded into memory and granted control over the rest of the process. For DOS, the files execute in the following order:

- IO.SYS

- MSDOS.SYS (this file is a text file under Windows 9X and ME)

- COMMAND.COM

- CONFIG.SYS and AUTOEXEC.BAT

Windows 9X/Me Boot Sequence

For Windows 95/98/Me, many more routines are executed afterwards to read the system Registry, initialize hardware devices, and start the graphical interface.

The following list summarizes the Windows 9X/Me boot sequence. Files are loaded in this order and their various tasks performed:

- *IO.SYS*: A small DOS core module that starts the Windows 9X/Me boot process and tells the PC to look for the MSDOS.SYS file.

- *MSDOS.SYS*: A hidden ASCII text file on the root device that contains information about the boot configuration.

- *DRVSPACE.BIN*: This program checks the integrity of the information in SYSTEM.DAT, which is part of the Registry. Note that DRVSPACE.BIN is also a compression program that allows for disk compression capability.

- *SYSTEM.DAT*: This file provides information about the setup of the system, including the different names, locations, and the corresponding drivers of the devices.

- *USER.DAT*: Another half of the Registry that contains user-specific information such as screen colors and icon choices.

- *CONFIG.SYS*: This file is needed if there are legacy devices to be loaded.

- *AUTOEXEC.BAT*: A file for setting system variables and loading TSRs and some other utilities. It is not a strictly necessary file for Windows 9X/Me.

- *SYSTEM.INI*: This file contains information about your computer's hardware settings, and is required for loading the various device drivers.

- *VMM32.VXD*: This is the virtual machine manager that runs after AUTOEXEC.BAT to load the other virtual device drivers it finds in the Registry and SYSTEM.INI.

- *WIN.COM*: This file switches the environment from real mode to protected mode, and then initializes the different devices and performs further file loading.

- *KERNAL32.DLL*: The 32-bit kernel for Windows.

- *GDI.EXE/GDI32.EXE*: The graphics engines for Windows.

- *USER.EXE/USER32.DLL*: The user interface engines.

- *WIN.INI*: File that contains application information configuration.

- *STARTUP Group*: The Startup folder that contains any programs to be run every time Windows starts.

Windows NT/2000 Boot Sequence

The following list summarizes the Windows NT/2000 boot sequence:

1. The file NTLDR, which is the NT Loader, is loaded and executed.

2. NTLDR switches the CPU to 32-bit flat memory mode.

3. NTLDR reads the BOOT.INI file that contains the list and paths of all the installed OSes, and shows you a menu of choices.

4. NTLDR loads NTDETECT.COM to build a hardware list.

5. NTLDR loads NTOSKRNL.EXE, which is the kernel file for Windows NT.

6. NTOSKRNL.EXE loads and initializes Windows NT using information from the Registry.

Speeding Up Your PC's Boot Process

The boot process can take a long time or at least it often seems like it. Can you shorten it significantly? Yes, you almost certainly can.

There are several ways to do this. The first way to explore speeding your PC's startup process is to find out whether your BIOS offers a setting to disable the memory test during boot, or one to enable "fast booting." The latter is a nickname that indicates that not only will the memory check be skipped, but also some of the other tests of hardware devices that don't often fail.

You don't want to use these settings unless you are pretty sure your PC's memory (and those other devices, such as floppy drives) is working correctly. Otherwise you are foregoing some valuable checks that might someday save your data. If you have booted many, many times without incident, however, you can select this setting in the BIOS, and from then on your PC will boot noticeably quicker.

Power-Saving PCs Seem to Turn On Faster

Battery-powered portable PCs have led the way in showing how much you might reduce a PC's power consumption. In this chapter I want to focus on one pleasant side effect of some of the common power-saving strategies used in those PCs.

The overall notion of power management is to power down all those components that are normally power hungry and that are not at the moment actually being used. Even at their best, modern PCs are not all that smart about how this is done, but some strides have been made toward this goal.

One obvious, and very effective, way to save power is to turn off the video monitor when it isn't being used. This makes the PC look as if it is off. Touch the mouse or press a key on the keyboard and the monitor wakes up.

Another step is to turn off the hard drive. Even more aggressive steps include slowing down or stopping the CPU clock, turning off the modem, and so forth.

How to Make a PC Hibernate

Portable PC makers have had the strongest motivation to deal with these issues creatively. Saving battery power is crucial. So they arrange to have as many pieces powered down as much of the time as possible. But they can't just turn off all the pieces and then turn them back on without requiring the PC to start everything all over again; that is to say, without requiring another annoyingly slow reboot.

The problem is that if you turn off power to RAM, it forgets its contents. Similarly, various peripheral parts in a PC can remember some important facts about their "current state" only while they are powered up.

So these PC designers created PCs that can be powered down and back, sometimes a piece at a time, under software control. Then they also made it possible to save the "state" of each piece and to restore that state when those pieces are awakened once more.

In effect, the PC pieces are put into "hibernation," in which state they forget (or don't notice) what is going on around them. Then, when they are "reawakened," they get briefed on whatever they might have missed.

There are several strategies for doing this; perhaps the most common being to write a file to the disk drive with all the required status information just before the PC is put to sleep. Of course, you must also arrange some way to detect that the PC was asleep the next time it starts, so it can "merely" awaken all its parts and reload their states before letting you get back to work.

This works pretty well, actually. But it doesn't work instantly. Some substantial amount of time (measured in tens of seconds, typically) is required to awaken all the parts and get them back to their original states. The "suspend file," as it often is called, also takes up a noticeable amount of disk space—over 70MB on one portable I have used.

Some Things to Try

Look at the screen during the boot process. Also watch the lights indicating disk access. See which parts of the boot process that I just described you can identify. A flashing of the access light for the floppy disk drives or the hard drive might indicate simply that the boot program is checking to see that those drives are responding to commands. If the access light stays on for several seconds, the boot program might be trying to read information from a disk in that drive. A "ka-thunk" sound from a printer probably means it was reset by a signal sent to it from the CPU at the boot programs behest. Of course, you should see the amount of main memory being counted onscreen as it is being checked (unless you have disabled that check in your PC's setup BIOS).

Explore your PC's setup BIOS screens. You can do this safely as long as you never answer yes to the question Save changes? before you exit from those screens. Determine which options your PC gives you and see what you can discern about its architecture from that set of options.

Common BIOS Tuning Options

This section briefly introduces some of the most popular BIOS tuning options. As stated before, changing the BIOS settings can affect the system performance, although the improvement might not be significant.

In any case, you must be extremely careful when performing such a configuration job. Your BIOS may have specific options to configure, which means you should consult your motherboard manual for details.

Before you proceed, locate the CMOS reset, which is a jumper or a switch that allows you to reset your motherboard to its factory default setting. If you later get into trouble by setting your BIOS improperly, you might be able to undo all the settings and start over. However, bear in mind that many custom systems (which today, includes most PC's sold) will not operate with the motherboard's default BIOS settings. If you're not certain what you're doing, the best way to proceed through an exploration of the BIOS/CMOS is "look, but don't touch."

Of course, knowing what you're doing is what it's all about. To that end, Table 16.1 explains many of the BIOS/CMOS settings that you're likely to encounter. These explanations won't necessarily tell you enough to make it safe for you to make changes, but they will be a step towards understanding what you're seeing.

Table 16.1 BIOS/CMOS Settings

DRAM Read Burst	Sets the timing for burst-mode reads from DRAM. The lower the timing number, the faster the system addresses memory. If you select timing numbers that are lower than the installed DRAM is able to support, memory errors can occur.
DRAM Write Burst	Sets the timing for burst-mode writes from DRAM. The lower the timing numbers, the faster the system addresses memory. If you select timing numbers that are lower than the installed DRAM is able to support, memory errors can occur.
DRAM R/W Leadoff Timing	Allows you to select the combination of CPU clocks the DRAM on your board requires before each read from or write to the memory.

Table 16.1   Continued

DRAM Fast Leadoff	Allows you to shorten the leadoff cycles and optimize performance.
Turbo Read Leadoff	Allows you to shorten the leadoff cycles and optimize performance in cacheless, 50-60 MHz, or one-bank EDO DRAM systems.
DRAM Speculative Leadoff	Allows you to enable Speculative Leadoff, which lets the DRAM controller pass the read command to memory slightly before it has fully decoded the address, thus speeding up the read process.
DRAM RAS# Precharge Time	Allows you to configure the precharge time. This precharge time value represents the number of cycles it takes for the RAS to accumulate its charge before the DRAM refreshes. If insufficient time is allowed, the refresh might be incomplete, causing the DRAM to fail in retaining data.
RAS# to CAS# Delay	Allows you to insert a timing delay between the CAS and RAS strobe signals; used when DRAM is written to, read from, or refreshed. When it is disabled, faster performance might be obtained at the expense of stability.
DRAM Page Idle Timer	Allows you to determine the amount of time in HCLKs that the DRAM controller waits to close a DRAM page after the CPU becomes idle.
DRAM Enhanced Paging	Allows you to instruct the chipset to keep the page open until a page/row miss.
SDRAM Speculative Read	Allows you to have your chipset speculate on a DRAM read address in order to reduce read latencies. This is actually done by having the controller issue the read command slightly before it has finished decoding the data address.
SDRAM (CAS Lat/RAS-to-CAS)	Allows you to configure a combination of CAS latency and RAS-to-CAS delay. You should not change the values in this field unless you change specifications of the installed DRAM or the installed CPU.
Refresh RAS# Assertion	Allows you to select the number of clock ticks RAS# is asserted for refresh cycles.

Table 16.1 Continued

DRAM Refresh Queue	Allows you to permit queuing of up to four DRAM refresh requests, thus allowing the DRAM to be refreshed at optimal times.
DRAM RAS Only Refresh	An older alternative to CAS-before-RAS refresh.
DRAM Refresh Rate	Allows you to specify the period required to refresh the DRAMs according to DRAM specifications.
Fast DRAM Refresh	Allows you to configure the refresh mode used by the cache DRAM controller.
Read-Around-Write	Allows you to optimize your DRAM settings. If a memory read is addressed to a location whose latest write is being held in a buffer before being written to memory, the read is satisfied by the contents stored in the buffer without being sent to the DRAM.
PCI-To-DRAM Pipeline	Allows you to optimize your DRAM settings by enabling full PCI-to-DRAM write pipelining. This technique makes use of the buffers in the chipset to store data written from the PCI bus to memory.
CPU-To-PCI Write Post	Allows writes between the CPU and the PCI bus to be buffered in order to compensate for the speed differences between the CPU and the PCI bus.
CPU-To-PCI IDE Posting	Allows you to post write cycles from the CPU to the PCI IDE interface, for the purpose of cycle optimization.
Peer Concurrency	Allows you to configure peer concurrency, so that more than one PCI device is allowed to be active at a time.
Passive Release	Allows CPU to PCI bus accesses during passive release.
Delayed Transaction	Allows you to support compliance with PCI specification version 2.1.

Understand that not all of these options will be available on your given system. Different BIOS versions deploy different options or use different names for the same options.

The level of control afforded by the BIOSes of different computers can vary widely. Mass-market systems made for entry level audiences are unlikely to let you go wild with the BIOS settings. In fact, major manufacturers prefer to err on the cautious side regarding hardware and system settings, in order to minimize the need for support. Small generic brand OEM computer vendors, on the other hand, tend to give power users the complete setup flexibility they need.

In any case, keep in mind that the performance changes you make through the BIOS are not going to make a big difference when running day-to-day business applications. The BIOS is only a control point that lets you adjust settings, but it can't extend the limits to which you can push your system. When you want to optimize your system, many factors come into play, such as the ratings of the individual components and the combination of these components as a team. There are always additional factors to consider when you push the system to the extremes.

CMOS Security

Due to the importance of the system's configuration settings, you must make sure that the CMOS cannot be easily tampered with. The following are the most popular options for securing your CMOS settings:

- User password
- Supervisor password
- User setup access
- Unattended start

The user setup access option allows the person with the user password to make BIOS adjustments. For security purposes, you should disable this option.

The unattended start option allows your computer to be booted up without a password. With this option enabled, you will still need to type your password before you can access the system.

You should always configure a password for CMOS access. Non-supervisory users should not be given access to the CMOS.

The Current BIOS Industry

A number of companies dominate the market for BIOS. They include:

- Phoenix Technologies, http://www.ptltd.com/
- American Megatrends, http://www.ami.com/
- Award, http://www.award.com
- Mr. BIOS, http://www.mrbios.com

In addition to these manufacturers, Intel has announced a System Management BIOS (SM BIOS)reference specification intended to ease and speed the implementation of management capabilities in desktop and mobile PCs, as well as servers. The goal of specifying the SM BIOS reference specification is to help PC manufacturers and BIOS and software vendors better define the key areas of BIOS support for managed systems, and to provide guidelines to ease integration of BIOS information into both operating systems and higher-level management applications.

Summary

When you power on your PC, a long sequence of events takes place. These tests make sure that all of the equipment in your PC is functioning properly. Configurations are checked, partly so that Windows doesn't try to use a piece of hardware that you've removed, and so that new hardware and resources are available to you. Any resources that need to be re-allocated are handled through plug and play, and, finally, the operating system takes charge.

With the PC up and running, you're ready to take an in-depth look at the PC's playground and working field: memory.

Understanding PC Memory

Many new PC users become very confused by the difference between storage and memory. And keeping these two clearly separate in your mind is crucial to developing a sound picture of how a PC is built and how it works. So we will say it for you once more: Memory and storage are two entirely different things. If you get these two confused, you will have no end of trouble trying to understand how your PC is built and how it works. Here's the difference in a nutshell: Memory is the collection of all the fast information holding places (made up of RAM and ROM). Storage is the collection of all the long-term information-holding places (often made up of magnetic or optical disks or tapes).

If you find analogies helpful, you might think of your entire computer as an office. The memory in your computer is like a desk; it provides space where all of the work can be performed. The storage in your computer is like a filing cabinet where information is kept for the long haul. As that information is needed, it can be placed on the desk (into memory), worked on, manipulated, changed, or used to create new information, and then all of that can be placed back in the filing cabinet (into storage).

Typically, a PC will have tens or hundreds of times as much capacity in storage as it does in memory. For example, a pretty good system these days might have between 64 and 256MB of RAM and it might have several gigabytes (GB) or tens of GB of disk storage. (Recall that one gigabyte is the same as 1024 megabytes.)

The CPU's Essential Playground

The PC's main memory is the collection of all the fast information holding places in a PC that can be "seen" by the CPU. That is, those places into which it can place information or from which it can retrieve information directly, without needing the information having to pass through any other holding places along the way. It is only in these places that programs can execute or data can be processed.

Most of these fast information-holding places are contained in the memory modules (DIMMs or SIMMs) that are most likely plugged into special slots on the motherboard. Those memory modules are small printed circuit cards that carry several integrated circuit (IC) memory chips, which are the actual holding places for information.

It is important to realize that the physical location of these holding places is not critical to your understanding of how your PC knows their logical locations. Your concern should be more on their logical locations.

Why Memory Is "Where the Action Is"

Storage devices are good at holding information for a very long time, which is why information is kept there. Most are capable of accepting alterations to their contents, yet hold those contents very well. That is unlike the behavior of memory chips, which, with a few exceptions, "forget" whatever they are holding the instant the power fails or your PC is reset.

Almost every type of storage device is much slower than the memory chips used in a PC's main memory. And this speed difference is why the memory, and only the memory, is the CPU's essential playground. It must have all the information it is going to use readily available at electronic speeds.

Having the CPU constantly fetch all its information from a disk drive and store intermediate values there while it is computing some result is extremely impractical. The only practical approach is to bring your information (both data and the programs that specify how that data is to be processed) into the PC's main memory. Then, and only then, can the CPU be asked to process it.

The difference in speed between storage devices such as hard drives and memory becomes obvious when you take a glance at the numbers. Hard drive access time is commonly measured in milliseconds (ms) that is, 1/1,000 of a second. A typical hard drive has an access time of between 9-12ms. Memory, on the other hand, has access times measured in nanoseconds (ns), that is, one-millionths (1/1,000,000) of a second. Memory access times are typically around 50ns. In other words, memory access is commonly about 180 times faster than storage access. Would you rather walk across the country at one mile per hour or fly at 180 mph?

What You Must Know About Memory Chips and Modules

There are at least three reasons to understand memory chips and modules. Each of them is valid, and all of them might apply to you. One is simple intellectual curiosity. They are, after all, some of the most intricate devices designed and built by human beings. There almost certainly are more memory *bit cells* manufactured and sold each year than any other product. (This is virtually guaranteed by the fact that most memory modules now sold contain literally millions of bit cells. And many millions of those modules are sold annually.)

A second reason is that understanding memory at the chip level and at the module level helps you understand the overall PC design. This includes such key ideas as the notion of banks of memory and what parity memory and error correction are and how they are used.

Third, you must understand the key parameters that describe memory chips or modules if you are going to buy more and insert them into your PC. (And knowing what they look like is also handy when it comes to finding them, and perhaps removing or inserting them, if appropriate.)

First, this chapter tells you a little bit about the many ways memory has been packaged for use in PCs. Then, it goes into some of the different "flavors" of RAM now available, and describes which kinds you might be using in your PC.

ROM versus RAM

Electronic memory is made in integrated circuit (IC) chips. These are tiny, tremendously complex, creations crafted from silicon, some trace impurities, and a little bit of metal, built in super-clean (and super-expensive) factories.

IC memory chips come in two main types and, within each type, in many flavors. The two types are read-only, or non-volatile, memory chips and random-access, or volatile, memory chips.

The non-volatile memory chips either have their data permanently manufactured (ROM chips) or they are relatively rarely reprogrammed with new data (NVRAM, or non-volatile random-access memory). In either case, they hold whatever data is put in them essentially forever, even when you turn off your PC.

The volatile memory chips (RAM), which are by far the more numerous in almost every PC, are meant for holding information temporarily. They can be written to as easily as they can be read from, but they forget whatever information they were holding when power is turned off (intentionally or not).

RAM Packaging

As previously described, electronic memory is made in integrated circuit (IC) chips. Each memory chip can hold up to several tens of millions of bit cells, and each bit cell, as the name implies, can hold one bit of information. These chips are made on large hyper-pure single crystal silicon wafers; each wafer holds perhaps a dozen to as many as a hundred chips. Only after all the chips on the wafer have been completely manufactured and tested are the chips cut apart. The good ones are used and the bad ones discarded.

With regards to RAM, the integrated circuits are mounted and packaged in a variety of ways. In one of these cases, groups of the chips are mounted on what amount to tiny printed circuit boards that can be plugged into a socket. The earliest of these were the *Single Inline Memory Modules*, or SIMMs. These were common when PCs used a 32-bit wide memory bus, because each SIMM normally has 32 (or 36) data lines. The SIPPs, which resembled SIMMs, were a variant of this form. They were connected with motherboards using pins (like those on the back of your hard drives or on the underside of your CPU) instead of the SIMM card connector.

Currently, the most common memory module is the DIMM, which stands for *Dual Inline Memory Module*. The physical difference between a SIMM and a DIMM is an obvious one: DIMMs have a separate set of leads on the back surface of their connector, and SIMMs either don't have contacts there or, if contacts are there, they are merely duplicates of the ones on the front. The RIMM, or *Rambus Inline Memory Module,* refers to something that resembles a DIMM, but that differs in some very subtle and enormously important ways. For example, a RIMM has its notches in different places than a DIMM (to keep you from inserting the wrong kind into a memory module socket).

Figure 17.1 shows a typical set of DIMM sockets.

FIGURE 17.1
*DIMM memory
sockets.*

Serial Presence Detect

You might have seen a message when your PC is booting up telling you something about the Serial Presence Detect data it has found. If you have, no doubt you have wondered what that is.

With all the variations in memory modules, many of which fit into the same standard DIMM sockets, the industry has developed an automatic way for a PC to ask the memory modules what kind each one is, and what speed ratings it has. This method involves another special-purpose bus.

This is yet another use for a new, but little known, serial bus inside your PC: the I2C bus (Inter-Integrated Circuit bus). Because it is a serial bus, it conveys information one bit at a time. It is a very low-speed bus, in computer terms, although pretty speedy in human terms. The clock speed of this bus is less than 1/1,000 of the speed of the memory bus yet that is still fast enough to handle every task within a small fraction of a second.

The particular I2C bus connection that is relevant for the Serial Presence Detect function is between the motherboard chipset, and in particular the Northbridge chip, and the memory modules. The chipset sends commands across this bus. Mainly when it uses this bus for Serial Presence Detect business, it is interrogating the DIMMs to learn what memory capacity each has, what technology it uses (for example, EDO, or SDRAM, or RDRAM), and how fast it can safely be clocked. When it knows these things about all the modules you have installed, it can choose a compatible means for sending data to the RAM or retrieving it from the RAM. (For example, if you have some slower DIMMs installed, the chipset might need to insert wait states, whereas if all the DIMMs are speedy SDRAM, it can dispense with those time-wasters altogether.)

Not all DIMMs have the Serial Presence Detect circuitry. If you have installed some that don't, the chipset cannot learn about those DIMMs, and it will simply have to make some assumptions. Often, you can set those assumptions by setting some jumpers on the motherboard or by choosing some settings in the motherboard BIOS setup screens.

What Is Parity?

IBM's original specification for the PC indicated that all RAM used in the main memory have a *parity bit*. This means that in addition to storing the 8-bit values (1s or 0s), a ninth bit is also stored. The value of this bit is chosen so that there is an odd number of 1 bits.

According to this strategy, before a PC writes to memory a special circuit on the motherboard calculates the correct parity bit value for that byte and then all nine bits are sent to the main memory location. Correspondingly, whenever such a PC reads a memory location, it again computes the parity bit from the eight data bits it finds there, and then compares that to the parity bit it also read. Only if they are the same value (1 or 0) will the PC let you continue. Otherwise, it comes to a complete halt with an onscreen message announcing this parity error.

IBM's decision to use parity bit protection for all data stored in a PC's main memory reflected its belief that data integrity is of the highest importance. IBM felt it was the best plan simply to prevent you from computing with any known-to-be-incorrect data.

Modern RAM is very reliable. This is particularly true in light of the next significant development in memory error-protection: ECC.

What Is ECC?

Although parity RAM certainly is still in use, its successor, Error Checking and Correcting (ECC) (sometimes wrongly called Error Correction Codes, not that it matters in the least) has widely pushed parity RAM out of use for a variety of reasons. Economically, ECC RAM is generally less costly than parity RAM. Functionally, ECC RAM just does more. Although parity RAM can detect errors, that's all it can do, and it generally halts the system when errors are encountered. ECC RAM can *correct* errors without interrupting your work. This difference is absolutely vital in mission-critical applications such as network servers, which simply cannot go down. Let's look quickly at how ECC does what it does.

There are a number of ways in which errors in RAM can occur, and there are several types of RAM errors. At the simplest level, individual bits get "flipped," storing the electrical equivalent of a 0 when they should be storing a 1 (or vice versa). As you can probably already surmise, even a 1-bit error can be fatal to your system (and multibit errors certainly occur, too).

ECC memory uses a set of extra bits to store a special code, known as a *checksum*. This is an encrypted version of the actual data you store in memory. For each binary word of data, there is a corresponding ECC code. The number of bits required to produce this

ECC code depends on the length of binary word your system is using. For example, 32-bit words require an ECC code seven bits in length; 64-bit words require eight bits of ECC. When data is requested from memory, the actual data *and* its ECC code are retrieved and quickly compared. If everything is in order, the actual data is passed to the CPU. If the code and the data don't match, the structure of the ECC code allows for the errant bit (or bits) to be identified. The error is then corrected as the data is sent to the CPU. The errant bit (or bits) in memory isn't changed. If the same data is requested again, the error is simply corrected again. Of course, in actual practice, the contents of memory are over-written again and again. Unless there is truly a physical flaw in one of the RAM chips, the error will simply disappear. ECC corrections can be logged for review by a system administrator who will check for errors happening repeatedly in the same parts of memory. These generally indicate hardware in need of replacement.

How Memory Chips Are Organized Internally

Many ROM (read-only memory) chips and some NVRAM (non-volatile random-access memory) chips have their bit cells arranged in groups of eight. These groups are always accessed as a unit. This means these chips must have eight wires for data to flow out of those locations (and for an NVRAM chip that can be reprogrammed, another eight wires for data to flow into them) in parallel. In addition, they must have several "address" wires over which the chip can be informed which of its many groups of eight bits is being accessed at this time. This type of a chip is called a *byte-wide memory chip*.

This strategy is not commonly used for (the usually much larger capacity) RAM memory chips, simply because a large capacity means more address wires are needed to point to the desired memory location, and the chip designers would rather have only a pair of data in/out wires instead of 16 of them. So RAM chips most often have their bit cells individually addressed. Or, at most, you can address groups of four bits at a time. The former kind of chip is called a bit-wide memory chip, and the latter is a *nybble-wide memory chip*.

How might these chips be combined into a usable amount of RAM? That depends on the number of parallel data wires in the memory bus (from the CPU to the main memory). If your PC has 16 (bidirectional) data wires, you need to use 16 bit-wide memory chips (or 18 if you want to hold parity information too), or else you might use four nybble-wide memory chips (plus a pair of bit-wide chips for parity). Each of those memory chips would hold its 1 (or 4) bit of information for each of some large number of locations and for the same number of locations in each chip, of course. This collection of memory chips is referred to as a *bank* of memory for that PC.

Modern PCs have many more data wires, and so their memory banks must be correspondingly wider. A Pentium, for example, has 64 data wires. Its banks of memory must, therefore, store 64 bits of data (and perhaps also eight bits of parity information) for each of some large number of locations.

If you use memory chips that are all bit-wide and each can hold 1,048,576 bits (1MB), you can hold a total of 64MB of data in one memory bank in a Pentium-class PC. This arrangement of 64 or 72 chips takes up a lot of room, and any time you want to change those chips it is quite an arduous task. Fortunately, there is a better way to do this, which is the topic of the next section.

As mentioned earlier, the first memory modules used in PCs were called SIMMs. These simply are small printed circuit cards with anywhere from three to nine memory chips soldered in place on one side of the card. The complete module typically was organized as a byte-wide memory module. That is, it had enough contacts on it to enable you to load or recall one byte (all eight bits, plus perhaps a parity bit) at once. These contacts are located along one edge of the card, which slips into a socket at an angle and is then tipped upright to lock into place.

You can plug one of these SIMMs into a socket much more easily than you can plug in all of the chips it contains, and the manufacturer that assembles them can guarantee that the several memory chips on that SIMM are compatible with one another. These features account for the great popularity enjoyed by SIMMs from almost the moment they were introduced, and for the near-total disappearance of individual plug-in memory chips from modern PCs.

SIMMs proved very popular, but they too have been replaced, for the most part, by DIMMs. The reasons for this are not hard to find.

As explained earlier, a bank of memory is considered enough memory chips or modules to hold or supply in parallel as many data bits as there are data lines on the PC's CPU. Having all the memory chips in a single bank fairly well matched is important. In particular, they must be able to hold the same number of bits of information. Furthermore, they should all respond to requests to hold or recall data in about the same time and should need similar signals to do so. These things can be readily guaranteed if you use identical memory chips or modules in all the sockets that make up one bank. But doing that with multiple chips or modules per bank takes conscious effort on the part of whoever puts in those memory chips or modules.

One simple way to guarantee that each bank will be properly filled with matched memory chips is to make up larger memory modules. These will have 64 data lines, and so a single one of them will serve as an entire bank of memory. Of course, such a memory will need to have many more contacts than a byte-wide SIMM where it plugs into its socket. To fit all of those contacts without making the module unduly large, the manufacturers put contacts on both sides of the printed circuit card that carries the memory modules. (They also can put the memory chips on both sides.) These modules are called DIMMs.

Plug in a DIMM and you have plugged in an entire bank of memory for your PC. Everything in that bank is automatically matched, with no further effort on your part. (Furthermore, these modules come with notches that "key" them in a way that prevents you from plugging a DIMM designed to work at 3.3 volts into a socket meant for a 5-volt DIMM, and vice versa. Also, DIMMs have many more ground wires than a SIMM, which is becoming crucial as you begin to run your memory modules at ever higher speeds.)

In any case, when you are about to install memory into your computer, read the manual first. Every PC motherboard or system comes with a manual that specifies, among other things, just which types of memory chips or modules it can accept. Please read this document carefully before you buy additional memory for your PC. You must follow the manufacturer's recommendations or your PC might malfunction. This also means that there might be some pretty severe limits on how much (or how little) RAM memory any particular PC can have. If you want to upgrade your PC, you might be able simply to get and plug in a new DIMM, or you might end up having to remove and replace all the memory chips or modules it now contains with new, more capacious ones. Which course you must follow will naturally affect the cost of the upgrade.

Another aspect to this is the question of parity versus nonparity memory. If your PC requires parity memory, you must supply it with memory chips in groups storing nine bits at each location. Similarly, if it uses memory modules, you must have ones that store and return that ninth bit for every byte location. (Some PCs enable you to specify whether you are using parity or nonparity memory modules by a jumper setting on the motherboard. For them, of course, you must make that jumper setting agree with the kind of memory modules you use, and you must use all the same kind, in this regard, in every bank.)

However way your PC is built, that is how it is built. You cannot change this aspect of its design without replacing the motherboard. So, again, know what you have and know what it uses. Then, if you want to upgrade your PC's RAM you will know what you must buy.

Various Flavors of RAM

Ordinary, volatile RAM comes in a variety of types, but one distinction separates all (volatile) RAM chips into two main groups. One group is called *static RAM* (SRAM), and the other group is called *dynamic RAM* (DRAM). The DRAM group is further broken down into several additional categories.

Static RAM (SRAM)

The earliest electronic memory chips used at least two (and sometimes as many as four) transistors per bit cell. In this design, one transistor—let's call it transistor A—is *on* (carrying current) when the cell holds a 1, and another transistor—let's call it transistor B—is on when the cell holds a 0. The circuit is arranged so that when one of these two transistors is on, the other one is forced to be off. This arrangement has two stable states: A on and B off, or A off and B on. The additional transistors, if they are used, are there to help you switch the circuit from one of its stable states to the other.

This works very well, and SRAM chips can be very fast. It isn't the best way to make massive amounts of memory, however, because dynamic RAM (DRAM) chips can have as much as four times as many bit cells formed in a given amount of silicon. By the economics of IC manufacturing, that means DRAM can be about one-fourth as expensive for a given data-holding capacity.

Still, when you need the fastest possible RAM, for example, in a PC's L2 memory cache or any time you need only a modest amount of RAM, SRAM is the way to go.

Dynamic RAM (DRAM)

Constant pressure is on the makers of RAM chips to come up with newer designs that will hold more bits of information. One way to do this is to reduce the number of transistors required to hold each one.

In dynamic RAM chips, only a single transistor is used to hold each bit. This must be a field effect transistor, and its *gate* electrode must be enlarged a little in order to serve as a *capacitor*, which is an electrical device that can hold an electrical charge. Because a field effect transistor needs no input current to control its output, it is possible for this capacitor, when it is charged or discharged, to control whether the transistor is on or off for a (relatively) long time. Using techniques similar to those used in EEPROMs, it is possible to put charges onto those gate capacitors or remove charges from them whenever you want.

There is only one fly in this ointment. Nothing in this world is perfect; in particular, the capacitor formed on the gate of the field effect transistor isn't perfect. It will, over time, leak away its charge. Does this mean DRAMs can't be made to work? Clearly not. The computer on which this chapter was written has hundreds of millions of bits of DRAM information storage, and it works very well.

We can best explain how this happens by using an analogy. Suppose you have a team of people who are going to help you remember some numbers. Suppose you arrange those people into an array with some number of rows and columns (also known as ranks and files, which is the source of the term *rank and file* for referring to a mass of workers).

Now tell each person what number he or she is to remember. If you don't let these people write down their numbers, and if you engage them all in small talk, within just a few minutes many if not all of the people will have forgotten the number they were told to remember. However, if you do one special thing they will all be able to remember their number essentially forever. Here is what you do.

Have a helper go to each row in the array of people and have that person call out just to that row, "All right, people. Listen up. Get ready to tell my buddy your special number if he asks." And have another helper go to one of the columns and call down that column, "Okay, if you are in the active row, tell me your number."

Only one person will call out his number. But every person in that row will bring it into the forefront of his mind and thus "refresh" his memory. Do this to every row often enough and no one will forget the number he or she was told to remember.

This is a very good analogy to how a DRAM chip works. If it contains, for example, one megabit of information, those 1,048,576 bit cells are arranged into 1,024 rows with 1,024 cells in each row.

When you read from this chip, you tell it which cell to read by activating one *row address* and one *column address*. (This could take 20 wires, but more often it uses the same 10 wires in two steps.) Every cell on the selected row is activated. Doing this means that if its voltage is high, it makes its voltage higher. If its voltage is low, it makes it even lower. In that way, all the content in these cells is refreshed, and they place that output value on the corresponding column output line. Only the one selected column line's value is reported to the data-out line of the chip.

If you will remember to read some cell from each row in every DRAM chip often enough, your PC's DRAM memory will work, but if you fail to do this for too long (and it turns out that *too long* in this context means for more than about a thousandth of a second), some of those bit cells will drift to a voltage where it isn't clear whether they are high or low, and thus they cannot be refreshed accurately.

You say you don't remember doing this with your PC? You might not even touch the keyboard for many minutes, and still it keeps remembering information in its RAM. How does it do this? It has a special *DRAM refresh* process going on all the time, in the background. This happens no matter what else the PC is doing. In fact, it is the very highest-priority task performed by your PC, because keeping those DRAM cells working properly is crucial to everything else it will be asked to do.

This DRAM refresh process takes some effort and time, but not much. If you had only a small number of DRAM bit cells to refresh, it wouldn't be worth the overhead. That is one reason why for a small amount of memory (as in an L2 cache, for example) SRAM is often used instead of DRAM. The other reason is that SRAM is often faster than DRAM, and its premium price can be affordable if you use only a little bit of it.

If you have hundreds of millions of bit cells to refresh (as is the case in a modern PC with tens of millions of bytes of RAM), it is most assuredly worth the overhead in time and cost of special circuitry for the savings in the cost of all that RAM. This is why DRAM is used exclusively in the PC's main memory.

The DRAM Alphabet Soup: from FPM and EDO Through VRAM to SDRAM to DDR SDRAM

Now for the confusing part: all the many subflavors of DRAMs. This is where the alphabet soup comes in. In an effort to make DRAM chips that work even faster, manufacturers have enhanced them in many ways. Each one carries its own fancy name and some special advantages.

A year ago, the only types of DRAM you were likely to encounter in a modern PC were EDO and SDRAM. Today, with the releases of the many new high-speed processors on the market, demand for memory bandwidth is huge. For any system that runs at an external bus speed of 200 or 266MHZ, DDR SDRAM or Rambus RDRAM might be your only choices.

One early way that manufacturers sped up DRAM, called *fast page mode* DRAM, was possible because normally DRAM chips have only half the number of address lines they need. They use the same wires for row and column addresses, distinguishing between the different values on those wires for a row and a column address by when those values are placed there. To speed things up, if the processor is accessing several memory locations in successive, or even nearly adjacent, locations, it need only tell one of these chips a row address once; then it can go ahead and access all the columns it wants. Only when it must move to a new row will it have to reissue the (new) row address.

Another strategy (used in EDO DRAM) is to have the data produced by the chip linger a while on the output. This *extended data out* design enables you to access a location, and then while you are still busy reading the information you just accessed, the chip will be getting ready to supply the next bit of data. This approach is now no longer the best one for desktop PCs, but for various reasons, involving both the history of the manufacturing processes used for making DRAM, and the marketing history of various flavors of DRAM, EDO DRAM is still the predominant form of DRAM in large servers.

Dual-ported DRAM chips enable you to access two locations at once. They do this by having two complete sets of circuitry for reading data from locations in the bit cell array. When millions of bit cells are on a single chip, this additional overhead can be built in for a minor additional cost. These devices are not symmetrical. That is, whereas one of the input-output ports enables you to access any place you like at random (and it also has the input circuitry for writing data to those locations), the other port is used just for reading data out, and then only an entire row at a time. These dual-ported DRAM chips, also sometimes called video RAM (VRAM) are especially useful for video frame buffers because those are inherently used for random-access writing and reading by the CPU and linear readout (by the video display circuitry).

Windows RAM (WRAM) is a special version of VRAM that is optimized for the types of access that are common in PCs running Windows and Windows applications. These include such things as filling in all of a region's bits devoted to a single color with a constant value, and easy ways to move a block of data from one region to another (*bit blitting*).

Synchronous DRAM (SDRAM) is currently the most popular kind of DRAM for use in desktop PCs. The essence of what is special about SDRAM is shown by its name. These chips can operate in lock-step with the clock signals on the memory bus. Thus they can accept or retrieve information in a single clock cycle. It means a much higher performance compared to the other memory types. A SDRAM module running at 133MHz is about three times faster than conventional Fast Page Mode RAM, and is about twice as fast as the EDO DRAM.

The Faster SDRAM

The original SDRAM modules were designed to work with systems whose memory bus (front-side bus) clock ran at 66MHz. Now, the most common performance PCs all use a 100MHz or higher front-side bus, and of course, there are SDRAM modules that can keep up with that faster rate as well. These DIMMs are labeled PC100/PC133/PC150 SDRAM. Usually, this fact is noted by a paper label that is stuck on an otherwise ordinary-appearing SDRAM DIMM.

Nowadays it is common to have a processor running at 133MHz front-side bus. This configuration requires a bandwidth of about 1.06GB per second for optimizing the performance. Apart from the processor, the PCI bus and the AGP port are also bandwidth hungry. It is obvious that a new memory type with a higher bandwidth is needed.

The speed of the memory was typically described in nanoseconds. However, because SDRAM has its performance strongly tied with the speed of the motherboard's front-side bus, it is more accurate to present the speed rating as 66MHz, 100MHz, 133MHz or 150MHz, and so on.

Intel invented the PCXXX standard. Basically, the PCXXX SDRAM label indicates that the SDRAM meets the PC100/PC133/PC150 specification. This specification was defined by Intel to allow the various RAM manufacturers to produce memory chips that would work with Intel's latest processor chipset that runs at a 100MHz/133MHz system bus speed. This set of specifications has been endorsed by most of the memory manufacturers worldwide, and thus became the "de facto" standard.

The PC133/PC150 standard enjoys a broad support base by industry giants, including Compaq, Dell, and HP. PC133 and PC150, with the exception of a higher speed, are fundamentally identical to PC100, both in terms of architecture and the physical pinout. This provides flawless backward compatibility, and is the major reason why they can obtain support from the industry players.

PC100 works at 100MHz while PC133 works at 133MHz and PC150 works at 150MHZ. The memory works synchronously with the processors bus, avoiding any delay in transfer rates. This does not mean zero delay. There is still a delay for processing the initial data. After the first piece of data is processed, the rest is processed at equal speeds.

In theory, 100MHz SDRAM has a speed rating of 10ns. However, in the real world, SDRAM DIMM with –10ns components are used for running at 66MHz only, as they might not function consistently in a 100MHz environment. It is recommended that, when you purchase SDRAM for your 100MHZ system, you buy the modules that use components marked with -8A, -8B, -8C, -8D, or -8E. These ratings indicate that, in theory, the modules can run at 125MHz, which will be safe and adequate for a 100MHz front-side bus setting. And, for the SDRAM to run at 133MHz, a 7.5ns or better rating is a *must*.

PC600, 700, and 800

You might have heard of speed grading like PC600, 700, and 800. In fact, they have nothing to do with SDRAM. They are actually the speed grades that describe Rambus RDRAM. You'll learn about RDRAM shortly. Meanwhile, you might want to know what is going on with these speed grades.

PC600 is the cheapest and slowest of all three. It is too slow to be used extensively by the major system manufacturers. On the other hand, PC800 is the fastest. To the manufacturers, PC800 RDRAM is almost an unattainable goal in the manufacturing process, making it an unpopular choice for use by the OEM systems. PC700, so far, is the most reasonable choice.

Rambus

Up to now, all PCs have used clock signals in the same way. The clock for some portion of the PC's circuitry "clicks" and that signal is sent to all the relevant circuits. They do whatever they are supposed to do when that happens, and the results of those actions are sent wherever they are supposed to go. This all happens and everything settles down before the next clock tick occurs. But PC clocks are getting faster and faster. Soon people will have no choice but to do things in a rather different manner. After all, electrical signals cannot travel any faster than light, and we are now getting to the point that even at that speed, signals can barely make it from the CPU to the other side of the PC system unit within much less than a clock cycle.

Rambus offers a solution to this problem. The whole idea of Rambus is to use memory chips that are fast, but not all that much faster than the best SDRAM chips. Yet, they will be made to act as if they were much faster. This offers the promise of stepping up the memory bus clock speed from its present 100MHz to 800MHz (and later on, even further). That is an enormous step up.

Figure 17.2 shows the picture of an RDRAM module.

FIGURE 17.2
An RDRAM module; RAMBUS's proprietary DRAM.

The Background of Rambus

Founded in 1990 by Mike Farmwald and Mark Horowitz, Rambus signed a contract with Nintendo to develop the memory technology for the Nintendo 64 game console. This helped the company gained widespread notoriety at that time.

Shortly after that, Intel entered into an agreement with Rambus in December 1995 to develop the next generation memory technology. The agreement with Intel was special. The deal was proprietary in nature. By pushing Rambus as the memory of choice for the next generation Pentium platform, Intel can profit from the production of Rambus RAM through licensing fees.

The key idea behind Rambus is a realization that it isn't necessary to wait for all the effects of one clock tick to die out before launching the next one. All you need to do is ensure that there are never two clock ticks passing by any given circuitry at once. Then each circuit sees a steady procession of clock ticks and responds to them as it should. The results of those actions make their way back to the rest of the PC as they should, following alongside the clock tick signal that triggered them.

Figure 17.3 shows the typical RIMM sockets used by RDRAM.

FIGURE 17.3
RDRAM requires a proprietary socket as well.

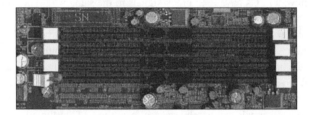

Architecture Comparison

Prior to the Rambus era, the CPU communicates with the DIMMs that make up the system RAM via the Northbridge chip. The CPU-to-Northbridge bus is 64 bits wide, as is the bus from the Northbridge to the DIMM sockets. The Northbridge chip also connects the CPU to the rest of the PC, mainly over a 32-bit wide PCI bus.

The memory system clock, which also provides the timing signals for the front-side bus between the CPU and the Northbridge chip, simply broadcasts its signal for all to hear. The delays that are incurred between when the signals are sent out and when they are received must be small compared to the time between those signals. Mainly for this reason, that system clock frequency is now topping out at 100 or 133MHz.

With Rambus, the memory system clock is trapped inside a box. The only way any circuits can "hear" the ticks of the clock is through the signals that flow out of the box through the indicated pipe. This pipe travels through each of the RIMM sockets in turn before arriving at the Northbridge chip. It then returns through each of the RIMM chips again, ending finally in the bus and clock terminators box. The clock will initially run at either 600 or 800MHz, and the front-side bus will run at one-sixth of that speed (100 or 133MHz). At this high speed, the time taken for the clock signals to traverse the entire path from clock to terminator is likely to be much longer than the time between clock signals. Because every trace in the clock and data lines is closely matched in length, width, capacity, and loading, the data signals and clock signals will travel alongside one another at exactly the same speed.

When the Northbridge chip (the Rambus Master) wants to write data to RAM, it can send the data and the addresses into which it is supposed to be stored out in parallel whenever a clock tick passes through the Northbridge chip. When the data arrives at the correct RAM chips on the RIMMs, it will be stored. In the meantime, the Northbridge chip might be furiously writing other data to different addresses, and those commands will already be traveling on their way toward the RIMMs.

When the Northbridge chip wants to read from memory, it will send out the signals indicating what addresses it wants to read. It can send out new addresses each time it sees a clock tick, even though it hasn't yet heard back the answers from the previous requests. When the requests arrive at the appropriate DRAM chips on the RIMMs, the RAM chips serve up the requested data, which then flows back along the data bus to the Northbridge chip.

The Rambus data path is broken into four byte-wide paths, so four independent transactions can be going on at once, accessing different portions of the DRAM on the RIMMs. The DRAM on each RIMM is actually broken into 16 blocks to further facilitate nearly simultaneous accesses to locations in adjacent blocks.

A very important point to understand is that although in a conventional memory architecture there can be, more or less, any number of SIMM or DIMM sockets, in the Rambus architecture there are exactly three. And whereas in the conventional architecture you need not fill all the sockets, with Rambus, you absolutely must fill every one.

What if you don't need that much memory? Then you must at least put a special *continuity module* or C-RIMM in any RIMM socket that isn't going be carrying DRAM. A C-RIMM is simply a RIMM without the DRAM chips. Its purpose is to carry the clock and data signals just as if it had DRAM chips.

In principle, the Rambus solution is a wonderful breakthrough. No longer does it matter how long it takes for electrical signals to propagate through your PC. The clock speed can go arbitrarily high, without regard to those time delays. In practice, things are, as you might imagine, just a little bit different.

Mostly, the designer and manufacturer of all the pieces has to be incredibly careful to match every wire that is going to carry data or clock signals with every other one. Otherwise, these signals can get out of step. Holding the required very tight tolerances is just barely do-able with modern manufacturing techniques.

When two signals propagate on parallel wires and yet get a little bit out of step, they are *skewed*. Controlling clock skew (or clock-to-data skew) is, therefore, the key to making Rambus work. The folks who developed this technology claim that we soon will be able to run the clock at 1.6GHz (1600MHz) or even faster. But before we can try that, we (the whole industry) will have to get the kinks out of running the Rambus clock at considerably lower speeds.

The Market Reality of Rambus

As of year 2001, several companies have agreed to produce RDRAM. Their combined output, however, is very small compared to the total output of SDRAM. Even worse, RDRAM production this year might lag the production of DDR SDRAM, which is discussed shortly. In fact, as the premier manufacturer of memory products in the market, Micron has openly preferred DDR SDRAM over RDRAM.

Most of the memory manufacturers do not eagerly participate in the RDRAM party because of the high licensing fees and the costly yet complex process of producing RDRAM. On the contrary, DDR SDRAM is a high-performance alternative that's built on an open standard.

RDRAM might not be welcomed by the end users either. It is due to the fact that RDRAM is not backward compatible with systems using the traditional SDRAM. An upgrade to use RDRAM is a costly option; users have to replace the motherboard as well.

DDR SDRAM

DDR (double data rate) SDRAM is the newest variation of SDRAM. What is so special about this "double data rate" technology? Traditionally, memory data is fed to the processor in "synchronous" fashion, meaning data arrives to the tick of the memory clock, which is essentially an electrical signal that bounces between two voltage levels. With SDRAM, data is transferred from the memory to the processor when the clock signal bounces from low to high. With DDR, data is transferred when the clock signal goes from low to high *and* when the clock signal goes from high to low.

Figure 17.4 shows a picture of a DDR SDRAM module, whereas Figure 17.5 shows the typical DDR SDRAM sockets.

Figure 17.4
DDR SDRAM is another variation on PC DRAM.

Figure 17.5
DDR SDRAM fits into these types of sockets.

PC1600 and PC2100

DDR increases memory bandwidth by clocking data on both edges of the DRAM clock. As suggested by its name, the maximum data rate of DDR is twice that of the traditional SDRAM. This also leads to an interesting naming convention scheme. A 200MHz DDR module is known as PC1600 to indicate a bandwidth of 1600 megabytes per second. With this formula, a 266MHz DDR module can be presented as a PC2100 part!

This naming convention is somewhat misleading. A 200MHz DDR module is running twice as fast as the conventional PC100 SDRAM. A 266MHz DDR module is running twice as fast as the conventional PC133 SDRAM. The names PC1600 and PC2100 are heavily inflated.

The Market for DDR

With the new design of DDR, the physical pin count has changed. A standard SDRAM uses 168 pins, whereas a DDR module uses 184 pins.

The deployment of DDR SDRAM requires new motherboard design, both in terms of physical layout and chipsets. Currently there are three major players in the market that supports the DDR standard. AMD's 760 chipset supports DDR. VIA's DDR266 chipset supports DDR. Ali is supporting DDR in its coming new chipsets. And even Intel—yes, Intel will incorporate support for DDR in its upcoming i84X chipset series.

DDR Performance Expectation

Is DDR SDRAM going to make your system twice as fast? The answer is somehow sad: no. In fact, whether or not DDR can dramatically increase the system performance depends on the CPU it works with.

Consider Pentium 4 as an example. P4 is known to have a small cache size but a long pipeline, and is very bandwidth hungry. It relies heavily on the second memory transfer rates. In this case, technology like DDR can be beneficial.

On the other hand, for cache-rich processors such as AMD Athlon, the need for high memory bandwidth is of lesser concern. Even if your CPU is bandwidth hungry, your application might not be. For most of the general business or day-to-day applications, there is no need to constantly transfer large chunks of data between the memory and the processor.

The Future of DDR

In any case, you should not expect a performance gain greater than 10% by using DDR SDRAM. However, due to its open standard nature and its relatively low price (compared to RDRAM), its future is guaranteed. There are motherboards on the market that can accommodate both SDRAM and DDR SDRAM. It seems like people are seeing DDR SDRAM as the next logical step after SDRAM.

Various Flavors of ROM and NVRAM

Like RAM, all ROM chips are simply arrays of transistors that are wired together in a particular pattern to do a specified job. The wiring used is actually created by etching that pattern in the last (or last few) metal layers put on the wafer.

When a CPU (or other part of a PC) reads data from a ROM chip or collection of memory chips, it supplies an address and then waits for the binary values to show up on the data pins. Internally, the chip activates a particular subcircuit specified by the address values on its input address lines, and then causes the output from that subcircuit to show up on the data output lines.

Mask Programmed ROM

The earliest read-only memory chips, called *mask programmed ROM*, were wired at the factory in a way that forced them to produce the binary data corresponding to the information they were supposed to contain. This hard-wired information content is, clearly, permanent. This was a simple and effective means of making ROMs, and it is still used whenever you need many chips that each contains exactly the same information.

The Oxymoron Chips: EPROMs

The makers of mask-programmed ROM chips knew that some of their customers wanted to have different information permanently held in different chips, and they wanted to have only a relatively few chips with each set of information. This is not economically feasible by the mask-programming method, simply because creating the mask used in the fabrication process typically costs many thousands of dollars, which is affordable only if you need many thousands of chips created using that mask.

The first solution to this problem was an insightful use of one of the ways a ROM chip can fail. The wiring that connects the circuits is composed of extremely fine traces of metal. If you run too much current through one of them, it will melt or vaporize.

Someone realized that if you make the points of failure in predictable places (by thinning the traces at those points), the circuit will have some initially manufactured-in data, but will still allow you to alter data simply by overloading selected points. In essence, these chips are manufactured to hold data that consists of all 1 bits. You can "blow out a fuse" to convert a 1 to a 0 wherever you need a 0 in the data in a particular chip. Manufacturing in the 1 bits is done at the factory. Blowing some of them to 0s can be done anywhere and any time you like.

Thus was born the electrically programmable read-only memory (EPROM) chip. Think about it. This name is surely an oxymoron. If you can program it, you are, in effect, writing data to it. But it is true that almost all the time you can only read data from these chips. You must use a special, over-voltage circuit in a special fashion to program them.

Battery Backed Up RAM

When PCs were young, you could easily buy mask-programmed ROM (and even EPROMs) or RAM. You couldn't buy any kind of simple, inexpensive devices that would act like a ROM most of the time, yet enable you easily to change the contents from time to time. That is exactly what PC makers wanted for one special role in their machines.

In the IBM PC and PC/XT (and clones of those machines), switches on the motherboard stored configuration information. This was awkward, and meant that any time the PC configuration was changed, someone had to open the PC and alter some switch settings.

IBM decided in its PC/AT to include more configuration information than in an XT, some of which might change at times when you didn't otherwise want to have to open up the case. IBM also wanted to include a *real-time clock* circuit, so you wouldn't have to tell your PC the time and date each time you turned it on.

IBM's solution was to include in the PC/AT's motherboard a special integrated circuit chip that held both a clock circuit and some RAM to store the current time and the configuration data. Near this circuit was a battery to keep it working even when the rest of the PC was off. To keep the demand for power from the battery low (so it would last a long time), IBM chose to use the then relatively expensive CMOS technology for that chip.

This technology soon adopted the name *the BIOS Setup CMOS,* or simply *the PC's CMOS.* Now, even though virtually all PC circuits are made using the CMOS technology, people still often refer to the subsystem of a CMOS chip plus battery used for the real-time clock and configuration storage as the PC's CMOS. (Recently, some manufacturers have begun using a more general, and more precise, term by calling this the PC's NVRAM, which stands for non-volatile RAM.)

This combination is such an attractive one that some manufacturers now sell modules that look just like any other integrated circuit package, but that actually have a long-life battery built into them along with the semiconductor integrated circuit chip.

EEPROMs, Flash RAM, FERAM, and other NVRAM Technologies

Now we have some better solutions to these problems. Clever engineers found several ways to make a chip that acts like a ROM most of the time, yet can have its data altered on demand. Generally these chips can have any specified collection of 1 bits changed to 0s, but they can have the 0s changed back to 1s only in a mass operation that affects all locations on the chip, or all of the locations in one block on the chip.

These chips carry many names. Electrically Erasable Programmable Read-Only Memory (EEPROM, usually pronounced *double-e-prom*) chips was an early name. Accurate, but cumbersome. These chips use a newer strategy than the fusible-link EPROMs. In an EEPROM, each bit cell stores its data as an electric charge on a capacitor. By one of several strategies, the manufacturer makes it possible to alter that charge with a suitable electrical signal. A newer design uses a ferro-electric effect bitcell. These FERAM (or FEROM) chips act pretty much just like RAM, except that they don't forget the information they hold when you remove power.

These devices can accurately be called non-volatile random access memory (NVRAM) chips, and because the PC user really doesn't have any reason to care which technology is used, this name is coming into vogue for referring to the function, and not to the technology by which it is achieved.

Addressing Memory: Intel's Segments

You read earlier that the contents of memory chips are addressed by voltages on the wires that attach to them. That is the physical level at which the circuitry actually works. From the programmer's point of view, the important issue is how memory is addressed from a logical perspective. In real mode, memory is addressed in a peculiar way called segment:offset addressing.

The segment:offset addressing strategy simply means that every reference in a program to a memory location uses two 16-bit numbers. One is called the *segment value* and the other the *offset*. The segment number, multiplied by 16, is added to the offset to determine the actual physical address.

One consequence of this design is that in real mode, a PC can address only about 1MB of memory. That is the size of its real-mode memory address space. When this design was first created, this seemed to many people a generous amount. It was, compared to the mere 64KB address space in all the previous microcomputers. Now it is positively stifling. Of course, PCs are now programmed to go into protected mode early in their boot process, and when they are there they can access as much RAM (and ROM) as you have installed.

> **Technical Note:** By a "trick," it is possible to address 1/16th of a megabyte in every PC that has some extended memory. This extra 64KB is called the *high memory area*. But for most purposes, it is adequate to say that a PC can address only 1MB in real mode.
>
> There is one other trick that you can use to let PCs with a 286 or 386 CPU access up to 32GB of memory, which is the full amount it can access in protected or real mode. This involves cheating, because it uses an undocumented command to manipulate the contents of the page descriptors in a way that Intel never intended and does not sanction. This isn't often done, but for completeness (and only for the very technically inclined readers), we thought we should mention it here.

In the late 1970s, Intel chose to make its first x86 CPUs access memory in this two-step fashion (using segments and offsets) so that converting programs originally written for the previous generation of microprocessors to run on these (at that time) new CPUs would be easier. Users have been stuck with this design ever since.

In protected mode, conversion of a logical address to a physical one is more complicated. Several steps are required to combine the selector value (which is the protected-mode name for what was the segment value in real mode) with the offset and pass that address through the page translation tables before finally coming out with a physical address.

The important point of this section is that when any PC starts booting, it has only about 1MB of memory address space. This implies some things that are critical to memory design and usage in PCs even when they aren't running in real mode.

IBM's and Intel's Limiting Choices

Intel made some other choices that forced the hand of any PC designer. It made all its x86 family of CPUs go, after they wake up, to a particular address (FFFF0h) that is just 16 bytes shy of the bottom memory address space. The CPU assumes that the number it finds there is the first instruction it is to execute. This means that you need ROM at this defined (FFFF0h) address and at least a few addresses beyond it. If you don't, the CPU cannot find any instructions and it won't be able to start the boot process.

At the other end of the memory address space, Intel put the interrupt vector table. Again, this is only a real-mode issue, but because all PCs start out in real mode, it affects memory design for every one of them.

In this case, RAM is required. This enables the PC to store numbers that point to interrupt service routines and to change those numbers when new ISRs are loaded.

ROM at the top, RAM at the bottom; it's actually a pretty simple picture. Then IBM went on to make some more decisions that slightly complicated the picture. IBM had, in its previous mainframe computers, reserved half of the memory address space for system uses and left the other half for users to use however they wanted. That is, the operating system and hardware had exclusive use of half the memory address space. Applications could use some portion of the other half.

IBM apparently realized that Intel's 1MB of memory address space wasn't all that generous, so it reserved only 3/8 of it for system use and left the remainder for applications to use. Five-eighths of 1MB is 640KB, which is where the infamous *640KB barrier,* discussed shortly, came from.

The Newer, Flatter Memory Model

Doubtless you have run into the phrase "32-bit access" or perhaps "32-bit program," and you might have wondered just what these phrases mean. Unfortunately, their meanings are not always the same. You also might recall having run across some reference to a "flat memory model" and wondered what that is. This section explains all these things.

When a PC is running in real mode, it can access only about 1MB of memory address locations. This means it needs only a 20-bit address to point to any place in its memory address space. (Twenty-one bits are actually required if you include access to the high memory area.) That is true even for the latest and greatest Pentium III machine when it is operating in real mode.

Although Windows 98 is a protected-mode environment, the DOS operating system that is used to start Windows 98 (and is then sent to the antiquation bin, when Windows 98 is running) operates in real mode. This fact has two important implications. First, in order to maintain backward compatibility with outdated hardware, PC operating systems, including Windows, must retain the capability of switching back into real mode. When in real mode, the PC can access memory only in the first megabyte, so that space is always going to be precious until the next generation of hardware and operating systems completely passes and no one need worry about real mode any longer.

Second, while in real mode, all the protections that give protected mode its name aren't there. Whatever old driver or piece of hardware has forced you temporarily back into real mode must be a very trusted one; otherwise, your PC is vulnerable to all sorts of unexpected crashes.

There is one exception to this last problem. One of the x86 CPU's several protected modes is called *virtual 86 mode* (v86), and another in the most recent models is called *extended virtual 86 mode* (Ev86). In these modes, the CPU acts as though it is in real mode for most purposes, but actually it remains in protected mode with all of that mode's, well, protections. If the program attempts to do something prohibited, the CPU automatically transfers control back to a portion of the operating system called the *v86 monitor program*, and that program decides what to do next.

This is how a "DOS box" (or DOS window) inside Windows works. For a program that can run in this environment, the mechanism offers a lot of protection between that program and others running on that PC at the same time. Unfortunately, not all real-mode programs can run in virtual 86 mode, which is why Windows 9x provides its MS-DOS mode. In that mode, the CPU really *is* operating in real mode with no protections at all. (Of course, the real-mode program can't access extended memory and no other programs are multitasking, so at worst you'll simply have to reboot your PC to recover from crashes.)

For both these reasons, PC operating system designers have been eager to get past DOS and on to something better. The most common shorthand for this newer, better, protected-mode world is *32-bit*. When a PC is running in protected mode (provided its CPU contains at least a 386-compatible chip), it has access to a full 4GB of memory address space, for which 32 bits of address are a necessity.

Windows NT/2000 are full-blown 32-bit operating systems that take advantage of 32-bit memory addressing. The 64-bit version of Windows XP has an even more advanced addressing mechanism.

Earlier in the chapter, you read that in real mode, a program refers to an address in segment:offset form. In protected mode, the same form is used; the segment number (still a 16-bit number) is termed a *selector*, and the offset now is expanded from a 16-bit number to a 32-bit number.

The selector's value is not itself a part of the memory address. It is, instead, a pointer to a data table called a segment descriptor table. (There is one for all the programs running in the PC at a given moment, called the Global Descriptor Table (GDT), and there is another one for each program, called its Local Descriptor Table, or LDT.) Part of the information in that descriptor table is the base address for this segment, which can be anywhere in the CPU's 4GB memory address range.

Another part of the segment descriptor specifies its size, and that includes a bit called the *granularity bit*. If that bit is turned off, the maximum segment size is 1MB. It can be any size up to that large. If this bit is turned on, the size number (which is 20 bits long) is multiplied by 4,096. In this case the maximum segment size is equal to the total memory address space (4GB), and the size must be some integer multiple of 4KB.

It is possible, but by no means necessary, for a protected-mode operating system to set the granularity bit to 1 and the segment base address to 0 for all segments. If this were to be done, every program would see the full 32-bit address space. That is the ultimate in what a programmer would call a flat address model. In this case, only the (32-bit) offset portion of the address would have any significance.

However, PC operating systems don't do this, and for some very good reasons. The best way to protect one program from another is simply to ensure that each cannot see the other's memory address space. That requires that each of those programs use segments that are smaller than the total memory address space. (There are other considerations as well, but you get the idea.)

Not All Memory Is Equal

Most of the time, whenever people refer to memory in a PC, they are referring to some portion of the main memory. However, this section reminds you of some memory areas that are not part of main memory and also of some of the jargon used in reference to memory.

Recall that not every physical memory address has memory. Some addresses will be locations in ROM. More are locations in RAM. But in almost every modern PC, most (quantitatively) of the memory addresses the CPU can address simply point to nothing. Not even to an empty socket where you could plug in a memory module. Just to nowhere at all.

This means, of course, that the CPU better not address those locations. And it doesn't. It still uses the full range of memory address in its internal workings, however, because of the "magic" of page mapping.

Logical, Segmented, Virtual, Linear, and Physical Memory Addresses

This section brings together some concepts that have been scattered around various other places in this book and fleshes them out a little more. Four terms are used to describe a memory address, and they refer to different types of memory:

- Logical memory address
- Segmented memory address
- Virtual memory addresses
- Linear memory address

Logical Memory Addresses

Logical memory addresses are the addresses used in programs. This term can be applied no matter whether the program is running in real or protected mode. It simply means the numbers that specify where a program is pointing in the PC's main memory.

Segmented Memory Addresses

A *segmented memory address* refers to an address in a real-mode program. It is specified by a pair of 16-bit numbers joined by a colon, for example 1A35:0043. (Both numbers are assumed to be in hexadecimal notation whenever you see an address written in this way, even though there is no trailing h or leading 0x on either number.) The first number is the segment, and its value multiplied by 16 is added to the second number (called the offset) to get the physical memory address.

Virtual Memory Addresses

In protected mode, what was called a segmented address is now referred to as a *virtual memory address*. This is still a pair of (hexadecimal) numbers separated by a colon. Now, however, the first one (still a 16-bit number) is called the selector and it determines which segment is used by referring to a segment descriptor table. The second number is the offset and now is allowed to be up to a 32-bit number.

Linear Memory Addresses

Both segmented and virtual memory addresses are translated from two numbers into one. This single memory pointer is called the *linear memory address*. Its maximum size is also a 32-bit number. (Well, in the Pentium Pro and Pentium II it could be a 36-bit number, but so far that possibility is not supported in any PC operating system.)

Physical Memory Addresses

Beginning with the 386, all Intel's x86 processors and all their clone CPU chips have had a memory paging mechanism built in. This paging mechanism can either be enabled or disabled, under software control. If it is disabled, the linear address is placed on the CPU's address lines, and as such it becomes the *physical memory address*.

If, on the other hand, paging is enabled, the linear memory address is further translated into a (generally different) physical memory address by reference to a pair of tables in main memory. These tables are called the *page directory table* and the *page table*.

The most significant 10 bits of the linear address (bits 22–31) pick out a line in the page directory table. That line contains a number that points to the location in RAM where the relevant page table can be found. The next set of 10 bits in the linear address (bits 12–21) select a row in the page table. A number found there points to a page frame, which is a 4KB region of physical memory address space. The bottom 12 bits of the linear address (bits 0–11) point to an actual memory location within that page frame. The page table and the page directory table entries also hold some additional information.

Some Ways the CPU Saves Time When It Does Memory Address Calculations

All this translation from segmented or virtual address to linear address and linear address to physical address could take up a lot of the CPU's time. This is especially so because each translation requires reference to some table or tables in RAM. However, starting with the 386, Intel has included some special, hidden registers inside the CPU to cache the relevant information.

Each time a new selector is loaded into a segment register, the segment descriptor information from the corresponding global or local descriptor table (GDT or LDT) is loaded into an invisible portion of the segment register (called the *descriptor cache register*). That enables the CPU to use it for address validation and translation without repeatedly rereading the GDT or LDT.

Similarly, whenever a page table is read, its contents are cached in the Translation Lookaside Buffer (TLB) in the CPU. Therefore, linear-to-physical memory translations can also be accomplished without a constant need to reread that table from RAM.

Note that all this caching for the purpose of speeding up memory address calculations is in addition to the L1 (and perhaps L2) memory caching that is being used to speed up access to data and instructions. This combination of techniques is a substantial part of what accounts for the much faster operation of PCs using 386-or-better CPUs over their predecessors, even when the CPU clock speeds were comparable.

Finally, when the CPU wants to send data out or pull data in, it puts the physical memory address on its address lines as low and high voltages (standing for the 0s and 1s of the binary number that is the physical memory address value). From there, the external circuitry must route this memory reference to the correct memory chips or module.

Memory the CPU Can't See (At Least Not Always)

Not all memory in your PC is a part of its main memory. The following sections quickly run down some of the other kinds of memory you can have in a PC.

Cache Memory

In effect, the CPU doesn't "see" the memory that is actually closest to it physically. That is, it doesn't really see the cache memory. It uses it, looking through the cache to see the main memory beyond.

Video Memory

The video subsystem needs some memory in which to build the images it will display on your monitor. This memory is referred to as the *video frame buffer*. (If you have two monitors, each will likely have its own frame buffer.) Because memory always comes in powers of two, and because most frame buffers need some different amount of memory, it is common for the video subsystem to have some other memory under its control, in addition to the frame buffer.

When PCs were young and their video displays primitive, the entire video frame buffer showed up in the CPU's memory address space. That was fine for a 16KB, 32KB, or even a 128KB video frame buffer in a 1MB PC. But now, with high resolution and large color depth displays, a 16MB frame buffer is common, with even larger ones being used in high-end machines. In real mode, in particular, it just isn't possible to fit the frame buffer into the CPU's meager 1MB of memory address space. This is dealt with by making at most 128KB of the frame buffer show up at once. The CPU can command the video subsystem, via some I/O ports, to reveal whatever portion of the frame buffer the CPU must access. The rest of the time that memory is kept out of the CPU's direct field of view.

This means that different portions of the very large frame buffer will occupy the same region of the CPU's memory address space, but at different times. When such a portion is not occupying that portion of the CPU's memory address space, it is, as far as the CPU is concerned, simply nonexistent.

In protected mode, with the full 4GB of memory address space available, this need no longer be a problem. It is possible to have the full 4MB or more of frame buffer show up somewhere in the CPU's 4GB memory address space. But often this is not done, for simplicity and compatibility with the real-mode way of doing things.

Finally, the video subsystem might have some uses for memory that don't involve the CPU. The video subsystem's main use of the frame buffer is simply to store the image that is currently on the screen, and to pump out the pixels to the monitor repeatedly so it will continue to redraw that image. But it also might need to have some font bit-patterns cached somewhere, or might need some scratchpad space for performing various graphics acceleration actions. Often, that space is taken from the portion of the frame buffer memory that isn't being used for the actual frame image.

Expanded Memory

This isn't common anymore, but if you have a very old PC, you might have an expanded memory card in it. This was a way to make a large amount of memory (relatively speaking) available in a mere PC or PC/XT. In a manner analogous to modern video subsystems, which reveal just a portion of their frame buffer at a time, the CPU's address space could show 65KB at a time (in four groupings of 16KB each).

This EMS strategy was valuable in its day, but it is obsolete now. With recent models of the x86 CPU family and with modern software, even DOS programs can access all the memory they could possibly want (by using a so-called DOS extender program to enable them to access extended memory). Windows programs can inherently access all the extended memory in your PC, and thus they also don't need any EMS memory. Still, there are some of the old, EMS-using, DOS programs doing useful work today just because some folks need them, and they don't want or perhaps cannot get those services from a more modern program.

Today, EMS-memory using resources are simulated by the operating system. DOS users will know the parts that do this by the names HIMEM.SYS and EMM386.EXE. These are device drivers that augment DOS. HIMEM.SYS takes some or all of the extended memory in the PC (memory at addresses above 1MB) and converts it into something called XMS memory. EMM386 then converts as much of that XMS memory into what appears to a program to be EMS memory.

XMS memory is not a special, new kind of memory. It simply is some extended memory (some of the main memory RAM that is located at a physical memory address greater than 1MB), which is under the control of a special protected mode program called a *memory manager,* and which is accessible using that memory manager by a protocol described by the Extended Memory Specification (XMS). Microsoft's version of this sort of memory manager is called HIMEM.SYS, and it has included a version of that memory manager in every version of DOS and Windows 9*x* since the introduction of MS-DOS 5.0 in 1991.

After Intel 386 (and later x86) CPUs, it became possible for software programs to remap 16KB "pages" of memory from the extended region into portions of the first megabyte. That is the essential trick performed by EMM386 and similar memory management programs that simulate EMS memory by using extended memory (usually in the form of XMS memory). That meant it was possible to go on using DOS applications that were written to assume the presence of EMS memory even on PCs that didn't have an EMS memory card in them.

As DOS programs in general, and those that assume the presence of EMS memory in particular, are fading from the scene, even the EMS-simulator programs are becoming obsolete. Instead, modern software uses the XMS protocol or else a Windows memory allocation request API to get the memory it needs. Even when the occasional program does need EMS memory, it can now get the effect of that memory from Windows 9*x* without any user intervention. At least this is true if those programs are run inside a "DOS box." Only if you run one of them from the MS-DOS prompt might you have to include EMM386.EXE in your startup files (CONFIG.SYS and AUTOEXEC.BAT).

Disk Controller Card Memory

Some hard disk controllers have cache memory built in to them. This is a way to speed disk accesses that doesn't use any of your PC's main memory. The only advantage of this method over using a disk-caching program is that you relieve your CPU of the burden of managing your disk cache. Particularly with the clock speeds of today's CPUs, this usually isn't nearly compelling enough to justify the added cost. Again, this is a relatively rare kind of CPU-invisible memory, but you might have some of it in your PC.

Network Interface Card Memory

Some network interface cards (NICs) use a small amount of on-board memory to cache information on its way into or out of your PC via the network. This is another kind of memory your PC's CPU knows nothing about and cannot directly access.

Memory On an Add-In Slave PC Board

You can buy a PC these days in many forms. You can buy an entire PC on a plug-in card that's inserted into another PC. That way you can have a multiple keyboard, mouse, and screen setups attached to your PC. Each one has its own CPU, and each CPU has its own main memory. Naturally, the host CPU can't see any of this. It just communicates with the slave PCs through input-output ports via its input-output bus.

Printer Memory

You might have as much as several megabytes of memory in your printer. If it is a page printer (such as a laser printer), it probably has an internal buffer that enables it to compose at least most of an entire page image before it begins printing that page. The CPU cannot see this memory either.

External RAM Disk Memory

You can create a fictitious RAM disk inside your PC by running a program that uses a portion of your PC's main RAM to emulate a disk drive. That RAM is fully in the view of the CPU, and indeed the CPU under the direction of the RAM disk program causes that RAM to act like a disk drive.

But you also can buy external RAM disks. These simply are boxes that contain a large amount of RAM, a power supply (probably with battery backup to keep them running when power fails), and a small computer that causes this RAM to look to your PC just like any other (very fast) disk drive. Because it looks just like a disk drive, it doesn't look like RAM to your CPU.

Your PC's Memory Needs Managing

Memory is one of the main resources in a PC, and all of the PC's resources (memory, input-output ports, DMA channels, IRQ lines, drives, and so on) must be managed. That is, in fact, one of the defining characteristics of any computer's operating system. It is a means of scheduling and managing the resources in that computer for the benefit of the computer's users and the programs that they run on that computer.

DOS and Windows are mainly systems for managing the PC's resources. They make these resources available to your programs as and they arbitrate between competing requests for resources. DOS and Windows don't exist in a vacuum, however, and you might discover great benefits in actively helping the operating system manage your PC's uses of its memory. The next section discusses active participation.

How Windows Allocates Memory

First, you must understand how memory is assigned to various uses in a PC. You've already read about most of the story for protected mode. This section explains the real-mode portion of the story, and then finishes the protected-mode story.

Real-Mode Memory Allocation

In real mode, DOS manages memory by using a chain of *memory allocation blocks* (MCBs), also known as *memory arena headers*. Because in real mode no protections are operative, DOS cannot really manage memory in the same aggressive fashion possible in protected mode. It can, at best, control which programs are loaded where. Each program is capable of doing anything it wants after it is loaded and given control of the machine.

How the OS Core Gains Control of Physical Memory

When a PC first boots, the BIOS POST program has absolute control over everything. At that point, the only memory allocated for use is the first 1KB—it's reserved for the interrupt vector table (IVT).

During the POST process, some IVT entries are filled in with pointers to interrupt service routines (ISRs) located in the motherboard BIOS. Also, some data is placed in the BIOS and DOS data area, which is a region immediately following the IVT.

When the BIOS POST completes its work, it loads the operating system. Well, actually, it loads the boot sector program from the boot disk. That program is loaded into memory at physical address 700h (immediately after the BIOS and DOS data area). Control is then passed to that program to do whatever it was written to do.

Note that both DOS and Windows 9x use what amounts to a standard DOS boot sector except for hard disks formatted with a FAT32 file system under Windows 98, Windows 95B, or 95C, and even then the rest of this sentence still applies. If it is a DOS boot sector, it contains a program that loads the operating system files and enables them to prepare the in-RAM, ready-to-run version of the operating system. (It takes some initialization steps, and the program code to do those steps is discarded when they have been done.) At the end of that process, more of the IVT has been filled in, and the operating system core has been loaded into RAM, also starting at 700h (overlaying the boot sector program).

How the OS Core Builds the Memory Arena Chain

Now the operating system core starts to process the startup files (CONFIG.SYS and AUTOEXEC.BAT, or the Windows 9x Registry and then those files). At this point, some memory management becomes both possible and necessary.

Deep inside the operating system core, at a location that is both officially undocumented and quite widely known (and also has been very stable from version to version of DOS) lies a special table of pointers called the *list of lists*. One entry in that table points to the beginning of the first MCB, which is located just above the operating system core. Each MCB is "owned" by some program. DOS owns the first one, as well as every other block that "controls" an unallocated region of memory.

Any memory region (memory arena) that contains a program is owned by that program. Any other memory regions that are used by that program for data will also be owned by that program. (One program might end up having half a dozen MCBs that it owns or only one if that is all it needs.)

DOS's first MCB includes all the rest of lower memory (from where it is up to the infamous 640KB boundary). DOS loads programs into an empty memory arena (the area controlled by an MCB that belongs to DOS). Ordinarily. it will load any program into the first such block that it finds that is large enough to accommodate that program. Then, control of the PC is passed to that program.

Some programs (all application programs, for example) will do their thing and then exit, turning back to DOS all the memory they were using. DOS then reuses that memory to load the next program.

Some programs (device drivers, for example) will do some initialization work, and then return control of the PC to DOS but ask that they be allowed to keep some portion of the memory they were using. As mentioned previously, another name for such a program is one that terminates and stays resident (it is often referred to as a TSR program). In those cases, DOS shrinks the memory arena to whatever size that program declares it must keep and creates a new MCB to control the memory that it reclaimed from that program.

After this process goes on for a while, a chain of MCBs will develop. Each one says how large the memory arena it controls is, and because that arena always starts right after the MCB, figuring out where it ends is pretty easy. The next MCB in the chain comes right after that.

This is a fairly straightforward process, and enables you to take a look inside your PC. We suggest that you determine just how the first megabyte of memory is allocated in your PC when you are running several programs and yet have a command prompt. You can do this in any of three ways. The first is to load DOS (and not Windows), and then load some device drivers and TSR programs (perhaps by lines in a CONFIG.SYS and/or AUTOEXEC.BAT file), and then work at the DOS command prompt that will result from all that. Second, you can do the same thing, but also run an application program that permits you to *shell out to DOS*. When you have shelled out to DOS, you will again get a DOS command prompt at which you can do this exploration. Finally, if you are running Windows, you can open a DOS box (also known as an MS-DOS command prompt), either in a window on the desktop or in full-screen mode. Here, too, you will have a DOS command prompt at which you can begin to explore memory allocation.

After you learn how to decode the contents of an MCB, stepping through the MCB chain is pretty easy. Just use the DEBUG program to display the contents of one MCB. Then determine the length of the memory arena it controls and add that length to the address of this MCB (and don't forget to add in the length of the MCB itself) using hexadecimal arithmetic. This will give you the address of the next MCB in the chain. Use DEBUG to display its contents. Repeat until you find a chain with a block type of Z, which indicates the end of the chain.

Alternatively, you can get much of the same information, but not see the form in which it is held in memory, by using the MEM command with its optional /d command-line switch, which is described in more detail later in this chapter.

Secondary Chains of MCBs

One main chain of MCBs starts with the first one just above the operating system core and typically ends just below 640KB. There can be one or more secondary chains. One type of secondary chain is more commonly called a *subchain*. This is a chain of MCBs within one memory arena controlled by another MCB.

The other type of secondary chain is found in upper memory (at a physical memory address above 640KB, but below 1MB). Such a chain can be formed by a third-party memory manager, by any XMS-aware program, or by DOS if you use its memory managers and declare DOS=UMB in your CONFIG.SYS file.

A memory control block occupies exactly 16 bytes. It always starts at a physical memory address that is an integer multiple of 16.

What Real-Mode Memory Management Is and Isn't

Remember, in real mode there is no way for the operating system to force a program to stay within any particular memory boundaries. (Nor can it prevent that program from doing anything it likes at any of the input-output port addresses.) After control of the PC is passed to a program, that program reigns supreme. It can do anything at all. So memory management in real mode is more accurately described as cooperative memory allocation and use. Everything is on the honor system. Protected-mode memory management is altogether different.

Protected-Mode Memory Allocation

We have already told you about how memory addresses are specified in protected mode. You know that the segment portion of a logical address is replaced by something called a selector in a virtual address (*logical addresses* in protected mode programs). You also know that selectors designate one segment descriptor in either the global descriptor table or in a local descriptor table. That descriptor contains an actual linear memory address for the beginning of the specified segment, and it also contains a length for that segment.

We haven't yet told you about the protection mechanisms that are involved in all this.

Actually, the entire story is too much to tell here. It would take up far too many pages. Unless you are a budding CPU designer or operating system programmer, your eyes would likely glaze over! So we'll just give you the short version of the story. That's enough to illustrate, at least roughly, how memory is allocated and protected in protected mode, and to show what that means for programs running in that mode.

Intel's Rings

Intel defined four levels of privilege for programs running on any x86 CPU in protected mode. It pictures this with a diagram that looks like an archery target. Ring zero is at the center, surrounded by rings one and two with ring three on the outside.

Programs running at ring zero have full access to the entire machine. They are every bit as powerful as real-mode programs. In fact, they are a little more powerful because they can set the boundaries on what other programs, running at lower permission levels, can do.

In each ring outside ring zero, programs have less access to the hardware and more restrictions on their behavior. Programs in ring three are the least powerful. Still, with some help from some ring-zero programs, even a ring-three program can accomplish any task it must do, provided that some ring-zero program is willing to do the hardware accesses for it.

This model is splendid. In principle, you would have a very small operating system core, consisting only of modules that had been extensively tested and were highly trustworthy, running in ring zero. Ring one would contain other parts of the operating system. Ring two might contain helper programs applets, and that sort of thing. Ring three would be reserved for your application programs.

As it happens, this model is too much. All the mainstream PC operating systems use only rings zero and three, which turns out to be sufficient. More than that is too much sophistication (and complexity), or using that many levels would cost too much in terms of performance (because it takes at least a little bit of time to effect a switch in operating level).

Therefore, most of the operating system, portions of many third-party device drivers, and certain other kinds of modules run in ring zero. Everything else runs in ring three. This works, but it also helps explain why even after extensive testing, Windows and Windows applications manage to crash every once in awhile.

Protected-Mode Segments Are Special

In real mode, a segment (any segment) is just a region of memory that is exactly 64KB and starts at some memory address that is an integer multiple of 16. That's all. Protected-mode segments are much more than this. A protected-mode segment can start at any memory address. It can have any length it must have, and it will ordinarily not be any larger than it must be. But most importantly, protected mode segments have *properties*.

There are two main types of segment, and some subtypes for one of these. The main two types are *code segments* and *data segments*. These names suggest something of their purpose and imply some of their properties. Data segments can be further subdivided into *stack* segments (which can be identified as either 16-bit or 32-bit stack segments) and other data segments.

Code segments are meant to hold pieces of a program (which is necessarily held there in the form of machine code, so it can be directly used by the CPU). Because of that, the CPU is permitted to withdraw its instructions only from these segments. It is not possible to alter the contents of a code segment. (If you define another segment of a different type that just happens to cover the same stretch of linear memory, you can modify its contents, which are the same contents as those in the code segment. Although it sounds convoluted, this is exactly how one must go about modifying a program in memory and also be able to execute it.)

Stack segments hold information temporarily. A program normally directs the CPU to "push" the contents of some or all of its registers onto the stack before beginning a new task. At the end of that task, those values can be "popped" back from the stack into the registers from which they came. (This must be done in just the right way. Otherwise, a value might be placed back into the wrong register, and that could lead to much mischief.)

Necessarily, therefore, a stack segment must be a region in which it is both possible to write and read information. But it won't be used to hold instructions, so being able to execute the information held there as CPU instructions is not necessary. These rules are enforced by the CPU after it discerns that a particular segment is of the type stack segment.

Stack segments also come in two sizes, but in this context that size does not refer to how large a region of memory the segment contains, but rather to the assumption the CPU will make about what size numbers it is to push on and pop off the stack. The two sizes are, as you might have guessed, 16-bit and 32-bit.

Data segments comprise the remainder of the existing segments. These can be given a variety of properties. Like stack segments, data segments cannot have their contents executed as instructions. (Unless, of course, a code segment is defined that just happens to contain those same contents, because its memory region happens to coincide with this particular data segment.) But they can be set to be read-only segments, write-only segments, or read-write segments.

When One Program Calls Another

Things get really complicated when one program wants to ask another program to do something. This happens all the time. If the calling program and the called program both reside in the ring of privilege there is no special problem. But if they are in different rings, some very special care must be taken to ensure that the more privileged program isn't effectively conned into doing something it shouldn't, and that it doesn't in the process confer more privileges on the calling program when it returns control.

These matters are taken care of by some very clever and intricate features of the x86 processors. To understand them you must learn all about Task Switch Segments (TSSs) and gates, which is very arcane stuff. Just know that Intel's engineers figured all this out correctly. So if the operating system is also crafted correctly (as seems to be the case with all the popular PC protected-mode operating systems), the right things will happen and the wrong ones will be prevented.

The Bottom Line

Protected-mode memory management enables the operating system, with a lot of help from the CPU's protection hardware, to rigidly enforce limits on programs. It can keep them separate, or it can enable them to share some resources, but not others. The particular decisions on these matters differ from operating system to operating system, and are, in fact, the source of some of the most critical differences between, for example, Windows 9x and Windows NT/2000.

Understanding the MEM Command

DOS and Windows 95 provide a command that enables you to look at how memory is being used on your PC. This isn't a book about DOS commands, so we won't go into any detail on how this MEM command works, but note that it does enable you to see much of what we have just been discussing.

If you just execute the command, you'll get only a summary of the types of memory your PC has and how much of each one is in use. If you add a command-line switch of /? (a slash character followed by a question mark), you'll get a help screen that shows you what other switches you can use.

The /c switch is very useful for determining which programs are loaded into lower or upper memory and how much memory each one uses. The /d switch essentially presents the information you can get by walking the MCB chain. The form of this display has changed with different DOS (and Windows) versions. Earlier ones used only hexadecimal values in the /d display, which discouraged most folks from using it (although it was wonderful for programmers). The latest versions use only decimal values except for the segment addresses in the left column. That is more user-friendly, in general, but it does mean you might have to do some translations from decimal to hexadecimal if, for example, you want to add the size of one memory arena to its address to get the address for the next one.

The Infamous 640KB Barrier and How to Break Past It

Let's return for a moment to the relatively simple (if uncontrolled) world of real-mode PC operation. Here is where memory management (in the sense of something a PC's user could do to make it work better) all began.

We have told you about how DOS loads one program after another and lets each one keep some or all of its memory if it needs to. After a while, you can accumulate quite a stack of programs in your PC. Normally, you want to do this because those programs are the necessary pieces that extend the operating system so you can access your CD-ROM drive, a network, a mouse, and other things that you must use. It is also possible to have all these bits and pieces use up so much memory that there isn't enough room left over for that big application program you must run. That's when memory management comes into play.

The first 640KB of physical memory is what IBM decreed programs could use. IBM reserved the rest of the 1MB of real-mode memory address space for system uses. Only a fairly small part of that reserved space is actually being used by the video adapter and motherboard BIOS ROM in most PCs. This suggests an opportunity: If only you could use some of that extra, unused space in lieu of a portion of the lower memory region, you might leave enough room down there for your big DOS program.

We won't go over the many ways in which folks devised to take advantage of this unused space, but we will tell you briefly about the one used most often today.

By placing a 386 (or later model x86-compatible) CPU into its virtual 86 (v86 or Ev86) operating mode, you can make it act as though it is in real mode, and yet take advantage of extended memory and the CPU's paging mechanism. This is precisely what HIMEM.SYS and EMM386.EXE do and what Windows 95 and 98 do for DOS applications. They take control of the PC, put it into protected mode, and remap some of the extended memory so it appears to be located at physical addresses in upper memory (between 640KB and 1024KB). Then they run your DOS programs in v86 mode, so they think they are running in real mode. They don't actually make the memory move to a new physical address, but any program running in v86 mode thinks that the linear addresses it generates are actually physical ones. The paging mechanism can, in fact, make any correspondence between the two that it has been told to make.

That creates some available RAM in upper memory. The next step is to move some of the real-mode programs cluttering up lower memory into this newly available RAM. Starting with version 5, DOS enables you to do this quite easily. Just put the line DOS=UMB in your CONFIG.SYS file and then use the LOADHIGH, DEVICEHIGH, and (in DOS 6.*x*) INSTALLHIGH directives to put your resident programs up there. (The DOS=HIGH directive also helps because it moves some of the core of the OS up into the high memory area, just past the end of the first megabyte.)

If you find yourself needing to run lots of TSR programs and real-mode device drivers, and if you then run low on available lower memory, this is the best approach to use to get more free lower memory.

If you are running Windows 9x, it will take care of much of this problem. Mainly it does this by substituting protected-mode drivers for most of those real-mode drivers and TSR programs. Also, it solves some memory usage problems that Windows 3.x has. These problems were another reason many folks had to use DOS-level memory management on their PCs.

Understanding Windows Memory Use

DOS plus Windows 3.x, or Windows 9x is in many ways just DOS in a pretty dress (Windows NT and 2000, however, do not relate to DOS at all). So whatever DOS does with memory before Windows is started is something that Windows simply must deal with. Then Windows goes on to do more with memory on its own.

Most of the time, Windows does an admirable job of using memory for its needs and those of the programs it is called upon to run. But when it doesn't, you will get an out of memory message. That doesn't mean that all your PC's RAM is in use. It just means Windows needs more of it than it is able to get right now. That is when memory management (in the sense of your involvement in the issue) makes sense for Windows users.

The most important point to remember is that Windows (version 3.x or Windows 9x) is a protected-mode environment. That means that after you start Windows, your PC is running in protected mode until you shut Windows down. Well, it will revert to real mode from time to time to perform some low-level DOS system actions, but then it immediately springs back into protected mode. (Windows 9x goes back to real mode much less often than Windows 3.x, but it still will go back typically many times each second.) This means that Windows will allocate memory for programs from the entire pool of RAM on your PC. It can access all the RAM you can give it. (And it would probably benefit from having more!) It uses memory from every range of available addresses, both in the first megabyte and beyond.

Some of its uses are for system-level things, such as a disk cache to speed up access to your disk drives. Other uses are for pieces of programs and portions of the data with which they are working. Windows is quite clever about swapping out to disk chunks of data and overlaying chunks of programs with other program chunks whenever it starts to run low on free memory. But it still isn't always capable of running programs you'd think it could. The reason sometimes is that Windows is running low on some specialized pool of memory it needs.

Windows Has Some Special Memory Needs

Whenever Windows loads a Windows application, it must use a small amount of the first 1MB of real, physical RAM to hold some information about that program. This special region that is normally called *lower memory plus upper memory*, or *conventional memory* when we are talking just about DOS, is now called *global DOS memory*. This is one of the precious memory regions Windows must use. Especially if you have a lot of TSR programs and device drivers cluttering up your global DOS memory, Windows might find it hasn't enough room there for its needs. In that case, you will get a "not enough memory, close some applications and try again" message.

Windows also uses some other and much smaller special memory regions called *heaps*. Heaps are where Windows stores the elements of the dialog boxes, windows, and other things you see on the screen. These also are places Windows programs store some of the many small data structures they use. They are most often described as the GDI and User resource heaps, but in fact, several heaps are being referred to by each label.

Different versions of Windows use different numbers of heaps, and their sizes can also differ between versions. Under Windows 3.*x,* there were clearly too few heaps and they were too small. Running out of heap space (which in Windows jargon became running out of *Windows resources*) was an all-too-common way of finding yourself simply unable to run the programs you wanted to run.

Windows 9*x* has mostly solved this problem. You still can run out of resources, but it happens less often. The most common situation in which it might occur is when you run programs that have *resource leaks.* These are programs that ask for portions of the heap space, and then when they are finished with them, forget to tell Windows it is okay now to take that memory back. Run enough of these guys and you are sure to run out of resources.

DOS Virtual Machines Under Windows

Whenever you run a DOS program under Windows 9*x* or ME, you are actually running it in a special environment called a *DOS Virtual Machine* (DVM). Another name for this is the DOS box or the DOS window mentioned previously. This is true whether you see the DOS application running literally in a window smaller than your whole screen or you see it running in full-screen mode.

The only exception to this rule is that if you run a DOS application under Windows 9*x* that must run in MS-DOS mode, Windows 9*x* will first shut down all the other programs that are running, shut itself down, and then run your DOS program in true real mode. (You can, if you want, run that program from a batch file that could load a memory manager and then run your DOS program not in real mode, but this isn't commonly done. The point of MS-DOS mode is to enable you to run DOS programs that just can't tolerate the protected-mode environment created by Windows.)

Under Windows 3.*x* and Windows 9*x*, you can have as many DVMs running at once as you want. Well, each one of them can use up just a little more than 1MB of your RAM, so how much RAM your PC has will limit the number of DVMs you can have running at once. Don't forget: Windows still needs some memory for itself.

Each DVM is actually an instance of v86 protected mode. It gets what it sees as a megabyte (or with the HMA 17/16 of a megabyte) of what it thinks is physical memory address space starting at address zero. Indeed, the interrupt vector table appears at the bottom of this space and the BIOS ROM near the top. Actually, this is some remapped RAM (courtesy of the CPU's paging mechanism) into which Windows has copied these portions of the real first megabyte's contents. This allows each DOS program to do whatever it likes in that megabyte of memory with utterly no impact on any other program running on the PC at the same time, whether it's a Windows program or another DOS program in a different DVM.

Any time this DOS program tries to access the screen, keyboard, or some I/O port, or other similar action, the Windows v86 monitor program will intervene. It "virtualizes" the screen memory (the frame buffer) so the DOS program thinks it is writing to the real screen. Windows then copies over that portion of the frame buffer's contents that it needs to make the appropriate window appear on the screen to show you what that DOS program is doing. (Of course, if the DOS program is minimized, Windows won't show you any of its frame buffer.)

Similarly, the DOS program gets to see only the real keystrokes when that DVM has the focus. The rest of the time Windows gets the keystrokes and uses them for itself or passes them to some other program.

Almost all DOS programs can be run this way, and this is the best way to run them on a Windows machine because they are protected in this fashion from one another. This is *real* memory management.

The Windows Virtual Machine

Curiously, Windows 3.x and 9*x* don't do nearly as good a job of protecting Windows programs from one another, for a simple reason. Only one Windows virtual machine exists. All Windows programs share that one simulated PC.

Windows NT/2000 is different in this regard. At least it can be. You can decide whether to run 16-bit Windows programs, such as those written for Windows 3.x, in a single Windows virtual machine (WVM) or to run each one in its own virtual machine.

Another way that Windows fails to fully protect one application from another is that it uses a message-passing model that enables one ill-behaved program to stop all the rest from working. If such a program doesn't properly receive and respond to messages sent to it by the operating system, that program is likely to "hang" or "freeze." Windows 3.11 and 9*x* partially solves this problem by making it relatively easy to use a local reboot (the Ctrl+Alt+Del key combination) to force that errant program to quit.

Some Ways to Help Windows Manage Memory

You can do several things to help Windows use memory more successfully. Undoubtedly the most important one is to buy and install all the RAM you possibly can. You can do some other things as well. If you are getting any out-of-memory messages from Windows, the first thing you must do is determine which kind of memory is in short supply. The most probable kinds are global DOS memory and heap space (resources).

The first stop should be the information that Windows offers on the topic. Look at the Help/About dialog box in Windows Explorer (Windows 9*x*) or File Manager (Windows 3.*x*), or in almost any other Microsoft program. They all will tell you something about the program, but they also will tell you about the available memory and available resources—just one number for each one.

That might be enough. If the free resource percentage gets low, that can be the problem. Sometimes something as simple as not loading a huge wallpaper image will free up enough of the heap space to enable you to get on with your work. If that doesn't do the trick, however, you might have to dig a little deeper.

Another way to find out what is going on is to use a system monitor program. One is built into Windows 9*x*, and Windows 3.*x* has one included in the resource kits you can buy. These Microsoft tools require resources of their own and don't quite do the job when it comes to finding out about the amount of free global DOS memory.

The Norton Utilities for Windows 9*x* has Norton System Doctor among its many tools. Among its many "sensors" are ones for (global) DOS memory and separate ones for User and GDI memory. You can configure various gauges or sensors to display many details about your system.

If you determine that you are running low on global DOS memory, go back to the section in this chapter entitled "The Infamous 640KB Barrier and How to Break Past It." When you have done what you can at the DOS level, there will be at least one more thing you can do.

Windows NT's Performance Monitor as well as Windows 2000's System Monitor provides you with the counters and objects necessary to monitor memory usage as well as memory paging performance. Regular monitoring is strongly recommended.

Memory Management Software

Windows 9x are often considered poor performers in terms of memory management. Users frequently receive "not enough memory" error when running multiple applications.

Microsoft does not provide any advanced memory management utility. However, there are several third-party utilities that do the job well.

Some of the better-known memory management software include:

- MemTurbo
- MemBoost
- WinRAM Turbo
- MemMax
- RAM Idle

Try performing a software search on the Web to obtain the evaluation version.

So How Much RAM Do You Need, Really?

We'd like to close this chapter with the one question we get asked most about memory in PCs: "How much RAM do I need?" Our favorite answer is, "It depends."

And it does. You must consider what you are doing with your PC (or perhaps what you are attempting to do, or want you could do, if low RAM is preventing you). Also look at how much RAM your PC can accept and what it now has in it. You might also look into the capabilities of your PC's L2 cache system. Certain motherboards support L2 caching of memory only up to a specified maximum. In the cases of these boards, this maximum cacheable memory is less than the maximum amount of RAM the board will support. With more memory installed than can be cached, the performance of your PC will seriously degrade. Finally, look at your budget and think about your plans for possibly getting a newer, bigger, better PC someday soon. After you considered all those issues, you are ready to address head-on the question of how much RAM to have.

If you want to run several large Windows applications at once, and especially if you will be manipulating large graphic files or video presentations, you almost can't have too much RAM. If you're running Windows 9x, start with 64MB. For Windows NT/2000, start with 128MB. Fortunately, RAM prices have been coming down recently. Adding lots of RAM to your PC has never been less costly. (Memory for portables is sometimes still pretty pricey, however.)

When you are considering the cost of adding RAM, also remember to think about what *not* adding it is costing you. Every time your PC must use the swap file (also known as virtual memory), things are being slowed. Add more RAM and that won't happen nearly as often.

Summary

This chapter included an in-depth technical look at the short-term storage places found within PCs—memory, that is. In the next chapter, we'll take a similar look at long-term storage of a variety of types, from magnetic to optical, from disk to disc to tape, to card and chip.

Storage: How Does Data Get There?

In the previous chapter, you read about how data gets into memory, how it's maintained and manipulated there, how it's used and moved from one location to another, and how it's finally removed from memory when it's no longer useful.

This chapter will continue that theme, answering many of the same technical questions for long-term storage. We'll look into the workings of hard disks, first on the physical level, and then on the logical level. (In other words, we'll examine how the hardware works, and then how your PC works *with* the hardware and the data it maintains for the long –haul.) In the course of this exploration, you'll learn about several types of *file systems*, which is a term that means logical structures that the OS and disks use to store and locate data reliably. We'll talk about the differences between a physical drive and logical disks, and between ways of *compressing* data to reduce its use of your available storage. You learn about the different formats used to write onto the variety of optical discs, why they're useful, and a good deal more. We'll finish off the chapter with a look at the cutting-edge of storage technology, both in terms of hardware innovation and new logical methods. Welcome!

Hard Disks

Back in Chapter 7, "Disks and PC Data Storage," we talked about the different types of disks, how they magnetically store data on either floppy material or hard platters, and how they connect to the PC so that data can be useful. If you're not familiar with those topics, you might want to take a look at that chapter before you continue here. We're going to assume you don't have questions about how magnetic drives actually *work*, and will jump right in to how drives are physically configured for actual use. Because the majority of PC users are running some form of Microsoft Windows, this discussion focuses on the specifics of that operating system. In order to focus on Windows, however, it's necessary to take a step back in time and see where Windows came from.

You're probably already well aware that Windows came from MS-DOS, the character-based operating system developed first by Microsoft in 1981. DOS (the Disk Operating

System) was named as it was to identify that DOS was a step away from older operating system for personal computers, most of which supported data storage only on slow, cassette tapes, just like are used to record music. DOS was an operating system for disks—a Disk Operating System.

It actually requires two layers of configuration for a disk-oriented operating system to work with disks. The first is a hardware layer. This identifies fundamental characteristics such as the number of platters, or recordable surfaces, and the number of recording heads. It also defines certain characteristics about how the disk can be used; this involves issues such as where data can be stored and so forth.

The Physical Structures

The most fundamental unit of information storage on a disk is called a *sector*. (This is true for any operating system, not just Windows or DOS.) A sector is a contiguous section of disk that has sufficient magnetic space to record 571 bytes of data. Of this, 512 bytes are available for use by the user, and the remaining space is used to store a header and trailer, or footer, if you like, for each sector. Among other things, these contain checksum information that helps your PC automatically verify that the data in the main part of the sector has been stored properly.

Look back at Figure 9.1, and then also look at Figure 18.1. In each of these figures, the short arcs of darker gray on the disk represent individual sectors. All the sectors around a disk at a given distance from the center form a *track*. The number of sectors in a track varies from one disk capacity to another, but every disk of every type stores its information as some number of concentric tracks, each made up of a different number of sectors.

Most floppy disks have data recorded in sectors and tracks on both sides of their magnetic surface. Hard disks have more than two recordable surfaces because they usually have multiple platters mounted on the same spindle with two recordable surfaces on at least most of those platters. (Sometimes the outermost surfaces—the top side of the top platter and the bottom side of the bottom platter—are reserved for special purposes and cannot be used to store the user's data.) The collection of all the tracks at the same distance from the spindle on all the recordable surfaces is called a *cylinder*.

DOS and the PC BIOS were designed from the outset with the notion that the various disks they would manage might have differing numbers of heads, differing numbers of sectors per track, and differing numbers of cylinders. What the original versions of DOS and the early PC BIOSes couldn't innately comprehend was a disk that had a different number of sectors on different tracks. And yet that is, in fact, just how most modern hard disks are built.

In these disks, because the outer tracks are longer than the inner ones, it's possible to put more sectors on those longer, outer tracks than on the shorter, inner tracks without crowding the individual bits together too closely in either place. Manufacturers commonly divide the tracks into two or more zones and put the same number of sectors on all the tracks within a zone, but a different number on the tracks in neighboring zones.

FIGURE 18.1

The location and numbering of disk heads (surfaces) and cylinders on a logical hard disk.

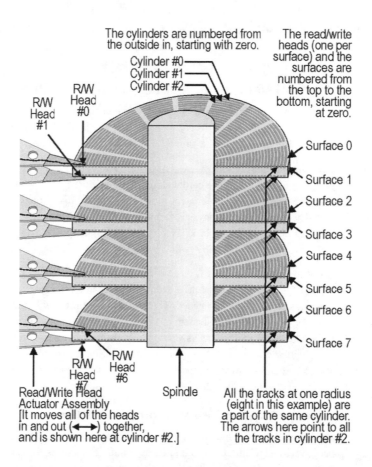

The cylinders are numbered from the outside in, starting with zero.

Cylinder #0
Cylinder #1
Cylinder #2

The read/write heads (one per surface) and the surfaces are numbered from the top to the bottom, starting at zero.

R/W Head #1
R/W Head #0

Surface 0
Surface 1
Surface 2
Surface 3
Surface 4
Surface 5
Surface 6
Surface 7

R/W Head #7
R/W Head #6

Read/Write Head Actuator Assembly [It moves all of the heads in and out (◄─►) together, and is shown here at cylinder #2.]

Spindle

All the tracks at one radius (eight in this example) are a part of the same cylinder. The arrows here point to all the tracks in cylinder #2.

There are two ways that such a disk can be made to work. One is by making the disk somehow pretend to be constructed differently than it really is. The other, more modern, method is to use *Logical Block Addressing* (LBA) to connect it to the PC.

In the first strategy, the disk controller electronics first organize into one long chain all the locations on the disk at which information can be stored. It assigns a logical block number (starting with 0) to each of those locations. Next, the drive electronics creates a fictitious drive geometry. This fictitious drive has an almost arbitrary set of numbers representing its supposed number of heads, sectors per track, and cylinders. Every logical block number is converted into an equivalent location on the fictitious drive, and that is the pseudo-physical address used for that information when dealing with DOS.

In the second strategy, an extra layer called the INT13H Extensions is added to the BIOS to let it deal directly with a disk that is organized as a one-dimensional chain of logical blocks. That avoids all the messiness of fictitious drive geometries and, more importantly, it allows you to use much larger disks than DOS and the original-style PC motherboard BIOS can natively understand. Older PCs can have their BIOS updated to reflect this methodology. All current PCs come with this support.

With tracks, sectors, and cylinders defined, let's focus on how this lowest-level information structure gets imposed on a disk. We'll then go on to see how it's further organized into logical subsections by the operating system.

Physical Versus Logical Formatting of Disks

Users commonly get confused when they first encounter the distinction between what is called the *physical* or *low-level formatting* and the *logical* or *high-level formatting* of a disk. Both processes consist simply of storing some special data on the disk, but the data is used for different purposes.

A freshly made diskette or hard disk has nothing stored on it. In that state, an operating system can't use the disk. Two (or in the case of hard disks, three) steps must be taken first. The first step is the physical formatting of the medium. The second step for floppies, and the third step for hard disks, is the logical formatting. Hard disks add a step in between these two called *partitioning* (which we'll talk about later in this chapter).

All of the information that is placed on a disk during the physical or logical formatting is used exclusively to help the drive store your data in an orderly manner, so it can retrieve your data again when it's needed. Think of a new, completely unformatted disk as a huge room where people can mill about randomly. Trying to locate a given person in such a room without disturbing all the others would be a rather unpleasant—and utterly inefficient—task. A formatted disk is more like a large theatre during a performance. All the people in attendance are seated where they belong and, with the proper reference of who bought which seats, you could at least locate parties with ease.

How the Physical Format Information Is Used

So the first step in converting a huge room into a structured theatre is setting up where people will sit. Naturally, you do this by bringing seats into the room and securing them in neat and orderly rows. On a disk, it's accomplished by recording empty sectors of information in each of the places where information is to go. This level of organization is called the *physical formatting* of the drive.

After the physical formatting is complete, every sector in which information might ultimately get stored is written to the disk surface. Each sector has a header region that includes numbers indicating where on the disk this sector is located. Each sector has a data section that's 512 placeholder bytes. And each sector has a section at the tail end that are used for error-checking and correction.

Writing the OS Logical Formatting

The second step in preparing a floppy (and third for a hard disk) is imposing the *logical format*. That means simply putting some special information that the operating system needs to manage the disk for data storage. If you'll indulge our continued use of the theatre analogy, this is like putting a number on every seat and hiring a staff of ushers to seat people properly and resolve ticketing disputes. An operating system *must* keep careful track of every file it stores on the disk so it can get that file's contents back whenever you, or a program you run, wants it.

On a disk, this job is achieved by putting a special program at the start of the disk and then building some special data tables both there and elsewhere on the disk. The special program and the associated data table located at the very start are called the *boot record*. The system uses this program and its data table to learn about the size of this disk and some of its other properties, and also to facilitate loading of the operating system from this disk, should that be desired.

The next special table is called the *file allocation table* or FAT. On most disks, Windows also creates a backup FAT to be used if the first FAT is damaged. The last of the special data tables that must be created is the *root directory*. We'll look at both of these in depth in just a moment. Let's first look at how these formatting structures are physically created.

How Each Kind of Format Is Installed

Floppy disks are supplied from the factory either with no formatting, or with both low- and high-level formatting already in place. In either case, you can redo both levels of formatting quite simply by running the operating system's disk-formatting command. Hard disks are different. It used to be that they came from the factory completely unformatted, which was necessary because the low-level format had to be whatever was needed by the electronics in the hard disk controller to which the disk would be attached.

Now, with all the disk controller electronics integrated onto each hard disk drive, hard disks have the low-level formatting already in place. After a hard disk is installed in a PC, and before it can have the DOS formatting installed, it must be *partitioned*. This is true even if the whole disk will be used as a single partition. (You'll learn why this is true and more about partitioning later in this chapter.)

Because hard disk makers aren't sure how you will be using their disks, and in particular don't know how you want them partitioned, they rarely do either the partitioning or the logical formatting for you.

When the partitioning information is in place, the logical format can be put on the disk, one partition at a time (if it has more than one) using the operating system's formatting command. Because the low-level formatting has already been done, this command need only insert the operating system-specific data into the defined physical sectors.

Dealing with Defects on a Disk

No physical systems people build, and certainly none as complex as a disk drive, turn out exactly as planned. There are always some defects inherent in the device. But PC users like to demand total perfection in the performance of their disk drives. When you store information there, you want it to come back 100 percent accurate, right down to the very last bit. Anything less, and some—perhaps a vital—part of your PC's operating system might fail, or you might lose some critical document. How can this gap be bridged?

The Two Tricks Used in Disk Data Storage to Ensure Integrity

In terms of disk storage, the digital circuits essentially guarantee that the data you send through them gets to its destination unchanged. Disk drives also have special provisions to ensure that when information is stored and then later read back, it can be checked to ensure its integrity.

Disk drives do this in two ways. First, the manufacturers of disk drives check all the information-holding places on each disk during the low-level formatting (and you would be checking it again if you were ever able to force a repetition of that step—which is something you only do by use of certain, specialized data recovery programs) to be sure that each sector will hold and return information faithfully. Any sectors incapable of doing this are marked as bad and are never used. Second, some extra, redundant information (called *error correction codes* or, on floppy disks, *error detection codes*) is stored along with your real information. When your data is read back from the disk, the drive checks it against the extra information to be sure that what it thinks it stored there is valid.

How Bad Sectors Are Tracked

There are several important differences in the ways that these things are done on floppy disks and on hard disks. On a floppy disk, any bad sectors are simply marked as bad and the disk's actual capacity is reduced by the number of bad sectors.

Modern hard disks, however, almost always appear to be perfect. They accomplish this by having more sectors for information storage than they tell you about. Some spare sectors are held in reserve, and whenever the disk controller detects a bad sector, it can replace that sector, in a functional sense, with one of the spare sectors. Different disks and different disk controllers use slightly different strategies. Some, for example, have a few spare sectors at the end of each track. Others just have a pool of spare sectors at the end of the entire chain of logical block addresses. Either way, the disk controllers usually manage to hide the defective sectors completely.

In fact, the only way you're likely to see any bad sectors on a hard drive is if it's a very old one, or if a sector goes bad while it's holding some of your data. A very old hard disk might not have been built with all the modern hardware for hiding defects, and if a sector goes bad while it's holding some data, the drive might not be capable of substituting another sector for it without losing the data that had been stored in the failed sector.

We said just a moment ago that, on modern drives, disk controllers usually manage to remap bad sectors, hiding them *completely*. Actually, that isn't quite true. Completely implies that you'll never notice the difference. But if you work with streaming data of any kind—sound, music, or, especially, video—you'll very likely discover quickly that remapping defective sectors can wreak havoc on your throughput performance. (Actually, you might notice a difference even with data that isn't of a streaming type, but less dramatically.) You can probably intuit why this is so. For much streaming content, the tolerances between what is being required of your PC's performance and the best it can give are very small. In the amount of time required to move a drive's read/write heads to the spare sectors where your data has been relocated, your video and audio could become completely out of sync. To compensate, your PC will start either dropping frames or skipping audio content, and the video will look or sound dreadful.

Fortunately there's a solution to this problem, assuming you have enough free space on the defective drive to manage it. High-end disk defragmentation tools will effectively undo this time-taking sector remap. The sectors that are known to be bad will, of course, remain marked bad, and no new data will be placed there. In the meantime, the defragger will collect all the data in the remapped file and reorganize it—it *optimizes* the data— into contiguous sectors. In a worst-case scenario, where the bad sectors fall right in the middle of the space required by a large file, the data is separated as unobtrusively as possible, so that only the slightest of head movements is required to jump to the sector where the file continues.

As a rule of thumb, if you're working with data that might be impacted by the remapping of bad sectors, get that data off the drive with the bad sectors. If that's not doable, strict disk defragmentation can give you the best of an imperfect world.

Integrity Maintenance

The beginning of each sector on a floppy disk contains a few bytes of data for the sole use of the disk drive. These are the address of the sector, plus an indication of whether the sector is bad. Then come 512 bytes of space for your information. Finally, two bytes make up a special, extra number, called the *cyclical redundancy check* (CRC) number. Each time your information is written, this extra number is added.

Each time your information is read, the disk controller first checks the lead-in bytes to be sure it's reading the correct sector. Then it reads the data and re-computes what the CRC value should be. Finally it looks at the actual CRC value on the disk. If the two numbers are equal, the controller concludes that it read that sector correctly.

If the CRC drive reads doesn't equal the CRC it computes from the data it read, it might try re-reading that sector. But after doing that a few times and still getting the same mismatch, the only thing the disk controller and operating system can do is announce their failure and prevent you from using the damaged data.

Hard disks handle much more data than floppies, both because hard disks can store so much more, and also because they can move information onto and off of their disks much more rapidly. They also encounter many more errors than floppies, but if a hard drive just gave up whenever it misread data, it wouldn't be a useful device. Fortunately, PC hard drives hide at least 99 percent of all mistakes they make.

Instead of merely calculating a CRC value for each sector, hard disks compute a short string of *error correction codes* (ECC). When a read error occurs, the most likely cause is a pinpoint defect on the disk's surface. That defect will mess up just a few bits in the 4,096 bits that make up a sector's 512 bytes. More importantly, the bad bits will all be close together. Some very clever mathematicians and engineers worked out a scheme for ECC that would allow them to not only detect when a mistake is made, but to know exactly what and where the error is. Each bit must be either a 1 or a 0; if you know exactly which bits are wrong, you can compensate for them just by reversing those individual values.

This is why it seems like hard disks work perfectly almost all the time. Errors actually occur several times a day, typically, but they're are fixed automatically and transparently. On an average PC, no more than a few times per year does a real error get through and actually cause some problem.

Figure 18.2 shows the anatomy of a hard disk sector. This picture is also a good representation of the anatomy of a sector on a floppy disk, except that the region that's labeled in this figure as containing ECC numbers is a little shorter on a floppy and holds only a CRC number.

FIGURE 18.2

The anatomy of a hard disk sector.

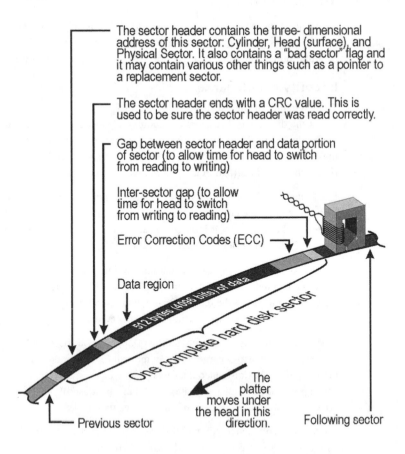

The sector header contains the three-dimensional address of this sector: Cylinder, Head (surface), and Physical Sector. It also contains a "bad sector" flag and it may contain various other things such as a pointer to a replacement sector.

The sector header ends with a CRC value. This is used to be sure the sector header was read correctly.

Gap between sector header and data portion of sector (to allow time for head to switch from reading to writing)

Inter-sector gap (to allow time for head to switch from writing to reading)

Error Correction Codes (ECC)

Data region

512 bytes (4096 bits) of data

One complete hard disk sector

Previous sector

The platter moves under the head in this direction.

Following sector

SMART Hard Disks Tell You When to Fix Them

SMART is an acronym that stands for *Self-Monitoring And Reporting Technology*. Most hard drive manufacturers now build this feature into at least some of their drives. These SMART drives constantly monitor their internal "health" and set some internal flags whenever they detect some incipient failure. Some BIOSes can read those flags during the boot process and report on what they find. Such drives are popular in large data centers, where foreknowledge of drive failures can be of inestimable value.

The Logical Structure of a Windows Disk

Now you know how sectors get on disks in the first place. You know something about the internal structure of each sector. What you haven't learned yet, though, is how Windows manages to keep track of all the files you have loaded into all those sectors. We told you the names of the structures it builds a few pages ago (the boot record, FAT, and root directory). The next several sections of this chapter explain just what each one is and how Windows uses it.

Figure 18.3 shows the logical structure that every formatted Windows diskette or hard disk has. The FAT12 structure is the complete description of what is on a Windows-formatted floppy. A hard disk drive can be logically divided—partitioned—in such a way that it appears to actually contain several hard disks, each of which might have either the FAT12/FAT16 structure, the FAT32 structure, or Windows 2000/XP's NTFS file system. Thus, your C: drive and your D: drive can both exist inside the same physical hard disk case. We'll talk more about partitioning in a few moments.

FIGURE 18.3

The essential regions within any Windows-formatted logical disk drive. The upper portion of this figure shows the layout used on the older FAT12 and FAT16 formats. The lower portion shows the corresponding information for the newer, FAT32 format.

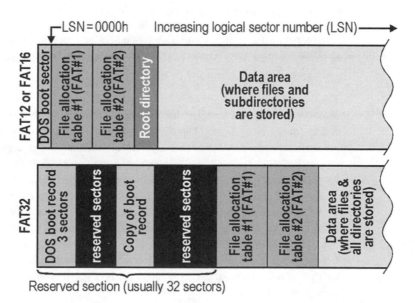

The Boot Record

The very first sector on any floppy, and the very first sector in each logical drive on a hard disk is where the operating system puts the *boot record*. (Or, more precisely, that is where the OS puts at least the beginning of the boot record.)

Every boot record written by any given version of Windows to a FAT12 or FAT16 disk is precisely the same, except for the contents of a small data table. (Because that table holds information on the size of that drive, and some other things, that part of the boot record must be different on different drives.) With that one exception, a floppy's boot record is the same as that on a hard drive. (All standard floppy disks use the FAT12 format.)

Because this boot record for FAT12 and FAT16 is exactly 512 bytes long, it also is sometimes called the *boot sector*—or, to distinguish it from the *master boot record* (MBR), it might be called the *DOS boot sector*. (You'll meet the MBR in detail in a moment.) The boot record on modern FAT32 hard disks is quite a bit different from that on a FAT12 or FAT16 disk, and is much larger, and so cannot properly be called a boot sector.

Most of the boot record is made up of a program used to help start up your computer, assuming we're talking about the disk you're booting it from. That's why it carries the name *boot record*. If the disk doesn't have the operating system on it, and if you try to start from it anyway, the program will put up the message: "Operating System Not Found".

Figure 18.4 shows how Norton Disk Editor (NDE) displays this boot record's information of a hard disk partition formatted using the FAT32 structure. Here you see just the contents of the data table for the DOS boot record, displayed in an easily readable form, for the C drive of the primary hard disk of our example desktop system. (We did have to cheat in one sense. The table is too big to see all at once on a normal 25-line display. If you were using NDE on this hard disk and went into this display, you would have to scroll down in order to see all the lines. We wanted to show you the entire table's contents in this figure, and so we did some cutting and pasting.)

The data table in the DOS boot record, which is called the *BIOS parameter block* (BPB), records some essential numbers that DOS must know about this disk. This is the data that you see displayed by Norton Disk Editor in Figure 18.4. It includes the number of bytes per sector, the total number of sectors on the disk, the number of copies of the FAT, the type of FAT (12-, 16-, or 32-bit), the number of sectors per FAT, the number of sectors in the root directory, plus a few miscellaneous other facts about this disk. In the FAT32 form of the BPB there are many additional fields. Some are to increase the reliability of your PC. (For example, the fields that specify where to find the root directory and where to find a backup copy of this boot record.) Others are included to increase its performance. (For example, the fields that show the Free Cluster Count and the Next Free Cluster number.) As you can see, this data table is basically telling Windows where on the disk to find its special data structures, and how much other space there is in which to store your data.

FIGURE 18.4

FIGURE 18.4

The DOS boot record from the primary hard disk's C partition on our example desktop system as it is displayed by the Norton Disk Editor. (Note that the large number of hidden sectors reflects that this drive has been configured to support multiple operating systems and boot environments.)

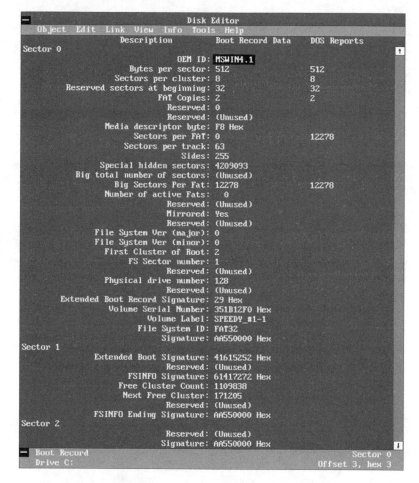

```
┌─────────────────────────────────────────────────────────────────────┐
│ ─                           Disk Editor                               │
│  Object  Edit  Link  View  Info  Tools  Help                          │
│              Description              Boot Record Data    DOS Reports  │
│ Sector 0                                                            ↑ │
│                          OEM ID: MSWIN4.1                             │
│                 Bytes per sector: 512                    512          │
│                Sectors per cluster: 8                    8            │
│      Reserved sectors at beginning: 32                   32           │
│                      FAT Copies: 2                       2            │
│                        Reserved: 0                                    │
│                        Reserved: (Unused)                             │
│             Media descriptor byte: F8 Hex                             │
│                   Sectors per FAT: 0                     12278        │
│                 Sectors per track: 63                                 │
│                           Sides: 255                                  │
│            Special hidden sectors: 4209093                            │
│     Big total number of sectors: (Unused)                             │
│             Big Sectors Per Fat: 12278                   12278        │
│           Number of active Fats:   0                                  │
│                        Reserved: (Unused)                             │
│                        Mirrored: Yes                                  │
│                        Reserved: (Unused)                             │
│         File System Ver (major): 0                                    │
│         File System Ver (minor): 0                                    │
│           First Cluster of Root: 2                                    │
│               FS Sector number: 1                                     │
│                       Reserved: (Unused)                              │
│         Physical drive number: 128                                    │
│                       Reserved: (Unused)                              │
│    Extended Boot Record Signature: 29 Hex                             │
│          Volume Serial Number: 351B12F0 Hex                           │
│                  Volume Label: SPEEDY_#1-1                             │
│                 File System ID: FAT32                                 │
│                       Signature: AA550000 Hex                         │
│ Sector 1                                                              │
│        Extended Boot Signature: 41615252 Hex                          │
│                       Reserved: (Unused)                              │
│              FSINFO Signature: 61417272 Hex                           │
│          Free Cluster Count: 1109838                                  │
│             Next Free Cluster: 171205                                 │
│                       Reserved: (Unused)                              │
│        FSINFO Ending Signature: AA550000 Hex                          │
│ Sector 2                                                              │
│                        Reserved: (Unused)                             │
│                       Signature: AA550000 Hex                       ↓ │
│ ─  Boot Record                                         Sector 0       │
│    Drive C:                                     Offset 3, hex 3        │
└─────────────────────────────────────────────────────────────────────┘
```

Note: One of the numbers in the BPB that often confuses people is the number of reserved sectors. This is the number of sectors at the beginning of this logical volume reserved for the boot program.

For all versions of Windows prior to the introduction of the FAT32 format for disks, the boot program was only one sector long. On those disks there's usually just one reserved sector (which contains the boot record). Rarely, if ever, will there be more than one, but the existence of this entry in the BPB shows that having more than one is a possibility, even if it never has been used.

With the OSR2 release of Windows 95 came a new way to format disks, called FAT32. Any disk formatted this way has a DOS boot record that takes up the first three sectors on the disk (or partition). It also usually stores a backup copy of that boot record (most often in the seventh through ninth sectors), and the format has been redesigned to allow for possible future extensions. For these reasons, on FAT32 disks you'll normally (but not always) find 32 reserved sectors.

The hidden sectors number might also seem strange. This is the number of sectors on the disk before the first logical volume.

The Data Area

The next area of the disk we'll look at is the last area in sequence, and by far the largest one. But until you understand this area's function and structure, the other two areas won't make much sense. The data area is where the OS stores your data. In fact, it includes all the space in the logical disk drive that isn't taken up in one of the system structures (the boot record, FAT, and root directory).

Sectors Versus Clusters on a Disk Drive

Your PC's hardware can only send data to, or retrieve it from, a disk one sector at a time. (Well, sometimes it can handle multiple, consecutive sectors in a single operation, but at the very lowest hardware level, the disk drive itself is only capable of handling individual sectors, neither more nor less.) Windows and other operating systems use logical sector numbers to address everything on the disk (including the system information in the boot record, FAT, and root directory). This numbering starts at zero (0) for the first logical sector (which, on a hard drive, contains the partition's boot record) in a physical disk drive.

Incidentally, don't confuse the operating system's logical sector numbers with the disk drive's logical block numbers. The difference is this: The disk drive tracks the logical block numbers for the entire drive. So this is ultimately the unit in which the BIOS must talk to the disk drive if it is using the LBA access strategy. (If it uses the fictitious geometry strategy, the BIOS uses a combination of three numbers, representing the cylinder, head, and sector (CHS) on that fictitious drive while the disk drive itself always uses the logical block number.)

An operating system, on the other hand, tracks the logical sector number within a partition (which is usually the same as a logical disk drive—in other words, something that gets its own drive letter). That partition takes up some portion of a disk, but not necessarily all the disk. Thus, an operating system's logical sector numbers and the drive's logical block numbers will be somewhat offset from one another. The only time the two are the same is on a floppy disk, or some other medium that is mimicking a floppy disk.

In the system areas of the drive—those reserved for the partition table, master boot record, and so on—the drive is capable of reading data one sector at a time. However, when it comes to keeping track of the files stored on the main or data portion of a disk, a different strategy is used.

This strategy entails using what is usually a considerably larger unit of data called a *cluster* or an *allocation unit*. A cluster is a collection of adjacent sectors of data (and the sectors do, in fact, contain successive blocks of data in a particular file). A cluster is the minimum amount of space that can be allocated to a file by the operating system—

whatever operating system it happens to be. Therefore, a file's data will use as many complete clusters as are needed to store the file. Consequently, if a cluster on a certain drive is 4KB, and a file's data is 3KB long, the file will still occupy a full 4KB cluster. The unused 1KB portion of the cluster is commonly referred to as *slack space*. If the file later grows to use this 1KB of space, it will fill the entire cluster. However, if the file later grows to 6KB, it will then require two full clusters—or 8KB, on our example disk—because it cannot share a partial cluster with another file.

So, in the Windows view, a logical disk drive consists of the system areas (boot record, FAT, and root directory) followed by some number of identical-size clusters into which it can store data. The purpose of the FAT and root directory is simply to hold the records that let Windows keep track of the information stored in the disk's data area clusters.

The File Allocation Table (FAT)

The *file allocation table* (FAT) is the principal structure by which Windows keeps track of what is using which portions of a logical disk. Every Windows logical disk drive (that is, each thing to which Windows assigns a drive letter designation) has a FAT. In fact, each such drive usually has two copies of that FAT. All FAT12 and FAT16 disks have two copies of the FAT. Most FAT32 disks also have two copies, but they are used somewhat differently and it's permissible to have only one or more than two of them.

Having two copies of the FAT protects you against certain types of problems that might lead to data loss. Every time Windows must access a file on a FAT12 or FAT16 disk, it checks the entries in the first FAT to see where to go. If it's writing data onto the disk, it updates both the first FAT and the second FAT.

However, if Windows gets an error reading the first FAT, it will automatically try to get the information it needs from the second FAT. Because it never reads the second FAT until it really needs it, Windows might not notice if the second FAT is damaged until it's too late to do anything about it.

The only ways you can learn about a problem with reading or writing the first FAT is if there's also an error in reading the second FAT—in which case the problems are very serious and you might well never recover your data—or if you run a utility such as Microsoft ScanDisk or Norton Disk Doctor to diagnose disk problems.

If there are any problems with reading either FAT, or if they aren't identical, the program will alert you to this problem. Depending on which tool you use—and assuming that only one of the FATs has been corrupted—you might be able to repair the FAT with the incorrect contents and thus make the two copies identical (and correct) once more.

It is prudent to check for problems on your disk drives on a regular basis, and Windows allows you to do this automatically at intervals you establish. If problems are fixed shortly after they occur, your data might never be endangered. If you never check for trouble, you still might not be totally out of luck—but it will require a lot of time and some skill using a tool like Norton Disk Editor to try to recover your data.

This story is slightly altered for FAT32 disks. Although normally things work exactly as described, it is possible for a program to change some values in the BPB inside the boot record, and thereby change how the FATs are used on that disk. (There is no major piece of software that works in the way you're about to read, but the capability exists, nevertheless.)

One change that is possible is to designate a different one of the FATs from the first one as the *primary* or *active* one, which then is the one that's used for all file accesses as long as that FAT is readable. Another change is to turn off mirroring of the FATs. If you do this, all updates to the FAT will be written only to the primary FAT.

These additional possibilities were included to help deal with damaged disks. By default these new features are turned off and two FATs are treated exactly like the FATs on a FAT12 or FAT16 disk.

But if a problem develops with the first (and therefore, by default, the primary) FAT, mirroring can be turned off and the system can be directed to use just the other FAT. A utility program that utilized these features might permit one to recover the data from such a disk quite easily in situations that otherwise would present major difficulties for data recovery. Then, after you have copied all the valuable data, the disk could simply be reformatted. That will usually fix the problems and you can then resume using the disk normally.

The FAT is simply a huge table of numbers, each of which, in most cases, is simply the address of another cluster. These address numbers are assigned consecutively, starting at 2 as the address number for the first cluster after the root directory on a FAT12 or FAT16 disk, and for the first cluster after the last FAT on a FAT32 disk. The FAT has an entry for each cluster from that beginning point to the end of the disk, and inspecting their contents tells DOS or Windows the status of all those clusters.

On a FAT12 disk each of these clusternumbers is twelve bits (one and one-half bytes) long. On a FAT16 disk they are each sixteen bits (two bytes) long. On a FAT32 disk they are each thirty two (four bytes) long. This means that on a FAT12 disk (a floppy disk), each three bytes in the FAT holds two cluster numbers. That can make reading them from a hexadecimal display of the disk contents (such as when using DEBUG) quite challenging. Fortunately, the Norton Disk Editor displays them as decimal values, each cleanly separated from its neighbors, no matter which format (FAT12, FAT16, or FAT32) is used.

The number contained in each location in the FAT normally is the address of another cluster, and it is this linkage that lets DOS or Windows find all the pieces of a file stored on the disk. But the number stored in a cluster location can also have one of several special values. If the value is 0, the cluster is currently unused and available. An End of File (EOF) value means that this cluster is in use, and the file using it has either all or the last portion of its information stored here. A third special number signals to DOS that this cluster is bad—meaning it cannot safely be used to store information. Any other number in the FAT is a signal that the cluster is in use, storing information from a file, and that the information for that file continues in another cluster—specifically the one whose address number is stored at this location in the FAT. (On a FAT32 disk, the bad cluster number is 0FFFFFF7h, but that number can also be used as a valid cluster number in a cluster chain. The only ways to tell for sure whether a cluster with this value is bad are these: First, if there is some other cluster entry in this FAT that points to this one, this is not a bad cluster. Second, if this number is too large for the size of this disk, it must be a bad cluster.)

Figure 18.5 shows a portion of a FAT table with some typical values in it. (This display is another screen capture from Norton Disk Editor and it also was taken from the FAT32 formatted C drive on our example desktop system.)

FIGURE 18.5

A portion of a typical FAT—one showing high levels of file fragmentation— is displayed by the Norton Disk Editor program.

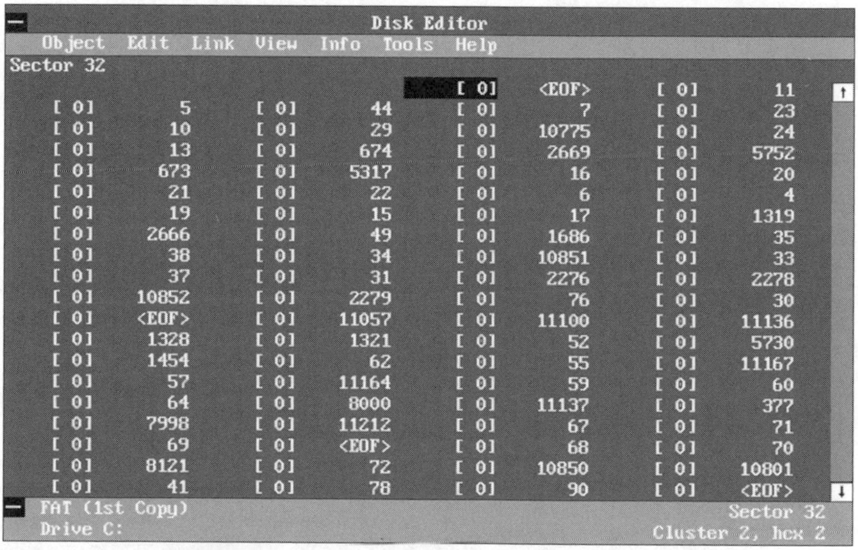

Here you see two numbers for each entry in the FAT. The first number (which is always a zero in this figure) is enclosed in square brackets. This is the high-order portion of the cluster contents. The low order portion is to the right of that, not enclosed in brackets.

The black highlight surrounding the first entry in brackets shows that we are now looking at the most significant half of the very first cluster number in the FAT. The information at the bottom of the screen shows that we are looking at the first copy of the FAT table, and in particular, at cluster number 2, which is the address of the first entry in that table. From Figure 18.4 you can see that this is the root directory for this disk, and from the fact that <EOF> appears in the rest of this cluster entry (just to the right of the highlight) you can see that the root directory for this disk is, so far, limited to a single cluster.

The fact that the root directory appears in the FAT as just another file is one of the major differences between a FAT32 formatted disk and FAT12 or FAT16 formatted disks. On a FAT32 disk, if the area that would normally be used for the root directory gets damaged, it is possible to relocate the root directory to some undamaged area. Of perhaps more importance, there is now no harsh limit on the size of the root directory. This is in stark contrast to the situation on all FAT12 and FAT16 disks, whereby the root directory size must be specified when it is formatted, and is usually held to a rather small number (commonly 512 filename or folder entries, or fewer). This number is further reduced if you use long filenames, as each long filename uses up multiple directory entries.

You might have wondered why the first line of numbers starts in the middle. The blank region at the left represents where you would find the cluster values for cluster addresses zero and one—but because there are no such clusters, this region is blank.

Technical Note: Why do cluster numbers start at two? The more usual choice for counting is to start at one or—if you are a mathematician or computer engineer—perhaps at zero. We can't start at zero, because the entry value must point to a cluster address, and zero is disallowed, because a zero entry value for a cluster means that cluster is available for data storage. But we could start with one. Why not do so?

The answer is that DOS wants to see a very special signature byte at the beginning of a FAT to let it know that this is a FAT, and what kind of FAT it is. The designers of DOS decided to use the first two cluster-entry-sized places in the FAT for this purpose. (If the cluster entry size is 1 1/2 bytes, they add a hexadecimal value FFFFh to the end of the signature byte. If the cluster entries each occupy 2 full bytes, the signature byte is augmented by FFFFFFh, and for four-byte cluster entries the first two cluster locations are filled with the signature byte plus FFFFFFFFFFFFFFh.) Now, when you multiply the cluster address value by the cluster size, you get the position within the FAT where that cluster's entry starts.

If you now turn your attention back to the entry in Figure 18.5 for cluster number three, you can begin to trace out the spaces on this disk used by a particular file. In this case the number in cluster 3's location in the FAT is 11. That means that the file that starts in cluster number 3 continues in cluster number 11. Checking the table, you will see that in cluster number 11 (two lines below cluster number 3) is the value 24. Thus the file goes on from here in cluster 24. If you continue this process you can determine that this file has its data spread over thirteen clusters in this order: 3-11-24-19-20-21-22-6-7-23-4-5-44. Looking at which groups of these numbers are in numerical order, you can also see that the file is broken into eight fragments (3, 11, 24, 19-20-21-22, 6-7, 23, 4-5, and 44).

Another file you can trace out in its entirety in Figure 18.5 starts in cluster number 66 (third column, fourth entry from the bottom). This file is spread over six clusters (comprising four fragments) in this order: 66-67-71-70-68-69. All the other files represented by entries in this figure are only partially contained in the first 80 clusters, which is all you can see represented here.

If your head seemed to spin while you were reading the last couple of paragraphs, be assured that the disk drive's heads also have to do quite a dance when they are asked to retrieve fragmented files like those shown here—a severely fragmented hard disk can force the drive head to zip back and forth repeatedly to read or write a file. Head movements use a comparatively huge amount of time, and a badly fragmented disk will definitely reduce your system's performance.

How Big Is Your PC's FAT?

We said that there are three kinds of FAT (FAT12, FAT16, and FAT32) supported by Windows and its predecessors. What we haven't told you yet is how Windows decides which kind to use on a specific disk, and how large those disks and their FATs can be.

The Original FAT12

The original DOS FATs used 12-bit numbers for each cluster entry, and Windows still uses 12-bit FATs for all floppy disks. (This is crucial, for it lets you read very old floppies that have data stored on them from the early days of DOS.) Furthermore, Windows also uses 12-bit FATs for any hard disk volume of less than 16MB.

A number with 12 bits suffices for storing values from zero to 4095. Several of these values are reserved, so all cluster addresses must be in the range from 2 to 4086. If Windows tried to keep track of every sector of data individually, this limit would mean that it could manage data only on a disk whose data capacity was quite small. You can get the actual value by multiplying 512 bytes (the amount in one sector) by 4085 (the maximum number of clusters)—and the answer comes out to be just a little more than 2MB. That's larger than most floppy disks, but a lot smaller than any hard disk.

So, Windows can keep track of every single sector of data on a floppy disk. But on a hard disk it must clump the data together into larger blocks (clusters). For simplicity, on hard disks of any size up to about 16MB capacity, Windows uses a cluster size of 4KB (eight sectors per cluster). Notice that 16MB is about the largest disk that Windows can track with 12-bit FAT entries and this size of cluster. That was fine when hard disks were commonly no larger than 16MB. Now, with hard disk capacity measured in GB, this strategy would mean using ridiculously large clusters.

Upping the Ante: FAT16

Starting around DOS version 3, a second style of FAT was introduced. (The exact point in the development of DOS varied with the many clone-specific versions introduced around that time.) These FATs use 16-bit numbers for cluster entries. For any disk volume that can hold more than 16MB—but less than 2GB—of data, Windows used 16-bit FATs.

The Windows designers decided to use clusters with at least four sectors in them (thus, a cluster size of at least 2KB) for all FAT16 hard disks. That size suffices for any hard disk with less than a 128MB total capacity. After that, every time the total capacity doubles, Windows doubles the cluster size. The largest logical disk drives that Windows can handle comfortably have capacities of up to 2GB. For such a large volume, the cluster size is 32KB. That means that even if a file contains only a single byte of data, writing it to the disk uses one entire 32KB region of the disk, making that area unavailable for any other file's data storage.

Non-FAT Windows: NTFS

The ever-increasing size of hard disks has caused PC operating system designers to face the limits imposed by the 16-bit FAT structure. A solution was introduced by Microsoft with the Windows NT File System (NTFS). It performs FAT-like tasks in completely new ways.

Unfortunately, disks formatted with the NTFS file system are largely inaccessible to DOS or Windows 9x/ME programs. Microsoft's latest version of Windows, Windows XP, is the first to bridge this gap in any convenient fashion. It's always been possible for NTFS and FAT volumes to exist in different partitions of the same physical hard drive. However, if you boot into Windows Me, or any earlier version of Windows, the data on the NTFS partition is inaccessible. In fact, those versions of Windows won't even recognize that the NTFS volume exists.

Under Windows XP, NTFS and FAT32 can co-exist rather nicely. And that's a good thing, because Microsoft has intentionally crippled the FAT32 file system under Windows XP. In every version of Windows prior to XP, the FAT32 system can support a single drive of up to 2TB (two terabytes, or 2,000 gigabytes). Under Windows XP, FAT32 will only support a drive size of up to 8GB. Although you won't encounter a 2TB drive any time soon, most PC's today come with drives of 50GB or more. This artificial restriction—and we call it artificial because the only reason it exists is to "encourage" people to use NTFS— is a tremendous inconvenience. If you use Windows XP and you don't want to use NTFS, you need to partition your drive into what today could be called tiny 8GB chunks. Why wouldn't you want to use NTFS? You might be dual-booting into a previous version of Windows to use a piece of legacy software or hardware that XP doesn't support. More fundamentally, you might just not like having someone else make such a fundamental decision about your PC.

On the other hand, NTFS provides features available from no other Windows file system. File-system-level security—practically non-existent under any of the FAT file systems— is a central feature of NTFS. Access to volumes, folders, or files can be controlled on a logon-password basis. You can automatically encrypt and decrypt individual files or entire folders or volumes, too. NTFS is generally held to perform better than the FAT systems. There are two reasons for this. First, an NTFS volume's directory is stored in the middle of the volume, which makes for more efficient access. (The read/write heads need to move less than they do if the directory is all at the start of the disk.) Second,

NTFS tends not to need defragmenting. That keeps file access as fast as possible, and also eliminates the time (usually hours) it takes to run a defragmenting utility and optimize a large FAT volume. If you're using your PC for any kind of server, NTFS is your only Windows-based choice.

FAT32

The most recent solution to these large-disk problems was introduced by Microsoft in its OSR2 release of Windows 95—and it is named FAT32. As the name suggests, FAT32 is pretty much like the earlier 12-bit and 16-bit FAT structures, expanded to accommodate larger cluster entry values (each using 32 bits, or 4 bytes, of space in the FAT) and with many new features (some of which were described previously) that make this quite an exciting new way to format disks. Windows 2000 also supports FAT32, although Windows NT 4.0 did not. Linux, too, can be installed on a FAT32-formatted disk.

The minimum size for a FAT32 volume is 512MB. What about the maximum size? Before you start calculating, you need to know that Microsoft has reserved the top four bits of every cluster number in a FAT32 file allocation table. That means that there are only 28 bits for the cluster number, so the maximum cluster number possible is 268,435,456.

If you work it out, this means that a FAT32 FAT table can, itself, grow to a maximum size of 1GB and at that size it contains just barely enough entries to represent all the locations on a 2048GB hard disk—assuming that standard sector size of 512 bytes. That is, for now, the maximum size disk volume (single drive letter) that you can have on a PC.

The Root Directory

The final part of the system area on a Windows logical disk drive is the *root directory*. The root directory is a part of the system area for FAT12 and FAT16 disks, but not for a FAT32-formatted disk. As noted previously, a FAT32 disk treats the root directory just like a subdirectory (with some minor exceptions).

The root directory serves much the same purpose for file access on a disk as the directory board that you can find in the lobby of most large office buildings for locating offices. The directory board tells you the office number to use to enter a specific set of offices. It doesn't mean that this room is the only one that a company uses, but that this is the company's reception area or entry point. Similarly, the root directory entries in a Windows file system point to the beginnings of several files. In addition to those pointers, the root directory entries also hold the names of those files, their sizes, and some additional information about them.

What the root directory doesn't do is tell you the details about all the places on this disk drive where a given file's information are stored. That is the purpose of the FAT. There can be several kinds of entries in a directory. We'll describe all of them in a moment, but we want first to focus on one special kind: the subdirectory.

Subdirectories

Large hard disks hold lots of files—far too many to keep track of sensibly if all their names were listed in a single place. The designers of Windows/DOS allowed for this by including (starting with DOS version 3) the notion of subdirectories. These are files that are pointed to by entries in the root directory (or in some other subdirectory), but their contents are treated as an additional file directory listing.

In almost all respects, the contents of these subdirectory files have a form that's identical to that of the contents of the root directory. But there are a few key differences. One difference is that only the root directory can have an entry for the logical volume's name (the volume label entry). Another is that every subdirectory (other than the root directory under FAT32) contains two special pseudo-directory entries.

The names of these pseudo-directory entries are very odd. One has the name "."—by which we mean its full name is simply a single period. The other has the name ".."—two periods. The single-period entry is a synonym for the subdirectory in which it's found. The double-period entry is a pointer to the directory (root or sub-) that is the parent of this directory. That is, the directory that contains an entry pointing to the file whose contents are this subdirectory. Figure 18.6 shows this relationship. Shown here in the root directory is a volume label (whose starting cluster number has the unreal value of zero) and one subdirectory entry (SUBDIR1). On the right you see a portion of the contents of SUBDIR1, including its two special pseudo-directory names and another subdirectory entry (SUBDIR2). Finally, you see that SUBDIR2 also contains a similar set of two pseudo-directory entries. The arrows show you where each directory entry points—that is, it indicates where each of the starting cluster numbers shown in this figure actually points.

The Different Types of Windows Directory Entries and What They Contain

Regardless of how you view the contents of a Windows directory, you aren't seeing all of what's contained in those directory entries. And you certainly aren't seeing how that information is arranged.

The information in a subdirectory is stored in exactly the same format as is used in the root directory. Figure 18.7 shows a subdirectory's contents using the DOS DIR command, but using a command prompt in a DOS window within Windows (what used to be called a *DOS box*, and now is just "the command line"). This figure shows the contents of a full-screen DOS box directory command in a special subdirectory on our G drive.

The directory listing in Figure 18.7 shows the names of the files and subdirectories in this directory (including the two, special pseudo-directory entries with the names "." and "..") and a size for each item, plus a time and date on which it was last modified.

Notice that no size is shown for the directory entries. Subdirectories are files and they each have some length, but that length just isn't shown here. You can determine their lengths by looking in the FAT to see how many clusters each directory occupies.

Root Directory
Name and Ext.
Other Info.
Starting Cluster
MYVOL
0
SUBDIR1
17
Subdirectory Named SUBDIR1 stored in cluster 17
Name and Ext.
Other Info.
Starting Cluster
.
17
..
0
SUBDIR2
45
Subdirectory Named SUBDIR2 stored in cluster 45
Name and Ext.
Other Info.
Starting Cluster
.
45
..
17
Every subdirectory is pointed to by its parent directory, by itself and by each of its children (which are the sudirectories pointed to by entries in this subdirectory)..

FIGURE 18.6
How subdirectories point to their parents and to their children.

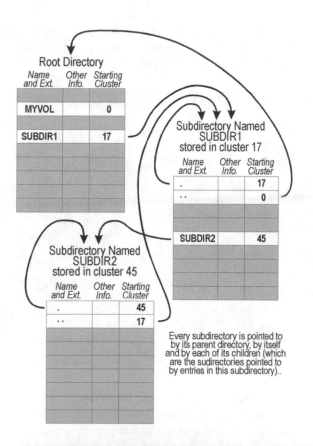

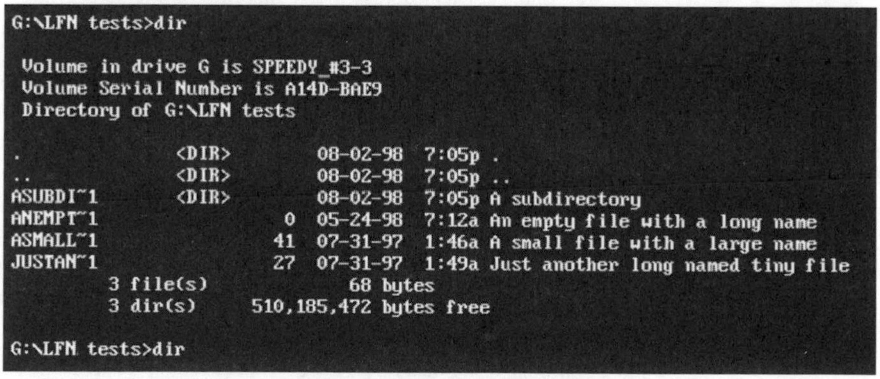

G:\LFN tests>dir
Volume in drive G is SPEEDY_#3-3
Volume Serial Number is A14D-BAE9
Directory of G:\LFN tests
.   <DIR>   08-02-98 7:05p .
..   <DIR>   08-02-98 7:05p ..
ASUBDI~1   <DIR>   08-02-98 7:05p A subdirectory
ANEMPT~1   0 05-24-98 7:12a An empty file with a long name
ASMALL~1   41 07-31-97 1:46a A small file with a large name
JUSTAN~1   27 07-31-97 1:49a Just another long named tiny file
3 file(s)   68 bytes
3 dir(s)   510,185,472 bytes free
G:\LFN tests>dir

FIGURE 18.7
The DOS DIR *command issued inside a DOS window also shows the long filenames (in the right column), but still much information is invisible. The same* DIR *command issued in real-mode DOS (in MS-DOS mode) on this disk would show everything exactly as it is here except for the long filenames.*

Figure 18.8 shows the same subdirectory shown in Figure 18.7, but this time you see its contents displayed in as human-readable a form as possible. This is the default way that Norton Disk Editor shows directory listings.

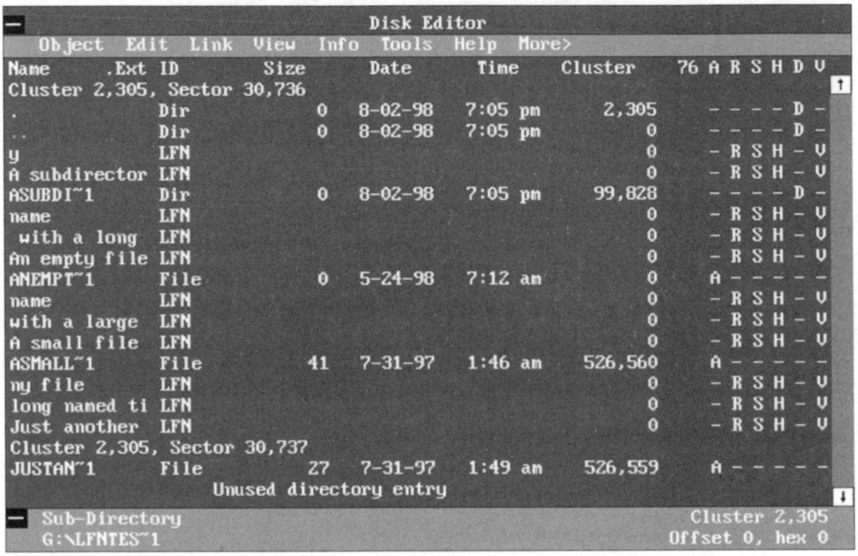

FIGURE 18.8

Norton Disk Editor can display the information in this same subdirectory in a readily human-readable form.

Name	.Ext	ID	Size	Date	Time	Cluster	76	A	R	S	H	D	V
Disk Editor													
Object Edit Link View Info Tools Help More>													
Cluster 2,305, Sector 30,736													
.		Dir	0	8-02-98	7:05 pm	2,305		-	-	-	-	D	-
..		Dir	0	8-02-98	7:05 pm	0		-	-	-	-	D	-
y		LFN				0		-	R	S	H	-	V
A subdirector		LFN				0		-	R	S	H	-	V
ASUBDI~1		Dir	0	8-02-98	7:05 pm	99,828		-	-	-	-	D	-
name		LFN				0		-	R	S	H	-	V
with a long		LFN				0		-	R	S	H	-	V
An empty file		LFN				0		-	R	S	H	-	V
ANEMPT~1		File	0	5-24-98	7:12 am	0		A	-	-	-	-	-
name		LFN				0		-	R	S	H	-	V
with a large		LFN				0		-	R	S	H	-	V
A small file		LFN				0		-	R	S	H	-	V
ASMALL~1		File	41	7-31-97	1:46 am	526,560		A	-	-	-	-	-
my file		LFN				0		-	R	S	H	-	V
long named ti		LFN				0		-	R	S	H	-	V
Just another		LFN				0		-	R	S	H	-	V
Cluster 2,305, Sector 30,737													
JUSTAN~1		File	27	7-31-97	1:49 am	526,559		A	-	-	-	-	-
Unused directory entry													

Sub-Directory   Cluster 2,305
G:\LFNTES~1   Offset 0, hex 0

Here you can see that the directory entry contains more than just the name and extension, the file size, and the date and time of last modification that you saw in the DIR listing. In particular, the NDE display shows that each directory entry also contains some file attributes and a cluster address where this file's contents begin on the disk. In fact, because these are FAT32 format directory entries, they have even more information in them than is shown here. The More> you see on the menu bar at the top of the figure shows how you access additional views of these directory entries from within NDE. We'll tell you in a moment the rest of what these directory entries specify about the files they represent.

Notice that the entry with a single period as its name points to cluster 2,305, and that this directory entry is in cluster 2,305. Also notice that the entry with the double period as its name points to cluster number 0. In reality there is no such cluster, but this means that this directory's parent directory is in the root directory. For a FAT32 disk (such as this one), the root directory is located in an addressable cluster (in this example, and most commonly, in cluster 2). However, because on a FAT12 or FAT16 disk the root directory is not in any numbered cluster, the designers of DOS decided to show the root directory location as cluster zero in all of the different FAT disk formats.

Also notice that here the size of the subdirectories are all shown as zero. The explanation for this is the same as for the missing lengths in Figure 18.7. The actual lengths of the subdirectory files simply aren't recorded in these directory entries. The DIR command omits showing any value; NDE shows it as a zero value.

Directory Entry Structure and File Attributes

Now you've seen a subdirectory in different ways, and it's time to look at the contents of a single entry in detail. Each entry in the root directory, and each entry in any subdirectory, is exactly 32 bytes long in all three FAT formats. Some of those entries hold filenames and information Windows needs to find that file's content, plus other information about the file. Some entries hold similar information about subdirectories. And some entries serve other purposes, including storing pieces of the long filename that belongs to a file pointed to by some other entry in this directory. We will explain first the entries that point to files and then those for long filenames. Figure 18.9 shows schematically the three variations on what a directory entry can hold, depending on which FAT system is in use, and on whether the entry is for a *short filename* (SFN) or a *long filename* (LFN).

The top chart in Figure 18.9 shows all the fields in a short filename directory entry on a FAT12 or a FAT16 formatted disk. The next chart shows the same information for a FAT32 formatted disk. Below that are charts showing the bit-by-bit details of how the file attributes are stored as well as how the date and time entries are stored. At the bottom is a chart showing how a long filename entry is stored. This format is identical for all three versions of the FAT file. Below each of the charts you see numbers running from zero to 31. These are the byte-offset values indicating how far into the directory entry a given field is found. This shows that the locations closest to the start of the disk are at the left in this figure.

Short Filenames in the FAT12, FAT16, and FAT32 Disk Formats

The first 11 bytes of this type of Windows directory entry are used to store the *short filename* (SFN) of the file to which this entry points. This SFN used to be called simply *the* filename before DOS and Windows were given the capability of handling long filenames.

Each SFN is broken up by Windows into two parts. The first eight bytes hold eight characters (letters, numerals, or certain symbols) that form the name. The next three bytes hold a three-character extension of that name. The Windows file-naming rules require the name to have at least one non-space character, and they permit a maximum of eight characters. If the name is fewer than eight characters long, it is padded with space characters to fill out the eight locations in the directory entry. Similarly, the extension can have anywhere from zero to three characters. The remaining locations in the directory entry are simply filled with space characters. Because all the 11 spaces are accounted for, there's no need to show the period that one conventionally types between the filename and the extension. It is merely implied in the directory entry.

FIGURE 18.9

The three forms of a directory entry on a Windows FAT disk.

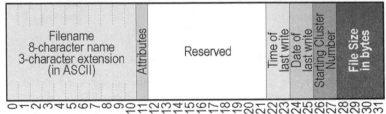

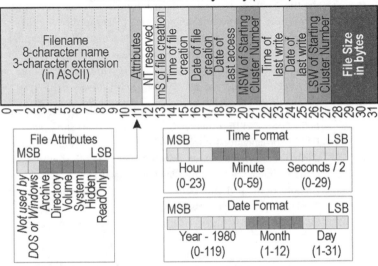

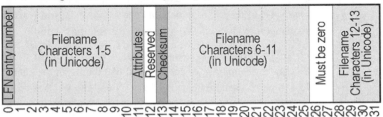

The 12th byte in the directory entry stores the file attributes. Of these eight bits, Windows uses six. The Windows attributes include:

- *Archive attribute (A)*—Indicates a file that has been opened by a program in a fashion that enabled the program to change the file's contents. Windows sets this archive bit to ON when the file is opened. Backup programs frequently turn it OFF when they back up the file. If you use this strategy, only the files with this bit ON must be a part of your next incremental backup.

- *Directory attribute (D)*—Indicates that this directory entry points to a subdirectory rather than to a file.

- *Volume attribute (V)*—Used on just one directory entry in the root directory. That one holds the name of this disk volume. (This attribute also is used with long filenames, as you will learn in the next section.)

- *System attribute (S)*—Indicates a file that is a part of the operating system (Windows) or it can be a file that has been flagged in this manner by an application program (for example, this is often done as a part of a copy-protection scheme).

- *Hidden attribute (H)*—These files (and those with the S bit set ON) are not to be displayed in a normal DIR listing.

- *Read-only attribute (R)*—Indicates to Windows that this file is not to be modified. Of course, because this is only a bit in a byte stored on the disk, any program could change this bit, and then Windows will freely let it modify this file. This is mostly used to protect against human error—that is, to help keep you from inadvertently erasing or altering key files.

Notice that having a file labeled with one or more of these attributes can make perfect sense. For example, most files that are tagged as system files are also tagged with the hidden and read-only flags. But it makes less sense (or so it would seem) to make the volume label have any other attributes, except perhaps the read-only attribute. In fact, just such an implausible combination of attributes (RSHV) is used by Windows to flag directory entries that are part of a long filename.

On a FAT12 or FAT16 disk the next 10 bytes are unused. They ordinarily will be filled with zeros, and they are considered reserved values. On a FAT32 disk these 10 bytes hold a variety of information about the file. The byte marked NT reserved is, as the name suggests, a field not used in Windows 9x or Me, but that is used by Windows 2000.

For compatibility reasons the fields that occur in FAT12 or FAT16 short filename directory entries are also found in the same places in the FAT32 short filename directory entries. The remaining fields that only occur in FAT32 short filename directory entries fall within what was a 10-byte-long reserved region in FAT12 and FAT16 short filename directory entries.

The fields labeled LSW of Starting Cluster Number and MSW of Starting Cluster Number contain the least significant word and the most significant word of the double-word (four byte) cluster number that is required to point to a location on a FAT32 formatted disk volume.

The byte at offset 13 (the 14th byte in the directory entry) holds what Microsoft calls the "millisecond stamp at file creation time." It can be used to determine to a rather high degree of accuracy which of two versions of a file were created first. The other time fields only hold the time to an accuracy of two seconds, as is shown in the Time Format details chart in Figure 18.9. The time and date formats are referred to as *packed binary* because in each case they fit several binary numbers into a single sixteen-bit location, simply putting each of those binary numbers into a specified group of adjacent bit locations within that sixteen-bit word.

The last four bytes of each directory entry hold a 32-bit binary number that indicates how long this file is in bytes. That would seem to suggest that Windows can handle files that are up to 4GB long.

On a FAT32-formatted disk you can actually have individual files with sizes up to just four bytes fewer than 4GB. Further, because the maximum disk size is 2048GB, you can even have a lot of these maximum size files on a single disk.

On a FAT12-formatted disk, in contrast, the total disk size is limited to around 16MB maximum total disk capacity, and some of it must be used for the boot sector, FATs, and root directory that constitute the disk's system area. Clearly the maximum size of any one file is somewhat less than 16MB.

Similarly, a FAT16 formatted logical drive cannot be any larger than 2GB, so the maximum size for any one file is somewhat less than that. And you cannot have more than one nearly maximum size file on such a disk.

In addition to the directory entries that point to files and those that point to subdirectories, there can be just one directory entry, and only in the root directory, of the third type: a volume label. In this directory entry, the name is used as the volume name (without a period inserted between the eighth and ninth characters, as is done for filenames and subdirectory names). The rest of the fields in this entry are not used.

Starting with Windows 95, there is a fourth kind of directory entry. This is one that holds a portion of a long filename.

How Long Filenames Have Altered Things

Before Windows 95, both DOS and Windows 3.x limited all filenames to the old *8.3 standard*. That is, they could have up to eight characters in the filename itself, plus up to three characters for the extension. Windows 95, in contrast, finally allowed filenames to be anything you like, up to 255 characters long. This file-naming scheme was first introduced in Windows NT, version 3.1, for NTFS disk volumes and in Windows NT, version 3.5, for FAT volumes. The Windows 9x implementation of long filenames is essentially identical to the one used with FAT volumes in Windows NT, version 3.5 or greater.

The old DOS standard lets you use only uppercase letters, A–Z, numerals, 0–9, and any of the following symbols:

$ % ' - _ @ ~ ` ! ( ) { } ^# &

Any time you entered a lowercase letter in a filename, DOS would simply convert it to uppercase. It was possible to use a space within a DOS filename or extension (as well as at the end of the name or at the end of the extension), but many DOS programs were unable to deal with the resulting filename appropriately. (Certain other ASCII and extended ASCII characters can also be used without causing DOS any problems, but many programs fail to recognize those names and might do unpredictable things to the corresponding files. Understandably, Microsoft recommends against trying these tricks with filenames.)

The new standard for long filenames adds the following symbols to the list of allowable characters:

+ , ; = [ ]

Furthermore, in a long filename you are allowed to mix upper- and lowercase letters freely, embed spaces wherever you like, and use as many periods as you like. (It is important that you realize, however, that when Windows looks at those long filenames it ignores case in deciding whether this filename matches some other filename.)

Windows became capable of working with long filenames by a rather clever strategy. For every file with a long name (LFN), it automatically creates an alias, which is also called the generated short filename (SFN). That short filename conforms to the old DOS file-naming rules, with the additional constraint that it cannot contain any embedded space characters.

Then, when Windows is creating that file, it makes a principal directory entry for that file whose name field is filled with this generated short name. That directory entry is preceded by one or more special directory entries that hold pieces of the long filename.

Each 32-byte LFN directory entry can hold at most 13 characters of the long filename. This is because those entries store the filename in a 2-byte Unicode format, and because some of the 32 bytes are used for other purposes. (You can read more about Unicode back in Chapter 4).

The first byte of the directory entry includes a number that counts the pieces of this particular long filename. (That is, the LFN directory entry that comes just before the SFN entry carries a value of 1 in this location.) The last entry for each LFN has the ordinal number you would expect (one more than the one just below it), but with 128 added to its value. (This just means the most significant bit is set to 1 instead of 0.) Windows 9x uses this fact to help it find the end of a LFN.

The attribute byte in an LFN entry (the 12th byte in the directory entry) now holds the special combination of attributes RSHV, and the 13th byte (now called the *type* byte) always contains a 0. This last statement is true for now, but Microsoft has firmly declared that there will be other types of LFN in the future, for which this value will not be zero. So far they have not hinted at what those other types of LFN might be.

The 14th byte carries a checksum based upon the SFN. This is another tool Windows uses to help keep LFNs associated with the right SFN.

The 27th and 28th bytes of the directory entry in an SFN entry hold the starting cluster in the data area where this file's content is stored (or the least significant 16 bits of that starting cluster number on a FAT32 disk). In the LFN entries this field is always set to 0. All the remaining 26 bytes in the directory entry are used to store the LFN in Unicode, 2 bytes per character. This is the only place in the directory where you will see Unicode characters.

How Short Filenames Are Generated

You learned that Windows creates a short filename (SFN) alias for each file with a long filename (LFN). But how Windows does this isn't so obvious, and certainly can cause you some grief if you don't understand it.

If the file's long name is short enough that it fits in the old-style 8.3-naming scheme, Windows just uses that name as its SFN, changing any lowercase letters to uppercase in the process. If the name is longer, or if it includes spaces or multiple periods, the SFN gets more complex.

There absolutely must not be two files in the same directory with the same short filename or the same long filename. And in fact, there cannot be a short filename that matches a long filename in the same directory. If there were, Windows wouldn't know which one you meant to use when you wanted to access one of them. This rule forces Windows to do some pretty odd things with the SFNs.

Windows starts with the long filename. It first strips out the spaces, underscores what remains, and then uses the first eight characters of the name and three characters of the extension to form the SFN. For these purposes, if a name has only one period and that one is the very first character—which is a legal LFN—then Windows treats it as having a name with no extension. The SFN is, therefore, built from the first eight characters of the long filename after that initial period. If the filename has one or more periods after the first character position, Windows treats the long name after the last period as the extension, and forms the SFN extension from the first three characters of whatever follows that last period.

If the SFN it generates is not unique in this directory, Windows forces it to be by lopping off two or more of the final characters of the name and substituting a tilde character (~) followed by a one, two, or more digits number. The number chosen is as small as possible while forcing the SFN to be unique. So, for example, the long filename `Program File List.DOC` might have a corresponding SFN of `PROGRA~1.DOC`. `Letter to Mother on 10-11-01.DOC` might SFN as `LETTER~1.DOC`. (In this second example, you can see that if you have several letters to mother, and you name them all the same, except for the date, you would have difficulty telling the files apart if you did a directory listing of this disk using a DOS box.) All of the first nine long filenames in this directory are given short filenames of the form LETTER~*x*.DOC, where *x* is the number of LETTER files in the directory. If you have more than nine such files, subsequent SFNs appear as LETTE~*xx*.DOC, where *xx* is a two-digit number, and so on.

The most subtle, and in some ways most confusing, aspect of the way Windows generates short filenames is that it will not necessarily generate the same name for a given file in two different locations. So when you copy a file from one directory to another, its long filename will go across unchanged, but its short filename might change, depending on the other files in the target directory.

Following all these new rules requires Windows to do a lot more writing and rewriting of the directories. In the past, when a program altered one file, the operating system only needed to rewrite the one disk sector in which the directory entry for that file resided. Now it might have to rewrite the entire directory, depending on just what changes have been made to the file in question. Normally, however, once the directory has been created with its short and long filenames, any subsequent renaming that doesn't extend the length of the long filenames will very likely be accomplished with no more sectors needing to be written than was the case under earlier versions of DOS and Windows.

To see how bad this can get, consider what must happen the first time you access a floppy disk that was formatted and loaded with files on a computer that was using an earlier version of DOS or Windows that didn't support long filenames. If you do this you'll find that the disk drive does a lot of thrashing about as the directory gets converted to the long filename format. After this is finished you'll find approximately twice as many directory entries have been used (which could present a problem if the root directory were already close to full).

Similarly, many programs, such as word processors, open a temporary file, work in it, close it and after deleting the original file, and then rename the temporary file to the original file's name. That was pretty simple when each file involved only one directory entry. Now, if the file in question has a long filename, lots of entries might have to be rewritten, potentially involving more than a single cluster on the disk.

Sorting and Searching with Long Filenames

The somewhat arbitrary and variable SFNs associated with long filenames also lead to some oddities in sorting files or searching for them. The old DOS command DIR /O:N, for example, was supposed to list the files in a directory in alphabetical order. It does so, but it uses the short filenames in deciding what that order should be. This can, and often is, different from what you get when you look at the long filename.

And, a search for a wildcard name such as *1.* will match all files with a numeral one as the last non-space character in their short filename as well as any that have a numeral one followed by a period in their long filename. So you must be attentive to these and similar details if you want to understand why programs that search for short filenames under Windows 9x produce the results they do.

What Windows Does When You Delete a File

When you delete a file, Windows doesn't erase it from your hard disk. Instead, it does two simple things. First, it sets to 0 the value in all the cluster locations in the FAT that belong to that file. Second, it changes the very first entry in the (SFN) directory entry for this file from the ASCII value representing the letter, number, or symbol in the filename to the special value E5h. In decimal, this value is 229, and it is the extended ASCII value for the Greek lowercase sigma ([gs]) in the most commonly used code page.

These two steps tell Windows that this directory entry and those clusters in the data area are now available for reuse. But until they are reused, almost all the directory information and all the file's contents are still in place on your disk.

So, if only you could replace the first character of the filename, and then guess correctly which clusters used to belong to this file, you could make it appear once more. Starting with version 6, DOS let you set up *deletion sentry*.

Deletion sentry actually moves files you think you are deleting to a special, hidden directory. Then, if you want to undelete them, it simply moves them back. (Moving a file doesn't actually involve any moving of the file's contents. It just means creating a new directory entry in the target directory that points to the original file's chain of clusters, and then deleting the original directory entry.)

This is how the Windows Recycle Bin works. Any file you delete from within Windows will simply be moved into the Recycle Bin. Any file you delete from the command prompt is deleted in the manner described in the first paragraph of this section. But there is a downside to this strategy. It means that when you delete a file you aren't actually freeing up any space on your disk. To do that you must also empty the Recycle Bin.

> **Note:** The only time you are likely to have trouble undeleting a file is when you try to do it just after deleting a whole bunch of files, and then only if the file you want was fragmented. Or, of course, if you have written something else to the disk in the places formerly occupied by the file you want to undelete. You can make your computer run faster and also make it easier to undelete files whenever you want no matter what deletion protection strategy you're using (if any), simply by periodically defragmenting all the files on your hard disk.
>
> Windows includes a tool to do this called Disk Defragmenter. It's in the Accessories subdirectory of your Programs entry under the Start menu.

Hard Disks are Different from Floppies

You know very well that there are physical differences between floppy disks and hard disks. Hard disks have rigid platters and use feedback servomechanisms to position the read/write heads, which enables you to store data much more densely on them. Floppy disks protect data with a cyclical redundancy check (CRC) value; hard disks go an extra step and use error correction codes (ECC), enabling them to not only detect errors but also usually to correct those errors on-the-fly.

Now we'll cover the logical differences between floppy disks and hard disks as they are seen by the motherboard BIOS and Windows. All other disk-like devices are made to look either like floppies or like hard disks in these respects, so understanding these differences is quite important.

Master Boot Record and Partitions

The most important difference between a floppy disk and a hard disk, from the perspective of the boot process and how data storage is structured on that disk, is that the BIOS assumes all disks contain a single logical volume or logical disk drive. But the boot program the BIOS loads from the start of a hard disk is different from that on a floppy disk. On a hard disk, this boot record is not called the DOS boot record. Instead it is called the hard disk's Master Boot Record (MBR). This program "knows" that all PC hard disks are supposed to be divided into one, two, three, or four partitions. Each of those partitions can be a primary logical volume, a hidden partition, or an extended partition. Extended partitions are ones that can contain multiple logical volumes.

If you have more than one primary partition on a single hard disk, only one of them may be designated as "active" and the remaining ones will be hidden. There can be only one active partition and only one extended partition on a single, physical disk drive. (A *logical volume* simply means all of the storage space that is referred to by a single drive letter. This might be a fraction of one physical hard disk, or it can even be the aggregate of several hard disks in certain circumstances.)

It is possible for a partition to have zero size, but the MBR assumes they are all defined in a data table (called the *partition table*) located within itself, and it looks first for those definitions before it begins to use any of the volumes.

Figure 18.10 shows Norton Disk Editor's default view of an MBR, which is simply a display in human-readable form of the contents of its partition table. In this case, you see that only two of the four partitions have any size, but all four lines in the data table are present.

FIGURE 18.10

The partition table in the master boot record of the second physical disk in our example desktop PC, as shown by Norton Disk Editor.

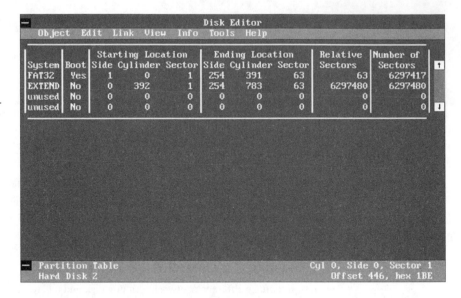

The first column in the following table shows you the type for each partition. This is stored in the actual table as single 8-bit number. Here are the possible values for the type numbers that Windows can understand, and the corresponding permissible sizes those partitions can have. The names listed for the partitions are Microsoft's; NDE uses slightly different names for these partitions types (DOS-12, DOS-16, EXTEND, BIG-DOS, FAT32, FAT32X BGDOSx, and EXTNDx, respectively) and NDE also recognizes many other type numbers that are used by other operating systems.

Partition Type Number	Partition Type	Permissible Size
01h	DOS primary partition 12-bit FAT (DOS2)	0 to 2MB
04h	DOS primary partition 16-bit FAT (DOS3)	32MB
05h	DOS-extended partition	Any size
06h	DOS primary partition 16-bit FAT (DOS4)	32MB up to 2GB
0Bh	DOS primary partition 32-bit FAT (DOS32)	512MB up to 2048GB
0Ch	DOS primary partition 32-bit FAT (DOS32X)	512MB up to 2048GB (Uses INT13h Extensions)
0Eh	DOS primary partition 16-bit FAT (DOSX13)	32MB up to 2GB (Uses INT13h Extensions)
0Fh	DOS extended partition (DOSX13X)	Any size

The partition table always shows the partition boundaries in terms of the cylinder, head, and sector numbers. Another newer strategy, particularly for drives larger than 2GB in size, assigns a unique, sequential number to every sector, ignoring the cylinder, head, and physical sector numbers. This creates what is, in this case—and for all disks for which you are accessing by use of the logical block address (LBA) strategy—an artificial "equivalent" of the actual disk drive. So it may well turn out that the start of a "cylinder" in this table has no relationship whatsoever to the actual beginning of a cylinder on the physical hard disk drive.

In the case represented by Figure 18.10, the disk is assumed to have 255 sides and 63 sectors per track. The maximum cylinder number then becomes whatever it must be to get the right total capacity. Partitions other than the first one always start at the beginning of a cylinder (side 0); the first partition always starts at cylinder 0, head 1, which leaves the entire first track (cylinder 0, head 0) for the MBR (and, in this case, 62 unused sectors). (An exception to this scheme is the somewhat specialized circumstance of logical partitions that exist inside an extended partition. In such a case, logical partitions begin on side 1, not size 0.)

This disk—the second physical drive on our system; used for temporary backups—has a total capacity of 6GB. You can see that from the total of the two numbers in the right column (which shows the number of sectors in each partition) multiplied by 512 bytes. Also, noticing that the two numbers in that column are about equal, you can see that half the disk has been allocated to a FAT32 partition, which makes this region a single logical disk drive (which is D: on this machine). The remainder of the disk has been allocated to an extended partition, which could potentially contain many logical disk drives.

The second column shows that only the first of the four partitions is flagged as *bootable* (a synonym for *active*). This is the partition in which the PC BIOS will look for a boot sector and operating system files to boot your PC. If you were to mark more than one of the four partitions as active, the MBR program wouldn't know which one you meant for it to use. (In fact, it would simply use the first one that was marked active and ignore the active mark on any other partition.) If you don't mark any of them as active, the MBR program won't attempt to boot the PC from this hard disk.

Most PC BIOSes can boot only from the first hard disk or from a floppy or, in some cases, from a CD-ROM. A major exception to this are PCs that use SCSI hard disks, either alone or in conjunction with IDE drives. In that case, a special BIOS on the SCSI host adapter can be enabled that allows the PC to boot from one of the SCSI devices. In the past, a PC that contained both IDE and SCSI drives most commonly could boot only from an IDE device or floppy—the PC's internal BIOS wouldn't give up control to the SCSI BIOS if it saw that any IDE hard drive was available. If none of the IDE drives was bootable and no system floppy disk was present, the PC would not boot at all. Today, most system BIOSes let the user select which of the IDE drives to boot from or whether to boot from a SCSI drive, if one is present.

For example, our example desktop system from Dell lets us choose the order in which we want to attempt to boot—with our choices being from a fixed disk, a removable disk, a CD-ROM drive, or from a network connection. Then, it lets us choose which of the selected class of devices will be the one it attempts to boot from when it tries that category of device.

Windows will allow you to create a single primary DOS partition only on a given physical hard drive. Third-party utilities can create additional primary partitions; however, all but one will be hidden. Other operating systems also can create primary partitions, but still only one primary partition can be active. An inactive partition will be totally inaccessible (until you change it to the active partition and reboot your PC).

Fortunately, Windows can also understand and access exactly one additional partition, of the type *DOS-extended*. (The name remains for historical reasons.) That partition can contain within it any number of logical disk volumes—limited only by the number of letters in the alphabet—which are in fact a kind of partition within a partition. Figure 18.11 illustrates this and shows how a hypothetical hard disk might be divided into three partitions, and how it might get a total of seven drive letters assigned to it by Windows. (This figure shows only the portions of the disk that are assigned each drive letter, or in the case of the first and last blocks, are reserved for the master boot record or for use by an operating system other than Windows. The details of how this subdivision can be accomplished are explained more fully in the next section.)

In Figure 18.11, the first partition is the primary partition. The second partition is the DOS extended partition that contains six logical disk drives. The third partition shown is a UNIX partition, which cannot be seen by Windows. If it is marked as bootable, the primary partition will disappear, and the PC will boot into UNIX. Some operating systems can see—and use—Windows partitions. Windows 2000, Linux, and some other versions of UNIX all have their own native file systems, but each of them has also been designed to work with most Windows partitions.

DOS-Extended Partition Tables

We said that you could divide a DOS-extended partition into multiple logical disk drives. How is this done? Simply by extending the notion of partitioning. Figure 18.11 shows another hypothetical disk, this time with just two partitions (one primary and one DOS-extended) and with only two logical drives within the DOS-extended partition.

The first sector in a DOS-extended partition is a special sector called an *extended partition table*. This is similar to the MBR with some significant differences. For example, there is no boot program in an extended partition table. Also, although its partition table has four entries (just like the table in the MBR), only the first few entries are used. The first entry describes a logical drive; the second one (if it is used) points to another extended partition table (still within the same DOS extended partition) in which an additional logical disk drive is defined.

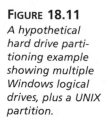

FIGURE **18.11**
A hypothetical hard drive partitioning example showing multiple Windows logical drives, plus a UNIX partition.

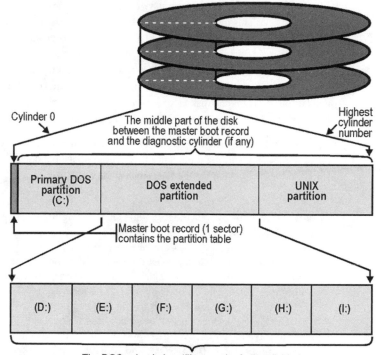

Cylinder 0

The middle part of the disk between the master boot record and the diagnostic cylinder (if any)

Highest cylinder number

| Primary DOS partition (C:) | DOS extended partition | UNIX partition |

Master boot record (1 sector) contains the partition table

| (D:) | (E:) | (F:) | (G:) | (H:) | (I:) |

The DOS extended partition may be further divided into logical drives (if this were your only hard disk, these would become, in this example, D: to I:)

Making Sense out of Chaos

Now you know how drives are physically and logically formatted, and how Windows organizes the data on them. But how are the drives, themselves, managed? What happens to the drive letters? These are serious questions with less-than-obvious answers. Fortunately, they are not difficult to answer.

How Windows Assigns Drive Letters

Floppy disk drives normally show up as drives A: and B:. This is unalterable in most PCs (although a few enable you to select which floppy will be A:). Hard disks and other disk drives get drive letters beginning with C:. Windows will assign C: to whatever drive it determines is going to be the boot device according to the specification in the BIOS. (That is, it will do this if that is anything other than a floppy disk drive.) If your BIOS doesn't have an option for boot device order, Windows will assign C: to the first hard disk it finds. As mentioned previously, because it looks first at the primary IDE or EIDE channel for a master device, that is where you ordinarily will want to put your main internal IDE or EIDE hard disk.

Windows will assign D: to the primary partition of the next physical hard disk, if it finds more than one. This includes both other hard drives on the IDE chains and SCSI hard disks. Windows keeps this up for as many physical hard disks with active (and thus, not hidden) primary partitions as it can find. Windows then assigns the next drive letter to the first logical drive inside any DOS-extended partition it finds on the first hard drive. The next letters go to any other logical disk drives in that same partition. Then Windows goes through the logical disk drives inside the DOS-extended partition on the second hard disk, and then on to the third hard disk, and so on.

Only after it has assigned drive letters to all the hard disk volumes it can find will Windows allow the assignment of a drive letter to any other disk-like devices. These include super-floppy drives that attach via the IDE chains, CD-ROM drives, and so on.

> **Note:** If you are using Windows, you can alter the drive letter assignments for any disk-like devices other than hard drives. Just go into the Device Manager tab in the System applet in Control Panel. Then click on the device whose drive letter you'd like to change, select Properties, and the Settings tab. There you'll see the current drive letter assignment and have the option of setting the lowest and highest letter you want Windows to use for this device the next time you boot. If you set those two letters to the same value, that will be the drive letter Windows will use. But it won't let you choose a drive letter that is currently assigned to a hard disk. We often find it helpful to use this feature to set the drive letter of our DVD, CD-ROM, and other such devices to something past the last hard disk we have installed. That way, if we want to install more hard drives, the optical drive letters won't change.

How Big Should Your C: Drive Be?

Many people wonder how large to make their C: drive and whether to create additional logical disk drives (logical volumes) on the first physical hard drive. Many PC vendors ship their products with just a single partition (that is C:) on the installed hard drive.

Keep several important considerations in mind when you are looking at this issue. None of them is a simple decision. You will have to make some judgment calls. This is okay because likely there are no really right (or wrong) answers.

First, having too many files and directories on one disk can make finding things much harder than necessary. If you partition your disk drives and put like files together in each partition or logical disk drive, they will have a level of organization one higher than the subdirectories off the root directory. You might think of this as putting file cabinets that contain material on different subjects or purposes into different rooms.

What about the option of making each volume very small and using a lot of volumes? This might be a good idea, but there are some drawbacks. First, remember that nearly every Windows application will put some data onto the drive that holds your Windows directory, even if you install the application to some other drive letter. Second, enlarging a logical volume after you realize you've made it too small can be tough. Be sure you allow enough room for growth in every volume, and especially in the one into which you install Windows. Additionally, you could easily end up running out of alphabet for your disk drives! Windows can assign letters only to a maximum of 26 drives, including the floppies that get A: and B:. (Adding even more pressure in this regard, if you want to map some network drives to local drive letters, you have to reserve some portion of the alphabet for that use.)

What about the opposite extreme? Suppose your files are, on the average, really large, so you don't worry much about cluster size. Can you make a single volume as large as you like? Earlier versions of Windows 95 would not work well with any volume over about 2GB, but today there is no such limitation.

RAID Systems—Sense and Sensibility

Redundant arrays of inexpensive (or independent) disks (RAID) is an idea for enhancing the reliability of a PC by having it store data on more than one disk, in a fashion that enables you to avoid or minimize downtime and the risk of data loss when one of those disks fails.

At least twelve levels of RAID are formally defined. They range in complexity and in the degree of safety they offer. The highest level stores data and ECCs across several disks in a way that enables you to replace any disk at any time with almost no chance of losing any of your data.

Some RAID implementations enable you to exchange, or *hot swap*, disk drives or power supplies whenever they seem about to fail or have failed, all without shutting off your PC system. This is especially critical for large companies that are running their mission-critical applications on such a PC.

Formerly RAID was used only on mainframe computers and large servers for networks because, despite the name, implementing RAID is more expensive than just buying a hard drive or set of hard drives with the same total capacity. Now, with hard drive prices plummeting, and with inexpensive RAID controllers available for desktop systems—and with some level of RAID support inherent in the latest versions of Microsoft Windows— it might be time to consider adding RAID to your desktop PC.

Optical Discs

Windows was originally designed to work only with floppy and hard magnetic disks. That means that it could not do *anything* with any optical discs. Fortunately, the designers of Windows included the possibility of *installable file systems*. Originally, they did this to support the use of networked drives as if they were local hard drives, but they also did this in order to allow possible future extensions of the types of (local) drives that might be attached to your PC.

When CD-ROMs came on the scene, Microsoft simply created another extension to Windows to support what are, in fact, rather differently formatted collections of files. CD-ROMs arrived with a format that was not like that of a magnetic disk. It also wasn't standardized across platforms or operating systems. Most CD-ROM titles originally worked either on a PC or on a Macintosh, but not both. (A large part of the reason for this was that the Macintosh supported long filenames, but DOS, at the time, was limited to one-to-eight-character names plus extensions of up to three characters—the so-called *8.3 file-naming convention.*)

Soon we began to see titles that had been made with two versions of the same material on the same disc so that these discs could be used on either a PC or a Mac. These hybrid discs stored the names of all the files in two ways: once in what was to become the ISO9660 format for PCs, and once in Hierarchical File System (HFS) format for Macs. Although this served the needs of CD creators for the moment, the industry realized that this nonsense couldn't be allowed to persist.

Romeo and Joliet Visit the High Sierra

A meeting ensued, held at a place high in the Sierra mountains. At this meeting, a compromise was reached and a new standard was born. Thereafter, CD-ROMs made to the new *High Sierra* standard worked with both PCs and Macs. This standard was later blessed with official status by the International Organization for Standardization (ISO) as ISO9660. This standard worked well for several years. Then CDs started to change, with the introduction of Photo-CDs, CD-R, and then CD-RW. The standard needed to grow along with the times.

Even before we had these new types of CDs, there were folks who were unhappy with the ISO9660 limitations on CD formats. In particular, the strict ISO9660 format includes a limitation on the filenames to something very much like what ancient versions of DOS supported. In particular, ISO9660 specifies all filenames have no more than eight characters and no more than three in the associated file extension. It even proscribes use of some of the characters that were allowed in old-style DOS filenames.

UNIX users wanted a way to record CDs with UNIX-style long filenames. So they devised a supplement to the ISO9660 standard called the *Rock Ridge* extensions for this purpose.

When Windows 9x came along with its support for long filenames, people wanted to be able to use that type of long filename, with its Unicode support, on CDs. This was the inspiration behind the *Joliet* supplement to the ISO9660 standard. This permits the use of long filenames, complete with Unicode support, up to a maximum of 64 characters including spaces.

Not everyone wanted Unicode support in the filenames. So yet another extension to the ISO9660 standard was created, this time called *Romeo*. This system uses long filenames consisting only of ASCII characters (up to 128 characters if the disc is only for use on a PC) that are readable by any version of Windows, and also are readable (if all the filenames are no longer than 31 characters) on a Macintosh.

This was, and is, a rather confusing state of affairs. The authors of CDs who use these approaches must know what machines and operating systems are going to be used to read the CDs they create. Otherwise, they might make them in a form that would be readable by only some of their target audience. Also, the ISO9660 standard with, perhaps, its Rock Ridge, Joliet, or Romeo extensions (all of which are mutually incompatible) doesn't deal well with discs that are to be written to in multiple sessions or those that are going to be erased and rerecorded. So with the emergence of CD-RW, and then of DVD, it was clear that some unifying generalization of these standards was needed.

Universal Data Format (UDF)

What resulted is the Universal Disk Format (UDF) specification, currently in version 2.01. The Optical Storage Technology Association promulgated this new format. It defines a new file system (that is a subset and expansion upon an earlier definition) for optical storage media. It explicitly addresses the special needs that arise when you are using a write-once medium, including the possibilities that occur when you can write only once to each location, but can write many times to the disc as a whole. It also provides a proper foundation for read/write optical storage organization and, of course, covers the manufactured all-at-once ROM discs.

Further, the UDF standard has been upgraded to cover how each of these issues changes when one considers DVDs as well as CDs. In particular, it allows for the many types of data storage you might want to store on a DVD and their differing needs for access. One particularly interesting addition is that of *named streams*. These are a generalization of the notion of a file's attributes to allow any amount of information of any kind. Each named stream is associated with one file, through its extended file entry. Thus, you will see only one file, but you can access either its actual contents or the named stream associated with it that contains supplementary information about the file.

The advantage to UDF is that it is explicitly a platform-neutral, operating system-neutral way of addressing files on a storage device. Thus, a UDF-formatted disc can be read quite nicely, thank you, on a Macintosh, a PC, or a RISC machine, a mainframe, and so forth—and these machines can be running the Mac-OS, DOS, Windows (most any flavor), UNIX, Linux, OS/2, MVS, or whatever you might want. All you need is a driver (installable file system) that understands UDF.

You don't have to go this route. Many CD writers still support the ISO9660 standard, with or without one of its extensions. Or, you can (with the use of appropriate drivers) treat most writable optical media as if they were simply additional hard drives, putting on them a FAT-style file organization. That mostly won't serve you very well. The UDF standard is the "proper" way to go for optical media—and using it is crucial if you want to be able to share the discs you create with others, or even to read them on a different machine's CD drive (where a UDF disc is what the most modern software will expect and the only kind it will accept).

What Are All Those Colored Books?

When the two companies that created CD technology, Sony and Philips, met, they kept their meeting notes in a red notebook binder. When those notes matured into a full specification for how CDs would be created and how they would be read, that first standard was called, accurately if unimaginatively, the *Red Book* spec.

Red Book is the specification that defines all of the most fundamental aspects of CDs. The fact that a CD can have up to 99 tracks, that they hold (in the main) 74 minutes of digital music, and that their data will be read from the center of the disc first, and then spiral outwards are all defined by the Red Book. Red Book also established how an audio CD's directory (actually called a *Table of Contents*) works, and how CD data is stored. This actually is quite different from other types of disk. Audio data is stored in logical structures called *frames*, and the smallest addressable collection of frames is called a *block sector*. This standard also establishes that error correction will be used in such a way that up to 220 audio frames in each sector can be unreadable without causing any degradation in the output sound quality.

> **Note:** Incidentally, at normal audio playback speeds—also known as 1X, or 150K/sec—75 sectors are read every second. From this you can deduct that approximately 2KB of data fits into each sector. In fact, each sector actually contains 12 bytes of data used to keep the player properly synchronized, 8 bytes of data which serve as a header that identifies that sector's exact location on the disc (in terms of minutes, seconds, and sectors), and 284 bytes of error-detection and error-correction data that follows the actual 2KB of content. A second sector type, developed as an extension to the Yellow Book standard, defines sectors slightly differently, allowing for an additional 8 bytes of header data. It also separates the error-correction data (284 bytes) from the error-detection data (an additional 4 bytes). This later development is called *Mode 2*.

Then, in 1983, a second standard was developed and stored in a yellow notebook. Thus, the Yellow Book standard expanded on the capabilities of initial CDs by allowing digital audio and digital computer data to be stored together on a single disc. Error correction techniques were improved in Yellow Book, and a method of interleaving different types of data was created so that video, audio, and computer data could be accessed quickly enough so as to seem simultaneous. CD-ROM discs comply with the Yellow Book standard, and the ISO9660 standard you've already read about was defined as part of Yellow Book. As part of the Yellow Book standard, computer data could be stored in the audio equivalent of Track One, and actual music could be stored starting with Track Two. In this way, a computer video game could load into memory and then accompany itself with real CD-quality music while you played.

Four years later, the Green Book standard was developed to allow for the creation of interactive compact discs (CD-I), which are used exclusively in video games. Although all other types of CD adhere—at the least—to the ISO9660 file system, CD-I uses the ISO9660+ file system, which is an extension of its namesake. CD-I also provides exclusively for reduced-quality (but greatly compressed) audio, which uses as little as 12.5% of the disc space that would otherwise be required.

The major development in CD standards occurred in 1990 when the *Orange Book* was put on the shelf. The Orange Book defines the characteristics of CD-R and CD-RW discs and drives, as well as magneto-optical technology. The Orange Book standard includes all that came before, and it's therefore possible to burn a CD-R that functions like an audio CD, a mixed-mode CD, or is even a copy of a CD-I video game. The primary purpose of Orange Book was to create an environment in which the largest number of discs would be usable on the largest collection of hardware.

The White Book defines VideoCDs and Kodak PhotoCDs, and the Blue Book defines CD-EXTRA or "Enhanced CD" discs. You'll appreciate the value of the Blue Book in particular if you've ever put an older mixed-media (Yellow Book) CD into your audio CD player and nearly gone deaf from the static created by your player trying to "sing" the computer data in what was once Track One. The Blue Book prevents compliant audio hardware from "seeing" the computer data on a mixed-media disk, and the Table of Contents identifies the first piece of digital music as Track One. This benefit was achieved through the creation of *multisessions*. Audio is stored in the first session, which is backwards-compatible with all older CD players. Computer data is stored in a second session, accessible only by Blue Book-compliant CD-ROM drives. This second session functions a bit like a CD within a CD, and consists of its own encapsulated ISO9660 or HFS file system.

The Purple Book is a standard that defines a double-density CD, capable of storing 1.3GB of data in a read-only, recordable, or rewritable format.

Finally, the Scarlet Book is the newest standard. It defines the implementation of what is being called the *Super Audio CD*. This is, in reality, an all-audio DVD (not to be confused with the DVD-Audio spec that you'll read about in a moment). Scarlet Book discs also comply with a digital watermarking and copy protection process that is, allegedly, unbreakable by any currently known process.

CD Data System Details

The total useable area of a CD is split into three main sections: the *Lead In*, the *Program*, and the *Lead Out* sections. The Lead In section contains synchronization data that helps the player's lens system lock on to the spiral of pits and lands that make up the disc's data. Also in the Lead In is the Table of Contents. This is a directory of the different tracks that make up the CD (in the case of audio). Somewhat analogous to a hard disk's FAT, the CD Table of Contents records the start time (and, thus, the exact disc location) for each track of music. The size of the Lead In area is fixed at the amount of data necessary to keep track of the CD's maximum number of 99 tracks. In a multisession disc, each session has its own Lead In area and functions as if it were a unique physical disc. (This is somewhat analogous to a hard drive containing multiple partitions.) The Program area is simply a continuous body of data that can store up to 80 minutes of digital music, or the computer data equivalent (about 700MB). This area can be subdivided into tracks. Finally, the Lead Out area simply contains zeros (the digital equivalent of "nothing") and entry into that area tells the drive's lens mechanism that the end of the disk has been reached.

DVD Book Standards

Apparently, the various optical storage companies have run out of colored notebooks, because the five "book" standards that define DVDs are simply named by the letters "A" through "E".

The DVD A Book standard was not the first, despite its name. DVD B Book has that honor, being the standard for DVD-Video discs, the original DVD format. B Book establishes the format for a read-only disc that uses the Universal Disc Format (UDF) file system you read about earlier. DVD-video discs were created for the sole purpose of playing full-screen, full-motion video in accordance with the MPEG2 standard (the same digital standard used by digital satellite broadcast systems). The B Book format provides sufficient data capacity for 135 minutes of high-quality synchronized video and audio. It also established standards for including captioning, alternative soundtracks, and copy protection. (Interestingly, it also mandated a manufacturing process that makes DVD-video discs no more costly to produce than simple audio CDs.)

A Book, in fact, defines the standard for DVD-ROM discs. These use a combination of the ISO9660 and UDF file systems, and are the DVD analog to enhanced CDs. They can be used exclusively for computer data or video/audio, or can support a combination of the two.

C Book is a specification for DVD-audio discs, a format that has yet to have any noticeable appeal. Audio for these discs is sampled at as high as 192kHz (as opposed to 44.1kHz with current audio CDs) with as many as 24 bits per sample (opposed to CD's 16). Up to six discrete channels of audio can be maintained. The format was first proposed in 1996, and players were expected on the market by 1999 but, frankly, no one yet seems to care.

D Book and E Book are probably the most important to PC users as they define all manner of recordable or rewritable DVDs, respectively. You can read about these technologies at length in Chapter 8, "Removable Storage." They all use the UDF file system, and some use *UDF-Bridge*, which is a combination of UDF and ISO9660. Although these two books initially defined only DVD-R and DVD-RAM formats, other recordable and rewritable formats like the very promising DVD+RW from Hewlett-Packard comply with their respective book.

Learning About File Formats

To round off this chapter, we're going to move from how files are stored to the files, themselves. Files store your data, but not every file stores just what you think it does. This section explains some of the variety of file formats, and suggests some ways you might explore them on your own.

ASCII Text Files

The simplest files contain almost exactly what you might expect them to. These are called *pure ASCII text files*. Examples include your PC's startup files, CONFIG.SYS and AUTOEXEC.BAT. Other ASCII text files are the various INI files used by many Windows (and some other) programs to store their initialization data. The distinguishing mark of these files is that, in addition to being pure ASCII files, they have a structure very much like that of WIN.INI and SYSTEM.INI. They are composed of blocks of text with each block beginning with a title enclosed in square brackets.

You can see what is in a pure ASCII text file if you're running Windows by loading it into Notepad or WordPad. Every operating system today provides some way of viewing ASCII files. Displaying ASCII text files works so well because they contain almost nothing but simple, displayable text characters taken from the ASCII character set.

We say *almost* only ASCII displayable text characters, because there are some exceptions. They almost always include some special control characters to indicate the end of a line of text. In text files prepared for PCs, that usually means the lines are terminated by a pair of control characters, one to say "move back to the left margin" and one to say "move down a line." These are termed the *carriage return* (CR) and *line feed* (LF) control characters and they have the ASCII values of 13 and 10, respectively (which are Dh and Ah in case you're looking inside the file with a snooping tool that displays the contents in hexadecimal).

Many text files also contain tab characters that have an ASCII value of 9. These characters stand for a variable number of space characters—whatever is needed to move the next character in the file to a column just past the next tab stop. Not all programs that use ASCII text files interpret these tab characters in the same way. Many text-based word processors assume a default spacing of five characters, and most of them also let you set the tabs wherever you want.

One other control character that is often used in text files is the *end-of-page character*. Another name for this is *form feed* (meaning that it signals a printer when to eject a page and start a new one), from which it carries the abbreviation FF. Its ASCII value is 12.

It used to be universal that all text files would end with a special end of file character. That is the Ctrl+Z (Control+Z) character, which has the ASCII value of 26 (1Ah). Before DOS, in CP/M machines there was no other way to know where the end of a file was. Now that the DOS directory entry keeps track of the file length right down to the byte, it isn't necessary to include a Ctrl+Z character. But if that character is present, a text-based ASCII file viewer, such as the old DOS TYPE command, will assume that it is an end-of-file mark and stop processing the file there.

ASCII text files also vary in how they represent paragraphs. Some put all of a paragraph on a single line, and then put a single pair of CR and LF control characters after it to indicate the beginning of the next paragraph. Others use a CR-LF pair to signal the end of a line within a paragraph and a pair of CR-LF pairs to signal a new paragraph. Still others use tabs to indent paragraphs or lines. All of these still qualify for the name pure ASCII text files, but they also go by names such as MS-DOS text, DOS text with layout, or some other variation.

Non-ASCII (Binary) Files

In the universe of files on PCs, ASCII text files are a small minority. All the rest are called *binary files*. They contain at least some non-ASCII characters (they have bytes of data whose most significant bit is set to one, and thus they represent an extended ASCII character) or they contain some control characters other than the simple CR, LF, TAB, and FF. You can use the DOS TYPE command on them, but if you do the results might startle you. (Incidentally, everything that follows is true not only of TYPE, but of almost any operating system's text-based ASCII file viewer.)

Your computer might display some of what you expect, plus a lot of other strange characters. Also, it might beep at you many times. And it might stop displaying information before it reaches the end of the file.

If a binary file contains only ASCII characters and extended ASCII characters (and the usual control characters CR, LF, TAB and perhaps FF), it's possible to display their contents with the TYPE command. But what you will see might not be what you would expect. This is because there are many definitions for the extended ASCII characters. If the file was prepared using one definition and if the TYPE command uses another, you might be surprised by what shows up on the screen.

The cause of the beeps, huge blank areas, and perhaps a sudden termination of the output is likely to be the presence of some other control characters. The Bell code (ASCII value 7) causes your PC to beep. The Vertical Tab character (VT) with ASCII value 11 (Bh) can move the cursor vertically on the screen. And, if the TYPE command encounters a Ctrl+Z (EOF) character (ASCII value 26, or 1Ah), it will stop right there.

All those things are perfectly normal. They just mean that the TYPE command is not the optimal way to look at the contents of those files.

Sometimes you will know something about how the file was created. For example, if it is a Microsoft Word document file it will have an extension of .DOC, although extensions are usually hidden in modern Windows file displays. The best tool to use to look at this or any other word processing document file is the word processor that created it. Spreadsheet files are best looked at in the spreadsheet program that created them, and so on.

Because of this more-or-less constant association of file extensions and the application programs that created them, Windows implements a set of File Associations so that you can simply double-click on a filename in Windows Explorer and that file will be loaded into the appropriate application program. Naturally this only works for file extensions that Windows knows about. Each time you install an application program, it will ordinarily register all the extensions it understands with Windows, so you can use this convenient means of accessing the files it understands thereafter.

Not every program that creates a binary file uses a unique file extension in its name. Often these programs insert a signature of some sort near the beginning of the file to indicate the kind of file it is, what application created it, and in a few cases, even which version of that application is required to load it. Many programs depend upon that signature to validate the files they are about to load, even if the extension might have told them.

Why Binary Files Are Different

Binary files aren't like ASCII files for the simple reason that they hold something other than just text. Even the word processing files, for which text is the main point, also hold other things.

Word Processing Files

Why aren't word processing document files just what you typed into the document? A word processing document file must contain not only the textual content, but also the formatting information. And many modern word processors go further by including pictures, drawings, outline headings, and summary information.

Database and Spreadsheet Files

Database files must keep information in records. That can be done in any of several ways. Some special ASCII control characters seem to have been designed for just this purpose. They bear names such as record separator and group separator. But the fact is that most PC database programs don't use them. Some database programs format the records into fixed length blocks. Others separate the records with special characters— just not the ones the ASCII code says they should.

Spreadsheet files are simply special-purpose database files. Their records are displayed differently, but the essential file storage ideas are very similar. Of course, the format particulars vary with the particular spreadsheet program you use. (One reason so many programs use their own file formats is to inhibit competitors from decoding their file formats and thus be able to use those data files with a competing product.)

If you have a database file you want to snoop inside, use a disk editor and look for things you recognize. If you find blocks of discernable text separated by regions of garbage, and if the distance from one discernable block to the next is constant, most likely you are looking at a fixed-length record database (or spreadsheet) file. The apparent garbage is actually numbers stored as binary values rather than as the ASCII representation of the numerals.

Program Files

Another important type of binary file you will encounter is a program file. Program files contain instructions to the PC in the language it understands: machine language instructions. So, of course it is not readily readable by humans. One easy thing to look for is the first couple of characters. If they are MZ, this is likely to be an EXE file, which is to say either an old DOS program or a Windows program. (If you see a message a short distance into the file that reads either `This program requires Microsoft Windows` or `This program cannot be run in DOS mode` then, naturally, you are looking at a Windows executable.)

Some of these program files have the extension .EXE. Others are .DLL files or .OVR files or some other extension. But all of them are programs. (Files with extension .COM are a simpler kind of program file. They don't have the MZ signature at the start, and they are supposed to be no larger than 64KB. They are, in fact, simply images of the bytes that are deposited into the RAM when you run them. EXE files, on the other hand, have a relocation header at the beginning that specifies what parts of their content go where in memory when they are loaded.)

Other Binary Files

There are still other kinds of files that are essentially binary. These include image files, sound files, and more.

The essential thing to know about all these binary files is that their *precise content* matters. You must not alter even one byte or they can become unusable. (This is in sharp contrast to a pure ASCII text file, for which in most cases a minor alteration is no big deal.)

So feel free to snoop around your PC's disk drives, looking inside all manner of files, but to save yourself much grief, be sure to use a tool that won't alter their contents. Or else be *very* careful!

Data Compression

One of the most important aspects of storage is how much you have, and how much useful information you can force into it. A popular way to get more for your money, as it were, is to make the information you want to store fit into less storage room. This can be achieved by *compressing* the data.

The compression being referred to in this context can also be called "squeezing out redundancy." Ordinary speech contains a lot of redundancy, and so do most PC program and data files. If you could create from one file another, smaller file that contained the same information as the source, and from which the source could be exactly reproduced, you could store only the non-redundant form of that file and save space on your disk drive. And, in fact, you can.

There are two complementary strategies for doing this. One uses a utility program (or operating system support) to compress individual files or groups of files whenever you choose. The other strategy builds the data compression (and decompression) engine into the PC's operating system so that every file is compressed when it goes to the disk and decompressed when it returns from the disk. This way takes no thought on your part, and so is much more convenient.

A downside to using a separate compression utility program is that you must consciously use it twice on each file or group of files for which you want to save disk space. You use it once to compress the file and another time to decompress it back to its original form. If you don't do the second step, you will find that the non-redundant form of your file looks like gibberish. The advantages of this approach include these: You can compress only certain files that you know will compress well. You can combine compressed versions of multiple files into one file called an *archive*. That file can then be sent over a modem in less time than the collection of uncompressed files, and you have the advantage that all the different, related pieces can be kept together.

The downside to using operating system compression is that when you have your PC compress or decompress a file, some time is required for the PC to do that work. If you do this for every file going to or from a disk drive, you might slow down your computer.

On the other hand, after the file is compressed there are fewer bytes to be written to or read from the disk drive, so perhaps you'll actually see a speedup. What you see on your PC will depend critically on the balance between the speed of the processor and the speed of the disk drive.

Generally, the decompression is much quicker than the compression, so almost always you will see a speedup of your PC for reading files that have been compressed.

The advantage to the integrated OS approach is simply that you don't have to think about it. It works automatically for every file you copy to the compressed drive, and it works just as automatically to decompress those files when you read them from that drive. So, there is a place in our world for both programs to do compression of files on demand, and also for an operating system-level data compression engine. Fortunately, both kinds of data compression are available. Even more fortunately, the plummeting cost of long-term storage is making compression all but unnecessary in terms of saving space on your hard disk. (It is still very useful to reduce the size of files you want to move over the Internet, or even those you want to put on a floppy or other removable disk to give to someone else.)

Standalone PC File Compression Programs

Many programs that can scrunch files down to a fraction of their original size are now available. These programs come in two basic flavors. One flavor is the lossless compression program. The other is the lossy compression program.

Lossy Compression

Lossy compression programs are useful for making an approximate representation of an original file. That is fine if the file was an image and you don't mind a slight degradation of the image when you reconstitute it from the compressed file. Lossy compression programs usually can compress files by differing amounts, depending on how you want to trade off degradation versus space saved on the disk. Often, you can compress an image (or a video clip and so on) by a factor of 10 without much noticeable degradation. But if you compress it by a factor of 100, you almost certainly will notice that the reconstituted images are not the same as the originals. Examples of this type of compression create JPEG image files, RealAudio/RealVideo streams, and MPEG movie files.

Lossless Compression

The more interesting programs for most uses are those that can create a non-redundant version of a file and then, upon demand, can re-create the original file *exactly*—that is, *lossless compression programs*. Make no mistake: When you are compressing a program file, you must be able to get it back again exactly as it was, right down to the very last bit. Otherwise, it is worse than useless. A program that is incorrectly reconstituted might simply not run—but it also might do something horribly different from what the original would have done.

Typical compression ratios achievable with program files are a little less than two to one. That is, the non-redundant form of the file might be only a little more than half the size of the original. Some spreadsheet and other data files can be compressed by much more than that, with the non-redundant copy sometimes taking only a tenth of the space needed for the original file.

The most popular type of lossless compression on a Windows-based PC is the familiar ZIP format. Windows now supports this at the operating system level through the construct called *compressed folders*. Essentially, compressed folders make support for zipped files a native part of Windows. With no additional software, you can simply double-click any .ZIP file and it will open like a regular Windows folder. You can compress or decompress files by simply dragging and dropping them in or out, respectively. To create a new empty compressed folder, you simply right-click on the desktop or in any Windows Explorer window and select New, Compressed Folder. It's extremely handy.

Compression Realities

The fact is, with ever larger, huge amounts of storage becoming more and more affordable, and with broadband networking heading inexorably towards ubiquity, compression is a lot less important than it was even two years ago. Compression takes time, and operating-system level compression takes time every time a compressed file is opened *or* closed. (The file decompresses while opening and is temporarily written to disk; it's then re-compressed when you close it and the temporary file is deleted.) You should take these issues into consideration when you're deciding what type of compression to use and how many files to keep compressed.

We don't use operating system level compression at all, and we use Windows' compressed folders simply to make files that we're keeping in long-time archival storage take up less room. Of course, even with broadband Internet access, compression can so dramatically reduce file size that it's worth the bother. Some of the graphic images you see in this book, for example, took up over 16MB of disk space before they were compressed down to a more manageable 400KB. Successful compression to this degree (a ratio of 40:1) is pretty uncommon, but some graphics formats are particularly space-hungry.

Speaking of graphics formats, don't expect to get much compression from a collection of JPEG images or MPEG movies. These files are already highly compressed (using lossy methods) and further lossless compression won't make them smaller. Indeed, in some instances, using lossless compression on a complex JPEG image can even make the file *larger*. This is because the original file has very little redundancy, so the lossless compression tool ends up making a redundancy table that reflects nearly every pixel in the final image. Naturally, the size of the non-redundant file *plus* this table is larger than the size of the file alone.

Summary

Disk and disc storage is an exceptionally broad topic. Not only could an entire book be devoted to it, entire books have been devoted to individual aspects of it, like the intricacies of DVD-video or techniques for recovering data from damaged devices. It's simply not possible, therefore, to give you coverage here that is both comprehensive *and* complete. The chapter focused here on "comprehensive," hoping that reading about these technologies will excite your own interest and lead you to delve more into the topics you find particularly exciting.

Advanced Networking

In this chapter, we'll take a deeper look at networking technologies. We'll first explore the layers that make up a network model and then talk about network operating systems. From there, we'll jump with both feet into a thorough exploration—as thorough as the scope of this book allows—of TCP/IP and how the Internet actually works. We'll augment the chapter with a forward-looking perspective on the next generation of TCP/IP addressing—Ipv6.

Layers in the Network Strategy

The overall network strategy must include more than simply specifying the wiring scheme and data packet handling protocol. You read about those two factors earlier if you read Chapter 11, "Networking—Wired and Wireless." A network strategy also must consider how programs within each connected computer communicate over that network. The OSI model (which stands for Open Systems Interconnection) is a well-defined, seven-layer model for networking.

This model divides networking tasks into seven fundamentally different layers to make it easier for the industry to explain the different operations that take place in successful networking. The seven layers are shown in Figure 19.1 and are most easily remembered with the mnemonic *All People Seem To Need Data Processing*.

The application layer is the interface to network services—it interacts with the user. The presentation layer translates between the application layer and all others. It also provides redirection, encryption, and compression. The session layer establishes the rules used for communication between two machines, and the transport layer—as the name implies—handles network transmissions. The network layer is where addressing and switching take place, and the data link layer handles error checking and other elements related to link control. The physical layer interfaces with what you can actually see and touch: the NIC, cable, and so forth.

Layer 7	Application Layer
Layer 6	Presentation Layer
Layer 5	Session Layer
Layer 4	Transport Layer
Layer 3	Network Layer
Layer 2	DataLink Layer
Layer 1	Physical Layer

Chapter 11 explored the two lowest-level layers in the OSI model. The other layers are all components of the network operating system (NOS) software that runs on top of this enabling hardware connection. Understanding those higher layers means taking a quick look at what, exactly, a NOS is and does.

The NIC Needs a NOS

Whenever you add new hardware to a PC, you must also add some software to enable the PC to use that hardware. Network software is no exception. Having a BIOS ROM on a network interface card is common. That ROM contains some basic device driver programs to activate the hardware on the card. However, the job that a network does is so much larger, and so much further abstracted from the role of mere hardware, that a simple device driver is not enough.

What Is a NOS?

A network brings into a PC a whole new realm of resources and possibilities. To manage this new realm, one needs support from the operating system through a set of routines commonly called a *network operating system* (NOS).

At the server side of the network, this NOS support is responsible for managing the many requests for resources that the server will receive from its attached clients. At the client side, NOS support simply means providing fundamental connectivity to the network.

Big problems face the designers of network operating systems. First, they must keep track of all the connected resources. Second, they must deal with many different kinds of connected computers and to make sense of the file systems on each one, translating filenames and path locations as necessary to make the distant computer's files look as if they are just like the local ones. Then, when a file is transferred, there might be an additional translation task to make the foreign file show up in the format and in compliance with the naming convention expected for that type of file on the local machine. (This sort of translation and reformatting falls under the aegis of the presentation layer's code conversion services.)

For small LANs this job isn't too bad, but for a very large WAN it can be tough. The Internet is so large and so dynamic (and without any central control) that the directory job has in some ways proven to be beyond our present ability to solve it fully.

> **Technical Note:** The step of translating file formats isn't always done. However, it is an important one if you want to give the local computer user the illusion that those foreign files are just like the ones stored on the local machine. One example is that on a UNIX computer, text files normally have only a line-feed character at the end of each line, whereas on a Windows machine, text files always end each line with a two-character combination (carriage return plus line-feed). This seemingly trivial difference has a big impact on the way the data in the file is displayed.

Some Common NOSes

Many network operating systems are in use today, but only a few of them have a significant market share. The first to be developed for DOS-based PCs were add-ons to the PC's operating system, whether that was DOS or DOS plus Windows. Later generations of PC operating systems have included all of the functionality of a NOS within the basic PC OS.

Most networks can be classified into one of two categories. The first use a file server and workstation model (also called client/server, but a more correct use of this term is discussed in the section "Client/Server Computing," later in this chapter). The second are peer-to-peer networks. Any modern NOS can support either architecture.

File Server and Workstation Networks

The notion of a file server and workstation model of networking is this: All the important files reside on one or more central computers (called file servers). Each person uses a workstation, which is a computer connected to the file server(s) by the network.

When you do some work on your workstation, you get the needed data files, and perhaps some of the applications as well, from the file server. You load them into your PC and do your work with them by running application programs in your machine. When you finish, you save your data files back onto the file server. Often these networks also have central printers, and any user wanting to print a document will direct it across the network to the printer.

Windows 2000 Server is the best-known NOS today, and it has replaced Novell's NetWare as the leading product. UNIX, with its decades-long history of supporting many different kinds of computers and its robust built-in support for networking, is the most popular network operating system for networked computers other than Windows PCs. Both of these NOSes are primarily intended for use on a file server and workstation model of network.

There are several advantages to file server-based networking. One is that all the critical files live on just a few, central machines. Professionals can oversee these machines, keeping them running smoothly, and those professionals can be counted on to do all the prudent file-management tasks, including backups. The users of the workstations needn't concern themselves with those pesky details that can be so crucial—and whose omission can be so tragic when a PC's hard disk crashes.

This arrangement also neatly separates the work of serving as librarian to many (the job of the file server) from working with the individual files' contents (the job of each workstation). This helps balance the workloads of the different computers in the network. The file server might have very little work to do for any one user—just retrieving a few files—but it must do that same job for many, many other users at the same time.

Another advantage is that a user can log in to the network from any workstation and do the same things pretty much anywhere. Because the files all live in the central repository, they can be accessed from any connected workstation just as well as from another.

Of course, this is not a perfectly true statement. Some workstations might have more RAM than others. That can matter if the task you want to do requires a huge amount of RAM, such as when manipulating large graphic files. Also, to save time and network traffic, the network administrator might have installed many of the more popular applications on local hard disks in the workstations. But if the one you need hasn't been installed on all the workstations, that can limit your freedom to log in from anywhere and still do the same kinds of work. One solution is to have a central copy of every application that can be used if there doesn't happen to be a local copy on a particular workstation.

Another problem with the connect-anywhere paradigm is access management. Windows 2000, in particular, is designed around the workgroup organizational principle and organizes workstations and servers into workgroups and domains. If a user does not have access to a given domain, he or she will not be able to log into a server in that domain.

Peer-to-Peer Networks

The other general kind of network uses a peer-to-peer model. This means that, in principle, all the computers that are hooked together are equal. In particular, any computer on the network can be configured to share some or all of its local resources with the users of the other computers on the network. That means each computer can become a file server (or a printer, scanner, or modem server). But at the same time, those computers are also workstations.

You don't have to share any resources you don't want to share in this type of network. That is, each workstation can be configured to have none, some, or all of its resources shareable. When you do share a resource, you can attach a password to it, and only those other users who know the password for that particular resource can access it. Some peer-to-peer networking systems do allow passwords to be assigned to the user, not to the resource, but they are rare.

Windows 9x/Mx/XP has a further refinement of having two kinds of access control: user-level, in which passwords are specified for specific users and groups, and share-level, in which a password is assigned to each resource. User-level access control in Windows is available; however, only if you have either a Novell or Windows 2000 server that can authenticate passwords. This is something that a traditional peer-to-peer network wouldn't have. Peer networking support for PCs was included in Windows for Workgroups 3.11 and every successive version of Windows.

One advantage to peer-to-peer networking is that users can exchange files among themselves directly. With the file server model, file sharing between workstations can happen only in a two-step fashion: First, one user uploads the file to the server. Then the second user downloads it from the server. By using passwords that are shared selectively, one can share files with only some of the other workstations. (This can also be accomplished on a file server, but it requires that the administrator of the file server set up differing access rights for different directories, and that the users be grouped according to which access rights they have. This discourages an ad hoc decision by one user to share files with another user, yet keep them private from all the rest.)

Another important advantage to peer networking, from the user's standpoint, is that it is closer to what the PC revolution has been all about: getting away from central control of the computing resource. There is another side to this, of course. The people in a company who are responsible for all the computing hardware and services have a much harder time keeping track of who is doing what on a peer network. Often, the central system administrators choose not to back up files stored on individual workstations, in which case users must assume that responsibility for themselves.

Some Networks Blur this Boundary

Windows 2000 is marketed in three versions: two intended for file servers and one for workstations. The intention is to support the file server plus workstation type of networking and also enable you to set up peer networking if you want.

Windows 2000 Server not only supports workstations running Windows 2000 Professional, but also workstations that are running Windows 9x or DOS plus Windows for Workgroups, Windows Me, Windows XP, as well as Macintosh and UNIX boxes.

In a mixed network, some machines might be designated as file servers. They can be repositories for most of the shared files, and perhaps also for many shared applications. But the individual workstations can also be configured to share some of the files, printers, and modems that they have locally with any other workstation user. So, with the built-in NOS functionality of these operating systems, you can have the best of both worlds. (Or, from the point of view of a curmudgeonly computing services manager, the worst of both worlds!)

TCP/IP: The Internet's Babelfish

In the late Douglas Adams' creation, *The Hitchhiker's Guide to the Galaxy*, a marvelous—though deity-challenged—creature appears. The "babelfish" lets you understand anything said to you in any form of language. All you have to do is stick one in your ear. What the babelfish does for hitchhikers trying to see the wonders of the galaxy for less than forty Altairian dollars a day, TCP/IP does for the Internet.

And, the Internet needs all the help it can get. Very few things, if anything, have grown so rapidly and continued to do so for so long. Today it has changed virtually everything about the world of PCs. Tomorrow it might change virtually all aspects of our lives. The next section covers briefly some of the technologies that are behind the Internet and its amazing growth and impact.

What Is the Internet?

The Internet is a network, in many ways just like the office network. It connects many computers together for the purpose of exchanging data. What's so different about the Internet is its scope. It is an interconnection of many smaller networks. Its scope is global. The number of connected computers is almost unimaginable, and its penetration into the ways we use our PCs to work (and play) is getting deeper by the day.

Also the Internet—unlike every network of which it is composed—is not something that is under anyone's control. No single person or organization is responsible for the Internet. Aspects of it have been entrusted to this group or that, but overall it is one of the most amazing demonstrations of a functional anarchy—quite possibly one of the few in all of human history.

The Internet Both Is and Is Not Like Any Other Network

At the technical level, the Internet is very much like any other network. It consists of computers connected together that exchange packets that carry information. Some of these computer-to-computer links are permanent ones; others are made temporarily to facilitate a particular data exchange and then broken once more.

One way in which the Internet is unlike many networks is its degree of massively redundant interconnectedness. For any given two locations in most networks, there are at most a few paths to get from here to there. On the Internet, however, there are usually a huge number of alternative paths. (Still, in some key places a substantial portion of the Internet can be temporarily severed from all the rest by just one mistake on the part of a backhoe operator.)

One way to understand the Internet is to look at it as having a central core, of sorts, and a huge ring (or edge) around the core. The central core consists of the primary routers that make up the backbone of the entire Internet. They are responsible for the movement of data across the farthest distances. Outside of the central core are the thousands of ISPs, called points of presence (or POPs), which connect first to even larger ISPs, which connect directly to the backbone. The design of the Internet is such that, should any part of the backbone fail, or should there be a failure or congestion anywhere within the network, data will simply automatically re-route to another path. In this regard, the idea of "bringing down the Internet" is next to impossible. (The Internet started life as ARPANET, a network system for the US military to use and that would continue to function after a cold-war nuclear disaster.)

Another difference is the wide variation in the value of the data stored in the connected computers. Most other networks connect computers belonging to a single company or organization, and those computers mainly store similar kinds of data with similar value to the people who make up those organizations. The Internet is, to put it bluntly, a mess in this regard.

Although you can't trust everything you find on the Internet, it is one of the most universally accessible, if not the richest, lode of information on the planet. After you learn to navigate around and validate what you find there with a combination of careful consideration of the apparent source of the information and cross-checking with other sources, you might find that you turn to the Internet more often than to almost any other information resource—simply because it proves to be the fastest way to answer most of your questions.

Furthermore, many people are now finding their natural communities of like-minded people via the Internet, without regard to their actual, physical locations. People who share interests on such divergent topics as flower arranging and terrorism have set up discussion and information sharing forums on the Net that span the planet. Whether this is a wonderful or a regrettable development for our society is something we will leave to sociologists to debate.

Protocols for All

Although the Internet is, in general terms, like any other network, it also has some things about it that are special. For example, the Internet was built around a data transmission protocol that was designed just for it. Furthermore, most of the higher-level protocols used to control various kinds of network-mediated transactions were first developed for use across the Internet or its predecessors.

Of course, like almost any great success in any field, these have now been adopted for use in a wide assortment of networks, including some that aren't connected to the Internet. One of the hottest areas of development in many businesses now are *intranets*, which simply copy the Internet model on a smaller scale for use within a single organization.

Transmission Protocols, Gateways, and Firewalls

Just about any network carries data from place to place in packages called *packets*. You can think of them as being in many ways like letters inside envelopes. The letter is the data load being carried. The envelope provides information on the source and destination of the packet. One way that network data packets differ from most letters carried in envelopes is that the packets are too small to hold an entire message. So almost all files that are transferred over networks—and a file is what corresponds to a letter in our analogy—must be broken into many small pieces. As Figure 19.2 shows, each one is enclosed in its own "envelope," (packet) and includes as header information the addresses of source and destination, as well as the sequence number of this particular piece of the "message" (file).

FIGURE 19.2

The envelope analogy as it relates to data.

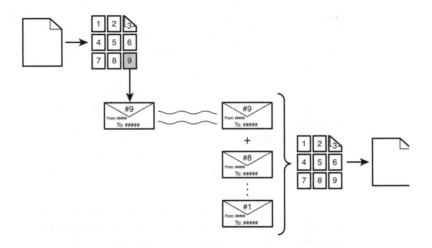

Note: Another analogy to help you understand what is going on is to think of shipping boxes instead of envelopes. If you order a large number of items from your favorite online shopping site, your order comes in a number of different boxes. Each box contains a portion of your order, and has the destination and sender address on it. Additionally, there is a sequence number on the box ("3 of 7") to easily let you determine whether all of the order came or not.

There are many ways for a packet to find its way from the source to the destination. Because any one of those routes can be more or less congested at any given instant, it is possible for the packets that make up a single message to travel from the source to the destination via many routes.

The implication is that the packets might arrive out of order. This is where the sequence number comes into play. The receiving software examines the envelopes and sorts them into the right order. It also acknowledges receipt of each one. If the sending software doesn't get an acknowledgement within a reasonably short time, it will assume the packet got lost and it will resend it.

One way this strategy can fail is if the link between sending and receiving programs has a high *latency*. This means simply that packets take an unusually long time to get from one point to another. That can happen even though the rate of data flow is very high, just because the overall distance to be traveled is very, very long. This is one of the salient characteristics of any link that must bounce off a satellite, for example. In this case the sending program might get tired of waiting and resend and resend packets ad nauseam. This, of course, doesn't really help things. Instead, it just clogs up the channel.

One way around this difficulty is a strategy called *TCP spoofing*. Here an intermediary is set up to receive and acknowledge packets midway, or just before the high latency portion of the link. The intermediary then forwards the packets over that high latency link and waits more tolerantly for the ultimate receiver to acknowledge their receipt. The satellite ground station responds to the sender in a timely manner and then, in what amounts to a separate conversation, sends the packets to the ultimate recipient and listens for acknowledgements with due allowance for latency.

The main protocol is actually a set of related protocols that describes how the Internet carries packets of information and is called Transmission Control Protocol/Internet Protocol (TCP/IP). Like most of the other standards that describe how aspects of the Internet work, this one was developed by an individual or a committee and then published (on the Internet, of course) for comment before it finally is adopted as a standard. The survival of the Internet as an operating medium of communication has depended upon the voluntary compliance with those standards by all the organizations, companies, and individuals whose computers make up the Internet.

Routers connect the different network segments. When the packets traveling on the different segments use different transmission protocols, the router is responsible for translating between them. In effect, the router hardware opens the "envelope" of each packet, extracts the contents, and then places it in a new envelope that is properly addressed for travel on the next network segment.

Some routers are more than just packet shufflers; they also serve a security function. (Think of them as a combination postal worker and security guard.) Some of these routers are called *firewalls*. They examine each packet they receive and test it against various rules. If it passes, they send the packet on to its destination.

Some of these rules might involve not passing packets coming from certain, untrusted source locations. Other rules might actually look inside the envelope and decide which packets to pass based on the data they contain. The person who configures the firewall has the responsibility to set up the correct set of rules to give the owners of that firewall the level of security they bought it to provide.

A side effect of a firewall might be to disguise the true source of packets when it forwards them. This can be both helpful and a great inconvenience. Here is one common example: A company can give the appearance to the outside of having only a few Internet addresses, but in fact have on the inside a great many more. This allows the company to better control the flow of information in and out of its networked systems. Their marketing Web site can remain easily available to the general public while their confidential financial information remains accessible to a knowledgeable few, but safe from the prying eyes of most. This sort of firewall router is often termed a firewall with *proxy server* functionality. The essential difference between it and a simpler firewall router is that the proxy server version will also set up a correspondence between the internal and external addresses for each conversation it permits to pass through its wall of safety. This correspondence will last only as long as that conversation does. Therefore, the external addresses can be reused as much as necessary while the "true" internal addresses of the users remain fixed.

Additionally, selected IP addresses are reserved exclusively for private, internal use. All routers are programmed to ignore any packets destined for these IP addresses. In effect, you can use these addresses locally, but they "don't exist" with respect to the larger, public Internet. Under the current version of TCP/IP, reserved addresses are from 10.0.0.0 to 10.255.255.255, 172.16.0.0 through 172.31.255.255, and 192.168.0.0 through 192.168.255.255. (We'll explain IP addresses in just a moment.)

This hiding or re-addressing of packets can be inconvenient when you want to carry on a conversation over the Internet with a computer that insists on knowing who you are. The firewall simply might not allow that type of conversation. The conversation you wanted to have might prove to be impossible to hold, unless you have a way of working around this roadblock. (Often such workarounds are available; you just have to ask your network administrator to learn about them.)

IP Addresses

You probably recall from reading about networks in Section II that each computer on a network has its own, unique identifier. On an Ethernet-based network, the MAC address of each PC's NIC (essentially, each network card's serial number) is used as that PC's official address. MACs are used on a TCP/IP network, too, but indirectly. Each PC's MAC is mapped to an address—called *IP addresses*—that the TCP/IP protocol understands natively.

In order for data to move around the Internet, every computer on the entire worldwide network must have a unique address. IP addresses are 32-bit numbers, which means that there are only four thousand million IP addresses available. Because it's very common for large corporations, schools, and governmental bodies to reserve huge groups of IP addresses for their own use, it turns out that four thousand million IP addresses isn't, in fact, enough. We'll talk about the solution to that problem in a moment.

IP addresses aren't usually expressed in the form of a 32-bit number, however. They're represented as four numbers separated by decimal points, sometimes called dotted-decimal notation. Each of the four numbers is a decimal expression of the value of one of the four bytes that make up the total 32-bit IP address.

IPv6 Addressing

In the next few years we can expect a new generation of IP addresses (referred to as IPv6) to arrive with double the number of bits. Ipv6 addresses are 16 bytes long, written as eight hex numbers separated by colons (each hex number standing for 16 bits). This new system should provide 340,282,366,920,938,463,463,374,607,431,768,211,456 unique IP addresses.

The US Census bureau estimates that approximately 110 thousand million people have lived on planet Earth, since the beginning. If there are, as currently estimated, 100 trillion cells in the human body, and 40,000 genes in each cell, IPv6 addressing would provide 773.3 million IP addresses for each gene in each cell in the body of every human who has ever lived. Surely *that* number of address possibilities will suffice for a very long time—even if the Internet continues its exponential growth for the foreseeable future of humanity.

These 128-bit IP addresses will, of course, look very different from those used today. An IPv6 address might be FEDC:BA98:7654:3210:EAFF:A19E:7A51:1AAA. Quite different from 191.2.32.12!

Host Names and Domains

Overlaid on top of—and completely independent from—the IP address scheme is a more human-friendly naming scheme for computers and their users. Rather than referring to a computer as 11001110 01010101 01011100 01001111, or even as 206.85.92.79, it is easier to remember it by a name such as SALES, GOOFY, or any other one you want to assign it. This text value is known as a *host* name, and can be used when referring to the computer in such things as e-mail. Thus, someone's e-mail address might be drew@ruppy.com. This says that his username is drew, and his mail account is accessible at the computer host named ruppy.

Ruppy, as it turns out, is located in the top-level domain com. Domains are human-friendly logical constructs within the Internet for organizing the different host names that are out there. There are a limited number of top-level (also called *generic*) domain names, and mostly they indicate either the fundamental purpose of computers in that domain or the country where the computer is located. The most common top-level domain name is com, which stands for some type of commercial entity. The net top-level domain refers to computers belonging to companies that provide Internet services. The gov top-level domain name includes most US government entities. The edu top-level domain includes most colleges and universities.

DNS, The Domain Name Server

Any time you specify a computer's domain name, as in ruppy.com, that name must be translated into the computer's IP address. This is done by sending a message to some Domain Name Server (DNS), which will either know the translation or will know which computer to ask. This whole process makes use of a sophisticated hierarchy among all DNSs on the Internet in which a smaller, local DNS is first searched. Only if it does not know the translation for a domain name is the search passed to a larger DNS server. That way, impact on the entire network is kept to a minimum. As soon as a map between the domain name and an IP address is found, the search stops and whatever DNS was last accessed returns the value.

Eventually, this process brings back to the requestor an IP address that it should use in place of the host and domain name. Then, when messages for a user at a certain computer arrive there, that computer looks in its table of usernames to determine in which actual mailbox it is to put that message.

DHCP and NAT

DHCP, or Dynamic Host Configuration Protocol, and NAT, or Network Address Translation, are two protocols that are subordinate to the greater TCP/IP protocol. They're necessary because IP addresses are expensive to obtain and their number is limited. A business might be able to afford only one IP address, but it might need to connect 10 computers to the Internet. Something has gotta give.

Enter DHCP and NAT. A NAT server (built into most NOSes and routers) can map literally thousands of internal IP addresses onto the company's single actual IP address. The NAT server maintains a translation table that maps the actual network ID of a PC to its internal IP address and that maps to the actual, external IP address, so that data moves as though the company could afford as many IPs as it needs.

DHCP provides IP addresses on an as-needed basis. Consider that you might own a small ISP that has 20 actual IP addresses assigned to it. Unfortunately, you have 200 customers. How do you provide them each with an IP address? As each user dials in to your system, your DHCP server assigns them an IP address for a fixed period of time. This is called a *lease*. Your customer can use this IP number until the lease expires (or until they disconnect). When the leased IP address is released, the DHCP server makes it available to another user who logs in, and so forth.

Ports and Sockets

It takes more than just IP addresses to make TCP/IP communication work. Two other primary structures organize and regulate the flow of data. These are ports and sockets.

You can think of ports as being like a collection of old-fashioned cubbyholes or mailboxes. In this case, each mailbox doesn't direct mail to a different user, but instead allows a different type of mail to be received. One box might accept only magazines, another bills, still another newsletters, all of them addressed ultimately to the same user.

The many ports that are open on a TCP/IP-connected PC work similarly. One port—and only one port—allows data to come in to the PC via the HTTP protocol that makes the World Wide Web function. Another port is available exclusively for e-mail. In general, these ports are open, and the computer is listening for data to arrive. (The software that does the actual listening is called a *socket*.) For each port, many sockets can exist. This, too, is key to how the World Wide Web works. On a Web server, one port is available for communication using the Web's HTTP protocol. Every user who connects to the server connects through the same port. In order for all of these simultaneous connections to be maintained and managed, each "plugs-in" to the server's single port through a different socket behind that port.

The following table names some of the most common ports and gives their number:

Port Number	Port Name
21	FTP (File Transfer Protocol)
22	SSH (Secure Shell)
23	Telnet
25	SMTP (Outgoing e-mail)
42	DNS (Name Servers)
80	HTTP (World Wide Web)
110	POP3 (Incoming e-mail)
113	IDENT
443	SSL (Secure Socket Layer)
6667	IRC (Internet Relay Chat)

Port Security

Two ways that security can be provided to systems behind a firewall are by shutting down ports, sockets, or both. If, for example, you don't want anyone on your corporate network to be able to retrieve e-mail from the big, wide world—which might contain a disastrous virus—or send e-mail—which might give your trade secrets to a competitor— you can simply program your corporate firewall to shut down port 25 and port 110. All other Internet traffic will flow normally, but e-mail services will simply be unavailable.

Similarly, if you don't ever use Internet Relay Chat, closing port 6667 and its related port 113 can close a hole that many hackers have learned to exploit. Closing all the external ports on your network basically hides your entire network from the world outside. You can't get out while the configuration is set in that manner, but no one can get in, either. Indeed, from outside, it appears that your network doesn't even exist.

Other Common Internet Protocols

The TCP/IP set of protocols handles the problems of routing packets from place to place and reassembling messages in an adequate manner.

Other Internet protocols deal with higher-level transactions. For example, the File Transfer Protocol (FTP) specifies how one computer can ask another computer to send it a copy of one or more files. Various mail protocols deal with how to handle e-mail. (These include protocols for addressing messages, and maintaining virtual mailboxes.) The Gopher protocol lets you access information on a remote computer arranged into a hierarchical menu. The rlogin and telnet protocols are for remote logins; they specify a way that you can convert your computer into a terminal to some remote computer (provided you have an account on that remote computer). rlogin stands for "remote login" and is used from one server to another on the same network, whereas telnet stands for "terminal network" and is used from one server to another regardless of whether they're on the same network.

Some of the more recent additions to the family of Internet protocols are ones used in connection with the World Wide Web. Even more protocols are being proposed all the time, and no doubt some of them will be adopted as official Internet protocols at some future time.

One standard whose popularity is growing is "multicasting." This means that when you send a digital video to multiple recipients, instead of sending actual copies of each data packet to each recipient, the data packets can carry multiple addresses and be sent to all those places in the most efficient possible manner. (That is to say, a packet might travel over most of the distance from you to your recipients before being copied into the video player program at each recipient's location. Thus on almost all the links only one copy of each packet would have to be transmitted.)

As TV and radio broadcasting over the Internet continue to grow in popularity, the importance of multicasting will continue to grow along with it. Right now there are many Web sites that offer something very much like a radio or TV broadcast. But the way they work today requires that a separate copy of every data packet be sent from that site to each of the (most likely huge number of) receiving computers. The consequent growth in the Internet's total traffic could be sharply limited if almost all of those duplicate packets could be avoided—which is precisely what multicasting promises to do.

Keep in mind that all these protocols are voluntary standards. Someone proposes one, a committee of volunteers discusses and publishes it for additional commentary, and then it gets adopted and published as an official Internet standard. However, that doesn't ensure that anyone will actually use it. Still, this process has proven to work remarkably well. The truly useful protocols do get widely supported by hardware and software vendors soon after (or in some cases well before) their official adoption.

Assuring a Quality of Service— Tomorrow's Internet

The new Internet that is being developed today will have a number of important new features. One of the most eagerly awaited is support for Quality of Service (QoS). This is a new protocol that lets users tag packets by the importance of their getting where they are going in a timely manner.

There are at least two reasons why you might want to use this feature. One is if you are sending a "streaming" multimedia file. This could be a movie, a TV show, a song, and so forth. Whatever it is, the intention is that the recipient will play it immediately, as it is coming over the Internet.

If you are going to enjoy playing such a streaming multimedia file it better keep coming all the time until it is through. Likewise, to enjoy talking to someone in a telephone conversation, you don't want any long delays in the transmission of your speech or that of the other party.

The other reason for wanting quick and consistent packet delivery might simply be that you value your message very highly, and in particular its timely delivery. Think, for example, of an order to your stockbroker to buy or sell a security that is rapidly changing its price. Any inadvertent delay might cost you a great deal of money.

Of course, everyone would *like* to have their messages go over the Internet at the ultimate possible speed. But are you willing to pay extra to get that service? Some people will be willing to pay for higher QoS, at least some of the time. This is why it is important to have a way to differentiate those packets whose quickest possible delivery is important from the others. Then users and ISPs can negotiate what level of service they'll get, and what they will have to pay for that service.

Summary

The subject of the Internet is huge. Thousands of books have been dedicated to it, and we've no doubt that thousands more are in our future. In trying to keep the chapter's goals realistic, we've not tried to use this chapter to exhaustively explain "how the Internet works." What we have done here is take the TCP/IP stack of protocols—which, collectively, enable the Internet to do what it does—and shown how it and a few of its key pieces function. You've seen IP addressing, which empowers the actual trafficking of data from place to place. You've encountered core routers that direct that data all over the world and are capable of avoiding network congestion or failure. We've touched on some of the sub-protocols of the Internet, such as HTTP, which facilitates the functioning of the World Wide Web, and talked about ports, which let those protocols function. We've also spoken about firewalls, which are the primary source of security against inappropriate and undesirable data movement.

Now, it's your turn. If networking fascinates you, explore. You'll find a lifetime of learning waiting for you.

Video Acceleration

In the early days, the VGA display systems were very slow. On one hand, the CPU had to spend lots of time processing the graphics data. On the other hand, the bus is flooded with the massive amount of data that was transferred. All these are excessive system burdens. Even worse, for the adaptors that use DRAM as the graphic memory, data reads and writes could not be performed simultaneously, causing serious delays.

With current multimedia and 3D application demands, traditional video cards can no longer deliver the performance needed. To provide the graphic power needed, you need a special type of video adapter that contains its own processor to boost performance levels. Called graphic accelerators, these cards have processors specialized for computing graphical transformations for achieving much better results than the general-purpose CPU.

Without a graphic accelerator, the majority of the workloads are placed on the computer CPU. The basic CPU is not designed for graphic processing. With a graphic accelerator, the computer's CPU is freed up to execute other commands while the accelerator's processor is handling the graphics computation works. Instead of transferring an entire raw screen image to the frame buffer, the CPU only needs to provide a small set of drawing instructions. The accelerator's driver will interpret the instructions and have the card's on-board processor execute the instructions. Operations that can be "accelerated" include:

- Line drawing
- Polygon drawing
- Font scaling
- Bitmap transfers
- Bitmap painting
- Window resizing
- Window repositioning

Figure 20.1 shows the 3dfx Voodoo2 graphic card's driver software configuration screen.

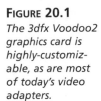

FIGURE 20.1

The 3dfx Voodoo2 graphics card is highly-customiz-able, as are most of today's video adapters.

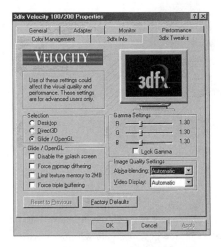

For 3D applications, there are even more elements to be accelerated. We will look into that after we go through the "fundamentals" of the current display technologies.

Vector Versus Bitmapped Images: Rasterizing and Rendering

Computer graphic images can be generated and stored inside a PC in two radically different ways: One is called vector art lines, circles, and curves and the other is referred to as bitmapped or raster pixel images. A piece of *vector art* is a file that contains mathematical descriptions (often called a *display list*) that specify how to generate the image but not the actual image itself. These descriptions break an image into its comprising component lines, rectangles, and curves.

A vector graphics file must be *rasterized* (reconstructed out of those components) before it can be presented as an actual image, either onscreen or on paper. Vector images are created with mathematical formulas. For example, to represent a circle, a vector image file includes the circle's position within the graphic (center point) and its radius. Your computer uses these two inputs to draw a raster version of the circle on the display adapter's screen.

One of the biggest advantages of vector graphics is that they can be enlarged or reduced without any loss of quality or definition, so they're resolution-independent. Because the graphic image is defined as a mathematical formula, all the computer needs to do is modify the input parameters as needed to create the appropriate size change when the image is rendered. Vector image files are also normally smaller than raster files. This is because only the data needed to reproduce the image is stored, not the image itself.

A *bitmapped* image, in contrast, has in the file the actual pixel image data. Each dot on your display is represented by a specific amount of data in the file. The actual amount of space that each pixel requires depends on the number of colors per pixel used in the image. For example, a 256-color image requires 8 bits per pixel (2^8 color combinations). Your PC's video display adapter simply pumps those pixels to the screen display or printer to have them show up as a visible image.

Some bitmapped images are stored in a compressed form, which means that by any of several means, much or all of the redundancy in that image has been removed. For example, the TIF file format enables you to compress the graphic image using one of several compression methodologies. The compression method you choose is important because some methods provide superior results. Some methods produce a very small file that is easily transferred over the Internet.

Unfortunately, some of the most aggressive compression methods also lose a small amount of the graphics data. These are known as *lossy compression methods,* and you should use them only when space is the prime consideration and some loss of detail is acceptable. Naturally, your PC must reverse any compression process to recover the original pixel data before the image is shown on the screen.

A bitmapped or raster file contains individual pixels similar to a real photo. An artist can generate one by using a paint program or scanning an image in from a printed original. Raster, bitmapped art is resolution-dependent. The resolution of the art determines the size of the file and the "sharpness" of the reproduction. This type of digital art cannot be enlarged or reduced at will without some deterioration of its quality. (Diagonal lines become jagged if you enlarge the image; detail is lost if you reduce its size.)

A *raster* is a name given to the way in which a PC display (and television sets) makes its images. The display device sweeps across each line of the image, working its way down the screen from line to line. Eventually, all the picture elements (pixels) on each line are drawn, which completes the raster. (The word raster comes from the Latin word for a fork. Think of a fork being dragged from side to side of a region of dirt. It would leave lines in the ground similar to the raster image lines on a video display.) The *rasterizing engine* is a software program or a piece of hardware that takes in the vector art descriptions and produces all the pixels needed to paint the raster.

There is one other major consideration when choosing between vector and bitmapped graphics: display speed. The rasterization process for vector art requires relatively more computer power. A graphics coprocessor or an accelerated video card can do much of the work, but some must be done by the PC's CPU. This means there are fewer CPU cycles available for other tasks, which might slow some applications, such as an animated presentation, to a crawl and ruin the effect that you're trying to create. Bitmapped files have an advantage because they're ready to show. All the computer needs to do is send the pixel data to the video screen, and the image quickly appears. As a result, bitmapped images are often faster to display as animated sequences.

It would be easy to choose between bitmapped and vector graphics at this point if it weren't for another problem. Generally, bitmapped images provide a good appearance only at the resolution at which they were prepared. This means that your 800×600 pixel animation might lose some crispness and detail when displayed at 640×480 pixels and might look stretched at 1024×768 pixels. (Some image display programs can scale these images, but unless they are specifically directed to do so, bitmapped images will display as received pixel-for-pixel.)

3D Vector Images

Another kind of vector image is one that specifies objects in full, three-dimensional (3D) form. For example, if the drawing you created were a sphere, the vector image file would describe the sphere using a center point and a radius, just as you would with the circle. In this case, however, you'd need to specify an X, Y, and Z axis location for the center point. In addition, you would need three radius measurements for height, width, and depth. (Theoretically, you could get by with a single radius measurement for a sphere, but supplying all three radius measurements enables you to create elliptical shapes as well.)

3D vector images are representational art, just like any other image that we've discussed. The image file contains a 3D description of how to draw an object, not the object itself. However, 3D image files often go beyond the descriptions found in 2D files to create realistic-looking objects onscreen.

Drawing a 3D image requires a substantially more complex process called *3D rendering*. In addition to size and positional information, a 3D image file often includes information about object surface textures, the positions of all of the light sources in the scene, and the point of view from which it is being viewed. The 3D scene-rendering engine then uses all those facts about the objects to construct an image that corresponds to what you would see if you were looking from the specified point of view at the prescribed objects.

There are other considerations with 3D images as well. For one thing, even though an object is fully rendered, the viewer might not be able to see it in its entirety. The object might be partially obscured by other objects in the scene. With both rasterizing and rendering, the work proceeds from the background toward the viewer. This enables the drawing program to create a realistic image that takes the viewer's perspective into account.

In rasterizing, perspective is handled by simply drawing objects in place, and then allowing "nearer" objects to replace those pixels with their own, thus overwriting the hidden portions of farther-away objects. Rasterizing has the advantage of allowing a programmer to create a 3D effect with relatively simple programming methodologies. The main problem with rasterizing is that the program will waste time drawing pixels that it doesn't need.

In 3D rendering, an attempt is made to decide before actually rendering an object whether it will be obscured or outside the field of view. It is worth spending the effort of rendering only on objects that are at least partially visible. The advantages and disadvantages of this method are the direct opposite of rasterizing. 3D rendering is harder for the programmer to create, but more efficient in operation.

How PCs Create Compelling Visual Images

You probably think that when you look at something you see it, but you don't. *No one ever sees any objects.* We see, at the literal level (by which we mean our retinas receive), a constantly changing pattern of colored light. Hidden in this pattern are clues from which we can learn about the world "out there." Those clues are almost always ambiguous. We cannot infer with certainty what is really out there just from those clues, but we can and do make reasonable guesses. Indeed, we must do that, for without a clear notion of what probably is out there, we wouldn't be able to function.

So if a PC's video display shows a pattern of colored light that resembles something that would come to us from some arrangement of objects, we are likely to interpret that scene as if it actually contained those objects. The more accurately the PC display simulates natural light patterns, the more realistic we say it is; the more we believe what we see. In terms of multimedia, this mostly means that we need enough total pixels, with enough possible colors per pixel, and the capability of changing those pixel colors quickly enough for moving images.

If you see something and soon thereafter see a modified version of that same thing, you are likely to interpret what you have seen as movement or change in a single object. You needn't see every stage of the movement or change; just seeing several successive stages in the process is sufficient. This fact, known as the *persistence of vision*, is what makes motion pictures work.

Decades before the invention of the first motion picture film, inventors of devices such as the Phenakistiscope and Zoetrope discovered that still images, displayed under the right conditions in rapid succession, could produce the illusion of motion in the viewer's mind. (Most of us have seen these, and similar, early devices in children's museums. Phenakistiscopes, for example, are those slotted disks that spin in front of a mirror. You look through the slots to see apparent movement created from still drawings on the backside of the disk.)

Early developers of movies experimented with display rates until they found a minimum number of images per second that would enable most people to see a continuous motion instead of a succession of snapshots. For the first few decades of motion picture history, movie makers displayed images at approximately 16 frames per second (fps). Standard film in modern movies runs at 24fps. In the United States, analog television runs video image sequences at 30fps (most of the rest of the world uses 25fps). The 30fps number for video and the 24fps number for film is a little deceptive. The reason is that film and video, due to the way they capture images, introduce natural motion blurring into each frame. The motion blur, as it progresses from frame to frame, adds something to the viewer's illusion of motion.

All of these schemes work for the viewer and seem natural, but higher frame rates produce smoother illusions of motion and less flicker thus, brighter, more convincing images.

Why is all this important? Because it suggests how to fool the brain into thinking you are seeing things that aren't actually there. An early digital artist, John Whitney, once said, "He who controls the pixels controls the image." He simply meant that if you could digitally compute and control each pixel in every frame of a moving picture, you could control the viewers' illusions about what they were seeing. At the time he said this, back in the early 1980s, computers weren't powerful enough to do that for more than a very rudimentary type of image. Now they are powerful enough, and we see evidence daily of just how much image manipulation is thereby made possible. (It used to be said, "Seeing is believing." That is simply no longer true or at least you are well advised not to take that point of view uncritically as you are probably well aware.)

The patterns of light that fall on each of your retinas are 2D patterns, but the world we invent in our minds to explain those stimuli is in 3D, just as is the physical world by which those patterns were generated. How do we get the extra dimensionality? We can do this in many ways. The most obvious one is by using our two eyes. The patterns on our two retinas differ slightly in ways that hint at the 3D quality of the world at which we are looking. But we don't really need those clues to see the world in 3D. Just cover one eye and look around. Do you have any trouble picking out which objects are nearer and which are farther away? Probably not.

We infer depth from a single eye's view by using what are called *monocular depth cues*. These cues include such things as noticing which objects block the view of portions of other objects. The blocking objects are clearly in front of those they block from our view. Another clue is the relative size of objects. The farther away an object is, the smaller it appears to be.

You might wonder why this matters. After all, you don't normally cover one eye when you look at your PC. Ah, but both your eyes see the same image on the surface of the PC's video display. Yet, with appropriate use of monocular depth cues in that image, you can become convinced that you are looking through the screen at some 3D image.

It turns out that these monocular depth cues are more important than the stereoscopic (two-eye) ones. This is why a flat photograph of a scene can still give the illusion that you are looking at a 3D scene. Of course, adding stereoscopic information helps add to the sense of reality. That is why almost all virtual reality systems include a means of creating two independent images and sending each to just one of the viewer's eyes. Still, we can create some pretty compelling visual experiences, which is what we're often seeking to do using only a single video display monitor presenting the same image to both eyes.

Making Images with Visual Pizzazz

The simplest images are static ones, and if those images are sufficiently bold and detailed, they can be quite compelling. Adding even a small amount of apparent movement to an image, however, can add a great deal of excitement. For this reason, animation has become commonplace, especially in multimedia applications.

An image on a PC's display screen can involve a lot of information. At a minimum, it will have the standard VGA resolution image (640 pixels per line and 480 lines per image), with each pixel having 1 of 16 possible colors. Such an image has 307,200 pixels, and for each one, half a byte of information is needed to specify its color. This means that if you want to replace one image with another, you must move over 150,000 bytes of information into the video frame buffer.

Many modern PCs have SVGA displays with higher resolutions and higher color depth. To specify this type of image, you must have three bytes, or 24 bits, of color information for each of 786,432 pixels (assuming TrueColor images that have sets of 1024×768 resolution pixels that are described by red, green, and blue triplets). That is 2 1/4MB of data just to specify one static image.

Images with this many simultaneous colors are called *photorealistic,* because they can reproduce almost anything that you can capture on a photograph. Resolution is not nearly as important to the illusion of photorealism as is the number of colors. You can realize this by simply noticing that the resolution of normal TV images is relatively modest. At best, a TV can display about 550 pixels per line, and most TV sets don't really resolve more than about 300 to 400 lines in each image. If you want to animate a scene with images this complex and in particular if you try doing it by creating a new image for each sixtieth of a second, the video subsystem of your PC has a tough job cut out for it. Also, the CPU and main bus might be taxed in the extreme, shoveling new data to the video display system quickly enough to update that image as needed.

There are several ways to cut this task down to size. One way is to use less-detailed images (ones with either fewer pixels or with fewer colors per pixel). That works, but it often means settling for a less-compelling visual experience. Another way is to change the image less often or to change only part of the image at a time. One trick, called *palette animation,* sometimes can be used to cut the work down to less than 2/1000 of the original amount. We'll describe next some of these ways that animated or video images can be generated more economically.

For just the price of a bit more RAM in the video image frame buffer and a little bit of added switching hardware, you can create animated imagery much more easily. To prevent flicker, the video card normally redraws the entire screen image at least 60 times per second. You must change that image only about 10 times per second to simulate convincing, if jerky, motion. At 30 image changes per second, the effect is as smooth as normal television.

Suppose you have enough frame buffer RAM to hold two complete images. First, draw a complete screen image in one region, and then, while the video output circuitry is scanning through that region 60 times each second, displaying that image on the screen, the CPU can be using the other region of the frame buffer RAM to create the next image. When that next image is ready, the CPU directs the video output circuitry to switch its focus to that new region, and the new image will appear onscreen within 1/60 of a second. Meanwhile, the CPU can go back to work in the original region of the frame buffer generating the next image.

If the images are so complex that the CPU must spend a second or more on each one, you will get the effect of a slide show. If it can create wholly new images in less than about 1/15 of a second, the result appears to be a movie. Giving the CPU a whole fifteenth of a second to create an image, however, means cutting the required rate of data pumping from CPU to video frame buffer by four over that which would be required to keep up with the full 60-frame-per-second rate used by the video output circuits. Thus, a mere 34MB per second will suffice, even for a 1024×768 photorealistic (24-bit per pixel) movie.

Bit Planes and Color Depth

Color depth refers, indirectly, to the number of possible colors of each pixel in a graphic screen image. If all the pixels are either black or white, you need only one bit to specify in which of these two colors a particular pixel is to be shown. If the image allows each pixel to have any one of four colors, you need two bits per pixel to define which of those four colors is used. By similar reasoning, you can see that four bits suffice to select any one of 16 colors. Eight bits can specify any one of 256 colors. The color depth is simply the number of bits needed to specify the color of each pixel.

The most commonly used color depths in PC images have been 2, 4, 8, 15, 16, and 24. Some special-purpose video cards use 32 bits per pixel, but in this case only 24 are used to specify the color. The remaining eight bits are used for what is called *alpha channel information*. This includes such information as degrees of transparency to let an underlying image (perhaps from some external video source) show through.

The following table shows a list of color depth settings.

Color Depth	Description	No. of Colors	Bytes per Pixel
4-bit	Standard VGA	16	0.5
8-bit	256-color	256	1.0
16-bit	High color	65,536	2.0
24-bit	True color	16,777,216	3.0

A *bit plane* is simply an organization of the bits that store an image in a three-dimensional array. First you form a planar array of bits, with one bit for each pixel on each line of the raster-scan image. Then you replicate this plane as many times as there are bits per pixel, placing each bit plane behind its predecessor. The result for *N* bits per pixel is a collection of *N* planes.

To put some numbers to this, consider a common VGA graphic display. The resolution of the entire image is 640 pixels per line and 480 lines. This says there are 307,200 total pixels. Normal VGA specifies that each pixel can have any one of a specified set of 16 colors. That means that the color depth is four bits. So, for each pixel you must have 1/2 byte of video image RAM, for a total of 153,600 bytes (exactly 150KB). Because RAM chips always hold a number of bits that is some integer power of two, normally VGA video cards carry 256KB of video image RAM.

Video Image RAM

We just said that the video image RAM is typically on the video card. Is that always true and why? Screen images for a PC must be held in special memory locations. These locations must be accessible to the CPU, but they also must be accessible to the video image output circuitry. The CPU needs rapid access to them, but the video output circuitry needs even more rapid access. This dictates where the chips that make up that memory must be placed physically.

If you have a plug-in video card, because the video image output circuitry is on the card, it only makes sense to put the video image RAM there as well. If your PC has its video display adapter circuitry located on the motherboard, you will find the video image RAM somewhere very near it. In any event, the video image RAM consists of a separate set of chips from those that make up the PC's main memory. That is because of the special qualities this memory must have to enable it to be placed next to the video image output circuitry. (There are a very few exceptions to this, incidentally. Silicon Graphics, Inc. developed a Visual Computing architecture for their Visual Workstation systems that enables nearly the entire system's main memory to be used for video-related purposes. Of course, one aspect of how this is achieved is that all memory in these systems must meet the higher performance and tolerance specifications reserved for dedicated video memory in more standard-use PCs.)

Exceptions aside, the newest mainstream PCs separate things even a bit more fully. They use an advanced graphics port (AGP) into which you plug an AGP video card. This AGP connector, shown in Figure 20.2, carries the data from the CPU over a different set of wires than those that serve all the other plug-in cards, and it can do this both at the same time as other data is going to the other plug-in cards (for example, on the PCI bus) and several times more rapidly than the data flow in the PCI bus.

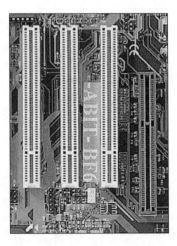

The video image RAM is located physically on the video card (or in the near vicinity of the video output circuitry). Logically, things seem quite different. From the perspective of the CPU, this block of RAM is just more RAM, like any other it can see in its memory address space. This block of memory in 386-and-higher CPUs can have its physical memory addresses remapped to any location within the CPU's logical address space.

Character-based images are prepared by the CPU. It stores the ASCII values for the characters to be displayed, with an attribute byte for each one, in the display adapter's video RAM. These are the simple images. Much harder to create are graphic images, simply because they have so much more information in them. One way to do this job and the only way it was done in early PCs is to again have the CPU compute the correct *color value* (the number of bits the color depth requires) for each pixel and then store those numbers in the video display adapter's video image RAM. This works, but it uses a lot of the CPU computing power.

A better solution for creating complex graphic images is to include a *graphics coprocessor* as part of the video display adapter. This is a small computer within the PC (located on the video display adapter option card, unless your PC has its video circuitry all on the motherboard). Its sole job is computing pixel color values for graphic images. The program that is creating the image can describe that image in fairly broad, high-level terms. For example, it might specify that a triangle is to be drawn and give the coordinates of the corners, the width, and color of the line to be used, and perhaps a color to use to fill the interior of the triangle. (This sort of sequence of high-level instructions of a graphic image is called a *display list,* as opposed to the detailed pixel image data otherwise required for a graphic image.)

If your PC has a graphics coprocessor, most of the time the CPU won't compute the image's pixel information, but it will instead pass instructions at this high level to the graphics coprocessor. That device will then compute which pixels in the image must be set to the color of the border and which are to be set to the fill color. And it will load all those pixel values into the video image RAM.

Perhaps the most significant point to make here is that the speed of data flow from graphics coprocessor to video image RAM and the flow from there to the screen are controlled only by the details of how the video card is built. If you have a high-end video card, it might use a very fast clock speed and a very wide data bus (up to 128 bits flowing in parallel) between the graphics coprocessor and the video image RAM. Furthermore, whenever the images being formed are very detailed (high-image resolution) and have a lot of color depth, the data flow from that RAM to the screen must also be tremendously fast. Naturally, the high-end video cards can support whatever rate they must to handle the images they are designed to create.

The following table shows the commonly used graphic memory types. Note that memory that supports dual port allows reads and writes to be performed simultaneously, leading to much higher performance.

	EDO	VRAM	WRAM	SDRAM	SGRAM	RDRAM
Maximum throughput (in MB/s)	400	400	960	800	800	600
Dual- or single-ported	Single	Dual	Dual	Single	Single	Single
Typical speed (in nanoseconds)	50-60ns	50-60ns	50-60ns	10-15ns	8-10ns	Depends on clock speed

The following table shows the possible combinations of color depth and resolution settings and their corresponding memory requirements.

Amount of Video Memory	Resolution	Color Depth	Number of Colors
1MB	1024×768	8-bit	256
	800×600	16-bit	65,536
2MB	1024×768	8-bit	256
	1280×1024	16-bit	65,536
	800×600	24-bit	16.7 million
4MB	1024×768	24-bit	16.7 million
6MB	1280×1024	24-bit	16.7 million
8MB	1600×1200	32-bit	16.7 million

The RAMDAC

We mentioned the DAC (Digital Analog Converter) previously. What exactly is a DAC? DAC stands for digital-to-analog converter. It is a single chip device that converts digital data into analog signals. DAC is used in many device types, including modems. The DAC used by a video adapter is called Random Access Memory Digital-to-Analog Converter (RAMDAC), which can convert digital data into analog signals for the monitor to process and display.

A RAMDAC consists of four components. The built-in SRAM is one of those. It is used for storing the color map. The remaining components are the three DACs that manage the monitor's primary colors electron guns. In fact, there is one DAC for each of the red, green, and blue colors the CRT uses to produce a complete color spectrum.

As mentioned, DAC converts data into signal. The rate at which the RAMDAC performs conversion determines the range of refresh rates and the number of colors at a given resolution that the accelerator card can support. The "speed" of the RAMDAC, to be true, does not contribute much to the overall display performance.

The Driver Software

The graphics card's driver software is essential to the acceleration performance. It translates what the application wants to display on the screen into instructions for the graphics processor to use. The way it performs the translation, together with the way it utilizes the graphics processor features, determines the card's ultimate performance.

Some accelerator cards work best at low resolutions, whereas some work best with high-resolution applications. Typically, a separate driver is used for each resolution or color depth. This means that, if a corresponding driver is not optimized, the graphics card might perform very differently at the different resolution modes.

The graphic chipset supplier usually provides the card manufacturers with the "model driver". It is then up to the individual manufacturers to customize or optimize the code for their derived design versions.

More About AGP: Is it Really Faster?

You might have noticed that almost all graphic accelerator cards are now using AGP bus. You might have been told that AGP is much faster than PCI. So, does it mean that an AGP graphic card will run significantly faster than its PCI counterpart?

First, let's look into the theory behind AGP. Technically, AGP is superior because:

- It offers higher data transfer rates when it is time to move the geometry stream from the CPU to the graphics card.

- It allows your operating system to manage large amounts of textures in off-screen memory as well as in system memory, allowing the graphic card to access these textures directly in either location, and resulting in more flexible memory management.
- It has faster clock speeds and bus pipelining.

First of all, is "texture" that important? Yes! All 3D objects are basically plain polygons. For these polygons to "model" a real world object, you must create 2D bitmap pictures, and wrap these pictures around the polygon. This is the process of texturing. Without good textures, the 3D objects will definitely look unreal.

AGP uses one of the following two ways to deal with textures: DMA mode and Execute mode.

In DMA mode, direct memory access is being used, and textures are stored and accessed mainly from the video RAM. In Execute mode, the graphic processor can access the texture information in main memory without first copying it to video RAM. In theory, DMA mode should be slightly faster because the graphics card can begin the process of fetching texture before it is needed to paint pixels onscreen. However, practically speaking, the effective bus throughput difference between Execute and DMA mode can be of great significance!

You can argue that DMA mode benefits from the fact that access to textures in high bandwidth local memory can generate higher performance. Execute mode forces textures to be accessed via the slower system memory, resulting in delay and bottleneck. Although this argument is technically correct, somehow it contradicts with the original purpose of AGP deployment.

In the good old days when video RAMs were extremely expensive, most cards had only 4MB or less on board. To support the massive amount of 3D textures, storing data in the main system memory was the ideal choice.

If you check the configurations of the modern 3D cards, almost all of them come with a minimum of 16MB video RAM, and 32MB and 64MB versions are popping up everywhere. In this case, the need for storing textures in the main system memory is minimal.

Many 3D applications are now built on the AGP DMA mode. Apart from performance, compatibility is the key issue. DMA mode requires that textures be copied to the video RAM first, which is architecturally compatible with the massive installed base of PCI accelerators. Execute mode, on the other hand, is a whole new mechanism that only runs with AGP.

AGP Texturing

The AGP Execute mode is also called "AGP texturing". Some people tend to believe that by fully "turning on" AGP texturing, performance can increase significantly. This is, in fact, quite misleading.

When AGP texturing is fully on, the graphics card has to take control of the system's main memory bus for the purpose of accessing texture data. When this happens, the system's CPU is locked out of main memory. This means the CPU might have to wait for its turn of memory access! Because many of the 3D applications are computational intensive, the overall performance can be adversely affected to a serious extent.

In 1997, Intel released the specifications for the second generation of AGP, which is AGP 2.0 (or AGP 2X). With AGP 2.0, things run at twice the speed of AGP 1.0. Under the new version, computers can process up to 1GB of graphics data per second, although the dedicated graphics bus will continue to run at 66MHz. And now, we are talking about AGP 4X, and probably 8X in the works. Still, with the increasing amount of installed video RAMs on the card, as well as the other factors associated with the system, this increase in "X" might not be of great significance.

AGP Pro

In the early days of AGP deployment, all chipset/motherboard designers used the PCI power recommendation for the AGP slot. That proved to be fine at that design stage and suited all available AGP cards.

As the performance of the video processors increase, this "old" AGP power design approach finally reached its limit. Many systems crashed or didn't start at all. The problem was that the AGP slot failed to provide the energy-hungry video processor with enough power.

To fix the power consumption problem, a couple approaches can be used.

- One easy way is to provide better power supply to the AGP slot. This requires a modification of the motherboard design, or that you connect the 3.3V AGP slot directly to the ATX power connector.
- Another way to solve the problem is to reduce the power consumption level of the video processor chip. The 3D chip makers are trying hard to shrink the graphics chip, so that the consumed power, the heat of the chip, and the voltage can all be reduced. In fact, this is the preferred way, as heat is also a big problem when the 3D chip is running at high speed with high power consumption.

It takes time for the 3D chipmakers to improve their chip designs. Meanwhile, for solving the current problem, AGP Pro has been introduced.

AGP Pro was released in April 1999. It provides the necessary power and consequent cooling by deploying a different connector design—the AGP Pro connector offers additional pins at the front and the back of the connector, although it is fully backward compatible.

The AGP Pro slot comes in different versions, including AGP Pro 3.3V, AGP Pro 1.5V, and AGP Universal. AGP Pro 3.3V and AGP Pro 1.5V have blocking pins to prevent insertion of an unsupported AGP card, whereas AGP Pro Universal does not.

So, what are those additional pins for? The original AGP standard can supply 25W to the graphics card. With the additional pins PRSNT1# and PRSNT2#, the AGP Pro cards can report its power requirements to the motherboard and provide a total of 50W or 110W—which is at the minimum, doubling the power supplied.

Of course, increasing power equals increasing heat. So, proper cooling methods must be deployed for the card and for the system.

AGP Levels of Performance

Quality 3D applications require frequent movement of textures, geometry data, and commands across the AGP bus. The AGP protocol offers four modes to accomplish the movement.

Frame mode is mainly used when data is written or read directly to or from the graphics controller. The type of data carried is mainly geometry data and command lists to a memory-mapped region on the 3D card. In some circumstances, texture data can be handled as well. In AGP frame mode, AGP pipelining mode, or sideband addressing mode, texture data that's written to or read from the main memory can be carried.

Each of these modes offers a unique level of AGP performance. Technically speaking, Frame mode offers only baseline level performance using the PCI protocol, whereas AGP pipelining mode offers relatively higher performance. However, maximum performance relies on the sideband addressing mode. As a summary, AGP frame mode can support the AGP 1X rate (66MHz, 264MB/s), whereas AGP pipelining and sideband addressing each can offer up to the 2X rate (133MHz, 528MB/s).

In AGP frame mode, data transfers occur at the rate of 264MB/s, which is twice the throughput of shared 33MHz PCI. In AGP pipelining mode, multiple outstanding transactions can be created to avoid bandwidth degradation produced by round-trips to main memory. The critical issue here is that, because pipelined transfers are not coherent with the CPU's cache, reads or writes can be performed without delay while the CPU caches are checked to see whether they contain the latest copies of the corresponding data.

Sideband addressing mode offers the highest AGP performance by introducing a separate address/command bus, which is known as the Sideband Address Port (SBA). This SBA can be used by the graphic controller to make data requests without interrupting the data bus.

AGP Sidebanding and Overclocking

Sideband addressing mode deploys SBA. So, what is SBA, and why does it exist?

One way to maximize the efficiency and throughput of the AGP bus is separate the address bus from the data bus. The sidebanding approach is to deploy an additional set of eight sideband lines, which are collectively referred to as the sideband address (SBA) port. The SBA port is 8 bits wide. It allows the graphics controller to issue new AGP requests and commands simultaneously while data continues to be transferred on the main 32 address/data (AD) lines.

Although the AGP bus can transmit AGP requests through the AD bus as well, the separation is logical in a sense that it can prevent the graphics controller from clogging up the AD bus with data requests. Remember one thing, sidebanding is a hardware level feature, meaning it is entirely transparent to your applications. Hence, you won't likely locate any special function marked with "sidebanding support" in your application.

So, what does the SBA have to do with overclocking? First of all, for achieving maximum performance, people like to overclock everything that is overclockable, from CPU to RAMDAC to the PCI bus, including AGP. Those who tried hard to overclock the AGP2X system frequently reported failed overclocking attempts.

In theory, overclocking the AGP bus is a logical step for improving the AGP performance, because it can bring about a substantial increase in AGP bandwidth. You do this by adjusting the bus speed (in MHz) of the AGP system from within your BIOS. However, do keep in mind that the act of overclocking is risky, because you are trying to run your hardware at a speed higher than that specified by the manufacturer. The AGP bus specification runs at a clockspeed of 66MHz for both AGP1X and AGP2X. Because AGP2X transfers data on *both* the rising and falling edges of the AGP signal, the increase of bus speed beyond 66MHZ can make your system unstable (you will have to push the limits on both sides).

It is widely known that, with AGP 1X, the overclocking margin can go as high as 60 to 70%. However, with AGP2X, a 12% margin is already difficult to achieve. In fact, SBA's timing sensitivity contributes partly to this "bottleneck".

Is there anyway to specifically enable or disable the SBA? That really depends. First of all, not every AGP2X card supports sidebanding. Some 3D card use chipsets that are sidebanding capable, whereas some do not. If it happens that your card does support sidebanding, you will need to determine whether there is any BIOS patch or any option in the card driver that allows you to enable or disable the feature manually. In any case, check with the manufacturer before proceeding.

The World of 3D

3D graphics and animations require lots of computing power as well as a large amount of memory. Because of the unique nature of 3D, the way acceleration is done is entirely different.

A 3D graphics chip takes the workload away from the CPU and performs the drawing and rendering processes in two major stages: geometry and rendering.

Polygons are the building blocks of the 3D images. At the geometry stage, all the objects in the 3D world are defined and arranged. Geometry set-up is the last stage of the graphics pipeline performed before the rendering stage. Massive calculations are involved, in particular, to scale the objects properly, to move the objects to their appropriate locations, to rotate the objects to their appropriate positions, and to coordinate the object interactions.

Triangle setup is the process that converts the data created by the geometry setup into a format that can be used by the 3D accelerator. After taking the inputs, the 3D accelerator starts the rendering process.

In the rendering stage, the 3D accelerator draws the pixels by reading them from the memory and writing them to the frame buffer. In a typical 3D animation scene, there are thousands of polygons on each frame. These polygons must be updated and transmitted through the memory at a rate of about 30 times per second. This frame rate, which is measured in frames per second (fps), indicates the capability of the accelerator. The higher the fps, the more powerful the accelerator is.

Before we continue our discussion of 3D acceleration, it is helpful for you to understand the following terminologies related to 3D rendering. *Texture mapping* is a process that wraps a 2D bitmap image over a 3D object. This is how we "paint" an object. *Z-buffering* calculates pixels and specifies the corresponding "Z" value, for determining the order of objects display. Put it this way, if the Z value of a particular pixel is bigger than another one, this pixel must be displayed later. *Anti-aliasing* reduces the "noise" present in an image by smoothing out the edges. *Gouraud shading* applies shadows to the surface of an object in order to make the outcome look more solid.

3D Acceleration

In the past, you could enjoy 3D acceleration by installing a dedicated add-on card that worked with the 2D card. That was the case with the first generation of the 3dfx Voodoo card. Part of the reason of this "separation of duties" is the fact that a combo 2D/3D chip might not be able to achieve satisfactory results on both ends.

Nowadays, the advancement in technologies allows the 3D acceleration functions to be integrated into the 2D chipset, and at the same time maintain a reasonable balance between 2D and 3D performance.

The following figures show the different generations of 3D chipsets on the market. Among them, GeForce is the most popular chipset, as shown in Figure 20.3. It incorporates a built-in GPU for geometry calculation, thus greatly reducing the load of the CPU.

FIGURE 20.3

At the time of this writing, the nVidia GeForce chipset is the state of the art.

Figure 20.4 shows the ATI Radeon graphic chipset.

FIGURE 20.4

Another of today's major contenders is the ATI Radeon.

Figure 20.5 shows the ATI Radeon graphic chipset combo with a cooling fan.

FIGURE 20.5

Almost all of the latest 3D graphic chipsets on the market require heatsinks and cooling fans to operate..

Fifth-generation chipsets include:

- 3dfx Voodoo 4/5
- ATI Radeon
- Matrox G450/550
- NEC Kyro II
- nVidia's GeForce Series

Fourth-generation chipsets include:

- 3dfx Voodoo 3
- 3DLabs Permedia 3
- ATI Rage Fury
- Matrox G400
- VideoLogic Neon 250
- nVidia TNT2
- S3 Savage 4

Third-generation chipsets include:

- NEC PMX1
- 3dfx Voodoo 2
- nVidia TNT
- S3 Savage 3D
- Matrox MGA-G200

Second-generation chipsets include:

- 3dfx Voodoo 2
- Intel i740/752
- 3D Labs Permedia 2
- ATI 3D Rage
- Rendition v2200

First-generation chipsets include:

- 3dfx Voodoo
- 3D Labs Permedia
- ATI 3D Expression

What Qualifies a 3D Card a Top Performer?

After all the discussions, you might be wondering what criteria you can use to define a "top-performing" 3D card? Based on various inputs, a qualified 3D card should:

- Support at least 32MB of local video memory: Local memory access is always faster than access via the AGP bus. With 16MB of video memory, it is just enough to run your 3D applications at up to 1024×768 in 32 bit color depth. If you want to run realistic 3D scenes, you should have at least 32MB of video RAM so that you can achieve a state of 1280×1024 with 32-bit color. The video memory bandwidth is another important limiting factor of the 3D performance. Get a card with the fastest memory possible.

- Support 32-bit rendering: 32-bit color rendering with 32-bit Z-buffering provides the best quality and the best 3D simulations of reality. However, not all 3D cards support 32-bit rendering. Take Voodoo3 as an example. Its 16-bit 3D architecture requires a reduction of color information when your application supports 32-bit rendering.

- Support multiple rendering pipelines: It used to be the case that, when a pixel was processed, it had to be rendered in two or more passes to reach higher realism. When there are multiple rendering pipelines, processing can be done in parallel. As a minimum, a 3D chip should have at least two rendering pipelines. However, the more pipelines a card has, the more powerful it will be.

- Use high-quality RAMDAC: RAMDAC links the frame buffer and the analog CRT. The higher the RAMDAC's bandwidth, the more pixels you can display on the CRT per second. A faster RAMDAC is crucial for decent refresh rates and high-quality pictures at a higher resolution.

- Support different-sized textures: To achieve more realistic 3D experience, textures are much more detailed than they used to be. A good 3D card should be capable of supporting large-sized textures. A texture with a size of 2048×2048 is considered "highly detailed".

The GPU Debate

nVidia was the first to introduce the first mainstream graphics processing unit (GPU) in 1999. Its GeForce series is popular because of its brute processing power. It has a dedicated geometry processor that takes over the geometry calculations from the main CPU. In fact, "Ge" represents geometry. The GeForce chipset controls the entire 3D data stream using its "real-time 3D geometry engine". Comprising nearly 57 million transistors, the GeForce 3 GPU is capable of delivering many millions of sustained polygons and pixels per second. The resulting performance, measured in terms of frame rate per second, is amazing.

However, not everyone is in favor of this approach. From a business perspective, if the GPU is strong enough to meet the computation needs, the demand for higher speed CPUs will be adversely affected. The CPU manufacturer prefers a "soft" approach, an approach that deploys enhanced instructions sets in the processor. Intel's Katmai New Instructions (KNI) and AMD's 3DNow! have been introduced as a result. The market, however, does not seem to appreciate these processor extensions. At least, most of the 3D games on the market do not include support for these extensions.

SLI

SLI stands for *scan line interleaved*. It means you connect two 3D cards from the same manufacturer, have one card count every other horizontal line, and the other count the line after that. Put it this way: You have one 3D accelerator render the odd lines, and the other renders the even lines. When finished, the two groups of lines are combined to display the complete image.

This solution effectively places two complete 3D renderers in parallel, with each processor working on a different part of the image. Because of this "separation of duties," screen rendering can take half as much time.

Why should the workload be distributed on a per-line basis? Why can't we just divide the screen into two halves and have each half handled by one 3D card? This approach isn't as easily optimized.

Assume you divide your 3D modeling application screen in two parts, with one processor rendering the top half and one processor rendering the bottom half. If the top half shows only the polygonal models while the bottom half shows the rendered animation sequences, all the detail and hard rendering work is located in the bottom part of the screen, resulting in one processor being very fast and the other being very slow. With scan line interleaving, the load is shared on alternate lines, which means processing is always divided evenly.

In theory, SLI delivers twice the 3D performance. However, in the real world, your applications might not need that much raw computing power. It is worth it to note that the entire line of 3dfx Voodoo cards support SLI. On the other hand, the GeForce series, as of the date of this writing, does not support SLI.

FSAA and TruForm

Other competitors try to compete with the GeForce series by improving the quality of image. This is, in fact, understandable. Even with the help of a GPU, there is always a tradeoff between image quality and throughput. A GPU is good at increasing the processing power. It is not designed to specifically enhance the image quality though.

3dfx, the producer of the Voodoo series, unveiled its T-Buffer technology on its Voodoo5 series. This technology focuses on enhancing the photorealism in real-time 3D by offering full-screen anti-aliasing (FSAA), a feature that makes the screen outputs look smoother and more realistic.

At the time of this writing, 3dfx has been taken over by nVidia. ATI now emerges as nVidia's primary competitor. ATI's Radeon line of chipset is comparable to the GeForce series in terms of performance and quality. One of the ATI advantage is the use of TruForm, a technology that has the potential to significantly increase the quality of 3D images without sacrificing performance.

In these days, all kinds of new 3D technologies are popping up almost on a daily basis. More and more competitors are entering the lucrative 3D graphics market. This means, as a consumer, you have more choices to choose from.

The 256-Bit Magic

When you're shopping for a 3D card, you'll likely encounter marketing that talks about "256-bit acceleration" and similar features. But the graphics processors don't use a 256-bit architecture, and the memory interface is only 128 bits wide. So what's "256" all about? According to nVidia, their 256-bit rendering engine (also called QuadPipe) is, in fact, four independent rendering engines that work in parallel across 64-bit wide data busses to collectively provide currently unsurpassed performance. This is an example of data pipelining, which you first read about in Chapter 5.

Benchmarking the 3D Performance

How can you tell if one 3D card is better than another? There are many 3D-benchmarking tools available in the market to evaluate 3D accelerator performance. Many of them, however, are being accused of having bias towards particular chipsets produced by particular manufacturers. Some hardcore gamers prefer to use 3D games as benchmarking tools instead.

The following list includes commonly used 3D benchmarking applications:

- Quake III Arena
- AquaMark V22
- 3D Mark 99
- Unreal Tournament 4
- Max Payne

Keep in mind that, when you run any of the benchmarking applications, your entire system is under heavy demand. The processor has a lot of computation works to do. The motherboard chipset has a lot of coordination works to do too. Simply put, the accelerator is *not* the only thing that is tested.

In general, a 3D benchmark is producing only one number—the frame rate. This result presents the complete unity of all the system devices. So, what does this mean? From a practical viewpoint, good 3D performance can be achieved only if you have a good combination of hardware components and configuration. The 3D card alone is not going to do the job.

What is the definition of *frame rate* anyway? It is defined as the number of frames that can be displayed in a certain amount of time (usually in one second). It reflects adequately the real-world performance of a 3D card without regards to the picture quality. The higher the frame rate a card can sustain, the more powerful the card is, in general. However, frame rate can't tell if the picture quality is good. You will still have to judge by your eyes. It is safe, however, to *assume* that a 3D card with strong raw processing power can handle textures of higher detail levels, thus producing higher quality screen outputs.

Different vendors might show you frame rate comparisons between different products. Be very careful about the numbers—make sure all scores are obtained from tests performed on the same platform with the same application at the same resolution and color depth mode. It is almost certain that a lot more rendering performance is required to supply a certain frame rate at a high resolution than at a low resolution. All 3D cards will for sure score high frame rates at 640×480 and lower frame rates at 1600×1200.

For the latest 3D benchmarking information, visit the following Web sites:

- Anandtech: http://www.anandtech.com
- Tom's Hardware: http://www.tomshardware.com
- 3D chipset: http://www.3dchipset.com/

Summary

It's our hope that this chapter has made you more fluent in the technology and systems that go into making today's high-end video function and function well.

With the completion of this chapter, you've actually completed your exploration inside the PC. If you've read through from Chapter 1, you've been introduced to and taken through an advanced understanding of all the systems that make up today's PC. In the next chapter, the last, we'll take a look at what the future might hold.

21

Inside Tomorrow's PC

Here, at the end of your tour inside the PC, we take a few pages to look towards the future. Predicting the future has always been difficult, particularly in the realm of technology. Just two years ago it seemed all but certain that we'd be talking to our PCs now, rather than using the mouse or keyboard, and that our cellular phones would be giving us affordable world-wide access to the World Wide Web. There were also experts saying that it would be impossible to produce a microprocessor that functioned above 800MHz.

Little did we know, eh?

Under the best of circumstances, it's hard to know which emerging technologies to embrace. When times are tough, as they say, it's anyone's guess.

A Changed World

When this book was just going to press, the world changed. On September 11, 2001, terrorists crashed two commercial jet airplanes into New York's World Trade Center. A further jet crashed through one side of the Pentagon, in Washington, D.C., and a fourth crashed in Pennsylvania thanks to the heroic efforts of its passengers to divert that plane from its true target: the Capitol building of the United States of America. Thousands of people were killed. Still more were terribly injured. The most of our entire planet stood behind the United States of America in declaring that tolerance for terrorists and for the views that lead to terrorism is over.

What has that to do with your PC? Just about everything. Let me explain why.

First, as you likely know, the USA is the center of both hardware and software development for the PC. It seems likely at the time of this writing that the USA is on the verge of formally declaring itself at war, possibly on a scale unprecedented. If that occurs—or if it has occurred, by the time you read this—then a switch to a wartime economy could dramatically change the PC's immediate future. Technologies currently under development could find themselves on the back burner as America's corporations switch their production and R&D efforts to support total war. At the same time, the needs of the military in conflict commonly lead to the creation of revolutionary devices and technology that then become available in the commercial market in times of peace.

Of course, on an even larger scale, the world environment of September, 2001, when I'm writing this, has individuals, companies, and governments rethinking technology on a multitude of levels. Where will this lead? No one can say. I will venture a few observations, however, trying to look at each issue from two sides.

One of the most significant recent developments in PC technology has been a dramatic push towards copyright protection and data encryption. You learned about this sort of thing on the hardware level when you read about MultiMediaCards and Secure Digital cards. On the one hand, the availability of such technology makes it worthwhile for content producers to actually produce content—it's harder to "steal" content that is encrypted, so anyone who wants to listen to, say, a hit song, will need to pay for it. On the other hand, a society that permits the widespread proliferation of encryption is making tools available that can help criminals keep their plans and secrets secret. So it might be that the same government agencies that have previously supported the availability of encryption technologies will come to feel, instead, that such things are best kept for the government. Making sure that teenagers don't copy audio CD's isn't really quite as important as making sure that terrorists fail in their efforts. It might be that these products will continue to exist, but at a much lower level of encryption. If that happens, it's likely that hackers will find ways of quickly defeating the technology, making it obsolete even as it tries to get a foothold in the market. The American public, too, has lashed out against the availability of encryption technology, which might have made the disaster of September 11 easier to perpetrate.

On the other hand, many Americans and lawmakers are calling for an increase in the use of encryption to make it harder for criminals and terrorists to break into the vital systems that keep society functioning. If this view prevails, a new branch of technological development could sprout leaves, and we might see PCs and servers that keep their data encrypted almost continuously—even in memory and across the variety of internal subsystems—decrypting it on the fly only to display it on screen or to print it. We could see the widespread development of high-speed, special purpose processors that would enable the necessary encryption and decryption without impeding the performance of your computing experience. We could even see a new subsystem (the security subsystem) added to the five I discussed in Chapter 1.

Other major developments in the PC world of late have targeted notebook and other mobile PCs. They're lighter than ever and have larger screens, longer battery life, and dramatic multimedia capabilities so you can watch movies or develop presentations during long business flights across the country—or the world. But what will happen to those technical developments if the majority of airports adopt the new security measures in place at Los Angeles International Airport, which has banned all carry-on luggage? What will be the ongoing need for highly portable PCs if more companies ban international air travel for business, as has General Motors Corporation?

One area that has traditionally driven the multimedia side of PC technology has been gaming. The reality of games is higher than ever before, and the demand for that reality has driven hardware and software development. Video processing must be faster to support lifelike motion at realistic levels of color depth and high resolutions. Similarly, displays have required ever-lower dot-pitch values to display high resolutions clearly, and ever-faster refresh rates to keep flicker out of motion. But recent comments, notably from Marc Prensky, the author of *Digital Game-Based Learning*, suggest that today's hyper-realistic games might be useful training tools for those who would assault a peaceable society. One company's flight simulator game provides such a high level of reality that commercial pilots are known to use it to keep their own skills sharp. Other games might be teaching the importance of mastering other skills, like killing. More subtle levels of teaching are happening, too. What is the long-term impact, Mr. Prensky has asked, of teaching children that enemies are everywhere, that there is always another enemy present as soon as one is conquered, and that success lies in a mastery of violence? It's impossible to see how technical development will change—but change it will—if we decide, as a society, that video games are, perhaps, too realistic, or if the most popular games— which, incidentally, are the most violent ones—seem imprudent to release.

Wireless technologies, too, are liable to develop in unexpected ways and possibly at an unexpected pace. Security concerns have led to a dramatic increase in the sales and use of cellular telephones. With so many more customers using so much more airtime, two things seem inevitable. One, it will be necessary to accelerate the development and deployment of high-end technologies which will support this increase in cellular traffic. Cellular providers are not going to allow thousands of new customers to live in frustration because carrier infrastructure is insufficient for the number of calls, messages, and cellular-Internet connections flying through the air. Scaled-down versions of these commercial subsystems could find their way into the wireless networks of tomorrow's homes and general businesses.

Two, the sudden existence of thousands upon thousands of new customers will provide the customer base necessary to justify an accelerated development of the wireless Internet technologies that have, up to today, served only a largely unaffordable niche market. If supply and demand makes wireless Internet access less costly, more developers will release products and services for users of that access. That, in turn, will lower the cost of service, and so forth.

The future of Internet evolution has taken on new levels of uncertainty, too. Technology that was embraced for its ability to shrink the world might now be shunned for that very reason. We might find ourselves embracing amazing new online capabilities to help keep us "close" to our loved ones, well educated, and competitive in business in a world in which travel doesn't seem as safe as it once was.

The fact is, it's probably not realistic to talk of a world that has "recovered" from the events of September 11, 2001. It's more reasonable to think in terms of a new world that "incorporates" the events of and the lessons learned on that date and in subsequent months and years.

Sure Bets

Amidst all of the world's current uncertainties, there are very few sure bets when it comes to our technological future.

But there are a few. The cost of long-term storage will continue to plummet while its capacity and speed soar like never before. Today's IBM Microdrive has a maximum capacity of 1GB on a single platter, which is one-inch in diameter and weighs 16 grams. At the time of this writing, its price dropped by one-third. These drives use so little power that they can be supported by a pair of AA batteries inside a digital camera. Consider that, only a year ago, portable storage of the same capacity required an AC-powered drive and a five-inch diameter cartridge. In other developments, Maxtor's new ATA/133 "Fast Drive" technology boots the transfer rate between drive and computer to a maximum of 133MB per second. The same company's "Big Drive" initiative (actually part of the larger ATA/133 development) makes it possible for hard drives to have over 100,000 times the maximum capacity of today's largest (137GB) drives. The speed and capacity of these drives will make it reasonable and affordable to take digital video to new levels on a new scale.

Wireless networking—both local and long-distance—is another technology that is doubtless here to stay and thrive. The benefits of connectivity without the annoyance and cost of wires are clear. In light of recent world events, however, companies will have to be more innovative in their use of available bandwidth, because it's unlikely that the FCC will release any of today's military bandwidth for public or commercial use. Necessity being the mother of invention, we might see new ways of manipulating and multiplexing digital signals that will open up entire new worlds of connectivity.

Other "sure bets" are those that have been forever present in the history of the PC. The speed of processors will continue to increase as will the performance of memory. The cost of all components will, in the main, drop. Although it's arguably uncertain whether the demand for portable technologies will continue to drive components to ever-smaller sizes, the drive for speed will do so. There is a limit to how fast electrical signals can move through space. At some point, the only way to reduce the amount of time it takes for a PC to perform certain tasks is to reduce the space over which those tasks must occur. That means smaller components, shorter distances between components and subsystems, and ever-thinner connections.

The drive for speed has also led to the recent development of silicon-gallium arsenide chips, by Motorola, which combine two existing methods of producing chips to produce new, affordable, and blazingly fast components.

The forthcoming 64-bit processors, like Intel's Itanium, are capable of performing at unheard-of speeds and addressing amazing amounts of memory—up to 16 terabytes. These changes will both fuel and enable the usefulness of other developments I've already mentioned—like the ongoing explosion in the capacity and speed of magnetic storage. They will also make it possible for Internet-based servers to process many times more transactions than is currently possible. When you combine these changes with the ever-increasing speed of affordable broadband connections to the Internet, you open up whole new worlds of online education, conferencing, transaction processing, and even entertainment. 64-bit processors will also be able to make the most of the AGP Pro graphic interface bus, which has four times the electrical potential of regular AGP.

Your Own Glass Box

If you've read through this entire book, you've gained strong insight into what, I hope, you now think of a your own "glass box," your PC. You know what's inside that box, now, and you know how all of those components and subsystems work. It's that knowledge that changes "black boxes" into "glass boxes." It's also that knowledge that gives you power over every aspect of your PC. By understanding how it works, you can maximize its performance and its potential. That maximizes your own productivity and can really improve the subjective quality of your computing experiences. That understanding also puts you in position to intelligently consider future developments against your own needs. You'll be able to see more clearly through the haze of marketing, and you'll recognize jargon and buzzwords for what they are. You'll get more out of every dollar you spend on your PC or PCs, and that will make you more comfortable with the idea of new technologies. You'll better recognize their real potential and will have much more skill in making meaningful personal and professional choices. Your computing experience will be more stable and more secure, too. And, I hope, more enjoyable.

Knowledge and understanding of what's going on inside the PC will make your computer more like your old baseball glove, or hammer; more like your own violin, or artist's palette; more like your favorite pen, or your car; more like an extension of yourself that fits right, feels comfortable, and is an inherently satisfying tool.

The world has changed, but it has changed before and will again. Whatever the shape of the future, computer technology will be part of it. I hope you have found that reading this book has made you more confident about facing the challenges of that future—and the challenges of today.

PART IV

Appendixes

Operating Systems: The Middleman Between You and Your PC

The topics covered in this appendix are a substantial departure from those in the main parts of the book. Those emphasized hardware. This one is all about software. But it's not about all kinds of PC software, just one very special kind that you use every day.

In fact, this chapter is about the most popular computer program ever created—and one that most of its users normally don't even think about as a software program. We are referring to the *operating system*. Until recently, in nearly all PCs ever made, the operating system underlying everything was called DOS. The majority of PCs today use the Microsoft Windows 2000, Windows Me, or Windows XP operating system, and DOS has become a thing of the past. That notwithstanding, understanding the past is an important aspect of understanding the present. So, we'll take a look here at the past, present, and future as we discuss operating systems.

Most PC users think of the software they use in terms of the application programs: Word, Excel, and so on. But you couldn't run any of those programs unless you first ran the program that creates the environment in which they are designed to operate. For the three programs just mentioned, that environment creator is some version of Windows. Of course, you might be running some other PC operating system. Popular choices include Linux or one of several versions of Unix. We'll discuss these in the section of this chapter near the end entitled "Understanding Your Choices for Your PC's Operating System." Let's first take a look at the operating system that has the various versions of Windows as its legacy. It's also the operating system that, until the release of Windows XP, was running under every version of Windows, whether you knew it or not. It's called DOS.

What Is an Operating System and Why Do You Need One?

Despite its widespread use, DOS is very much misunderstood. It was a computer operating system, but that might not mean a lot to you. What is a computer operating system and why must you have one? Those are important questions with answers that aren't obvious. We'll try to make them clear in this section.

The formal definition of a computer operating system is something that "manages and schedules the resources" of the computer. So what does that mean?

Let me put it this way: Think of your computer as a business you own. You have tasks you want accomplished. You hire workers who have specialized skills to do some of those tasks, but they need a good work environment. When they pick up the phones on their desks, they need to hear a dial tone.

When employees need supplies, they should be in stock and be deliverable. In an office, the office manager handles these tasks, sometimes with the help of a whole staff. This is very much like what an operating system is. It is a manager of the environment in which other programs work, and it also includes laborers ready to perform particular subtasks whenever they are directed to do so.

How You Can Avoid Having an OS—And Why That Is a Bad Idea

It is possible to avoid having an operating system for your PC, in the sense of a separate program you run first before you run your application programs. But doing that would be a very bad idea.

The way to avoid having a separate OS is simply to build into each application program all the instruction code necessary to accomplish all the things an operating system normally does.

That is, if you were going to be doing some word processing, your word processor program also would have in it the necessary detailed instructions to accomplish reading characters from the keyboard (and knowing when to do so). It would also need to know how to write them to the video display and access the disk drives to store your work in files and manage those files appropriately.

One reason doing this is a terrible idea is that it requires the authors of all application programs to know intimately how your particular PC's hardware works and is configured. That's really not their job. They must know how to write the word processor (or other application) and shouldn't be bothered with the nitty-gritty details of making a PC work.

The second reason this is a terrible idea is that each application would be very much larger than it now is, because each one would have to incorporate much of the same set of instructions for operating the PC hardware. Putting those common instructions into a separate program you run first (and that keeps on running "underneath" your application programs) is a much better plan.

Finally, if you did put all that operating stuff into each application, the only way you could shift from one task to another would be to reboot your PC with a new boot disk containing the next application you wanted to run. Major awkwardness! And what about multitasking? Under this scenario, it wouldn't be possible.

This is not a viable solution. There are just too many compelling reasons to have and use an operating system. Originally, this meant using DOS.

The Days of DOS

DOS stands for *disk operating system*. This means that DOS was an operating system that was particularly concerned with how to deal with disk drives.

In Chapter 15, "Motherboard Magic," we told you that the motherboard BIOS ROM contained some small programs to activate the normal PC hardware pieces. Those mostly are interrupt service routines that deal with the keyboard, the original PC video display options, the floppy disk drive(s), and some elemental actions on the hard disk drive(s). An operating system, like DOS, uses all these programs, but it also does much more.

DOS was—and, today, the various versions of Windows are—mainly concerned with how the disk drives were used at a higher *logical* level. DOS managed files and controlled how you stored and accessed them, also much as Windows does now. The BIOS routines, by contrast, deal only with the physical reading and writing of data at some absolute address (specified by a head number, cylinder number, and sector number within the single track at that head and cylinder location).

DOS was, however, concerned with much more than just disk management. It had the jobs that Windows now manages: allocating memory (RAM), scheduling tasks, and resolving competing demands for the PC's other resources. Thus, DOS launched programs, which in turn used DOS to access various features of your PC. For versions of Windows up to and including Windows 98, DOS actually enabled Windows to load. In this regard, Windows started out like just another program as far as DOS was concerned. After loading, however, Windows 9x managed almost all PC resources and devices and DOS effectively "slept". Today's versions of Windows—Microsoft Windows Me, Windows XP, and Windows 2000—do away with DOS altogether. This has tremendous advantages, as you'll see in the section, "DOS Is Dead! Long Live Windows!," later in this appendix. For the time being, let's explore how DOS interacted with PCs; this will give you a strong foundation for understanding how most operating systems work.

How Does an Operating System Work?

Operating systems provide an environment for the user and for other programs. Their job is to keep track of who—what application or data—is using what portions of memory, which spaces on the disk drives, and so on. They also have the job of coordinating the work of all those lower-level programs that respond to interrupts. These include the programs in the motherboard BIOS ROM, programs that come bundled with DOS, and programs that are added to your system by various device drivers.

What Are the Essential Pieces of an Operating System?

An OS such as DOS comes on several disks or on a CD-ROM. (Of course, it can also be installed on a new PC's hard drive by the manufacturer.) It contains a huge number of modules, each of which generally resides in its own file. This collection is a great deal more than what we would consider the essence of an operating system. The essence of DOS, for example, is a *kernel* and perhaps a *shell program* (which also is often called the *command processor*). Most of the remaining files function as *device drivers*, each of which integrates with the rest of the operating system to provide a specific type of functionality or access to installed hardware. Although these do integrate seamlessly with the operating system and might be distributed by the operating system manufacturer, they are, strictly speaking, external components. (DOS also included independent utility programs that functioned as if they were internal to DOS. These were known as *external commands*.)

The DOS Kernel

The kernel is the fundamental, central part of the operating system. (Think of a nut, such as a walnut or cashew, which has a shell on the outside and a kernel in the center.) For DOS, this kernel consisted of two components, each of which came in its own file.

Microsoft's names for the DOS kernel files were IO.SYS, and MSDOS.SYS. These are all files with the file attributes of *hidden, system,* and *read-only*. (Please do not confuse these DOS files with the Windows 9x files of the same names. They are different, although IO.SYS in Windows 9*x* contains most of the functionality of both the files IO.SYS and MSDOS.SYS in the now-ancient MS-DOS version 6.22.)

The DOS Command Processor

The only visible (not hidden) file on a DOS disk that might qualify for the description "an essential part of DOS" is the command processor, or shell program. This is the file called COMMAND.COM (in virtually all versions of DOS).

We mentioned previously that the kernel of DOS is like the kernel of a nut, namely the portion at the core that is hidden from view but that carries most of the value. This analogy is why the only visible-to-the-user portion of the operating system, the command processor, often is referred to as the "shell" program of the operating system. (This term is universal in references to Unix.)

The Essential Parts of an Operating System

The DOS kernel, as its name suggests, was at the core of the operating system, and as such it was involved in nearly everything DOS did. The kernel presented a uniform *application program interface* (API) by which other programs could ask it for services. It also supported the rest of the programs (including other parts of DOS) in doing their jobs. (In the case of Windows 9x, the Windows API performed these same tasks once Windows is running.)

Generally, a program that wanted some help from DOS caused a *software interrupt*. An interrupt causes the CPU to stop what it is doing within that program and go instead to an external program called an *interrupt service routine* (ISR), which resided somewhere within the operating system. That program does whatever it was designed to do, and then it returns from the interrupt. At that point, the CPU resumes executing the instructions in the original program. All of this happens very rapidly, and normally it does so without the PC user's awareness.

The command processor, or shell, was not only the only visible essential part of DOS; it also was the most visible portion of the operating system when it was running. This program presented the user interface—the command prompt in the case of DOS—and it accepted and processed commands.

As you can likely see, both parts of the operating system—its kernel and its shell—are required. Although the kernel provides underlying services, the shell (command processor) enables the user and the user's applications to interact with and benefit from those services.

In the case of DOS, the command processor also included several useful built-in command functions. These included the DIR command to display a directory listing, the VER command to report the DOS version, and several others, referred to collectively as "the DOS internal commands." Most of what you might know as DOS commands, such as FORMAT and FDISK, are not among them. Those are among the external DOS commands mentioned earlier.

What Does the Operating System Do for You?

An operating system such as DOS works in several ways. Some of these are apparent; others are fully hidden. In the next section, we'll use DOS as an example—because it's a delightfully straightforward and, for many users, familiar example—of how the operating system, and particularly its command processor shell, function.

What COMMAND.COM Did for Users

Have you ever started your computer using a Microsoft Windows startup disk, and selected to start up directly to the command prompt? Have you ever gone to the Windows Start menu and selected the MS-DOS prompt from the collection of accessories? If you have, you've doubtless seen the familiar DOS prompt, which usually looks something like this:

```
C:\>
```

Until the advent of Microsoft Windows Me, when you accessed the command prompt in one of these two ways, you were using DOS directly to control what your PC did. You type a command and press the Enter key; you expect your PC to do what you just told it to do. (Starting with Windows Me, what appears to be the familiar DOS prompt is, in fact, an emulation of DOS, provided fully within Windows.)

It sounds simple, doesn't it? But it's not as simple as it seems.

The command processor (COMMAND.COM) first presented you with this DOS command prompt and then watched the keystrokes. As you type, COMMAND.COM took each keystroke, converted it to the appropriate ASCII character, and sent that character to the screen for display. If it didn't do this, you would have never see what you typed. COMMAND.COM also kept track in an internal buffer of all the keystrokes you pressed in your current command (and, in a separate buffer, of the last command you issued).

If you typed a backspace, COMMAND.COM had a more complex job to do. First, it sent a backspace to the screen. That moved the cursor back one space (unless it was already back as far as it can go). Then COMMAND.COM sent a space character to wipe out the character that was at that position on the screen. As is the case with any other character it "prints" on the screen, this moved the cursor forward one space. Then COMMAND.COM sent a second backspace to the screen to move the cursor back again. Finally, it moved the pointer back one space.

If you pressed one of the function keys F1 through F6, COMMAND.COM took some special actions. These usually involved copying one or more characters from the last command buffer into the current command buffer and putting them on the screen.

All of this activity's complexity pales by comparison to what COMMAND.COM did when the Enter key was pressed. It had to switch roles from assisting you in typing a command to trying to determine what your command meant, and then doing that job.

First, COMMAND.COM *parsed* your command. Parse is a fancy word that means to determine which "words" make up this "sentence." Any valid DOS command had to begin with a verb (an action word), and it then could go on to add an object, or a subject plus an object, or some qualifying adjectives or adverbs.

COMMAND.COM was mainly concerned with determining what verb you typed, and it assumed that the verb was the first "word" on the command line. After it found the verb, it checked this word against its list of DOS internal commands. If there was a match, COMMAND.COM launched the appropriate mini-program, and then sent the rest of the command line to that program. This is, for example, how the program associated with the DIR command did its job.

If the verb doesn't match any of the entries in COMMAND.COM's list of internal DOS commands, DOS assumed that the verb was the name of a program that you wanted to run. So, it turned to the task of finding that program.

COMMAND.COM would look first for that program in what is referred to as the *current directory* on the current disk drive. DOS, in a portion of the kernel, maintained a pointer to the current disk drive and another pointer to the current directory on that disk drive. (What Microsoft Windows calls a *folder,* incidentally, is the same as a *directory* in DOS.)

COMMAND.COM assumed that the name specified by the verb is to be followed by .COM, .EXE, or .BAT unless it already has an explicit extension attached. It looked for files with the verb name as the filename and with one of these three extensions in the current directory. An example of such a file is AUTOEXEC.BAT, which—if it exists—runs automatically each time the PC is started.

When it found such a file, it used DOS kernel services to open the file and read it into memory. If it was a COM file, the contents of the file were simply copied into a region of RAM. If it was an EXE file, just the first 256 bytes of the file were read into memory initially. COMMAND.COM examined the contents of that small "EXE header" to determine where in memory to put the rest of that file's contents. Finally, if the file was a BAT file, COMMAND.COM read in just one line of that file at a time, treating each line as if it were typed at a new DOS command prompt.

When COMMAND.COM loaded a COM or EXE program into memory, it also put the remainder of the command line you typed (or that it found in a batch file) into a small block of memory provided for the program's use located just below the program in memory (RAM). Control then passed to that program. While the program was running, it interacted directly with the DOS kernel to obtain the resources that it required.

When that program quit, it asked the kernel to turn control of the PC back to COMMAND.COM, releasing the memory that program was using (unless that program asked for some of its memory not to be released, as device drivers did). This completed, COMMAND.COM presented another DOS command prompt and went back into the mode in which it could help you compose the next command.

If COMMAND.COM didn't find a matching file in the current directory (with an appropriate filename extension), it looked elsewhere. To do this, COMMAND.COM referred to a region of memory called the DOS environment and from that region it read an ASCII character string called the *path*. This is a collection of locations on your PC's disk drives that are specified in terms of disk volume letters and subdirectory names separated by semicolons. This path was parsed into its elements. For each of those locations, COMMAND.COM repeated the search it performed in the current directory until it found a program to run, or until it ran out of places to look. In the latter case, DOS displayed the message `Bad command or filename` and again presented you with a new DOS command prompt.

What Did DOS Do for Programs?

We've given you a summary of the things DOS did, more or less directly. But DOS was much more important to you than even that rather lengthy description suggests, because virtually every aspect of PC operation called upon DOS.

For all non-Windows programs, DOS allocated all the memory blocks in the first 640KB and often in upper memory as well. Other memory managers could also be called upon to allocate memory in what was once the upper memory region—640KB to 1MB—or beyond that in the High Memory Area or Extended Memory. Likewise, if an application program needed to access a data file, DOS helped it find the file and then either open and read the contents of it or put new or additional contents into it. There were a bunch of other tasks that DOS did for programs, ranging from the relatively trivial, such as reporting the time of day or the date, to fairly complex, such as launching another program and then returning control to the original program after that second program completed its work.

Of course, Microsoft Windows versions after 9x provide all memory and resource allocation services for Windows programs and for DOS programs that are run in a Windows DOS emulation. Windows, too, now controls disk access,, as you'll read later.

DOS Is Dead! Long Live Windows!

Windows has put DOS out to pasture. Although it's true that DOS was still used to start Windows 9*x*, even those versions of Windows have usurped nearly all the DOS functionality that users relied on in Windows 3.*x* and earlier DOS-based environments.

Originally, Windows was designed and marketed not as a replacement for DOS, but as an add-on "operating environment." That phrase was supposed to clarify its relationship with the underlying operating system. The earliest versions of Windows used DOS to manage most of the resources in the machine; Windows' only job was to manage the environment that the users and applications interacted with. Users got a graphical user interface (GUI); programs got a new and much richer collection of application program interface (API) calls that they used to ask Windows, or DOS, to do something for them.

As Windows evolved, each new version shrunk the boundary between Windows and DOS. Beginning with Windows 9*x*, particularly with Windows 98, nearly everything that DOS once did—from memory management, to displaying data onscreen, to providing access to external devices—was now done with 32-bit (protected-mode) modules within Windows. These modules are faster, more efficient, and more adaptable to the needs of specific devices and nascent technologies. With the exception of loading it when you boot your PC, Windows 9*x* hardly needed DOS for anything. Windows Me, Windows 2000, and Windows XP don't need DOS at all.

Note: Another way to look at this is that Windows 9*x* (95 or 98) was really two operating systems in one. At startup and a few other times, the real-mode DOS operating system was the dominant member of the team. The rest of the time—nearly all of the time—protected-mode Windows 9*x* was running the show. Current versions of Windows unify everything. DOS is dead.

Of course, nearly all programs run under Windows today. Indeed, even in the vertical markets of legal and financial software—long some of the most staunch holdouts for conversion from DOS to Windows—usability and training issues have escorted in wide-spread change. The latest versions of all of the most popular DOS legal applications, for example, are now Windows programs.

Variations on Windows Now in Common Use

Windows is not a singular thing. As you probably know, there are many versions of it. The earliest versions of Microsoft Windows are only of historical interest at this point. They were very limited functionally, and they have been rendered obsolete by the later versions.

The following sections recap briefly the different versions of Windows that are still being used in significant quantities.

Windows 95

Windows went through many successful incarnations—known variously as Windows 3.*x,* Windows for Workgroups 3.11, and so on. After a long period of development, Microsoft introduced Windows 95. This version was meant for ordinary desktop PC users, and it was a direct upgrade from Windows 3.11. (If you look deeply inside Windows 95, it will identify itself as Windows version 4.*x.*)

Windows 95 was different from Windows 3.*x* in many ways; at least, it certainly *looked* different. More accurately, Windows 95 represented two changes. One is that it exemplified a very substantial rethinking of the user interface. The other is that Windows 95 moved all the operating system support functions that could be moved from real mode (DOS) to protected mode. Ideally, almost nothing a Windows-specific application needs is likely to require switching the machine from protected mode to real mode and back again.

Windows 95 was generally a more stable operating environment than Windows 3.*x,* and it supported a very wide range of hardware and software, which goes a long way to explain why it was the desktop PC operating system of choice for a sizable number of PC users.

Even though Windows 95 took over most of DOS's functionality, DOS did still exist, operating in two ways, underneath Windows 95. One version of DOS under Windows 95 was the actual real-mode operating system that loaded before Windows starts. This is what you got when you booted to the Startup menu and selected the Command Prompt option. It is also what you got when you used a Windows 95 startup disk (for example, if you have a problem that prevents you from booting Windows from the hard disk). And it is very nearly what you got if you selected Restart in MS-DOS mode from the Shut Down menu. (This real-mode DOS was augmented by its HIMEM.SYS memory manager pro-gram, so in fact it ran in a version of protected mode after HIMEM has loaded. But this was a limited sort of protected-mode operation. All of the DOS real-mode API was avail-able, and very little else.)

The other version of DOS that ran under Windows 95 was provided in a so-called "DOS box" or "DOS command window" running while Windows 95 was also running. This could be a full-screen DOS window or it could be a smaller window running on top of the Windows 95 desktop. This was actually a simulated DOS, provided as an aspect of the protected-mode Windows operating system. The VMM32.VXD program created this DOS instance, which also "virtualizes" all the hardware aspects of the PC so that DOS programs running in this mode cannot do any damage either to Windows or to other DOS or Windows programs running at the same time. You'll read about this point a little more fully later in this appendix.

The protected-mode simulated DOS had different functionality than the real-mode DOS. In particular, it supported Windows 95 long filenames, and some of the DOS commands (such as XCOPY) had several added command-line switches (revealed if you ran the program with the command-line switch /?).

Both of these Windows 95-embedded DOS versions were missing many of their external commands (in particular, commands that posed some danger to data when run in a multi-tasking environment such as FORMAT). That functionality was moved into protected-mode (32-bit code) modules within Windows 95.

We'll describe Windows 95's inner working in some detail shortly. First, though, we want to mention some of the other versions of Windows on the market.

Windows 2000

Before Windows 95 came on the scene, Microsoft came out with a version of Windows that was a really different animal. This was Windows NT, and its current version is known as Microsoft Windows 2000 Professional.

Windows 2000 truly is a different operating system, built from scratch rather than on top of an earlier combination of DOS and Windows 3.*x*. Compatibility was much *less* of an issue for its developers, and stability was much *more* of one. As a result, Windows 2000 is among the most reliable operating systems out there. It is fully 32-bit, and although it makes some attempt to run older 16-bit Windows applications and DOS applications, it has some very stringent requirements on those it will accept. Some of the older programs just won't run on Windows 2000 at all—certainly none that attempt to access the PC hardware directly (as many did to improve their performance). But then, that is the price of its far greater stability and security.

> **Note:** The change from 16 to 32 bits might seem like a subtle difference, but it has a profound impact on the complexity of the program. The 32-bit code does away with the segmented memory architecture. It also enables the CPU to run in protected mode, thus protecting the operating system from poorly written applications.

Windows 2000 comes in several flavors, including server and workstation versions. Microsoft's original notion was that Windows NT (and, now, Windows 2000) would be the high-end, commercial version of Windows, and Windows 9x would be the consumer version. In fact, Windows 2000's greater stability has caused many companies (and not a few individuals) to adopt it. With the dramatic increase in hardware support that came with Windows 2000, this version of Windows is gradually finding its way onto desktops everywhere.

Windows 98 and Windows Me

With the release of Windows 98, Microsoft originally hoped that most consumers would opt to upgrade from Windows 95 (or Windows 3.x, for those stragglers), and that large corporations would upgrade, instead, to Windows 2000. Windows 98 addressed, in particular, the growing need for the operating system to support the many new types of hardware—particularly multimedia hardware—that were beginning to appear in households and small offices. Many corporations have, in fact, upgraded to Windows 98 and Windows Me.

What was different about Windows 98? First, it (and its underlying real-mode DOS) was capable of working with the new FAT32 formatted partitions. (In fact, this capability was introduced before Windows 98, in the OSR 2 release of Windows 95, also known as Windows 95B or version 4.00.950B or 4.00.1111.) Real-mode DOS *must* have the capability of accessing and storing files on a FAT32 volume in order to enable you to boot from a FAT32 disk and then access any other disk volumes formatted in that manner.

Many of the functional changes from Windows 95 to Windows 98 were anticipated in the steady stream of updates and upgrades to Windows 95 that Microsoft made available online. Many of those upgrades were also bundled into the Windows 95A Service Pack upgrade and later into the Windows 95B (or OSR2) version it supplied to original equipment manufacturers (OEMs) for installation on new PCs. Some functional changes were not available however; t DirectX technologies were first integrated into the OS in Windows 98.

> **Note:** OSR2 and the FAT32 support it provided were never available as an installable upgrade for users. Therefore, for most users, Windows 98 was an important upgrade because it enabled them to reap the benefits of implementing FAT32.

One area in which there was an obvious difference in Windows 98 is in its level of integration of the Internet. This integration enabled users to use the Internet Explorer Web browser as their default shell program for Windows 98. In this way, working with Web-based content and working with files on your local drive required that the user learn only one set of skills. However, this integration was not mandatory. Many users preferred to retain the familiar Windows 95 appearance and launch a Web browser when they wanted to access the Internet. This change in integration reflected the ever-growing importance of the Internet. Microsoft realized that to keep its dominant position, it essentially had to expand its next-generation operating systems in a manner that would make the Internet appear to be a part of the OS, built in seamlessly (or apparently so).

The idea was, and is, that all resources you want to access—whether they are on a drive on your PC, on another PC across the room connected to yours via a LAN, or on some PC clear across the globe connected via the Internet—should look just like a folder on your PC or a page on the Web. So the distinction between the Windows Explorer and the Internet Explorer wasn't as clear. Of course, there is great difference between accessing your own PC's hard disk or a disk attached to a PC on your local area network and accessing some remote computer halfway around the globe. After all, you can count on the integrity and safety of files on your hard disk in ways you simply cannot trust files on some distant machine belonging to a total stranger. With the blurring of the line between what is local and what is remote, it is important to keep those security issues in mind.

With Windows Me, DOS was finally dead and buried. Windows now starts up directly and there is no MS-DOS mode to boot into. DOS applications and commands can still be used, of course, but through virtual DOS environments that are actually emulated within Windows Me. Windows Me also began the process of borrowing code and routines from Windows NT and Windows 2000, moving the two platforms ever closer to unification.

Windows XP

What can you expect in the future? Well, all roads lead to Windows XP—all roads. Windows XP is the current generation operating system for users of Windows 9x, Windows Me, *and* Windows 2000. The core of Windows XP is the familiar Windows NT/Windows 2000 kernel, which should make migration less painful. And Windows XP expands on the device support that distinguished Windows 2000 from the previous, and rather device-unfriendly, Windows NT 4. You can read more about Windows XP in the following section entitled "Windows 2000 and Windows XP."

Windows Is an Event-Driven Environment

So far in this chapter we have pointed out that DOS and Windows have been the dominant PC operating systems and have described the various versions of Windows that are in use today. We also told you a little bit about how DOS worked, both in terms of what you could see it do for you, and what it did behind the scenes.

This section discusses one of the most important ways that Windows, as an environment, differs from DOS. Understanding this is crucial to understanding how any Windows program works.

When a programmer sat down to write a DOS program, he or she started with a desired procedure. Then the programmer wrote instructions that followed each step of the desired procedure. This is called, not surprisingly, *procedural programming*.

Windows is different. The programmer first must think about the appearance of the program. The next concern is to define all the events that might occur—for example, a mouse pointer being moved across a certain region or a mouse button being pressed while that pointer was at that location. Then, for each event, a separate procedure is written. The collection of all these event handlers is the Windows application.

Windows must send notice of all these events to all the programs that need to react to them. After all, only one mouse pointer is on the screen, and many programs can be running. So the underlying Windows program will notice where the mouse moves, when the mouse's buttons are clicked, when keystrokes occur, and so on. For each such event, Windows sends a message. This is routed to every Windows program in the same manner that a magazine might make the rounds at a company with a checklist of readers stapled to the front cover.

Each Windows program must receive the message, decide whether it is supposed to act on it, and if not, pass it along to the next program.

If any one of the Windows programs becomes stuck, messages can't be passed around this loop—and that can stop Windows as a whole. There are, however, usually several loops going, and some of them might still continue to work. This is why often even when your PC seems to freeze, you can still move the mouse pointer around the screen as freely as you like.

For these reasons, Windows programming is not generally considered procedural in character (even though Windows programs are full of procedures). Instead, it is called *event-driven* or *message-based*.

Cooperative versus Preemptive Multitasking

Now we have set the stage so that you are ready to learn one more important aspect of how Windows works, and also how this aspect of Windows has evolved. This involves cooperative multitasking versus preemptive multitasking.

Multitasking means running several programs at once. In fact, it means having the CPU spend some time running one program, stop that and spend some time running another program, stop that and go on running a third program, and so on. If all those times add up to a very short time, so that the CPU gets back to each program many times each second, it will seem to the users as though all the programs are running simultaneously. But actually they are simply doing what is called *time sharing, time slicing,* or *time domain multiplexing*.

There are two ways this can be accomplished. In both cases, you need some supervisor program that handles the context switching for the CPU from one program to the next. (Each time a context switch is about to occur, the CPU must be instructed to save enough information about the task it has been doing so it can resume that work later, and then it must reload the previously saved information about the next task.)

The two strategies for multitasking differ in how they determine when it is time to make a switch to the next program. *Preemptive multitasking* means having the supervisor program set strict time limits on each program. At the end of its *time slice*, that program simply gets cut off, no matter where it was in its process. This is okay, because the CPU will complete the current instruction, and it will save enough information so it can resume exactly where it left off, as soon as it returns to running this program.

Cooperative multitasking, on the other hand, means that each program is asked to relinquish control on its own. Windows programming guidelines suggest a maximum time that any Windows program should be allowed to hold control before it relinquishes it, but it is up to the programmer who writes that program to be sure that those guidelines are not violated. Microsoft specified that Windows programs include code that would let them relinquish control to Windows, and thus to other Windows programs, on a regular basis. But this is simply not always done.

Anyone who has run any number of Windows programs in the past has seen many of them share the machine most of the time, yet on occasions grab the machine in a viselike grip and not let go until they are good and ready. Worse yet, sometimes a Windows program will "hang" and be unable to let go of control, at which point you have no choice but to reboot your PC. Microsoft has noticed this behavior, as is obvious from how later versions of Windows handle things. Whereas Windows 3.*x* used only cooperative multitasking for all Windows applications (and preemptive multitasking for DOS applications), Windows 95 used cooperative multitasking only for the older, "legacy" 16-bit Windows applications. All newer, 32-bit programs are preemptively multitasked, as are all DOS applications running under Windows.

Windows 2000 and Windows XP go even further, using only a preemptive multitasking model. That prevents any one program, no matter how badly (or maliciously) written, from taking control of your PC and not letting go.

Understanding Your Choices for Your PC's Operating System

During most of this book we have acted as though you are running Windows 98 or Windows Me, because statistically speaking, most readers are. However, there are many other choices for your PC operating system. This section briefly lists some of the more popular options and explains why you might want to choose each one.

Windows 98 and Windows Me

When Windows 98 came out, it was the focus of an enormous amount of media coverage. It was the hot new thing, but moving up to it often meant having to add to or upgrade your hardware. It did, however, give developers some new features to exploit for users' benefit. Subsequently, all the top-of-the-line PC products have been written or rewritten to run on Windows 98 or later, or almost all major applications can now run on Windows 9x, Windows Me, or Windows 2000.

Windows 9x and later versions support more hardware options, most notably including USB support. Windows Me added support for IEEE-1394 FireWire, and Windows XP supports the new IEEE 802.11b standard for wireless networking.

All of these versions center on the issue of compatibility: compatibility with the past and with the present cutting edge of technology. They support nearly any Windows program ever written, and, through Windows Me, support even a lot of shady game programs. They also support the latest efforts from the major PC software publishers and offer built-in support for more hardware than any other PC operating system. Occasionally, you still must go to the hardware gadget's manufacturer for a suitable device driver, but out of the box, Windows 9x and Windows Me support so much stuff—and with their plug-and-play aspects even recognize the stuff—which means you spend less time searching for third-party drivers.

Windows 2000 and Windows XP

Windows 2000 is Microsoft's crown jewel. Windows 2000, as the direct successor to Windows NT, is stable and secure, so it is a safe choice even for large corporations with vast amounts of critical data to manage. But Windows 2000 is also the most finicky Windows version. You simply cannot run that old DOS game program on it. And you might be surprised to discover that some other, seemingly ordinary Windows or DOS programs also have problems under Windows 2000. Before you commit to this operating system, be sure it will support programs and hardware devices that you simply *must* be able to use. (Alternatively, check out the last part of this section where we explain how you can have your cake and eat it too, by running your PC both with and without Windows 2000.)

The successor to Windows 2000, Windows XP, was supposed to be the best of all worlds, bringing the reliability and security of Windows 2000 together for the first time with the widespread and encompassing support for peripheral devices that Windows Me—as the successor to Windows 98—enjoys. For example, Windows XP provides full native support for USB and IEEE-1394 standards, as well as new standards for wireless networking, image acquisition, and multimedia performance. Windows XP is also available in a 64-bit version, designed to support Intel's Itanium processor, which you can read about in depth in Chapter 15. In fact, Windows XP has fallen far short of its promise, proving to have some of the most severe security holes in any operating system ever commercially available.

Windows XP's user interface looks a good deal different from anything that has come before, but existing users of Windows 2000 will recognize familiar options and technologies, particularly in the areas of file and document maintenance and organization. A delightful element of the interface is the new Compatibility Mode system. If you have a piece of software that won't work properly in Windows XP, you can simply launch an emulation of any previous version of Windows that you require—back to Windows 95—and run the program inside the emulator.

Linux

Linux is a marvelous program and an unbeatable value. It is free! Linux is a version of Unix that first was crafted as a work of love by one programmer and then augmented by many others. You can get the whole operating system, source code and all, plus a variety of Linux-compatible software, for nothing more than the price of a download. Or you can buy it on a CD-ROM for the cost of the disc.

Linux is maintained and improved by an even larger, international team of programmers than Microsoft can field. Although they aren't working under anyone's central direction, Linus Torvalds (the originator of Linux) is still working to maintain some sanity in terms of which new features are included in successive versions of Linux.

The existence of this body of knowledgeable advocates of Linux means that if you run into a problem using it you very likely can get some free help fairly rapidly from the Internet—at least if you are familiar with the use of Usenet newsgroups. Or, you can buy versions of Linux that are supported by several companies (RedHat and Caldera being a couple of them). This might be a better option if you aren't a hacker at heart and would rather ask questions than work things out independently.

Given its heritage (Unix), it is not surprising that Linux is a suitable choice for a PC operating system that serves as a Web server. In fact, this or some other flavor of Unix is the best choice for any system that must be extremely reliable and flexible or that must do a lot of *real-time* work. (That is, where the PC must respond in a time-critical fashion to events in the outside world.)

Unix

If your task is to set up a PC to do a critical real-time job (for example, a numerical controller for a machine tool), where it simply must keep working at all times and must be able to respond in a timely manner to many very fast external events, DOS, Windows 9x, Windows Me are all bad choices; Windows 2000 or Windows XP might do the job, but almost any flavor of Unix will be better.

Advantages to Unix are several. For one thing—and one of the primary reasons it's used today—its parallel processing capabilities are phenomenal, and this comes in particularly useful if you're hosting Web or other Internet content. You can have the server host your content while, at the same time, firewalls and antivirus software are doing their own jobs behind the scenes to keep your enterprise safe from hacking. Unix's security features overall—by which we mean at workstations, at servers, and at remote machines—are, frankly, some of the best around, period.

Unix is also an excellent choice for handling workgroup computing, and it's masterful as an environment for database management, whereby you will likely have many—perhaps hundreds or thousands—of employees accessing the same massive database file over and over, all day long. This *scalability*—the ability to work equally efficiently and reliably on a desktop and on a supercomputer—is unique to Unix.

A great number of applications exist for running under Unix, including some of the most sophisticated graphics tools available, such as those used by medical imaging, drafting, architecture, and the motion-picture industry.

On the other hand, Unix is commonly known as "user surly," rather than user friendly. When used in command-line mode, rather than hidden under X-Windows or a similar graphical environment, many Unix commands are cryptic and the learning curve for beginners is steep. What in DOS was the EDIT command becomes vi in Unix. The familiar DOS DIR command is ls under Unix, and if you want to remove a directory, what in DOS is the rather intuitive DELTREE command mutates in Unix into rm -rf.

And yet, what Unix does well, it does superbly. It might be just right for you.

How You Can Avoid Making a Choice

In reality, you really don't have to choose. You can have them all. Yes, really, you can run one PC with several operating systems. Naturally, you will be running only one of these operating systems at a time, but you can change to another OS simply by rebooting your PC.

Several strategies exist for doing this. Windows 9x, Me, and Windows 2000 come with a version of *multibooting* built in. This strategy enables you to choose between their native operation and another OS. Usually, this involves some batch files that replace critical system files for one operating system with the corresponding files for the other system.

> **Warning:** We'd be remiss if we didn't end this discussion with a cautionary note. Some of these PC operating system choices use the old DOS FAT12 and FAT16 formats for their file systems. All of them can read those file systems (and almost all of them can write to them). But many of these operating systems also support some alternative file systems.
>
> Windows 9x, Me, and XP support the FAT32 file system, but the other operating systems can't make any sense out of disks formatted in that way. Windows 2000 and XP also support a file system that only they can access, called NTFS.
>
> Linux normally uses several disk volumes, some with their own proprietary format and others with a DOS-like format. Many other Unix flavors do something similar.
>
> If you choose to load several operating systems on your PC, you must have enough disk space for all of them. Each one wants some space for its files—and in modern versions, those are some pretty substantial requirements. The only

shared spaces will be those that use a commonly accessible file system. Any nonshared spaces are in addition to that. Thus, you'll need a large hard drive to make this strategy practical. (Fortunately, these days, that doesn't have to cost you very much money.)

Therefore, the bottom line is this: If you want to boot your PC into any of a number of operating systems, you have to give some careful thought to which file systems you will be using under each one. Be sure that each OS can access the files you want it to see (and perhaps also assure yourself that it won't be able to access the files you want it not to touch). You can do this, but it does take some careful thought and planning.

Summary

This chapter explained a topic you might never realized you would want to understand. We hope you found it interesting and illuminating reading. After you make your decision as to which operating system to use, you will be able to go back to ignoring your PC's operating system much of the time. Still, this knowledge will serve you well whenever you find that your PC's OS isn't working quite the way you want it to.

Understanding How Humans Instruct PCs

This appendix is all about the many ways in which you can tell your PC what to do. That covers a broad range of subjects, from the careful crafting of assembly-language programs and the ins and outs of object-oriented computer languages to simple macro definitions that customize how some application works.

Harnessing the PC's Power to Help Mere Humans

The first digital computers were programmed in a very laborious manner. The only "language" they understood was an appropriate collection of binary numbers, so their human makers had to insert these numbers by hand. In those days, every time a computer operator turned on a computer for the first time (or had to restart it for some reason), he or she would have to set a group of switches to represent the 1s and 0s of a binary instruction word, and then press another switch to enter that instruction. This process had to be repeated many times until an entire short program was entered. Finally, pressing yet another switch would start that program, which would prepare the computer to read and then run a longer program from punched cards or a tape drive.

Fortunately, we no longer have to worry about all that. Our PCs know how to start themselves, and modern methods of program generation enable us to create computer programs in a much easier way. There are, in fact, several ways people program computers. The rest of this chapter describes the most popular ones.

Assembly Language Saves Mental Effort

People are good at different things than computers are good at. Computers excel at keeping track of details. People excel at seeing the big picture or, in general, at seeing patterns.

Using assembly language is a strategy for using the computer to do what it does well, in ways that make it easier for humans to do the work of building computer programs. This strategy is the closest to the original method of computer programming of all the ones we will describe for you. It also was the first strategy devised. But it still is extremely useful, because it is in certain ways the most powerful way to program a computer. Because it illustrates most of the characteristics of all the other ways to program computers, we will spend more time describing this kind of language than on any of the others.

The General Characteristics of All Computer Programs

A computer program is simply a long list of instructions, perhaps with some data values mixed in. The CPU reads the instructions and performs the indicated actions. If some data is mixed into the program, there must be some instructions in that program that tell the CPU when and how to use those data values. There also must be some other instructions that will cause it to skip over the data values as it is reading the program so it can find the next instruction it is to perform.

Some instructions contain data within themselves. Others reference data the CPU will find in a specified register or at some designated memory location. Some instructions are simple, taking only one byte to state. Others are much more complicated, and expressing them might require more than a dozen bytes of program code.

That means that a list of the binary numbers that make up a computer program will almost certainly make little sense at a glance to any human. People see the meaning a whole lot more easily when the program is broken into its individual instructions. If each instruction is further broken into the action to be done and the data to be acted upon (or an indication of where that data is found), the intent of those instructions is much easier to see.

The next section goes into an example in great detail. If you already know how an assembly-language program is structured and how it corresponds to the machine language program it represents, or if you simply can't be bothered, you can skip the next section. However, if you want to understand how assembly language works, in at least this very simple case, take some time to study this example.

A Very Simple Sample Program

Figure B.1 shows a very short (15-byte) program as the CPU would see it. People see numbers here. The CPU sees this as *code,* which means that these numbers *encode* the actions we want the CPU to perform. Every pair of hexadecimal values in this figure specifies the value of one byte of the program code. So, for example, the hexadecimal values 8E (for the fourth byte) imply a byte whose binary content is 10001110 (8h = 1000b, Eh = 1110b—where the trailing *h* implies a hexadecimal number, and the trailing *b* implies a binary number).

Now we will show you how that short program would look as an assembly-language program (see Figure B.2). All the numbers in this figure are, like those in Figure B.1, hexadecimal values, even though we didn't put a letter *h* after each one. That is simply the assumption you must make whenever you read any assembly-language program, at least in the forms in which they usually are presented.

FIGURE B.1

A very short program as it is seen by the CPU.

```
BA 00 00 8E C2 26 80 36-17 04 20 B4 4C CD 21
```

Note: Sometimes programmers use a suffix letter *b* for binary numbers, *o* for octal, *h* for hexadecimal, and *t* or *d* for tens for decimal. Other times you are simply expected to know from context the number base that is being used.

FIGURE B.2

The same information shown in Figure B.1, but expressed in assembly language.

```
MOV     DX,0000
MOV     ES,DX
ES:
XOR     BYTE PTR [0417],20
MOV     AH,4C
INT     21
```

This is a small real-mode program. You could run it at the DOS prompt. But before you do, it would be nice to know what it would do to your PC if you did. We will explain that in some detail right now.

The first instruction (MOV DX,0000) "moves" (copies) the explicitly stated value of 0 into the 16-bit wide data register (DX). The second instruction (MOV ES,DX) copies the contents of the DX register (which we now know is 0) into the extra segment register (ES).

Note: Situations like this, in which two instructions are needed to accomplish a single goal—moving 0 into ES—are necessary because the CPU doesn't allow you to directly move a 0 into the ES register. Issues like these are why programming can become so complicated.

Notice that the structure (syntax) for a line of assembly code such as this is that the first "word" is the verb, specifying the action to be taken. The next word is the destination, and the last word is the source of the data to be used in this action—or in the case of the first line, it is the actual data value to be used in the action.

Then comes a line that asserts that the currently active segment (for purposes of reaching out into main memory) will now be the extra segment. This assertion applies until it is countermanded by another, similar, assertion, or until the program ends.

The line that begins with XOR (XOR BYTE PTR [0417],20) is an *exclusive or* statement that determines whether the values of two bytes are the same. Just what this statement tells the CPU to do takes a little explaining.

First, you must know what an exclusive or (XOR) of two *bits* means. If either of the bits is a 1, but not both of them, the result is a 1; otherwise, it is a 0.

Another way to look at this is to notice that if one of the bits is a 0, the result is going to be the same as the value of the other bit being compared. But if the first bit is a 1, the resulting bit will be the opposite of the other bit you are comparing.

When you do an XOR of two *bytes,* you just go through each position in the two bytes. First, you compare the least significant bit in each byte and put the XOR result into the least significant bit of the result byte. Next, you move to the second bit in each byte, and then on to the third, fourth, and finally the eighth, or most-significant, bit in each byte.

The part of the assembly-language line that says BYTE PTR [0417] indicates that one of the bytes to be compared is whatever number is located at address 0:0417—and here we are giving the address in the usual *segment:offset* form—which always means that one implying hexadecimal numbers before and after the colon. (You might wonder why we put the number 0 before the colon. Remember, the segment value was set to be whatever value is in ES in the line just before this one, and we just loaded it with a 0 value in the lines before that.)

The final portion of this assembly-language line gives an explicit value to the other byte in our comparison. That value is 20h, which is the same as the binary number 00100000b.

There is one more not-so-obvious thing you must know about this assembly-language instruction: The result of the comparison of the two bytes will be put into the memory location from which the first byte value being compared was taken. That means that this instruction reads into the CPU the value that was stored at 0:0417 in main memory, XORs that 8-bit value with the 8-bit value 20h, and then puts the resulting byte back into main memory location 0:0417.

Now, from what we just told you about what the XOR operation does and the fact that one of the bytes being compared is 20h, you can now see that this instruction just reverses the value of the sixth bit in the byte at main memory location 0:0417, leaving all the other bits in that byte unchanged.

As it happens, this particular memory location has a special significance. It is the byte in which the BIOS stores the current state of the shift keys on the keyboard as well as the *shift state* of the system corresponding to each Shift key. The first (least-significant) bit has the binary value 1 if—and only if—the right Shift key is depressed. The next bit is a 1 if—and only if—the left Shift key is depressed. The next bit tells whether either Ctrl key is pressed (1 = yes; 0 = no), and the fourth bit does the same for the Alt keys.

The upper four bits show whether the system is in the Scroll Lock, Num Lock, Caps Lock, or Insert states. That is, a 1 in any of these positions corresponds to that state being on.

Aha! Remember that our program is going to change only one bit, the bit in the sixth position. Now you know enough to see that when you run this program it will reverse the value of the bit that says whether the Num Lock state is on. Thus, running this program will set the Num Lock state off if it is on, and on if it is off. That is just what pressing the Num Lock key does. So this program is a way to press the Num Lock key without touching the keyboard.

But the program does something more. The next line (MOV AH,4C) says that it moves the byte value 4Ch into the upper half of the AX register (which is also known as the AH register, meaning the higher portion of the A register). The last line (INT 21) produces a software interrupt of type 21h. This is perhaps the most commonly used DOS interrupt service. It handles a significant portion of the calls a program makes to DOS. The value of AH tells DOS that this program is finished with its work and that DOS should return control to whatever program had it before this program was loaded. Normally, that means to let COMMAND.COM put up another DOS prompt and wait for you to tell it what you want to have your PC do next.

This was just a simple program. It is actually a useful one (in case you want a way to achieve the effect of pushing the Num Lock key in a batch file), but by no means does it show you the range of things you can do with an assembly-language program.

In particular, many assembly-language programs enable the programmer to refer to locations in memory or locations within the program by symbolic names. The assembler keeps track of where these locations are (actual RAM address or offset from the beginning of the code segment and actual line of code). The programmer then can use meaningful names for each block of code, based on what it is supposed to do. When an instruction tells the computer to jump to a new block of code to do some new task, that instruction will read something like JMP CloseFile instead of JMP 0A35 or some other arbitrary numerical address.

The Power of Assembly-Language Programs

You can see from this example how detailed and "close to the hardware" an assembly-language program really is. It actually must specify each and every byte of *machine-language code* (the binary numbers the CPU will read) that is going to become a part of the final program. That is in marked contrast to what a programmer does when using what we call a high-level programming language, as we will explain in more detail in a moment.

This low-level characteristic of assembly-language programming means that a person who writes a program in assembly language has total control over what the PC will do. It is logically exactly equivalent to writing down the exact bytes of machine code the program is to contain. But writing assembly language instead of machine language code is much easier for humans to do.

The main reason to write in assembly language instead of in actual machine language bytes is that it is so much more *mnemonic* (which means suggestive and memorable) to write MOV DX instead of writing simply BAh, which is the actual byte that means that action to the CPU. If there were only a few instructions that you had to remember, memorizing them all might not be too tough. But when there are as many instructions as there are for a modern x86 processor, plus a large number of possible modifications to those instructions, it all becomes a bit much for mere humans to memorize.

After an assembly-language program is completed, the programmer *assembles* it. This means running a special "assembler" program that takes the assembly-language statements as input data and generates the actual machine-language bytes that the CPU must see in order to know what it is supposed to do as its output.

Consider that concept again: A programmer writes assembly-language statements. An assembler program converts them into machine-language bytes with a nearly one-to-one relationship between the programmer's assembly-language commands and the final machine-language code. It stores the result in a file. That file is the final program the programmer set out to create. When it is run, the CPU reads those bytes and does what they direct it to do.

The Problem with Assembly-Language Programs

The power of assembly-language programming is the control you have to specify *exactly* everything that is going to happen and *exactly* where and how it will happen. This is also the problem with assembly-language programming.

It is a problem simply because humans are not very good at keeping huge amounts of detail in their minds at once. You can keep track of which numbers are where in a short program, but when the program becomes really large, there simply is too much to keep track of. Or, at least, doing so without making mistakes from time to time becomes very hard.

It would be so much nicer if you could somehow let the computer keep track of the details and just focus your attention on the bigger picture. So, for example, you might want not to have to decide which numbers are placed into which registers, or when to put a number into a memory location instead of into a register. And when writing information to a disk, you certainly don't want to have to be concerned with all the things DOS must do to manage files. That's the function of DOS.

Indeed, you can let the computer do more of the work, but as always, there is a price to be paid when you do so. Still, most programmers, most of the time, are more than happy to pay that price in exchange for using a higher-level programming language.

Working at a Higher Level: Letting the PC Do More of the Work

A popular piece of advice to managers is "don't micromanage." That means to tell your workers what results you want, but don't tell them exactly how to do their jobs. Assume they know what they are doing, unless you have a pretty good reason to think that they don't.

The Notion of a High(er)-Level Language

This also describes the goal of higher-level programming languages, which embody a lot of detailed programming knowledge. They are like workers who know how to do a job. We call them tools, because they help people do jobs with less effort.

The programmer who uses one of these tools is acting like a manager, specifying a desired result without having to go into the details of just how that result will be achieved. The program then determines a means of accomplishing the specified result and generates a machine-language code sequence that will do that.

In effect, this notion enables you to break up the work of writing a complex computer program into two steps. One is the step of deciding which overall actions are to be performed, in what order, and so on. That is the job of the programmer at the higher level. The other job is deciding how each of the specified actions will be carried out. That is the job of the author of the programming tool that the first programmer is going to use.

After a program is completed, if it is going to be used often, a good programmer will examine how the tool did its job in at least those areas of the program that are used most extensively. Then, depending on the programmer's judgment about how well the tool constructed that portion, he or she might redo it using a lower-level tool that gives the programmer more control over just how that task is carried out. In this way, the portions of the program that are executed most often can be made as efficient and speedy as possible, without the programmer having to spend an equal amount of effort on all the other parts of the program that are only rarely invoked.

Higher- and Lower-Level Programming Languages

Many "higher-level" programming tools have been constructed. They differ in a number of ways. Some are barely higher-level than machine language. That is, they make it pretty easy to specify almost exactly what the machine is going to do at every step of the way, yet they manage to take off the programmer's hands at least a little of the grunt work.

Other high-level programming tools are much further away from what actually will happen. They enable the programmer who uses them to specify actions in much more general terms, and then they do those specified actions in whatever way the author of the tool deemed best. Using one of these tools makes writing complex programs easier, but it also makes those programs less predictable in terms of exactly how they will do whatever it is they are to do. Generally, even the best of the programs written using the higher-level languages are less efficient and run more slowly than equivalent programs with equivalent functionality that have been carefully crafted in a lower-level language. There is at least one major exception to this: Programs written in high-level languages need only be recompiled with a compiler that supports a new processor's extensions to take advantage of those instructions, whereas assembly-level programs must be rewritten.

Classifying Computer Languages by Generations

Observers of the industry have come up with a classification of computer languages according to how low- or high-level they are. These levels are called *generations* (which partly reflects the fact that it was not very feasible to develop a yet higher-level language until the immediately preceding generation of programming tools was available). Many computer languages exist in each generation, each optimized for a certain kind of programming task.

The lowest-level, or *first-generation,* languages are simply the actual binary machine languages "understood" by the various CPUs. Each different kind (or model) of CPU has its own machine language. (The machine languages used for all the models in Intel's x86 family of CPUs are sufficiently similar to one another that rather than refer to each one as a completely new language, you can think of them as simply different dialects of a common tongue.)

The *second-generation* languages are assemblers. This includes both the very basic assemblers, such as the one built into the program DEBUG and much more powerful macro assemblers that enable you to use symbolic names and also to name whole blocks of code as macros and invoke them simply by using their names. Generally, you need a different assembler for each new kind of CPU with its own new machine language. Each assembler typically is upgraded when new *models* of that kind of CPU come out; then it can understand and assemble correctly the new dialect of machine language understood by the newest model of the target CPU and still be able to handle assembly-language programs written for earlier models in that CPU family.

The *third-generation* languages enable a programmer to create programs without having to know much about how the target computer is constructed. In particular, you don't have to know how many registers the CPU has (let alone their specific names or sizes), whether there is a memory cache, and so on. Typically, each of these languages is available in several dialects, each dialect being designed for use in generating machine language code for a particular kind of machine. The programmer might be able to write the program once and then compile it several times, using different dialects of the same programming language to create versions of the program to run on each of several kinds of computer.

An enormous number of third-generation computer programming languages has been created. Some that are commonly used on PCs include FORTRAN (*Fo*rmula *Tran*slator), COBOL (*C*ommon *B*usiness *O*riented *L*anguage), BASIC (*B*eginners *A*ll-purpose *S*ymbolic *I*nstruction *C*ode, to give it the original full name), Pascal, Lisp, APL, C, Ada, C++, C#, and so forth. (These names appear roughly in the historical order in which the languages were developed.)

The most popular third-generation languages for writing commercial software today are probably C++, C, COBOL, BASIC, and FORTRAN in descending order of popularity. There are so many different languages and so many in widespread use because each language has its own strengths and limitations. Some of the highlights:

- FORTRAN was originally created to help scientists program computers for technical calculations.

- COBOL was developed by a committee as the best all-purpose computer language for business programs. It is widely used for accounting programs and other financial applications in large corporations.

- BASIC was developed as an instructional language for students at Dartmouth University, so it stresses ease of program crafting with minimal need to remember arcane details.

- C is intended as a very powerful language for writing operating systems and other incredibly complex software. Because it is intended for use mainly by professional programmers, you must master a lot of arcane detail to become an expert C programmer. Also, it has enough low-level manipulation possibilities that it almost could be described as both a third- and a second-generation computer language bundled together.

- A variant form of C that has had many object-oriented features added to the base language is called C++ and it is the dominant language used to craft commercial programs. (We'll explain just what *object-oriented* means a bit later in this chapter.)

- Closely related to C++ is Java. It has become quite popular for Web site programming. Also related to C++ is C# (pronounced "C Sharp"), which is the language core of Microsoft's entire .NET scheme.

The *fourth-generation* computer languages are designed to minimize the effort necessary to create a program. Often, these are intended for use by nonprofessional programmers. Examples of fourth-generation languages (or 4GL languages as they are sometimes denoted) include dBASE, Forth, Perl, Clipper, and Visual Basic.

Finally, a *fifth-generation* computer language incorporates knowledge-based expert systems, inference engines, natural language processors, or other kinds of *artificial intelligence* (AI). These are only now being developed, and therefore there aren't many good ones in widespread use on PCs.

Choosing a Computer Language Requires Compromise

From all this diversity, you might be getting a notion that there are some trade-offs you must make—and that would be exactly right. Sometimes a programmer wants nearly total control. Other times, programmers must relinquish some of their control in order to focus their attentions on larger issues and leave the lower-level work to others. Some applications involve lots of higher mathematics. Others simply do an enormous amount of simple arithmetic. Still others are primarily concerned with organizing and managing large databases. Choosing the right programming language for a particular task is, therefore, an exercise in balance and compromise.

Sometimes the right choice is to first work in some very high-level language to get a working program no matter how inefficient it might be. Then you can redo portions of that program using a lower-level tool to create greater efficiency. This sort of strategy is closely related to the reasons why there are both interpreters and compilers for many of the higher-level programming languages. But to explain that, we must first tell you what those things are.

Interpreters

We have told you that, after you have written a program in a higher-level language (anything above the first generation), it must be translated into actual machine language (binary) code before the CPU can understand and use it. This translation step can be done in any of several ways.

One way that has a lot of utility is to run a program that will translate one line of the program and then ask the CPU to execute that line (in its translated form, of course). Only after that step is done will the program translate the next line. Such a program is called an *interpreter*.

The advantage to this approach is simplicity for the user. You write a program and then run it immediately and see exactly what each line of the program causes the computer to do. If you must alter a line or two, you can do so and immediately rerun the program, reinterpreting it each time you do so. But when you finally finish the program and then intend to run it many, many times, this is not the optimum way to do the translation.

Compilers

Think of the human language parallel: we are writing this book in English. Suppose the publisher wants to sell many copies in certain foreign countries; the sensible plan for the publisher is to hire interpreters to translate the whole book one time into each target language, and then print and sell copies of each translation.

The alternative, which would resemble the use of a computer language interpreter, would be to let customers rent only the English language book accompanied by a skilled human translator and have that translator read it to the foreign language–speaking customer. Obviously, this isn't the least expensive or most efficient way for the publisher to distribute the work.

So people have crafted *compiler* programs. After a program is completely written out in the high-level language, the compiler reads it, generates a machine-language program, and saves it in a file. Then, as a totally independent step, that file (the executable program) can be run once or as many times as you want.

Almost all commercial programs are created this way, and usually only the executable (translated) program is shipped to the customer. The programmer and publishing company keep the *source code* (the high-level language version of the program) to themselves, in part to keep others from seeing just how they wrote it and perhaps writing a competing program more easily.

The advantages of doing this are clear. The disadvantage to this approach is also clear: If you must alter even one byte of the higher-level language program, you must recompile the entire program before you can test it.

P-Code

In an attempt to get the best of both worlds, some tool builders came up with what they term *p-code* (or *pseudo-code*). In this approach, you write the program in a high-level language, and it is immediately processed into an intermediate form that is close to machine language, but not actually machine language. (The particular form the p-code takes can be generated relatively quickly, and that in turn can be very rapidly interpreted into actual machine code.) Then, when you want to run the program (to test it, for example), the corresponding p-code interpreter is invoked to do that final step in the translation.

The advantage to this approach is that the p-code translator has a relatively simple job to do, and thus it can be much faster than a full interpreter. But it can enable you to alter just a portion of the program (and recompile just that portion to its p-code equivalent) and then quickly test the whole program once more.

This approach was used for Pascal when IBM introduced it as one of the initial PC programming languages. BASIC was introduced for the PC only in a fully interpreted (and relatively slow) version. Later, various companies (including Microsoft) came out with compilers for BASIC. Eventually Microsoft introduced QuickBasic, which is a p-code interpreter and editing/compiling environment for BASIC that functions in much the way the early Pascal tools did.

Visual Basic is a direct descendent of QuickBasic because it also provides an editing and debugging environment (and includes a p-code compiler and interpreter) for generating a variant form of the BASIC computer language. It differs because it was designed to create programs to run under Windows, and to facilitate this job it enables you to see the program under construction in a graphical user interface and to construct it in a more directly graphical manner than was possible before. Furthermore, because Windows programs operate primarily in response to "messages," Visual Basic programs—like all other Windows programs—are written in a more sophisticated modular fashion than was customary in earlier versions of BASIC.

Virtual Machines

In another variation on this theme, some high-level language developers have built special-purpose computers whose machine language instructions are essentially identical to the constructs in their particular high-level language. Then the programmer can write the program and directly execute it on this special kind of computer. No interpretation or compilation is needed.

This special kind of computer (its basic instruction set are the instructions that form a particular high-level computer language) can be, and occasionally is, actually built in a hardware form. Such a CPU chip has a dialect of Java as its native language.

More commonly this type of special computer is merely simulated by running a special program on a more general-purpose computer. For example, you can run a program called Pick on a PC or on a mainframe computer. Either way, the result is to make the computer act as though it were built in some different way as a "Pick machine." Then you run Pick programs on this "virtual Pick machine." Pick machines are special database engines, and they are optimized for that task. Pick programs access databases, using the special qualities of a virtual Pick machine. An important point to notice is that this strategy enables a user to run the same program on any virtual Pick machine, no matter what kind of computer hardware is actually doing the work.

Similarly, although it now is possible to build a computer with a CPU that executes Java directly, the more common approach—and what is now universally done in PCs—is simply to simulate the Java virtual machine in software running on the PC's normal CPU. Whether running on a virtual (simulated) Java machine or on an actual hardware Java computer, the main virtue of Java is precisely the relative hardware independence that it provides. A 100 percent pure Java program should run in exactly the same way (although at perhaps different speeds) on any computer—a Macintosh, a PC, or Sun workstation. It won't need to be rewritten or recompiled for each type of computer.

This approach is especially powerful when writing programs for use over the Internet, because the program author need not be aware of which types of computers the users of his or her program might be using. Anything Java permits is okay, as long as the user's computer has a Java virtual machine inside it.

Dividing Up the Work

We have mentioned several times the notion that programming a computer can be quite complex, and that often the best strategy is to divide the overall task into several subtasks, letting specialists work on each separate subtask. Now we want to go back over that notion in a little more detail and explain the distinction between BIOS programs, the operating system, application programs, and applets.

BIOS-Level Programming

BIOS (basic input/output system) is the name given to the programs in your PC that are designed to activate the various pieces of hardware. Someone must know exactly how each chunk of hardware works and therefore exactly what instructions the CPU must process in order to get that chunk of hardware to do some useful task. There is no need for everyone who writes any other type of PC program to have this detailed knowledge.

Instead, we let BIOS programmers write those very low-level, right-next-to-the-hardware programs to activate each gadget within our PCs. No matter how this particular keyboard (or video screen, modem, or whatever) operates, any other program can ask for it to be operated by using a standardized protocol called an Application Program Interface (API).

The motherboard BIOS includes hardware driver programs for all the standard pieces of PC hardware. Any nonstandard hardware must either have as a part of itself another BIOS ROM containing its driver programs, or you must load the appropriate programs off a disk into memory before the PC can utilize that nonstandard hardware.

No matter how nonstandard the hardware is, the application programmers don't need to know anything about how it really works. They can just write their programs to ask for standard "services" from that hardware and trust the BIOS driver to handle the details.

On the other hand, many modern operating systems (notably Windows NT and most variants of UNIX) tend not to use the BIOS programs for much of anything. One major reason for this involves concerns about security coupled with a need to make sure the operating system works in the same way, independent of the machine on which it is running.

Application Programs

Application programs do whatever it is you bought your PC to do. At least we don't know of many people who bought a PC just to watch the DOS prompt or read directory listings. Most people want to write things, keep track of our money, or communicate using their PCs. And they need application programs to accomplish those tasks.

The Operating System as Middleware

Between the BIOS and the application programs is the realm of the operating system. In a way, it can be termed *middleware*.

The operating system does many things, including, as mentioned previously, scheduling application programs, resolving conflicts among applications that want access to the same resources, and so on. It also has the task of handing off service requests from the application programs to the hardware device drivers in the BIOS that do the actual work.

Sometimes in the handing off, the operating system also must amplify those requests for service. For example, an application program can ask the operating system to open a file named C:\MyDocs\Drew and leave the task of finding that file up to the operating system. But the BIOS can't do that task, described in that way. It must know the exact head, cylinder, and sector numbers where the contents of that file are stored. So the intervening layers of the operating system have to do some work to prepare the request for the BIOS routines.

In this example, the operating system must ask the BIOS to perform several subtasks before it can proceed to the main task. The OS must find out, by using the services of the BIOS, which files are stored in which locations so it can determine from which locations to ask the BIOS to retrieve the required data.

There are many other instances in which the API used by the application program is stated in more general terms than the API understood by the BIOS routines. Each time, the operating system must perform any necessary translation and amplification in order to get the BIOS routines to do whatever is needed to satisfy the application program's requests.

We have stated all this in very general terms. We didn't say whether the operating system was DOS or Windows, or perhaps Linux. It doesn't matter. All of them work in conceptually the same fashion, which is the point we want you to understand.

How Not to Keep On Reinventing the Wheel

Programming is detailed, hard work. Programmers love efficiency as much as the rest of us, so they have devised some clever ways to avoid the avoidable portions of the task of designing software. This section describes briefly some of those strategies. In the process, it also will help you understand one of the most misunderstood jargon terms of our time: object-oriented programming.

Programming Libraries

Almost all application programs must handle the same jobs, such as getting input from the keyboard and mouse, putting information on the screen, and opening files. By the division of labor described earlier, low-level driver programs handle all the picky details of these tasks . Even with that help, the application program must have at least a few lines of code to ask for that help, and those lines will be repeated in program after program.

To save time and effort, the obvious thing to do is save those lines of code in some form that lets them be reused as needed. This is the essential idea behind a *programming library*.

Such a library can be as simple as a single file that contains many lines of code, with the idea that the programmer will cut and paste sections from this file into the program currently under construction. Or it can be somewhat more sophisticated, with a directory portion that describes all the blocks of code it contains so that the cutting and pasting can be automated.

Program Linkages and Modular Programs

The next step beyond this is to build a mechanism for assembling programs out of building blocks. Those building blocks are pretested blocks of code in a library. But now, instead of cutting out each little program fragment he or she wishes to use and then pasting it into your main program, the programmer can simply include in the main program a pointer to that block. Then when the program is compiled, the compiler can know enough to open the library file, read the relevant blocks, and act as though they were a part of the main program.

This action is called *linking*. The compiler translates the main program into machine code (putting it in a file called an *object module*), with a description of where routines from the library must be inserted. Then a separate program, called a *linker*, reads the object module and extracts from the library the appropriate machine-language routines to complete the program. Notice that now the library doesn't contain blocks of high-level language code. Instead, each of those blocks must have been precompiled and ready for use.

There is another way to use a library of this type. You don't have to make the compiler actually include the machine language code fragments inside the compiled application program. Instead, you can have the program reach out and execute those code fragments from within the library program each time it needs them whenever that application program is executed. In order for this to work, of course, the library in question must be available to that running application program. Such a memory-loaded, instantly available, run-time library of code fragments is called a *dynamic link library* (DLL).

Object-Oriented Programming

Finally we come to that wonderful and frustrating buzzword phrase, object-oriented programming (OOP). This once meant something very precise. Now, however, it sometimes seems to mean whatever the speaker wants it to mean. If a company says its tools support OOP, it means the tools support what the company wants you to think OOP is. And each company's tools are likely to do slightly (or, sometimes, dramatically) different things.

We won't go into all the variations on this idea that are currently in use. Instead, we will try to give you a sense of the overall concept. It is a very powerful concept, even though the tools that put it into practice are still being refined in an attempt to make all the promise of this approach at last become real.

Before defining OOP, we must describe the old style of programming in a slightly different way than we have until now. In older programming languages, the programmer crafts some lines of code designed to perform a procedure on some data. The data is the object acted upon by the program—something that is outside the procedure.

If you were to create a new program based on an existing program, you would read over the details of the existing program, copy unchanged what you wanted to use, and write the new parts from scratch. Then, after compiling it, you would introduce this program to the data on which it is to work.

The essence of OOP is to create new kinds of programs. They are functional blocks that contain procedures and even some data, and you are supposed to view these blocks as being black or *opaque*. That is, you can activate a block (have it do one of the things it "knows" how to do) and yet have utterly no notion of how it works or what it contains.

This all sounds abstract, and it is. The next section gets a little more explicit, and in the process, introduces you to some of the OOP jargon.

Objects, Classes, Instances, and Libraries

In OOP programming, a key concept is a *class*. This is a *type* of a something. For example, you might define a class as a button in a dialog box on a computer screen. You can do something with this button (in particular, you can "press it" by clicking on it with your mouse or other pointing device), and it will react somehow. The class in this case is all the possible buttons that you can make appear on a computer screen and that can then be pressed.

When you have a class, you can define *subclasses* with some additional particulars. For example, you might define a subclass of buttons called rectangular buttons, green ones, or ones with labels. Each of these is a particular subset of all possible buttons. Of course, you could have among the rectangular buttons a subclass of buttons that also have labels, and within them a subclass of buttons that are red but turn green when pressed.

A particular button is an *instance* of a particular subclass of the class of all buttons. An instance of a button is also referred to as an *object*.

The definitions of various classes of objects (and also of some subclasses) can be referred to in the aggregate as a *class library*.

Attributes, Behaviors, and Methods

Each class (or subclass) will have some set of *properties*. Some of these are best called *attributes*. For example, a particular instance of the button class will have a particular size, shape, color, and value (content) for its label.

The attributes are stored in *variables*. The values in those variables are the attributes for this particular instance of this class; the variables themselves are the attributes of the class.

Other properties tell how the button behaves. For example, when it is pressed (by a mouse click) it will do something. Perhaps it will send a particular message to some other object. Behaviors are defined by *methods*. That is, you write a procedure to spell out just what a certain behavior is, and that procedure is now one of the methods for this class of object.

Notice that methods within a class can act upon objects outside that class. Thus, in the previous example, the button can send a message to some other kind of object (perhaps a window that is supposed to open or close when that button is pressed). This behavior is specified by a method within this class definition, even though it implies an action on an outside object.

Inheritance, Interfaces, and Packages

The payoff to all this begins with the concept of *inheritance*. After you have defined some classes, you can define a new subclass by naming the class of which it is a subclass and then spelling out the attributes and methods that this subclass has but its parent class doesn't have.

By the act of saying that a new object is an instance of a subclass of a certain class, you automatically imply that it has all the attributes and methods that characterize the objects in that class, plus the new ones that you are explicitly defining for this subclass. (If you don't want some subset of the attributes and methods in the class of objects you referred to, you can simply redefine those attributes or those methods in your new subclass definition.)

The jargon language for this goes thus: A subclass *inherits* the attributes and behaviors of its parent class of objects. The helps because you don't have to copy the sections of older programs that you like. Just name your new objects as subclasses of those older program's classes (with specified differences), and you will get the full attribute and behavior set you want. The older program is in a sense included by reference. (And you must build into your OOP program a pointer to that older program, which is to say to its class library.)

The *interface* to an object is just a list of the methods it contains (without the details of what those methods actually do). This list doesn't include the methods defined in the parent classes above this one in the hierarchy; only the ones defined in this class definition are listed in its interface.

Finally, *packages* are groups of related classes and interfaces that are bundled together, so you can refer to all of them by referring just to the package name, or to some of them by referring to the package name and the class name within that package. This allows different objects to have the same name and yet be different, simply by being contained in different packages.

Putting It All Together

Whew. That was a quick one. Let's now recap everything. Object-oriented programming is a formally defined way to access the capabilities of previously written programs within a new program. This strategy means that when you have a useful package of classes and interfaces, you can use it without needing to know the details of its contents. And yet you can override any of the attributes or behaviors of any of the individual classes within that package any time you need to do so.

There is nothing magic about OOP, nor is it necessarily a "better" way to program than the older style with its libraries and linking. Modular programming in some manner is almost a necessity, and certainly adds efficiency to the programming task. Which kind of modularity one uses is less critical.

Helping Ordinary People "Program" Their PCs Easily

Now for the last section of this chapter, the one that tells you how you, whoever you are, can and probably do engage in programming your PC. Often it is so easy that you won't even be aware that what you are doing is programming—but it is.

If you have ever written a DOS batch file, which is a list of commands you don't want to have to type over and over at the DOS prompt, you were programming. You put those commands into a file with each one on a separate line, gave the file a name (with the extension .BAT), and thereafter you could simply type its name at the DOS prompt and COMMAND.COM would do the rest. COMMAND.COM is, in this instance, acting as an interpreter of the DOS batch programming language.

If you use a spreadsheet program and write some macros to perform useful calculations, you are programming. The spreadsheet program is interpreting them, which is to say that, among other things, it is an interpreter for that macro programming language.

Early versions of Microsoft Word had a macro language (Word Basic). It was modeled upon QuickBasic, which is one of the older computer programming languages (well, at least in its earlier, interpreted form, usually referred to as BASIC). With this language, you could write macros to do all manner of things within Word. More recently, Microsoft has phased out Word Basic, but that functionality has been transferred to a more general language, subsets of which are available in all of the MS Office applications. This universal language is now based on the more GUI-oriented version of BASIC known as Visual Basic, and the form in which it appears in Office is known as Visual Basic for Applications (VBA).

> **Warning:** A side observation is in order here. Anyone can put a Word Basic or Visual Basic for Applications macro into a Word document file. If that macro is given the proper form and name, it will automatically be executed each time that document is opened in Word.
>
> This means that if you download such a document from the Internet (or load it off a floppy disk given you by a friend) and then open it up in Word, you might activate one or more macros within that document. These are potentially powerful enough to do great mischief.
>
> We call such rogue macros embedded in a Word document (or any similar file from a macro-enabled application program such as Excel) a *macro virus*. Before you open any such document from an unknown source, it's a very good idea to scan it with a virus scanner such as Norton AntiVirus.

With the growth of the power of these batch and macro languages, many people who never thought they would be programmers are writing some pretty serious PC programs. Now there is yet another kind of programming that "ordinary" folks might find themselves doing: HTML programming for Web or intranet publishing. If you run a Web page editor or word processor that can save your work as hypertext, you will seem only to be typing and formatting a page of text. Then you will highlight some phrases or words and indicate that they are links to some other pages. The program you are running will use that information to construct a Hypertext Markup Language (HTML) document, which is a kind of program. You can see this when someone viewing that page clicks on a link, and some *action* results (a new link appears or a Java applet or JavaScript program runs). In this context, your word processor or Web page editor is actually a fourth-generation computer language-programming tool.

Summary

This appendix explained a wide variety of ways that people write programs for PCs. It showed you some of the distinguishing features of different generations of computer programming languages and of different ways that these high-level language programs can be translated into machine-language instructions that the PC's CPU can understand and act upon. Finally, it explained what OOP means (and a lot of associated jargon), what Java applets are, and how creating a Web page—which is some serious programming—can be done as easily as writing a letter.

Glossary

100-BaseFX—100Megabit Ethernet across fiber optic.

100-BaseT (Or 100baseTX)—100Megabit Ethernet across twisted-pair wire.

10-Base2—10Megabit Ethernet across two-conductor coaxial wire, generally using BNC connectors.

10-BaseT—10Megabit Ethernet across twisted-pair wire.

3DNow!—An addition to the normal set of instructions for x86 processors introduced by AMD and now supported by several CPU manufacturers. These are mainly intended to accelerate processing of 3D intensive game programs. The 3DNow! instructions are similar in concept to the MMX instructions, but they support both integer and floating point instructions and data. They followed Intel's introduction of MMX and preceded its introduction of the KNI instruction group that does a very similar set of tasks. Microsoft DirectX multimedia driver (in version 6.0 and beyond) supports this standard.

A Book—The DVD specification that defines all characteristics of DVD-ROM discs and their supporting hardware players.

Access Time—See latency.

ACPI (Advanced Configuration And Power Interface)—The modern way for the operating system to control the power consumption of system components.

Active Directory—A directory service included with Windows 2000. Information regarding network resources such as users, computers, and printers are stored in the directory service database. The Active Directory makes it easy for users to gain access to resources located anywhere on the network using a single login ID. Administrators can manage their enterprise network from a single point of administration, including multiple domains.

ADPCM (Adaptive Differential Pulse Code Modulation)—An audio compression (lossy) technique used in CD-ROM XA and CD-I discs.

ADSL (Asymmetrical Digital Subscriber Line)—An asymmetric form of purely digital data delivery over conventional telephone lines. See *xDSL*.

AGP (Advanced Graphics Port)—A bus that connects the video processor to a portion of main memory through the Northbridge chip. This bus operates at full system bus speed and an AGP video card is, therefore, much faster than a PCI video card.

Aliasing—In a graphic image, the result of trying to display detail at a low resolution. In practice it has the effect, among others, of making diagonal lines look like stair-steps.

Alphanumeric Mode—See *character-based*.

ALU (Arithmetic Logic Unit)—The component of a CPU that is responsible for performing integer math functions as well as making logical comparisons.

Analog (also Analogue)—A signal, as with audible sound, that possesses continuous variances, as opposed to discrete variances.

APM (Advanced Power Management)—The first standard means of specifying system-level control of power consumption by various parts of a PC. This standard was introduced by Microsoft and Intel in 1995 with Windows 95. It has now been supplanted by ACPI.

AppleTalk—Protocol developed by Apple Computer for communications between the Macintosh computer system and other computers or peripherals.

Application Programming Interface (API)—A set of routines that an application program uses to request and carry out lower-level services performed by the operating system.

ASCII—See *text file*.

Asymmetric—In the context of data transmission, a scheme in which data can be received and sent simultaneously by dividing the total available bandwidth into two channels, each of which has a different throughput.

Asynchronous—Two or more events that are not synchronized in time. In the context of data transmission, a process by which data is sent or received at a variable rate. Contrast with *synchronous*.

ATA (AT Attachment)—A standard that defines how hard disks and similar devices can be attached to a PC (based on the ISA interface). This is the formal name for what is commonly known as IDE. See *ATAPI*, *EIDE*, *IDE*, and *ISA*.

ATAPI (Ata Packet Interface)—An extension to the ATA standard allowing support of devices other than hard disks (CD-ROM drives) over the ATA interface. See *ATA*, *EIDE*, *IDE*, and *ISA*.

ATM—In computer circles this refers to Asynchronous Transfer Mode, which is a communications protocol for packet-switched data communication that uses very small (53 byte) packets; often used for very high-speed networks.

ATX and MicroATX—Two of the standard designs for PC motherboards. These designs are based on the IBM PC/AT motherboard's design, but commonly feature smaller overall size and other improved features.

Availability—A term that refers to the fraction of the time that a computer system is available for useful work. A "high availability" system is a very reliable one. (This concept has been an important one for large computer systems for years; it only recently has become an issue for PCs, as they are now doing some of the jobs formerly reserved for mini- and mainframe computers.) Contrast with *performance*.

B Book—The DVD specification that defines all characteristics of DVD-Video discs and their supporting hardware players.

b Versus B—In this and many other books and technical magazines b stands for a bit and B stands for a byte (eight bits).

Back-Side Bus—Modern CPUs for PCs have two data buses communicating with memory at different speeds and for different purposes. One, termed the front-side bus or system bus, goes to the Northbridge chip and then on to main memory, AGP video, and the PCI bus. The second (back side) bus goes only one place, to the Level 2 cache memory. This bus operates at the full speed of the CPU core or at half that speed; the front-side bus operates typically at a small fraction of the core speed. See *DIB*.

Bandwidth—The capacity of any data path, whether digital or analog, to transmit data. With specific regard to PCs, bandwidth is commonly expressed in terms of bits or bytes per second.

Batch Program—An ASCII (unformatted text) file that contains one or more commands in the command language for Windows 2000. A batch program's filename has a .BAT or .CMD extension. When you type the filename at the command prompt, the commands are processed sequentially.

Battery Backup—See *uninterruptible power supply*.

Biometrics—The study of the means for measuring unique properties of the human body, and the devices that measure these properties. Examples include retinal scanners, fingerprint scanners, iris scanners, face recognition systems, and voice recognition systems. These devices are now becoming common authentication means to permit users access to a network or other restricted resource, alternative to passwords, keys, smart cards, or the like.

Bit rate—The rate at which data is moved from storage media to the storage device's output electronics.

Blue Book—One of several CD specifications, responsible for defining the details of the CD-EXTRA (or *Enhanced CD*) format.

bps—Bits per second, also written b/s. (Bps, on the other hand, stands for bytes per second). Similarly, Kbps and Mbps refer to thousands and millions of bits per second, whereas KBps and MBps refer to thousands and millions of bytes per second.

BRI (Basic Rate Interface)—One of two ways you can get ISDN pure-digital telephone service. In this protocol, two channels for data transmissions are defined, each of which operates at 64Kbps, in addition to a third channel that is used for control purposes, which operates at 16Kbps.

Bridge—A means of connecting two or more LANs, possibly converting between different data transmission protocols in the process, and also perhaps filtering which of the data packets received from any one connected LAN get passed to each of the others. Contrast with a *router*. In another usage this refers to a device that couples different busses inside a single PC, or linking two PCs or other, similar devices. A PCI-to-PCI bus is one example of this. A Northbridge chip serves as a bridge between the front-side bus, the AGP bus, and the PCI bus. The portion of a Southbridge chip's function that connects the PCI bus to an ISA bus is yet another example.

Bus—A formal specification of an interconnection between two parts of a PC that could, in principle, be manufactured by different vendors. A full bus specification must include the logical, physical, electrical, and timing aspects of the interface.

Bus Connection—A term used to describe a data path that joins a source with one or more destinations. Contrast with *point-to-point*.

Bus Contention—A situation in which two or more devices connected to a bus want to use that bus at the same time.

C Book—The DVD specification that defines all characteristics of DVD-Audio discs and their supporting hardware players.

C2 (C2 Orange Book)—C2 Orange Book Certification means that according to the United States government this operating system meets the criteria set forth by the National Computer Security Center (NCSC). See also *Orange Book*.

Cable Modem—A device that allows two-way data transmission over a CATV cable network, typically for access to the Internet. Contrast with *ISP* and *direct broadcast satellite service*.

Cache—A temporary holding place. Cache memory describes a very fast yet small amount of RAM that is used to hold data on its way into or out of the CPU. A disk cache refers to some RAM that is used to hold data on its way to or from a disk drive.

CATV (Community Antenna Television)—The formal name for what most people call simply cable television. These vendors string cable to homes and offices and then supply a combination of channels, some carrying copies of off-the-air television signals, some with signals from satellites, and others from local studios. Most vendors now also offer data services, including two-way access to the Internet, which is referred to as a cable modem. Contrast with *ISP* and *direct broadcast satellite service*.

CAV (Constant Angular Velocity)—A way of controlling the rotation of an optical disc so that the disc always spins at the same rate. Contrast with *CLV*.

CCITT (Comité Consultatif Internationale de Telegraphique et Telephonique)—The international standards committee largely responsible for defining the ways telecommunication systems interact and communicate.

CD, CD-ROM, CD-R, And CD-RW—These are all optical discs for storing digital data. The original type, CDs, are used to store audio information in digital form. CD-ROMs store digital data of a more general kind, including programs and any kind of data file. CD-R refers to a recordable CD disc whose content can be written by the user (on a suitable drive), but only once for any place on the disc. CD-RW refers to a different type of recordable CD disc that can be written and re-written, much like a very high capacity floppy disk. Contrast with *DVD*.

CDDI (Copper Distributed-Data Interface)—A protocol for high speed data transmission over copper-wire links, derived from FDDI. See also *HIPPI* and *fibre channel*.

CD-EXTRA—See *Enhanced CD*.

CDPD (Cellular Digital Packet Data)—An industry standard for transmission of digital data (currently at 19.2Kbps) over a cellular phone network.

Channel—Any pathway over which data moves.

Channel-Bonding—A term that describes using two or more data channels of an ISDN connection simultaneously to increase the data transfer rate. See also *Multilink-PPP*. Contrast with *modem-bonding*.

Character Mode—See *character-based*.

Character-Based—A mode of operation in which all information is displayed as text characters. Also called *character mode*, *alphanumeric mode*, or *text mode*.

Chipset—The electronic logic chips that are needed to connect and control the parts of a PC motherboard. In most modern PCs this is almost entirely contained in two VLSI chips called the Northbridge and Southbridge chips.

Client—A computer that accesses shared network resources provided by another computer (called a *server*). Contrast with *server*.

Client-Server—Refers to a way of partitioning the workload for a given application between a central machine (the server) and many attached workstations (the clients).

Clock—The PC's main, or system, clock is the circuit that synchronizes all actions of all of its principal parts. Normally this runs at the same speed as the CPU (or some multiple of the CPU speed), and a small fraction of this speed regulates the actions on the front-side bus. Yet-smaller fractions of that speed are used to control the steps on the *PCI* and *ISA* buses and elsewhere within the PC.

Clock Speed—the number of times, per second, that a PC's main, or system, clock "ticks." This is usually measured in MHz, or thousands of "ticks" per second.

CLV (Constant Linear Velocity)—A way of controlling the rotation of an optical disc so that the number of bits per second that pass before the laser is constant. In order for this to be possible, the speed of the disc's rotation is altered as the laser aims variously at data near the inner or outer edge of the disc. Contrast with *CAV*.

CMYK—The Cyan-Magenta-Yellow-Black model of color printing. Contrast with *RGB*.

Codec (compressor/decompresor)—A program or device driver that is capable of extracting viewable video or analog audio from a compressed, digital data stream.

Color Palette—A table of color values used to reduce the number of bits required to accurately display a graphic image. If an image contains, for example, only 256 unique colors, it can be palletted so that all of those colors are accurately represented using only eight bits, even if the original image was created at a 24-bit color depth.

CompactFlash Card—A standard bus and module design initially intended for add-on memory for handheld PCs, digital cameras, and other similar devices. This standard is now being extended (in its second generation form, referred to as CompactFlash Card II, or CFII) to include devices such as miniature hard drives, and for use in larger systems, such as the newest, very thin laptop computers. In contrast with SmartMedia, CompactFlash includes the flash memory controller circuitry in the removable module.

Compression—Reducing the size of a data file either by removing redundancy (lossless compression) or by removing both redundancy and some nonessential information (lossy compression).

Computer Name—A unique name that identifies a computer to the network. The name can't be the same as any other computer or domain name in the network, and it can't generally contain spaces.

Controller—Generically, any circuitry that provides an administrative function for some other circuitry, as in a "disk controller," or "game controller." In many cases, the term describes any of the various cards that plug in to a PC to provide additional functionality.

Copy Protection—A method of protecting content providers from piracy at the expense of law-abiding consumers.

CPU (Central Processing Unit)—The device within a PC that does the bulk of the information processing. This has within it many parts, including one to fetch information from external memory, one to decode instructions and then direct the actions of the other parts of the CPU, an arithmetic and logic processing unit, a floating point calculation unit, and perhaps others.

C-RIMM (Continuity RIMM)—A blank RDIMM module needed to fill any empty RIMM sockets before a Direct Rambus memory subsystem can be used. See also *RIMM*.

CRC (Cyclic Redundancy Check)—An error-detection method used in optical storage, among other uses.

CSMA/CD (Carrier Sense Multiple Access with Collision Detection)—The protocol that defines Ethernet. A method of utilizing a bus topology in which all devices have free access to the media (multiple access). Devices first listen to make sure the line is available (carrier sense), and then attempt to transmit. In the case of two devices transmitting and precisely, or nearly, the same moment, the error is detected (collision detection), and each device waits a pseudo-random amount of time before attempting to retransmit.

D Book—The DVD specification that defines all characteristics of DVD-R discs and their supporting hardware recorders and players.

DAC (Digital to Analog Converter)—Circuitry designed to convert a digital data stream into an analog one. For example, to convert the digital data on a CD into audible, analog music.

DAT—Digital Audio Tape, used for storing both music and computer data. The latter use is sometimes called *DDS*.

Data Throughput—The amount of data that traverses a given path per unit of time (usually a second).

DDR SDRAM (Double Data Rate SDRAM)—A standard for higher performance SDRAM that competes with *RDRAM*.

DDS—Digital Data Storage, a version of DAT used for computer data.

Deadlock—A condition in which two processes are each stalled, waiting for the other to complete.

Decompress (or Decompression)—Taking a compressed collection of data and returning it to its original, uncompressed state.

Demand Paging—A method by which data is moved in pages from physical memory to a temporary paging file on-disk. As a process needs the data, it's paged back into physical memory.

Desktop—The primary interface between the user and the operating system. A frame that allows the user to interact with tools that Windows provides.

Device Driver—A program that enables a piece of software or the operating system to activate and use (that is, transmit to and receive information from) a hardware device, or one that allows treating hardware as if it were something different. For example, a printer driver translates computer data into a form understood by a particular printer. See *DLL* and *VxD*.

Device—A generic term for a computer subsystem such as a printer, serial port, or disk drive. A device frequently requires its own controlling software called a *device driver*.

DFS—see *distributed file system*.

DHTML (Dynamic HTML)—An enhancement to HTML that permits defining pages whose content will change after they have been downloaded to the client machine. Specifically, it extends the capability of scripts to change the HTML page on which the scripts are hosted. The browser can read the DHTML code and display its content differently as the user takes certain actions (for example, passing a mouse over a "hot spot" on the page).

DIB (Dual Independent Bus)—Intel's name for the two buses going from the CPU to other parts of a PC. See *front-side bus* and *back-side bus*.

Digital Signature—A method of verifying the identity of a digital encoded piece of information sent by the originator.

DIMM (Dual Inline Memory Module)—A small printed circuit board (PCB) carrying multiple memory chips mounted on both sides of the board and with independent electrical contacts on the two sides of the PCB. Contrast with *SIMM*.

Direct Broadcast Satellite Service (DBSS)—This refers to satellites that broadcast signals directly to users. Originally developed as an alternative to cable television, now also includes providers of Internet customized data delivery to individual subscribers as well as broadcast data services. Contrast with *CATV*, *cable modem*, and *ISP*.

Disc—Within this text and throughout most of the industry, this spelling refers specifically to optical storage media.

Disc at Once—A way of recording an optical disc so that the entire disc is burned in one continuous process with the laser never turning off. When used with audio CDs, this format eliminates the two second gap that normally occurs between audio tracks. Contrast with *Track at Once*.

Disk—Used generically to refer to any data flat-media rotating storage device using magnetic techniques.

Disk Caching—A method used by a file system to improve performance. Instead of reading and writing directly to the disk, frequently used files are temporarily stored in a cache in memory, and reads and writes to those files are performed in memory. Reading and writing to memory is much faster than reading and writing to disk.

Distributed Application—An application that has two parts, a front end to run on the client computer and a back end to run on the server. In distributed computing, the goal is to divide the computing task into two sections. The front end requires minimal resources and runs on the client's workstation. The back end requires large amounts of data, number crunching, or specialized hardware, and runs on the server. A trend towards a three-tier model for distributed computing has begun in the last few years. That model separates the business logic contained in both sides of the two-tier model into a third, distinct layer. The business logic layer sits between the front-end user interface layer and the back-end database layer. It typically resides on a server platform that might not be the same as the one the database is on. The three-tier model arose as a solution to the limits faced by software developers trying to express complex business logic with the two-tier model.

Distributed File System (DFS)—Provides a single tree structure for multiple shared volumes located on different servers on a network.

DHCP (Dynamic Host Configuration Protocol)—Used to enable individual computers on an IP network to retrieve their configuration specifications from a server. In this way, a limited number of IP addresses can be utilized by a larger number of computers on an as-needed basis. Once a computer no longer requires an IP address, the address is released back to the DHCP server so it can be assigned to another computer on the network.

Dithering—A means of approximating a color that can't be represented directly on a display or printing device by printing adjacent dots of differing colors whose values average to the desired color.

DLL (Dynamic Link Library)—A file that contains one or more programs that can be referenced by some other program. A DLL can be loaded by the operating system only when needed, or it can reside in main memory indefinitely. See *VxD*.

DMA (Direct Memory Access) Controller—A controller that can be programmed by the CPU and then left to move a block of data from one region of main memory to another, or to or from an I/O port without further CPU attention.

DNS (Directory Name Server)—A computer that is programmed to supply actual IP addresses that correspond to a named resource on the Internet or any other network using TCP/IP as its data transmission protocol. See also *URL*.

Domain Name Service (DNS)—A hierarchical name service for TCP/IP hosts (sometimes referred to as the *BIND service* in BSD Unix). The network administrator configures the DNS with a list of hostnames and IP addresses, allowing users of workstations configured to query the DNS to specify the remote systems by hostnames rather than IP addresses.

DOS (Disk Operating System)—Originally named to contrast with the operating systems that preceded it, this term simply indicates a computer's OS, which is loaded from disk-based storage when the computer is powered up. Older computers had their operating systems loaded from tape or stored permanently in circuitry. Later, the term came to be used as a proper noun for the operating system created by IBM and Microsoft for use on Intel-based PCs.

DRAM (Dynamic Random Access Memory)—RAM modules (or chips) that can only retain information if they are clocked at frequent intervals. Contrast with *SRAM, flash memory*, and *ROM*.

DSP (Digital Signal Processor)—A special-purpose CPU that is designed specifically to support calculations appropriate to signal processing. DSPs are often used in modems and other devices within or attached to a PC, as well as in specialized instruments.

DTV (Digital Television)—A group of standards for purely digital television image transmission. This group includes various resolutions for the images.

Duplex—In printing this refers to printing on both sides of a page. In telephony this refers to data flowing in both directions over the link, thus full-duplex means data flows both ways at the same time, whereas half-duplex means the data flow alternates between one direction and the opposite, with only one direction active at a time.

DVD—Originally standing for Digital Video Disk, and then for Digital Versatile Disk, this term now is just DVD. An optical disc of the same size as a CD but capable of holding far more data.

DVD-R—An optical disc based on the DVD "D Book" standard. It is recordable and can be written to exactly once.

DVD-RAM, DVD-RW, DVD+RW—Different types of rewritable optical discs based on the DVD "E Book" standard. They can be written to, erased, and rewritten infinitely.

DVD-Video—The standard format for the commercial distribution of full-length audio-video content on DVD. Video is compressed using the *MPEG2* methodology.

E Book—The DVD specification that defines all characteristics of rewritable DVD discs and their supporting hardware recorders and players.

ECC (Error Control and Checking, or Error Control and Correction)—A methodology by which errors at the bit or multiple-bit level in RAM are intercepted and corrected as that data is being sent to the CPU.

EDO RAM (Extended Data Out RAM)—This variation of DRAM technology allows the CPU to address one location while still reading data from a previous one, thus increasing the speed with which data is read from memory. This has been the workhorse form of DRAM in high-end PCs for the past several years, but was replaced by *SDRAM*.

EEPROM (Electrical Erasable Programmable Read Only Memory)—An integrated circuit design for the creation of NVRAM modules. Functions as ROM (read-only memory) at all times, except under specific conditions in which content can be downloaded electronically.

EIDE (Enhanced Integrated Device Electronics)—An improved version of the IDE channel definition, permitting use of logical block addressing for very large hard disks, booting from CD-ROMs and similar devices, and so forth. See *ATA*, *ATAPI*, *IDE*, and *ISA*.

Encrypted File System—A feature of the NTFS 5.0 file system that allows data on-disk to be stored in an encrypted format.

Encryption —A method by which data is rendered secure and unreadable to anyone who does not possess a proper password or decryption key.

Enhanced CD—Also known as CD-EXTRA, a multisession CD format in which digital audio and computer data are combined on the same disc. The session containing the CD-ROM data "disappears" when the disc is played in a traditional audio player.

EPROM (Erasable Programmable Read Only Memory)—An integrated circuit design for the creation of NVRAM modules that require exposure to ultraviolet light to erase their contents.

Ethernet—A very common protocol for data communication (technically referred to as CSMA/CD) in which multiple devices attached to a bus are each permitted to send packets asynchronously, but must listen first to be sure no other device is using the bus, and then again while sending to be sure no collisions are occurring with that transmission. True Ethernet operates at 10Mbps data transmission speed. Ethernet-like standards have been developed that operate 10 and 100 times that speed, referred to often as Fast Ethernet and Gigabit Ethernet. Ethernet and Ethernet-like protocols have been implemented on various physical media. The most popular are referred to 10-BaseT (twisted pair operating at 10Mbps), 100-BaseT (twisted pair operating at 100Mbps), and 2-BaseT (coaxial cable, usually at 10Mbps).

Extended Partitions—Partitions that consume the remaining free space after primary drives have been established. You can have only one extended partition per physical drive. Extended partitions can usually be segmented into numerous logical drives.

Fast Ethernet—An Ethernet-like networking standard that operates at 100Mbps. See *Ethernet*.

FAT File System—A file system based on a file allocation table maintained by the operating system to keep track of the status of various segments of disk space used for file storage.

Fault Tolerance—The ability of a computer and an operating system to respond gracefully to catastrophic events such as power outage or hardware failure. Usually, fault tolerance implies the ability to either continue the system's operation without loss of data or to shut the system down and restart it, recovering all processing that was in progress when the fault occurred.

FC-AL (Fibre Channel Arbitrated Loop)—A redundant cable design for a Fibre Channel link to provide security against cable failure.

FDDI (Fiber Distributed-Data Interface)—A protocol for high speed data transmission over optical fiber links. See also *CDDI*, *HIPPI*, and *Fibre Channel*.

Fibre Channel (FC)—A standard for networking using primarily optical fibers as the physical medium. The Fibre Channel protocol continues to be developed with speeds of up to 10Gbps currently being tested.

File Sharing—The ability of an operating system to share parts (or all) of its local file system(s) with remote computers.

File System—In an operating system, the overall structure in which files are named, stored, and organized.

File Transport Protocol (FTP) —The protocol enables two computers, a client and a server (or other hardware device), to copy files back and forth over the Internet.

Firewall—A computer that buffers all accesses from a LAN to an external network (such as the Internet). This computer not only translates protocols, as a simple bridge would; it converts network addresses, as a proxy server would, and it also implements various filtering rules to keep "bad" packets of data from passing through it.

FireWire—See *IEEE 1394*.

Fixed Point—A way of storing and manipulating numbers that can be expressed within a predetermined number of bits, and with an implied decimal point location within that number. This method gives all numbers the same absolute precision (minimum difference between distinguishable numbers) and also implies a maximum size to those numbers. Contrast with *floating point*.

Flash Memory—A type of non-volatile, electronic, random-access memory. These modules hold data indefinitely even without power being applied to them continuously (although power is required to read those data). Using a special, generally slower, process the data held in a flash memory module can be changed. This latter process is termed "flashing the memory." See also *CompactFlash card* and *SmartMedia card*. Contrast with *DRAM*, *NVRAM*, *SRAM*, and *ROM*.

Flicker—A very annoying property of images on a display device (for example, a video monitor) that aren't refreshed frequently enough to fool the eye into thinking they are static (or continuously displayed moving) images. Too much flicker will cause severe eye strain and headaches. See also *refresh rate*.

Floating Point—A way of storing and manipulating numbers of almost any size.

Form Factor—Jargon referring to the physical size and shape of an object.

Fragmentation—Caused by data from the same disk file being dispersed across different areas of the disk drive. This can cause performance degradation of the disk I/O.

Frame Rate—A measure of how frequently the image on a display device is changed. Usually expressed in frames per second (FPS). See also *flicker* and *refresh rate*.

FSB (Front-Side Bus)—Another name for the system bus that connects the CPU to the Northbridge chip in a modern PC. See also *back-side bus* and *DIB*.

FTP Service—File transfer protocol service that offers file transfer services to remote systems supporting this protocol. FTP supports a host of commands allowing bi-directional transfer of binary and ASCII files between systems.

Full-Duplex—See *duplex*.

Fully Qualified Domain Name (FQDN)—In TCP/IP, hostnames with their domain names appended to them. For example, a host with hostname `ellephai` and domain name `goddess.com` has an FQDN of `ellephai.goddess.com`.

Gamut—The range of possibilities. Mostly encountered in PCs in connection with discussions of color, where the gamut for a given technology refers to the extent of its ability to show a wide range of colors.

GART (Graphics Address Remapping Table)—A mechanism used by AGP cards to permit them to find the data they use from main memory even as the linear addresses of those data are shifted by the CPU's page table mechanism.

GIF (Graphics Interchange Format)—One of the two most common graphic file formats in use on the Internet. This file compression format is copyrighted by CompuServe (now AOL), but is very widely used without apparent regard for its legal status. See also *JPEG*.

Gigabit Ethernet—An Ethernet-like network type that operates at 1000Mbps (1Gbps). See *Ethernet* and *Fast Ethernet*.

Global Descriptor Table (GDT)—A table that is built in memory before any x86 processor can go into protected mode. The contents of this table specify the regions of memory that every task can access.

Green Book—The CD standard responsible for defining the CD-i (Interactive CD) format, used primarily for the distribution of video games.

Half-Duplex—See *duplex*.

Hardware Abstraction Layer (HAL)—A structure that virtualizes hardware interfaces, making the hardware dependencies transparent to the rest of the operating system. This allows an operating system to be portable from one hardware platform to another.

HDSL (High-Speed Digital Subscriber Line)—See *ADSL, SDSL, xDSL*.

HFS—Hierarchical File System, found in the Apple Macintosh's operating system and used in conjunction with *ISO9660* to produce CD-ROMs that are compatible on both Windows and MacOS PCs.

HID (Human Interface Device)—A term referring to any object by means of which a human might interact with a computer. (Examples include the keyboard, mouse, telephone, and fax machine.) This term also refers to a standard that classifies such devices, to assist in supporting them in software.

High Sierra—A file system for CD-ROM, formalized as the *ISO9660* standard.

HIPPI (High Performance Parallel Interface)—A protocol for high speed data transmission a multi-wire link. See also *CDDI, FDDI*, and *fibre channel*.

Hot Swap—The capability of removing and replacing components of a computer (the hard disk drive) without having to shut down the PC. This capability is inherent in many devices attached via either a USB or an IEEE 1394 connection, and it can be provided for other devices by a special hardware interface.

HP PCL (Hewlett-Packard Printer Control Language)—See *PCL*.

HPC (Handheld PC)—A computer that is a PC (able to run a version of Windows, most commonly Windows CE) and yet is very small and highly portable. Contrast with *PDA*.

HSM (Hierarchical Storage Management)—A general term for a strategy that moves less often used data files off the hard disk onto some less-rapidly accessible storage medium, such as an optical disc in a jukebox, and then when the data are even less-often used, off-line to an external archive.

HTML (Hyper-Text Markup Language)—A subset of the Standard Generalized Markup Language (SGML) used in Internet- and intranet-based Web objects, this standard has gone through several generations, each one taking more features from SGML and allowing for more elaborate and precise Web page definition.

HTTP (Hyper-Text Transfer Protocol)—The standard way that Web browsers request pages of HTML code from a Web server.

I/O Manager—Defines an orderly framework within which I/O requests are delivered to file systems and device drivers. The I/O Manager doesn't actually manage I/O processing. Its job is to create an IRP that represents each I/O operation, pass the IRP to the correct driver, and dispose of the packet when the I/O operation is complete.

I/O Port—A hardware interface between the CPU and some external device. Each I/O port has an address, or a range of adjacent addresses (of which the lowest one is called the base address). These addresses form a separate address space from that of main memory. The devices attached to I/O ports might be inside the PC or outside of it.

ICC (International Color Consortium)—A standards organization as well as the standard they have created for color matching across multiple input and output devices.

IDE (Integrated Device Electronics)—The common name for the ATA standard. Originally a description of peripheral devices (such as a hard disk drive) that contained all the control and interface electronics necessary to connect them to a PC, this now (especially in its EIDE form) refers to a standard way of connecting any of a large variety of peripheral devices to a PC. See also *ISA* and *EIDE*.

IEEE 1284—The Institute for Electrical and Electronic Engineering's standard number 1284 is the formal description for the various forms a PC parallel port can take. This includes the original PC parallel port, the bi-directional parallel port, the EPP (Enhanced Parallel Port), and the ECP (Extended Capability Port).

IEEE 1394—The IEEE's (Institute for Electrical and Electronic Engineering) standard number 1394 is the formal description for what began as Apple Computer's FireWire very-high-speed serial bus.

IEEE 802.11b—The formal standard for what is also known as the Bluetooth wireless networking protocol.

Integer—A whole number (positive, negative, or zero) that has no fractional part. Integer arithmetic is a means for doing mathematical calculations in which all the numbers are assumed to be integers. Contrast with *real number*.

Interlaced Scan—Forming an raster-scan image by drawing every other line on the screen in turn (typically from top to bottom), and then going back and filling in the missing lines. This is the method prescribed in the NTSC standard for television images, which is the television standard in the US. Contrast with *progressive scan*.

Internet—The collective name for all the networks worldwide that are connected to one another and that use the TCP/IP protocol suite.

Interrupt—When an interface card in a PC wants to address the other pieces of the system, it must first interrupt the processor. The processor of interrupting the processor is done through the use of a message called an interrupt or *IRQ*.

Intranet—An Internet-like network, but one whose scope is limited logically and perhaps also physically so that it can only be accessed by users within one corporation or entity.

IP (Internet Protocol)—The standard method for communicating over the physical links that make up the Internet, this is in fact a collection of standards, each tuned to the needs of a particular transport medium.

IP Address—A number (currently 32 bits long but in IPv6 slated to be extended to 128 bits) that specifies a unique device in a network. Conventionally this number is written as four decimal numbers (each in the range 0 to 255) separated by periods (for example, 125.14.95.5). A DNS is used to "resolve" names of resources to their equivalent IP address. A reverse-DNS search refers to looking up the name of the resource by reference to its IP address. See also *URL*.

Ipv6—A standard proposed for the next generation Internet Protocol. Its primary purpose is to dramatically increase the number of servers and resources that can be made simultaneously available over the Internet and provide significant enhancements to Internet-related security technologies.

IRQ—See *interrupt*.

ISA (Industry Standard Architecture)—The design of the bus slots used by IBM for option cards in the original PC and PC-AT models, later adopted by all clone PC manufacturers as the standard way to attach peripheral devices to a PC. This also was the source for the design of the IDE and EIDE channels. The ISA bus doesn't support many features now considered essential (or at least highly desirable) to peripheral connectivity and so it has been phased out of new PCs.

ISDN (Integrated Services Digital Network)—This is a dial-up, but purely digital alternative to conventional, dial-up, analog POTS telephone service. It comes in two flavors, with BRI (Basic Rate Interface) service having two 64Kbps signal channels and PRI (Primary Rate Interface) service offering 23 64Kbps signal channels.

ISO9660—The International Standards Organization standard responsible for defining the file system used on a PC-compatible CD-ROM discs.

ISP (Internet Service Provider)—A vendor that offers a variety of ways to connect to the Internet. Usually these include a link that takes place over a leased or dial-up telephone line. Contrast with *CATV*, *cable modem*, and *direct broadcast satellite*.

Jitter—This term refers to the degree of inconsistency of the spacing of the "ticks" of a clock signal.

Joliet—An extended version of ISO9660 that includes support for Windows long file-names and Unicode.

JPEG (Joint Photographic Experts Group)—This term refers to a standards body, and to a digital still-image compression standard they have created. See also *GIF* and *MPEG*.

Kerberos Protocol —The Kerberos protocol offers greater security compared to previous methods of authentication as passwords themselves are encrypted when sent over the line.

Kernel—The portion of an operating system that manages the processor and provides the most fundamental level of services.

LAN (Local Area Network)—A connection between multiple PCs created in order to facilitate the sharing of application programs, data files, and resources (such as printer or modems) within a restricted geographical region, such as within a single building. Compare with *WAN* and *VPN*.

Lands—The raised surfaces of a DVD or CD which, together with *pits*, define the data the disc contains.

LAPM (Link Access Procedures For Modems)—Now the primary protocol for asynchronous-to-synchronous conversion, flow control, and error detection and correction in V.42 modems. These modems also support the Microcom Networking Protocols (MNP) Classes 1-4 as an alternative way of accomplishing these same tasks.

Latency—The delay after issuing a command before it begins to take effect.

Lead In—The area at the beginning of a CD or of each session of a multisession CD. It contains the CD's or session's table of contents, which is used to identify files stored on that disc or in that session.

Lead Out—The area at the end of a CD or of each session of a multisession CD.

Linux—A very popular "open source" operating system for PCs created by Linus Torvalds and based upon Unix. The pronunciation is "Lih-nucks."

Local Descriptor Table (LDT)—A table that is built in memory for each task running on an x86 processor before it can go into protected mode. The contents of this table specify the regions of memory that task can access.

Local Printer—A printer that's directly connected to one of the ports on a computer.

Local Procedure Call Facility—Processes running in the different application subsystems must communicate with one another in order to accomplish anything. For processes in the local machine to communicate with one another, they must use the local procedure call facility.

Locale—The national and cultural environment in which a system or program is running. The locale determines the language used for messages and menus, the sorting order of strings, the keyboard layout, and date and time formatting conventions.

Logon Authentication—Refers to the validation of a user either locally or in a domain. At logon time, the user specifies his or her name, password, and the intended logon domain. The workstation then contacts the domain controllers for the domains, which verify the user's logon credentials.

Lossless Compression—A compression methodology that guarantees that the compressed content can be restored to its exact original condition.

Lossy Compression—A compression methodology that prevents compressed content from ever being restored to its *exact* original condition, but that attempts to delete only redundancies that do not noticeably impact the usefulness of the resulting file.

LS-120—Also called a "super-floppy" disk, this is a disk (and corresponding drive) that can use either traditional magnetic means for recording data (in the same format as a standard floppy disk), or with enhanced positioning assistance from an optical head. This optical head follows prerecorded optical tracks on special floppy disks and it can record approximately 100 times as much data.

LVDS (Low Voltage Differential Signaling)—A common means for sending signals across some of the more advanced, high-speed busses inside a PC. This uses a pair of wires with signals that move in opposite directions to represent each data transition. The receivers for this system look only at the difference in voltage on each such pair of wires to sense the arrival of each data transition, thus helping them ignore any superimposed noise signals (which commonly are going to be similar in size and sign on both wires).

Magneto-Optical Discs—A rewritable optical disc. A laser is used in conjunction with a magnetic recording head to store data digitally. The laser is then used to read the data. Also known as MO discs.

Main Memory—The pool of RAM and ROM that the CPU can address directly. Some of this is on the motherboard; portions can reside on a video card or some other option card. (Various devices in a PC can also have some RAM or ROM, but if it isn't addressable by the CPU then it isn't a part of main memory.)

Memory—The space, comprised of a variety of types of RAM chips, in which a computer performs its work.

Memory Address—Every location in main memory where data is held has an address. This binary number is used by the CPU, the DMA controller, the cache memory controller, and any other hardware that must read or write those data from or to that location. The collection of all the memory addresses the CPU can address is called its memory address space.

MicroATX—See *ATX*.

Microcom Networking Protocols (MNP)—Originally a proprietary set of protocols used only in Microcom modems, many of them are now available to all and they have been adopted widely. Classes 1-4 are officially approved as an alternative to LAPM within the V.42 modem standard. Class 5 provides a standard for data compression during transmission. MNP 10 was a special version that supports cellular phone connections, which often suffer from brief interruptions that otherwise would cause the modems to lose their connection.

MIDI (Musical Instrument Device Interface)—A standard way of connecting music generation, recording, and playback devices such as synthesizers with each other, with keyboards, with other input devices, and with PCs over a low-speed serial bus. This also refers to a way of encoding music and other audio program material so that it can be sent over a MIDI bus and played back by a synthesizer.

MIME (Multimedia Internet Mail Enhancements)—A broad and extensive standard for attaching data objects of any kind to an Internet mail message (or a message traveling over any network using the Internet protocols). This includes compressed files, audio files, video files, and more. The standard includes a means for defining new types of attachments as desired.

Mirroring (RAID 1)—A form of drive fault tolerance that involves adding one hard drive for every one hard drive that you want to protect in your system. The same data is then written to both drives or groups of drives. In the event of a hard drive failure, the system will switch to the other, mirrored, hard drive for data.

MMX (Multimedia Extensions)—Intel's extension to the x86 instruction set using the SIMD technique to speed certain types of calculation. This standard was adopted by the industry and these instructions were eventually available on all of the newest clone CPUs as well as on Intel's CPUs.

MO—See *Magneto-Optical Discs*.

Modem (Modulator and Demodulator)—Technically this name refers to a device that converts digital data into analog tones and back again. It now has been extended, however, to include some purely digital devices, such as cable modems and ISDN modems.

Modem-Bonding—Refers to using simultaneously two analog modems connected to two separate voice-grade POTS telephone lines in order to double the achievable data transfer rate. With the advent of xDSL, this method has been all but abandoned.

MP3 (Motion Picture Experts Group, Audio Layer 3)—A subset of MPEG1, this standard defines a way to compress audio files very effectively without losing much of the quality. It rapidly became the standard way to distribute and share high-quality audio over the Internet, but its future remains in doubt as new standards are developed to provide copy-protection features for the recording industry. See also *MPEG*.

MPEG (Motion Picture Experts Group)—This term refers to a standard body of engineers and others in the movie and television industries, and to several compression standards they have promulgated for digital motion picture data compression. MPEG2 is now the standard for digital television and DVD-based motion images. MPEG4 is the latest standard, based largely on QuickTime, and used for low-bandwidth transmission. See also *JPEG*.

MPEG2—The compression standard for digital video used in digital broadcast satellite systems and *DVD*s.

Multilink-PPP—The protocol most commonly used to "bond" two ISDN digital channels or two analog modem channels together to achieve double-rate data transfers. This capability was first included in OSR2 of Windows 95. See also *channel-bonding* and *modem-bonding*.

Multiprocessing—Using multiple processors to perform one or more processes simultaneously. Contrast with *multitasking*.

Multisession—A recordable CD format in which multiple sessions of data can be written at different types. Each session contains its own lead in, lead out, and program areas.

Multitasking—A single CPU working on more than one task at the same time. The central processor (CPU) is switched between the different tasks so frequently that it gives the illusion that all are being attended to all the time, even though in fact, only one is being worked on at any given instant. Contrast this with *multiprocessing*.

NAS (Network Attached Storage)—Storage devices that can be attached directly to a network and then accessed by all the other devices (for example, PCs) on that network. Contrast with *SAN*.

NBF Transport Protocol—A descendant of the NetBEUI protocol, which is a transport layer protocol, not the programming interface NetBIOS.

NDS (Novell Directory Services)—Novell's proprietary means for providing and accessing directory information over a network.

NETBEUI (NETBIOS Extended User Interface)—Microsoft's standard for locating resources on a network in which data packets are formatted according to the NetBIOS standard.

NETBEUI Transport—NetBEUI (network basic input/output system) extended user interface. Used primarily in small or workgroup networks.

NETBIOS Interface—A programming interface that allows I/O requests to be sent to and received from a remote computer. It hides networking hardware for applications.

Netware—A 32-bit network operating system produced by Novell Corporation.

Network Device Driver—Software that coordinates communication between the network adapter card and the computer's hardware and other software, controlling the physical function of the network adapter cards.

Network File System (NFS)—Originally developed by Sun Microsystems, allows directories and files to be shared across a network. It is the *de facto* Unix standard for network file systems and has been ported to many non-Unix operating systems as well.

Network Interface Card (NIC)—Adapter card added to the computer to provide access to the local area network (LAN).

Network Operating System (NOS)—Any operating system whose primary function is to provide network services and resources to client machines.

NFS—See *network file system*.

NIC—See *network interface card*.

NNTP (Network News Protocol)—A service used to distribute network news messages from servers to clients.

Northbridge Chip—A VLSI chip (part of the motherboard "chip set") that connects the system bus (from the CPU) to the AGP port, main memory, the PCI bus, and the zoomed video bus.

NTFS (Windows NT File System)—An advanced file system designed for use with the Windows XP and Windows 2000 operating system. NTFS supports file system recovery and extremely large storage media, encrypted file systems, in addition to other advantages. It also supports object-oriented applications by treating all files as objects with user-defined and system-defined attributes.

NTSC (National Television Standards Committee)—The standard video signal format used in the United States. It specifies interlaced scan, 30-frame per second images. See also *interlaced scan*, *progressive scan*, *DTV*, and *PAL*.

NVRAM (Non-Volatile RAM)—A general term referring to any of a wide variety of technologies that support electronic data retention even when external power is removed, yet permit those data to be changed when that is desired. Some of the technologies this encompasses include EPROMs, EEPROMs, flash memory, and battery-backed up RAM.

OBE (Out Of Box Experience), also called OOB—Refers to how easy or hard a customer finds it to set up a new computer.

OLE (Object Linking and Embedding)—A way to transfer and share information between applications.

OLTP (On-Line Transaction Processing)—Large database applications such as airline or theater ticket reservations systems that are simultaneously accessible from many terminals or connected PCs.

OOP (Object-Oriented Programming)—A style of programming that bundles data and procedures (called methods) into "black boxes" with defined interfaces but hidden interiors. These program boxes are arranged in a hierarchy via the concept of classes and inheritance.

Operating System—The software that manages and schedules resources within a computer; the underlying programs that enable application programs to operate the hardware. DOS, Windows, and Linux are some of the popular operating systems for PCs.

Orange Book—The CD standard that defines the characteristics of recordable and rewritable CDs (*CD-R* and *CD-RW*, respectively) and of *magneto-optical* (MO) discs.

Packet—Specified arrangement of data and address information. A packet is the basic building block of a protocol. Many formats of packets have been defined for various packet-delivery data communication protocols. In the most general sense, a packet is a single unit of information transmitted as a whole from one device to another on a network.

Packet-Switched Data Services—A means of carrying many messages on the same circuits by breaking each one into many small packets. All the packets are sent, serially, across the circuit, one after another, and each is routed correctly to its own destination based on address information carried within the packet. Contrast this with *PSTN*.

Page—A fixed-size block in memory.

PAL (Phase Alternation Line)—A television signal format used in video equipment in some parts of Europe and Asia. With 25 frames per second it is incompatible with NTSC (30 frames per second) signals used in North America. See also *interlaced scan*, *progressive scan*, *DTV*, and *NTSC*.

Parallel—Sending data more than one bit at a time by the use of separate wires for each of those bits. Contrast with *Serial*.

Partition—A portion of a physical disk that functions like a physically separate unit.

PCB (Printed Circuit Board)—An card made of an insulating material coated with metal that is then etched to form a circuit, or several such cards laminated together to make a multi-layer PCB. This is the technology used to create motherboards, plug-in option cards, and memory modules.

PCI (Peripheral Component Interconnect)—An Intel-sponsored standard, now very widely deployed, for connecting peripheral components to computers. Originally only a 32-bit bus operating at speeds up to 32MHz, it now supports both a wide (64-bit) and fast (66MHz) version.

PCL (Printer Control Language)—Hewlett-Packard's page description language. Originally designed as a limited program for their first laser printers, it has now, by its present version 6, become a very competitive alternative to Adobe's PostScript. Printers with support for PCL built in can be sent a much more compact description of a page to be printed than is possible for a "dumb" printer than can only put pels on a page. See *pel*, *pixel*, and *PostScript*.

PDA (Personal Digital Assistant)—A common term for small, extremely portable digital devices that provide less overall functionality than a PC. One of the most popular examples of this class of device is the Palm. Contrast with *HPC*.

Pel—The smallest physical unit of an image that a given device (display or printer) can produce. Contrast this with *pixel*, which is the smallest unit of image information in a file or that is delivered to that output device.

Performance—A relative term indicating how quickly a computer can perform some task. A higher performance PC will do more in less time than a lower performance one. Contrast with *availability*.

Phase Change—The technology that makes rewritable CDs and DVDs possible. It uses a material that can be in one of two states, or phases—amorphous or crystalline. One state is used to represent a digital 0 while the other is used to represent a 1. A laser beam changes the state of each bit area to represent these 1s and 0s as needed.

PhotoCD—A CD format created by Kodak and defined as part of the *White Book* standard.

Pipelined—A term describing any process in which several steps start before the first one is finished. It provides a way of speeding up calculations by beginning later steps while earlier steps are still being worked upon. This is applicable to many component parts used in a PC.

Pits—The hollowed area of a DVD or CD that, together with *lands*, define the data the disc contains.

Pixel—The smallest logical unit of an image. This is an "atom" of the image, and can be specified in terms of its color according to any of several color models. Contrast this with *pel*.

Pocket PC—The version of Microsoft Windows designed to run on handheld devices and the collective name of those hardware devices.

Point-To-Point (PtP)—Describes a data path that joins a source with a single destination. Contrast with a bus connection, in which the source broadcasts a message to several destinations simultaneously.

Port—A connection or socket used to connect a device to a computer, such as a printer, monitor, or modem. Information is sent from the computer to the device through a cable.

PostScript—This page description language by Adobe was introduced with the first Apple LaserWriter. This is a full computer operating system (complete with file system and I/O control, and so on), but it is designed specifically to address the needs of a printer, video terminal, or other two-dimensional imaging device. A variation of PostScript called the Portable Document Format (PDF) is commonly used to create files that will display in a PDF viewer (Adobe Acrobat) with all the graphical details exactly as its designers intended them to appear.

POTS (Plain Old Telephone Service)—Analog telephone service (voice grade line) using a separate single pair for the connection to each telephone. The normal sort of telephone service used in homes and offices for the past century. Contrast with *xDSL*.

PPGA (Plastic Pin Grid Array)—A standard packaging methodology for integrated circuits in which the contacts are formed as a rectangular array of pins on the bottom of the package. These packages can then be installed in a socket, in particular of the ZIF design.

PPTP (Point To Point Tunneling Protocol)—A protocol used to create a Virtual Private Network (VPN) over a public packet-switched network (such as the Internet).

Precision Graphics Markup Language (PGML)—An application of XML to support a more graphically precise specification of the appearance of Web pages and documents destined for a printer than is possible within normal HTML. Providing an alternative way of specifying formats to that included in the CSS standard, PGML was developed by Adobe, and is based on their PDF (Portable Document Format) and PostScript page description languages, but extends them in several ways that are important for Web pages such as progressive rendering and transparency.

PRI (Primary Rate Interface)—One of two forms of ISDN. Provides 23 64Kbps data channels and one 64Kbps signaling channel. See *ISDN*.

Primary Partition—The bootable partitions that you create on a bootable hard drive in the system. Partitions that can be set to take the lead position during the starting of the PC and can be used to boot the operating system.

Print Device—Refers to the actual hardware device that produces printed output.

Progressive Rendering—Drawing an image first in low resolution, and then refining it one or more times at successively higher resolutions. This strategy is often implemented in GIF and JPEG files used on the Web to enable viewers to see the basic image quickly. If viewers stick around, the image appears in its full resolution. See *GIF*, *JPEG*, *PGML*, and *resolution*.

Progressive Scan—Forming an raster-scan image by drawing each line on the screen in turn (typically from top to bottom). Essentially all PC video displays use progressive scanning to form their images. Contrast with *interlaced scan*.

Protocol—A set of rules and conventions by which some goal is achieved. Networking software usually implements multiple levels of protocols layered one on top of another to support the transport of data throughout the network or across multiple networks.

Proxy Server—A computer that links a LAN with an external network (such as the Internet), and hides the network addresses of internal machines from the view of anyone connected to the external network. Contrast with *firewall*.

PSTN (Public Switched Telephone Network)—The normal telephone network used for dial-up calls. One circuit connection is established for each call and maintained for the call's duration. The PSTN also is often referred to in data communications circles as POTS service. See *POTS*. Contrast this with *packet-switched data services* and *xDSL*.

Public Key Cryptography—A method of data encryption in which a publicly known key is used to encrypt data, but that data can only be decrypted by the intended recipient who knows a secret key, which is mathematically related to the original public key. In this way, it is possible for many individuals to send secure content to an individual who—being the only person who knows the secret key—is the only person able to read that content.

Purple Book—The standard that defines double-density CDs.

Qos Or QOS (Quality of Service)—A somewhat nebulous term, covering various means of guaranteeing that a data link will manage to provide a given application that uses it with at least some specified minimum level of data throughput and some maximum latency. The USB and FireWire standards include QOS provisions for some devices while allowing others to send data on an as-bandwidth-is-available basis. Some Internet ISPs offer special, higher-cost services with some QOS guarantees and Ipv6 will include QOS support in its design.

QuickTime—An Apple-developed compact file format for encoding video and audio program material. Now the basis for the MPEG4 standard.

RAID (Redundant Array of Inexpensive Devices)—A collection of hard disks attached to a special controller that distributes the stored data across those disks in a way that maximizes speed of access to the data or minimizes the risk to those data when one of the disks fails. There are many arrangements in common use: RAID 0 (sharing data non-redundantly across multiple disks to improve performance, but not reliability), RAID 1 (also known as disk-mirroring, which improves reliability, but not performance), and RAID 5 (which provides an economical balance of redundancy with capacity, and works well in disk arrays with any number of disks from two up) are the most popular.

RAM (Random Access Memory)—This is the electronic, read-write, random-access memory that is used mainly to hold programs and data while they are being used in your PC (as opposed to disk storage where those files reside when they are not in use). See also *DRAM, EDO RAM, SDRAM, SRAM*, and *RDRAM*. Contrast with *ROM* and *flash memory*.

Raster-Scan Image—Any image that is formed by drawing lines of dots. This term is generally applied to a video display device, but it can also be used to describe the output from most printers. See also *interlaced scan* and *progressive scan*.

Real Number—Any number (positive, negative, or zero) including both whole numbers (integers) and ones with a fractional part. (Examples: 4.17, -0,0025.)

Red Book—The original CD standard, responsible for defining the characteristics of read-only audio CDs and their supporting player hardware.

Refresh Rate—How frequently the image on a display device is redrawn. See also *flicker* and *frame rate*.

Remote Administration—Management of one computer by an administrator located at another computer and connected to the first computer across a network.

Resolution—How finely an image is defined, spatially. This can be separately defined for the image and for the image display (or printing) devices. See also *pel* and *pixel*.

Resource—Any part of a computer system or a network, such as a disk drive or memory, that can be allotted to a program or a process while it's running.

RFC (Request For Comment)—The name given to proposed standards when they are posted on the Internet for comment. Each one is numbered. Later—and possibly after revision—when it is adopted as an official standard, the RFC remains on the Internet as the definitive description of that standard. When it is replaced with an upgraded form of that standard, it remains available for review, and the new form is given a new RFC number.

RGB—Red, Green, and Blue. A model for the onscreen display of graphic images. Unlike CMYK, which uses positive amounts of black as a "primary" color, RGB uses reduced brightness of its three primary elements to create dark tones.

RIAA—A species of bottom-feeder.

RIMM (Rambus Inline Memory Module)—A DIMM that carries DRAM modules for use in a Direct Rambus memory subsystem. These devices are designed to let data and clock signals flow through them in parallel paths with carefully matched lengths and propagation delays. See also *C-RIMM*.

Ring 0—The lowest level (most privileged) at which programs can operate on an Intel x86 processor. This is where the kernel of an operating system must run, and in Windows it also is the location of a number of additional operating system components. Compare with *Ring 3*.

Ring 3—This is the highest level (least privileged) at which program can operate on an Intel x86 processor. This is where user programs run (including all Windows application programs.) Compare with *Ring 0*.

RISC-Based Computer—A computer based on a reduced instruction set (RISC) micro-processor. Compare with *x86-based computer*.

Rock Ridge—An extension of the ISO9660 CD file system that supports long filenames but not Unicode. Used primarily for Unix operating systems and their derivatives.

ROM (Read Only Memory)—This term is applied to several, very different things. When it is applied to electronic memory it refers to the memory chips that hold programs and data that do not change and must always be accessible to the processor in a PC, or to the memory chips that hold programs and data in, for example, a modem. Applied to a CD or DVD this refers to a version of those digital storage media that can only have data manufactured into them at the factory (as opposed to –R, -RW, or -RAM variations whose data can be written by the user).

Router—A means of connecting two or more LANs that use the same protocol together, filtering which of the data packets received from any one connected LAN get passed on to each of the others. Contrast with *bridge*.

SAN (Storage Area Network)—A standard, based on fibre channel, for connecting multiple data storage devices (typically large hard drives) to multiple hosts. This arrangement is commonly used in very large server or "server farms" as it permits very high speed data transfers and redundant access, thus insuring both high performance and high availability for the storage system.

Scalability—The ability of an operating system or an individual piece of software to either take advantage of the presence of multiple processors (as on a supercomputer), or to operate on progressively smaller systems without losing fundamental capacity to function.

Scarlet Book—A CD standard that defines the characteristics of the SuperAudio CD, which is, actually, an all-audio DVD that incorporates complex copy protection.

SCSI (Small Computer System Interface)—This standard for connecting peripheral devices to a computer has gone through many generations of improvement. SCSI1, SCSI2 (including its Ultra- and Wide- variants), and SCSI3 devices are all in common use today. Further, this standard formed the basis for other, more advanced interconnection standards, such as *USB* and *FireWire*.

SDRAM (Synchronous Dram)—This is the latest generation of DRAM memory modules, supplanting EDO RAM first in workstation and other desktop PCs, and later in servers. SDRAM chips can transfer data in a single clock cycle because their operations are synchronized with the system clock. See also *RAM, DRAM, RDRAM,* and *SDRAM.* Contrast with *SRAM, flash memory*, and *ROM*.

SECC (Single Edge Contact Cartridge)—Intel's method of packaging CPUs in modules that contain the CPU and Level 2 cache memory.

Secret Key Encryption —A method of encryption in which the same key is used for both, encrypting and decrypting the information. Also called symmetric cryptography. Contrast with *public key cryptography.*

Segment—Network-level term used to describe a single subnet.

SEPP (Single Edge Processor Package)—Intel's name for a board-level packaging that fits into a Slot 1 or Slot 2 CPU module socket. Used as an alternative to their Socket 370-compatible designs for certain Celeron and Pentium processors. There are also third-party adapters that use this form factor to support CPUs that plug into a Socket 5, Socket 7, or Super7 socket on motherboards with a Slot 1 socket.

Serial—Sending data one bit at a time. Contrast with *Parallel.*

Server—A term commonly used to denote a computer (which might be a PC, a mini-, or a mainframe) whose main use is to store and "serve up" information for use on attached workstations. In client-server applications this central machine might also perform some significant portion of the data processing workload.

SGML (Standard Generalized Markup Language)—Subject of a formal, international standard, this is an elaborate scheme for "marking up" a document to indicate the nature of various elements in a textual document, including how they are displayed on a printed page or display screen. The Web was initially designed to use pages that were defined using a small subset of the SGML markup codes, called *HTML.*

SIMM (Single Inline Memory Module)—A small printed circuit board carrying multiple memory chips. Although there are usually electrical contacts all along one edge on both sides of the PCB, the contacts that are directly opposite one another are electrically connected together and do not function independently. Contrast with *DIMM* and *RIMM.*

Skew—Refers to the amount by which a data signal might get out of step with its associated clock signal. See also *jitter.*

Slot 1—The Intel standard for SECC CPU modules first used in the Pentium II. This is a 242-pin socket and all the CPU modules that fit into it run their L2 cache memory at half the processor core frequency. See *Socket 7.*

Slot 2—The Intel standard for SECC CPU modules. This is a 300-pin socket and all the CPU modules that fit into it run their L2 cache at the full speed of the processor core.

SMART (Self-Management and Reporting Technology)—Hard disks are able to inform the operating system when errors occur in a way that suggests the drive might soon fail altogether. When this is supported by a utility program (or by the OS), drive failures can be anticipated and data saved from loss.

SmartMedia Cards—Cards that only contain flash memory chips, and not the controlling electronics required to access those chips. Contrast with *CompactFlash*.

SMIL (Synchronized Multimedia Integration Language)—An extension to HTML to support multimedia documents in which synchronizing the sounds with the video portion is critical.

SMTP (Simple Mail Transfer Protocol)—A widely used protocol for exchanging messages, not restricted to mail, nor used only on the Internet.

SNTP (Simple Network Time Protocol)—A simple protocol for synchronizing clocks (including PC clocks) across a network, or worldwide.

Socket 7—The standard socket used by Intel Pentium processors and by their clones from AMD, Cyrix, and IDT-Centaur. This was the last of the Intel specified CPU socket designs that it licensed to its competitors.

SODIMM (Small Outline Dual Inline Memory Module)—An industry-standard miniaturized version of the DIMM used in mobile PCs.

Southbridge Chip—A VLSI chip (part of the motherboard "chip set") that connects the PCI bus to the ISA bus, mouse port, keyboard port, USB and IEEE 1394 (FireWire) ports, IDE (or, usually, EIDE) channels (to hard disks, CD-ROM drives, DVD drives, and so on), and any floppy disk drives in the PC. Contrast with *Northbridge chip*.

SRAM (Static Ram)—Memory chips or modules in which data can be held indefinitely without clocking (but only so long as power is applied to the chips). Because this is a relatively expensive kind of memory to make and it can be made to operate very rapidly, it is most often used in PCs in relatively small quantities in the system's cache memory. Contrast with *DRAM*, *flash memory*, and *ROM*.

Stripe Sets—A RAID technique in which the combination of 2 to 32 volumes can allow for more speed due to the fact that they alternate the writing of data across numerous drives at one time.

Subnet—Portion of an entire network that includes only devices sharing the same network address and/or collision domain.

Super-Floppy—See *LS-120*.

Super-Scalar—Referring to the increase in computing power in successive generations of a CPU, PC, or other device or system that increase more rapidly than simply in proportion to their internal clock speed, or any similar single-dimension measure of their "size" (for example, amount of RAM, amount of storage, number of CPUs).

Synchronous—Two or more events that occur at the same time. In the context of data transmission, a process whereby data is transmitted or received at a fixed rate. Contrast with *asynchronous*.

System Bus—The primary electronic path across which data moves in a PC. Sometimes called a front-side bus..

TCP/IP (Transmission Control Protocol/Internet Protocol)—The basic protocol used for data transmission on the Internet, and now on many Intranets and other LANs. This is a reference to both a physical layer control and the next higher-level control of the process of communication over a data link. It still refers to a fairly low-level of control of the communication, and is normally "supervised" by higher-level protocols such as SMTP.

TDI—See *transport driver interface*.

Telnet Service—The service that provides basic terminal emulation to remote systems supporting the Telnet protocol over TCP/IP.

Text File—A file containing only letters, numbers, and symbols. A text file contains no formatting information, except possibly linefeeds and carriage returns. Text files are also known as *flat files* and *ASCII files*.

Text Mode—See *character-based*.

Thread—An executable entity that belongs to a single process, comprising a program counter, a user-mode stack, a kernel-mode stack, and a set of register values. All threads in a process have equal access to the processor's address space, object handles, and other resources.

Topology—The cabling and physical protocol scheme of a network.

Track At Once—The ability of a CD recorder to write a portion of a CD's content and then pause, turning off the laser. This method of writing is responsible for the two-seconds of silence heard between tracks of commercial audio CDs. Contrast with *Disc at Once*.

Translation Lookaside Buffer (TLB)—A special hidden register inside the Intel x86 CPUs that holds values read from the Local or Global Descriptor Tables (LDT or GDT) in memory and that are used to calculate addresses for future accesses to memory.

Transport Driver Interface (TDI)—In the networking model, a common interface for network components that communicate at the session layer.

Transport Protocol—Defines how data should be presented to the next receiving layer in the networking model and packages the data accordingly. It passes data to the network adapter card driver through the NDIS interface, and to the redirector through the transport driver interface.

UDF (Universal Disk Format)—The file system used for DVDs and magneto-optical discs.

Ultra-DMA—A variation on DMA hardware in which data transfers are permitted on both the falling and rising edges of the clock signal, thus effectively doubling the speed with which data can be moved. See also *DMA controller.*

UNC (Universal Naming Convention, also known as Uniform Naming Convention)—A standard way of specifying a resource (typically a file or peripheral such as a printer) on a network, it consists of two parts. The first identifies the host computer's name; the second identifies the shared resource's share name. Example: \\computer\resource.

Unicode—A fixed-width, 16-bit character-encoding standard capable of representing all of the world's scripts.

Uninterruptible Power Supply (UPS)—Device that provides continuous power to a server or other mission-critical device in the event of a power failure. Usually a battery contained in a metal case that the devices are plugged into (also called a *battery backup*).

Universal Plug-and-Play (UPnP)—A Microsoft-proposed standard to extend plug-and-play behavior from PCs to a host of diverse devices including traditional consumer electronics (TVs, VCRs, and so on) and data-enabled appliances.

URI (Uniform Resource Identifier)—A standardized way of representing resources, especially on the Internet. There are two broad classes of URI, and some resources fall into both categories. The first and most well-known is the URL (Uniform Resource Locator). This specifies a resource by how you get to it. The other broad category is the URN (Universal Resource Name). This names a resource that must continue to have a globally unique and persistent name even when the resource ceases to exist or becomes unavailable. See also *URL.*

URL (Uniform Resource Locator)—A special case of a URI (Uniform Resource Identifier). A URL specifies an accessible object on the Internet, primarily by describing how to access it. A URL consists of three parts. The first names a protocol for accessing that object. The second is the name of a host. The last part names (specifies as a path) which object on that host is being addressed.

USB (Universal Serial Bus)—A medium-speed serial bus using a transmission derived from the SCSI bus protocol, but permitting "hot plugging" of devices. The preferred way to connect peripheral devices to a PC, except for those few that require super high-speed connections. (Those peripherals at present are usually connected via a SCSI or IEEE 1394 FireWire bus.)

UTP (Untwisted Shielded Pair)—The formal name for the kind of cable used in Ethernet networks.

VBA (Visual Basic For Applications)—A Microsoft programming language, based on Visual Basic, included in Office applications. This facility allows any user of these programs to automate their operation and, in some ways, to modify their functionality.

Virtual Memory Manager—Responsible for mapping the virtual memory addresses needed by the applications into actual memory.

Virtual Memory—Space on a hard disk that the operating system uses as if it were actually memory. Windows does this through the use of paging files. The benefit of using virtual memory is that you can run more applications at one time than your system's physical memory would otherwise allow. The drawbacks are the disk space required for the virtual-memory paging file and the decreased execution speed when significant swapping is required.

VLSI (Very Large Scale Integration)—A manufacturing technique that allows making very complex integrated circuits. Commonly used for CPUs, PC chip sets, DSPs, and certain other very complex logic circuits. Complexity in these circuits is measured in numbers of logic gates they include. SSI (Small Scale Integration) circuits contain only a few dozen gates at most. MSI (Medium Scale Integration) contain a few hundred or thousands. LSI (Large Scale Integration) circuits contain tens of thousands of gates, whereas VLSI circuits now routinely include several million gates.

VoIP (Voice Over IP)—An umbrella name for an assortment of hardware and software products aimed at moving most or all voice telephone calls off of the analog public switched telephone network (PSTN) and onto data networks using Internet Protocol (IP).

VPN (Virtual Private Network)—A strategy for using the Internet to connect two or more LANs in physically distinct locations in a way that ensures a high level of security for data traveling across this link. Contrast with *WAN*.

VxD (Virtual Device Driver)—The x in this name stands for "anything." (Thus a VKD could be a virtual keyboard driver, or a VDD a virtual display driver.) These are small programs that augment the operating system at its lowest level (Ring 0) and thus can be made to do anything and to directly access any portion of the hardware.

W3C—See *World Wide Web Consortium*.

Wake On LAN—A strategy for making it possible for a PC that is in a powered down state to be returned to full power-on status when it receives a signal across a LAN. This is useful for managing many PCs from a central location.

WAN (Wide Area Network)—A very large area network arrangement similar in function to a LAN, but typically extended over a much broader geographic region. A WAN will typically use dedicated wire or microwave links to connect the constituent LANs, as opposed to the connection of LANs over a shared medium that is characteristic of a VPN.

White Book—The CD standard responsible for defining the Video CD format and its related recording and playback hardware.

Windows—Microsoft's overall name for its most popular family of PC operating systems. This family includes the original Windows 1.0-3.11 programs that were simply graphical user interfaces (GUIs) loaded on top of DOS; Windows 95 and 98 which were more complete integrations of DOS with the GUI; Windows NT, Windows 2000, and Windows XP which are fully 32-bit (and, optionally for Windows XP, 64-bit) operating systems based on the Windows model for user and program interactions' and Windows CE, which is the reduced version of Windows for use on handheld PCs (HPCs).

Windows CE—The version of Microsoft Windows that is intended for use on handheld PCs. Now called *Pocket PC*.

Wizard—Small applications found within larger applications that, generally, step the user through some task.

Workstation—A term commonly used to denote a computer attached to a central server. This often implies a computer with more power (speed, amount of RAM, size, number, and/or resolution of the attached video display or displays, or other significant attributes) than the usual desktop PC.

World Wide Web Consortium (W3C)—A membership organization, jointly hosted by MIT in the USA and CERN in Europe, which adopts and publishes standards for the World Wide Web (and, by extension, for any LAN, intranet, or extranet using Internet and WWW protocols).

WWW (World Wide Web)—This term refers to the collection of machines connected via the Internet that serve and use information in accordance HTML and related protocols. This is essentially an application using the Internet as infrastructure, and it has become one of the most commonly used of those applications (along with e-mail and file transfers).

x86—The family name for the Intel CPUs used in various generations of PCs (starting with the 8088, and continuing through the 80286, 386, 486, and Pentium family of processors). This name also includes all the compatible CPUs made by other manufacturers.

x86-Based Computer—A computer using a microprocessor equivalent to an Intel 80386 or higher chip. Compare with *RISC-based computer*.

xDSL—Any one of several standards for digital communication over normal copper twisted pair telephone wires from a home or office to some convenient (for the telephone company) point where analog POTS signals can be separated from the all-digital xDSL ones. See *ADSL* and *SDSL*.

XML (Extensible Markup Language)—A standard way to describe database objects for display within a Web page. This standard augments HTML (with or without CSS, PGML, and so on) to make Web pages that can be automatically updated with data extracted from a database in any of several standard database formats.

XSL (Extensible Style Language)—An extension to XML to enable, among other features, search engines to access and index text contained within a Web page graphic.

Yellow Book—The CD standard responsible for defining the CD-ROM format and its related player hardware.

ZIF (Zero Insertion Force)—A socket design in which there is a lever that removes all pressure on the pins while the device is inserted or removed, and then applies pressure to them concurrently to provide reliable connections.

Index

laptops, 27
mobile PCs, 37
peripheral devices, 186
serial ports, 185-190, 192-193
small networks, 217
Southbridge chips, 339
user accounts
ISPs, 210
setup access, 368
unattended start option, 368
User memory, 409
user-level access control, 465
USER.DAT file, 362
USER.EXE/USER32.DLL file, 362
utilities
data compression, 457
Disk Editor, 79
UTP (Unshielded Twisted Pair), 214

V

V.32 standard, 227
V.34 standard, 224, 226-227
V.42 standard, 227
V.90 standard, 227, 230
v86 monitor programs, 392
Vaio laptop, 32
values, 103, 302
variables, object-oriented programming, 542
vector images, 123, 269, 478, 480
vendors, industry standards, 96-97
versions
BIOS, 357
DOS, 513
PCI buses, 331
vertical signals, 124-125
vertical tabs, 70, 75
Very Large-Scale Integrated Circuit (VLSI), 184
VESA (Video Equipment Standards Association), 331
VGAs
color, 126
images, 130
laptops, 25
VIA chip, 291-292
ViaVoice (IBM), 255

video
accelerators, 336
AGP buses, 335-337
BIOS, 352
BIOS ROM, 323
DVDs, 452
frame buffers, 396
graphics coprocessors, 128
images, 127-128
memory, 14, 114, 396
mobile PCs, 37
modes, 129
motherboards, 114
multicasting, 474
output circuitry, 130
RAM, 381, 485-387
streaming, 15
upgrades, 114
Video Equipment Standards Association (VESA), 331
VideoLogic Neon 250 chipset, 495
viewing BIOS configuration, 365
violence in video games, 503
virtual 86 mode, 111, 392
interrupt vector tables (IVTs), 320
monitors, 304
physical addresses, 304
virtual machines, 537
addresses, 302, 401
DOS (DVM), 407-408
Java, 538
Windows, 408
virtual memory, 305, 312, 394, 410
viruses
boot sectors, 356
macros, 544
Visor (Handspring), 56, 58
VisorPhone, 56
Visual Basic, 535, 537, 544
Visual Workstation, 127
VLSI (Very Large-Scale Integrated Circuit), 184
VMM32.VXD file, 362
Voice over IP (VoIP), 229
voice recognition, 251-255
voice-capable modems, 228-229
VoIP (Voice over IP), 229
volatile memory chips, *see* RAM

X

Y-Z